Beginner

Introduction to Plant Design 2024

Imperial

January 2024

Published by:

ASCENT Center for Technical Knowledge
630 Peter Jefferson Parkway, Suite 175
Charlottesville, VA 22911
866-527-2368
www.ascented.com

AS-PLT2401-ITR1IM-SG // IS-PLT2401-ITR1IM-SG

Contents

Exercise Files

To download the exercise files for this learning guide, use the following steps:

1. Type the URL ***exactly as shown below*** into the address bar of your Internet browser, to access the Course File Download page.

   Note: If you are using the ebook, you do not have to type the URL. Instead, you can access the page simply by clicking the URL below.

   https://www.ascented.com/getfile/id/macrognathusPF

2. On the Course File Download page, click the **DOWNLOAD NOW** button, as shown below, to download the .ZIP file that contains the exercise files.

3. Once the download is complete, unzip the file and extract its contents.

   The recommended exercise files folder location is:
   C:\Plant Design 2024 Practice Files

   Note: It is recommended that you do not change the location of the exercise files folder. Doing so may cause errors when completing the exercises.

Chapter 1

Introduction to AutoCAD Plant 3D

The plant design industry creates and communicates a vast array of information. Because the industry consists of many facets of design, the industry requires a broad solution. AutoCAD® Plant 3D and Autodesk® Navisworks® are two separate software applications that work together to meet the requirements of a broad solution. In this chapter, you learn about many of the general topics for plant design and the use of the AutoCAD Plant 3D software to create plant designs that meet your design requirements and workflows.

Objectives

After completing this chapter, you will be able to:

- Navigate the Project Manager and explain the purpose of a project and where the drawings and data are stored.
- Open drawings in the context of the project from the Project Manager.
- Identify the aspects of the user interface that are unique for plant design and the workflow for creating and modifying a P&ID or 3D plant design.
- Explain the philosophy behind layering and explain the project setup options for layers and colors.

Lesson: Working in a Project

Overview

This lesson describes how to navigate the Project Manager, the purpose of a project, and where the data and drawings for a project are stored.

Because a complete plant design project can be composed of many different drawing files, it is important to be able to efficiently access and create the files while keeping them associated with the project. The Project Manager is the central hub where you access all of the drawings. Along with providing easy navigation to the various drawings, you can also use the Project Manager to set up drawings, establish common project settings, import and export data, and create project reports.

Objectives

After completing this lesson, you will be able to:

- Describe how AutoCAD P&ID and AutoCAD Plant 3D projects work with data.
- Explain how data is organized in the AutoCAD Plant 3D software.
- Describe the Project Manager user interface.
- Explain the purpose of the Data Manager.

About Projects

A project in the AutoCAD P&ID software or the AutoCAD Plant 3D software is made up of a collection of drawings and other forms of data. When collected together, these data sources interact in the larger context of a project. When you work with any individual component of the project, such as orthographic or isometric drawings, you do so from in the project rather than by directly opening these drawings from outside the project. This approach maintains the integrity of the relationships between the components in the larger project. One of the primary reasons to use the AutoCAD P&ID software or the AutoCAD Plant 3D software instead of the AutoCAD software is that the AutoCAD P&ID software and the AutoCAD Plant 3D software create not just a simple drawing but data associated with drawings and the items in them.

Project Components

Some of the drawings that are used as components of a project are:

- P&ID
- 3D model
- Orthographic
- Isometric

Additional data that could be used as part of a typical project are:

- Process information, such as stream tables.
- Equipment and instrument cut-sheets.
- Catalog and specs for piping.
- Structural analysis, if required.

The following illustration shows how these components interact.

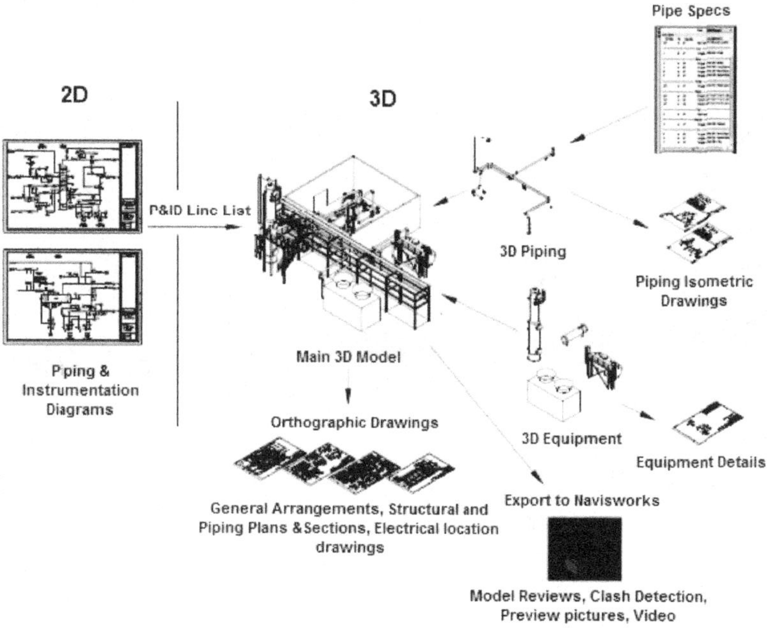

Project and Drawing Options

You can set options and other settings for the overall project or for individual components in the project. You find most of these settings on shortcut menus as shown in the following illustration. Properties of the overall project affect the project as a whole, and properties for individual components only affect those specific components.

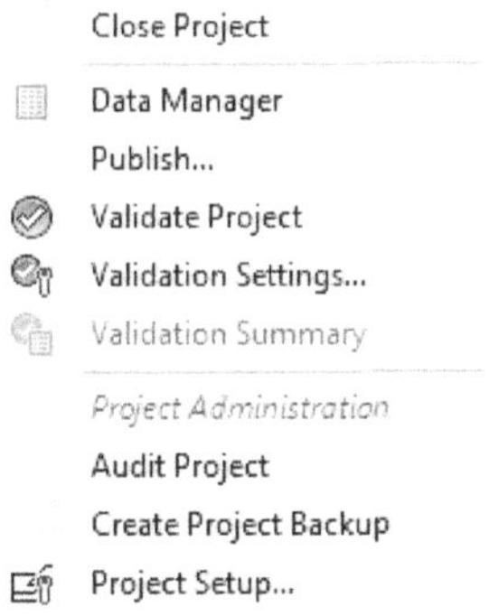

Project shortcut menu

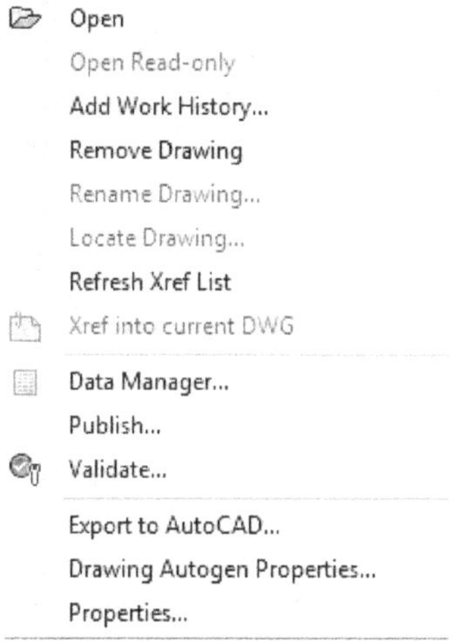

Drawing shortcut menu

Data Organization

Data that is used in a project is organized in a system of default folders. If you work in a multiple user environment, it is recommended that you manage Plant projects with Vault or store the data in a centralized network location. An example project folder structure is shown in the following illustration:

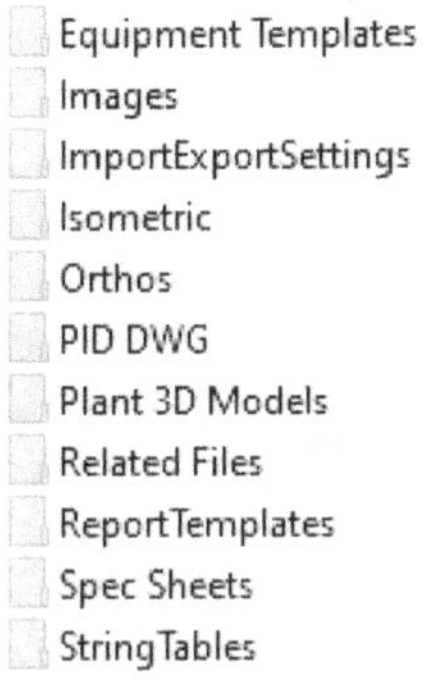

Project Files and Paths

There are several ways to organize the files for a project. Files are most often stored under the P&ID Drawings or Plant 3D Drawings folder, or sub-folders, with the equivalent folder structure created in the Windows project directory. A separate folder for templates can be created to store company or project standards.

When a project is created you do not indicate whether it should be stored as a relative or absolute path. This is only required when you are using the XREF command to attach drawings to one another. Project folders are all created relative to the *Project.xml* file.

Once the project structure is set up, you can copy existing drawings that need to be used into the project. The Copy command duplicates the selected file and places it into the project folder structure defined in the project settings.

The Start Window

When you open the AutoCAD P&ID software or the AutoCAD Plant 3D software, you are presented with the Start window (as shown in the following illustration). By default, the Project Manager is displayed on the left side of the window. The next division contains drop-down lists that have options for creating new projects and sheet sets, opening existing projects, and opening collaboration projects. There are three buttons: Recent, Autodesk Projects, and Learning. Clicking these buttons opens relevant options and information on the right side of the Start window. A list of links is also provided to access online services such as What's new in the software, Online help, and the Community forum.

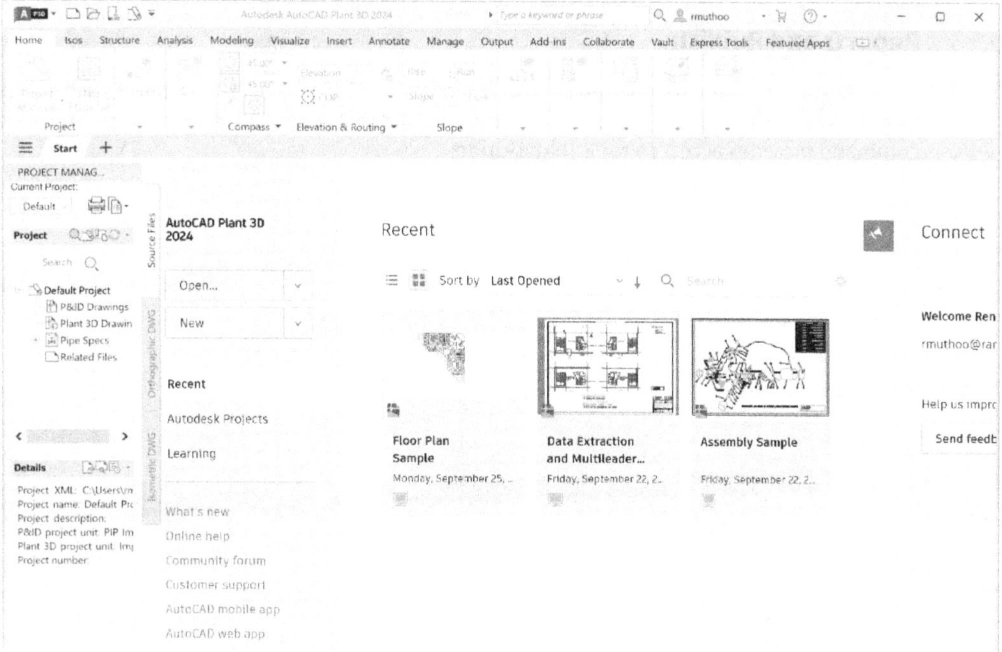

About the Project Manager

The Project Manager provides access to the project-wide settings and data, as well as individual data components in the project. By default, the Project Manager is located on the left of the screen.

Current Project

At the top of the Project Manager palette is the Current Project list, which shows the current project and enables you to select from other projects. Hovering over any of the project names in the drop-down displays a tooltip of the actual location of the project. Other options in the drop-down enable you to create a new project or to open an existing project, as shown in the following illustration.

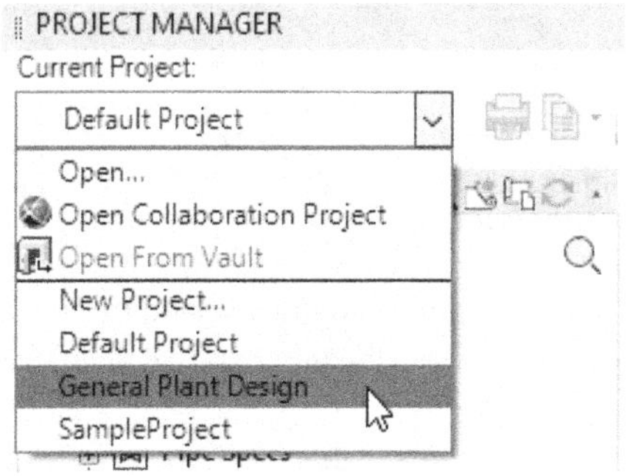

Reports and Publish

In the Project Manager, to the right of the Current Project list are the Publish and Reports commands, as shown in the following illustration. These commands are accessible project-wide. The Reports command provides access to tools that include:

- Data Manager
- Import/Export
- Reports

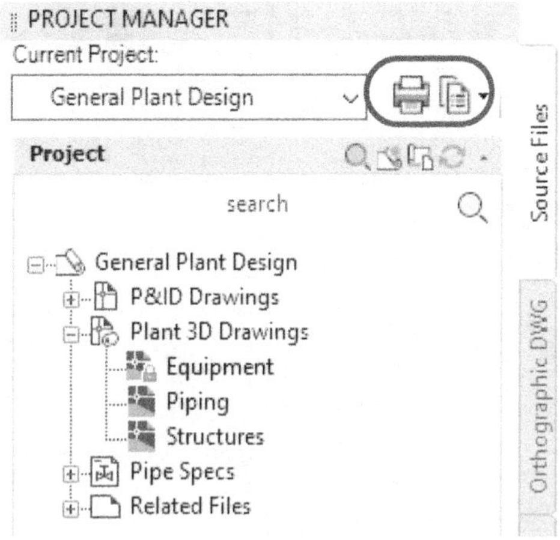

Project Panel

The Project panel displays a "tree-view" of the drawings in the project. The most common tab used is the Source Files tab, as shown in the following illustration. The drawings shown in the Source Files tab are P&ID drawings and 3D model files. The Orthographic DWG and Isometric DWG tabs contain output drawings generated from your 3D piping model.

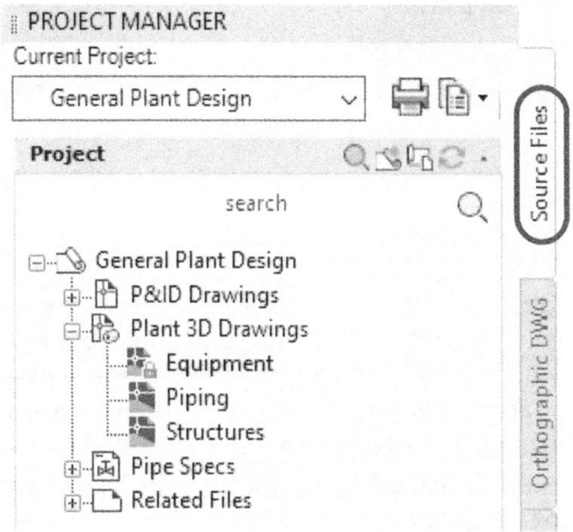

There are four fixed top level folders: P&ID Drawings, Plant 3D Drawings, Pipe Specs, and Related Files folders. All these folders, except for the Pipe Spec folder, can have additional sub-folders created to organize and store drawings or other related project documents inside. Drawings, folders, and other items in the tree can be arranged as required by using standard Windows techniques, such as dragging and dropping. The Pipe Spec folder contains a listing of all the 3D piping specs included in the current project. Piping spec files can be added, removed, or edited in a project from this branch of the Project Manager.

The Related files folder is a convenient place to put links to documents associated with the project, such as cut sheets, spreadsheets, etc. The folder can have additional subfolders added to organize these files.

The Search bar at the top of the project panel is used to find files in the Project Manager when working with a large number of drawings. Entering the filename, or a part of the filename, displays the files that match the search criteria by temporarily filtering out all the other files.

The Project Manager takes advantage of the fact that what you see in the tree is a representation of the folder or drawing in the project. The drawing icons change based on what is happening to the drawings in the project. Some icon changes could include the indication of locked or missing drawings.

Details/Preview/History Panel

The bottom panel of the Project Manager provides information about the drawing selected in the project panel. This panel toggles between basic drawing details, drawing preview, and drawing history.

- **Details** - Provides basic details of the item selected, such as drawing location and size, the status of the drawing, and who created and worked on it last.
- **Preview** - Presents a thumbnail preview of the drawing selected.
- **Work History** - Provides a work history of the drawing. This enables you to track the status and notes added to a drawing.

About Vault Projects

Projects can be stored in the Autodesk Vault software and are opened using the Project Manager. AutoCAD Plant 3D Project administrators need the Vault client for certain operations, but a plant user should only use the Project manager to work with Vaulted files. When opened, a local workspace is created and files are copied from the vault. Any additional users accessing the project have separate local workspaces created on their systems. The project database in the local workspace is updated (⚡) as you save files in the working folder, as shown in the following illustration. The project master database is updated when you check in files to the vault.

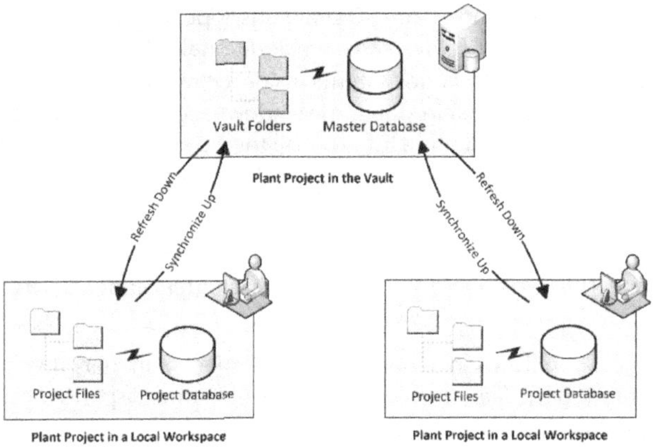

If you create a plant project in the vault, you can use the following vault-enabled features:

- **Local workspace** - Files are no longer kept on a network shared drive. Vault project files are modified in the local workspace and synchronized to the vault.
- **Check-in and check-out document management** - The Project Manager is fully integrated with the Autodesk Vault software. The Project Manager prompts you to check out the files as you work.
- **Automatic file versions** - You can view or restore the previous revision of a file.
- **Master project database** - Vault projects use SQL Server for the project database. The master database is always synchronized to match the files that are checked in to the vault.
- **User authentication and access control** - Administrators can manage access to a vault project using the Autodesk Data Management Console to set up user accounts and assign roles.

Getting Started with Vault

When your project administrator has provided you with a vault server location and credentials, you can use the Project Manager to open a project, as shown in the following illustration. The first time you open a vault project you specify the location of your working folder. Project files are then copied to your working folder from the vault.

Project files are initially read-only in your workspace folder. The Project Manager prompts you to check out files as you work. You can check in project files when your changes are complete. You can also synchronize to the vault to share your work-in-progress without checking in the files.

> **Important:** Do not use the Autodesk Vault Client to work with plant projects.

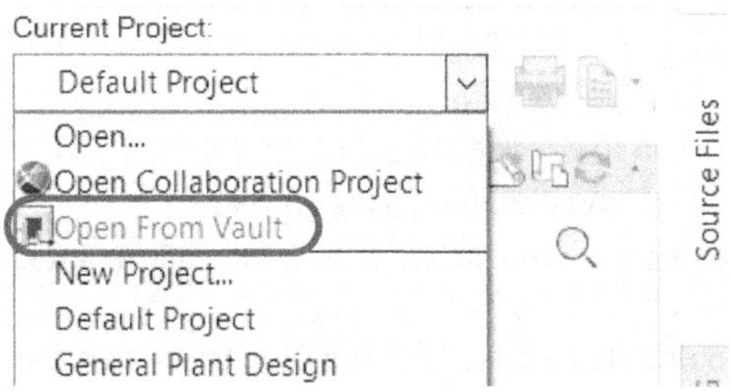

Project Manager

Vault project and file management features are integrated directly into the Project Manager. If a vault project is opened, the Project Manager displays a vault project type which displays next to the project name. Files in the project display for the check-out status when checked out. Hover the cursor over the filename to identify who has the file checked out, as shown in the following illustration.

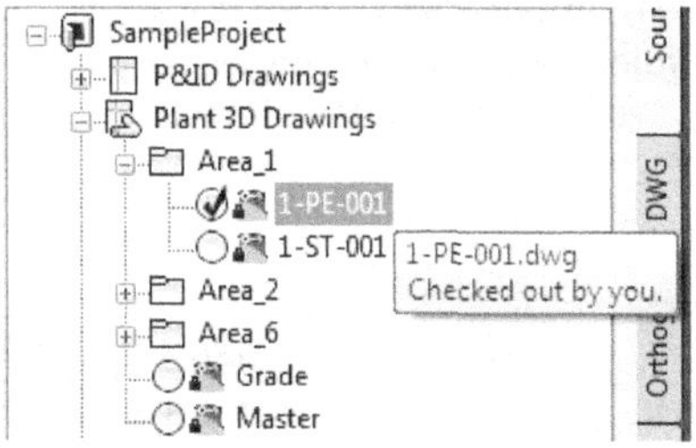

Vault Ribbon

You can manage your vault log-in session and vault project files from the ribbon, as shown in the following illustration.

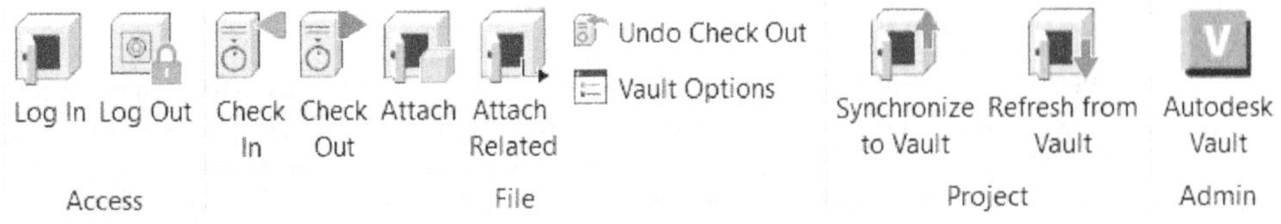

- When working with vault projects, the AutoCAD Plant 3D software prompts you to log in. Autodesk Vault log-ins are maintained for the duration of the drawing session unless you log out. If you want to access a different vault, you must log out first.
- The Log In/Log Out options in the ribbon enable you to log into and out of the vault.
- The Check In option in the ribbon enables you to check a file in for the first time or check a file back into the vault.
- The Check Out option in the ribbon enables you to check a file out of the vault.
- The Undo Check Out option in the ribbon enables you to undo a file checkout.
- The Synchronize to Vault option in the ribbon uploads the file's data to vault while maintaining the checkout.
- The Refresh from Vault option in the ribbon updates the file with the properties from the vault.

About Collaboration Projects

AutoCAD Plant 3D projects can be hosted on BIM 360 Team and are opened using the Project Manager. A project located on a BIM 360 Team hub can be accessed and edited, outside a company's network, by anyone connected to the internet. The project administrator can share projects from the BIM 360 Team hub and invite users with read-only or read/write permission to a project. Collaboration projects hosted in the cloud are downloaded to the local computer and edited in Plant 3D like any other project. Similar to a Vaulted AutoCAD Plant 3D project, collaboration project drawings are checked-out and checked-in as work is completed on them. A collaboration project must be created locally and then uploaded to BIM 360 Team.

Getting Started with Collaboration Projects

Once you have a BIM 360 account and you have been invited to join a collaboration project hosted on the BIM 360 Team, you use the Project Manager to open the project, as shown in the illustration below. You must first be logged in to Autodesk to open a collaboration project. Then, to open the collaboration project, select the Open Collaboration Project menu item from the Project Manager. If you have been invited to a project, select the project from the list of available Plant projects. Project files are then copied to your local computer.

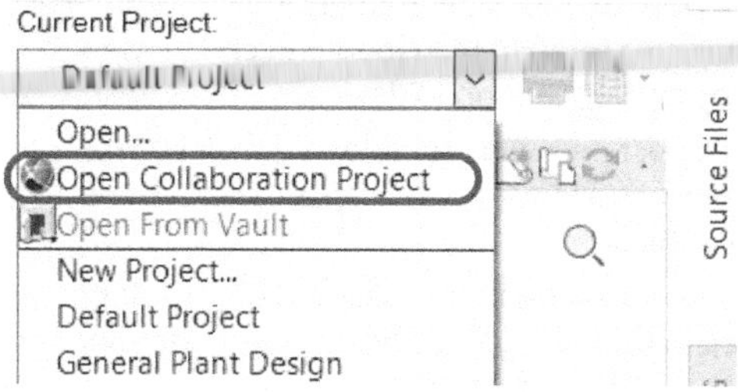

Project Manager

All Project files are initially read-only on your local computer. Opening a drawing from the Project Manager will automatically check-out the file for editing. After making any changes to the drawing file, saving and closing the drawing will automatically check the file back in and upload a copy to Autodesk Docs for all other users to see. You can also check-out and check-in files manually.

Collaboration project and file management features are integrated into the Project Manager. If a collaboration project is opened, the Project Manager displays the project type next to the project name. Files in the project display a check-out status when checked out. Hover the cursor over the filename, or view the details panel in the Project Manager, to identify who has a file checked out.

Collaborate Ribbon

You can share and manage project files to Autodesk Docs from the ribbon as well as perform other collaboration project commands, as shown in the following illustration.

- The Check In option in the ribbon enables you to check a new file in to the collaboration project for the first time or check a file back in after making changes. A check-in uploads the file to the cloud for others to view it.
- The Check Out option in the ribbon enables you to check out a file for editing. You can either check out the files manually or they automatically checkout when opened.
- The Undo Check Out option enables you to cancel changes and revert to the copy previously stored in the project.
- The Attach option enables you to Xref other drawings in the collaboration project to your open drawing.
- The Share Project button enables you to upload a local project to Autodesk Docs. Once uploaded, users in other locations can be invited to join the collaboration project.
- The Share Drawing tool enables you to collaborate with others by sharing a virtual link to a copy of the currently open drawing file with them. With the Share Drawing tool, you can share drawings along with all the relevant referenced files, such as Xrefs, images, and font file types. The copy of the drawing being shared is stored on the cloud and can be accessed anytime and from anywhere. The link to the drawing file can be shared with others, and they can review, mark up, and edit the drawing in the Autodesk® AutoCAD® web app. Recipients can make changes to the copy of the drawing file with no access to the original drawing file that is owned by the sharer.

- Shared Views creates views for sharing your designs with stakeholders and are a great alternative to printing .PDF and .DWF files. Shared views are stored in the cloud and can be viewed and commented on by any web enabled desktop, tablet, or mobile device.
- The Push to Autodesk Docs feature allows project members to upload drawing layouts from multiple drawings to an Autodesk Docs project as a PDF. This enables team members to view the digital PDFs of drawings while they are in the field.
- Trace provides a safe space to add changes to a drawing in the web and mobile apps without altering the base drawing. Traces are created in the web and mobile app interface and then saved on the cloud to be shared with other collaborators on the team.
- DWG Compare provides a way to quickly highlight the differences between two versions of the same drawing file or two different drawing files.

About the Data Manager

When you add items to a P&ID or to a 3D model, you are not just adding graphics to a drawing. Each item added to a drawing can contain properties in addition to the graphical symbol in the drawing screen. The Data Manager provides a database view into your project and the data in the project. You can access the Data Manager using the Reports command in the Project Manager. You can also access the Data Manager by right-clicking on the P&ID Drawings node or AutoCAD Plant 3D Drawings node in the Project Manager and clicking Data Manager, as shown in the following illustration.

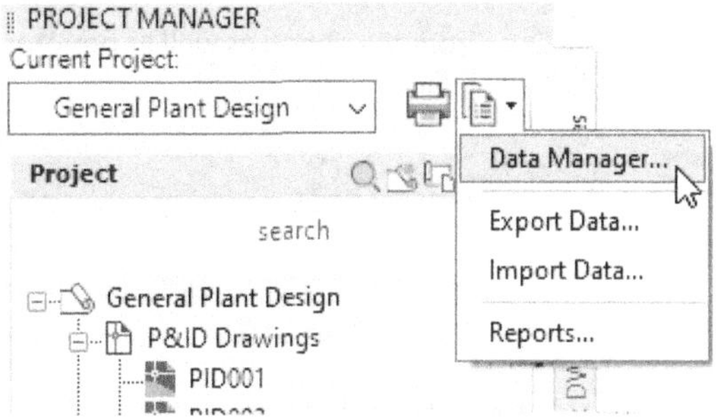

You use the Data Manager to create reports and import/output from your project data. You can also change the data in the drawing by entering required values in the Data Manager.

As shown in the following illustration, the Data Manager information can be filtered to present:

- Current Drawing Data
- P&ID Project Data or Plant 3D Project Data (varies depending on the selected drawing type)
- Project Reports

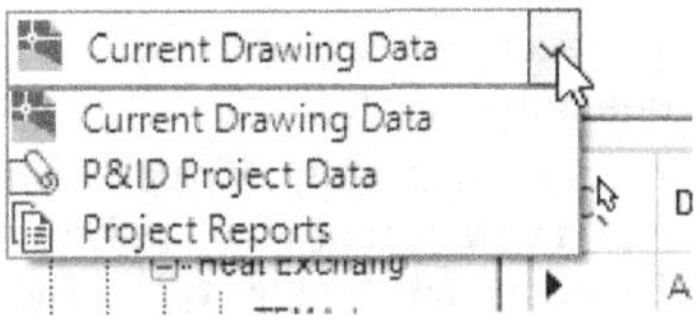

Data Manager with a P&ID drawing open

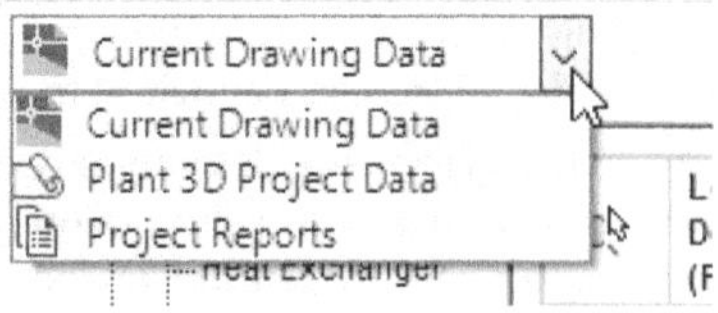

Data Manager with a Plant 3D drawing open

Exercise: Work in a Project

In this exercise, you open a project and examine the various settings and data in the project. You then explore project-wide options, and drawing-specific settings.

Import a Project

In this section of the exercise, you open a project and examine the various settings of the drawings and data in the project.

1. Start the AutoCAD Plant 3D software.
2. In the Project Manager, for Current Project, click Open.

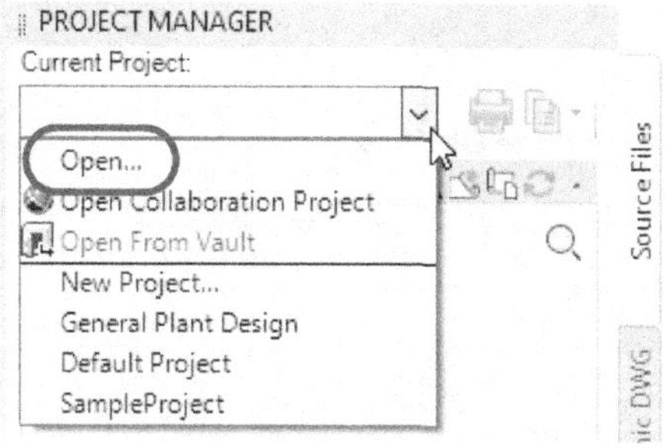

3. Set General Plant Design as the current project as follows:
   - In the Open dialog box, navigate to the folder *C:\Plant Design 2024 Practice Files\General Plant Design*.
   - Select the file *Project.xml*.
   - Click Open.
4. On the Source Files tab, expand P&ID Drawings on the Project panel. Double-click on PID001 drawing to open it. Save it.

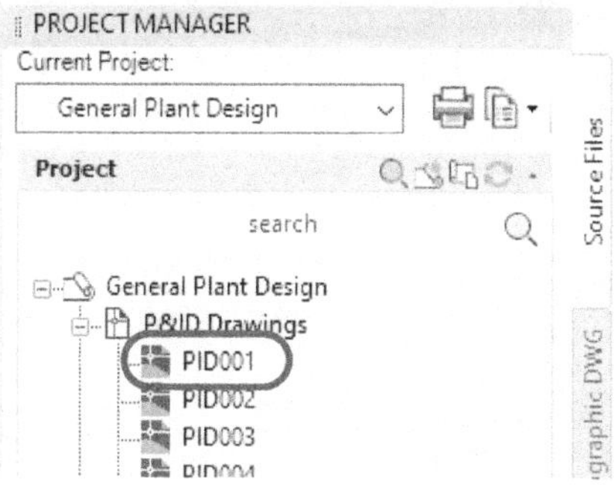

5. In the lower section of the Project Manager, examine the details of the drawing. The Details button should be selected.

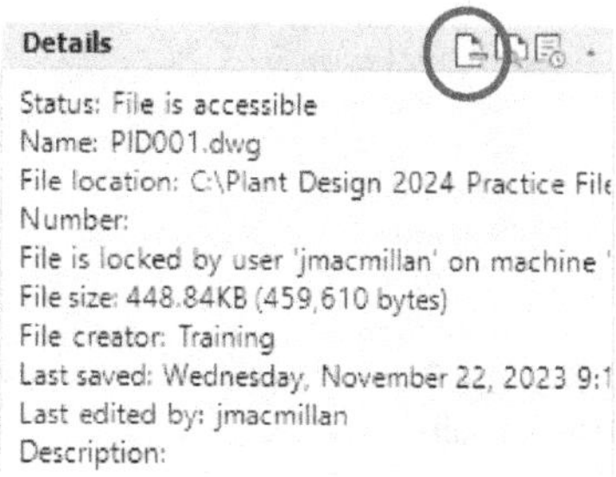

6. Click Preview to preview the drawing.

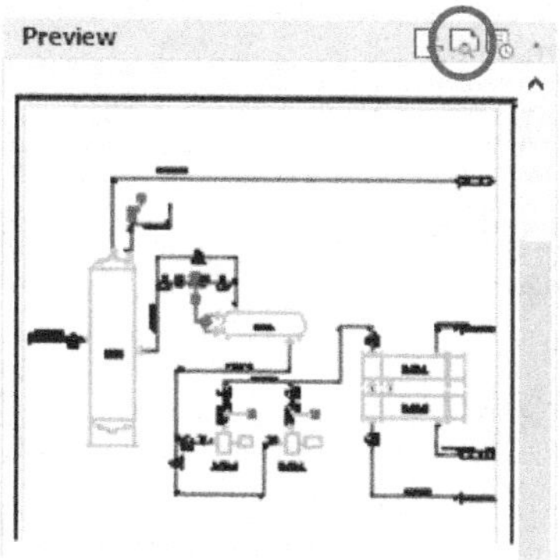

7. Click Work History to view the history of the drawing.

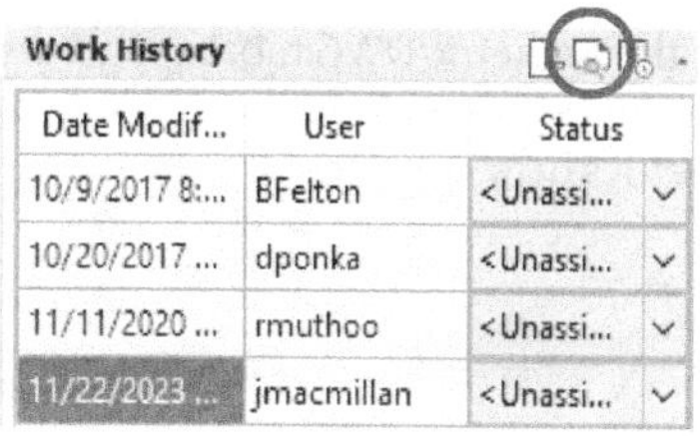

8. In the Search bar, type 004 and press <Enter>. Note that PID004 is displayed and all other drawings are hidden.

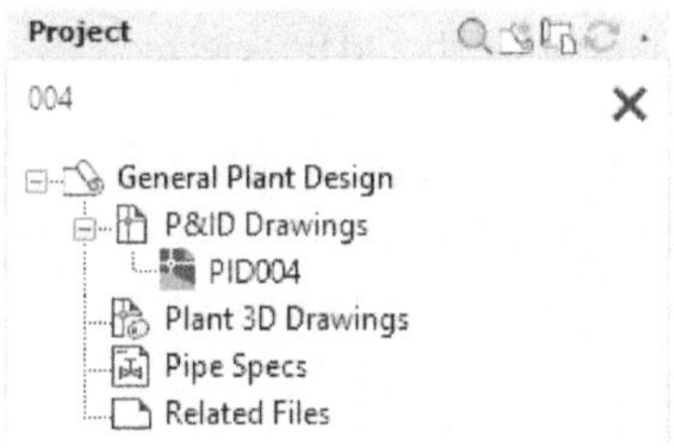

9. Click **X** in the Search bar to clear the search and display all drawings.

10. On the right side of the Project Manager, click the Orthographic DWG tab. Expand the nodes in the Orthos panel to examine the Ortho data.

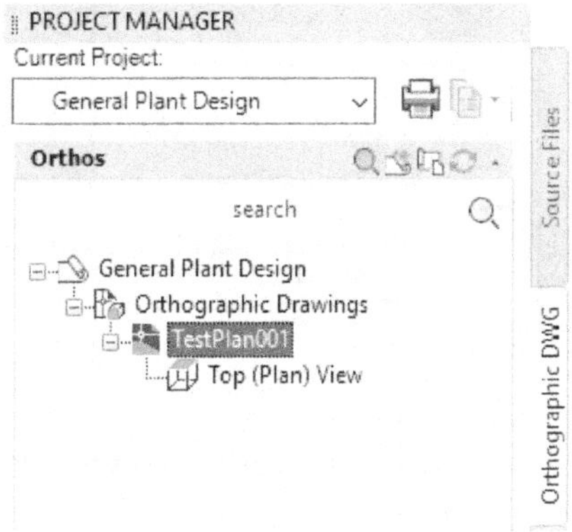

11. Click the Isometric DWG tab. Expand the nodes in the Isometrics panel to examine the Isometrics data.

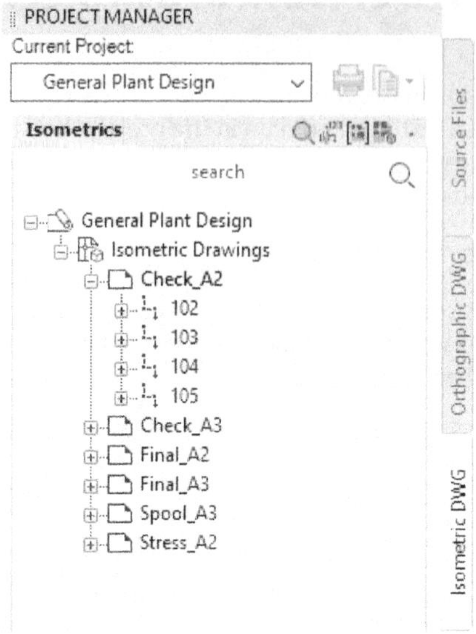

Project-Wide Options

1. In the Project Manager, for Current Project, click New Project to start the Project Setup Wizard.

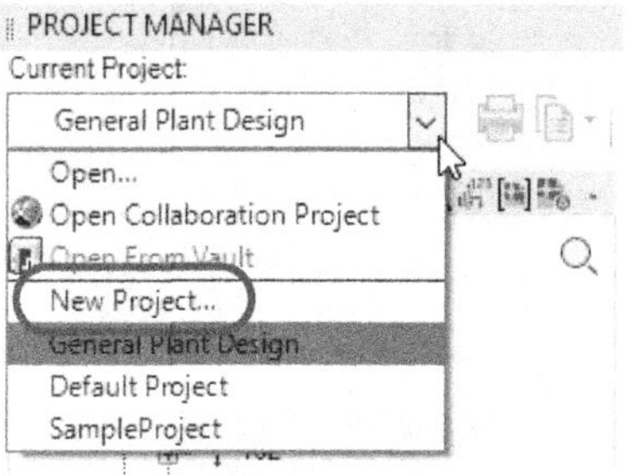

2. Examine the general settings available on the first page of the wizard.

3. Click Cancel. Click Yes. You do not create a new project in this exercise.

4. In the Project Manager, right-click on General Plant Design. Click Project Setup.

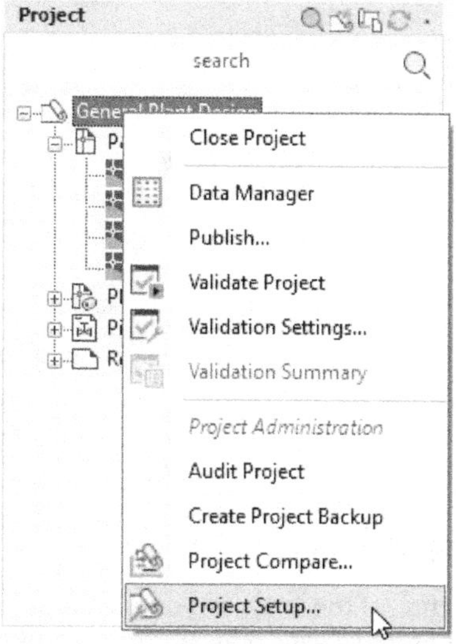

5. In the Project Setup dialog box, examine the settings and options available for the Project Details. When finished, click Cancel.

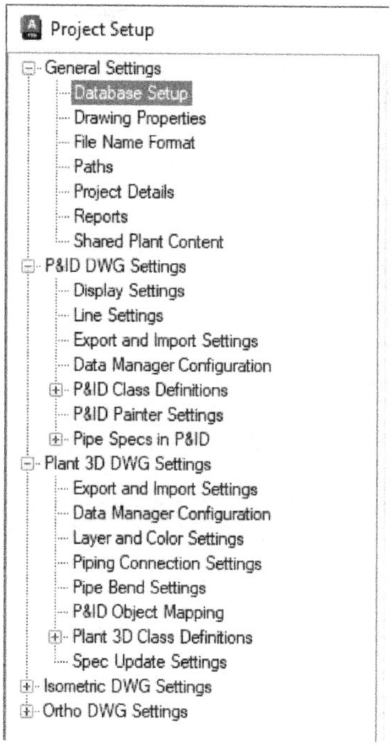

6. In the Project Manager, right-click on General Plant Design. Click Validation Settings.

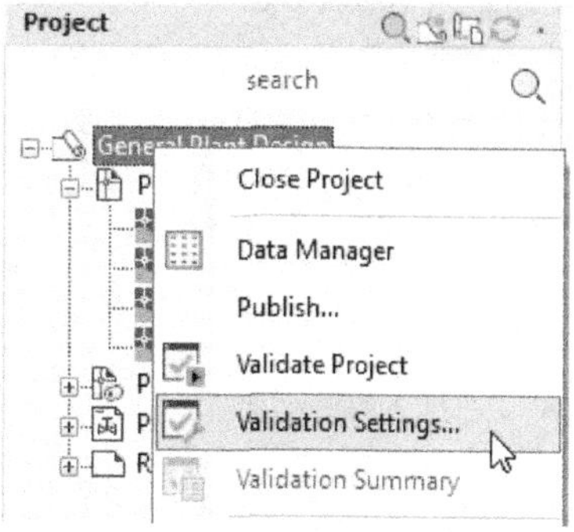

7. In the P&ID Validation Settings dialog box, select some of the error reporting conditions and review the descriptions. When finished, click Cancel.

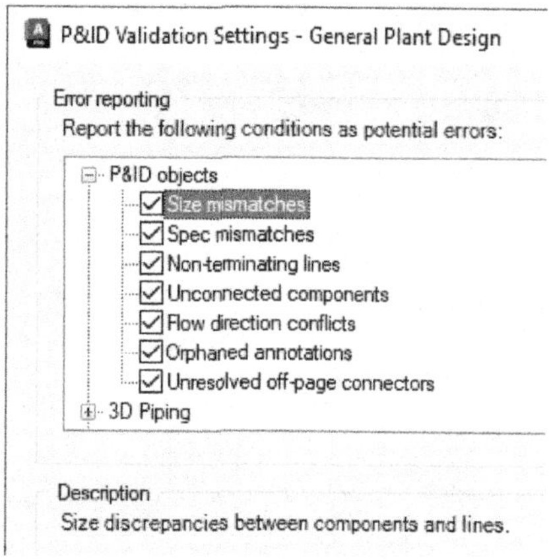

8. At the top of the Project Manager, in the Reports drop-down list, click Data Manager. The Data Manager that opens gives access to the database that is behind the drawings.

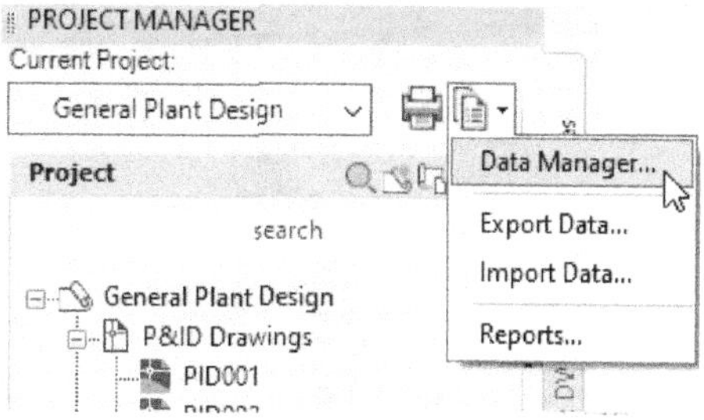

9. Examine the data in the Data Manager.

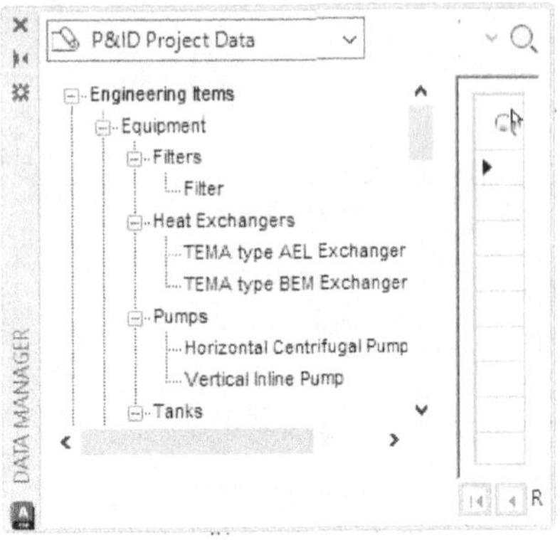

10. Close the Data Manager.

11. At the top of the Project Manager, under Reports, click Export Data. In the Export Report Data dialog box, examine the Reports available.

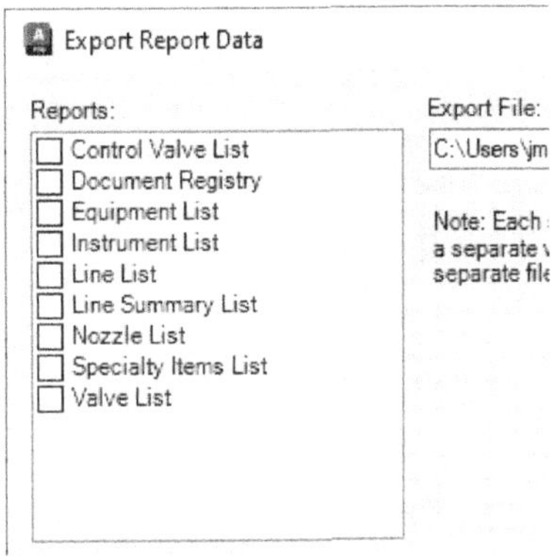

12. Click Cancel to close the Export Report Data dialog box.

13. At the top of the Project Manager, under Reports, click Reports. From the Project Reports list, select Equipment List. Examine the report data.

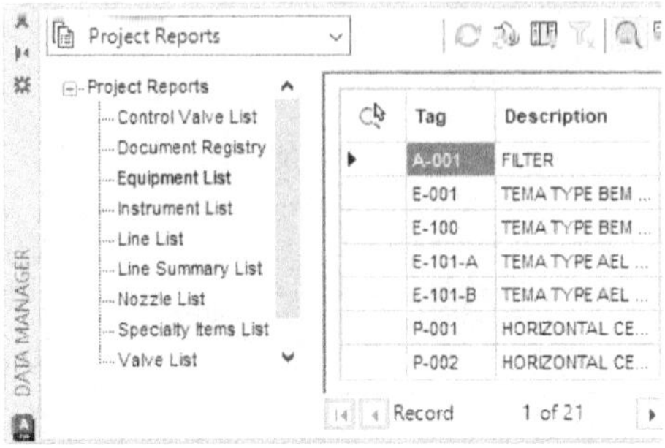

14. Close the Data Manager.

Drawing Options

In this section of the exercise, you examine settings and options for specific drawings in the project.

1. In the Project Manager, click the Source Files tab, if required.

2. Expand Plant 3D Drawings. Right-click on the Structures drawing. Click Properties.

3. Examine the Drawing Properties dialog box. When finished, click Cancel.

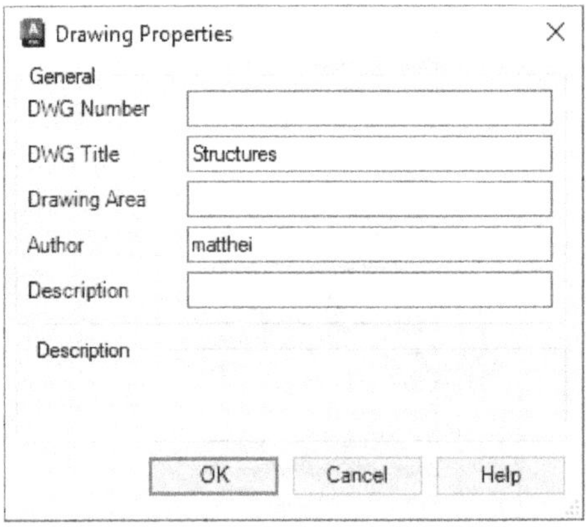

4. Right-click on the Structures drawing. Click Data Manager. The drawing is opened and the Data Manager is displayed. This is a filtered version of the Data Manager that shows only data from this specific drawing, and not the entire project.

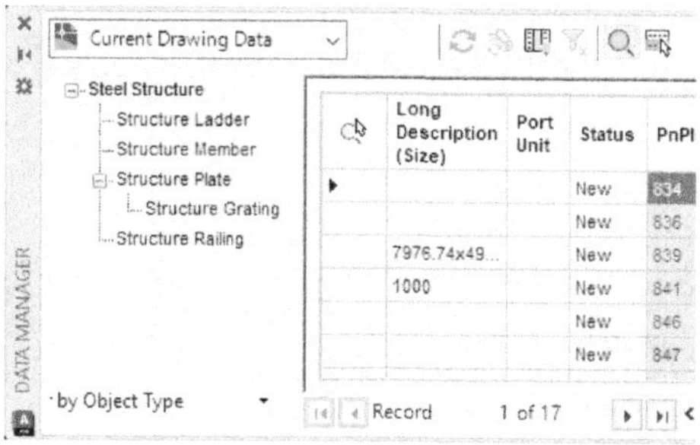

5. Close the Data Manager.

6. In the File tabs bar, click the X adjacent to the Structures name to close the Structures drawing without saving. If you are prompted to save changes, click No.

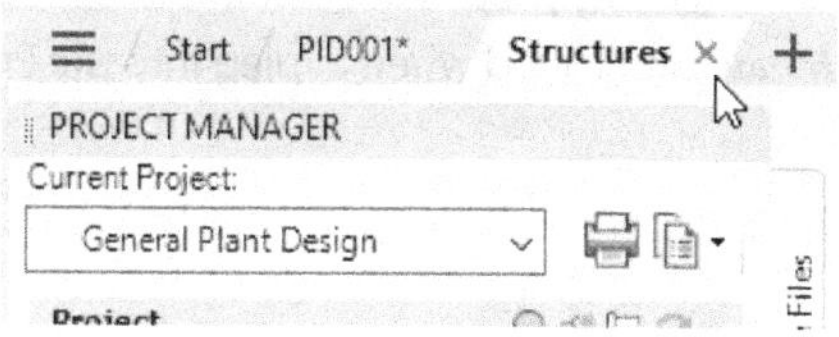

Lesson Review Questions

1. An AutoCAD Plant 3D project only consists of DWG files.
   a. True
   b. False
2. What are the types of 2D drawings generated from the 3D model? (Select all that apply.)
   a. Orthographic
   b. Process flow diagrams
   c. Isometric
   d. P&IDs
3. You can add and edit data fields in the Data Manager.
   a. True
   b. False
4. Which of the following statements are true regarding data organization for your projects? (Select all that apply.)
   a. Data for a project is organized in a set of system-defined folders.
   b. Drawings that are stored outside the project folder structure cannot be copied into the project.
   c. Drawings that are copied into a project are included in the project's folder path.
   d. Drawings that already exist in the project folder are duplicated when copied into the Project Manager.

Lesson: Opening a Drawing

Overview

When you are working in Windows applications, such as the AutoCAD P&ID software and the AutoCAD Plant 3D software, there are many different ways to open files. While there are multiple ways in which you can open a drawing file, the best way to access drawings is through the Project Manager. To realize the full benefit of projects and the Project Manager, you must know how to open drawings in the context of the project and from inside the Project Manager, as shown in the following illustration.

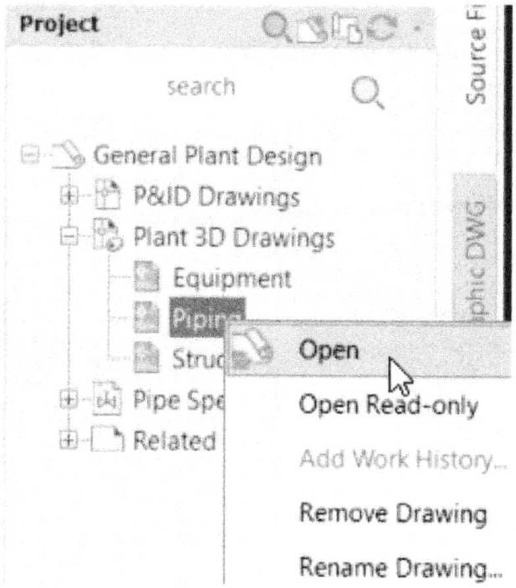

Objective

After completing this lesson, you will be able to:

- Describe how the AutoCAD P&ID software and the AutoCAD Plant 3D software work with drawings.

Opening Drawings

The best way to access the project and the drawings in the AutoCAD P&ID software or the AutoCAD Plant 3D software is through the Project Manager.

As shown in the following illustrations of the Project Manager, you open the drawings in the Project pane by:

- Using the shortcut menu.
- Double-clicking the drawing.

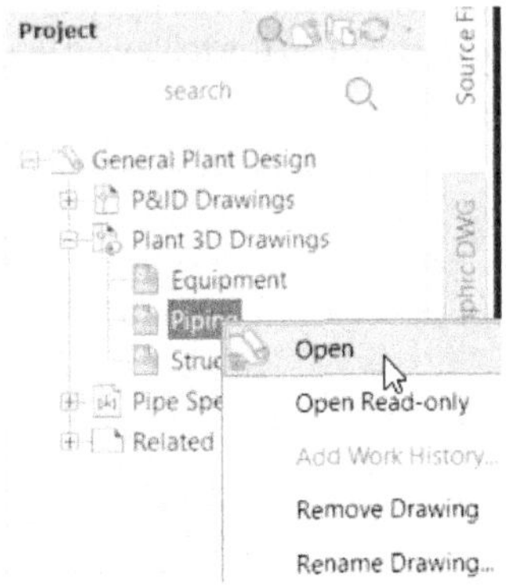

Right-click

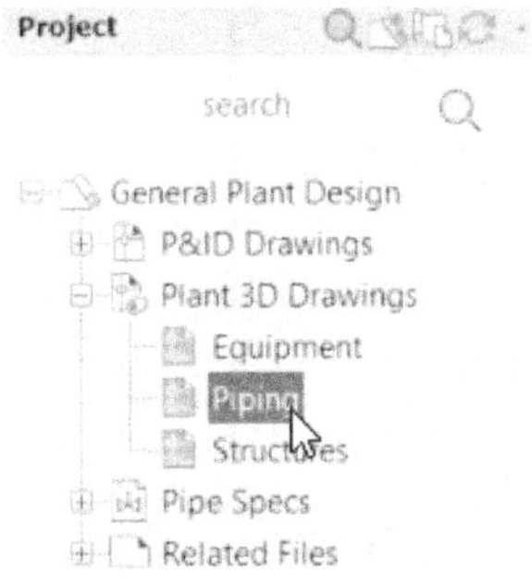

Double-click

Drawing History

If the project has been set up to prompt for work history when you open a project, a dialog box opens when the drawing is open in the editor to enable you to enter work history information, as shown in the following illustration.

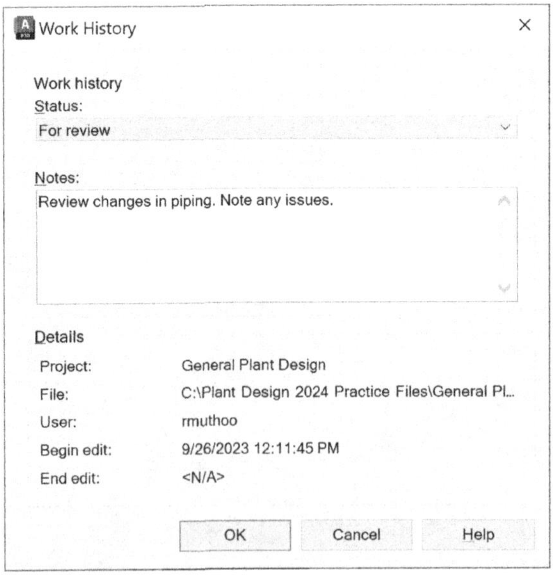

Renaming Drawings

Drawings can be renamed from the Project Manager. To do so, right-click on the drawing in the Project Manager and click Rename Drawing. The Rename DWG dialog box opens and you enter the new name. After clicking OK, the new name is displayed in the Project Manager and the file in the project is also renamed.

Access to renaming drawings from the Project Manager is shown in the following illustration.

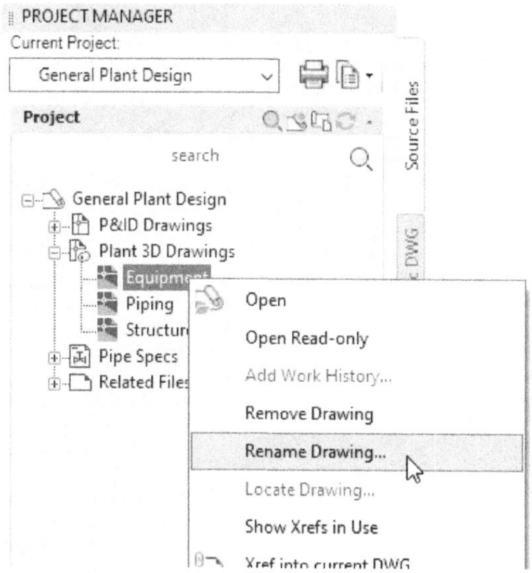

A drawing being renamed in the Rename DWG dialog box is shown in the following illustration.

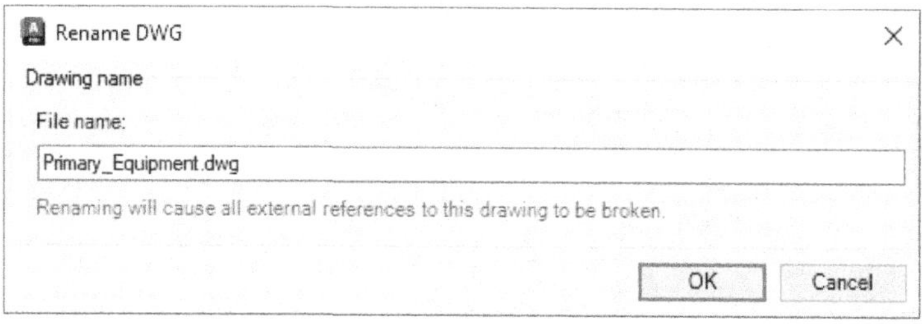

Removing Drawings

Drawings can be removed from a project using the Project Manager. To do so, right-click on the drawing in the Project Manager and click Remove Drawing. The Remove Drawing From Project dialog box opens. Click Remove the Drawing from this Project to confirm the removal of the drawing from the project. When removed, the drawing is not deleted or removed from the project folder. It is only removed from the project.

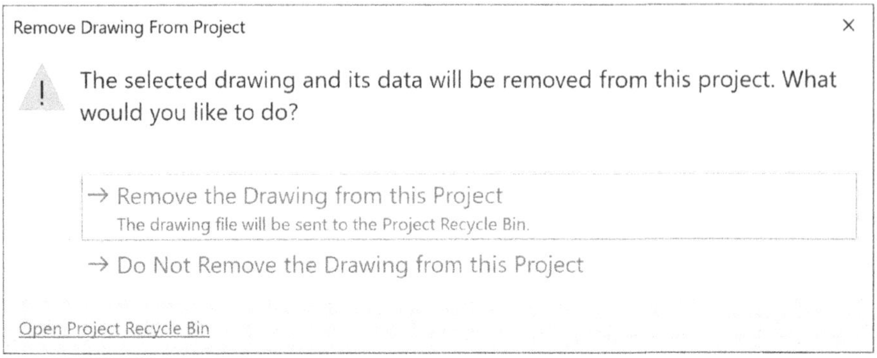

Exercise: Open a Drawing in AutoCAD Plant 3D

In this exercise, you open and close drawings in the AutoCAD Plant 3D software using various tools and options.

1. Start the AutoCAD Plant 3D software, if not already running.

2. Set General Plant Design as the current project as follows (if not already set):
   - In the Project Manager, Current Project list, click Open.
   - In the Open dialog box, navigate to the folder *C:\Plant Design 2024 Practice Files\General Plant Design*.
   - Select the file *Project.xml*.
   - Click Open.

3. Under P&ID Drawings, right-click on the PID001 drawing. Click Open. (You might have the drawing file already open.)

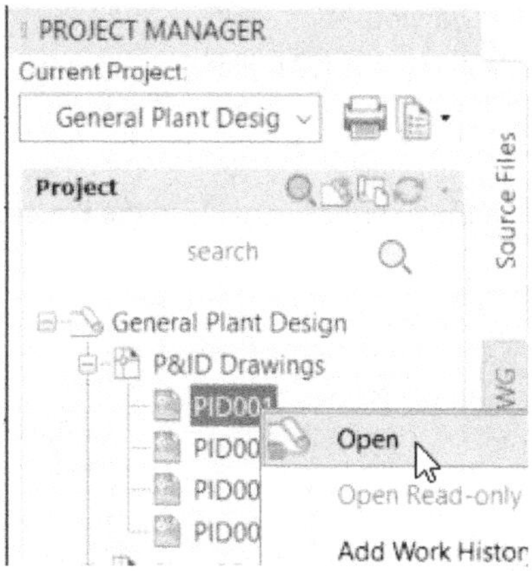

4. To close the PID001 drawing without closing the AutoCAD Plant 3D software, in the drawing window, click X (Close) in the top right corner of the drawing or click X with the PID001 filename in the File tabs bar. If you are prompted to save changes, click No.

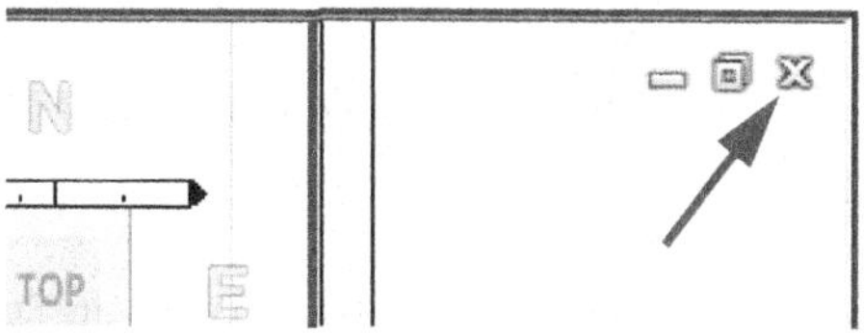

5. You can open a drawing by double-clicking the drawing in the Project Manager. Under Plant 3D Drawings, double-click on the Equipment drawing.

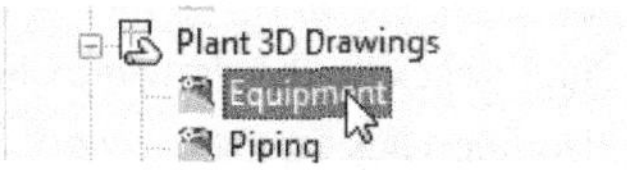

6. You can open multiple drawings. With the Equipment drawing still open, in the Project Manager, double-click on the Structures drawing.

7. You can switch between open drawings by selecting the drawing tabs above the Project Manager. In the tabs bar, select the Equipment tab to return to this drawing.

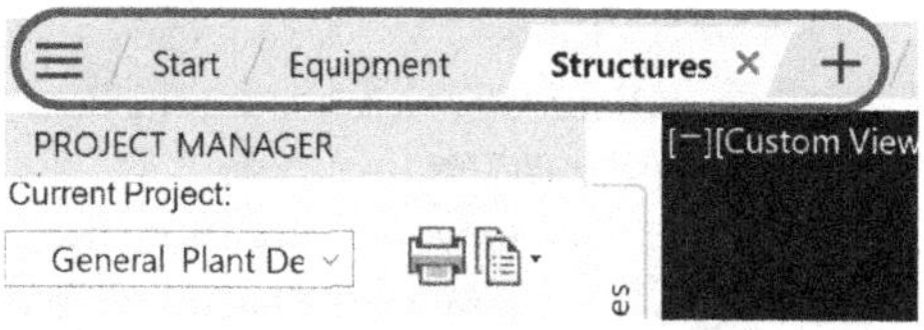

8. To close the Equipment drawing, click X (Close) on the Equipment tab. If you are prompted to save changes, click No.

9. Another option to close drawings is to use the Application menu () in the upper-left corner of the AutoCAD Plant 3D software. In the menu, hover the cursor over Close. This gives you the option to close either the current drawing or all drawings. Click All Drawings to close all the open drawings.

Lesson Review Questions

1. After you add a drawing to the project, it should only be opened using the Project Manager.
   a. True
   b. False
2. The AutoCAD Plant 3D software keeps a history of all the times a drawing has been opened and saved in a single session.
   a. True
   b. False
3. What are the ways a drawing can be opened from the Project Manager? (Select all that apply.)
   a. Select the drawing and enter O for Open.
   b. Right-click on the drawing. Click Open.
   c. Double-click on the drawing.
   d. Select the drawing and double-click on the drawing in the preview window.
4. What are the ways in which a drawing can be closed? (Select all that apply.)
   a. Click Close (X) in the program's Title Bar.
   b. Click Close (X) in the drawing's working window.
   c. Click Close (X) in the drawing's tab.
   d. In the Application menu, under Close, click Current Drawing.
5. You can have multiple drawings open at the same time in the AutoCAD Plant 3D software.
   a. True
   b. False
6. What happens if you use the Remove Drawing shortcut menu option on a file in the Project Manager tree?
   a. You remove the file from the project, but the file stays where it is on the drive.
   b. You remove the file from the project and the file is deleted from the drive.

Lesson: Exploring the User Interface

Overview

In this lesson, you learn how the AutoCAD Plant 3D commands are integrated into the standard AutoCAD user interface. The AutoCAD Plant 3D software is built on AutoCAD, and uses AutoCAD commands as a basis, with some AutoCAD Plant 3D commands added to the ribbon menus, Properties palette, and shortcut menus. The approach is the same for both the P&ID and the 3D parts of the AutoCAD Plant 3D software. Some of the commands are for different types of items, whether they are in 2D or 3D. You can use the Workspace command to set which commands you want to use.

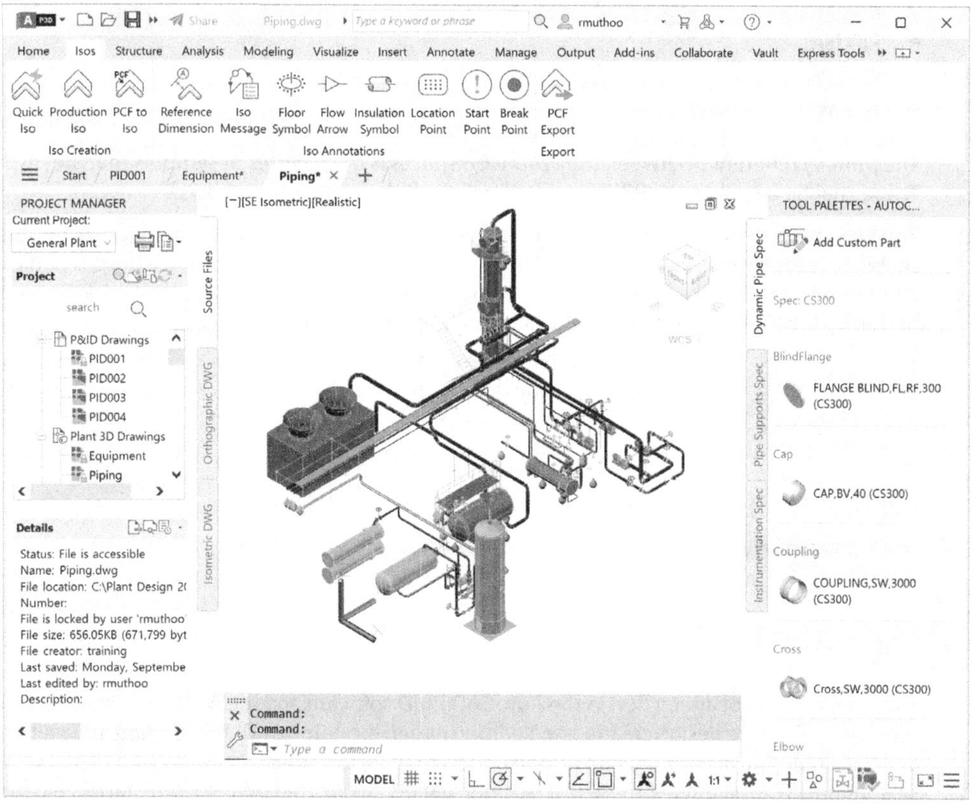

Objectives

After completing this lesson, you will be able to:

- Identify how different workspaces are organized.
- Explain how ribbons integrate AutoCAD Plant 3D and standard AutoCAD commands.
- Describe how tool palettes are organized.
- State the data that is added to the Properties palette.
- Describe on-screen tools added to the AutoCAD Plant 3D software.

Task-Specific Workspaces

In this section of the lesson, you explore how workspaces are integrated in the AutoCAD P&ID software and the AutoCAD Plant 3D software.

Workspaces Defined

The Workspace command enables you to set up and customize sets of commands so that they arrange the interface to meet your needs. The AutoCAD P&ID software and the AutoCAD Plant 3D software adds several new workspaces to the standard AutoCAD software:

- 3D Piping
- PID PIP
- PID ISO
- PID ISA
- PID DIN
- PID JIS-ISO

The primary difference between the P&ID workspaces is the palettes of symbols that are displayed. These change based on the P&ID standard on which the workspace is based.

You change the workspace using the Workspace Switching command on the AutoCAD status bar, as shown in the following illustration. Clicking on the arrow opens the Workspace drop-down list where you can select the workspace as required. Alternatively, you can customize the Quick Access toolbar to display the Workspace drop-down list and use this to assign the workspace.

Task-Specific Ribbons

The main method of interaction in the AutoCAD P&ID software and the AutoCAD Plant 3D software is the ribbon. To make design creation and editing easier, the commands for creating and editing a P&ID or 3D plant design are arranged in ribbon panels that are grouped by task, as shown in the following illustrations. The majority of these task-specific panels are located on the Home tab. The panels displayed on the Home tab vary based on the active workspace.

P&ID Home Tab (split for improved clarity)

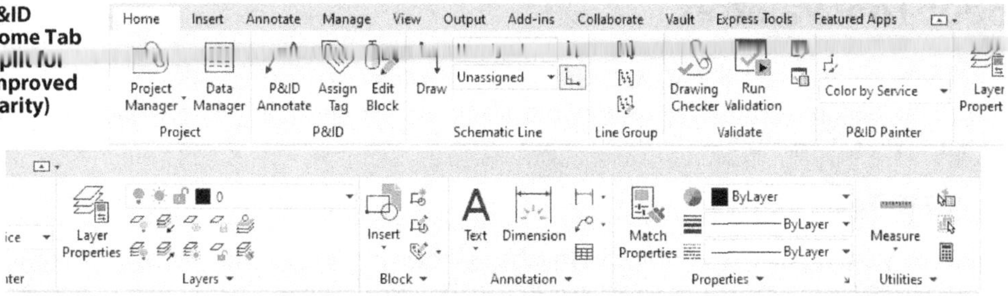

3D Piping Home Tab (split for improved clarity)

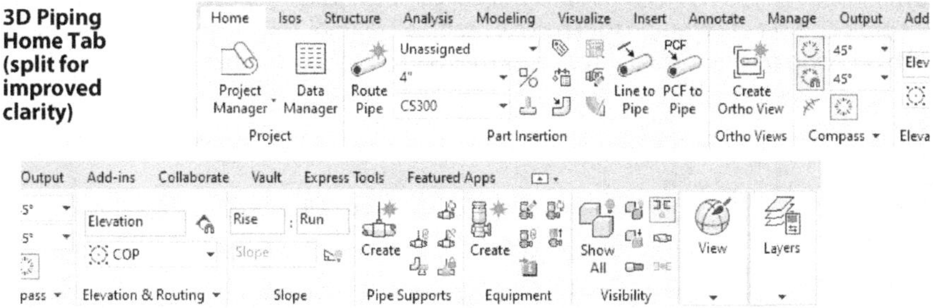

Isos and Structure Tabs

When the 3D Piping workspace is active, in addition to the panels on the Home tab, you can access the Isos tab and the Structure tab, as shown in the following illustration. The Isos tab contains commands dealing with isometric generation. The Structure tab has commands dealing with structural part generation in the 3D model space.

Isos Tab

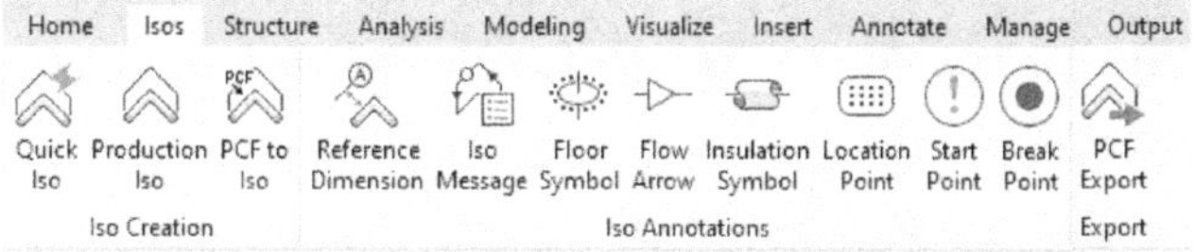

Structure Tab (split for improved clarity)

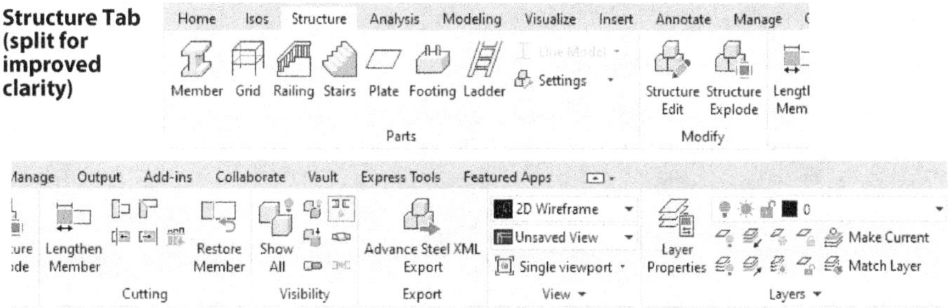

> You can drag a panel out of the ribbon and place it anywhere on the screen. This enables you to have the commands on that panel available, even though you might click on another tab on the ribbon.
>
> There are additional context tabs that appear when you are in an orthographic drawing.

About Tool Palettes

Tool palettes in the AutoCAD P&ID software and the AutoCAD Plant 3D software contain items specific to the workspace you are working in. The differences between the P&ID workspaces are primarily in the symbols available on the tool palettes.

P&ID Tool Palettes

The P&ID tool palettes are divided into tabs, as shown in the following illustration. The symbols on each tab are grouped to be similar in layout to the class definitions in the project setup. Additional custom symbols that are created for use in a project can be added to these palettes. In addition, in a multi-user project, a set of common tool palettes can be created. You change the palette that is displayed by clicking on the tool palettes properties and selecting another palette.

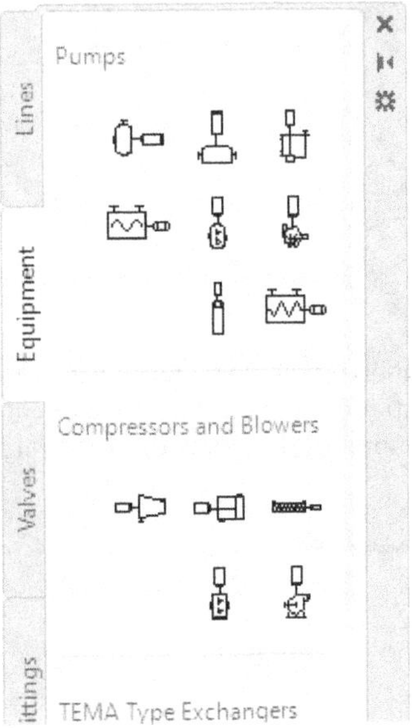

3D Tool Palettes

In the 3D Piping workspace, the Tool Palette is divided into three tabs: Dynamic Pipe Spec, Pipe Support Spec, and Instrumentation Spec as shown in the following illustration. Each tab contains a selection of items for the active specification. The Dynamic Pipe Specification tab contains specific information for the current pipe specification. The current pipe specification can be assigned using the Spec Selector list on the Part Insertion panel on the Home tab. To view the spec in more detail, click the Spec Viewer command on the Part Insertion panel. Once selected, the Pipe Spec Viewer Tool Palette is populated with the components in that specification.

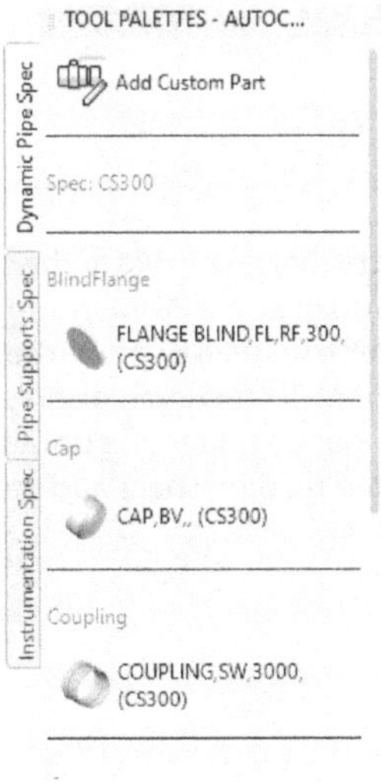

Changing Tool Palettes

You can switch between the tool palettes by right-clicking on the title bar, and selecting the tool palette from the menu, as shown in the following illustration. While you can switch to a different palette at any time, you typically do so if you switch from working on a P&ID to working on a 3D model. In this case, the tool palettes automatically change when you switch workspaces. Switching to a different standard in the same P&ID is not typically done nor required.

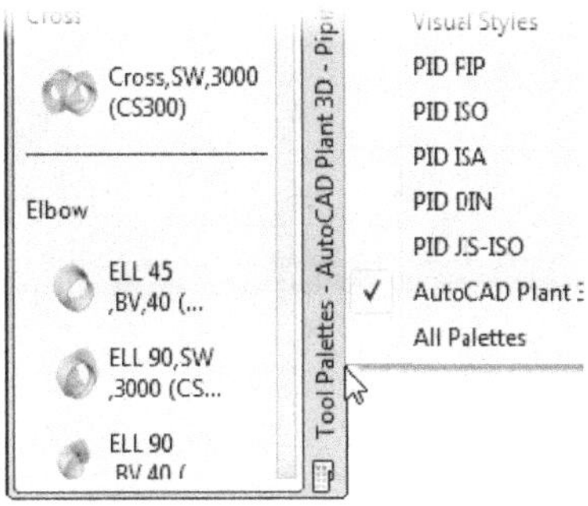

You can customize the tool palettes using standard AutoCAD customization commands.

About the Properties Palette

The Properties palette is a useful tool for viewing and changing properties of items that you select in the drawing. It is recommended that you leave the Properties palette open and docked, so that as you work with items you can view and access the properties of those items.

Accessing the Properties Palette

To access the Properties palette:

- Double-click on the item.
- Right-click on the item. Click Properties.
- Enter Properties in the command line.
- Press <Ctrl>+1.

The AutoCAD Plant 3D software adds a section to the Properties palette that is specific to the selected item, as shown in the following illustration. For example, if you are working on a P&ID and select a valve, a P&ID section is displayed at the bottom of the Properties palette with P&ID properties. If you are working on a 3D piping drawing and select a valve, an AutoCAD Plant 3D section is displayed with 3D properties of that object. The AutoCAD Plant 3D list of properties can be quite long because a lot of properties are involved with the 3D model, including but not limited to, pipe specs and part geometry.

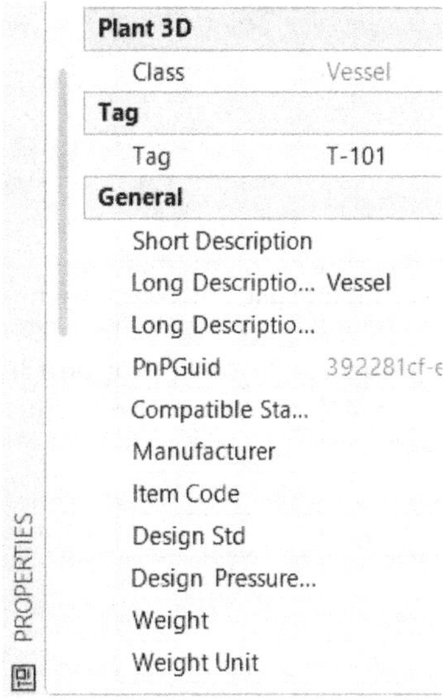

On-Screen Tools

The following commands and options are available when you select or hover over an item in the drawing window. These options vary based on the drawing type and item selected.

Grips

A single click on an item in the drawing window selects the item and displays any grips that are applicable to it. These grips enable you to modify the item in specific ways. Following is a partial list of some of the AutoCAD Plant 3D-specific grips available, depending on what item you have selected:

- Continuation grip
- Endline grip
- Substitution grip
- Add nozzle

> Refer to AutoCAD Plant 3D Help topics for a more comprehensive list and explanation of grips.

Examples of grips are shown in the following illustration.

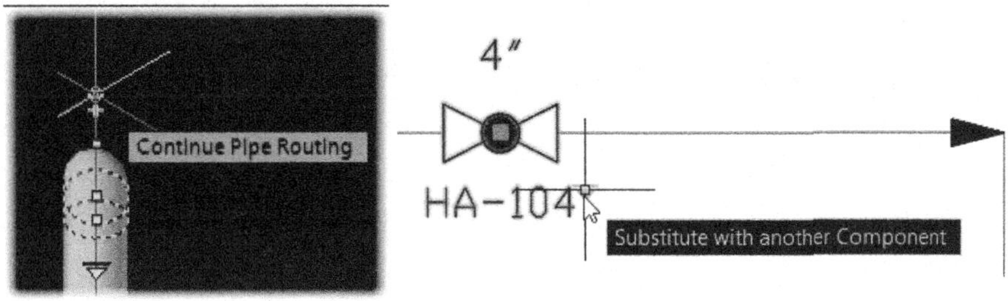

Shortcut Menus

Right-clicking an object displays an item-specific menu, as shown in the following illustration. This menu has the standard AutoCAD items, as well as additional AutoCAD Plant 3D menu items relevant to the selected object. Because these menus vary based on the drawing type and item selected, you can use this menu as a shortcut to the menu item you need.

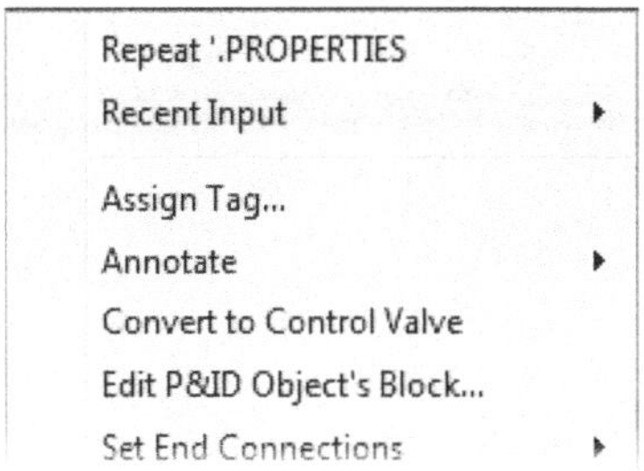

2D Grid and Snaps

It is strongly recommended that you use the standard grid/snaps in P&ID at all times. This assists in lining up items and making sure the layout is spread out and organized in a standard manner. If your P&ID is imperial, the industry standard snap spacing is 1/8". It can be helpful to first layout equipment on a 1/4" grid, and position text on a 1/16" grid. These options are available in the Status bar.

Object Snaps

While the use of object snaps is nothing new, one thing you might find different is that the node and near object snaps are enabled by default in the AutoCAD Plant 3D software. These object snaps are on by default because of their benefit in connecting a pipe to an existing one, connecting to nozzles, or positioning piping components on a pipe.

Exercise: Explore the User Interface

In this exercise, you explore the various commands that have been added to the AutoCAD software as part of the AutoCAD Plant 3D software. You examine tool palettes, ribbons, the Properties palette, and on-screen tools.

Tool Palettes and Ribbons

In this section of the exercise, you explore workspaces, tool palettes, and ribbons.

1. Start the AutoCAD Plant 3D software, if not already running.
2. Set General Plant Design as the current project as follows (if not already set):
   - In the Project Manager, Current Project list, click Open.
   - In the Open dialog box, navigate to the folder *C:\Plant Design2024 Practice Files\General Plant Design*.
   - Select the file *Project.xml*.
   - Click Open.
3. In the Project Manager, double-click on the PID001 drawing to open it (expand P&ID Drawings).

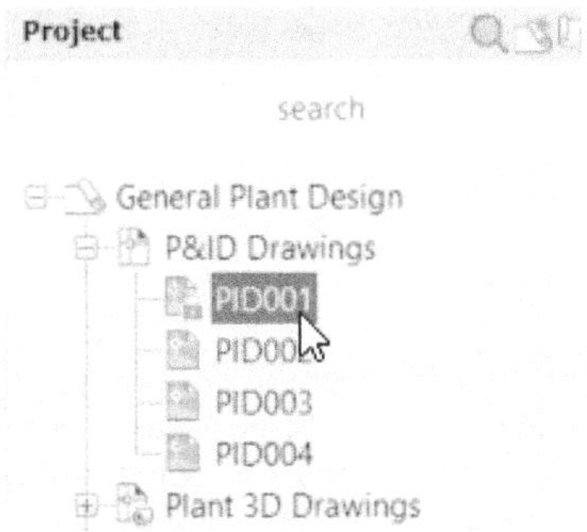

4. One of the first things you note is the tool palettes and ribbon layout. Examine the tool palette. Note that the AutoCAD Plant 3D software opens a workspace, tool palette, and ribbon for 3D design.

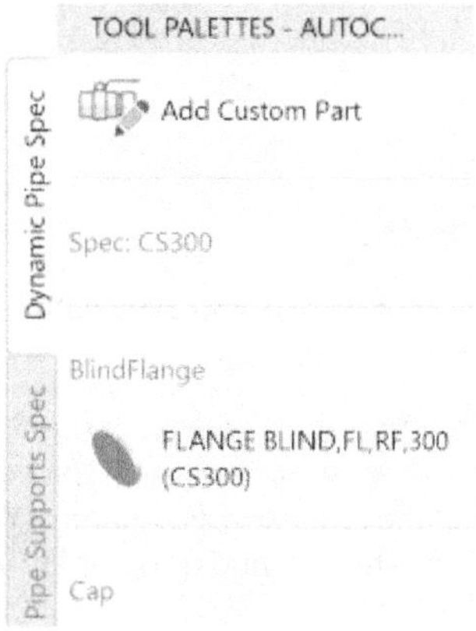

5. Examine the ribbon layout.

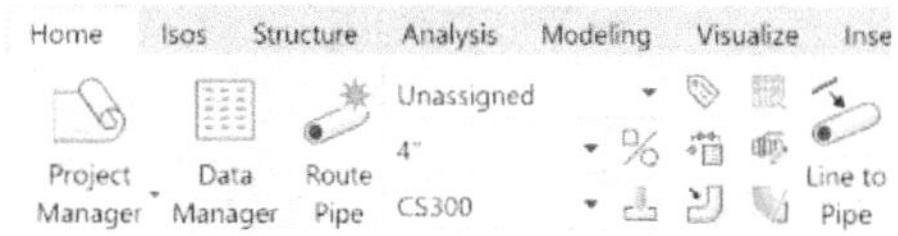

6. On the status bar, click Workspace Switching.

7. Select PID PIP, which is the P&ID PIP workspace.

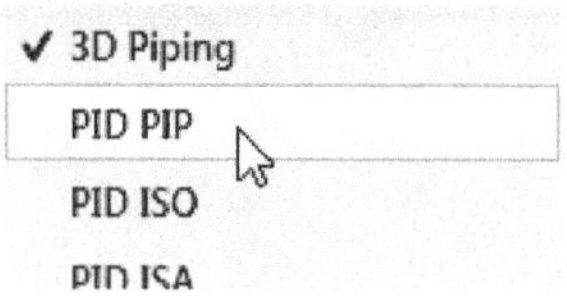

Alternatively, you can customize the Quick Access toolbar to display the Workspace drop-down list and use this to assign the workspace.

8. Examine the changes on the tool palettes and ribbon.

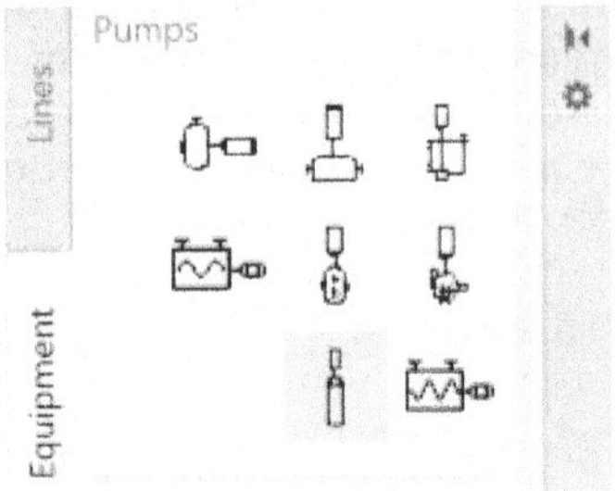

Properties Palette

In this section of the exercise, you view data for objects in the Properties palette.

1. To open the Properties palette, in the drawing window, double-click on the vessel as shown in the following illustration. (You can toggle off the drawing grid display in the Status bar.)

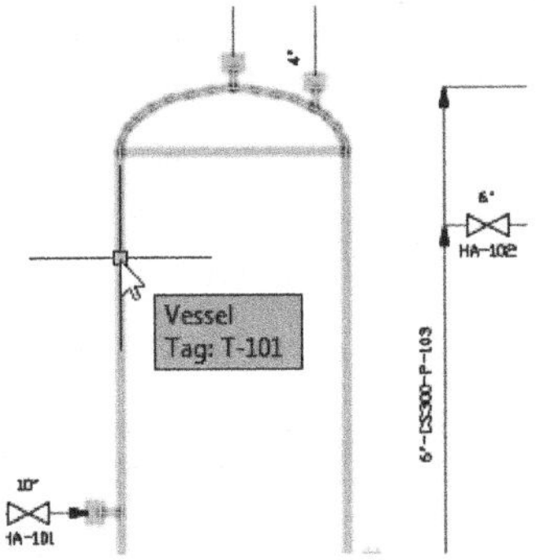

2. To dock the Properties palette, drag it to the side of the drawing window.

3. Examine the P&ID data that is specific to the vessel selected.

P&ID	
Class	Vessel
Tag	
Tag	T-101
Styles	
Graphical style	Vessel Style
General	
PnPGuid	bcc21ddf-ccf5-471e-b941...
Description	VESSEL
Manufacturer	
Model Number	

4. Select any other object in the drawing. Note that the data changes in the Properties palette to represent the object selected.

5. Press <Esc> to clear the selection.

On-Screen Tools

In this section of the exercise, you explore various tools that you access directly on the drawing screen.

1. Select the 4" valve as shown in the following illustration. Note the custom grips.

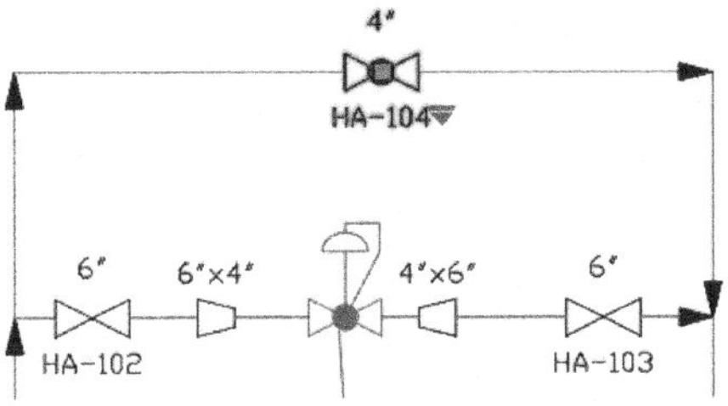

2. Hover the cursor over the arrow grip, as shown in the following illustration. Note that it is a Substitution grip. Click on this grip to display a component list. Here you can substitute this valve with another component. Do not make a change.

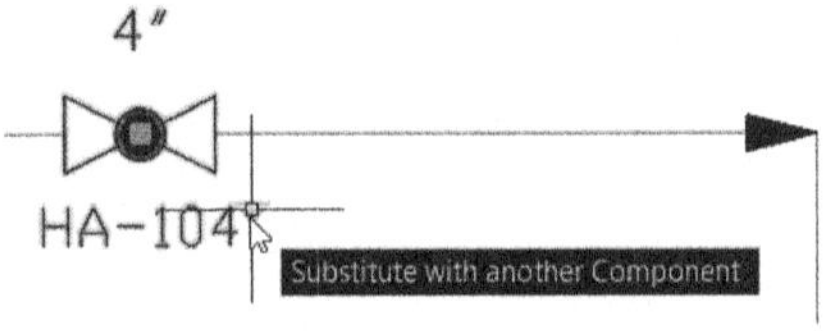

3. Click on the Move grip (square grip in the center of the circle) and drag the valve to another location on the line. Click to place it at the new location. This breaks the line at the new location.

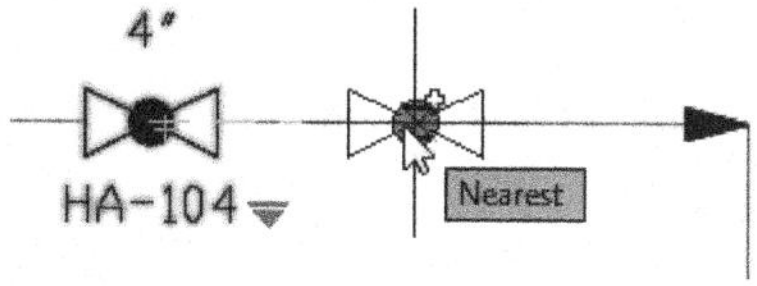

4. With the valve still selected, right-click and examine the P&ID-specific commands available on the context menu. Press <Esc> to close the menu.

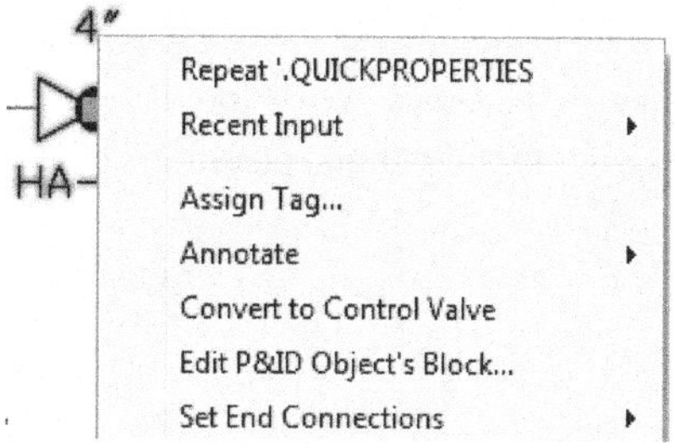

5. Hover over any object in the drawing to display a tooltip that provides information about that object, as shown in the following illustration. .

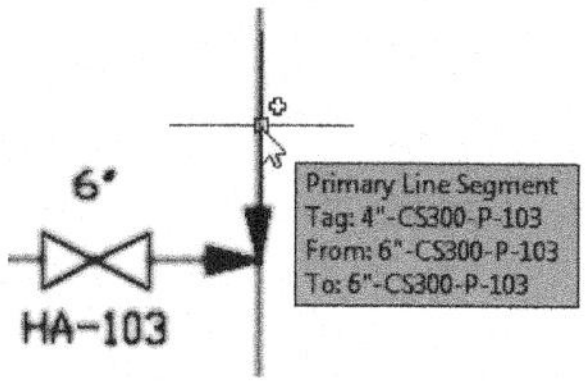

6. Save and close the drawings.

Lesson Review Questions

1. The AutoCAD Plant 3D software introduces a whole new interface to the AutoCAD software.
   a. True
   b. False
2. Tool palettes in the AutoCAD P&ID software and the AutoCAD Plant 3D software contain items specific to the workspace in which you are working.
   a. True
   b. False
3. Which of the following methods enables you to change the current tool palette that is active while remaining in the same workspace?
   a. Right-click on the item and click Properties.
   b. Right-click on the Tool Palette header and select a new tool palette.
   c. Click the Workspace Switching command in the Status Bar and select a new tool palette.
   d. Select a workspace from the Workspace drop-down in the Quick Access Toolbar.
4. What are the valid access points for commands and options for creating and editing objects in a drawing? (Select all that apply.)
   a. Properties palette
   b. Right-click shortcut menu
   c. Tool Palette
   d. Ribbon menu
5. Which of the following methods enables you to open the Properties palette? (Select all that apply.)
   a. Double-click on the item.
   b. Right-click on the item and click Properties.
   c. Enter properties at the command prompt with or without an item selected.
   d. Right-click on the drawing in the Project Manager and click Properties.

Lesson: Managing Layers and Colors

Overview

Layers and colors are an important part of efficiently managing and interacting with the plant design geometry. This lesson describes the layer palette and project setup options regarding layers and colors. This lesson also explains the basic philosophy behind layering in a P&ID drawing, 3D model, and 2D orthographic and isometric drawings.

Objective

After completing this lesson, you will be able to:

- Describe how layers are managed.

About Layers

Layers and colors in the AutoCAD Plant 3D software are organized using two separate methods:

- 2D drawings use predefined layers in templates.
- 3D drawings can generate layers automatically during the design process based on automation schemes.

Regardless of layer organization, it is recommended that you set the color of items to ByLayer. This has several advantages including ensuring that objects of a particular color can be operated on by all the options in the Layer palette.

2D Drawing Layers - P&IDs, Orthographic, and Isometrics

Layers in a 2D drawing are most closely associated with the organization, editing, and output of the drawing into a final form, such as a DWF, PDF, or hard copy. This means that the various objects on the drawing are organized into layers associated with that general class of item. You use colors to distinguish between the various objects so that you can tell each object at a glance. Depending on the plotting options selected (ctb or stb) the color is also used to determine the line thickness of the object on the output selected.

For example, on a P&ID drawing, you organize the instrumentation onto an instrumentation layer, the piping onto a piping layer, annotation onto an annotation layer, etc., as shown in the following illustration. On an isometric drawing, the geometry might be on different layers based on the size of the pipe or fitting or other special characteristics.

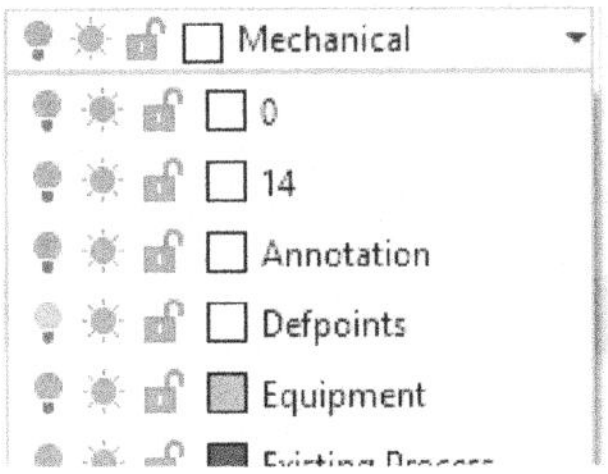

Layers in the 3D Model Files

In a 3D model file, layers are used to organize the various items in the model into easily manageable groups. This enables you to manipulate the model during the design process and to select items, such as piping, steel, or equipment, as required. Because every project in 3D is different, there are fewer set standards for 3D.

Most companies have standards for how they want designers to use the layers in 3D. Typical layer organization in 3D might be as follows:

- Every piece of equipment is on its own layer, named after the equipment number.
- The various types of structural steel have their own layers (stairs, supports, handrails), unless they are associated with a piece of equipment, in which case they are on a layer named after the equipment with the structure type appended to it; for example, P-100A_Supports.
- Piping is a special case. You can set up an Automated Layer and Color Scheme depending on your company standards. This enables you to automate the layers on which the piping and other inline objects are placed to meet company standards. A typical standard for piping might be to have the layer set to the line number, and the color of the layer set to the service of the line.

Access to the Layer and Color settings in the Project Setup dialog box is shown in the following illustration.

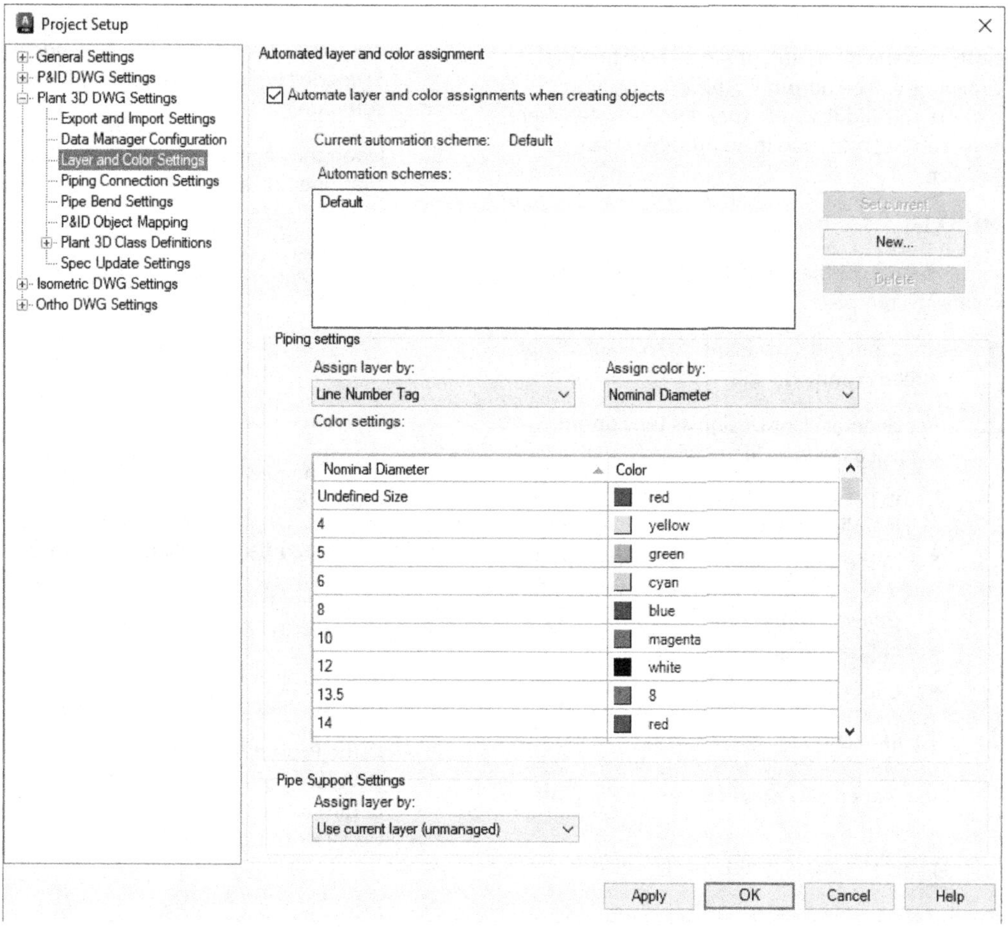

Exercise: Manage Layers and Colors

In the AutoCAD Plant 3D software, layers are used to both manage items and organize how the final drawings will be output. In this exercise, you explore the various areas that demonstrate where layers are set and used in an AutoCAD Plant 3D project.

P&ID Layers

In this section of the exercise, you explore P&ID layers in a template.

1. Start the AutoCAD Plant 3D software, if not already running.

2. Set General Plant Design as the current project as follows (if not already set):
   - In the Project Manager, Current Project list, click Open.
   - In the Open dialog box, navigate to the folder *C:\Plant Design 2024Practice Files\General Plant Design*.
   - Select the file *Project.xml*.
   - Click Open.

3. To open and examine the layers in a template drawing, click New in the Application Menu to create a new drawing using a template.

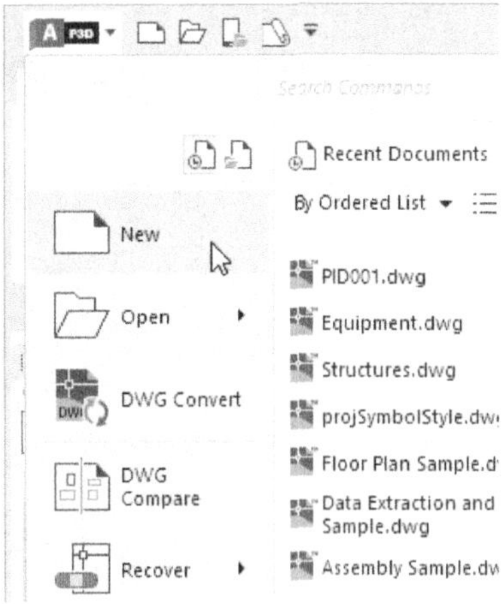

4. In the Select template dialog box, select and open the *PID ISO A1 - Color Dependent Plot Styles.dwt* which is available with the software.

5. Open the Layers Properties Manager. Examine the layers that are in this template.

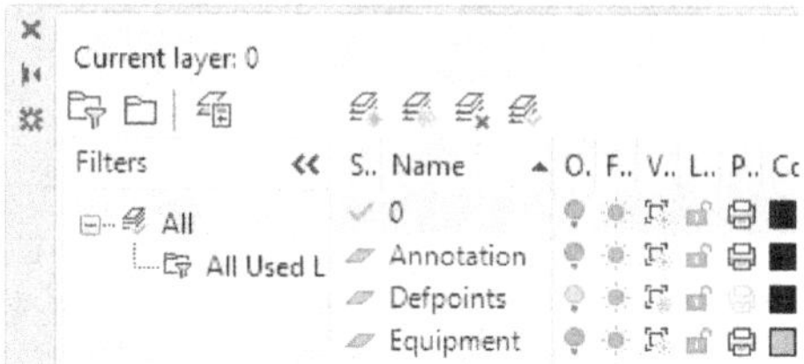

6. Close the new drawing and do not save if prompted.

P&ID Symbol Layer Management

In this section of the exercise, you explore how layers are used in P&ID symbol definitions.

1. In the Project Manager, right-click on the project name. Click Project Setup.

2. In the Project Setup dialog box, expand P&ID DWG Settings>P&ID Class Definitions> Engineering Items>Equipment>Blowers. Click Centrifugal Blower.

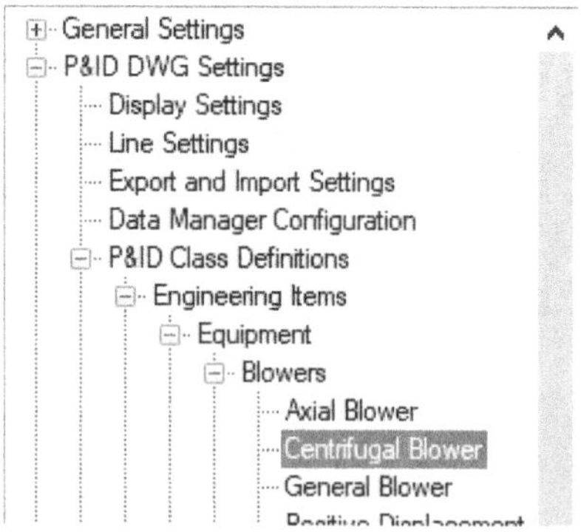

3. On the right hand pane of the dialog box, in Class settings: Centrifugal Blower, click Edit Symbol.

4. In the Symbol Settings dialog box, in the General Style Properties area, note that this symbol color is set to ByLayer, and the layer is set to Equipment.

General Style Properties	
Layer	Equipment
Color	☐ ByLayer
Linetype	———— ByBlock
Linetype Scale	---- Use Current ----
Plotstyle	ByColor
Line weight	---- Use Current ----

5. Explore the settings for some of the other symbols.

6. Close all open dialog boxes without making any changes.

3D Layers

In this section of the exercise, you explore layer settings in a 3D template.

1. In the Application Menu, click New to create a new drawing using a template.

2. Select and open the *Plant 3D ISO - Color Dependent Plot Styles.dwt* which is available with the software.

3. Open the Layers Properties Manager. Note this template has only one layer with the name **0**.

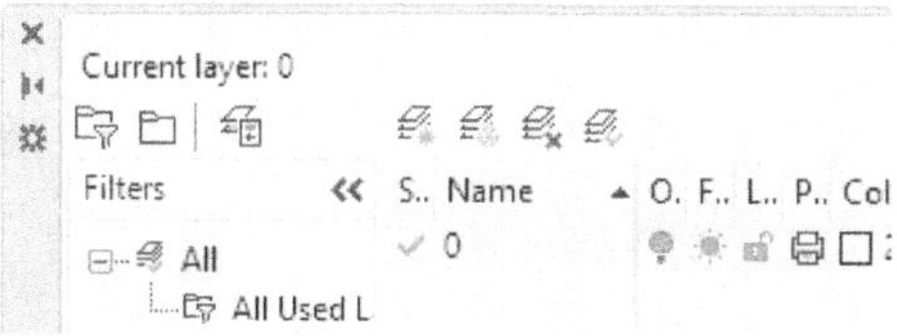

4. Close the Layer Properties Manager.

5. Close the new drawing.

3D Object Layer Management

In this section of the exercise, you explore how layers are used in 3D object definitions.

1. In the Project Manager, right-click on the project name. Click Project Setup.

2. In the Project Setup dialog box, expand Plant 3D DWG Settings. Select Layer and Color Settings.

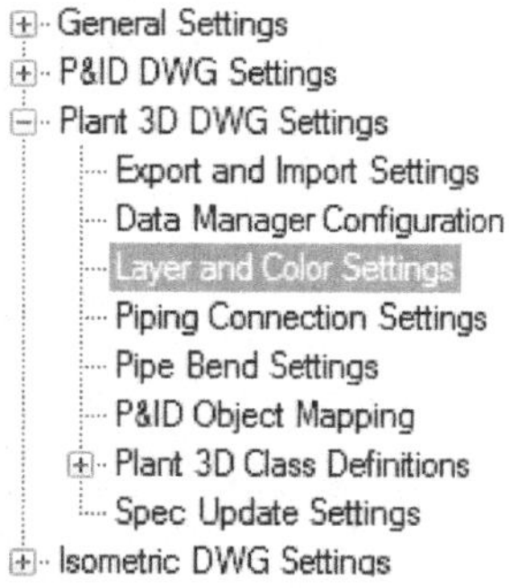

3. In the Automated layer and color assignment section, examine the settings:
   - Automation schemes is set to Default.
   - Assign layer by is set to Line Number Tag.
   - Assign color by is set to Nominal Diameter.

4. Under Assign color by, select Service. Examine the changes that are made to the Color settings.

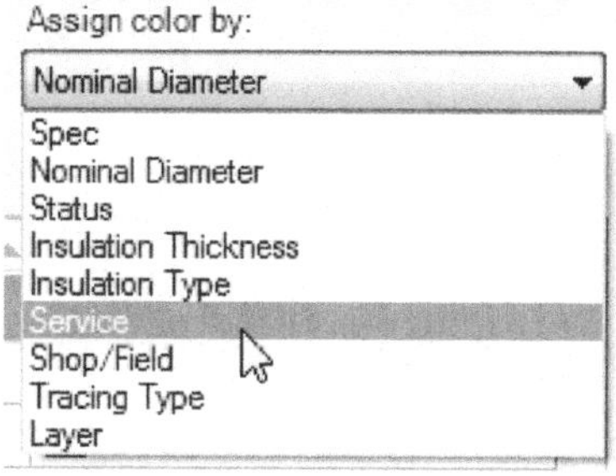

5. Use Cancel to close the Project Setup dialog box without saving the changes.

3D Layers in a Drawing

In this section of the exercise, you open a 3D drawing and examine the layers that have been generated.

1. In the Project Manager, under Plant 3D Drawings, double-click on the Piping drawing to open it.

2. Open the Layer Properties Manager and examine the layers. If the layers are filtered and do not display, select All on the left pane, to display them.

3. Close the Layer Properties manager and close all the open drawings without saving.

Lesson Review Questions

1. Layers in the 3D model are automatically assigned based on a property of objects being placed.
   a. True
   b. False
2. P&ID drawings can have a piping layer associated with each schematic line.
   a. True
   b. False
3. What is the recommended method for setting the color of AutoCAD P&ID and AutoCAD Plant 3D objects?
   a. ByLayer
   b. ByStandard
   c. ByObject
   d. ByBlock
4. Layer and color settings for P&ID drawings are configured the same way that layer and color settings are configured for Plant 3D drawings.
   a. True
   b. False

Chapter Summary

In this chapter, you learned about many of the general topics for plant design and the use of the AutoCAD P&ID software and the AutoCAD Plant 3D software to create your plant designs.

Having completed this chapter, you can:

- Navigate the Project Manager and explain the purpose of a project and where the drawings and data are stored.
- Open drawings in the context of the project from the Project Manager.
- Identify the aspects of the user interface that are unique for plant design, and the workflow for creating and modifying a P&ID or 3D plant design.
- Explain the philosophy behind layering and explain the project setup options for layers and colors.

Chapter 2

AutoCAD P&ID

When you are creating piping and instrumentation diagrams (P&ID), you are creating a schematic representation of the sequence of equipment and systems in a plant design. During the creation of P&IDs, there are many tasks that you need to accomplish before the design is complete. Some of those tasks include adding industry-standard symbols to the drawing, breaking and mending lines, ensuring flow direction, adding tags and annotations in industry-formats, identifying and correcting potential inconsistencies, and sharing project information. In this chapter, you learn how to use the AutoCAD® P&ID software to create, modify, and manage 2D piping and instrumentation diagrams for a plant design.

Objectives

After completing this chapter, you will be able to:

- Add drawings to a project by creating new drawings, linking to existing drawings, and copying them from another project.
- Place equipment, set the tag, see the predefined type, and make changes to a symbol like adding nozzles.
- Add pipelines to connect equipment, group pipe segments, assign tags and information to the line, and add and remove components to the line.
- Add general and in line instruments and set up an instrument loop.
- Describe the purpose of tags and create unique tags including a unique tag that links symbols over multiple drawings.
- Place annotations and modify the properties and data driving the annotations.
- Make changes and modifications to the generated PID using AutoCAD PIDs Sline grips and substitute arrow commands and with AutoCAD's move, copy and stretch commands.
- Use the Data Manager to create reports, review information in the PID, export the data to external files (XLS, XLSX, CSV) and import that same data again after revising externally. Also adjust the columns displayed in the Data Manager.

- Create one-off symbols by converting inserted blocks of symbols to PID objects.
- Add offpage connectors and connect these with other drawings and use them to navigate between drawings.
- Use of Report Creator to generate different reports of a plant design.

Lesson: Creating and Adding Existing Drawings

Overview

New design projects often consist of a combination of new designs and the reuse of aspects of existing designs. To have all of the required drawings correctly associated to your project, you need to know the correct way to create new drawings and leverage existing drawings. This lesson describes how to add drawings to the active project by creating a new P&ID drawing and copying an existing drawing from another project to the active project.

Objectives

After completing this lesson, you will be able to:

- Create project folders and subfolders in the current P&ID project.
- Create a new drawing in a P&ID project.
- Link or copy an existing drawing to the current P&ID project.
- Access the drawing properties for a drawing in the current P&ID project.
- Work with the Drawing Checker.

Creating Project Folders and Subfolders

To help organize your P&ID drawings in the Project panel, you can create folders and subfolders under the P&ID Drawings folder in the Project Manager.

Drawings organized into project folders and subfolders are shown in the following illustration.

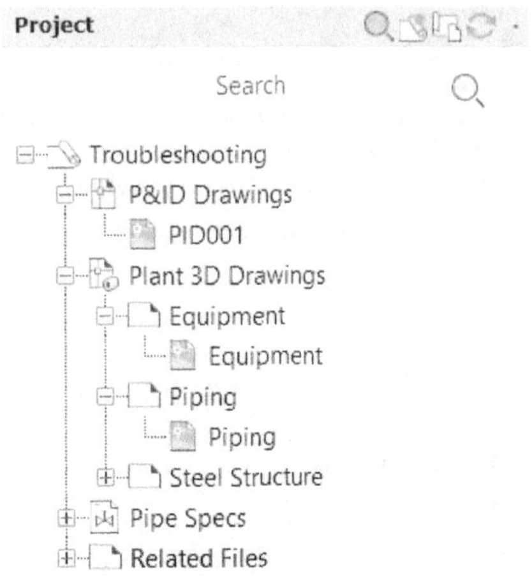

Process: Creating Project Folders and Subfolders

You create a project folder or subfolder by right-clicking on P&ID Drawings in the Project Manager and then clicking New Folder on the shortcut menu, as shown in the following illustration. In the New Folder dialog box, enter the name of the folder, specify which template to use, and specify whether you should be prompted for a template for each drawing to be created. A corresponding folder will be created in the project directory in Windows.

Renaming and removing folders in a project should be done using the Project Manager. To rename and remove, right-click on the folder name and select Rename Folder or Remove Folder, respectively.

Creating a Drawing

As a P&ID Project progresses, it is likely that additional drawings are going to be added to the project. The Project Manager enables you to quickly create a new P&ID drawing.

Process: Creating a New Drawing

You can add new drawings to the current project by right-clicking on the P&ID Drawings folder in the Project pane of the Project Manager and clicking New Drawing, as shown in the following illustration. The New DWG dialog box opens. Here, you can name the drawing, enter the drawing author, and browse to select a DWG template.

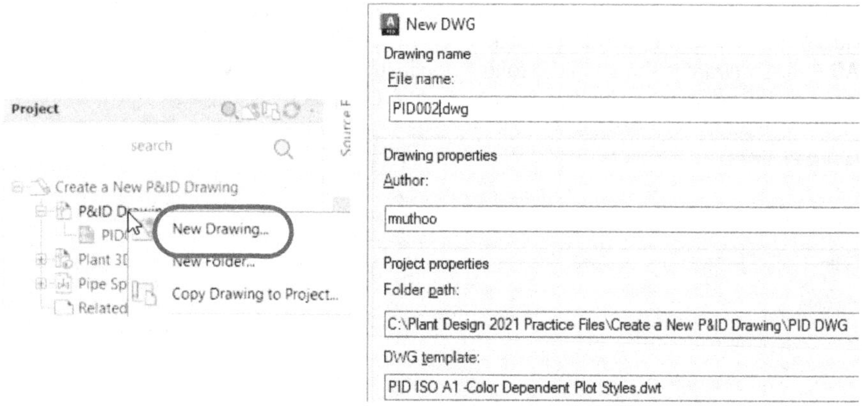

Adding Existing Drawings to the Project

You often need to include existing drawings in the current P&ID project. Adding existing drawings enables you to work more efficiently by reducing the amount of new data created. The Project Manager enables you to copy drawings to the current project.

Process: Adding Existing Drawings to the Project

To copy a drawing to the current project, you right-click on the P&ID Drawings folder and click Copy Drawing to Project, as shown in the following illustration. You then navigate to the drawing file location and select the required drawing file. When you copy a drawing to a project, the original drawing remains in its current location, and a copy of the selected drawing is made and added to the current project.

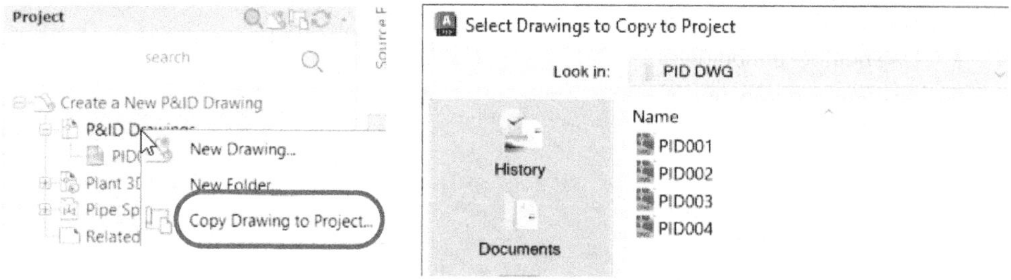

Moving Drawings

Drawings cannot be moved between the top level sections in a project. For example, they cannot be moved between AutoCAD P&ID Drawings, AutoCAD Plant 3D Drawings, and Related Files. To move the drawings between folders within the same section in the Project Manager, select the file and drag it to a different folder. This moves the drawing in the Project Manager but does not change its location on the drive.

Access Drawing Properties

You access the drawing properties of a P&ID drawing by locating the drawing in the Project pane of the Project Manager, right-clicking, and clicking Properties. The Drawing Properties dialog box for the AutoCAD P&ID software is shown in the following illustration. The Drawing Properties enable to you to assign basic information to the drawings in your P&ID project.

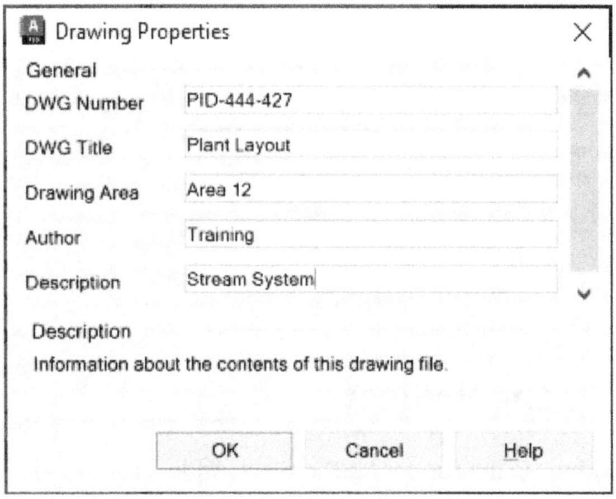

Drawing Checker

The Drawing Checker examines all of the text and annotations in the P&ID against the current project properties to find any discrepancies caused by changes made outside the drawing. The Drawing Checker Review dialog box prompts you when updates are required. Typically, the Drawing Checker identifies the following items as needing to be updated:

- Instrument bubble text
- Equipment tag annotations
- Line number annotations
- All other annotations

By default, when you open a P&ID drawing, the Drawing Checker is executed. If discrepancies exist, you are prompted to conduct the review now or later. When Review Now is selected the Drawing Checker dialog box opens indicating that Annotations in the drawing are out of date.

The Drawing Checker Review dialog box that opens if discrepancies exist when the drawing is open is shown in the following illustration.

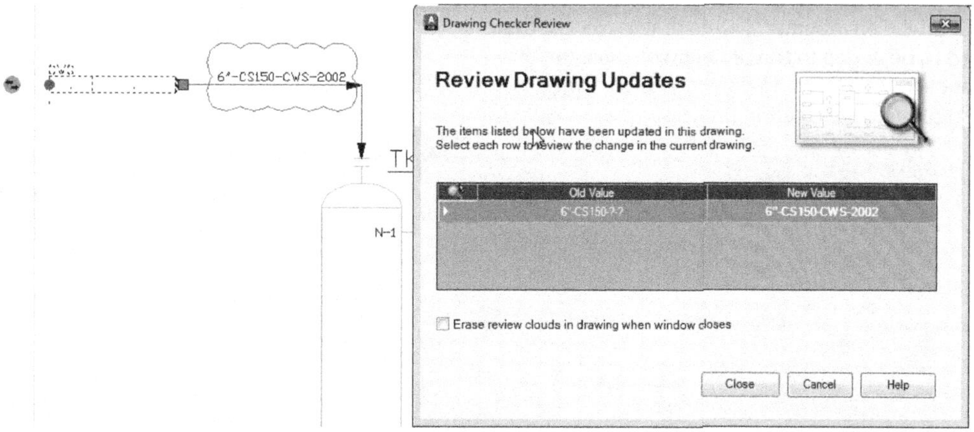

The Drawing Checker Review dialog box lists the items that have been updated. Select a row in the list to zoom to the update. A cloud displays around the update highlighting it. To accept the update you can select the Erase review clouds in drawing when window closes option. If there are multiple updates in the list, and some are to remain for checking later, clear the Erase review clouds in drawing when window closes option. You can manually delete the review clouds outside the Drawing Checker to accept the updates.

The Drawing Checker runs automatically when you open a drawing. Run the system variable PLANTDWGCHECKERAUTOCHECK to toggle auto-checking off when drawings are open.

To force the Drawing Checker to run when a drawing is already open, on the Home tab, on the Validate panel, click Drawing Checker, as shown in the following illustration.

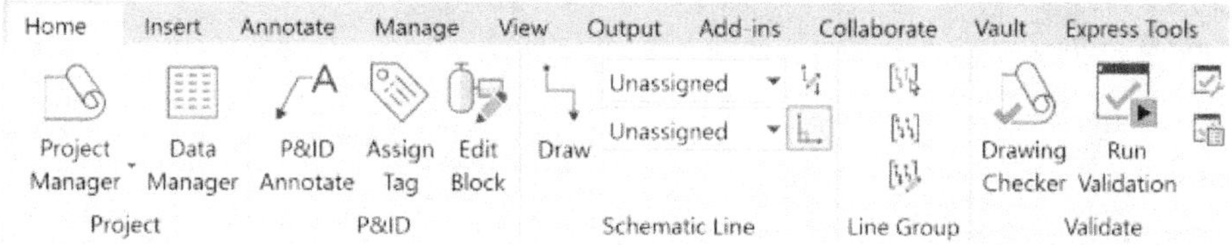

Exercise: Create a New P&ID Drawing

In this exercise, you learn to create a new drawing, link a drawing to the project, and copy an existing drawing from another project to the active project.

In a real-life environment, often drawings exist that need to be added to the project. You have the chance to reuse existing drawings and information to streamline the creation process.

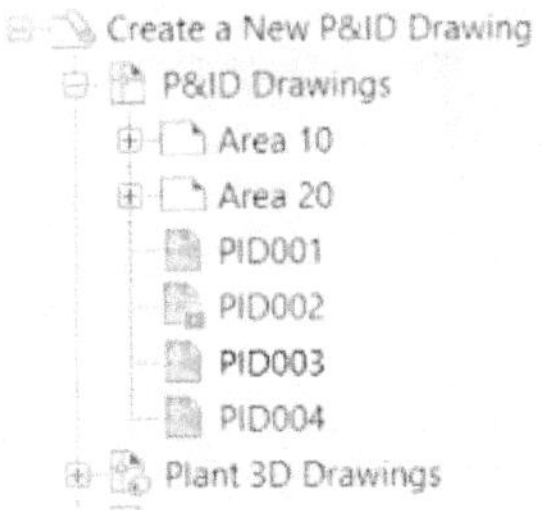

1. Start the AutoCAD Plant 3D software, if not already running.

2. Open the project as follows:

   - In the Project Manager, Current Project list, click Open.
   - In the Open dialog box, navigate to the folder *C:\Plant Design 2024 Practice Files\Create a New P&ID Drawing*.
   - Select the file *Project.xml*.
   - Click Open.

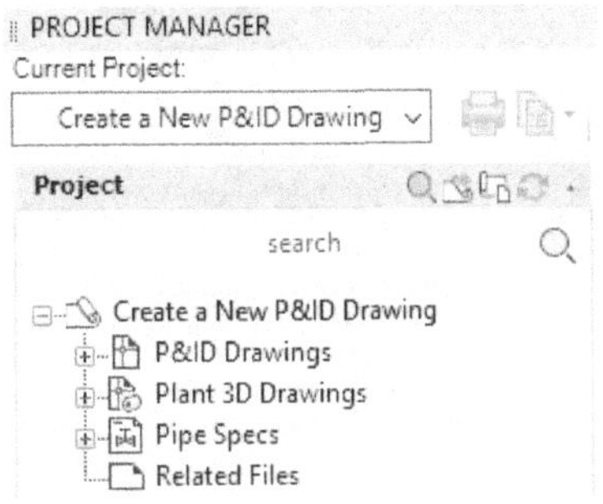

3. To open a P&ID drawing:

   - In the Project Manager, expand P&ID Drawings.
   - Right-click on PID001.
   - Click Open.

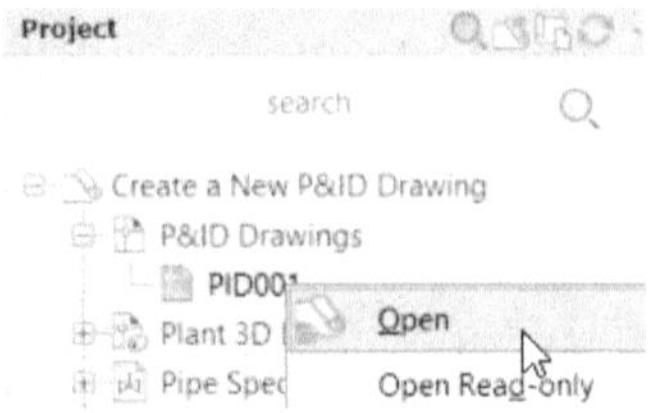

4. To create a new P&ID drawing:

   - In the Project Manager, under the Create a New P&ID Drawing, right-click on P&ID Drawings.
   - Click New Drawing.

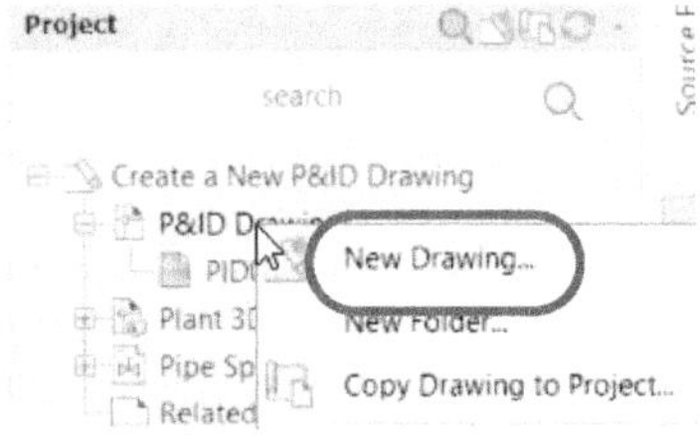

5. To define basic drawing properties:

   - In the New DWG dialog box, for the File name, enter **PID002.dwg**.
   - If required, under Author in the Drawing Properties, enter an author's name.
   - If required, select a DWG template.
   - Click OK.

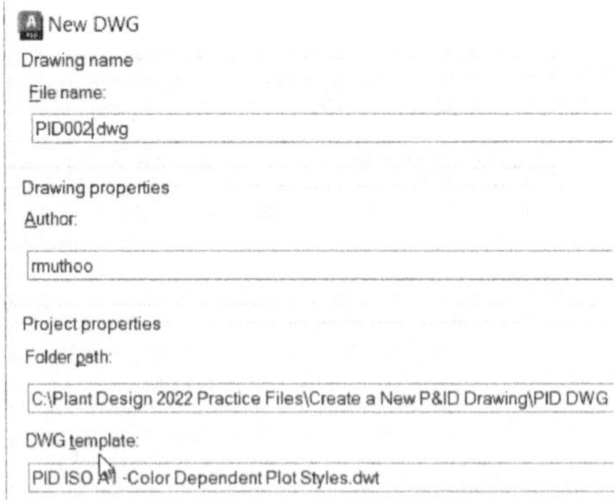

6. The new P&ID drawing is created and opened.

7. To edit the drawing properties:

- In the Project Manager, under the Create a New P&ID Drawing, expand P&ID Drawings, if required.
- Right-click on PID002. Click Properties.
- In the Drawing Properties dialog box, under General, for Description, enter **New P&ID Drawing**.
- Click OK.

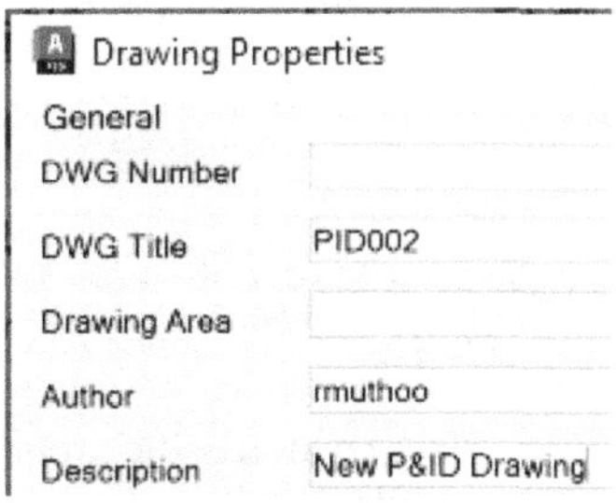

8. To create a project folder:

- In the Project Manager, right-click on P&ID Drawings.
- Click New Folder.

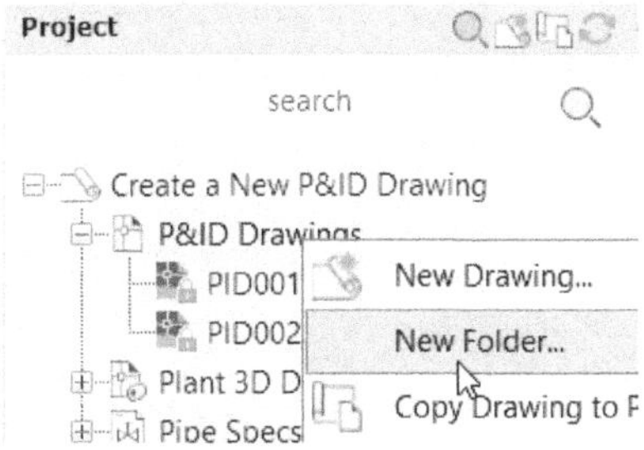

9. To assign the property information and folder on the hard drive:

- In the New Folder dialog box, for Folder name, enter **Area 10**.
- Note the change in the Folder path.
- Click OK.

10. Create another folder called Area 20. The folders are displayed in the Project Manager.

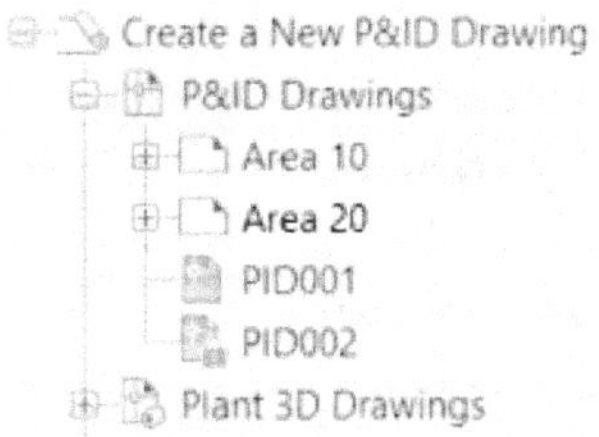

11. To copy a drawing to the project:

- In the Project Manager, right-click on P&ID Drawings.
- Click Copy Drawing to Project.
- Navigate to the *C:\Plant Design 2024 Practice Files\Create a New P&ID Drawing* folder.
- Press and hold <Shift> and select the *PID003.dwg* and *PID004.dwg* drawings.
- Click Open.

12. The drawings are copied to the project and displayed in the Project Manager. The PID003 and PID004 drawings in the project are located in the P&ID Drawings folder for this active project.

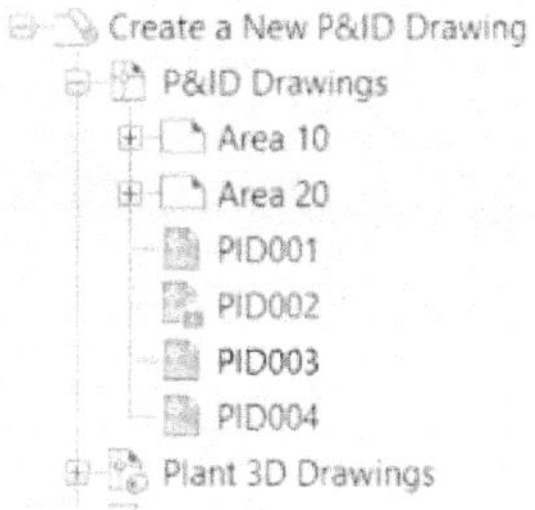

13. Close all open files. Do not save.

Lesson Review Questions

1. What drawing property fields are available by default? (Select all that apply.)
   a. DWG Number
   b. DWG Title
   c. DWG Revision
   d. Description
2. You can move drawings directly between the P&ID Drawings and Plant 3D Drawings areas while in the project.
   a. True
   b. False
3. How do you rename or remove folders from the project?
   a. Renaming the folder and/or the drawing with Windows Explorer is sufficient.
   b. Using the context menu (right-click) on the Project Manager.
4. When a drawing is copied to a plant project, a duplicate drawing file is created in the project directory. If the original drawing that was used to do the copy is moved in Windows Explorer, the copied drawing loses its reference in the Project Manager.
   a. True
   b. False

Lesson: Equipment and Nozzles

Overview

In this lesson you learn to place equipment, set the tag, see the predefined type and make changes to a symbol using the P&ID object edit function. You also learn how to manually add nozzles to a symbol without changing the original symbol.

Because P&IDs represent the piping, equipment, and control devices in diagram form, the place to start when creating a P&ID is to add the equipment to the drawing. After you add the equipment, such as tanks and heat exchangers, you are then able to connect the equipment with lines. To establish this starting point, you need to know how to add equipment to the drawing and manipulate it after it has been added.

The beginning of a design after equipment symbols have been added for two vessels, a tank, a pump, and an exchanger is shown in the following illustration.

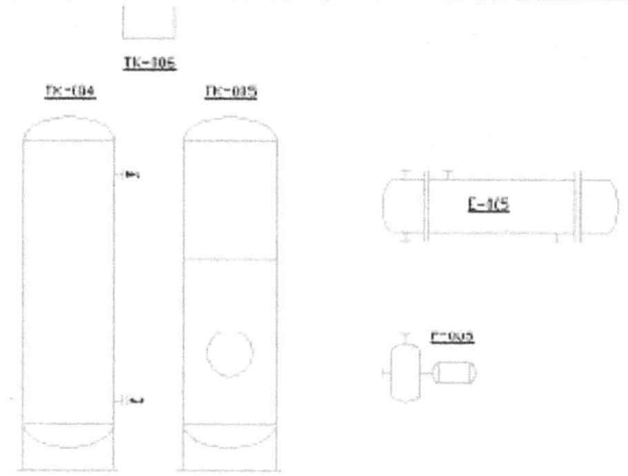

Objectives

After completing this lesson, you will be able to:

- Add P&ID equipment to a drawing.
- Modify an existing P&ID symbol.
- Add a nozzle to a P&ID symbol.
- Add Tag information to new and existing components in a P&ID design.

Adding Equipment

Knowing how to access the Tool Palette and then locate and insert objects enables you to create P&ID designs efficiently. The equipment required to create a P&ID design is located on the Equipment tab in the Tool Palette, which is divided into logical groups to enable you to quickly find the P&ID symbol required.

The Tool Palette -P&ID PIP palette with the Equipment tab active is shown in the following illustration.

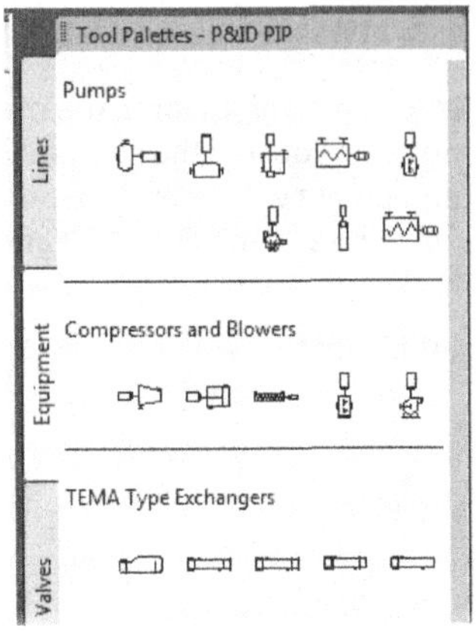

Process: Adding Equipment

The process for adding P&ID equipment to your design is very straightforward. To add equipment, you locate the required symbol in the appropriate group and click it, then click in your drawing where the symbol is to be located. Depending on which symbol is selected, you might be able to perform additional operations, such as scaling.

A Horizontal Centrifugal Pump being selected in the Equipment tab in the Tool Palette and then being located in the drawing is shown in the following illustration.

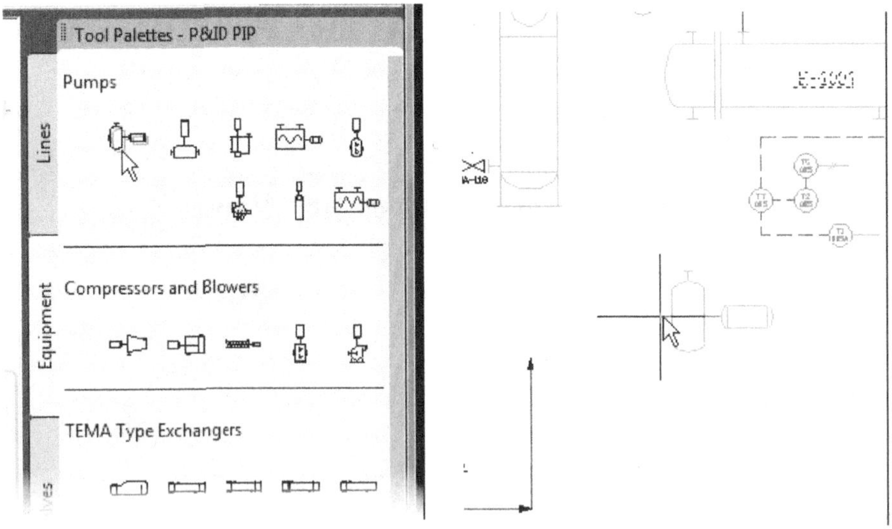

Modify an Existing P&ID Symbol

Often at some point in the design process, a P&ID symbol requires some type of change. Should this situation occur, it is important to know how to edit an existing symbol. Even though the edited P&ID symbol is an AutoCAD block, it remains independent of other similar symbols when edited.

A P&ID symbol being edited in the Block Editor is shown in the following illustration.

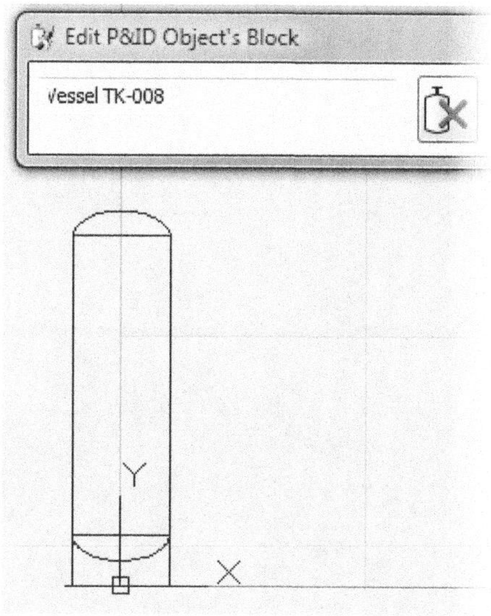

Process: Modifying an Existing P&ID Symbol

To edit an existing P&ID symbol, you open it in the AutoCAD block editor. To do so, select the required symbol in the drawing and right-click. From the menu, click Edit P&ID Object's Block, as shown in the following illustration. The block opens in the AutoCAD block editor in which you can modify the geometry to match your situation. You can also add geometry to the symbol.

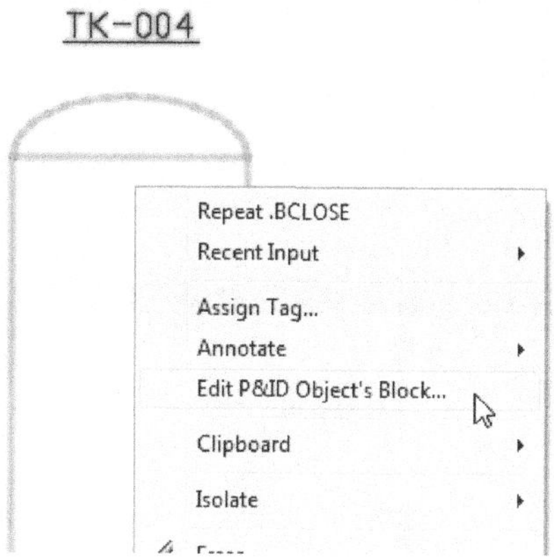

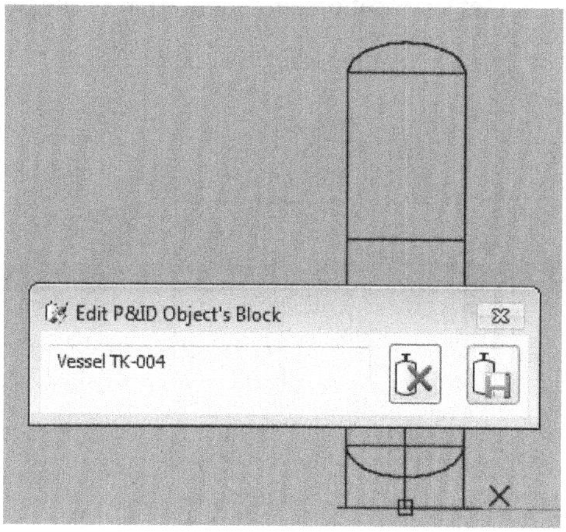

Adding Nozzles

A storage tank is not useful without the ability to add or remove contents. While some nozzles are automatically added to the design, such as when a pipeline is connected to a tank, often you need to manually add a nozzle to the design.

A typical P&ID design with various types of equipment, all requiring nozzles is shown in the following illustration.

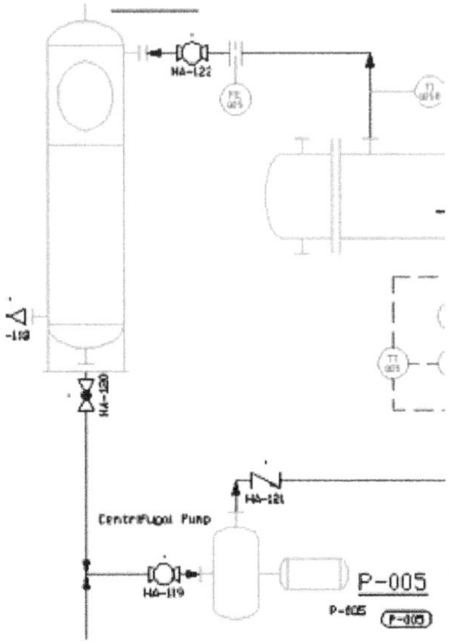

Process: Adding Nozzles

To add a nozzle to a component in a P&ID drawing, you need to access the available nozzles on the Fittings tab on the Tool Palette, as shown in the following illustration. You click the required nozzle, then click the component to which it is going to be attached. You then click or enter a numerical value to set the location and orientation of the nozzle.

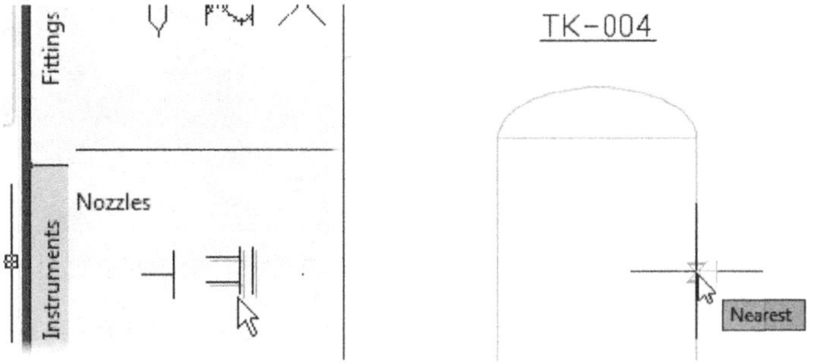

Adding Tag Information

Virtually every component of a P&ID design can have information assigned to it using a Tag. In some cases, when you insert a P&ID symbol the Assign Tag dialog box opens automatically, prompting you to enter or select tag information. In other cases, tag information can be added after the symbol is inserted.

The Assign Tag dialog box that automatically opens when a P&ID Tank was inserted is shown in the following illustration.

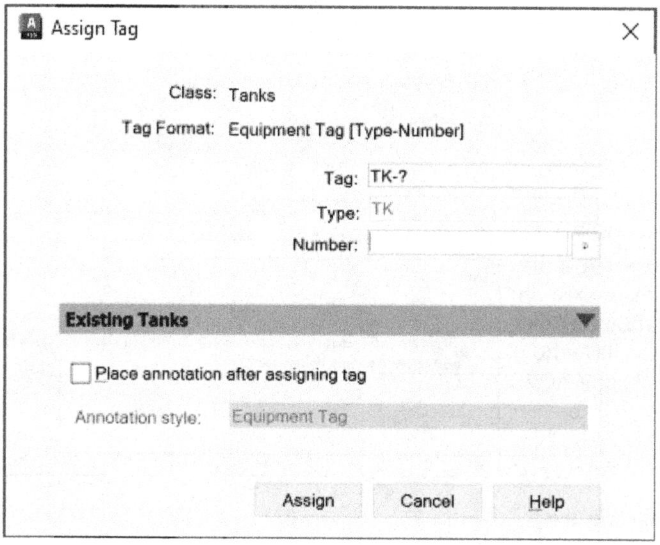

Process: Adding Tag Information

Tag information is added in the Assign Tag dialog box. This dialog box is automatically opened when you insert certain symbols. To edit Tag information or add it to symbols where the dialog box is not automatically displayed, you right-click on the symbol and click Assign Tag in the menu. From this point on, the process for adding or editing tag information is the same.

1. Open the Assign Tag dialog box.
2. Enter the Number value or select Number (arrow) to assign the next sequential number of that type of object selected.

   Hint: Select the Existing Pumps drop-down to review the tag numbers that have been used in the drawing. This helps to prevent the reuse of a previously used number.

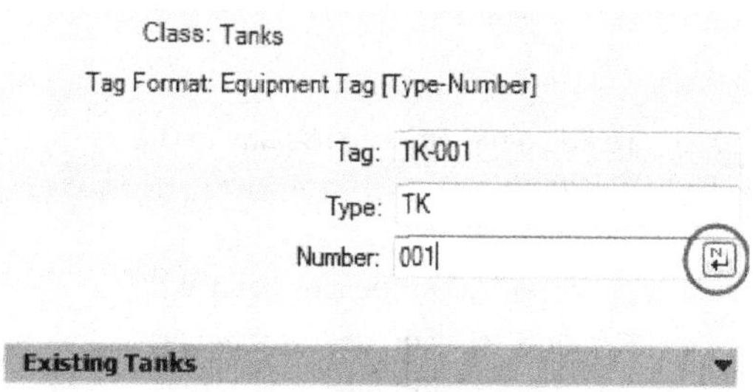

3. To display the tag information in the drawing, select the Place annotation after assigning tag check box.

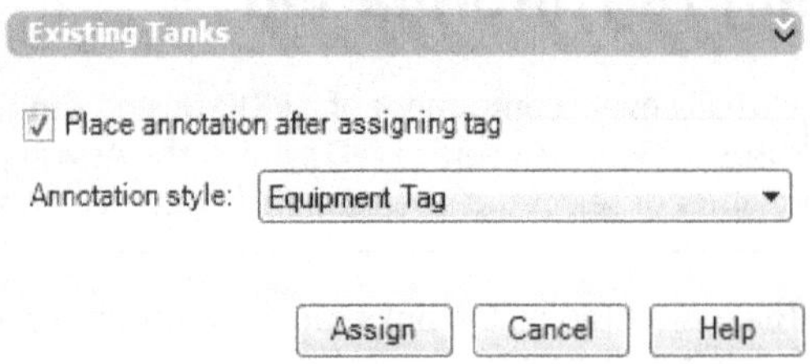

4. Select the Annotation Style.

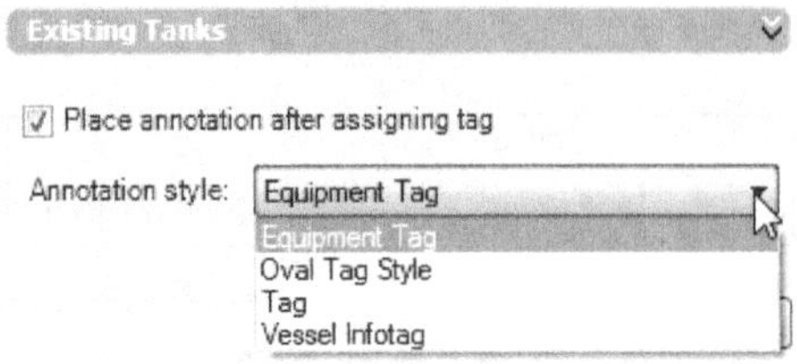

5. Click Assign to create the tag. If the current tag number already exists in the drawing you are prompted that no two components can have the same tag. Click OK to assign a new number.

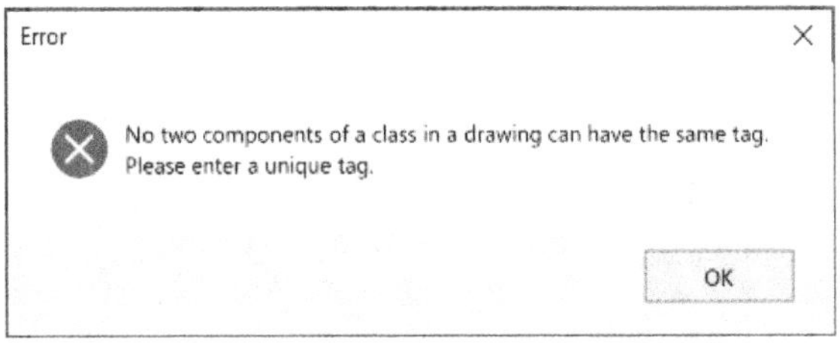

6. Place the tag in the drawing (if it is to be displayed).

   Any time the data is changed, the tag automatically updates with the changes.

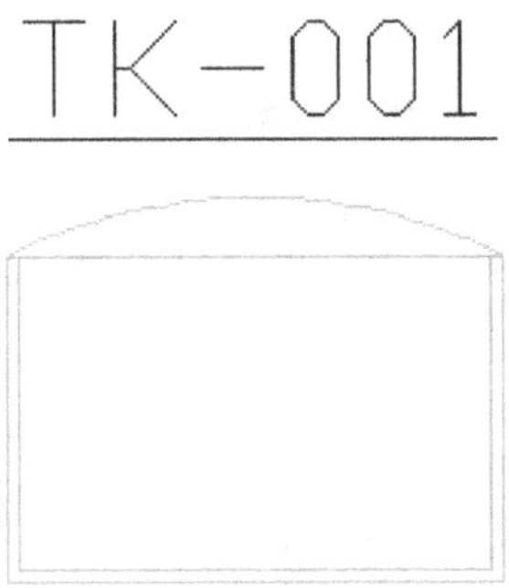

7. To edit a tag you can use any of the following:
   - Change the tag using the AutoCAD Properties palette.
   - Right-click on the symbol and select Assign Tag.
   - Double-click on the tag.
   - Select the tag and use the Move grip to move the tag.

Exercise: Equipment and Nozzles

In this exercise, you learn to place equipment, set the tag, see the predefined type, and make changes to a symbol using the P&ID object edit function. You also learn how to manually add nozzles to a symbol without changing the original symbol.

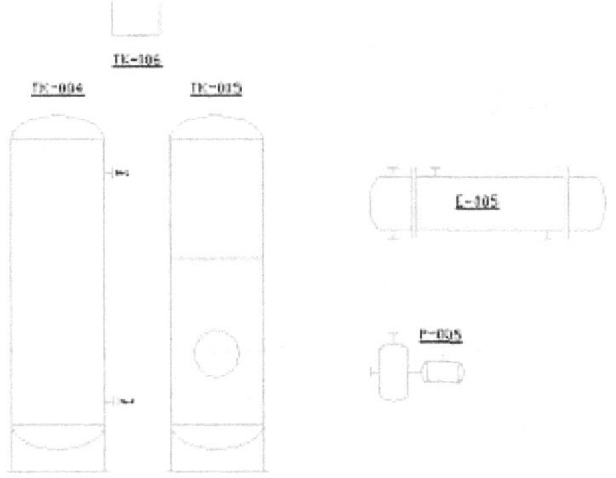

1. Start the AutoCAD Plant 3D software, if not already running.

2. Open the project as follows:
   - In the Project Manager, Current Project list, click Open.
   - In the Open dialog box, navigate to the folder *C:\Plant Design 2024 Practice Files\Equipment and Nozzles*.
   - Select the file *Project.xml*.
   - Click Open.

3. In the Project Manager>P&ID Drawings, open *PID002.dwg*.

4. In Workspace switching, click PID PIP, if not already active. If the P&ID PIP Tool Palette is not displayed, right-click on the header of the open Tool Palettes and click PID PIP.

   Note: This is always recommended to ensure that the correct Tool Palettes are displayed.

   Note: If no Tool Palette is displayed, click on Tool Palettes in the View tab>Palettes panel.

5. Ensure that you are in Model space. Model should be displayed on the status bar. If not, select Paper to switch to Model space.

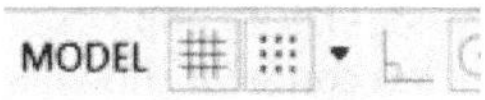

6. On the Tool Palettes - P&ID PIP, click the Equipment tab.

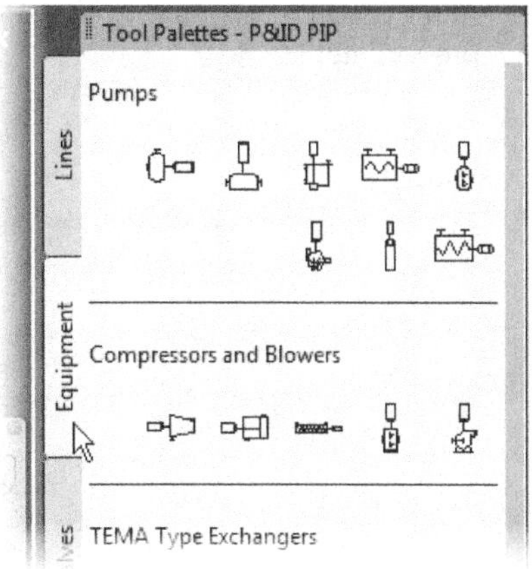

7. To begin to insert a vessel, on the Equipment tab in the Tool Palette, under Vessel and Miscellaneous Vessel Details, click Vessel, the first icon as shown in the following illustration.

   Note: The Vessel and Miscellaneous Vessel Details category is near the bottom of the palette. If it is not displayed, hover your cursor over the Tool Palette and use the middle mouse button to scroll down to locate it.

   Note: Hover over an icon in the Tool Palette to display its name.

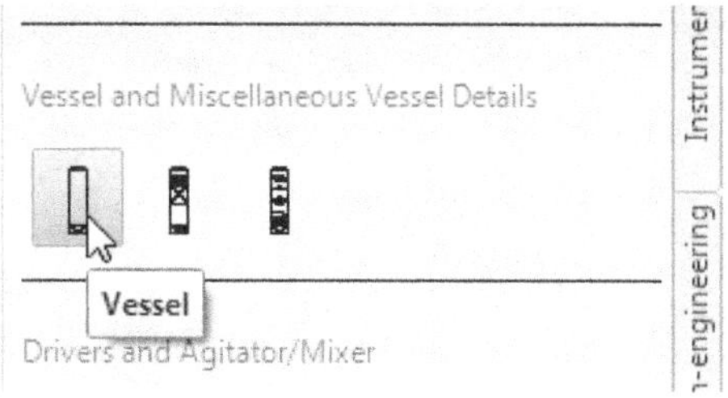

8. To locate and scale the vessel:

- Toggle the grid off (Gridmode in status bar).
- In the drawing window, zoom into the canvas near the lower left corner.
- To locate the vessel, click a point in canvas near the lower left corner as shown in the following illustration.
- To scale, move the cursor and note the change in size.
- At the Scale Factor prompt, enter **25** and press <Enter>.

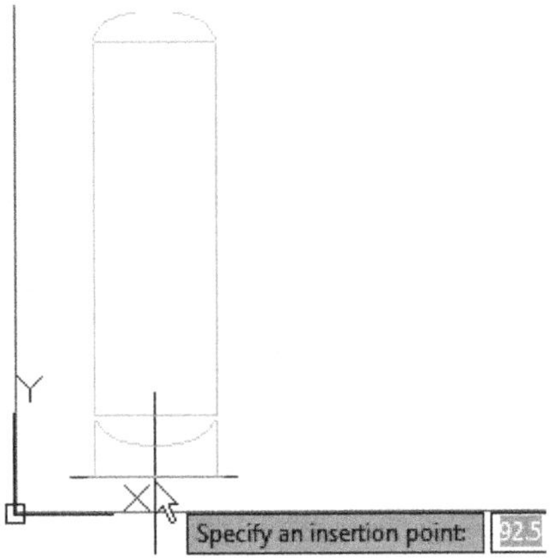

9. The Assign Tag dialog box opens. To assign tag information:

- In the Assign Tag dialog box, note the Tag, which originally displays as TK-?.
- For number, click the icon at the end of the field, as shown in the following illustration. The AutoCAD P&ID software searches the document and displays the next available number and replaces the Tag ?.

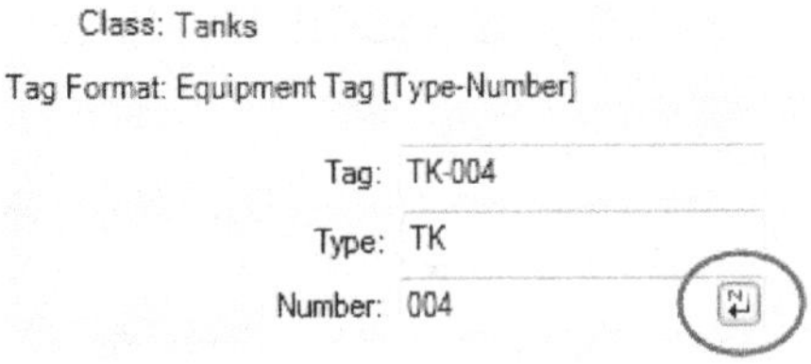

10. To place the annotation in the drawing:

- Under Existing Tanks, select Place annotation after assigning tag. (Checkmark is displayed).
- For Annotation style, select Equipment Tag, if required.
- Click Assign.

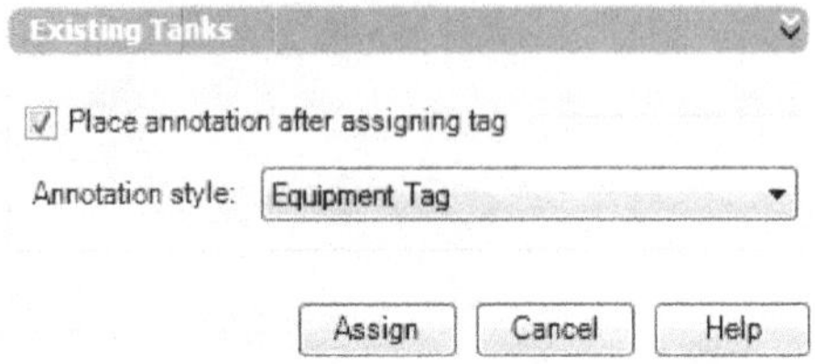

11. To place the annotation in canvas, click above the vessel as shown in the following illustration.

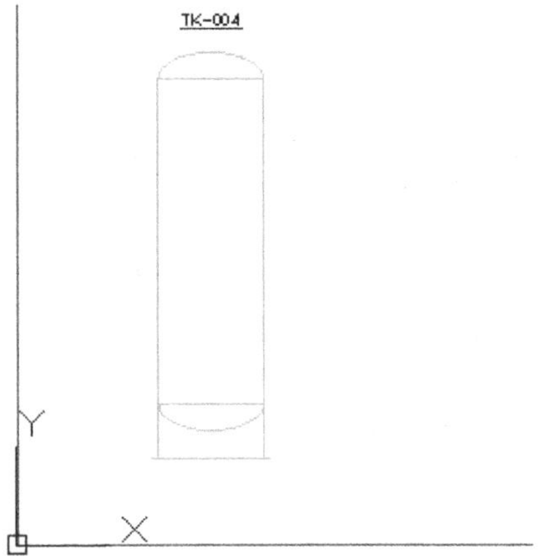

12. Copy the vessel using standard AutoCAD techniques as shown in the following illustration.

13. To update the annotation tag:

- Right click on the copied vessel.
- Click Assign Tag.
- In the Assign Tag dialog box, for Number, click the icon for the next available number.
- Under Existing Tanks, clear the checkmark for Place annotation after assigning tag.
- Click Assign.

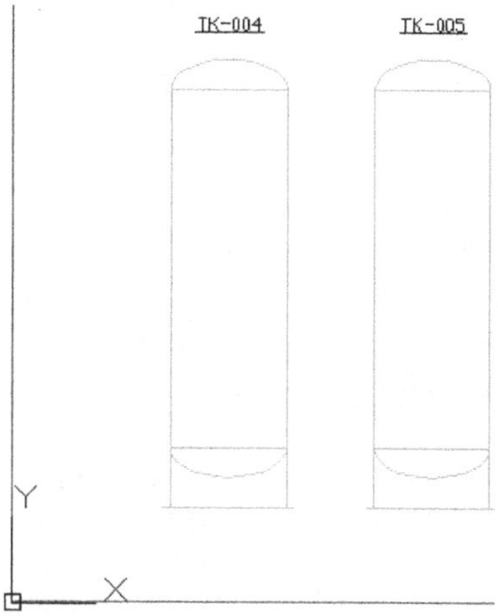

14. To place a storage tank:

- On the Equipment tab in the Tool Palettes, under Storage Tanks, click Open Top Tank.

Note: Hover over an icon in the Tool Palette to display its name.

- In canvas, click above the two vessels (approximate center of the 2 vessels).
- To scale, move the cursor and note the change in size.
- For scale, enter **10** and press <Enter>.

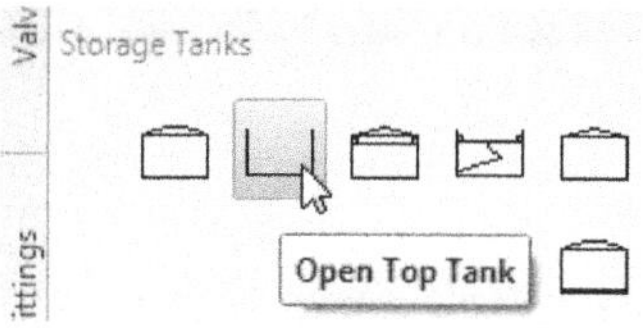

15. The Assign Tag dialog box opens. To assign tag information:

- For Number, click the next available number icon.
- Under Existing Tanks, select Place annotation after assigning tag to checkmark it.
- Click Assign.
- Locate the tag below the new tank.

Note: You can use the AutoCAD Move command if the tank needs to be re-positioned.

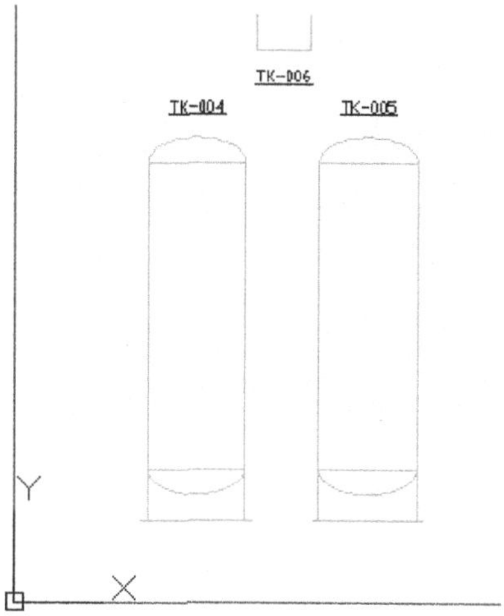

16. To place a pump:

- On the Equipment tab in the Tool Palettes, under Pumps, select Horizontal Centrifugal Pump.

Note: Hover over an icon in the Tool Palette to display its name.

- In canvas, click to place near the right of the tanks.
- In the Assign Tag dialog box, click the next available number icon and Assign.
- Place the annotation tag near the pump as shown in the following illustration.

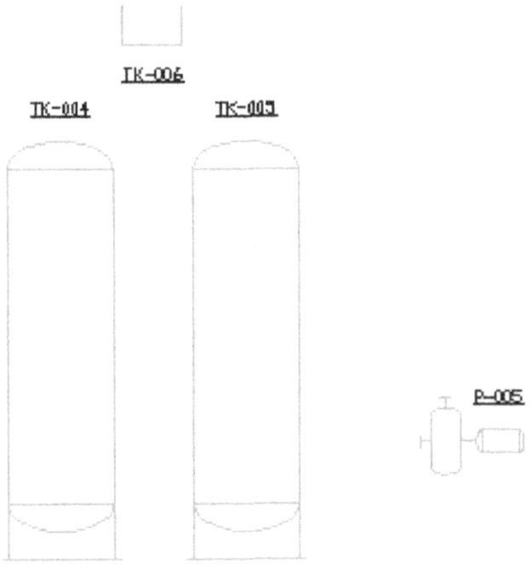

17. Using the same process as the tanks and pump, place a TEMA type BEM Exchanger (in TEMA Type Exchangers) next to the tanks. For Number, enter **005** and place it in the center as shown in the illustration.

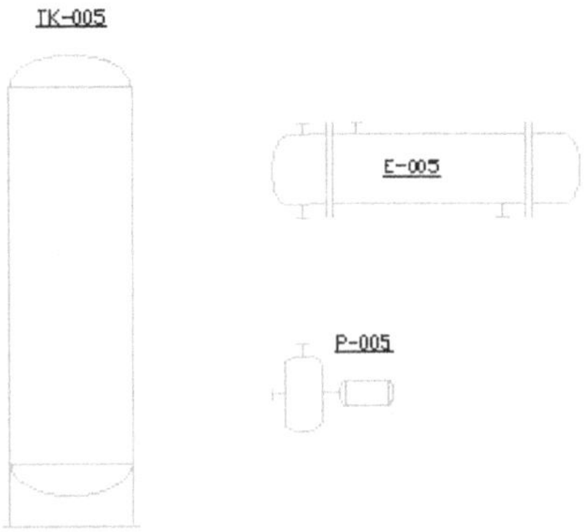

18. On the Tool Palette, click the Fittings tab.

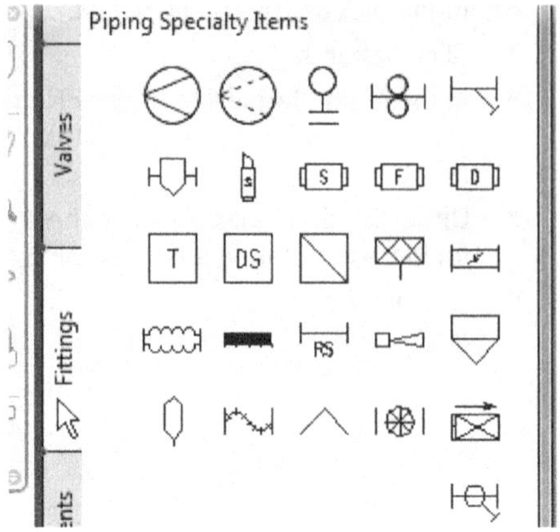

19. To add a nozzle to a tank:

- On the Fittings tab in the Tool Palette, under Nozzles, click Single Line Nozzle.
- To specify the asset, click to select the geometry that defines tank TK-004.
- To locate the nozzle, click the right vertical line of the tank near the top.
- To orient the nozzle direction, move the cursor directly to the right of the location. Click in canvas.

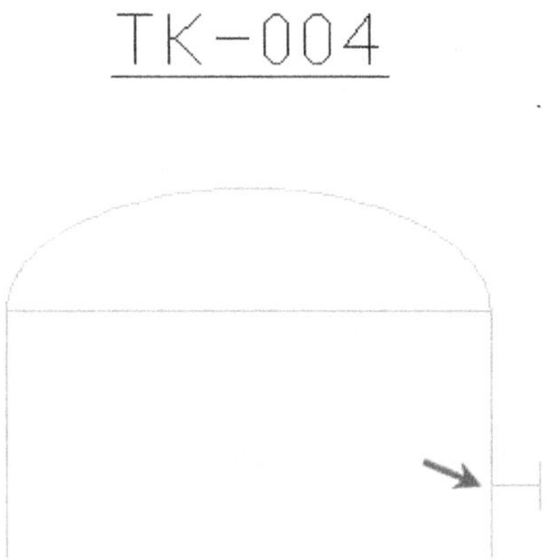

20. Using the same process as Step 19, add a Flanged Nozzle to the same tank (near the bottom) as shown in the following illustration.

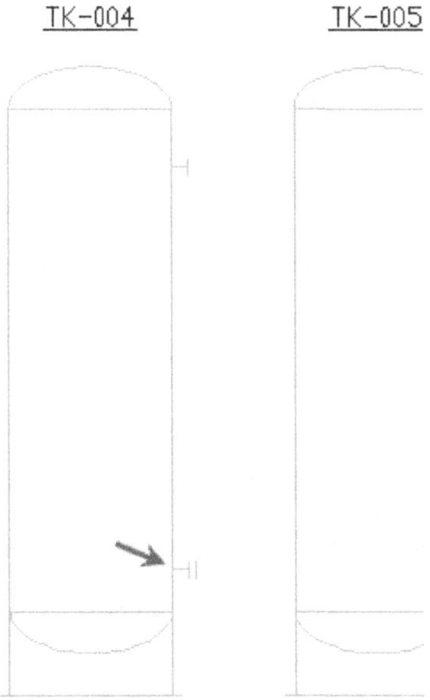

21. Hover the cursor over the first nozzle placed. Note the tooltip information. The tag information is already assigned.

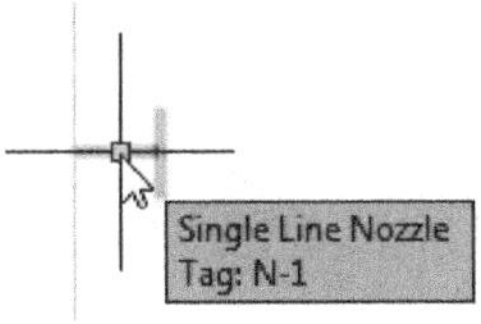

22. To display the tag:
- Right-click on the nozzle.
- Under Annotate, click Tag.
- Place the annotation tag next to the nozzle.

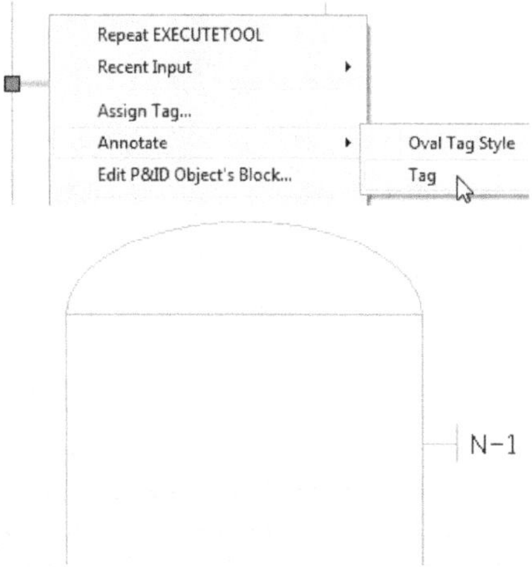

23. As in Step 22, add the tag to the lower nozzle.

24. To edit a P&ID symbol:
- Right-click on tank TK-005.
- Click Edit P&ID Object's Block.
- In the Block Editor, using standard AutoCAD tools, add the line and circle as shown in the following illustration.

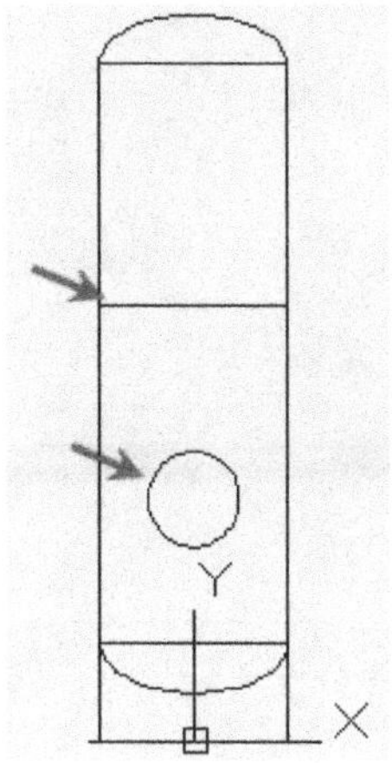

25. In the Edit P&ID Object's Block dialog box, click the Save Changes and Exit Block Editor icon. Note the changes to tank TK-005.

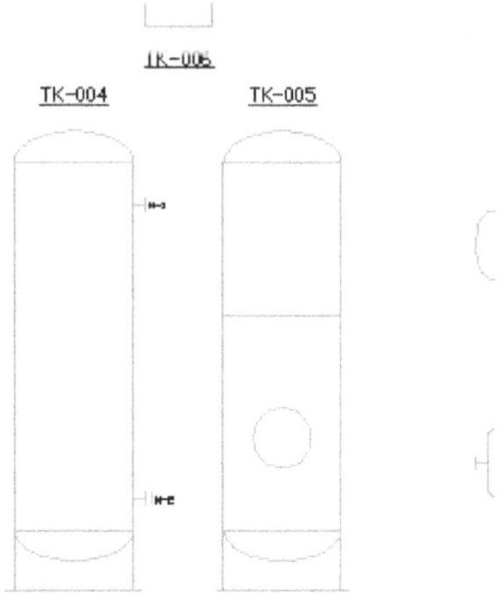

26. Move the symbols and tags, as required. To move a symbol or tag, select the item and use the Move grip (square grip) to relocate it. When moving a symbol, the tag moves with it. Moving a tag does not affect the symbol.

27. Save and close all drawings.

Lesson Review Questions

1. When assigning a tag to a symbol, are you able to see which tags are already in use?
   a. Yes. The Assign Tag dialog box shows the list of already used tags.
   b. No. The validation function prompts you if a tag is already in use.
   c. No. There is no way to check for existing tags while tagging.
2. When you modify a symbol using Edit P&ID Object's Block, the original symbol definition also changes and updates all instances of the same equipment already placed.
   a. True
   b. False
3. There is no limit on how many nozzles can be added to a tank.
   a. True
   b. False
4. How can you change the tag of a symbol? (Select all that apply.)
   a. The tag of a symbol cannot be changed. You have to delete the symbol and insert it again.
   b. The tag can be changed using the AutoCAD Properties palette.
   c. The Assign Tag option in the symbol's shortcut menu can be used to change the tag.
   d. The tag can be changed by double-clicking the tag annotation in the drawing.
5. What does the Place annotation after the assign tag option do when it is enabled?
   a. Places a piece of equipment in the drawing.
   b. Places a tag annotation for the symbol being placed.
   c. Edits a tag value.
   d. Deletes the tag annotation.

Lesson: Piping

Overview

Creating and modifying pipe and instrumentation lines in a P&ID drawing is an important task. In this lesson, you learn how to work with pipelines (Sline), including how to add pipelines to connecting equipment, group pipe segments, assign tags and information to the line, and add and remove line components. With each pipeline created, flow arrows display to indicate the direction of travel, as shown in the following illustration. These lines also dictate the orientation of check valves when they are used. Additionally, each time a line is attached to a vessel or tank, a nozzle is automatically displayed at the connection point.

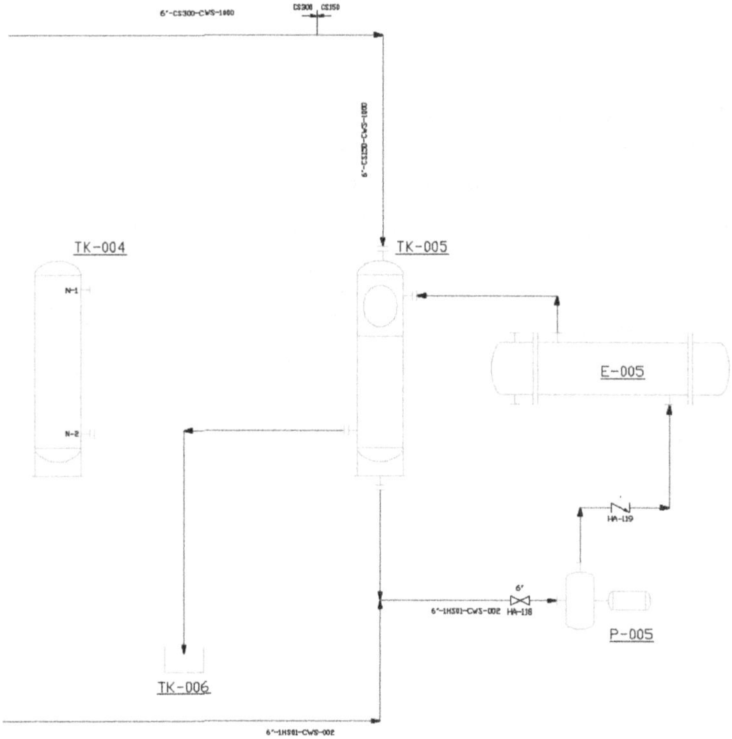

Objectives

After completing this lesson, you will be able to:

- Add pipelines to a P&ID design.
- Connect unassigned lines to a P&ID component.
- Annotate lines used in a P&ID drawing.
- Insert valves into a P&ID design.
- Group lines to a common line number.

Creating Lines

Every plant uses piping and instrumentation to complete the tasks it has been designed to do. Therefore, every P&ID design requires the use of pipe and instrumentation lines.

Pipelines are the arteries of a P&ID design. Without them, the required fluids and gases cannot move about the plant and perform the functions required to manufacture products. Knowing how to create pipelines, assign data to them, and edit them is essential to creating any P&ID Project.

Instrumentation lines are just as critical. Instrumentation enables you to monitor what is going on internally in pipelines, tanks, and other components in a plant. Correct implementation of instrumentation lines is critical to the everyday safety and operations of any plant.

The Lines tab in the Tool Palette and the Schematic Line panel in the ribbon are shown in the following illustration. This palette contains the tools to add both piping and instrumentation lines to your drawing. You add piping and instrumentation lines using a similar process, but the linetype and locations differ. When placing a pipeline, you can preset the specification and the size of the pipe, if required, from the drop-down list of properties in the ribbon. Once set, a pipeline drawn from the Tool Palette or the ribbon uses that size and spec set.

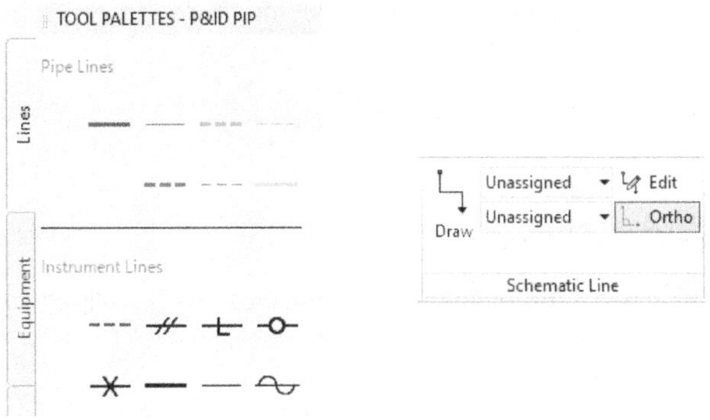

Process: Creating Lines

To add a line to a P&ID design, you first select the type of line to add on the Lines tab in the Tool Palette. From there you select the points to define a starting point (1). Since all lines are created orthogonally, you need to add any jogs (2) in the line to arrive at the termination point (3), as shown in the following illustration.

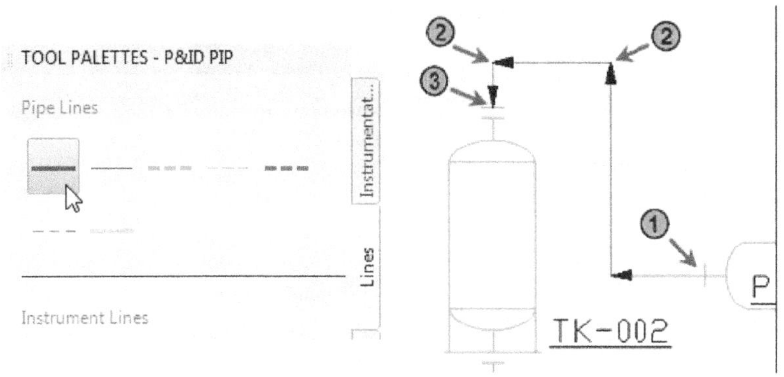

Attaching Lines to a Component

Generally, lines start and terminate at a component in the P&ID design. When that option is not available, you need to manually attach the line to the component.

A quick and easy way to review the from and to attachment information for a line is to hover the cursor over the line. Based on the information in the tooltip, you can determine if either end is not attached. The tooltip information for a line is shown before and after attaching the end to the tank, as shown in the following illustration.

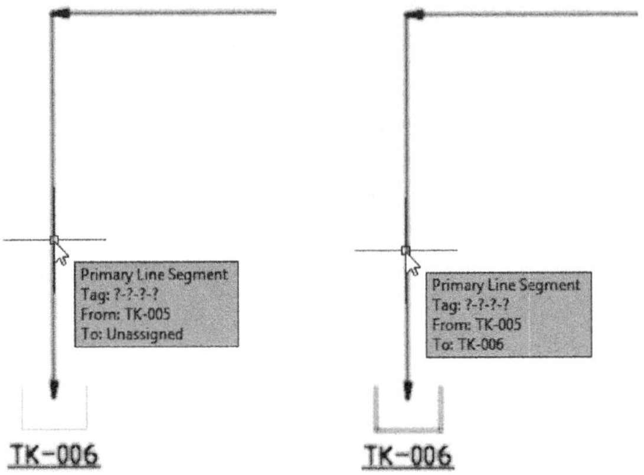

Process: Attaching Lines to a Component

The following steps describe how to attach a line when the line is not already physically attached to a component.

1. Right-click on the line. Under Schematic Line Edit, click Attach to Component.

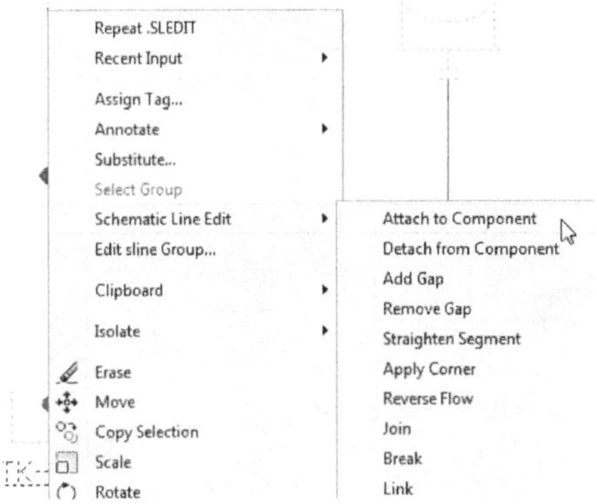

2. Select the Component and then select the endpoint of the line.

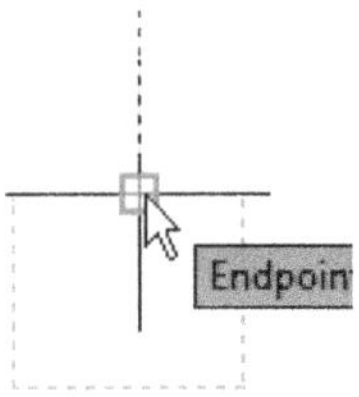

Annotating Lines

Each line placed in a drawing has a specific purpose. To ensure an accurate design, each line should be tagged with all pertinent information.

Click Assign Tag, as shown in the following illustration, to open the Assign Tag dialog box. The Assign Tag dialog box assigns tag information to different components in a P&ID design, and enables you to edit existing tags.

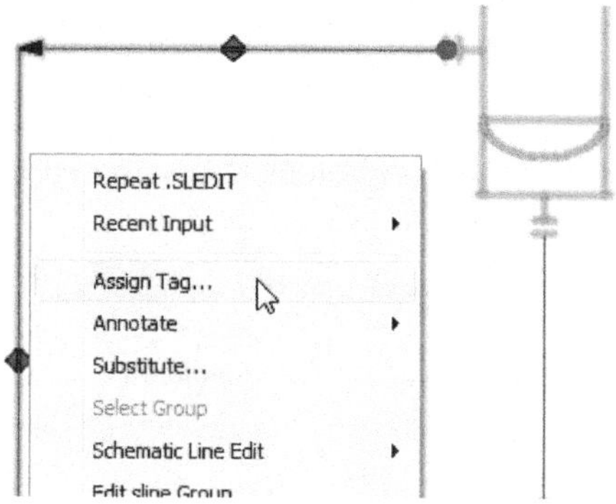

Process: Annotating Lines

The Assign Tag dialog box and the resulting tag applied to a pipeline are shown in the following illustration. After opening the Assign Tag dialog box, you select the required data from the drop-down menus or enter values to generate the tag. To display the tag on the drawing, you place a checkmark in the Place annotation after assigning tag check box. When you are satisfied with the data entered, click Assign and then click in the drawing to locate the tag, if displayed.

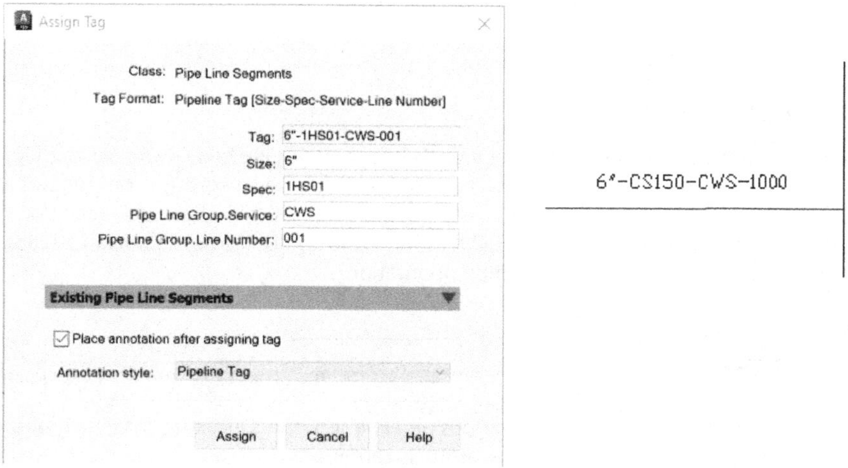

Inserting Valves

Valves are critical to a P&ID design because they control the flow through the different pipes. When valves are inserted into a pipeline, they automatically break the line and be oriented to the line. If the valve is a directional valve, it matches the flow direction of the line when placed.

Valves are inserted into P&ID designs in the same manner as most other symbols. To insert a valve, you locate the required valve on the Valves tab in the Tool Palette, click the valve, and then click where you'd like the valve placed in the P&ID drawing. To edit the Tag information, right-click on the valve and click Assign Tag.

For example, a check valve is selected in the Valves tab in the Tool Palette and then inserted in a pipeline in the design, as shown in the following illustration. The flow direction of a check valve is critical. Since the line has an assigned direction, the check valve is automatically inserted in the correct direction.

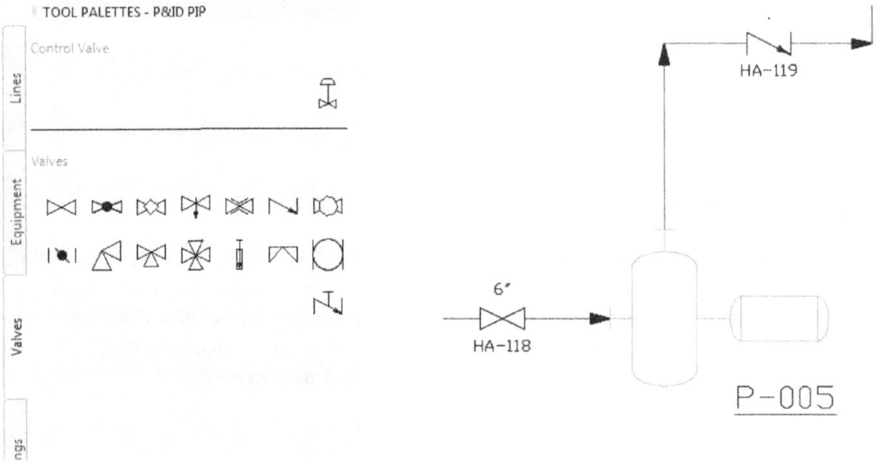

Change Flow Direction

To reverse the flow on a line, right-click on it and click Schematic Line Edit>Reverse Flow. Flow is reversed for all segments in the selected line, but not for the entire line group. Components along lines with a required flow direction, such as check valves, automatically change direction on lines in which the flow direction is reversed. Items, such as Reducers do not flip automatically because the flow direction of the pipe does not define their orientation.

Grouping Lines

You group lines when you want to group various pipeline segments into one pipeline group. The reason for grouping lines is that the pipeline group is carrying the line number and service information. Typically, a line list is created, which is made up of the pipeline group information. The line number is a vital part of that list.

When a line is started on an existing line, it is assigned to the line group of the existing line. However, if a line is terminated on an existing line, it is not automatically assigned to the existing group.

For example, two lines before and after the grouping process are shown in the following illustration. The tag information for the top line is automatically updated to display the Pipe Line Group Service designation and the Group Line Number.

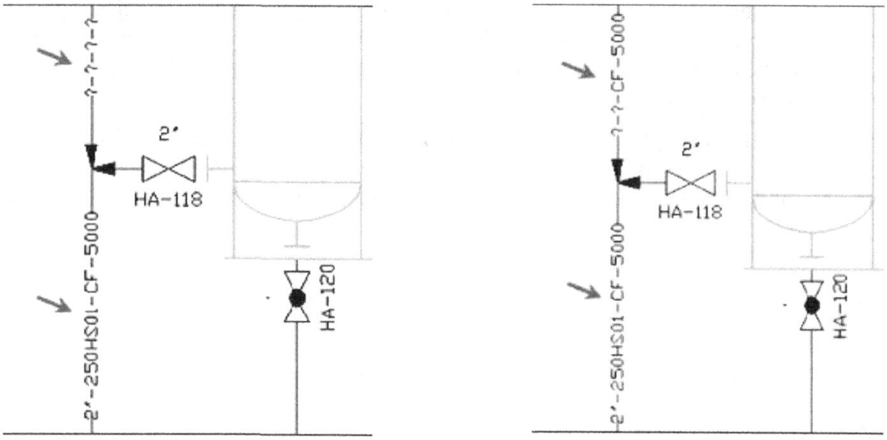

Process: Grouping Lines

To group lines, you start the Make Group command. You are prompted to select the source line. The tag information assigned to this line is the data used for both lines. You then select additional lines to be added to the group.

Accessing the Make Group command on the ribbon is shown in the following illustration.

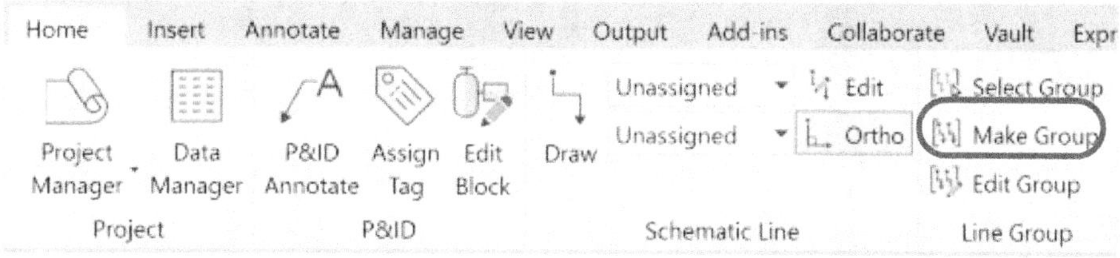

Guidelines

Follow these guidelines when creating lines and line groups:

- Pipeline groups carry line number and service information.
- A line started on an existing line is automatically assigned to that existing line's group.
- A new line terminating to an existing line is not automatically assigned to the existing group.
- When creating a new line group, the tag information assigned to the first selected line is the data used for all lines added to the group.

P&ID Painter

Colors for inline objects in P&ID drawings can be temporarily overridden to display information about pipelines using the P&ID Painter. Inline objects can be colored by properties by activating the Paint by Property command in the P&ID Painter panel on the ribbon. Colors can be selected in the drop-down list in the P&ID Painter panel. When the painter is activated, inline objects are colored according to a property value configured in the Project Setup.

Configuring P&ID Painter options is done using Project Setup by accessing the P&ID Painter Settings. Styles can be added to colorize inline items based on the value of properties. Only list type properties are available, and each listed value must have a color applied to it for display.

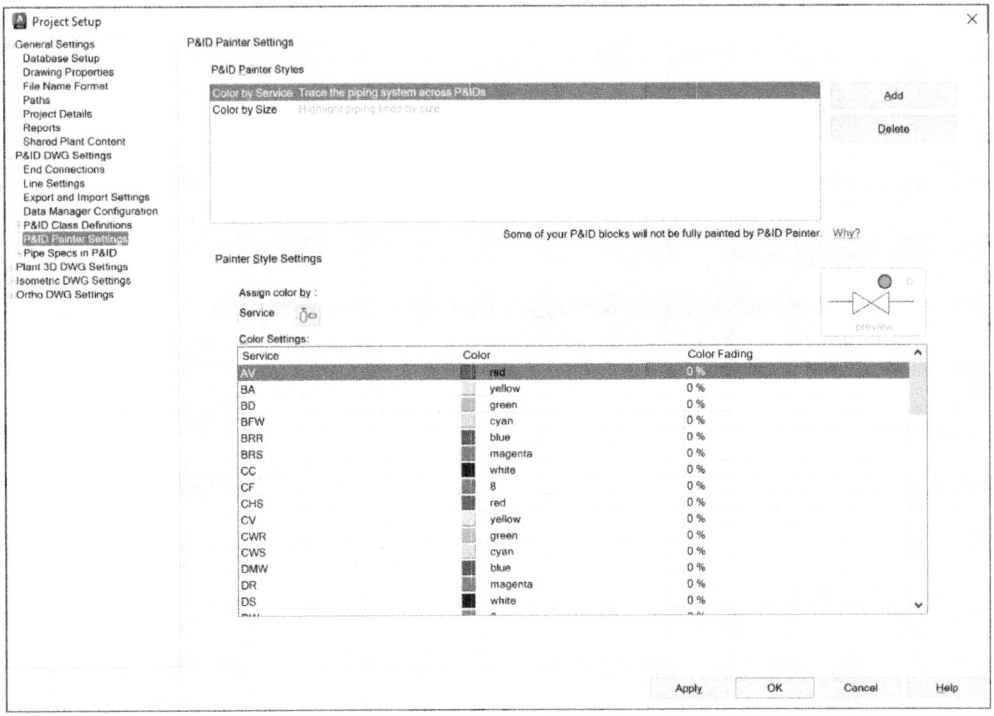

Exercise: Place Lines and Inline Components

In this exercise, you add pipelines to connect equipment and then add valves and reducers to the line to complete it. Finally, you place a spec breaker and delete a previously placed reducer.

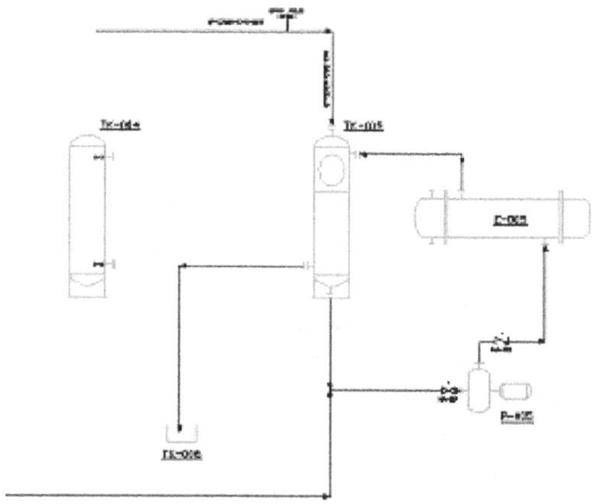

1. Start the AutoCAD Plant 3D software, if not already running.
2. Open the project as follows:
   - In the Project Manager, Current Project list, click Open.
   - In the Open dialog box, navigate to the folder *C:\Plant Design 2024 Practice Files\Place Lines and Inline Components*.
   - Select the file *Project.xml*.
   - Click Open.
3. In P&ID Drawings, open *PID002.dwg*.
4. Under Workspace Switching, click PID PIP, if not already active. In Tool Palettes, right-click on the header and click PID PIP to display the P&ID PIP Tool Palette, if required.
5. To make the Lines palette current, on the Tool Palettes, click the Lines tab.

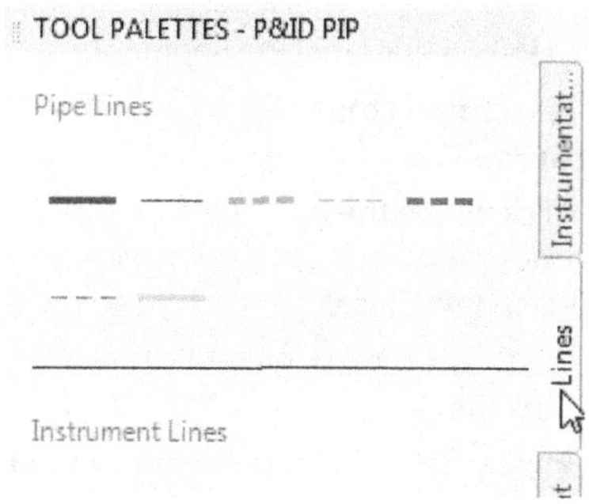

6. Add pipelines to the design, as follows.

   Note: The illustration shown below identifies the selections (1, 2, 3) with green numbered circles to identify where you should be making selections on the drawing.

   - On the Lines palette, under Pipe Lines, click Primary Line Segment.
   - Select a point above TK-004 (1).
   - Track from the midpoint of the top quadrant of tank TK-005 (3) and select the intersection of the line and the tracking point (2).
   - Select the midpoint of the top quadrant of TK-005 (3), as shown in the following illustration.

   Note that a nozzle is automatically added.

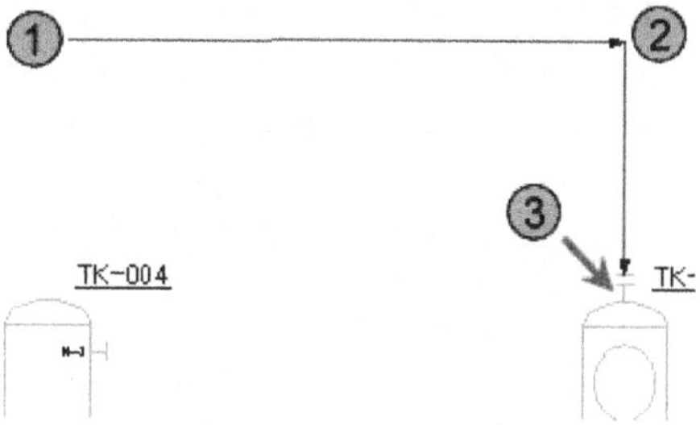

7. Add a line to the open tank, as follows.

Note: The illustration shown below identifies the selections (1, 2, 3) with green numbered circles to identify where you should be making selections on the drawing.

- Start the Primary Line Segment.
- Select along the left side of tank TK-005 as shown (1).
- Click above the open tank (2) (use tracking point from the midpoint of the open tank base).
- Click near the opening of the open tank (3).
- Press <Esc> to complete the command.

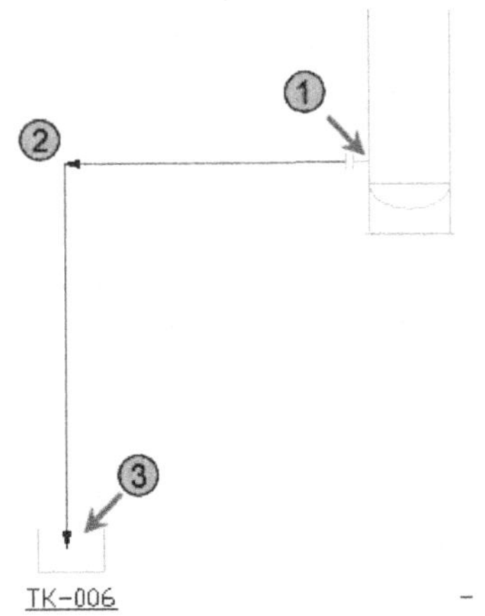

8. Using the same technique and tracking, add the following three pipelines to the design.

Note: The illustration shown below identifies Line numbers (1, 2, 3). The following steps require you to create all line segments.

- (Line 1) Starting from the base of TK-005 to the left nozzle of pump P-005.
- (Line 2) From the top nozzle of pump P-005 to the right nozzle on tank E-005. (Add a line to create a bend.)
- (Line 3) Starting anywhere from below the objects to the junction on line (1). (The arrows of the two lines at the junction should be pointing towards each other.)

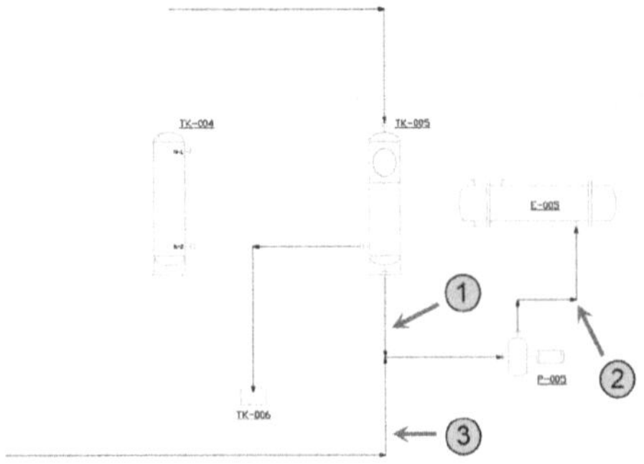

9. Assign presets for the size and spec properties for the line that will be created in the next step:

- In the Home tab, in the Schematic Line panel, select the first Unassigned drop-down list and select 4" as the size.
- In the second Unassigned drop-down list, select CS300 as the spec.

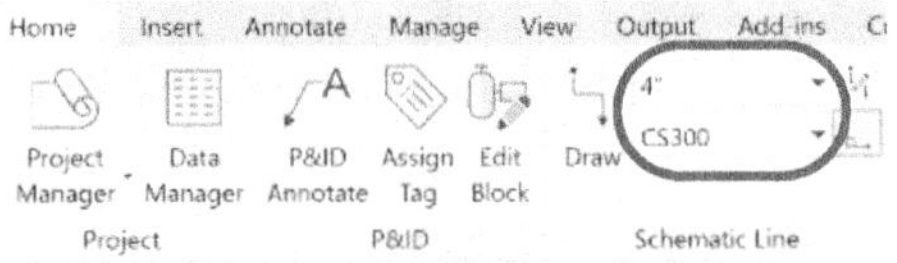

10. Click the Draw button or use the Tool Palette and draw a line from the top left nozzle of E-005 to the side of TK-005 as shown in the following illustration. Note that a nozzle is automatically created, and the new line drawn is 4" and CS300 spec.

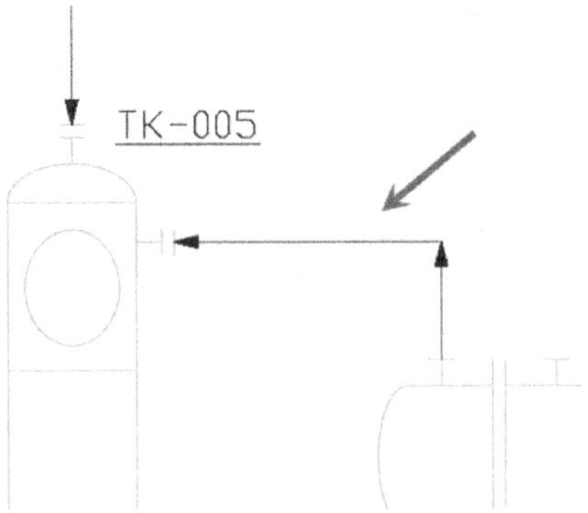

11. To assign tag data:

- Right click on Line 3 from Step 9. Click Assign Tag.
- In the Assign Tag dialog box, click in the size box and select **6"** from the drop-down list.
- Similarly, select the Spec (**1HS01**) and Pipe Line Group Service (**CWS**), as shown in the illustration below.
- Enter **001** in the Pipe Line Group Line Number.

Note how the tag is generated.

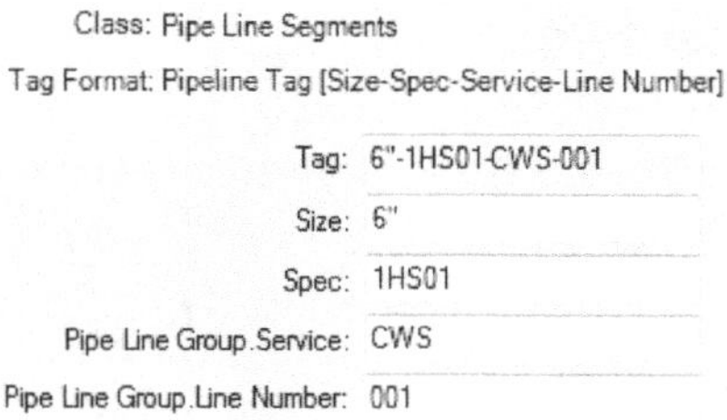

12. To place the tag:

- In the Assign Tag dialog box, under Existing Pipe Line Segments, select Place annotation after assigning tag.
- Click Assign.
- Place the annotation below the horizontal portion of Line 3.

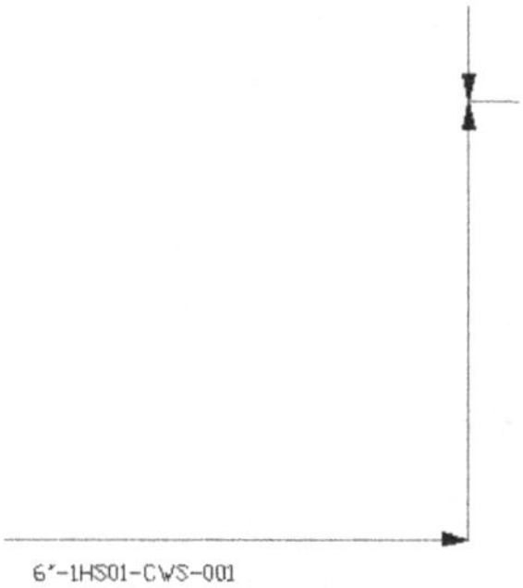

13. Assign tag data to the line going from TK-005 to P-005 (Line 1) and place it below the horizontal portion, as shown in the illustration below. In the Assign Tag dialog box, select the same values as before, except for Pipe Line Group Line Number, enter **002**.

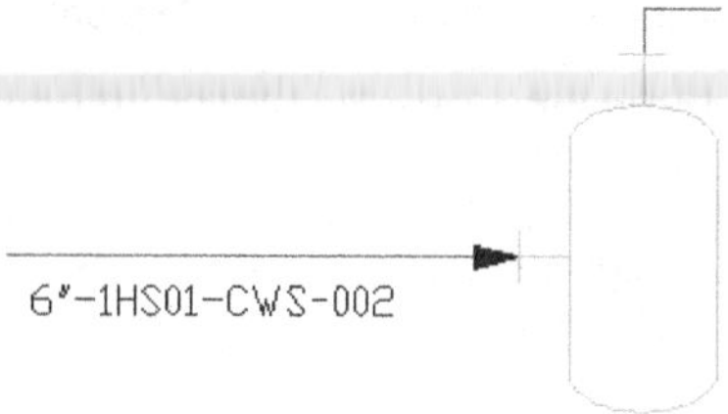

14. To group pipe segments:

- Hover the cursor over the line segment (1) from TK-005 to the pump P-005. Note the line segment that highlights and the tooltip information. Do not select the line segment.

Note: If the line does not highlight when you hover the cursor over it, right-click in the graphics window and click Options> Selection tab>When no command is active>OK.

- On the ribbon, on the Home tab, on the Line Group panel, click Make Group.
- When prompted to select the Source Line, select the line from TK-005 to the pump.
- When prompted to add lines, select the line that joins along the bottom to the junction of the initial line.
- Press <Enter>.
- Move the cursor over either of the lines. Note that they both highlight together and that the group numbers match in the tooltip.

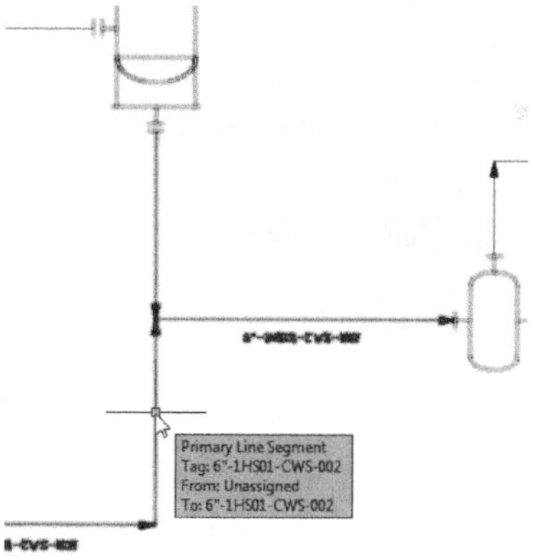

15. To access tag information for the pipeline:

- Hover the cursor over the line from empty space to the top nozzle of TK-005 (above all the objects). Note the information already assigned to the pipe with the Tag displaying ?-?-?-?.
- Right-click on the pipe.
- Click Assign Tag.

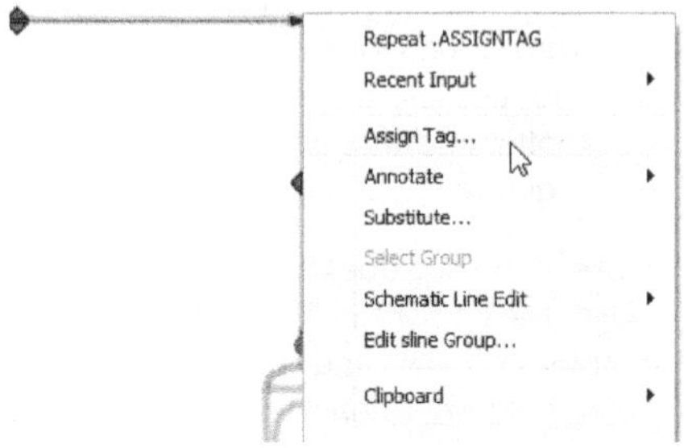

16. To assign information to the line:

- In the Assign Tag dialog box, select the information from the lists as shown and enter **1000** for Pipe Line Group Line Number.
- Under Existing Pipe Line Segments, select Place annotation after assigning tag, if required.

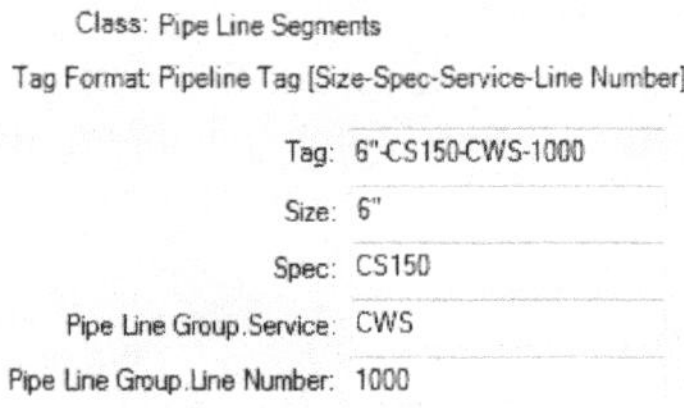

17. To add the tag to the design:

- Click Assign.
- Click above the horizontal line to place the tag information.

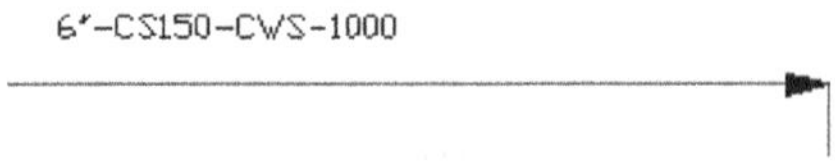

18. To add the same annotation to a different segment of the line:

- Right-click on the vertical portion of the same pipe just above TK-005.
- Under Annotate, click Pipeline Tag.
- Place the tag to the left of the vertical portion of the line. Note how it is placed vertically

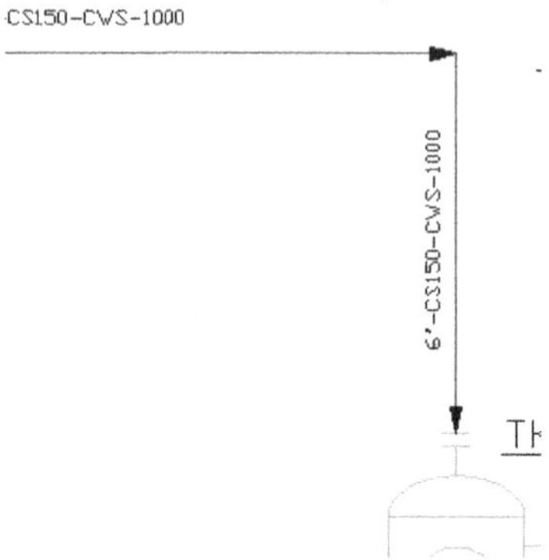

19. Click the Fittings tab in the Tool Palette.

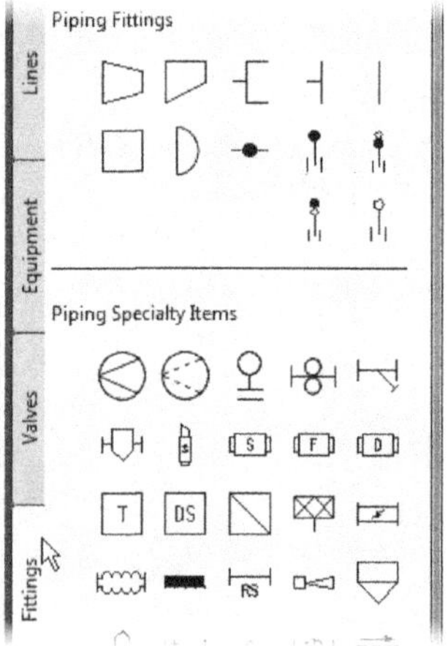

20. To add a reducer to the pipe segment:

- On the Fittings tab in the Tool Palette, under Piping Fittings, click Concentric Reducer.
- Click the pipeline to place the reducer as shown in the illustration.

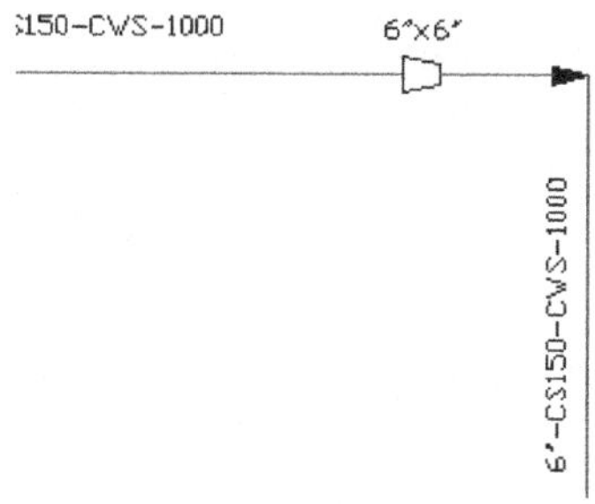

21. To edit the reducer size:

- Right-click on the pipeline to the left of the reducer.
- Click Assign Tag.
- In the Assign Tag dialog box, for size, select 4".
- Clear the checkmark for Place annotation after assigning tag.
- Click Assign.

Note the new values and the orientation of the reducer. Also note that the vertical tag is incorrect. It updated to show that it was 4" when it should be 6".

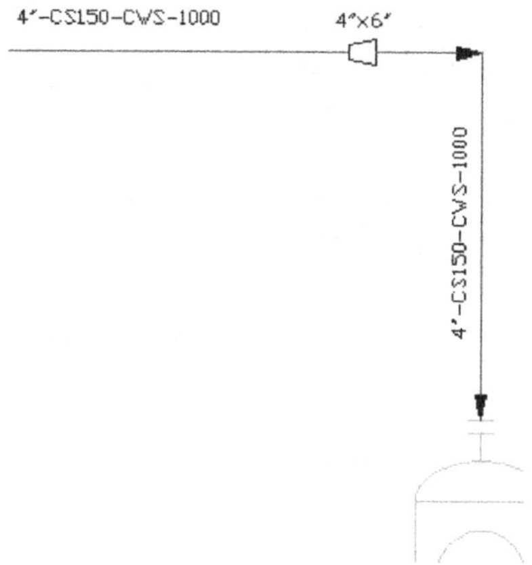

22. Delete the tag to the right of the Reducer that shows the pipeline as 4" (vertical tag)

23. Hover the cursor over the line on the 6" side of the Reducer. Right-click on the pipe and click Assign Tag.

24. Ensure that the Size is showing as 6". Enable the Place annotation after assigning tag option, click Assign, and place the tag. It updates to show the correct size.

25. To delete the reducer:

- Right-click on the reducer.
- Click Erase.
- In the Property Mismatch dialog box, click 6".
- Click Continue.

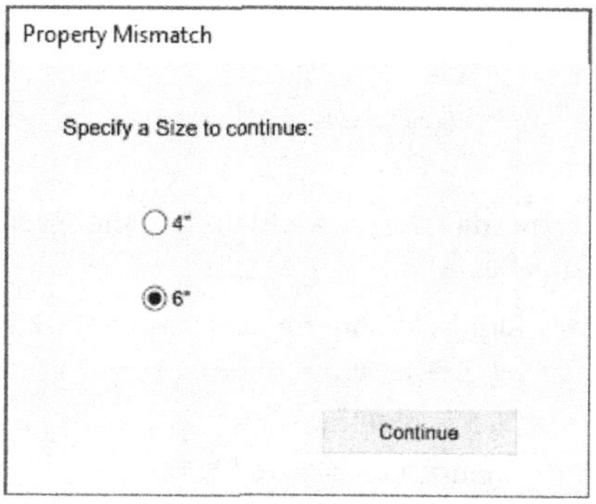

26. Click the Non-engineering tab in the Tool Palette.

27. To add a Segment Breaker to the design:

- On the Non-engineering palette, under Miscellaneous Symbols, click Segment Breaker.
- Select the pipe as shown in the following illustration.

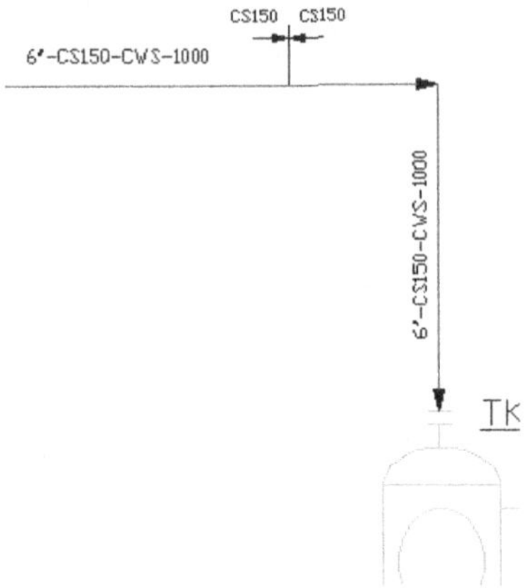

28. To modify the pipe and update the segment breaker:

- Right-click on the pipe segment to the left of the segment breaker.
- Click Assign Tag.
- Change the Spec to CS300.
- Clear the Place annotation after assigning tag.
- Click Assign.

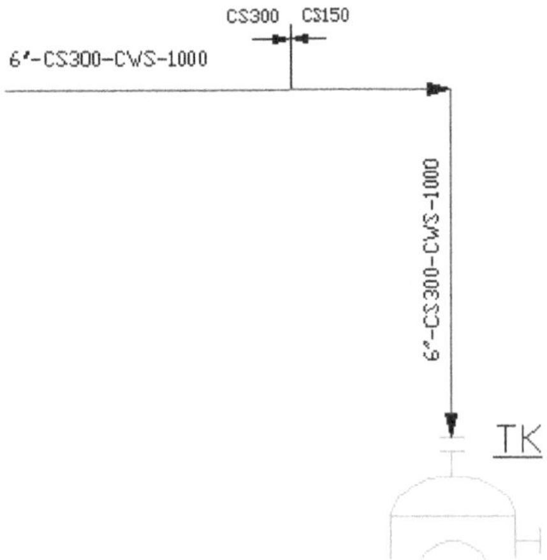

29. Note that the tag to the right of the segment breaker updated incorrectly. Erase the tag and recreate it to show the correct spec.

30. Click the Valves tab in the Tool Palette.

31. To insert a valve:

- On the Valves tab, under Valves, click Gate Valve.
- Select the pipe segment at the bottom left of TK-005 as shown in the illustration.

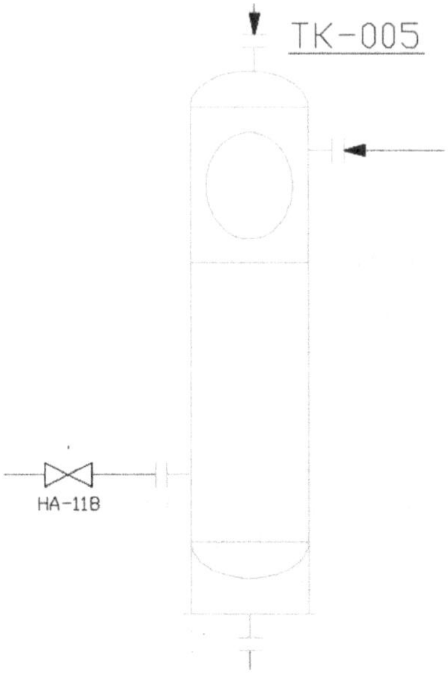

32. To move the valve to a different pipe segment (left side of P-005), select the square grip on the valve and drag it to the new location, as shown in the following illustration. Press <Esc> to clear grips.

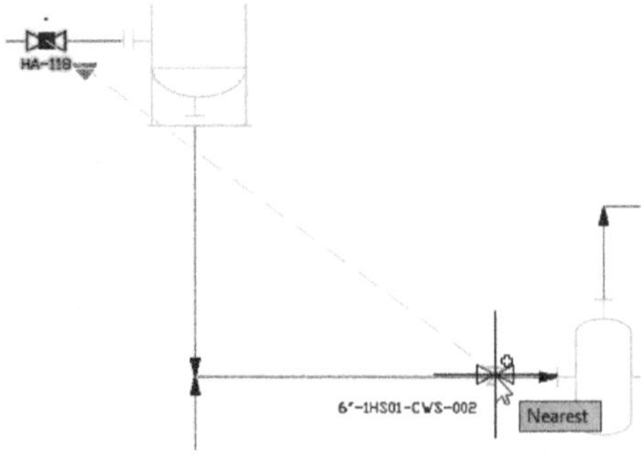

33. To place a check valve:

- Under Valves, click Check Valve.
- Select the horizontal pipe segment from the pump P-005 to E-005.

Note that the direction of the valve matches the direction of the pipe flow.

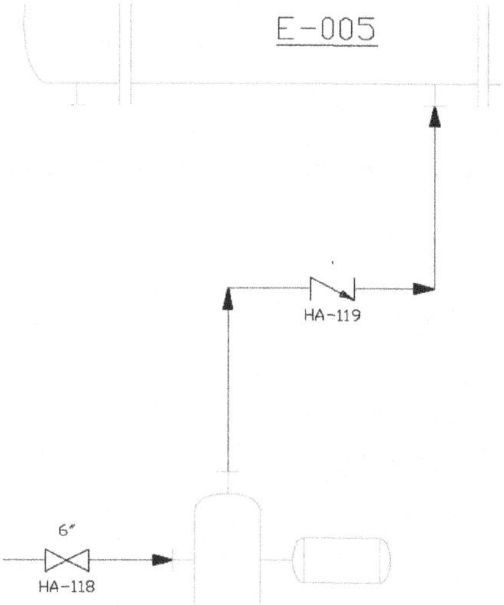

34. To review pipe information:

- Hover the cursor over the segment going from TK-005 to the TK-006 (Open Tank).
- Note that the line goes from TK-005 to Unassigned.

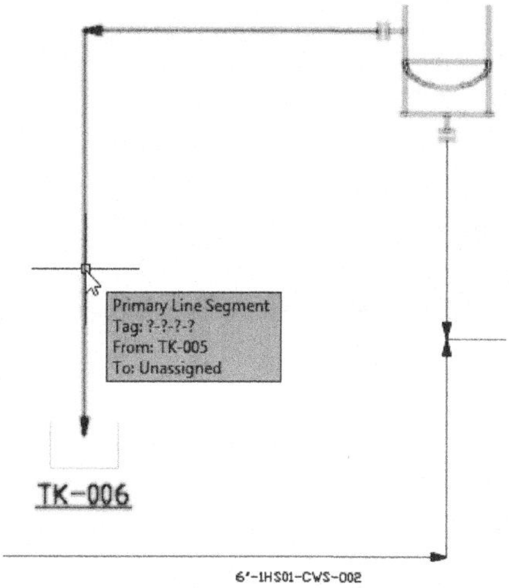

35. To assign a pipe to a component:

- Right-click on the pipe segment.
- Under Schematic Line Edit, click Attach to Component.
- Select TK-006 (Open Tank, not the tag).
- Select the endpoint of the pipeline.
- Hover the cursor over the segment again and note that the line goes from TK-005 to TK-006.

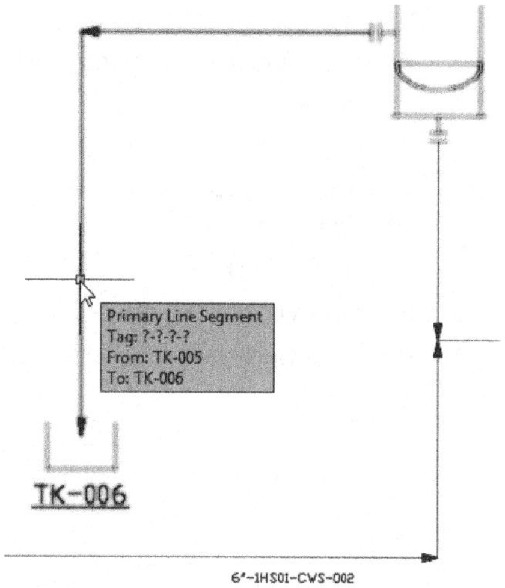

36. To paint the lines by property:

- In the Home tab of the ribbon, in the P&ID Painter panel, verify that Color by Service is selected in the drop-down list.
- Click Paint P&ID icon to enable the painter.
- Examine the color changes that occurred to the pipelines and other inline components.
- Click the Paint P&ID icon again to disable the painter.

37. Save and close all drawings.

Lesson Review Questions

1. When deleting a reducer or spec break, how do you determine which size or spec of the line remains?
   a. The line reverts to the size or spec prior to the addition of the symbol.
   b. A dialog box prompts you to choose between the sizes and the specs.
2. A placed check valve orients automatically based on the flow direction of the pipeline.
   a. True
   b. False
3. When the flow direction of a pipeline changes, the reducer on the line also changes its direction.
   a. True
   b. False
4. How can you change the flow direction of a check valve without changing the flow direction of the pipeline?
   a. Select the check valve and click the flow grip.
   b. Right-click on the check valve and select Change flow direction.
5. Which property information is applied to line tags in the pipeline group?
   a. Spec
   b. Size
   c. Line Number
   d. Service

Lesson: Instruments and Instrument Lines

Overview

In this lesson, you learn to place the different types of instruments and to set up a measurement loop using instruments and several different instrument lines. You also learn the difference between a general instrument and an inline instrument.

A section of the design before and after instruments and instruments lines have been added is shown in the following illustration.

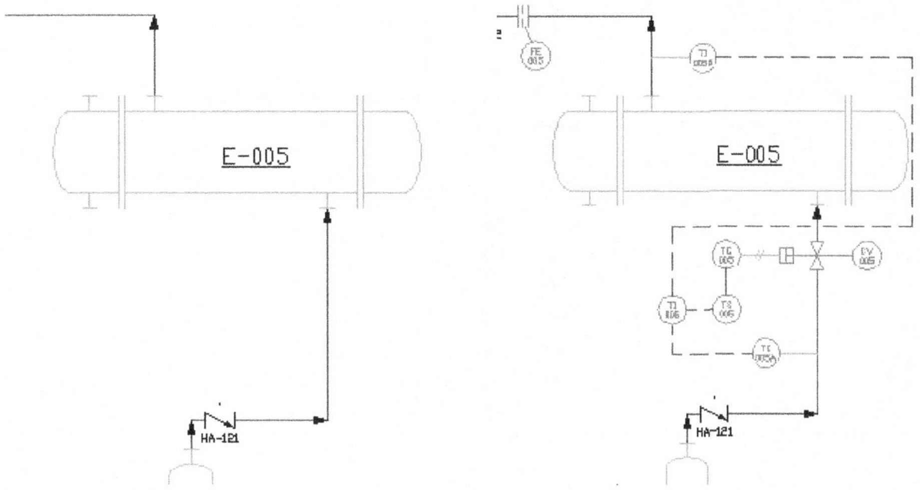

Objectives

After completing this lesson, you will be able to:

- Add general instruments to a P&ID design.
- Add inline instruments to a P&ID design.
- Add instrumentation lines to a P&ID design.

Adding General Instruments

General Instrument symbols are used in a P&ID design to represent instrumentation that monitors the various lines and components in the design. You access General Instruments on the Instruments tab on the Tool Palette.

The General Instruments on the Instruments tab on the Tool Palettes are shown in the following illustration.

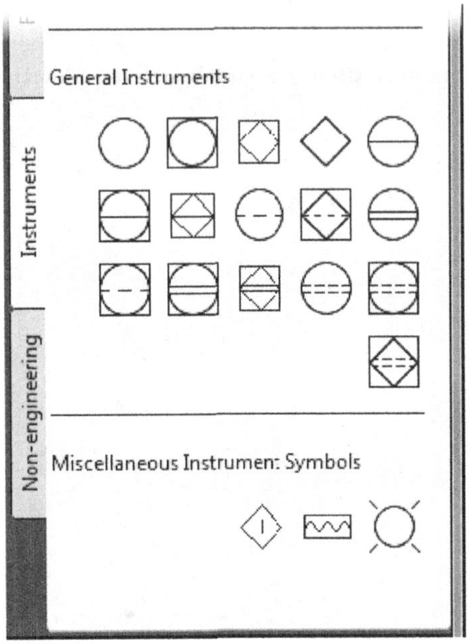

Process: Adding General Instruments

To add a General Instrument symbol to a P&ID drawing, in the Tool Palette, click the Instruments tab, and under General Instruments, select the required instrument symbol. You then click in canvas to locate the symbol. When adding a general instrument symbol, you can pick a random area in the canvas, or insert the symbol inline with existing instrumentation lines.

When the symbol is placed, the Assign Tag dialog box opens, enabling you to define parameters regarding the specifics of the instrument to be used in the design. By default, the instrument balloon displays. You can also display the tag information and pick the annotation style. The Balloon's information is a representation of the instrument tag.

The process after the instrument symbol has been placed in the canvas is shown in the following illustration. On the left, the data defining the instrument is entered and selected in the Assign Tag dialog box. On the right, the resulting instrumentation symbol and tag is displayed.

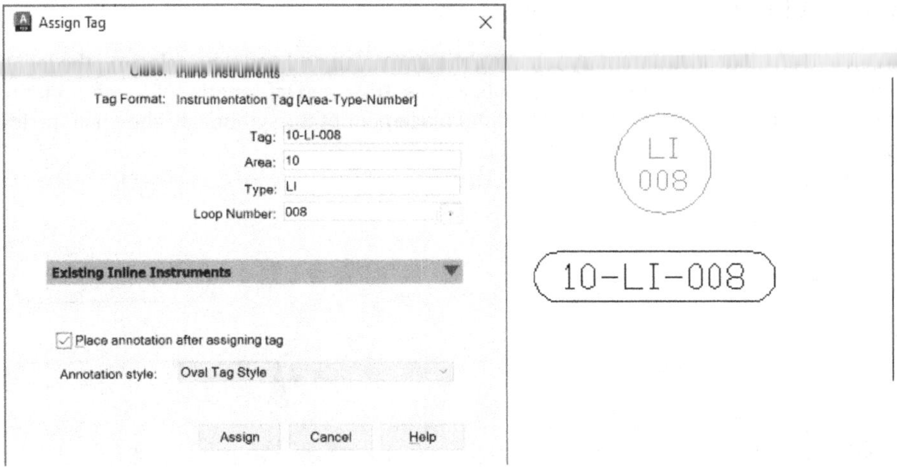

Adding Inline Instruments

Inline instrumentation is added to a P&ID design by selecting the required symbol on the Instruments tab, under Primary Element Symbols (Flow) in the Tool Palette. You then locate the symbol by selecting pipeline.

Like most other symbols, when you locate the inline symbol, the Assign Tag dialog box opens to enable you to specify data regarding the symbol. When complete, the AutoCAD P&ID software automatically breaks the pipeline around the inserted inline symbol.

The Instruments tab, under Primary Element Symbols (Flow) in the Tool Palette is shown in the following illustration. In the Tool Palette, the Restriction Orifice symbol is being selected.

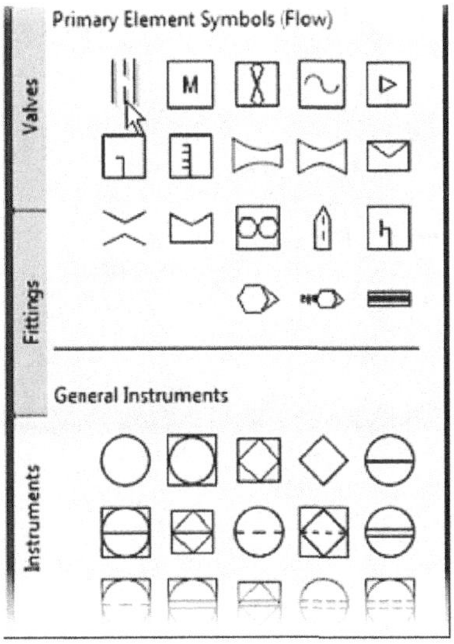

Process: Adding Inline Instrumentation

You can add an inline instrument by selecting the symbol to add and then selecting the location on the line. After specifying its insertion location, you assign its tag information. Tag information being added to an inline instrument and the resulting placement of the symbol are shown in the following illustration.

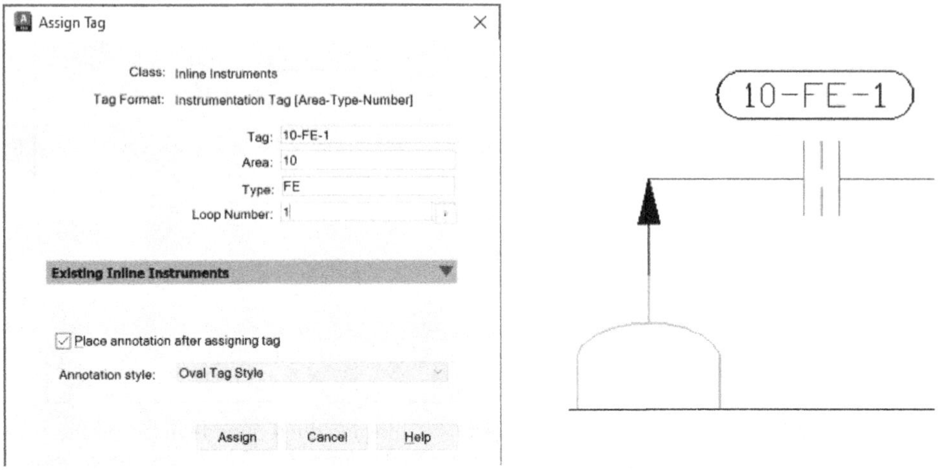

Using Instrumentation Lines

Instrumentation lines connect the general instrumentation symbols to the pipelines and other components comprising a P&ID design. Instrument lines connecting gauges to the plant components are shown in the following illustration.

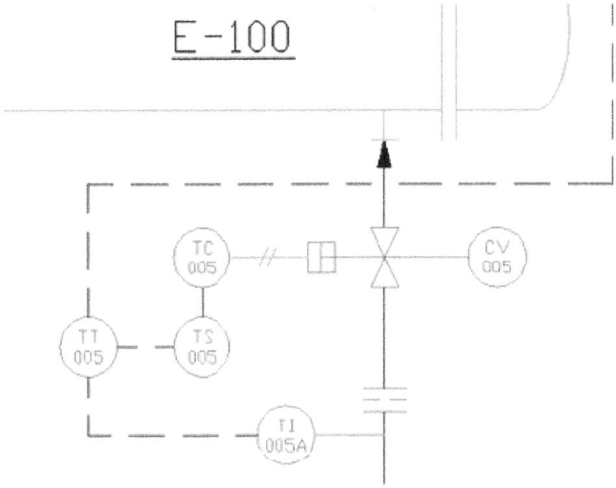

Process: Using Instrumentation Lines

To add Instrument Lines to your design, you select the type of line required in the Lines tab in the Tool Palette. You then select the starting and ending points of the line to connect the components. At any time you can add or remove components from the line. You cannot assign tags to instrument lines. The Electrical Signal instrumentation line being selected in the Lines tab in the Tool Palette, and the resulting line created to connect two general instrument symbols in the P&ID design is shown in the following illustration.

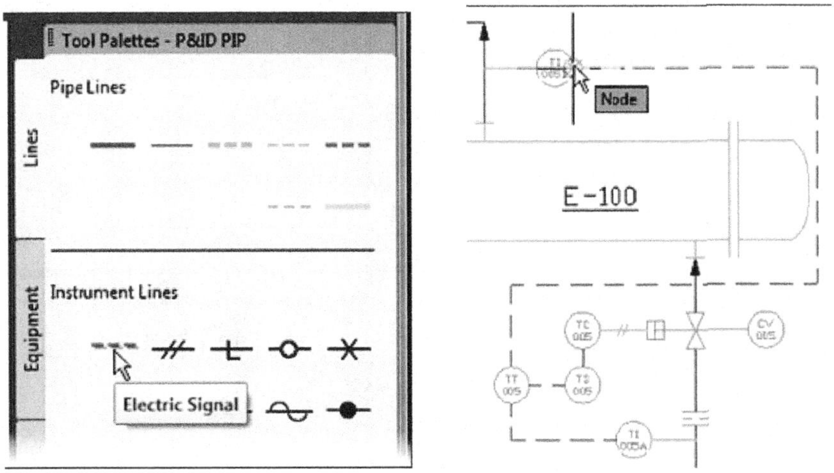

Exercise: Instruments and Instrument Lines

In this exercise, you place an inline instrument (orifice, flow instrument, etc.) and add the required tag that will be made visible with the instrument balloon. Next, you create a temperature measuring loop around the heat exchanger that measures the temperature difference in front of and after the heat exchanger. The signals lead to a control instrument that sends a signal to the control valve to open or close it.

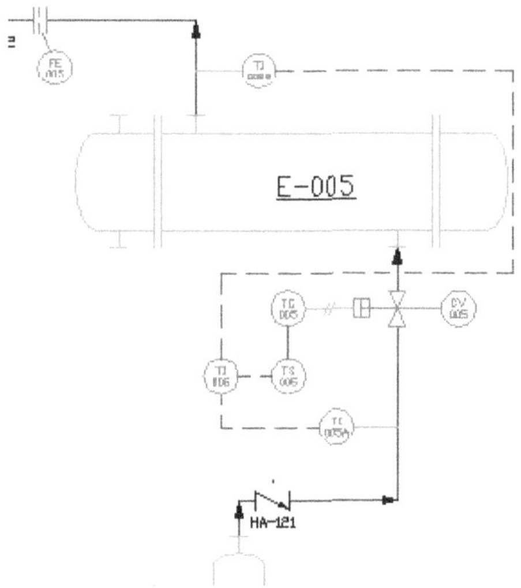

1. Start the AutoCAD Plant 3D software, if not already running.
2. Open the project as follows:
   - In the Project Manager, Current Project list, click Open.
   - In the Open dialog box, navigate to the folder *C:\Plant Design 2024 Practice Files\Instruments and Instrument Lines*.
   - Select the file *Project.xml*.
   - Click Open.
3. In P&ID Drawings, open *PID002.dwg*.
4. Under Workspace Switching, click PID PIP, if not already active. If the P&ID PIP Tool Palette is not displayed, right-click on the header in the Tool Palette and click PID PIP.
5. Click the Instruments tab in the Tool Palettes - P&ID PIP.

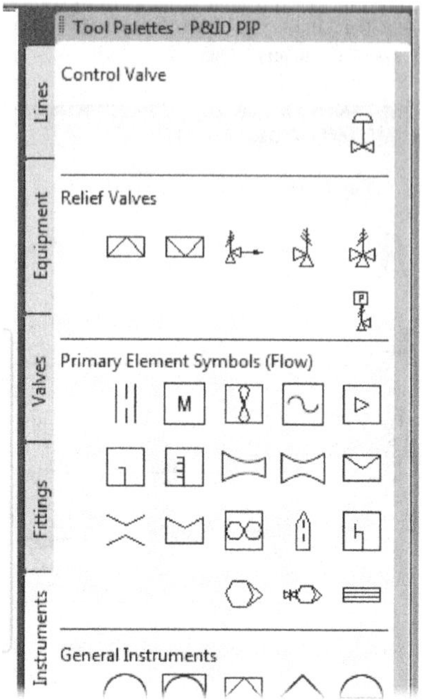

6. To add an orifice to the design:
   - Zoom to the area of Ball Valve HA-122.
   - In the Instruments tab of the Tool Palette, under Primary Element Symbols (Flow), click Restriction Orifice.
   - Locate the orifice by clicking the line to the right of Ball Valve HA-122 as shown in the following illustration.

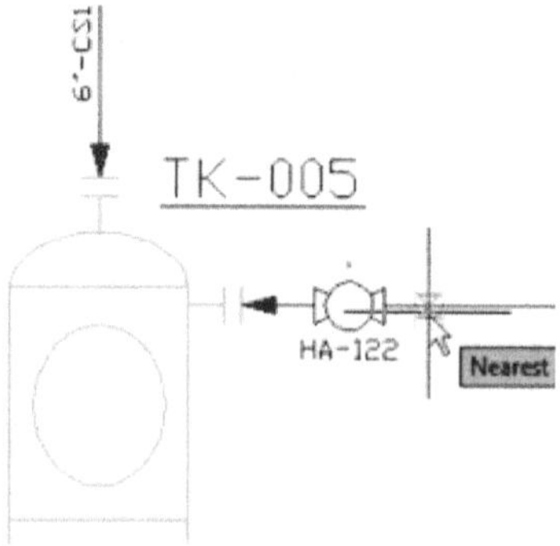

7. To assign tag information:
   - In the Assign Tag dialog box, for Area, enter **10**.
   - For Type, click in the field and select FE-Flow Element from the list, if required.
   - For Loop Number, enter **005**.
   - Under Existing Inline Instruments, clear the Place annotation after assigning tag option.

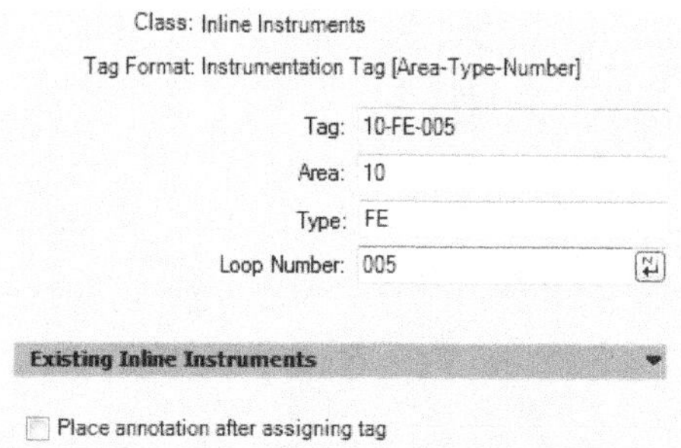

8. To complete the addition of the orifice:
   - In the Assign Tag dialog box, click Assign.
   - Click below and right to the symbol.

Note: Symbol color has been changed for clarity.

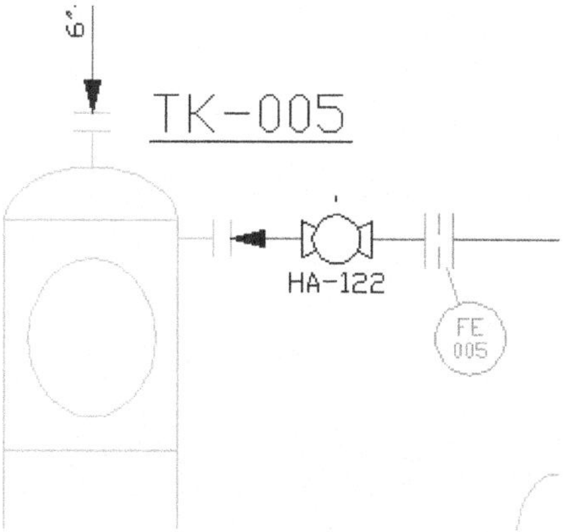

Note: If frames are displayed around the tag information you can set WIPEOUTFRAME to 0.

9. To define a control valve to add to your design:
   - In the Instruments tab of the Tool palettes, under Control Valve, click Control Valve.
   - In the Control Valve Browser dialog box, under Select Control Valve Body, select Gate Valve.
   - **Note:** Once the first Control Valve has been placed it becomes the default and the Control Valve Browser dialog box does not automatically open. To open the Control Valve Browser dialog box, right-click and click Change body or actuator.
   - Under Select Control Valve Actuator, select Piston Actuator.
   - Click OK.

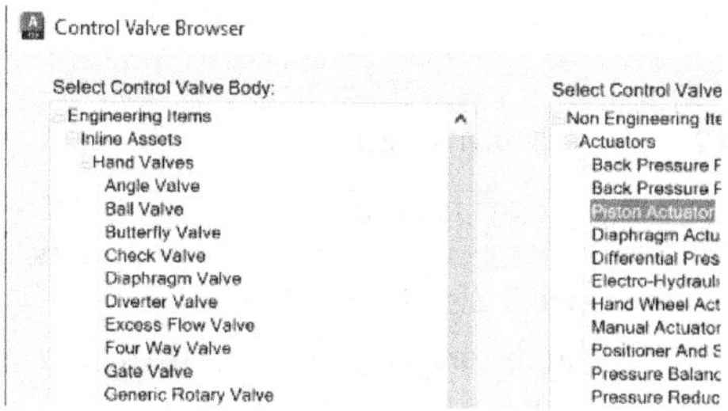

10. To locate the control valve:
   - Click the pipeline below E-005 as shown in step 11.
   - Click to the right of the valve to locate the tag.
   - In the Assign Tag dialog box, for Area, enter **10**.
   - For Loop Number, enter **005**.

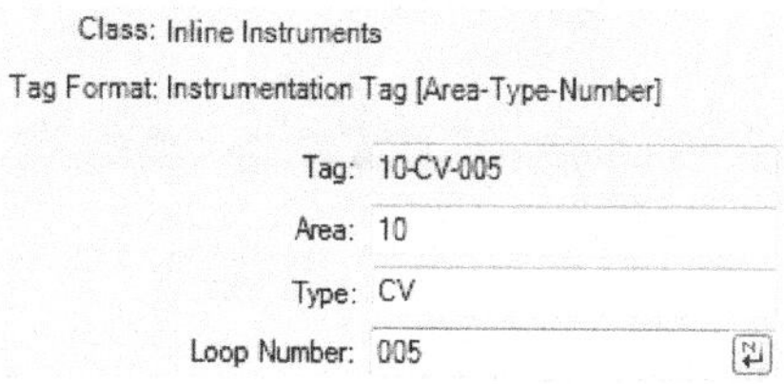

11. Click Assign.

Note: Symbol color has been changed for clarity.

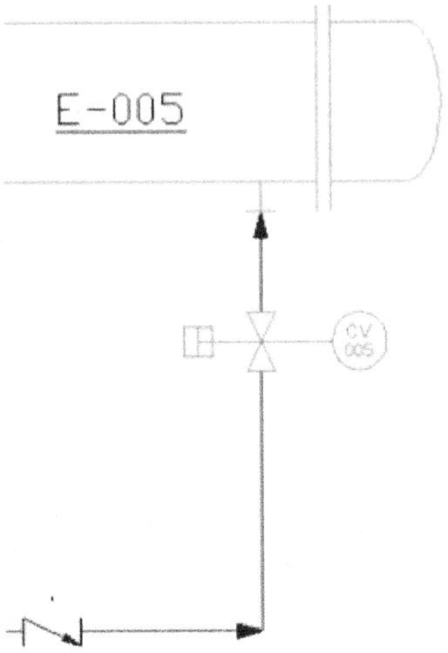

12. To add an instrument:

- On the Instruments tab in the Tool Palette, under General Instruments, click Field Discrete Instrument.
- In the drawing window, click to the left of Control Valve CV-005.
- In the Assign Tag dialog box, for Area, enter **10**.
- For Type, select **TC**.
- For Loop Number, enter **005**.
- Click Assign.

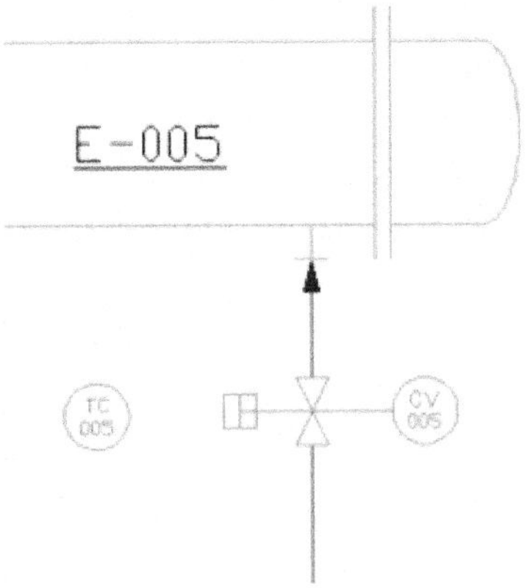

13. To add another instrument:

- Press <Enter>.
- Click below the first instrument.
- In the Assign Tag dialog box, for Type, select **TS**.
- Click Assign.

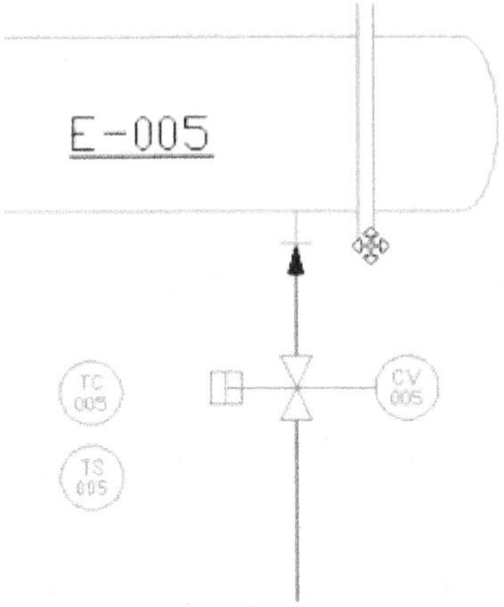

14. Place three additional instruments (TI- 005, 005A, and 005B) as shown in the following illustration.

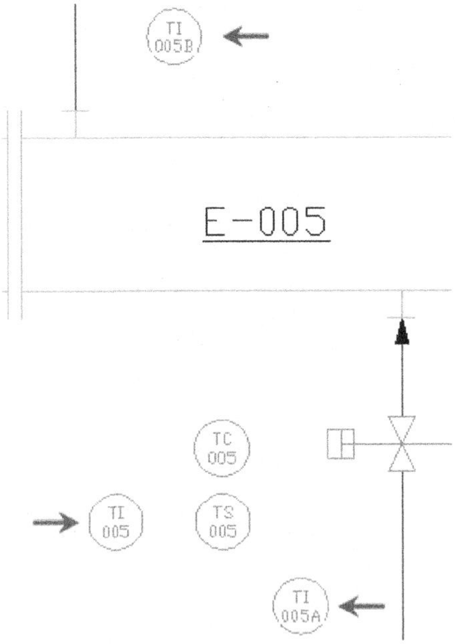

15. Click the Lines tab in the Tool Palette.

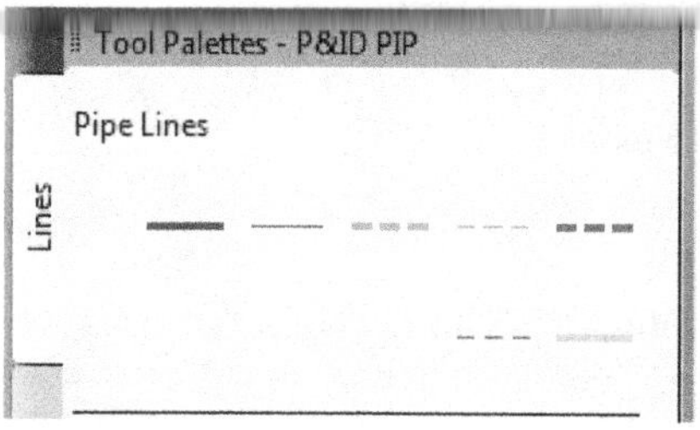

16. To add a leader line:

- On the Lines tab in the Tool Palette, under Instrument Lines, click Leader.
- Select the right quadrant on the TI-005A instrument to attach the leader line.
- Select the pipeline to the right.
- Create the leader line for the TI-005B instrument as shown in the following illustration.

Note: After completing the first line, press <Enter> to restart the command.

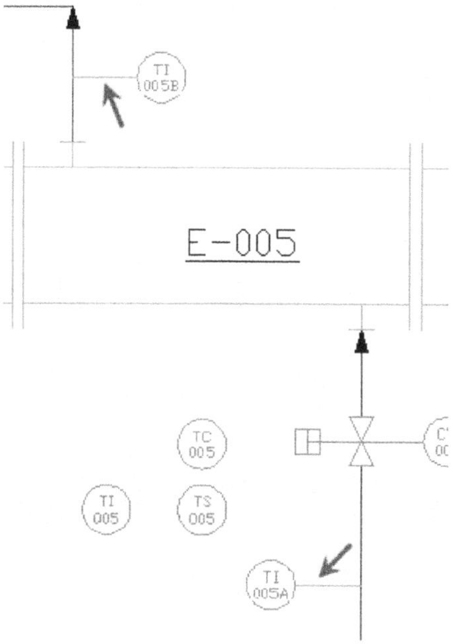

17. To add electrical lines:

- On the Lines tab in the Tool Palette, under Instrument Lines, click Electric Signal.
- Place the four lines as shown (arrows).

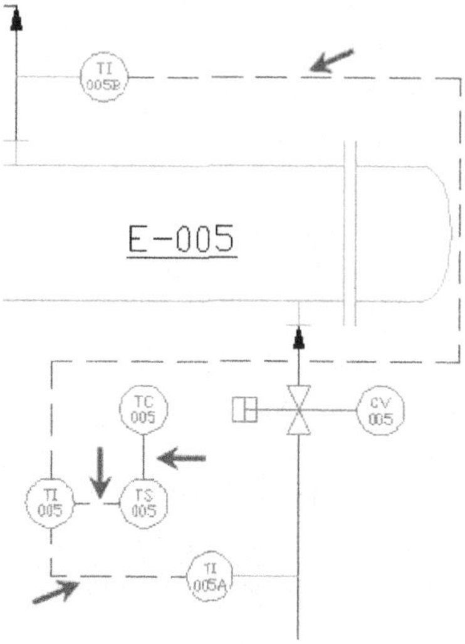

18. To add a pneumatic line:

- On the Lines tab in the Tool Palette, under Instruments Lines, click Pneumatic Signal.
- Click the control valve and the instrument as shown in the following illustration.

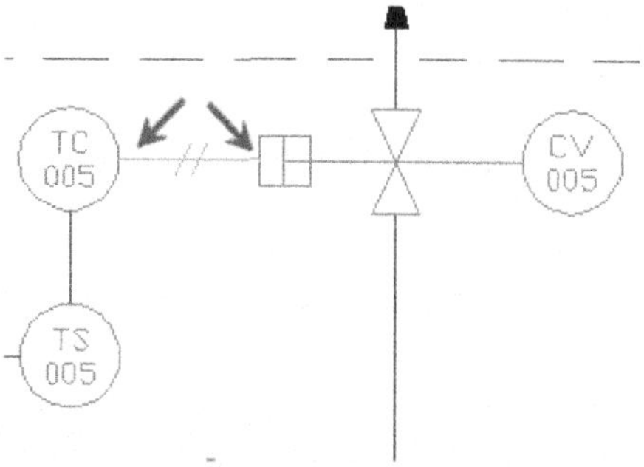

Note: If the Signal lines do not display with the linetypes shown in image, this might be because of the distance between the Instruments and the linetype scale of the drawing. Hover the cursor over the line to ensure the correct line type is used.

19. Save and close all drawings.

Lesson Review Questions

1. It is possible to place general instruments inline on a pipeline.
   a. True
   b. False
2. What are the named groups of instrument types in AutoCAD Plant 3D? (Select all that apply.)
   a. Primary Element Instruments
   b. General Instruments
   c. Valve Instruments
3. A general instrument balloon is a representation of its tag.
   a. True
   b. False
4. Do instrumentation lines carry a tag similar to the pipelines?
   a. Yes, they carry the same information as pipelines.
   b. No, the tag property is not available for instrument lines.
   c. Yes, the tag property is available for instrument lines.
5. Instrumentation lines are found on the Instruments tab in the Tool Palette.
   a. True
   b. False

Lesson: Tagging Concepts

Overview

In this lesson, you learn how tagging can be used to create unique tags and how it can be used to create a unique tag that is used to link symbols over multiple drawings.

You can assign tags to your components and lines, as shown in the following illustration. A tag is data that is never displayed on a drawing. However, an annotation often includes a tag property and displays that property on a drawing. To fully benefit from tags and tag data, you need to understand their purpose and where they are created and used.

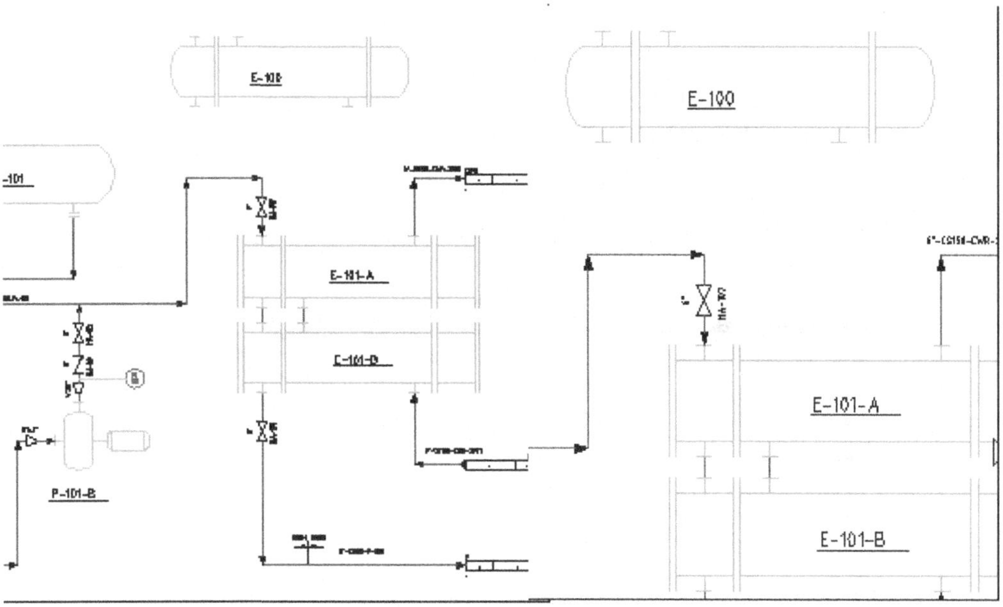

Objectives

After completing this lesson, you will be able to:

- Explain how to view existing tag data.
- Link tag data to symbols in multiple drawings.

View Existing Tag Numbers

Each time a drawing is added to a project, the data from that drawing is incorporated into the project. When you assign tag information in the Assign Tag dialog box, you can view the existing tags by expanding the dialog box.

Just below the Number field, a label that begins with Existing is displayed. The exact name depends on the component that is being assigned tag information. For example, when assigning tag information for a Heat Exchanger, the title is Existing Heat Exchangers. For a pump, it is Existing Pumps. By clicking the arrow at the end of the title area, you see all of the components of the same type listed with their tag numbers.

The Assign Tag dialog box with the existing component information displayed by expanding the Existing Heat Exchangers drop-down list is shown in the following illustration.

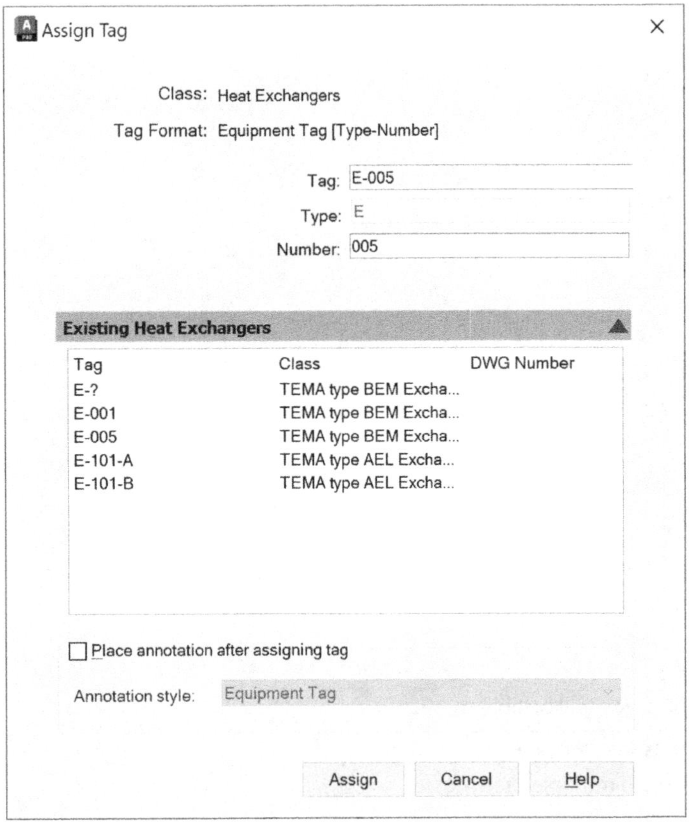

Linking Symbols to Multiple Drawings

Often the symbol for one component in the PID design has to be displayed in two or more drawings in the project. In these situations, you can link the tag information assigned to one of the symbols to the other iterations of it in the project. To perform this operation, each drawing to be linked needs to be open.

Process: Link Symbols to Multiple Drawings

The following steps describe how to link symbols in two drawings to each other.

1. Open all drawings containing the symbol in the project to be linked.

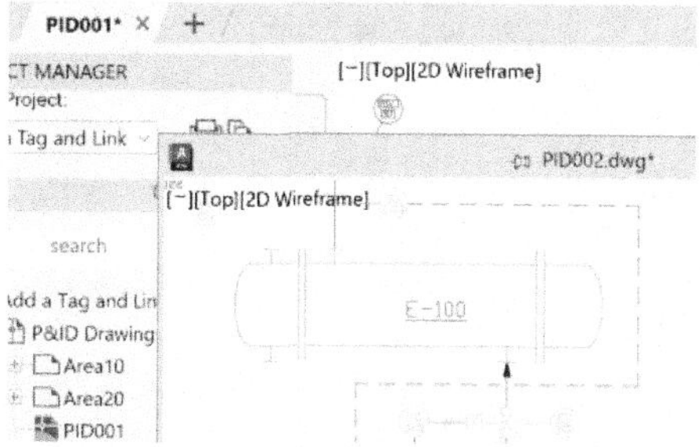

2. Insert a new symbol or go to the symbol in need of tag information.

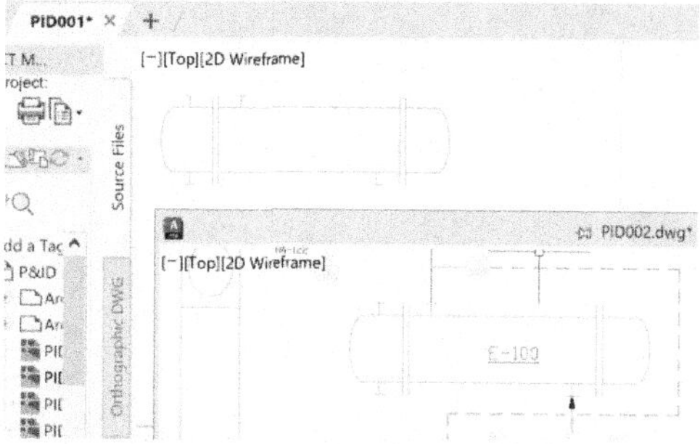

3. Open the Assign Tag dialog box and review the list of assigned tags by expanding the Existing... area.

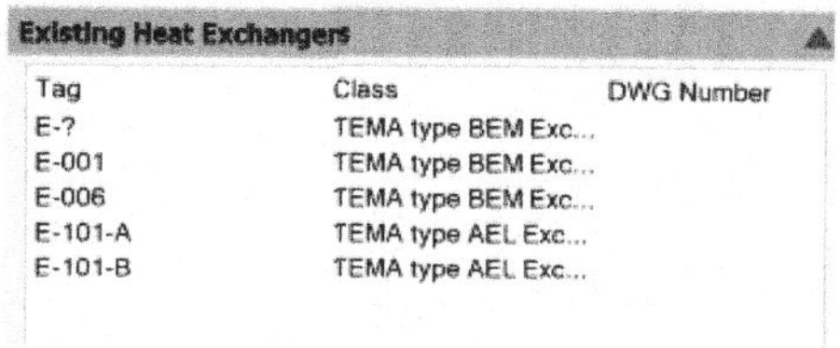

4. In the Number field, enter the number of the symbol to be linked, click Assign. In the Tag Already Assigned dialog box, click Assign this Tag to the selected component. Click OK.

   Note: To display the tag data, In the Assign Tag dialog box, be sure to check Place annotation after assigning tag.

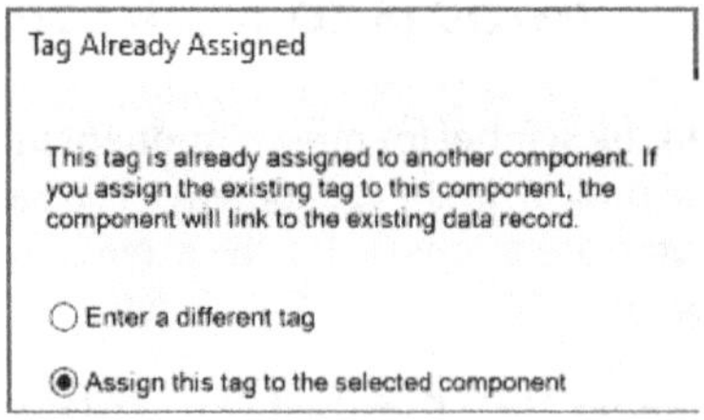

5. The two symbols are linked.

Exercise: Add a Tag and Link Multiple Symbols to a Tag

In this exercise, you review a tag to determine whether it is already in use and you link symbols over multiple drawings using the same tag.

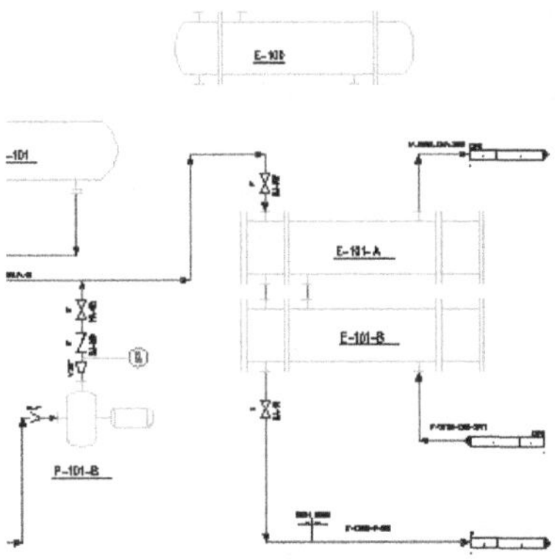

1. Start the AutoCAD Plant 3D software, if not already running.

2. Open the project as follows:
   - In the Project Manager, Current Project list, click Open.
   - In the Open dialog box, navigate to the folder *C:\Plant Design 2024 Practice Files\Add a Tag and Link Multiple Symbols to a Tag*.
   - Select the file *Project.xml*.
   - Click Open.

3. Open *PID002.dwg* in the *P&ID Drawings* folder.

4. Ensure that you are working in the PID PIP Workspace and Tool Palettes.

5. If not already displayed, press <Ctrl>+<1> to display the AutoCAD Properties palette.

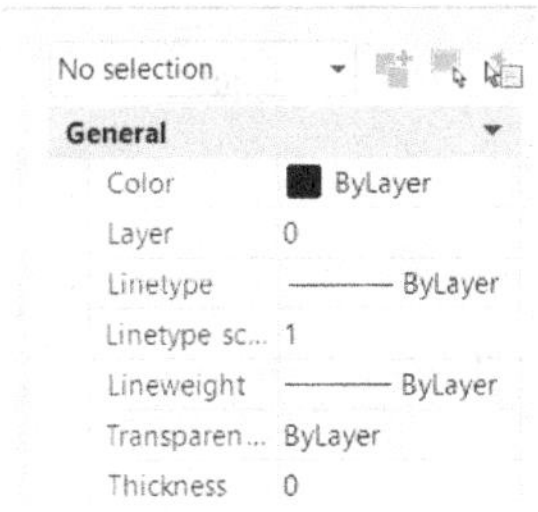

6. To edit a P&ID symbol tag using the Properties palette:
   - Select Heat Exchanger E-005.
   - In the Properties palette, under Tag, select Tag E-005. Once selected, click the More button.
   - In the Assign Tag dialog box, for Number, enter **006**.
   - Click Assign.

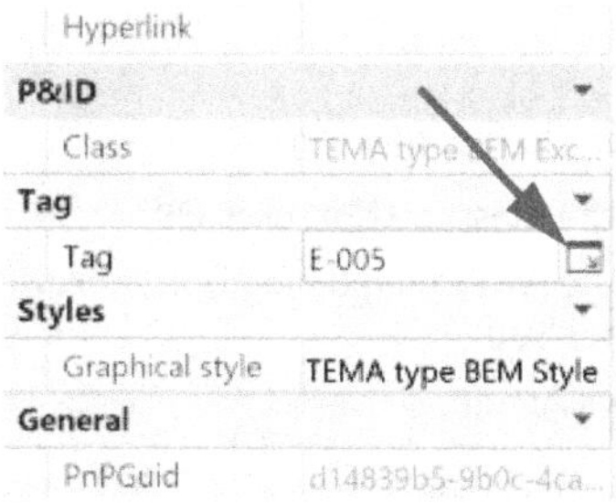

7. Close the Properties palette.

8. To view other tags:
   - Right-click on Heat Exchanger E-006.
   - Click Assign Tag.
   - In the Assign Tag dialog box, for Existing Heat Exchangers, expand the list by clicking on the arrow.

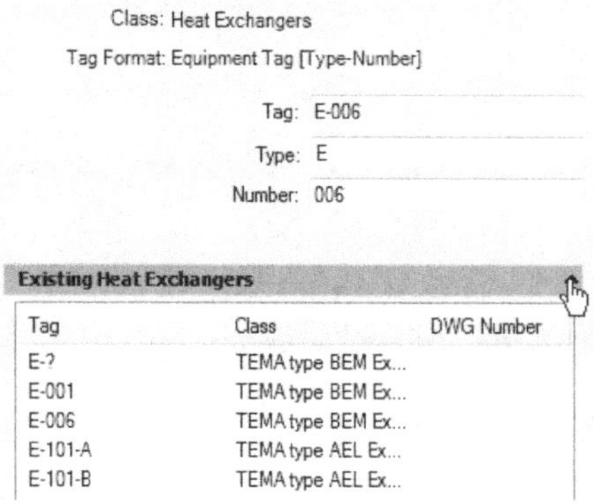

9. Note the presence of the E-001 Heat Exchanger.
   - In the Assign Tag dialog box, for Number, enter **001**.
   - Click Assign.
   - A message is displayed that indicates the number is already assigned to an asset.

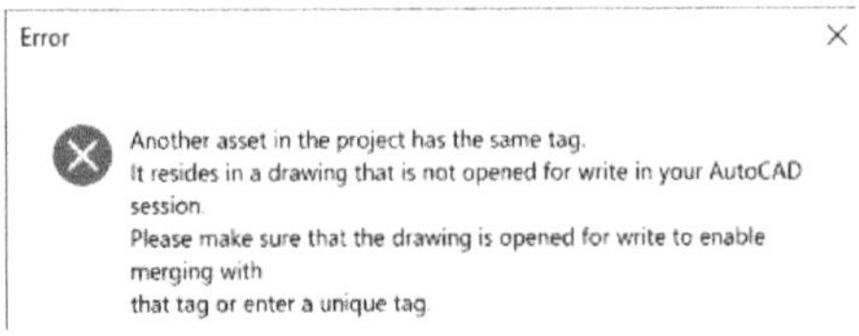

10. To return to the drawing:
    - In the message box, click OK.
    - In the Assign Tag dialog box, for Number, enter **100**.
    - Click Assign.
11. In the Project Manager, under P&ID Drawings, right-click on PID001. Click Open.
12. In drawing PID001, zoom into the area of the heat exchanger near the top right side as shown in the following illustration. Note that the heat exchanger has not been assigned a tag.

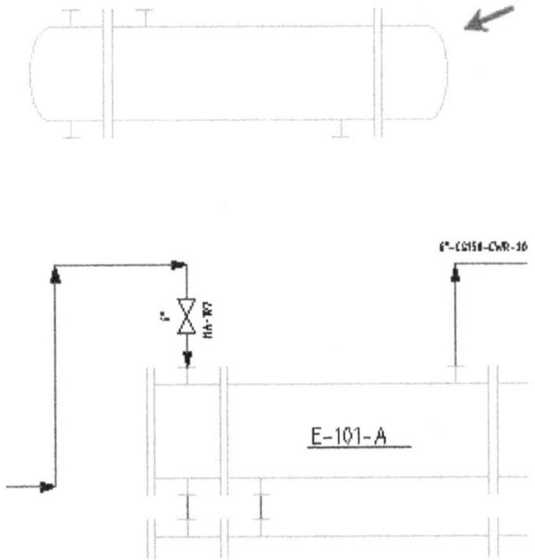

13. To assign a tag to the heat exchanger:
    - Right-click on the heat exchanger.
    - Click Assign Tag.
    - In the Assign Tag dialog box, for Number, enter **100**.
    - Click Assign.
14. To link the heat exchangers in the two drawings:
    - In the Tag Already Assigned dialog box, select Assign this tag to the selected component.
    - Click OK.

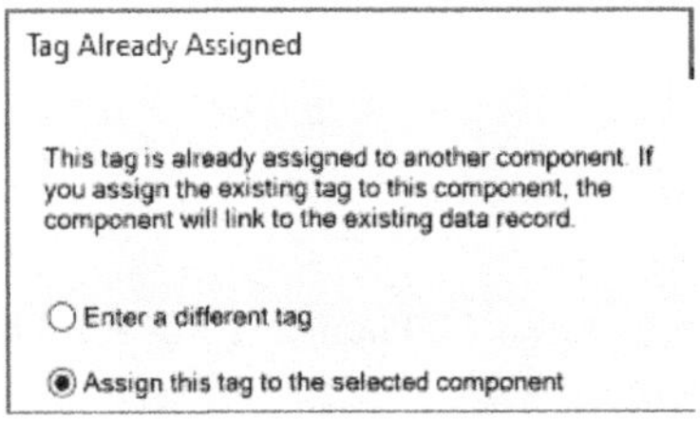

15. To display the tag:
    - Right-click on the heat exchanger.
    - Expand Annotate, and click Equipment Tag.
    - Click inside the heat exchanger.

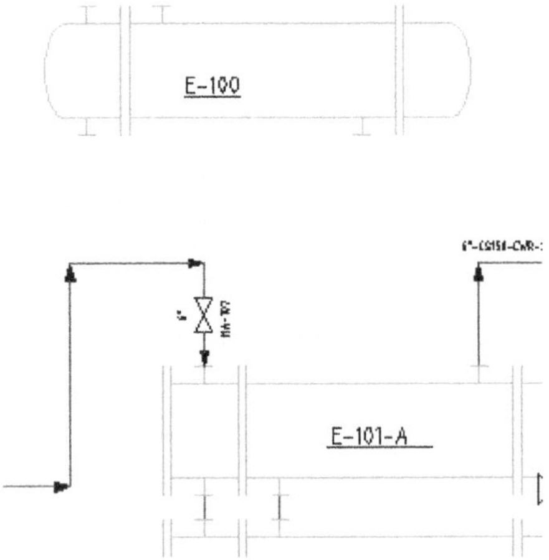

16. Save and close all drawings.

Lesson Review Questions

1. Is it possible to link symbols and reuse their existing tags?
   a. Yes. You can enter a tag used on other drawings and apply it to a symbol if all existing drawings already containing that symbol are open.
   b. Yes. Enter the tag again and the AutoCAD P&ID software does not prompt you about the duplicate assignment.
   c. No. A tag can only be used once on one drawing to protect the accuracy of project information.
2. Viewing existing tag numbers in the Assign Tag dialog box only shows tags in the open drawing.
   a. True
   b. False
3. A symbol with a linked tag can be displayed on...
   a. The same drawing as the original tagged symbol.
   b. A drawing in another project.
   c. An unlimited number of P&ID drawings in the project.

Lesson: Annotation Concepts

Overview

In this lesson, you learn how to place annotations and what types of annotations can be placed. This lesson also describes the difference between a tag and an annotation.

While a tag is a component's unique label, an annotation is the text on the drawing that communicates the tag and other vital information visually. Annotations display the properties or tag data of a component or line. Being able to leverage the tag data in an annotation is important for decreasing the time it takes to finalize a plant design and to eliminate mistakes.

A typical plant design with various P&ID symbols annotated with tag information is shown in the following illustration.

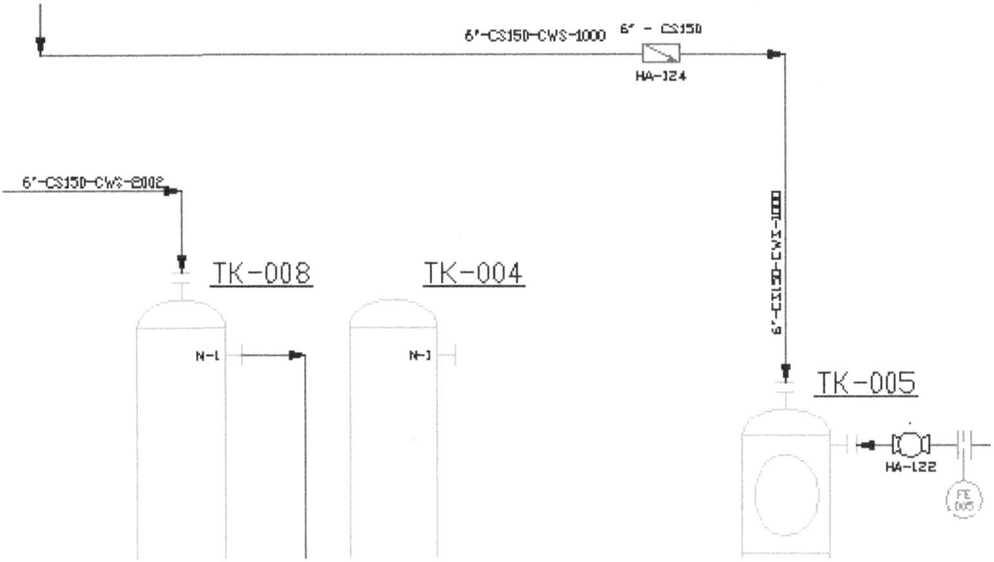

Objectives

After completing this lesson, you will be able to:

- Explain where tag data resides.
- Annotate symbols and edit annotations.
- Recognize and access different tag styles.

About Tag Data

Tag data can and should be assigned to most symbols in a P&ID project. While the specific information about the symbol varies depending on the object, the base information should enable anyone familiar with the project to determine specifically what component is required. This information enables those involved in the project to perform calculations and other engineering requirements, as well as helping purchasing to order the correct components.

Definition of Tag Data

Tag data is information assigned to a P&ID symbol to convey vital information about a component. A tag is a unique identifier used to label each unique component in a project individually. The data can be displayed in the drawing if required, but is always held in the Data Manager. From there, the data can be exported and shared with others in the project and used for downstream applications.

Example of Tag Data

A Centrifugal Pump in the P&ID design is shown in the following illustration. The tag P-005 is displayed under the pump and also in the Data Manager.

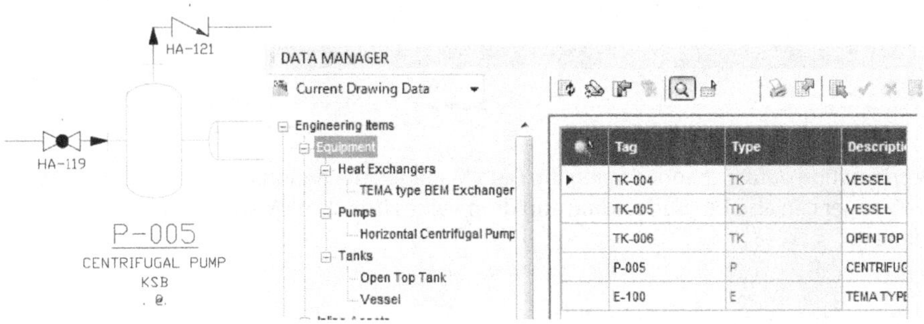

Annotating a Symbol

An annotation is the text information placed on the drawing. Annotations include the tag value and often include other properties about a component. To annotate an object in a P&ID drawing, right-click on the object and click Annotate, then pick the style you wish to use. You then click in the drawing to place the annotation.

The access to the Pump Infotag annotation is shown in the following illustration.

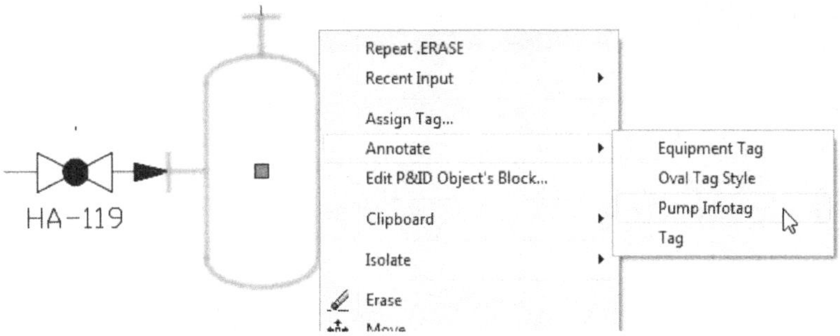

To edit an annotation, you can double-click on the annotation to open the Edit Annotation dialog box, as shown in the following illustration. Alternatively, you can open the Edit Annotation dialog box by selecting the annotation and in the Properties palette, selecting the edit button next to the Attributes of the tag when any of the fields are selected.

You can also use the Assign Tag dialog box to make the required changes to the tag if there are no other attributes displayed. If a symbol is already tagged and an annotation representing the tag has been placed on the drawing, then when you finish editing a tag, using the Assign Tag dialog box, clear the Place annotation after assigning tag option so that a new annotation is not added.

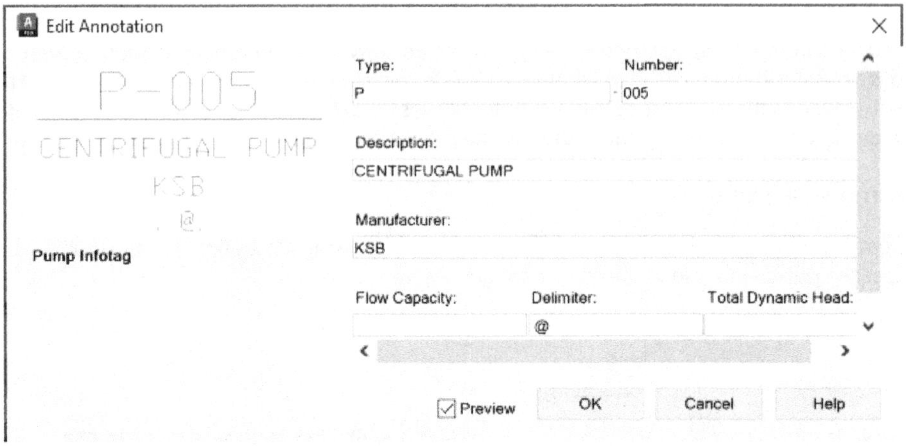

If the annotation data is changed using the Data Manager, the annotation updates automatically. The Data Manager can also be used to drag and drop values from Data Manager into the drawing to help annotate it.

Annotation Styles

You can display the tag data in the canvas of your design at any time during the design process. In many cases, the Assign Tag dialog box opens when the symbol is placed and you can select to display the tag information then. In other cases, or if the data was not displayed when placed, you can right-click on the item and click Assign Tag. The Assign Tag dialog box opens and you can display the tag then.

To change the style of displayed tag information, you can right-click on the symbol and click Annotate, then select a style from the available styles. The new annotation is added. If required, you might have to delete any existing annotations. Existing annotations are not replaced. Depending on the type of symbol selected, the available styles vary.

Two examples of the options available when annotating symbols in a P&ID design are shown in the following illustration. The illustration at the top shows the basic options available for most symbols. The illustration at the bottom shows the annotation options for a general instrument symbol.

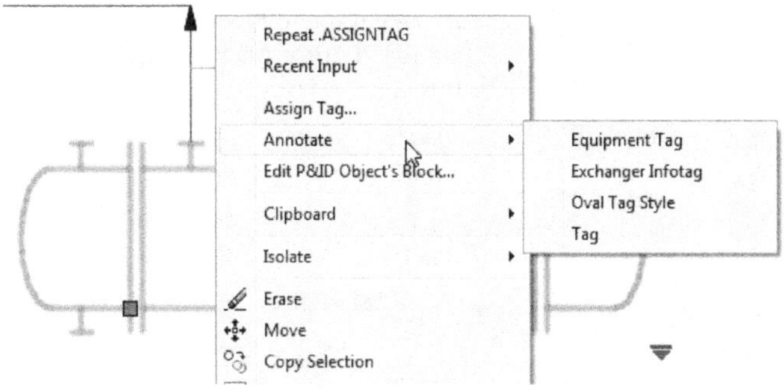

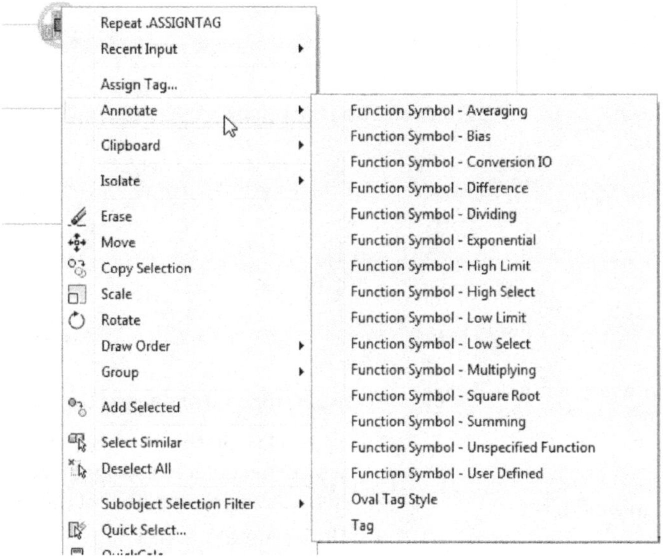

Examples of Annotation Styles

The default annotation styles available display tag data in your drawings are shown in the following illustration.

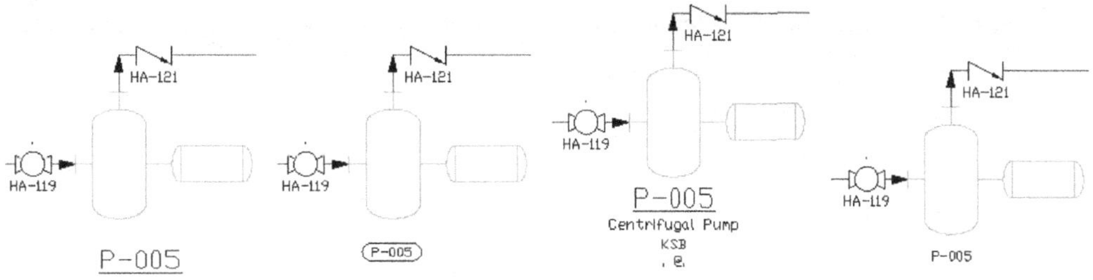

Exercise: Annotate Your P&ID

In this exercise, you place several annotations using the right mouse button functionality.

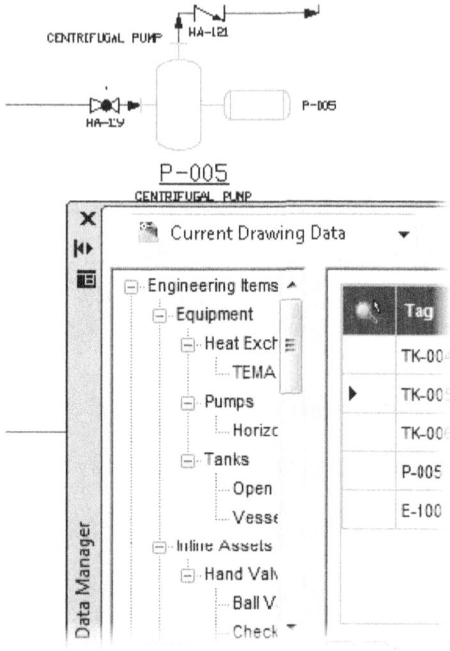

1. Start the AutoCAD Plant 3D software, if not already running.
2. Open the project as follows:
   - In the Project Manager, Current Project list, click Open.
   - In the Open dialog box, navigate to the folder *C:\Plant Design 2024 Practice Files\Annotate Your P&ID*.
   - Select the file *Project.xml*.
   - Click Open.
3. Open *PID002.dwg* in the *P&ID Drawings* folder.
4. Ensure that you are working in the PID PIP Workspace and Tool Palettes.
5. Note the three annotations shown with arrows in the following illustration. Using standard AutoCAD techniques, delete all three.

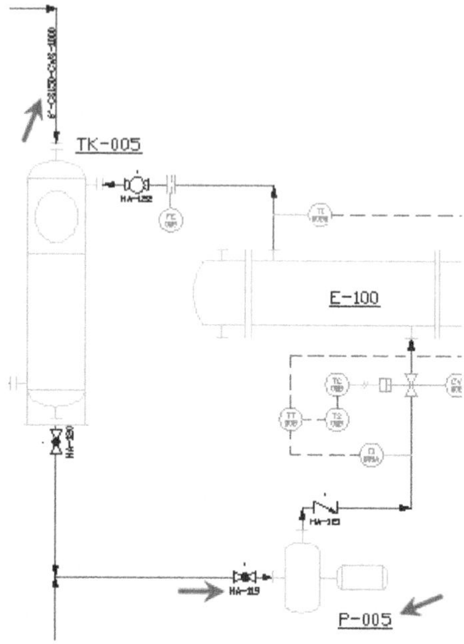

6. To display missing or deleted tag information:
   - Right-click on the pump symbol (for which you deleted the annotation P-005) in the lower-right corner of the design.
   - Under Annotate, click Tag.
   - To locate the tag, click to the right of the pump symbol as shown in the following illustration.

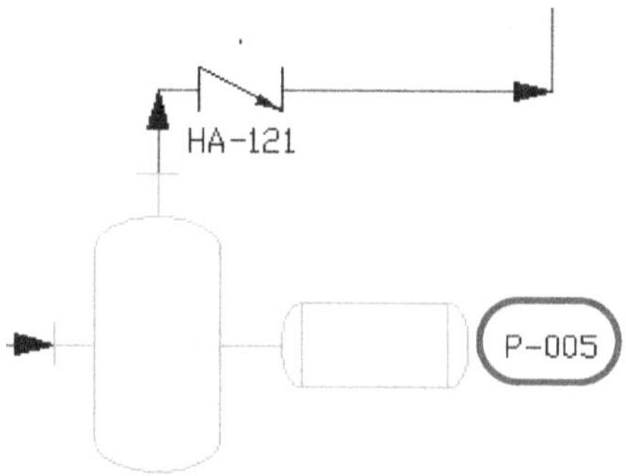

7. To add a different style tag to the same symbol:
   - Right-click on the pump symbol.
   - Under Annotate, click Pump Infotag.
   - To locate the tag, click below the pump symbol.

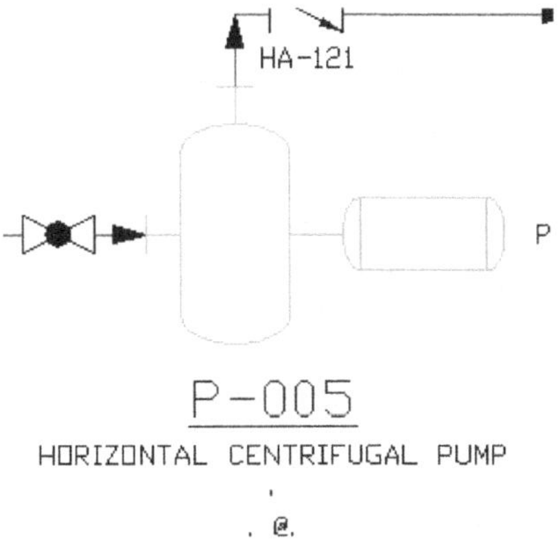

8. To edit the Pump information tag:
   - Select the last tag added (Infotag).
   - In the Properties palette, in the Attributes section, click in the value field for #(TargetObject.Description) and select its More button to open the Edit Annotation dialog box.
   - In the Edit Annotation dialog box, for Description, enter **CENTRIFUGAL PUMP**.
   - For Manufacturer, enter **KSB**. Note the dynamic update in the preview window.
   - Click OK.
   - Clear the selection by pressing <Esc>.

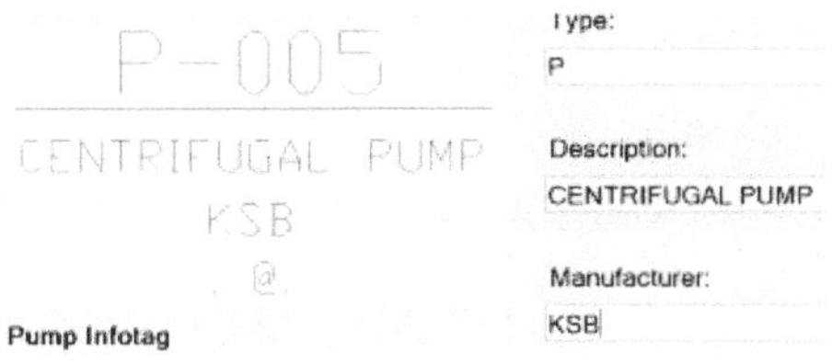

9. To display a valve tag if the annotation is not automatically placed:
   - Right-click on the valve to the left of the Centrifugal Pump P-005.
   - Under Annotate, click Valve Label. Note that it gets added below the valve.

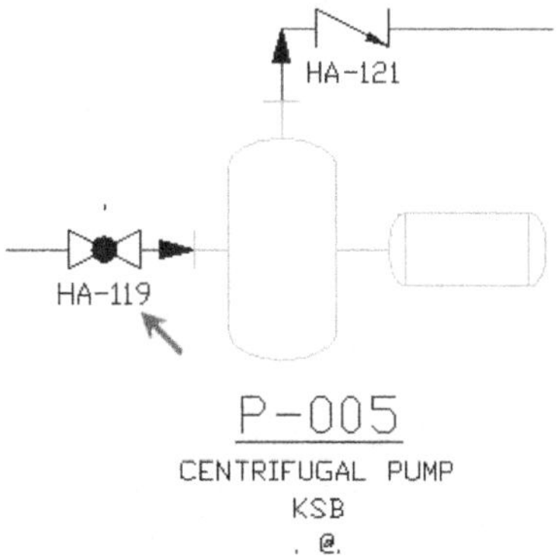

10. To display the pipe tag:
    - Select the pipeline going into the top of tank TK-005.
    - Right-click. Under Annotate, click Pipeline Tag.
    - To locate the tag, select the midpoint of the pipeline segment.

Note: Object snaps will affect the location of the tag.

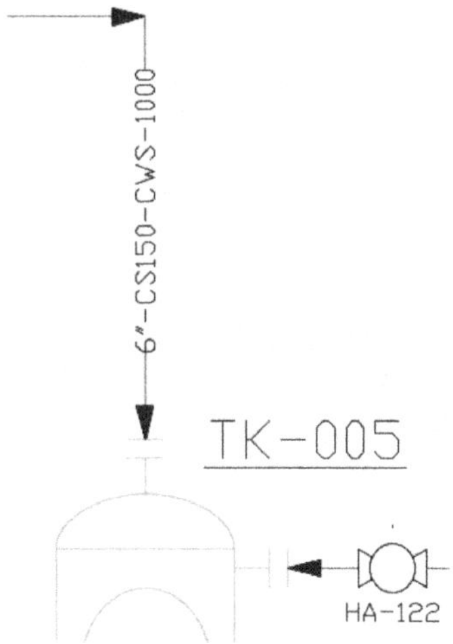

11. Note that the pipeline is broken. To resolve this, select the pipeline tag. Select the square grip and drag the tag to the left of the pipeline. Note that the line is reconnected.

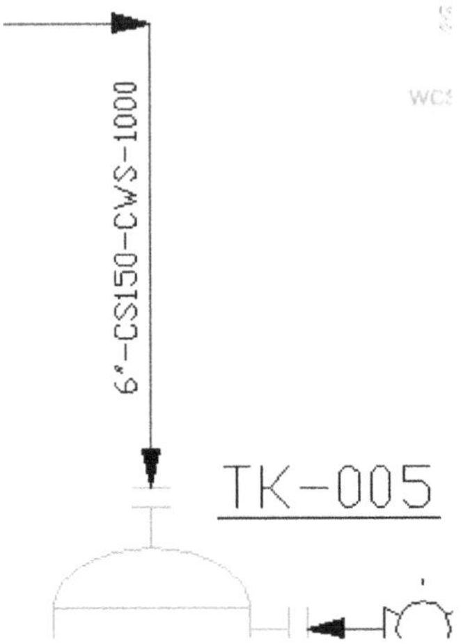

12. Save and close all drawings.

Lesson Review Questions

1. What is the preferred method for placing annotations for P&ID symbols?
   a. Placing the annotation when the Assign Tag dialog box is closed.
   b. Using the AutoCAD TEXT and MTEXT commands.
   c. Annotations are always placed automatically.
2. How do you place only one property next to the symbol that is not part of any annotation?
   a. Properties must be added to an annotation format.
   b. Drag and drop the value from Data Manager into the drawing.
3. How can you change the property values displayed in an annotation? (Select all that apply.)
   a. Data Manager
   b. Double-click on the annotation
   c. Properties palette
4. Which of the following annotation styles is shown below the pump in the following illustration?

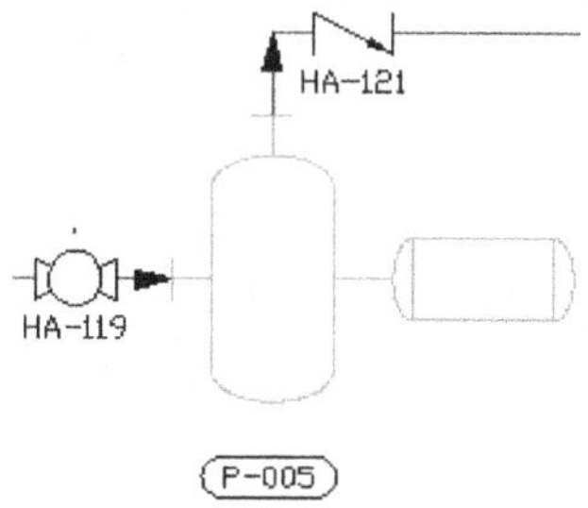

   a. Equipment Tag
   b. Oval Tag Style
   c. Pump Infotag
   d. Tag

Lesson: Editing Techniques

Overview

The way a design is initially created very rarely exactly matches the final delivered design. To go from the initial creation to the final deliverable, you must be able to make changes to the initial design. This lesson describes making changes and modifications to a generated P&ID using the AutoCAD P&ID Sline grips and substitute arrow commands and the move, copy, and stretch commands.

Objectives

After completing this lesson, you will be able to:

- Add line segments in the middle of a line.
- Link two lines that are not physically connected.
- In a P&ID design, create a gap in a line.
- Perform basic line edits using grips and standard AutoCAD edit commands.
- Access and substitute symbols.
- Change the flow direction of a pipeline.

Applying Corners to Lines

At times, it might be necessary to change the layout of a line. Since a single line is typically made up of multiple segments, to change the direction you need to apply a corner to the line.

You access the Apply Corner command from the Schematic Line Edit option on the shortcut menu, as shown in the following illustration.

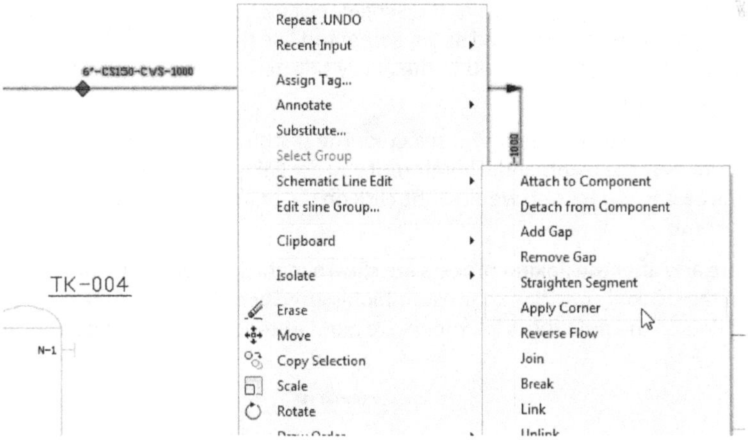

To apply a corner to a line, after starting the Apply Corner command, select a point on the line where the corner is going to begin (shown on the left in the following illustration). Then you select additional points (shown on the right) to define the new location of the line.

The path of the initial line was changed to go around the symbols by adding corners to the line, as shown in the following illustration.

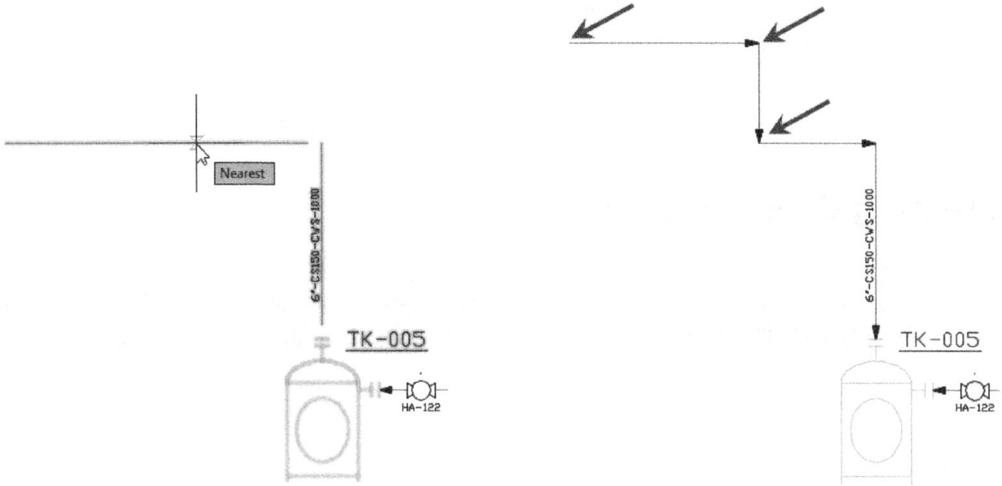

Linking Lines

Schematic lines are linked in drawings when you wish to have the tag data assume the values of the selected (source) line. You link lines when the line is a single line but cannot be displayed as a continuous line in the drawing due to space restrictions and inline components.

Process: Linking Lines

To link lines, right-click the link, select Link from the Schematic Line Edit option, and then select the line to be linked with. You are then prompted at the command line that the initial line is going to be deleted and the segment is going to be linked to the newly selected line. To complete the link you must respond Yes on the shortcut menu.

The controlling segment is the second segment selected. The first segment is selected when you right-click on the line to start the command. Therefore, if you are linking an unassigned line and a line with tag data, and the data is correct, you would right-click on the unassigned line first, then select the line with tag data second.

The same lines before and after the linking process are shown in the following illustration. Note that in the illustration on the left, only one line segment is highlighted and the tag data is all question marks. In the illustration on the right, both segments are highlighted and the tag data matches the linked line.

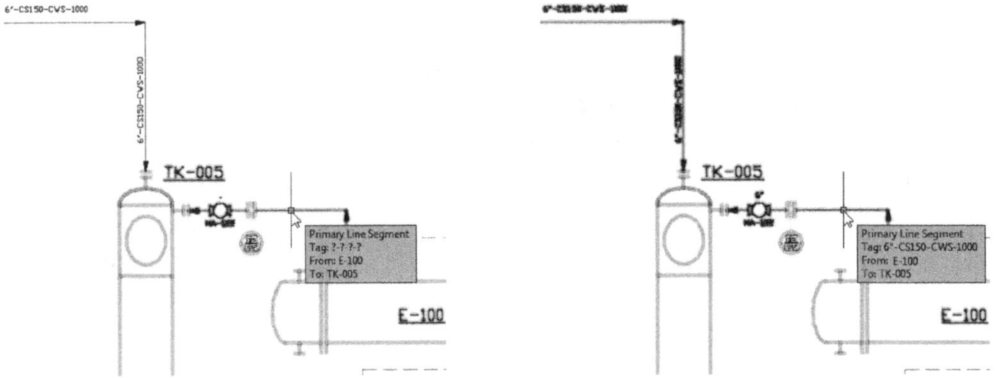

Creating Gaps in Pipelines

A P&ID drawing can become very congested. At times, it might be necessary to have a pipe or other lines cross a symbol. When this happens you can create a gap in the line while maintaining the integrity of the line data.

To access the Add Gap tool, right-click on the line and under Schematic Line Edit, click Add Gap, as shown in the following illustration.

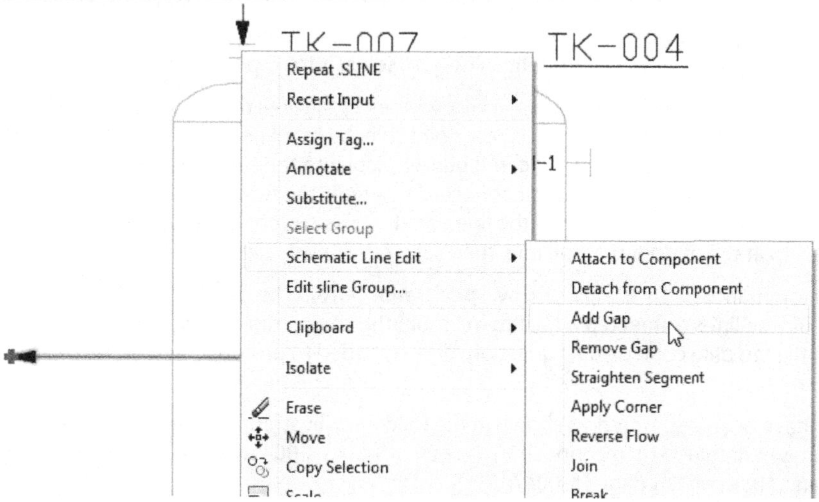

Process: Creating Gaps in Lines

After starting the command, to create a gap in a line, you select the line where you want the gap to start, then again where you want the gap to end. The section of the line between the two selected points is removed, and symbols are added to the two endpoints to indicate that the line is part of another line.

The Add Gap command is started and the first point is selected (left arrow), as shown in the following illustration. To complete the command, the second point is selected (right arrow). The result is shown in the illustration on the right.

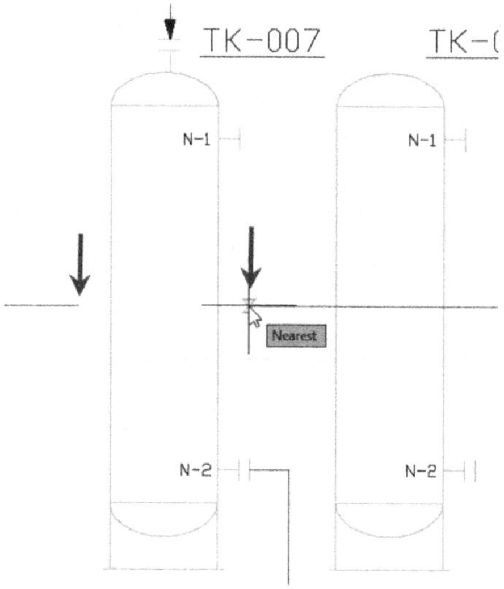

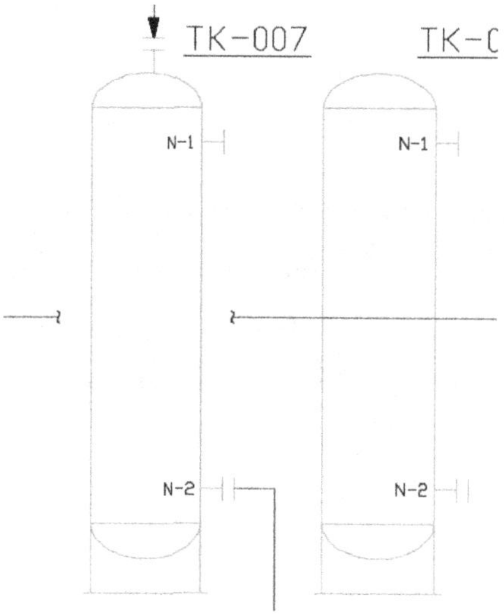

Basic Line Editing

AutoCAD P&ID lines respond to basic AutoCAD editing techniques. When you select a P&ID line, grips are displayed at specific points on the line. These grips can be used to edit the line, or you can use AutoCAD edit commands as well. To edit a line, you select it to display the grips.

If you need to change the end location of a line, you select the line, then select the endpoint grip. You then pick a new endpoint location. If the new point selected is inline with the existing line, the length of the line changes. If the new end is located perpendicular to the existing line, a new line segment is created. If the endpoint of the line was connected to a tank, the nozzle is deleted automatically, and added if connected to a tank. To move the line parallel to its current location, you select the line, then select the grip at the midpoint of the line, then select the new location.

AutoCAD commands, such as Move, Copy, and Stretch can also be used to edit P&ID drawings. If you move a tank, the lines connected adjust to maintain the connection. Copying a symbol produces a copy with the tag data copied and a question mark (?) added to prompt you that the data needs to be updated.

Two edits have been performed, as shown in the following illustration. Tank TK-008 was moved. Note that the lines maintained their connection. A copy of Tank TK-004 was placed just to the right of the original tank. Note the tag data: TK-004?.

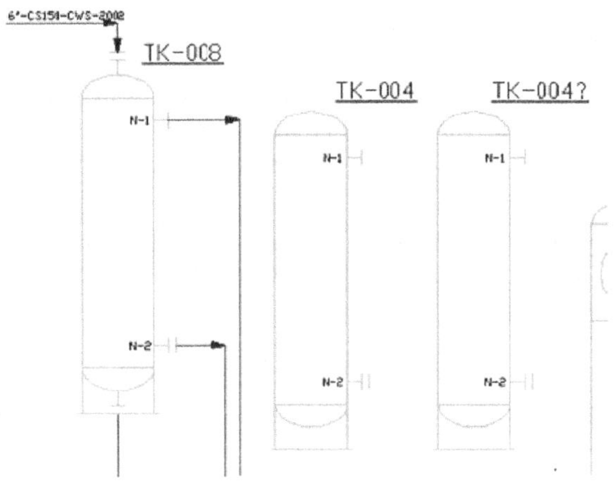

Process: Basic Line Editing

The following describe the use of basic grip editing techniques to edit lines.

1. Select the line to enable its grips.

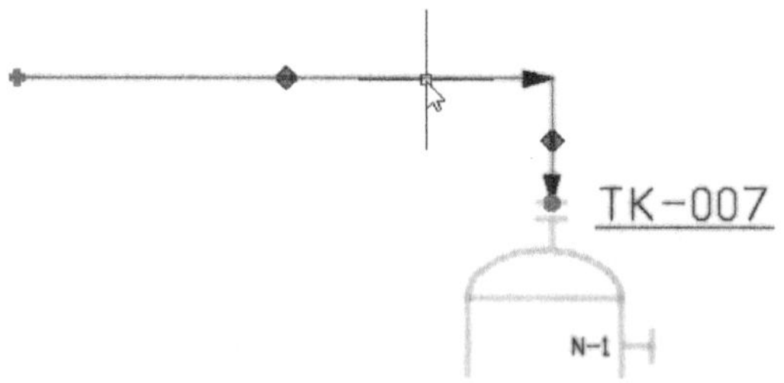

2. To disconnect from the tank and shorten the line:
   - Click the endpoint grip.
   - Click a new location inline with the line.
   - Note that the nozzle is deleted.

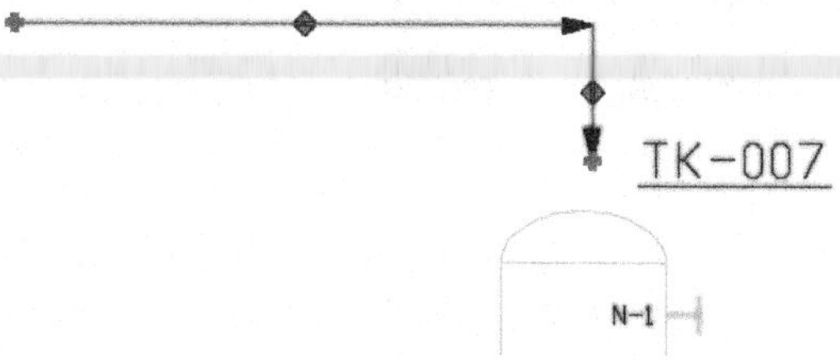

3. To move a line segment parallel:
   - Click the middle grip.
   - Click a new location.

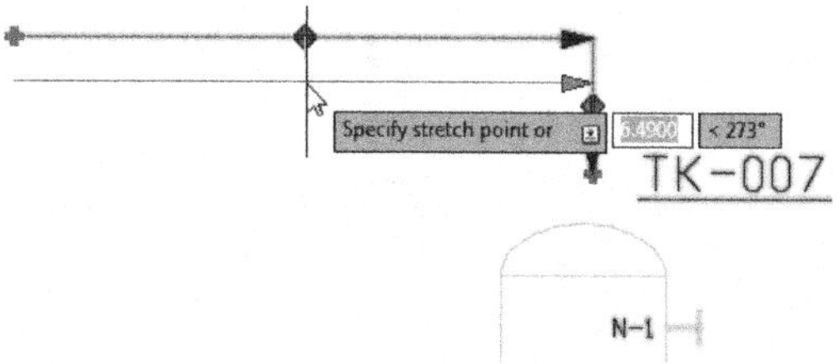

4. To add segments when the line is not connected to a symbol:
   - Click the endpoint grip.
   - Click the endpoint of the new segments.
   - Note how the nozzle is displayed when the endpoint specified is on the equipment.

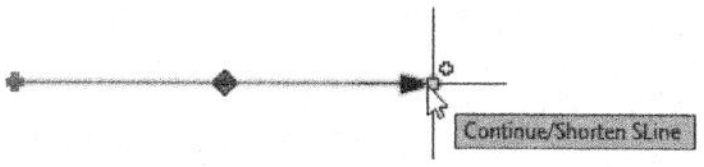

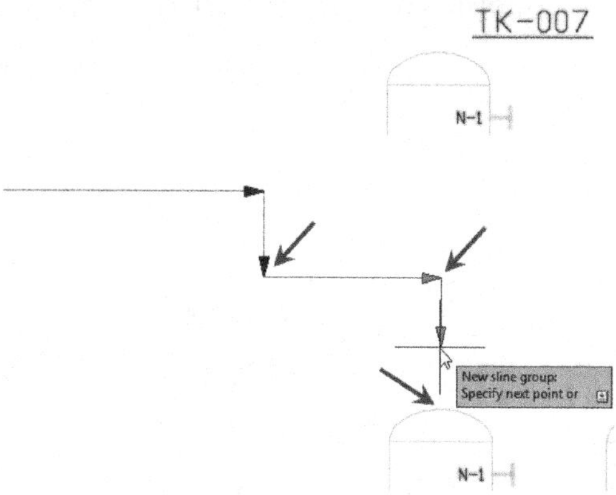

Substitute Symbols

After you have inserted a symbol into your design, you can change the symbol to a similar one without deleting the original and inserting the new one. If a symbol can be substituted and you select it with no command active, a substitution arrow displays along with the grip.

A valve is selected, as shown in the following illustration. In the middle of the valve is a grip that enables you to move the valve to a new location. At the bottom right is the substitution arrow. The available options are listed here.

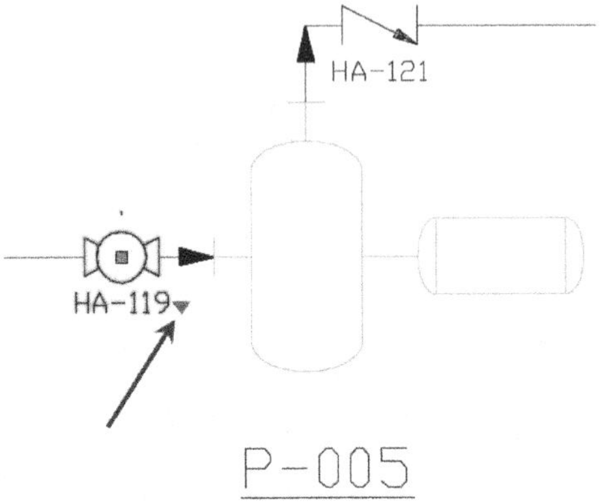

Examples of Symbol Substitution

Some of the substitution menus available when editing P&ID symbols are shown in the following illustration.

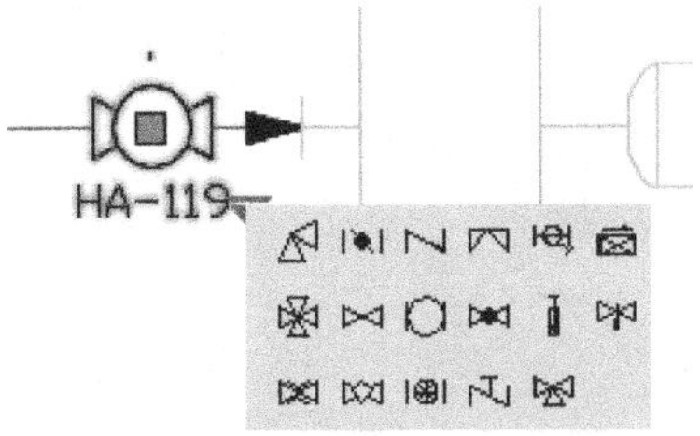

Valve Substitution

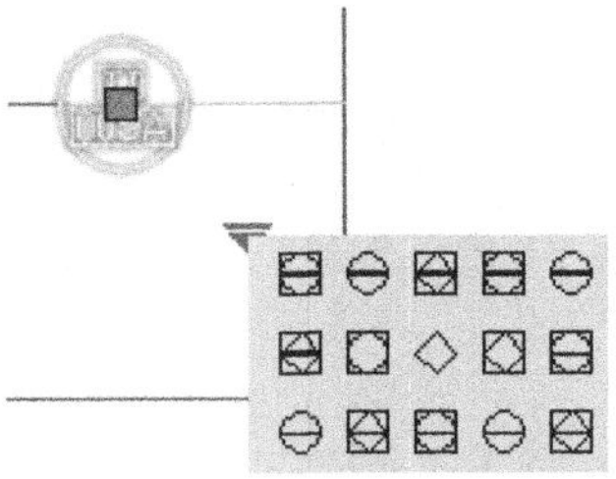

General Instrument Substitution

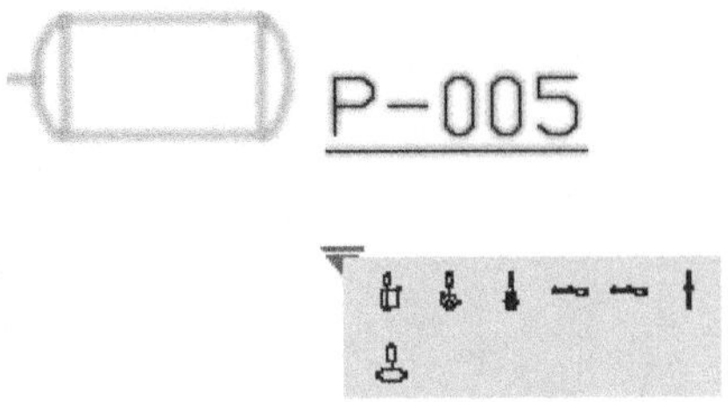

Pump Substitution

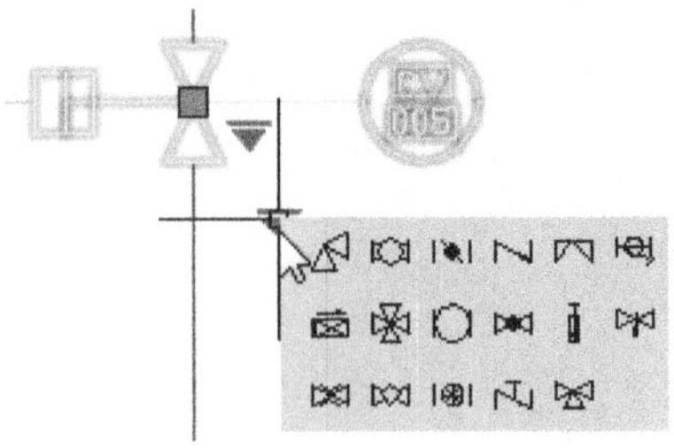

Control Valve Substitution

Flow Arrow

Certain components can only be installed in a specific direction in a pipeline. Typically, if the flow direction of the pipe is reversed, any flow-dependent symbols also change automatically. However, if you have a directionally dependent device in the wrong direction, you can change the direction without affecting the pipe flow direction.

A check valve direction does not match the pipe flow direction, as shown in the following illustration. The progression from left to right shows the valve direction not matching the pipe flow direction (on the left). The valve is selected and the Flip Component arrow is selected in the middle, and finally the resulting valve with corrected pipe flow direction, on the right.

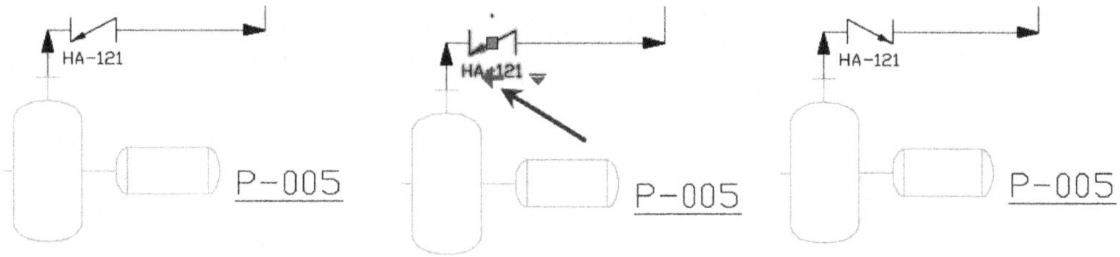

Exercise: Modify the Layout of Your P&ID

In this exercise, you make modifications to the layout of the P&ID using specific P&ID and regular AutoCAD functionalities.

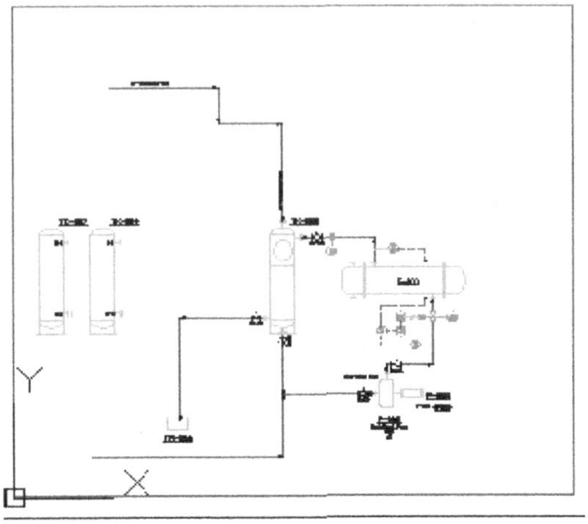

1. Start the AutoCAD Plant 3D software, if not already running.
2. Open the project as follows:
   - In the Project Manager, Current Project list, click Open.
   - In the Open dialog box, navigate to the folder *C:\Plant Design 2024 Practice Files\Modify the Layout of Your PID*.
   - Select the file *Project.xml*.
   - Click Open.
3. Open *PID002.dwg*.
4. Ensure that you are working in the P&ID PIP Workspace and Tool Palettes.
5. To move a pipeline parallel to its current position:
   - Select the 6 inch pipe that connects to the top of tank TK-005.
   - On the horizontal segment, select the diamond-shaped grip at the midpoint of the line segment.
   - Move the cursor up and click to relocate the pipeline.

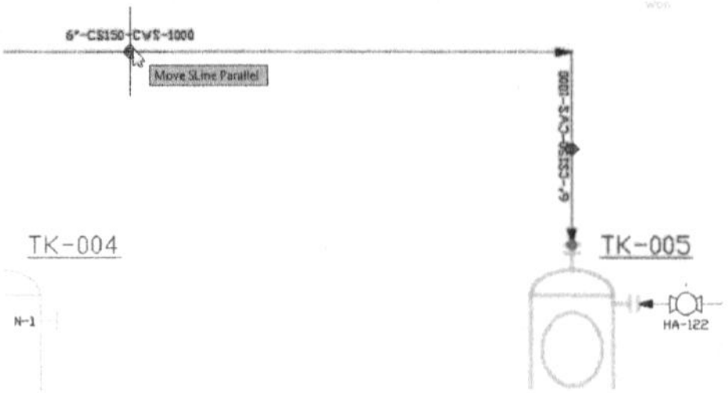

6. To change the length of a pipeline:
   - Select the left plus grip on the endpoint of the horizontal segment of the same line.
   - Move the cursor to the right and click to relocate the endpoint and shorten the pipe length.

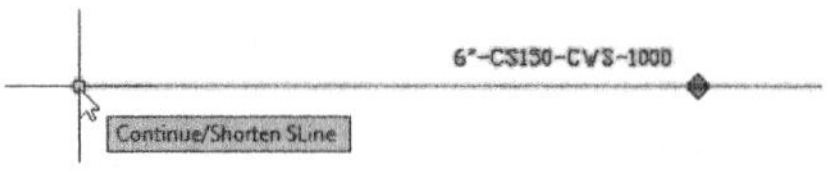

7. To add segments to the open end of a pipeline:
   - Click the same plus grip as in the previous step.
   - Click directly above the endpoint.
   - Click to the left.
   - Right-click and select Enter.

Note that a bend has been added.

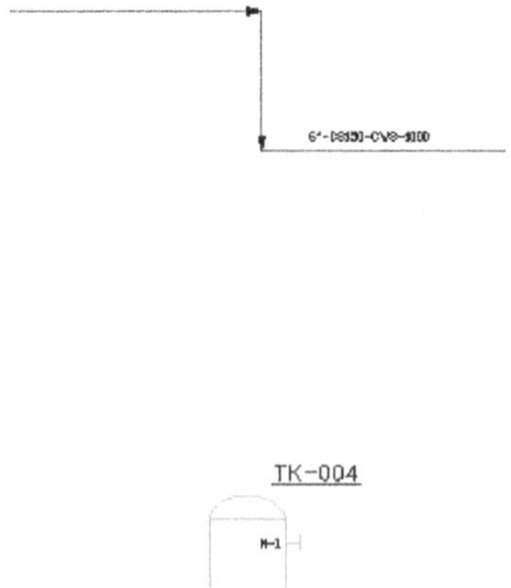

8. Zoom in to the connection to tank TK-005, as shown in the following illustration.

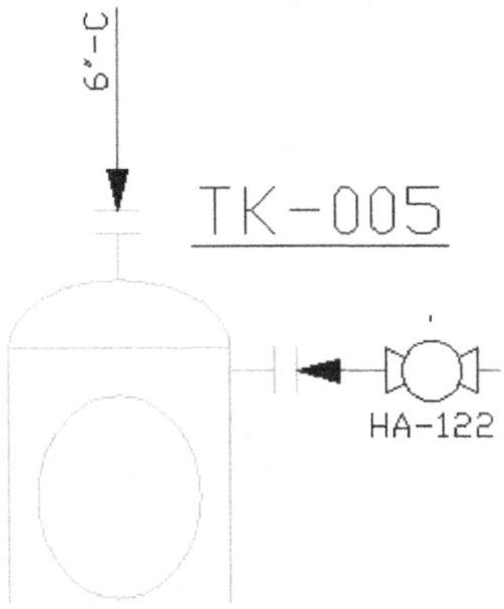

9. To disconnect a pipeline:
   - Select the 6" pipeline connecting to tank TK-005.
   - Select the round grip point at the nozzle.
   - Select a location above the connection.

   Note that the nozzle is no longer displayed on the tank and a connection is broken.

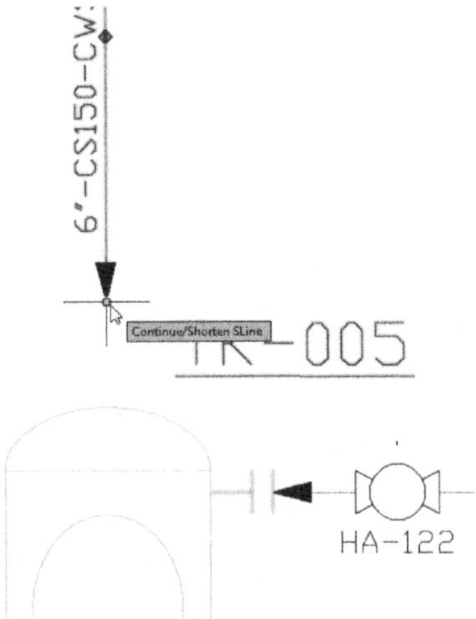

10. To connect a pipeline:
    - Select the plus grip at the same endpoint of the 6 inch line.
    - Select the top of the tank.

    Note that the nozzle is now displayed.

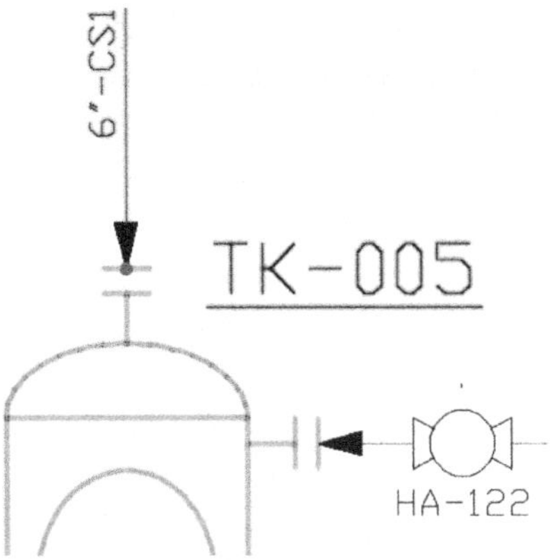

11. To remove a corner from a pipeline, select the line shown and select the midpoint grip of the far left segment, as shown in the following illustration.

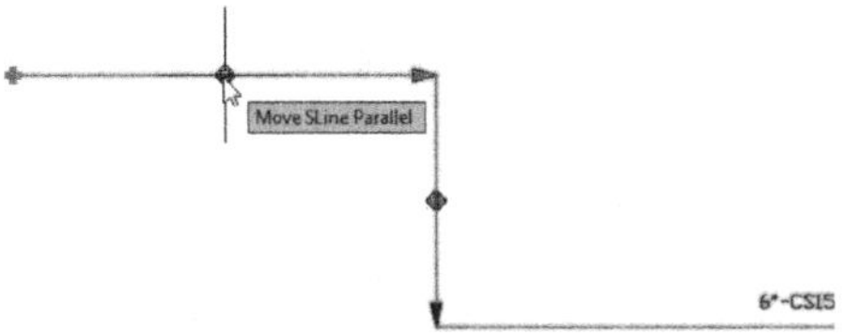

12. Drag the grip until both segments of the pipeline are collinear and click to place it.

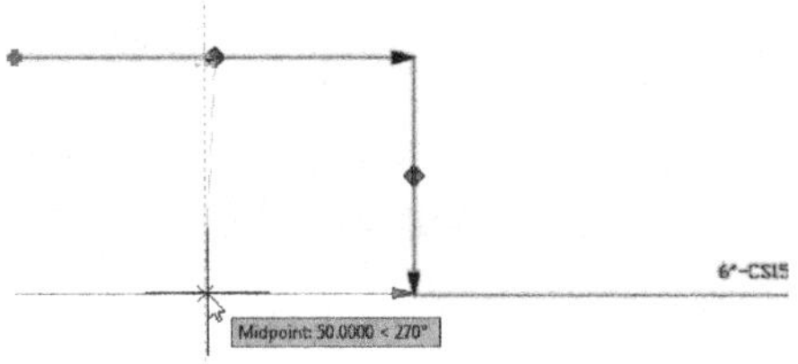

13. To add a corner to a pipeline:
    - Right-click on the 6 inch pipeline that connects to the top of tank TK-005.
    - Under Schematic Line Edit, click Apply Corner.
    - Select a point on the horizontal segment.
    - Click above the selected point.
    - Click to the left of the second selected point.

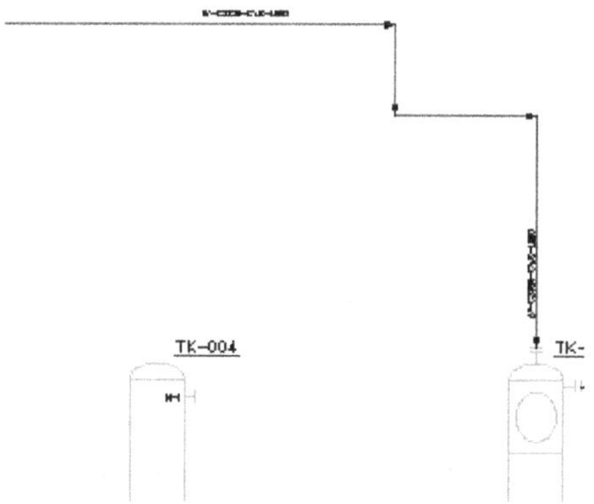

14. Zoom to the area of the E-100 Heat Exchanger.

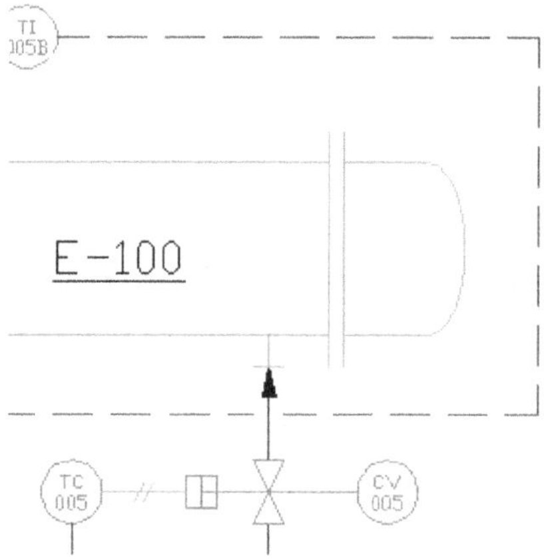

15. Select the vertical portion of the electrical line (red dashed line). Using the diamond grip on the vertical portion, move it over the heat exchanger as shown in the following illustration.

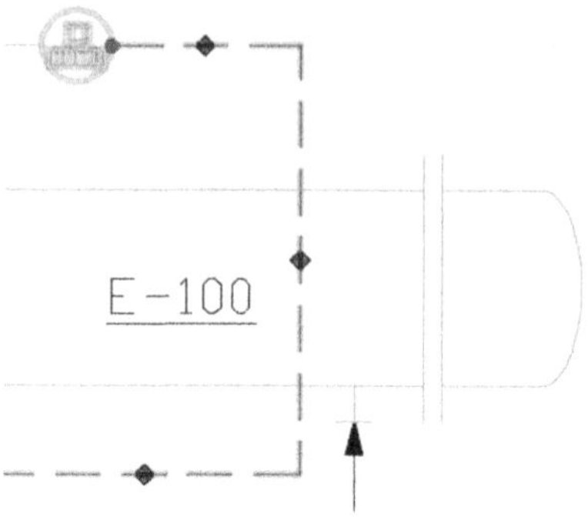

16. To create a gap in a line:
    - Right-click on the electrical line.
    - Under Schematic Line Edit, click Add Gap.
    - On the line, select two points outside (above and below) the Heat Exchanger.

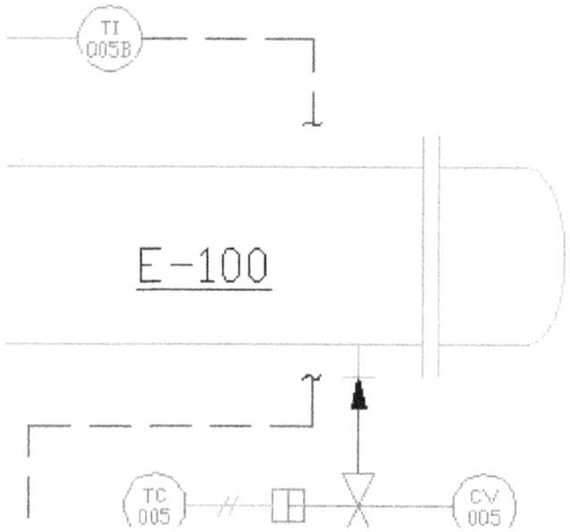

17. To link two pipelines:

- Right-click on the pipeline below heat exchanger E-100 (1).
- Under Schematic Line Edit, click Link.
- Select the line above heat exchanger E-100 (2).
- Click Yes in the heads up menu.
- Hover the cursor over one of the pipelines. They both highlight.

Note: If the line does not highlight when you hover the cursor over it, right-click in the graphics window and click Options>Selection tab>When no command is active>OK.

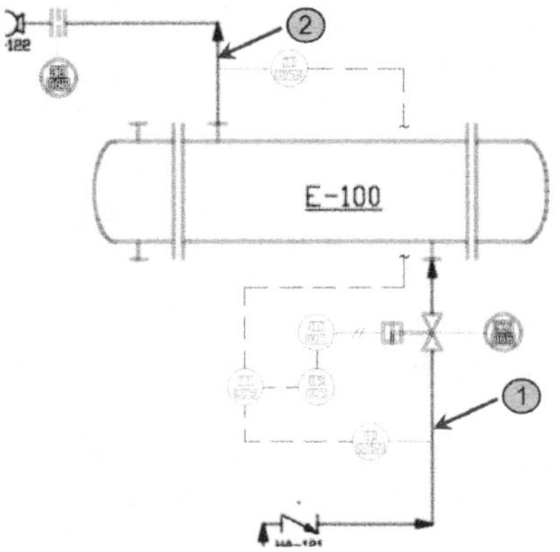

18. To substitute a P&ID symbol:

- Select the valve HA-119 (near P-005).
- Click the grip arrow near the right bottom.
- In the replacement options, click Ball Valve.

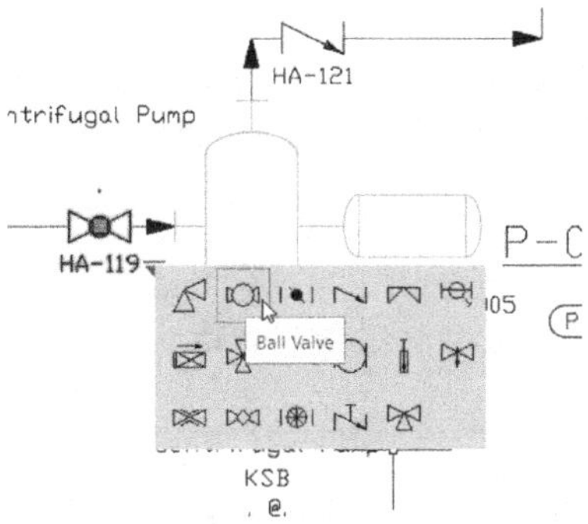

The valve is updated to a ball valve, as shown in the following illustration.

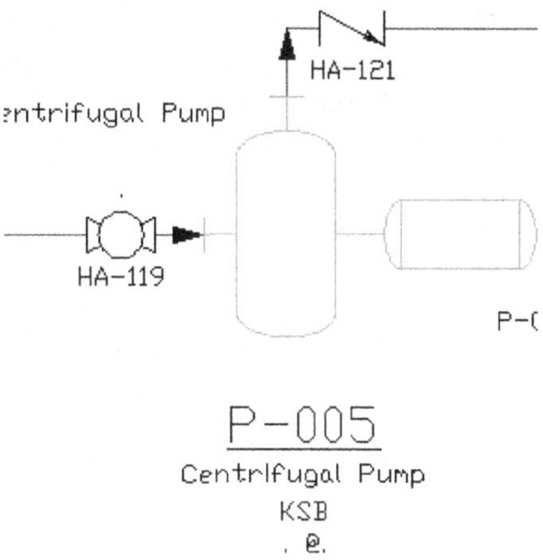

19. To copy a P&ID symbol:

- Select the tank TK-004.
- Right-click and click Copy Selection.
- Select a base point on the original tank.
- Locate the new tank to the left of the original.
- Press <Esc> to exit the command.
- Note that it displays a ? in the tag

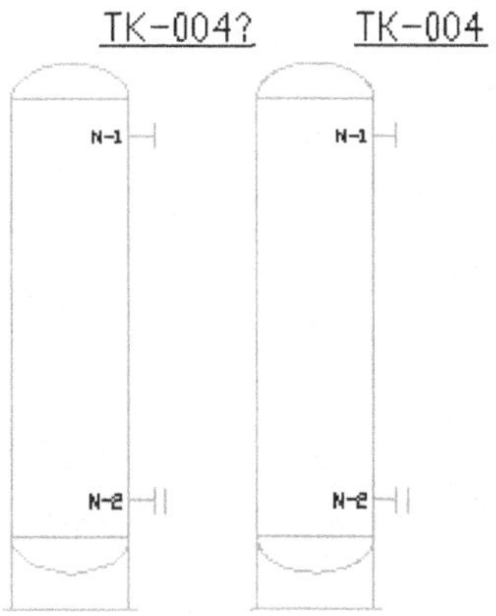

20. To update the tag information:

- Right-click on the new tank.
- Click Assign Tag.
- In the Assign Tag dialog box, for Number, click the button at the end of the field.
- The next available number (007) is automatically inserted.
- Click Assign.

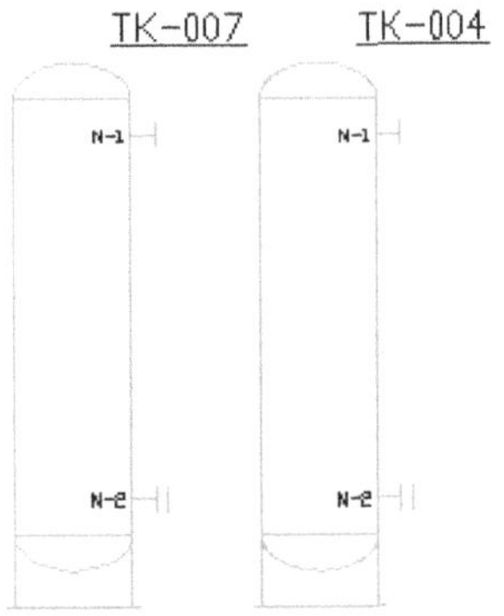

21. To move symbols:

- Select both the tanks TK-004 and TK-007.
- Right-click and click Move.
- Select a base point on one of the tanks.
- Locate the new tanks to the left of the original, as shown in the following illustration.
- Click to place the objects at the new location.

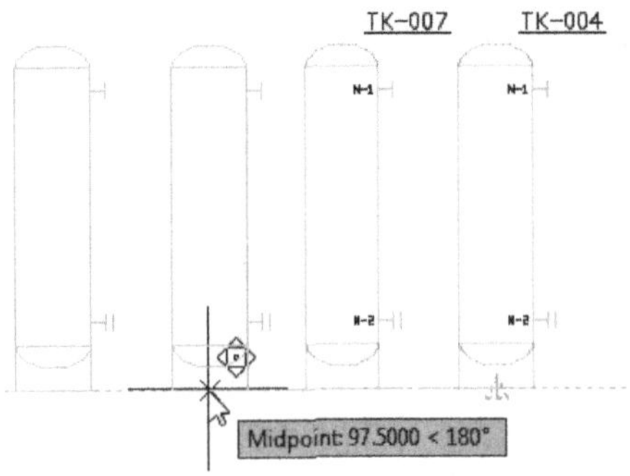

22. To begin to create more space for additional P&ID symbols:

- Start the AutoCAD Stretch command.
- Select the objects using a crossing window as shown in the following illustration.

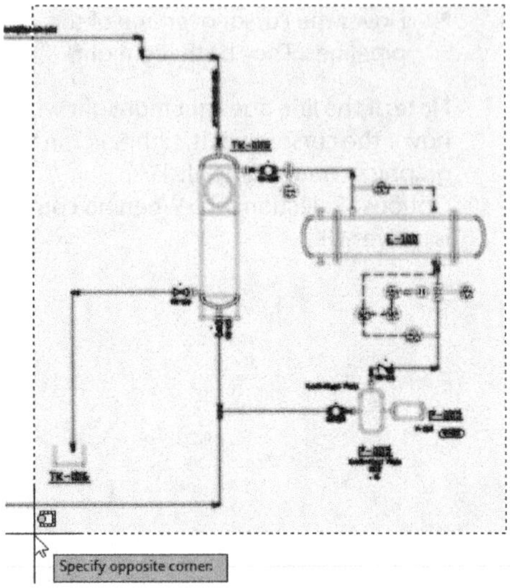

23. Stretch the selected components to the left, as shown in the following illustration.

Note: Be sure to have Ortho on or use another method to ensure horizontal movement.

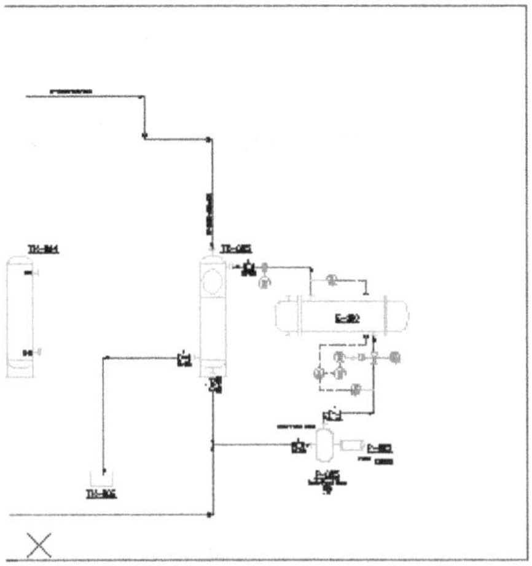

24. Save and close all drawings.

Lesson Review Questions

1. How can you move a line without having to delete and redraw it?
   a. Using the Move Sline Parallel grip.
   b. Schematic lines have to be deleted and redrawn.
2. When a valve is placed on a line and it turns out to be the wrong valve, how can you correct this without losing the valve's information?
   a. Right-click on the symbol and click the Replace option.
   b. Select the valve and use the Substitution grip.
3. If a line crosses a piece of equipment, how do you open the line without losing information?
   a. Use the AutoCAD Break or Trim commands.
   b. Right-click on the line and under Schematic Line Edit, click Add Gap.
4. Can you place a line and give it the same tag as an existing line without the lines connecting?
   a. Yes, using the Join option on the Schematic Line Edit context menu.
   b. Yes, using the Link option on the Schematic Line Edit context menu.
   c. No. Lines that are not physically connected on the same drawing cannot have the same tag.
5. The TK-004? tag indicates that its symbol was copied and the new symbol needs to be tagged.
   a. True
   b. False

Lesson: Data Manager and Reports

Overview

In this lesson, you learn how the Data Manager can be used to help create reports, look at the information in the P&ID, export the data to external files (XLS, XLSX, CSV), and import that same data again. To be able to view just the right information in the Data Manager, you also learn how to manipulate the column order and which columns should be visible.

Objectives

After completing this lesson, you will be able to:

- Explain the different types of data available in the Data Manager.
- Describe the different sections of the Data Manager and access the different classes.
- Access drawing, project, and report data.
- Export project data.
- Import project data.
- Access, apply, and remove filters in the Data Manager.

About the Data Manager

For a P&ID drawing to be effective, each object must be fully documented. This is done by assigning information with tags and properties. The number of objects typically found in a P&ID drawing results in a large amount of data. In addition, it is often possible to have many drawings in a P&ID design. To facilitate viewing, editing, importing, and exporting the data for drawings and the project, the data is stored in a single location.

The AutoCAD P&ID Data Manager is shown in the following illustration. In this instance, the data display is being changed from the Current Drawing Data to another data source.

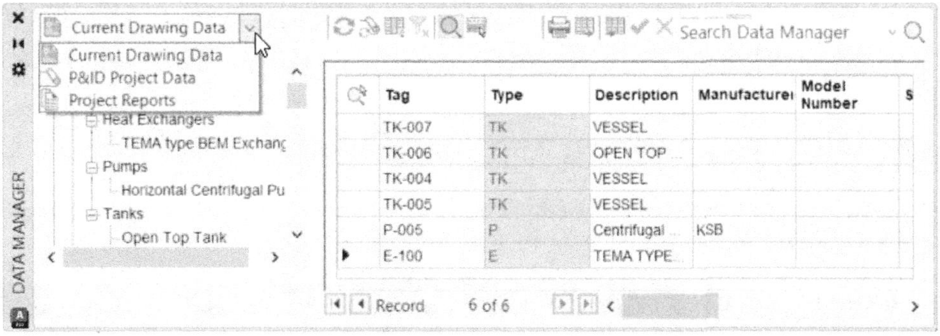

Definition of the Data Manager

The Data Manager is a centralized location that enables you to view, modify, export, and import drawing and project data. In addition, you can organize the information in the Data Manager into different configurations to generate reports.

The AutoCAD P&ID Data Manager displaying project data is shown in the following illustration. The illustration on the left shows the Class list (Engineering items) which enables you to show specific information.

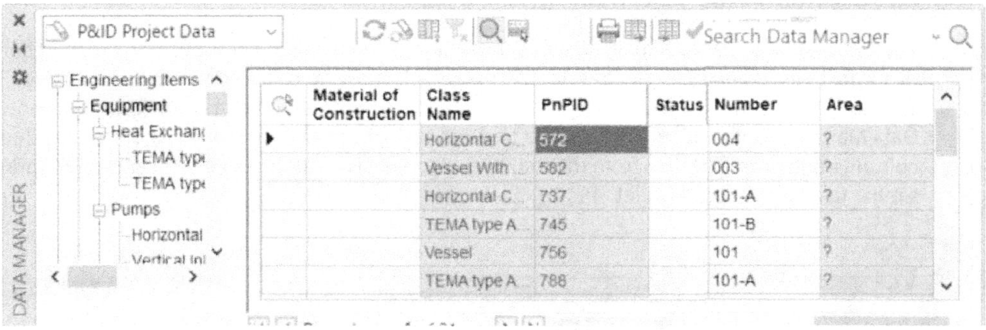

Using the Data Manager

The Data Manager is accessed on the Home tab, on the Project panel, on the ribbon. Once it is displayed, you can access data for the current drawing, project, or project reports.

Two iterations of the Data Manager are shown in the following illustration. First, the display is set to show all the tanks in the current drawing. Below that, all the tanks for the project are displayed.

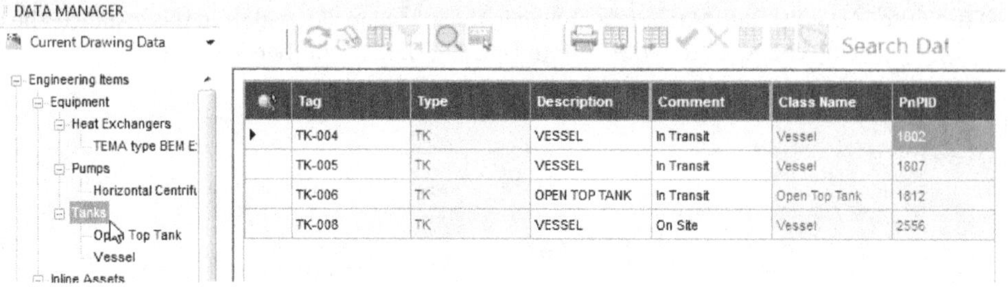

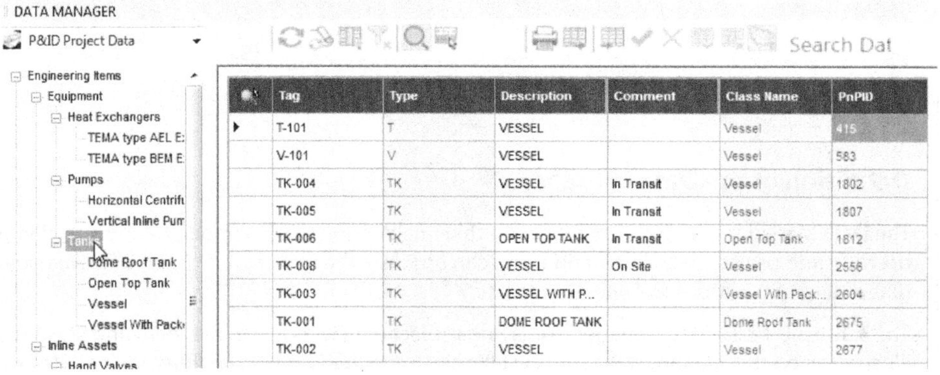

Description of the Data Manager

The Data Manager has four main areas, as shown in the following illustration. In the top left corner, the drop-down list (1) enables you to select from Current Drawing Data, Project Data, or Project Reports. The Class list (2) enables you to restrict the data displayed based on common P&ID components. The Data Manager toolbar (3) enables you to perform tasks, such as import and export of data, hide blank columns, and print. The data from the drawing or project is located in a column and row configuration similar to a typical spreadsheet (4).

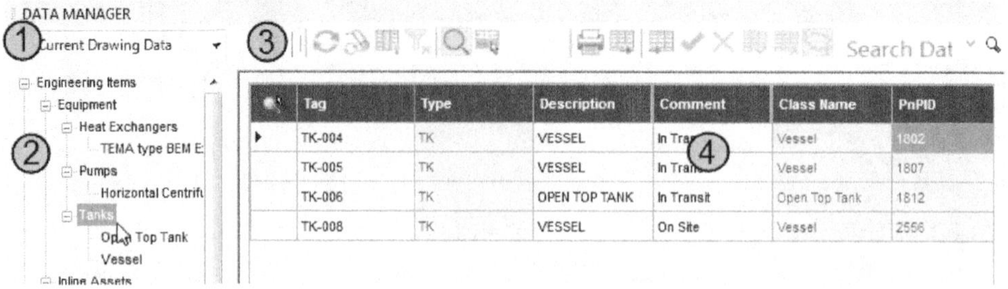

Process: Using the Data Manager

1. On the ribbon, on the Home tab, on the Project panel, click Data Manager to display the Data Manager.
2. Select to display Drawing, Project, or Report data.

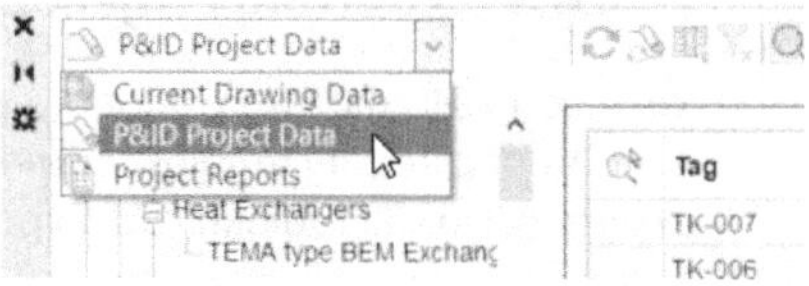

3. Select the required Class.

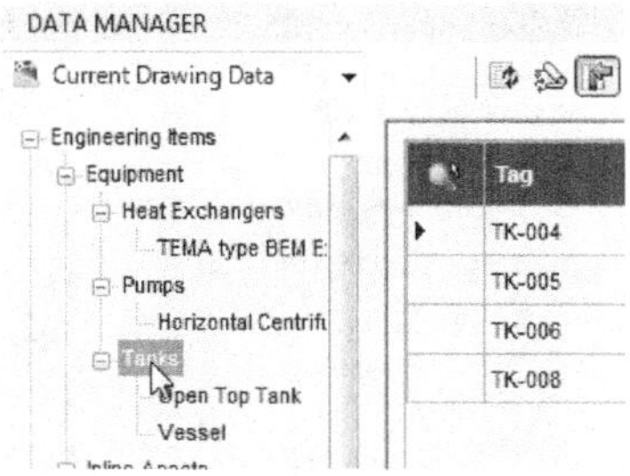

4. View the data.

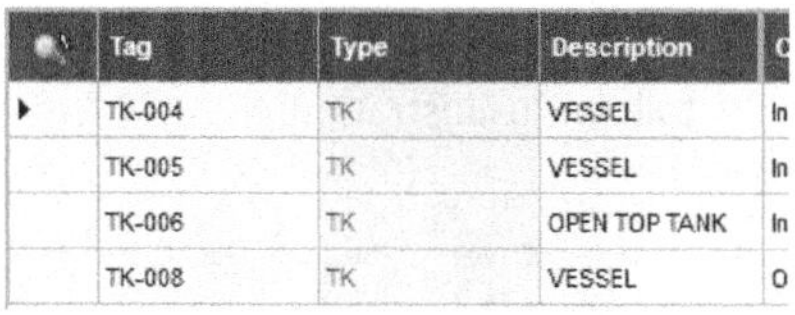

Drawing, Project, and Report Data

The Drawing Manager provides access to all of the data in the drawing or project. In addition, you can organize the project data into a variety of available reports as shown in the following illustration.

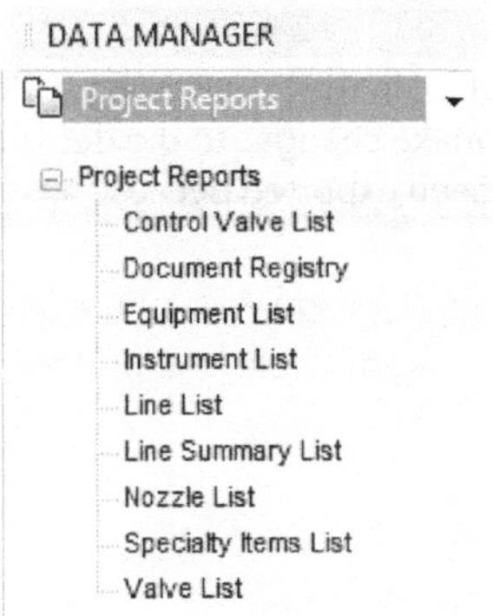

Exporting Project Data

Data is only useful if it is accurate and gets to those individuals who need it. To share Data Manager information with others outside the design team, you can export the data to an Excel spreadsheet or CSV file.

Process: Exporting Project Data

To export P&ID data from your project, you first access the Data Manager. In the Data Manager, select a report or category from the current drawing or project. The selected item defines what will be exported. On the toolbar, click Export.

The button in the Data Manager for exporting is shown in the following illustration.

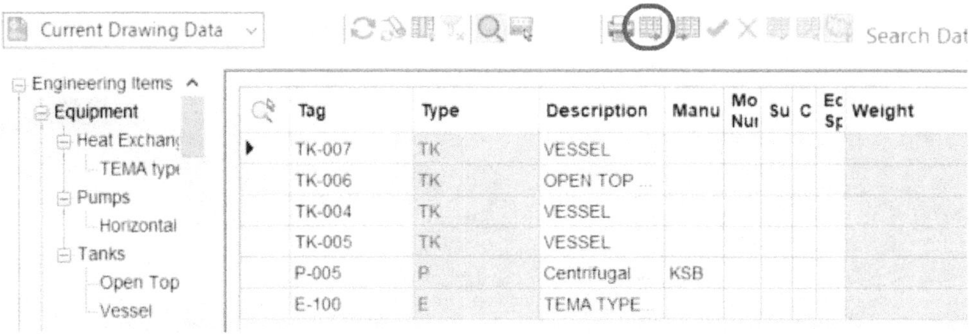

The Equipment list was selected for the example and the exported spreadsheet is shown in the following illustration.

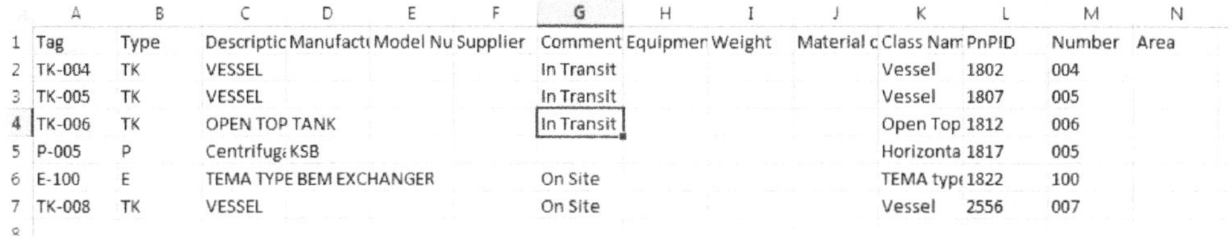

	A	B	C	D	E	F	G	H	I	J	K	L	M	N
1	Tag	Type	Descriptic	Manufactı	Model Nu	Supplier	Comment	Equipmer	Weight	Material c	Class Nam	PnPID	Number	Area
2	TK-004	TK	VESSEL				In Transit				Vessel	1802	004	
3	TK-005	TK	VESSEL				In Transit				Vessel	1807	005	
4	TK-006	TK	OPEN TOP TANK				In Transit				Open Top	1812	006	
5	P-005	P	Centrifug	KSB							Horizonta	1817	005	
6	E-100	E	TEMA TYPE BEM EXCHANGER				On Site				TEMA typ	1822	100	
7	TK-008	TK	VESSEL				On Site				Vessel	2556	007	
8														

Importing Project Data

P&ID data can be imported into your project using the Import option in the Data Manager. There are many reasons to import data into a P&ID project. Customers can make changes to the design, specifications on equipment can change, or the data could have been exported because it is easier to add and edit data in a spreadsheet.

When importing data, it is critical that the worksheet name and column headers match the view/classes and property names in the Data Manager. Therefore, it is advisable to export the current data to a spreadsheet, and edit the exported spreadsheet.

The Import button in the Data Manager, which is used for importing reports, is shown in the following illustration.

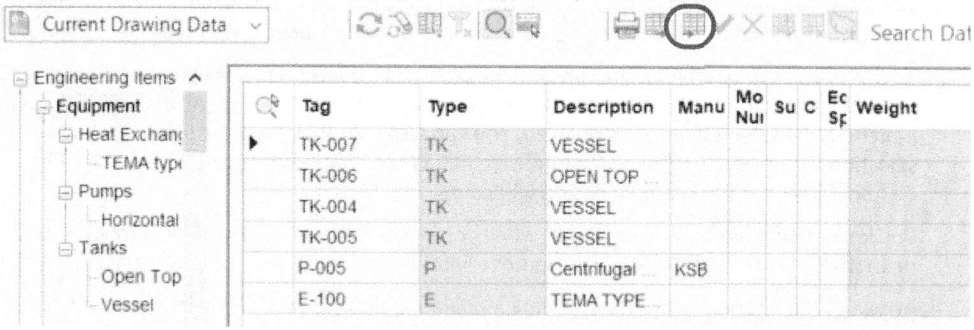

The Data Manager information following an import is shown in the following illustration. The cells of any data that changed are highlighted in yellow (1). If the data was changed in the spreadsheet, then hovering the cursor over the data reveals the previous value (2). And in the drawing, the symbol has a revision cloud placed around it (3) until the edited value is accepted or rejected.

For each edited value, you can right-click on the individual cell and accept or reject the edit. If you are sure that you want to accept or reject all of the edits, you can select the appropriate option in the toolbar.

Process: Importing Data

The following steps describe importing data into a P&ID project.

1. Access the Data Manager.
2. Click Import.
3. Select the spreadsheet or CSV file.
4. Review any edited data. Select to accept or reject the changes.

Filtering Data in the Data Manager

The Data Manager provides many classes to filter the data that is displayed. However, there might be times when you want to have even greater control over the data displayed in the Data Manager.

To do so, you can use filters. The simplest way to invoke a filter is to select any cell that contains the value that you filter by. You then right-click and click Filter By Selection. All items in the column matching the selected cell are displayed. You can also select to show the inverse of the cell by selecting the option to Filter Excluding Selection. When complete, right-click and click Remove Filter. Custom filters can be created by using wildcards.

You know that a filter has been added when you right-click and the Remove Filter option is available or, in the Data Manager toolbar, the Remove Filter option is active.

Access to the filtering options in the Data Manager is shown in the following illustration.

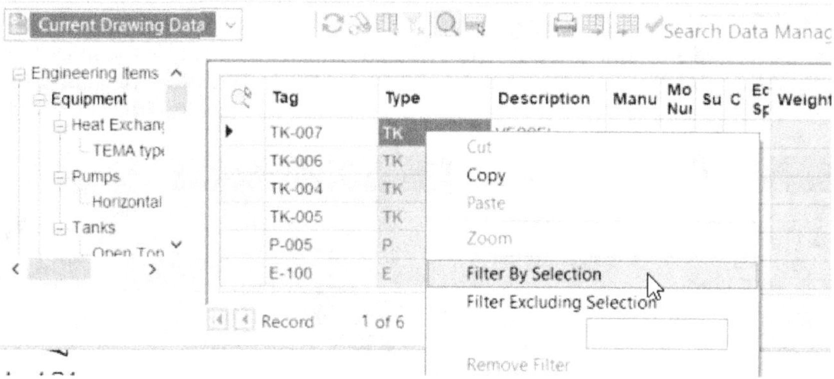

Filtering Example in the Data Manager

Data in the Data Manager before and after filtering by selection is shown in the following illustration.

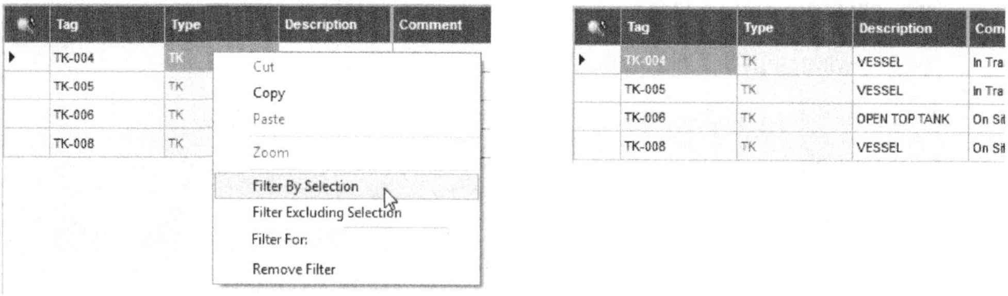

Exercise: Use Data Manager to Review, Export, and Import Data

In this exercise, you use the Data Manager to reorder columns, filter for the required data, and print project reports. You then export data to an Excel spreadsheet, modify the data in Excel, and import the modified data back into the design.

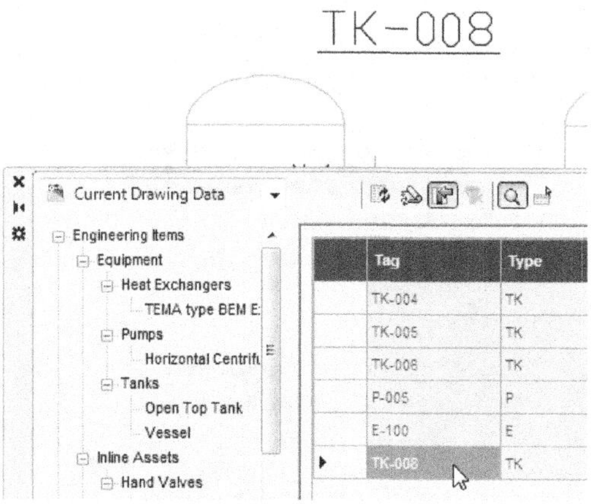

1. Start the AutoCAD Plant 3D software, if not already running.
2. Open the project as follows:
   - In the Project Manager, Current Project list, click Open.
   - In the Open dialog box, navigate to the folder *C:\Plant Design 2024 Practice Files\Use Data Manager to Review, Export, and Import Data*.
   - Select the file *Project.xml*.
   - Click Open.
3. Open *PID002.dwg*.
4. Ensure that you are working in the P&ID PIP Workspace and Tool Palettes.
5. To display the Data Manager, on the Home tab, on the Project panel, click Data Manager.

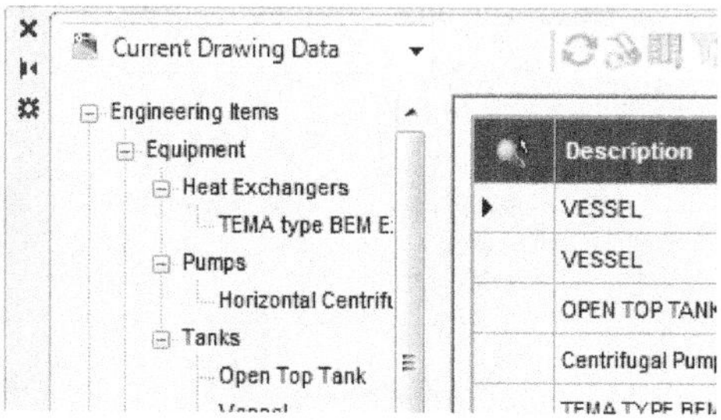

6. To view all the equipment in the project, from the Class List, select Equipment.

   Note: The order might vary from that shown.

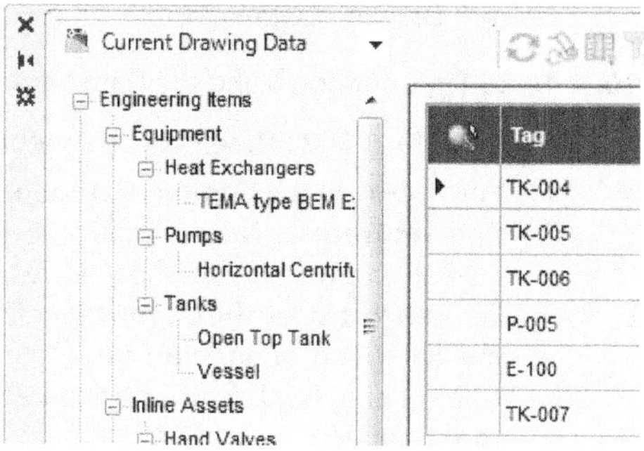

7. To view data for the project:
   - In the Data Manager, click the drop-down arrow next to Current Drawing Data, as shown in the following illustration.
   - From the list, select P&ID Project Data.

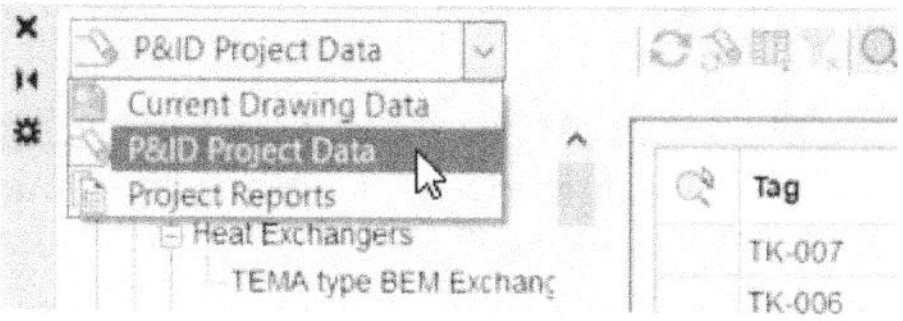

8. To view data for Project Reports:
   - Click Project Reports from the drop-down list.
   - From the Project Reports list, select Valve List, as shown in the illustration below.

   Note: The order might vary from that shown.

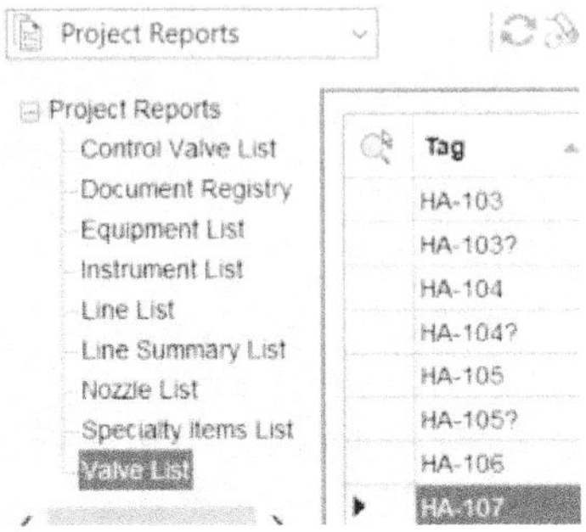

9. Return the Data Manager display to the Current Drawing Data.

10. To add information using the Data Manager:
    - From the Class list, select Equipment.
    - For TK-006, in the Comment column, enter **In Transit**. (**Note:** Expand the right side area or use the scroll bar at the bottom to display the Comment column.) If a dialog box opens after clicking in the Comment field, click OK and then enter the comment.
    - For TK-007, in the Comment column, enter **On Site**.

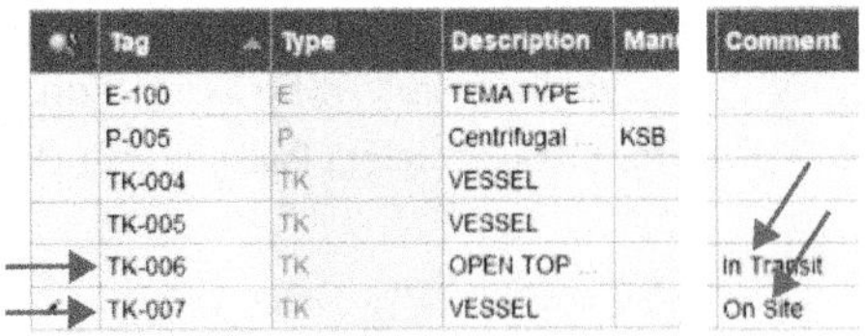

11. To view filtered data (for example, listing only TK types in the Type column):
    - Right-click on any TK cell in the Type column.
    - Click Filter By Selection as shown in the following illustration.
    - Note that only four TK data are displayed.

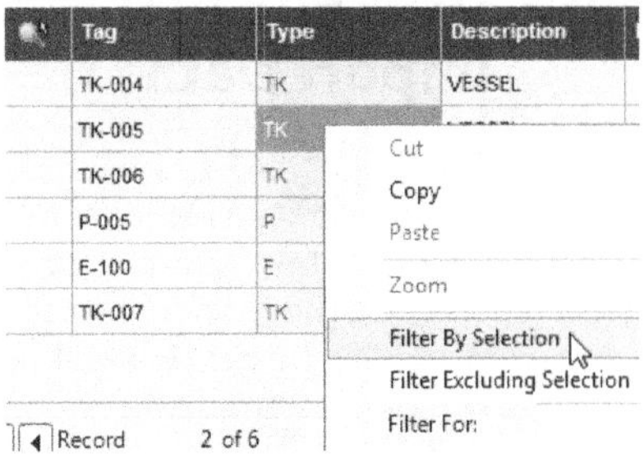

12. To remove any filter, right-click on any cell. Click Remove Filter.

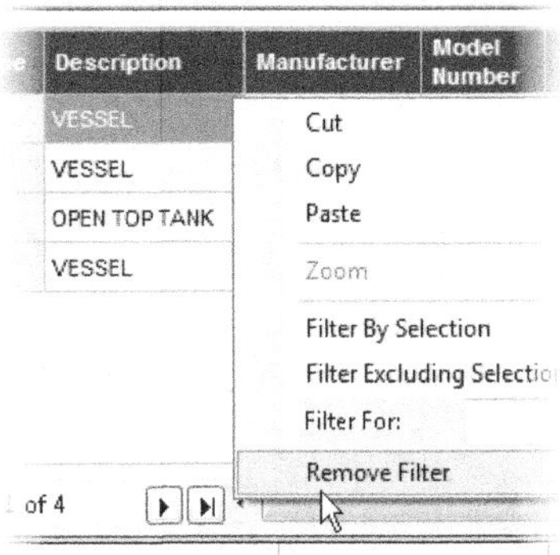

13. To filter all objects except selected ones:
    - Right-click on any TK type.
    - Click Filter Excluding Selection. Note that only two data are displayed.
    - Remove the filter.

14. To view only populated columns, on the Data Manager toolbar, click Hide Blank Columns.

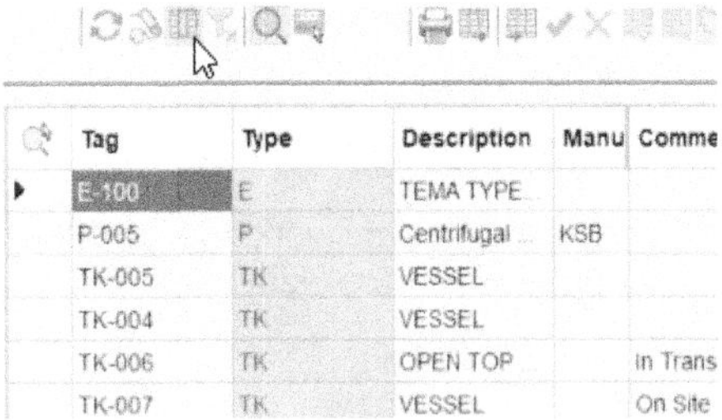

15. To begin to export data:

- On the Data Manager toolbar, click Export.
- In the Export Data dialog box, for Select export settings, verify Displayed Data is selected.
- Under Include child nodes, click Active node only.

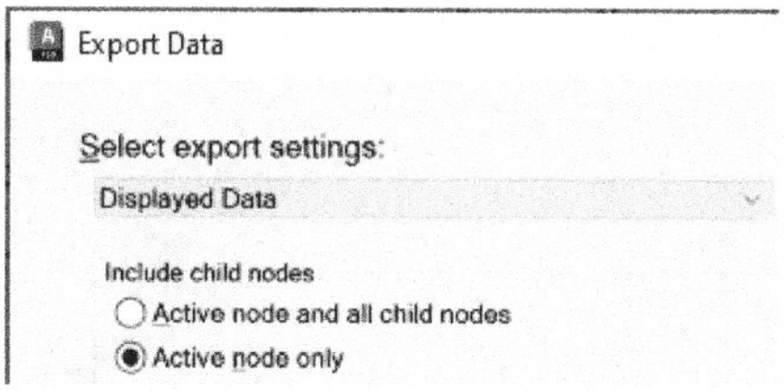

16. To export the data:

- For the location for exported data, click Browse.
- In the Export To dialog box, navigate to your Practice Files folder (or any other location) to save the file. Set the name of the file as **PID002-Equipment**.
- For Files of type, select the Excel Workbook (*.xlsx) option.
- Click Save.
- Note: If the file is read-only, use **Save As** to save the file.
- Click OK in the dialog box.

Note that XLS or CSV files can also be exported.

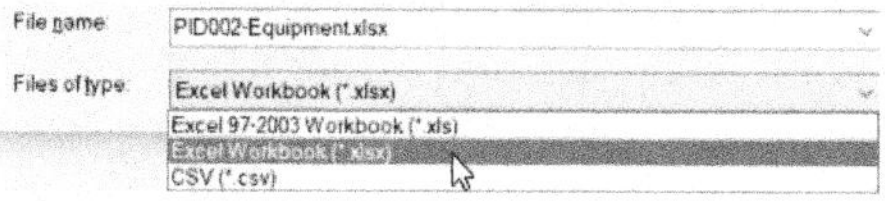

17. In Windows Explorer, navigate to your Practice Files folder or the folder where you saved the spreadsheet. Open it PID002-Equipment.

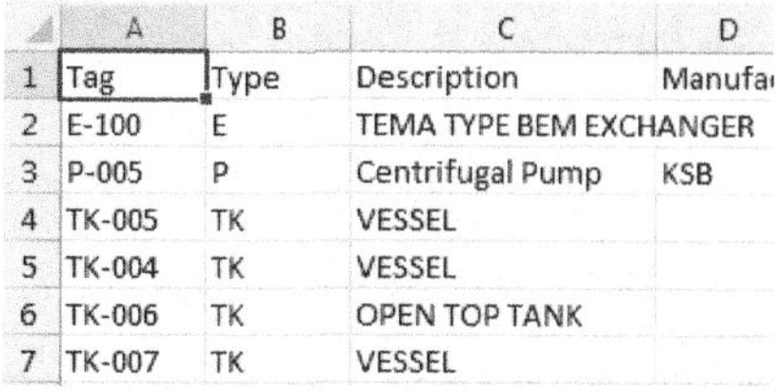

	A	B	C	D
1	Tag	Type	Description	Manufa
2	E-100	E	TEMA TYPE BEM EXCHANGER	
3	P-005	P	Centrifugal Pump	KSB
4	TK-005	TK	VESSEL	
5	TK-004	TK	VESSEL	
6	TK-006	TK	OPEN TOP TANK	
7	TK-007	TK	VESSEL	

18. To edit your drawing using the spreadsheet:

- In the spreadsheet, in the Tag column, change TK-007 to TK-008.
- In the Comment column, for item E-100, enter **On Site**.
- In the Comment column, for items TK-004 and TK-005, enter **In Transit**.

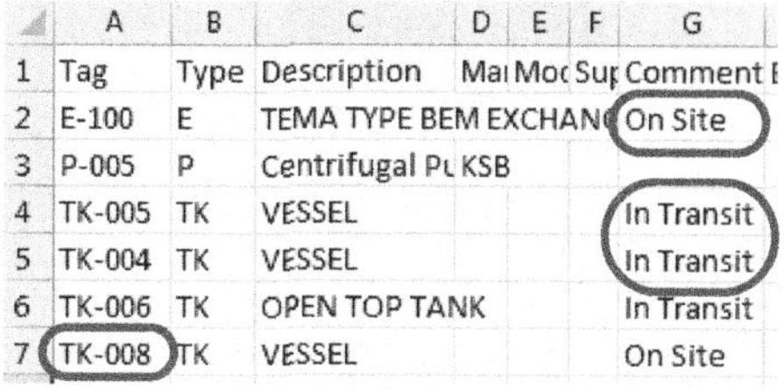

	A	B	C	D	E	F	G
1	Tag	Type	Description	Mai	Moc	Sup	Comment
2	E-100	E	TEMA TYPE BEM EXCHAN				On Site
3	P-005	P	Centrifugal Pu	KSB			
4	TK-005	TK	VESSEL				In Transit
5	TK-004	TK	VESSEL				In Transit
6	TK-006	TK	OPEN TOP TANK				In Transit
7	TK-008	TK	VESSEL				On Site

19. Save the spreadsheet. and close it.

20. To import the spreadsheet data:

- In the software, on the Data Manager toolbar, click Import.
- If prompted to accept a log file, click OK.
- Navigate to the spreadsheet **PID002-Equipment**. Click Open. (verify that the Files of type is Excel Workbook (*.xlsx).
- In the Import Data dialog box, click OK.

21. In the Data Manager, the yellow cells indicate that they have been edited.

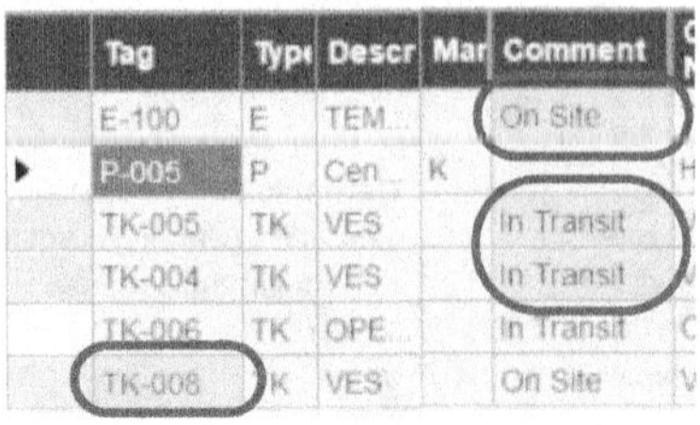

22. In the Data Manager, click the first row of Tag item TK-008. Note that the drawing zooms to that item which is originally TK-007.

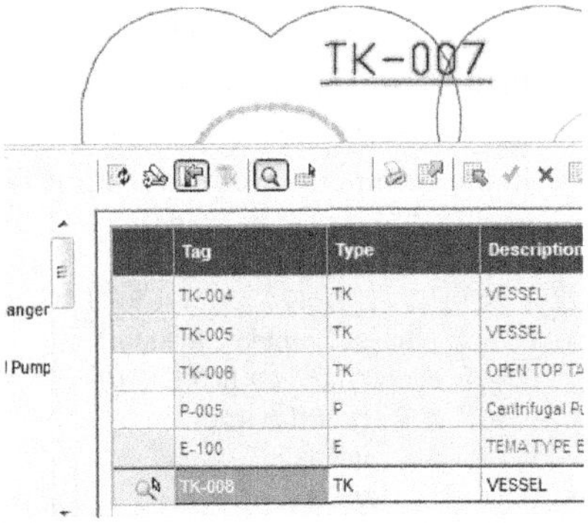

23. Zoom to extents. Review the drawing, and note that three edited vessels are outlined in red revision clouds.

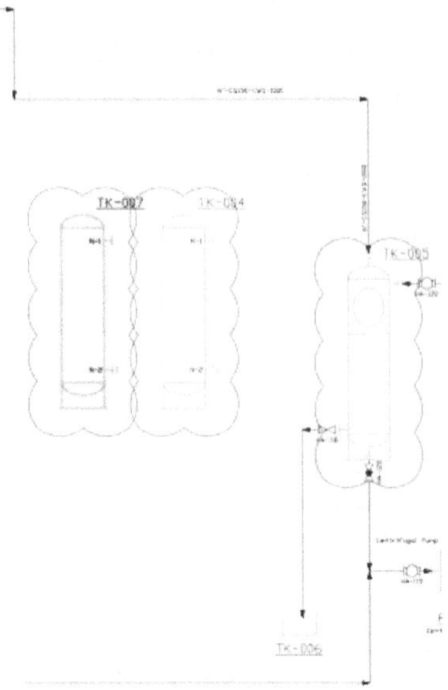

24. To accept edited data:

- In the Data Manager, Tag column, right-click on the TK-008 cell.
- Click Accept Edit.

Note the change in the Data Manager and the drawing.

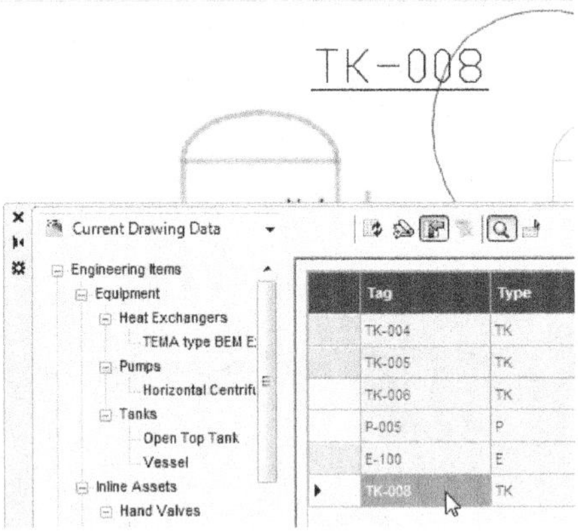

25. To accept all changes, on the Data Manager toolbar, click Accept All.

26. Save and close all drawings.

Lesson Review Questions

1. Can you import more than one Data Manager view at the same time?
   a. No, only the currently displayed view is imported into the Data Manager.
   b. Yes. All worksheets from the Excel file can be exported at the same time if the worksheet names are identical with the class name.
2. What types of documents can you export? (Select all that apply.)
   a. HTML
   b. DOC
   c. XLSX
   d. CSV
3. When importing data into the Data Manager, you need to individually approve every property that has changed.
   a. True
   b. False
4. What is essential when importing from Excel?
   a. You need to verify that the worksheet name and the column headers match the view in the Data Manager.
   b. Data cannot be imported from Excel, only from a CSV file.

Lesson: Custom One-off Symbols

Overview

This lesson describes how to create custom P&ID symbols from standard AutoCAD geometry, then convert a symbol to a P&ID object.

Creating custom P&ID symbols enables you to tailor your design to fit the exact needs of your customers, your company, and industry.

A custom P&ID symbol is shown in the following illustration.

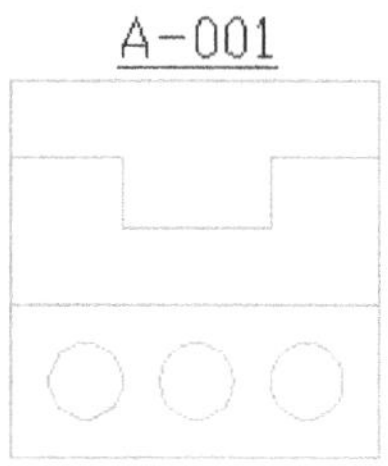

Objective

After completing this lesson, you will be able to:

- Create a custom P&ID symbol from standard AutoCAD geometry.

Create a Custom P&ID Symbol

The AutoCAD P&ID software enables you to create P&ID drawings that match your industry and company requirements. If a need for a symbol arises that the AutoCAD P&ID software does not already have, you can create a custom symbol.

A custom symbol (arrow) is inserted into a P&ID drawing, as shown in the following illustration.

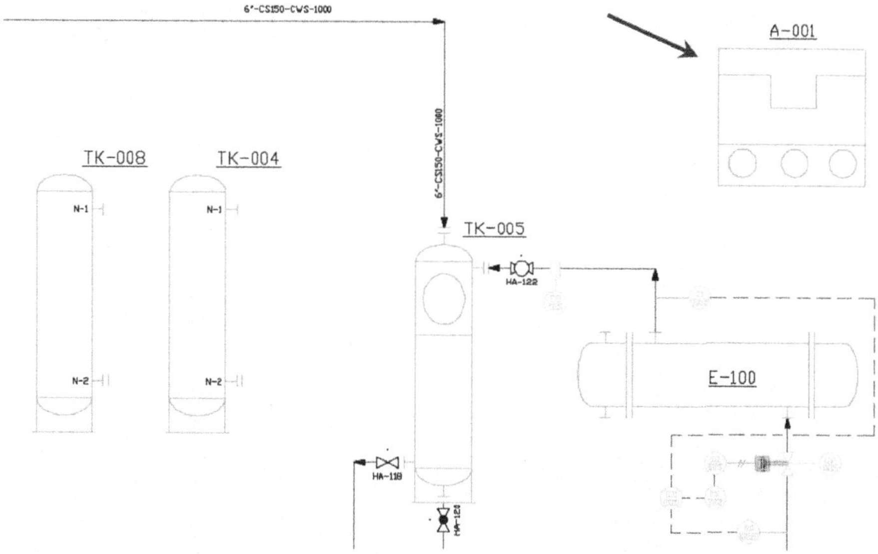

Process: Creating a Custom P&ID Symbol

The following steps describe the steps to create a custom P&ID symbol.

1. Using standard AutoCAD tools, create geometry that represents the symbol.

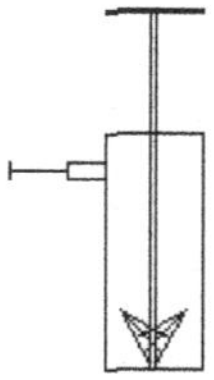

2. Select all the geometry.

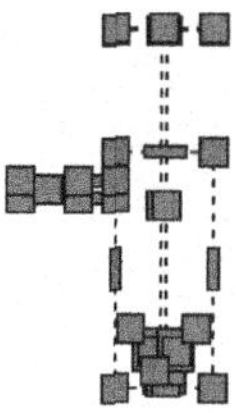

3. Right-click. Click Convert to P&ID Object.

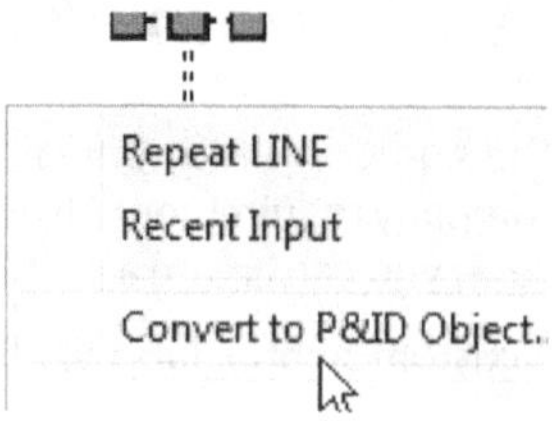

4. In the Convert to P&ID Object dialog box, assign a Class to the custom symbol.

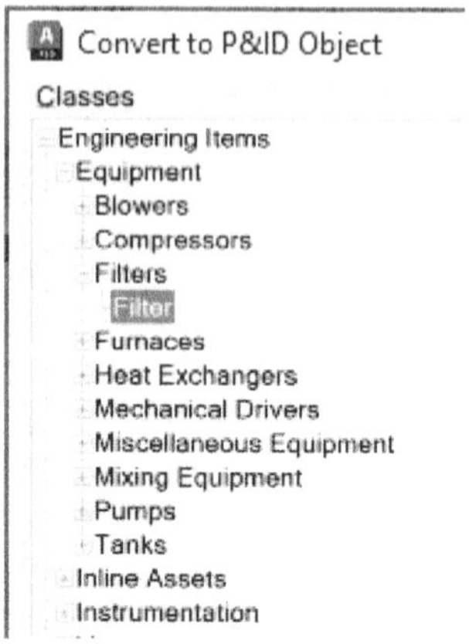

5. Select an insertion point. The color of the symbol updates to reflect the selected class.

   Once the symbol has been converted, you can edit the block definition by selecting it, right-clicking, and clicking Edit P&ID Object's Block. All entities can be edited using standard AutoCAD techniques.

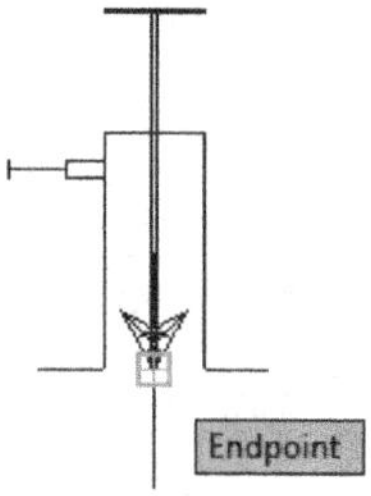

Exercise: Customize One-off Symbols

In this exercise, you use standard AutoCAD objects and drawing techniques to create a custom P&ID object.

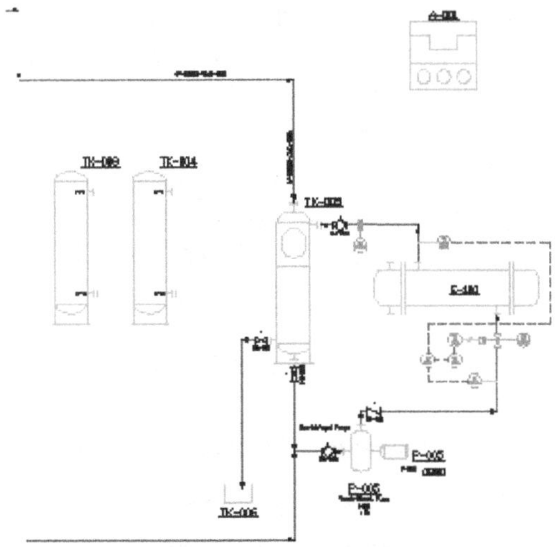

1. Start the AutoCAD Plant 3D software, if not already running.
2. Open the project as follows:
   - In the Project Manager, Current Project list, click Open.
   - In the Open dialog box, navigate to the folder *C:\Plant Design 2024 Practice Files\Customize One-off-Symbols*.
   - Select the file *Project.xml*.
   - Click Open.
3. Open *PID002.dwg*.
4. Ensure that you are working in the P&ID PIP Workspace and Tool Palettes.
5. Zoom to the empty area above Heat Exchanger E-100.

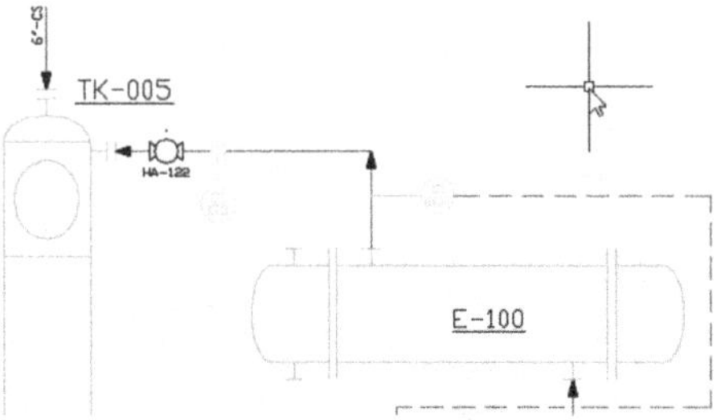

6. Using standard AutoCAD objects and techniques, create the following geometry to represent a filter.

   Note: Assume the dimensions. It might be beneficial to use Snap and Grid to quickly create the geometry.

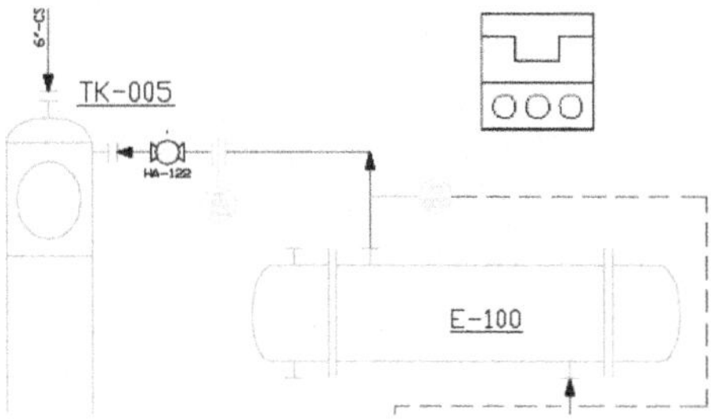

7. To begin to create a P&ID symbol:
   - Select all the geometry just created.
   - Right-click. Click Convert to P&ID Object.

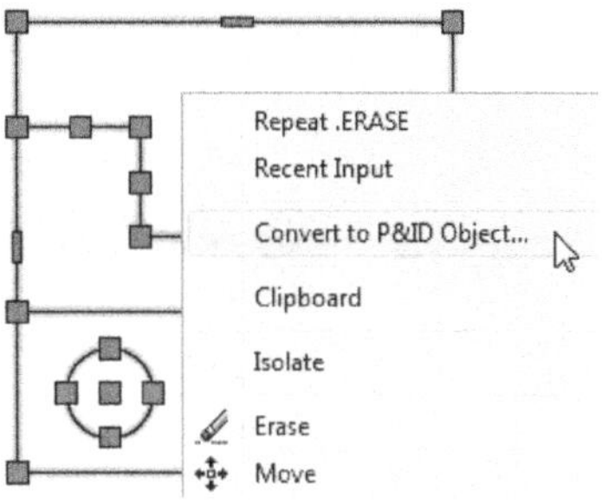

8. To define the P&ID object:

- In the Convert to P&ID Object dialog box, expand Engineering Items, Equipment, and Filters.
- Under Filters, click Filter.
- Click OK.

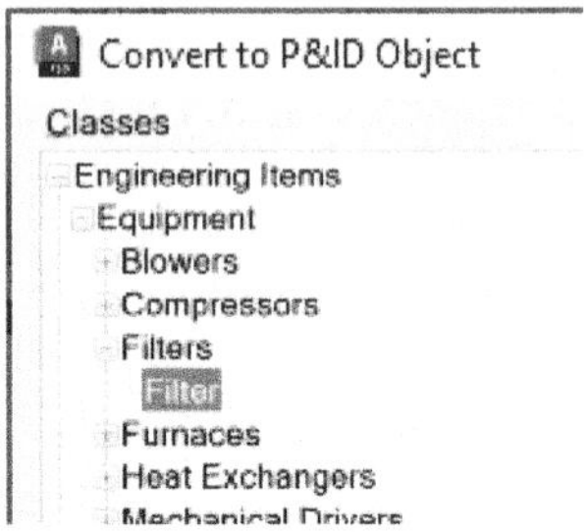

9. In the drawing window, select the insertion point at the midpoint of the bottom line.

Note the change in color to match other P&ID Filters.

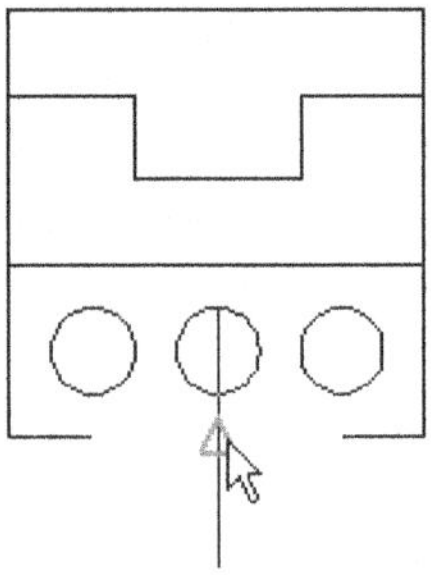

10. To assign tag information:

- Right-click on the new P&ID Symbol.
- Click Assign Tag.
- For Type, select **A**.
- For Number, enter **001**.
- Under Existing Filters, select Place annotation after assigning tag to display a checkmark.

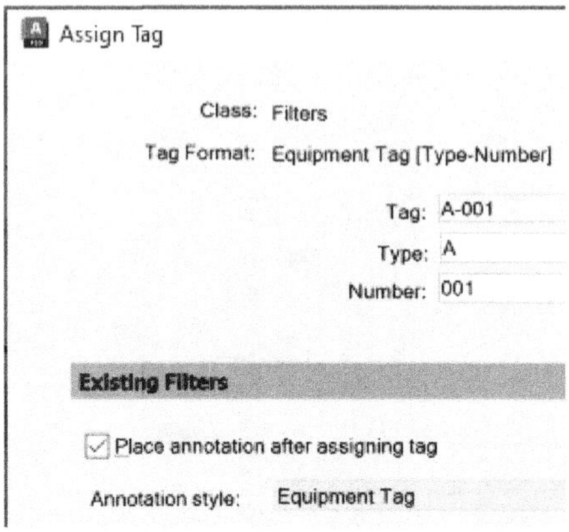

11. To locate the tag:

- In the Assign Tag dialog box, click Assign.
- Click above the new filter symbol.

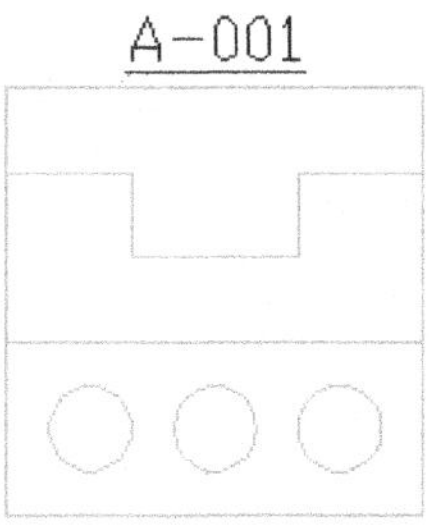

12. Save and close all drawings.

Lesson Review Questions

1. Custom symbols can be modified after they have been converted to P&ID symbols.
   a. True
   b. False
2. How do custom symbols know which tag format to use?
   a. The AutoCAD P&ID software analyzes the shape of the symbol and determines what it is.
   b. AutoCAD P&ID uses the tag format specified by the object class selected during the conversion process.

Lesson: Offpage Connections

Overview

In this lesson, you learn how to add offpage connectors and to connect them with other drawings. You also learn how offpage connectors can be used to navigate from drawing to drawing. Finally you learn how information on a line in one drawing is synchronized with the line on the other drawing.

The number of drawings required to document a P&ID for a plant design depends on the complexity and size of the design. The more complex the design, the greater the likelihood that it is going to require multiple drawings for complete documentation. For a line to span from one drawing to another, you need to use connectors, as shown in the following illustration. Offpage connectors are used in pairs: one in the originating drawing and one in the connecting drawing.

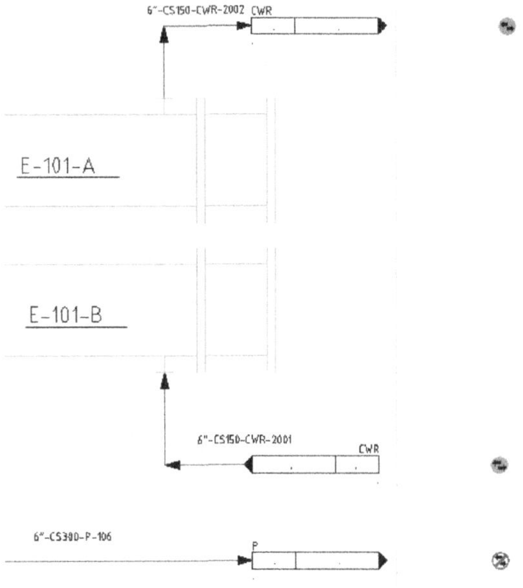

Objectives

After completing this lesson, you will be able to:

- Describe the purpose of Offpage Connectors.
- Add Offpage Connectors to a drawing.
- Connect Offpage Connectors.
- Reviewing the Offpage Connectors specified in a drawing.
- Specifying the Offpage Connector properties.
- Remove an Offpage Connector from a project.
- Review changes from the Data Manager in Offpage Connectors.

About Offpage Connectors

In the complex world of design and engineering, it is important to keep designs organized. An organized drawing enables all involved to read and find information efficiently. Organization also reduces costly errors and saves valuable time both during design, and during downstream operations, such as purchasing and manufacturing.

Since a P&ID design can span multiple drawings, it is important to connect lines going from one drawing to another with Offpage Connectors. Offpage Connectors enable you to organize your drawings.

Definition of Offpage Connectors

An Offpage Connector is a symbol inserted at the endpoint of a P&ID line that indicates where that line continues on another drawing. It alters the behavior of the connected lines in that any operation performed on one line is automatically applied to the lines in the other drawing. In other words, the lines act as if they were a single line in a single drawing.

An example of Offpage Connectors is shown in the following illustration. The pipeline data for both lines match from one drawing to another.

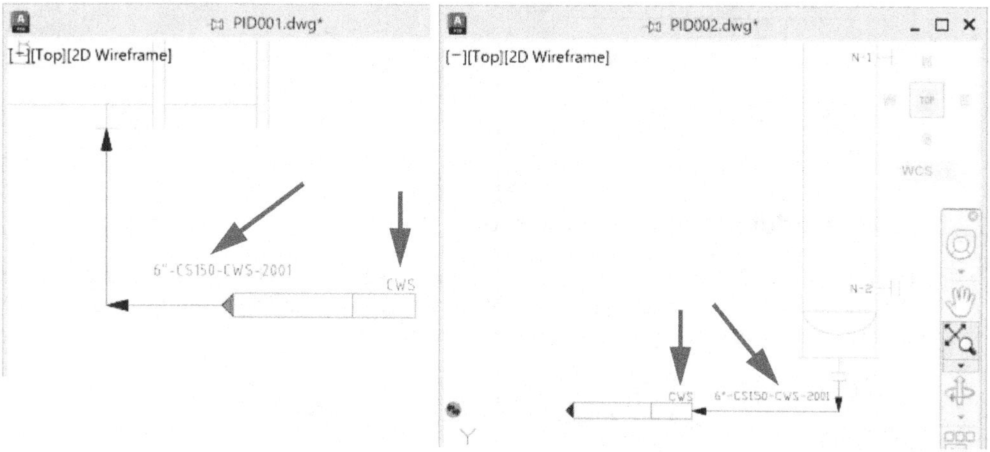

Adding Offpage Connectors

An Offpage Connector is added to a P&ID drawing the same way other symbols are added. They are accessed on the Non-engineering tab in the Tool Palette, on the Off Page Connectors and Tie-In Symbol panel.

The Non-engineering tab in the Tool Palette is shown in the following illustration.

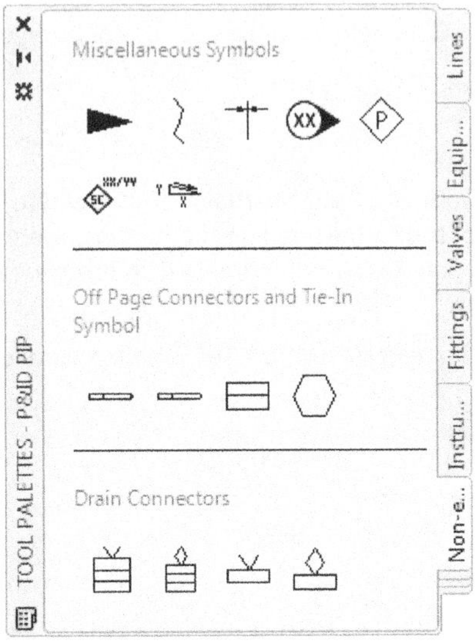

Process: Adding Offpage Connectors

The process for adding Offpage connectors to a drawing is shown in the following illustration. First, click the Non-engineering tab in the Tool Palette. Then, on the Off Page Connectors and Tie-In Symbol panel, click Off Page Connector and select the endpoint of the line.

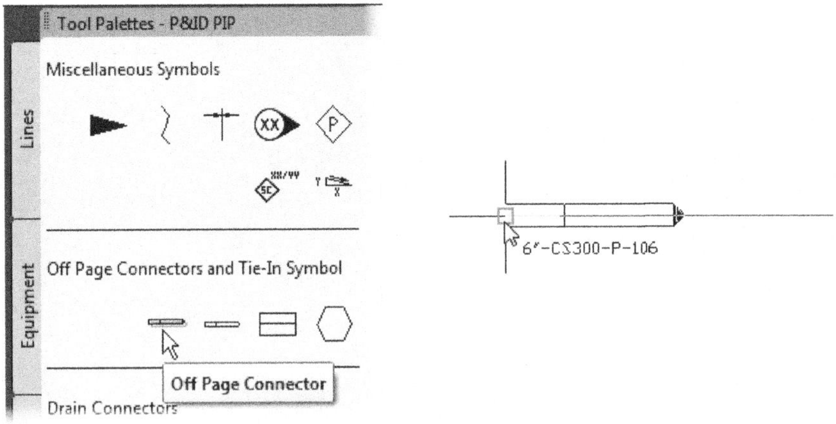

When a connector is initially added  displays next to the Off Page Connector, indicating that it has not been connected.

Connecting Offpage Connectors

After Offpage Connectors are placed on a drawing, they need to be connected to their counterparts. Typically this is in another drawing, but it can be in the same drawing if physically connecting the lines is not feasible.

To connect two lines with an Offpage Connector, you select an existing Offpage Connector in the drawing, which is connected to a line without a line number assigned, then click the cross grip on the Offpage Connector and click Connect To.

Access to the Connect To option for Offpage Connectors is shown in the following illustration.

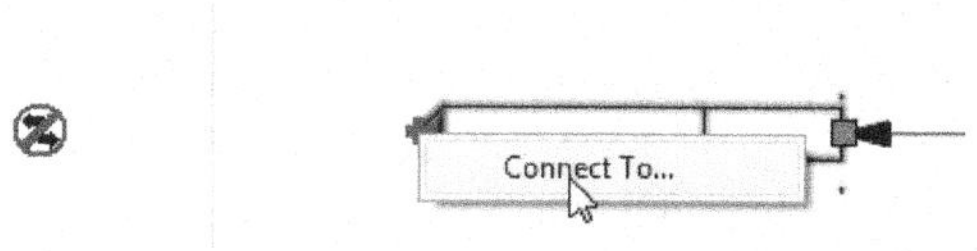

Create Connection Dialog Box

When you select the Connect To option on an Offpage Connector, the Create Connection dialog box opens. In this dialog box, you can select another drawing in the project to connect to. The available connectors are shown in the table at the bottom of the illustration. Lines that are grayed out represent connectors in a drawing that cannot be connected to. Selecting a connector zooms to the connector in the Preview area. You can pan and zoom inside the Preview area to get a better idea where a particular connection will be made.

Access to the Create Connection dialog box is shown in the following illustration.

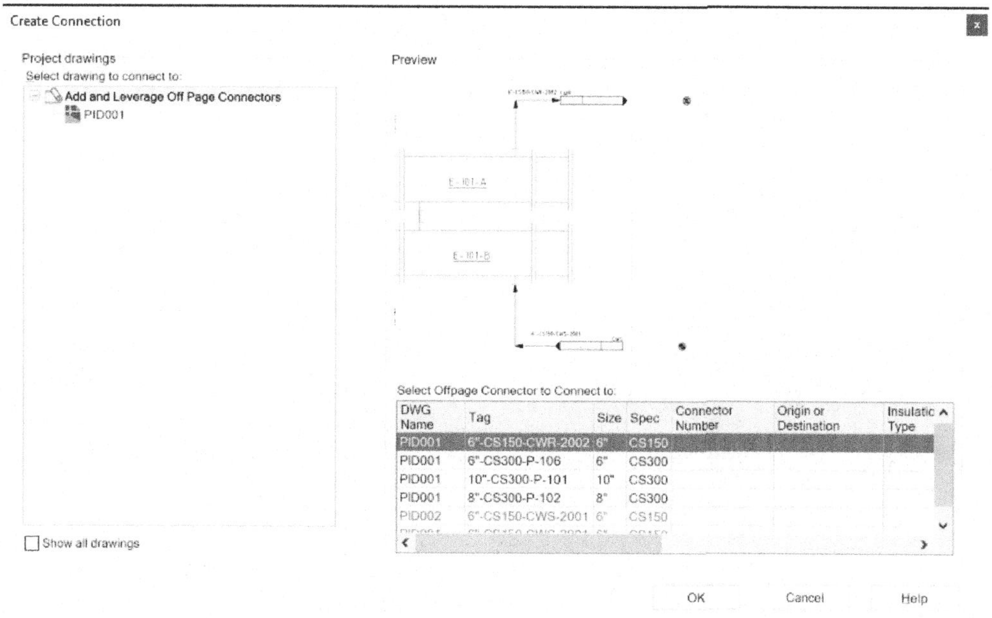

Process: Connecting Offpage Connectors

The following steps describe how to connect offpage connectors.

1. Add an Offpage Connector to a line.
2. Click the Offpage Connector and click the cross grip. Click Connect To.
3. In the Create Connection dialog box, click the drawing to be connected with. The drawing does not need to be opened to make the connection.
4. In the Select Offpage Connector to Connect to: area, select the Tag name to which to connect. Click OK.

   Note: You can connect an unassigned line Offpage Connector to an assigned line Offpage Connector, but not the reverse.

   Note: A connector must exist on the connecting pipeline to assign the connection.

Reviewing Offpage Connectors

Offpage Connectors can be reviewed in a dialog box or the connected drawing can be opened. To use either of these techniques, use the following:

- Select the Offpage Connector, click the round grip, and select View Connected. The connecting pipeline is shown in the View Connected Offpage Connector dialog box, as shown in the following illustration. Pan and zoom in the dialog box using the cursor to review the connected drawing.

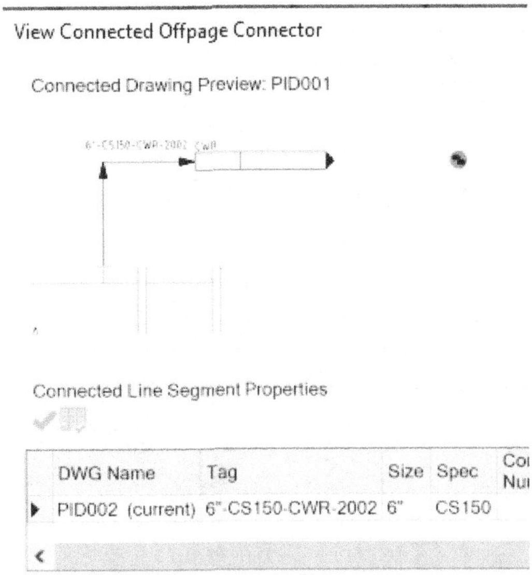

- Select the Offpage Connector, click the round grip, and select Click Open Connected DWG. The drawing to which the Offpage Connector is connected opens for review.

Offpage Connector Properties

You can tell at a glance whether a connector is disconnected, connected, or connected with mismatched properties. The appropriate status icon displays next to the connector, as shown in the following illustrations:

Not Connected **Connected (no mismatches)** **Connected (mismatches)**

To add additional properties to the Offpage Connector, use the following:

- To enter property values for a connector number or the Origin or Destination, right-click on a connector and click Properties. You can enter the Connector Number (e.g., **123**) and Origin or Destination (e.g., **TK-005**) in the appropriate field in the Properties palette.
- The drawing number, unlike the connector number, is a drawing property. If you right-click on the drawing name in the Project Manager and click Properties, you can enter a DWG Number. The appropriate Connected TO and Connected FROM Drawing Numbers are then displayed automatically in the connector when the connection is made.

An Offpage Connector with populated properties is shown in the following illustration.

Delete an Offpage Connector

To delete an Offpage Connector from a project, you use the standard AutoCAD method to delete objects from a drawing. The AutoCAD P&ID software deletes the selected Offpage Connector.

Data Manager Edits and Offpage Connectors

Data for Offpage Connectors is supplied from annotations on the lines that they connect. If you edit the tag information of a line, the information displayed on the Offpage Connector updates as well. This is also true for data edited using the Data Manager. Since the Data Manager edits the line data, in essence, you are directly editing the Offpage Connector.

Exercise: Add and Leverage Offpage Connectors

In this exercise, you place and connect multiple Offpage Connectors between a newly created drawing and existing drawings. You add information to the connectors using the Property dialog box and the Data Manager. You also navigate to the different pipelines using the Offpage Connectors.

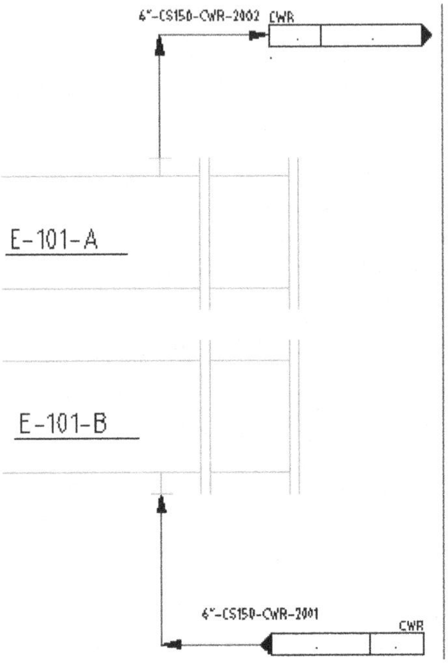

1. Start the AutoCAD Plant 3D software, if not already running.

2. Open the project as follows:
   - In the Project Manager, Current Project list, click Open.
   - In the Open dialog box, navigate to the folder *C:\Plant Design 2024 Practice Files\Add and Leverage Off Page Connectors*.
   - Select the file *Project.xml*.
   - Click Open.

3. Open *PID001.dwg* and *PID002.dwg*.

4. Ensure that you are working in the P&ID PIP Workspace and Tool Palettes.

5. To create pipelines in *PID002.dwg*:
   - Click the Lines tab in the Tool Palette.
   - Under Pipe Lines, click Primary Line Segment.
   - In *PID002.dwg,* create pipelines entering and exiting TK-008, as shown in the following illustration.

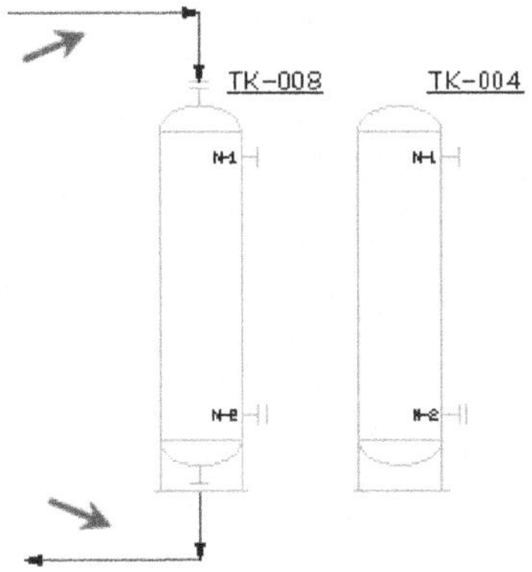

6. Click the Non-engineering tab in the Tool Palette.

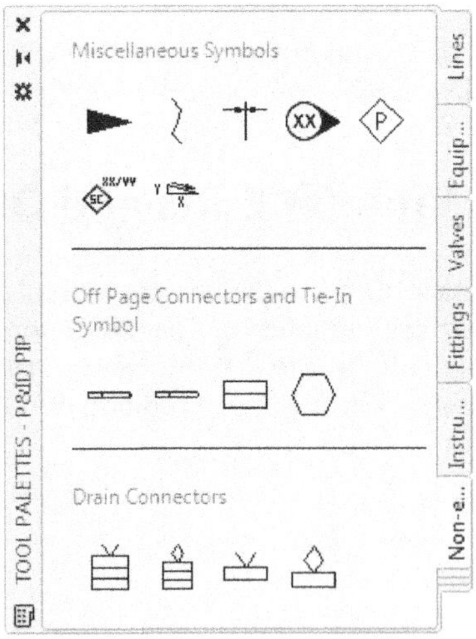

7. To add a page connector:

- On the Non-engineering palette, under Off Page Connectors and Tie-In Symbol, click Off Page Connector.
- Select the endpoint of one of the newly created pipelines.
- Add another connector to the other line, by selecting its endpoint.

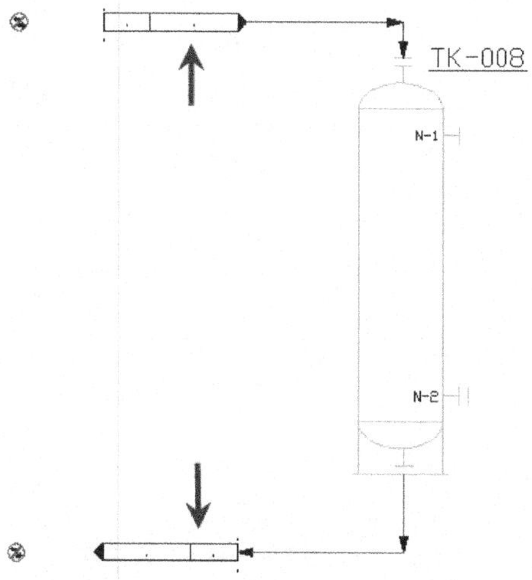

8. To apply an annotation tag to the pipelines:

- Right-click on the top pipeline.
- Under Annotate, click Pipeline Tag.
- Click above the line to locate the tag.

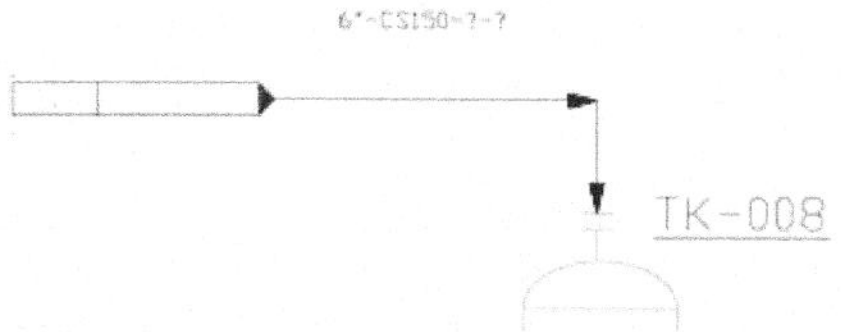

9. As in Step 8, add a tag to the lower pipeline.

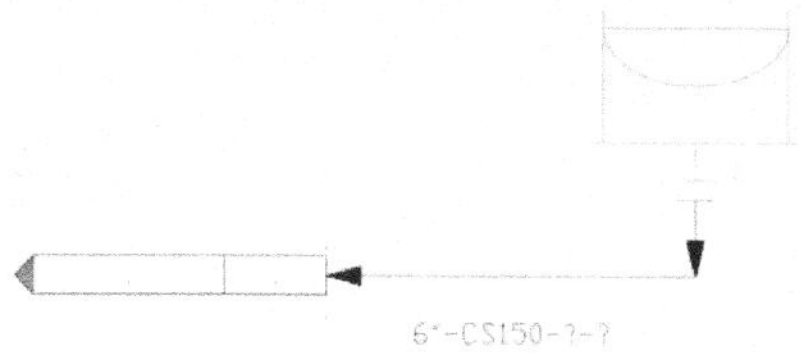

10. Activate drawing PID001.

- Zoom to the right side of the drawing where E-101-A and E-101-B are located.
- Note the two pipelines with Off Page Connectors.
- Also note that these lines have tags applied (6"-CS150-CWR-2002 and 6"-CS150-CWS-2001).

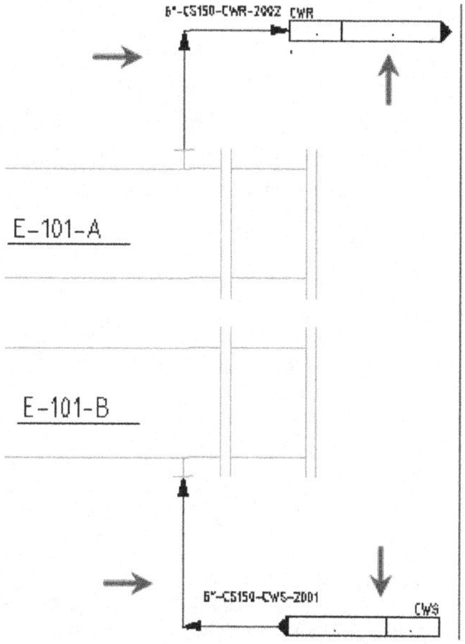

11. Return to the PID002.dwg drawing.

12. To begin to connect to another drawing:

- Select the Off Page connector that is at the bottom of the TK-008 tank. Note that the Offpage Connector symbol is (red).
- Click the plus sign at the left end of the connector.
- It turns red and click Connect To.

13. To connect to another drawing:

- In the Create Connection dialog box, select PID001.
- Under Select Offpage Connector to Connect to:, select the 6"-CS150-CWS-2001 connector in the list by selecting the Tag name. Note that the Preview of drawing PID001 zooms to this connector.
- Click OK.
- Note in PID002 that the Offpage Connector symbol turns (green) indicating that it is now connected and has no mismatches. The line tag also changes to display the selected connector.

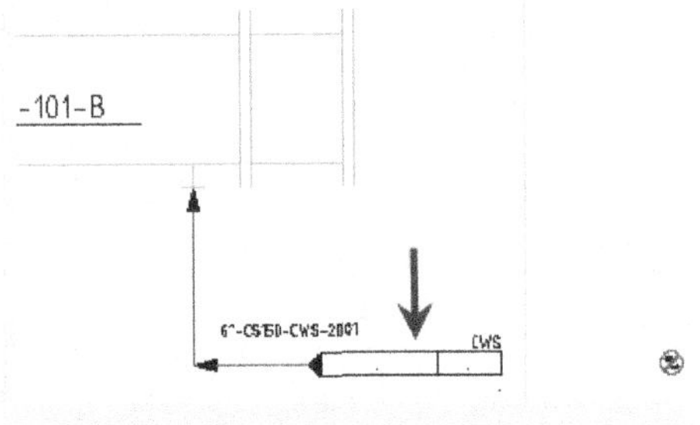

Select Offpage Connector to Connect to:

Tag	Size	Spec	Connector Number	Origin or Destination
6"-CS300-P-106	6"	CS300		
6"-CS150-CWS-2001	6"	CS150		
6"-CS150-CWR-2002	6"	CS150		
10"-CS300-P-101	10"	CS300		

14. In the PID002 drawing, make another connection to another drawing:

- Select the Off Page connector that is at the top of the TK-008 tank.
- Click the plus sign at the left end of the connector.
- Click Connect To.

15. To connect to another drawing:

- In the Create Connection dialog box, select PID001.
- Under Select Offpage Connector to Connect to:, select the 6"-CS150-CWR-2002 connector in the list by selecting the Tag name. Note that the Preview of drawing PID001 zooms to this connector.
- Click OK.
- Note in PID002 that the Offpage Connector symbol turns (green) indicating that it is now connected and has no mismatches.

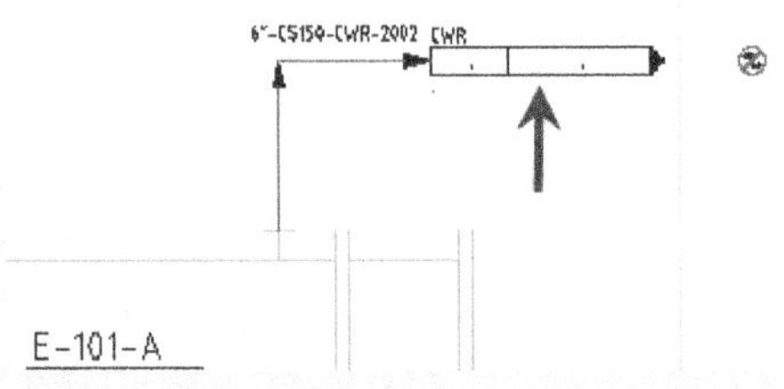

Select Offpage Connector to Connect to:

Tag	Size	Spec	Connector Number	Origin or Destination
6"-CS150-CWR-2002	6"	CS150		
6"-CS300-P-106	6"	CS300		
10"-CS300-P-101	10"	CS300		
8"-CS300-P-102	8"	CS300		

16. To review the connections:

- Activate PID001 drawing and select the connector leading from the E-101-A component.
- Hover the cursor over the round grip at the end of the connector (it turns green). Note that it is connected to PID002.
- Review that the connection on the lower connector is also set to PID002.

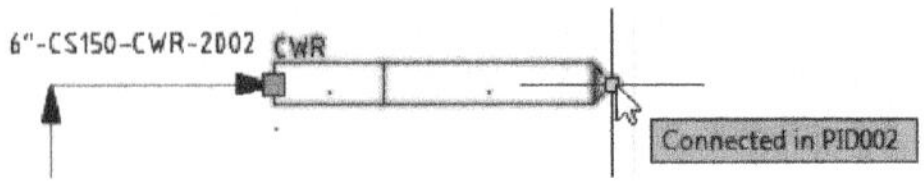

17. To review a specified connector in the View Connected Offpage Connector dialog box:

- Activate PID002.dwg.
- Select the Offpage Connector that connects to the top of TK-008.
- Click the round grip (turns red).
- Click View Connected to view the connecting pipeline in the View Connected Offpage Connector dialog box.
- Close the View Connected Offpage Connector dialog box.

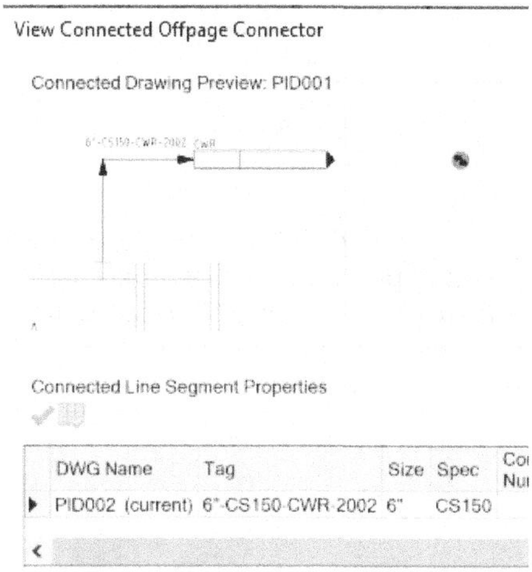

18. To open a drawing associated with a connector:

- Select the Offpage Connector that connects to the bottom of TK-008.
- Click the round grip.
- Click Open Connected DWG to open/activate the connected drawing. Note it zooms to the connector in PID001 drawing

19. Assign a third Offpage Connector:

- In the PID001 drawing, zoom to the offpage connector at the bottom right of the design. Note that (red) is displayed indicating a connection is missing.
- Select the connector.
- Click the plus sign grip (turns red).
- Click Connect To.
- Note that there are no connectors that have not already been assigned. Click Cancel.

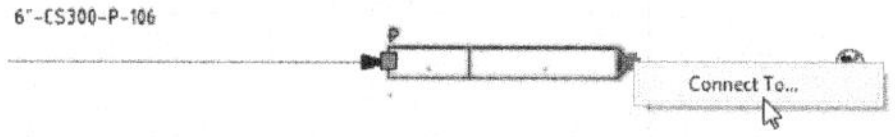

20. Complete the connection:

- Activate PID002.dwg.
- On the Non-engineering tab of Tool Palette, under Off Page Connectors and Tie-In Symbol, click Off Page Connector.
- Select the endpoint of the pipeline going to the bottom of TK-005.

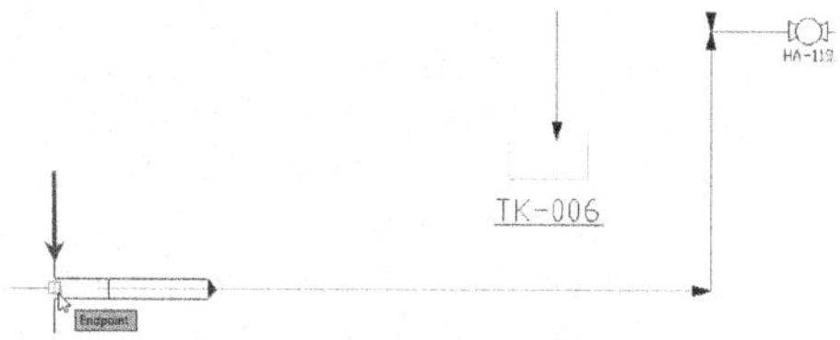

21. To make the connection:

- In PID002, select the Offpage Connector going to TK-005 (that you just inserted).
- Click the plus sign at the left end of the connector.
- Click Connect To.
- In the Create Connection dialog box, select the PID001 drawing, if not selected.
- Select 6"-CS300-P-106 tag and note that the drawing is zoomed to this connector in the drawing. Zoom out if required to verify that this connector is at the bottom right of the drawing.
- Click OK.

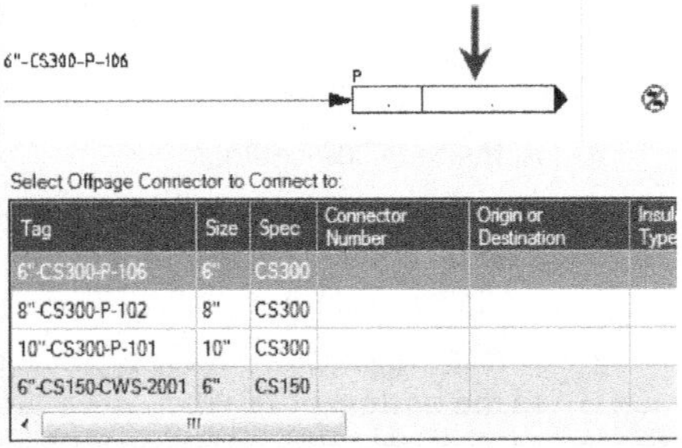

22. In the PID002 drawing, select the pipeline to the newly assigned Offpage Connector. Right-click and click Assign Tag. The values 6" for Size and CS300 for Spec should already be selected. In the Existing Pipe Line Segments, clear Place annotation after assigning tag. Click Assign.

23. To delete an offpage connector:

- In PID002, right-click on the off page connector that was just created (bottom of TK005).
- Click Erase.

24. In drawing PID002, on the Home tab, on the Project panel, click Data Manager.

25. To view drawing data:

- In the Data Manager, select Current Drawing Data.
- Under Engineering Items, click Lines, and click Pipe Line Group.

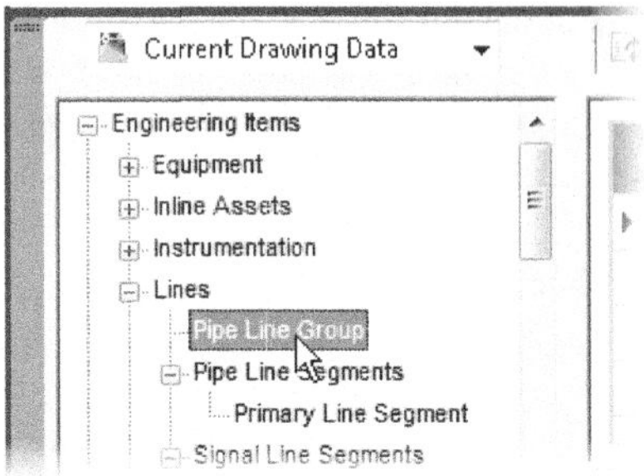

26. Adjust your drawing so that you can see the output pipeline from tank TK-008 in *PID002.dwg.* The Data Manager should be visible as well.

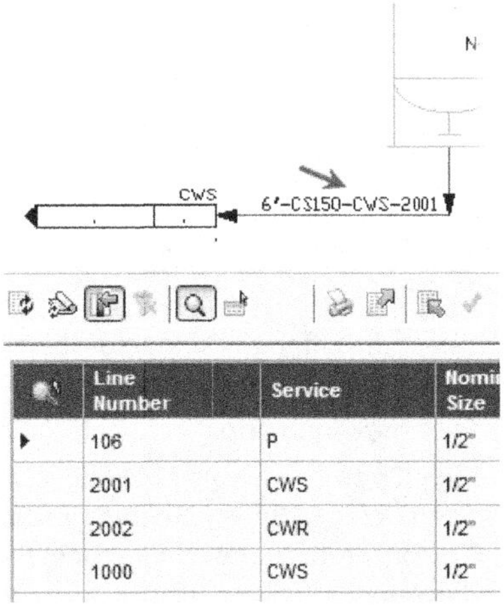

27. To change data:

- In the Data Manager, for Line Number 2001, click its cell in the Service column. If a dialog box opens, click OK. Click in the same column again.
- Note that it opens the drawing PID001 and zooms to the off page connector that connects to E-101-B.
- Using the Data Manager scroll bar, scroll down to display 2001. Click twice in the Service column to display the drop-down arrow. Click the arrow to display the list and select CWR - COOLING WATER RETURN.
- Click any other cell.

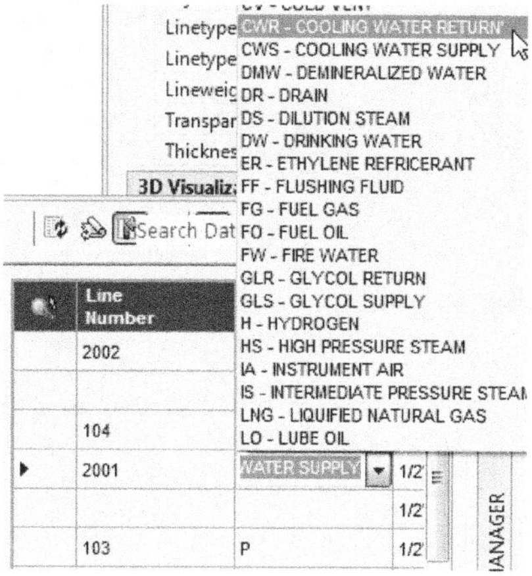

28. Note that the line data updated automatically. Close the Data Manager.

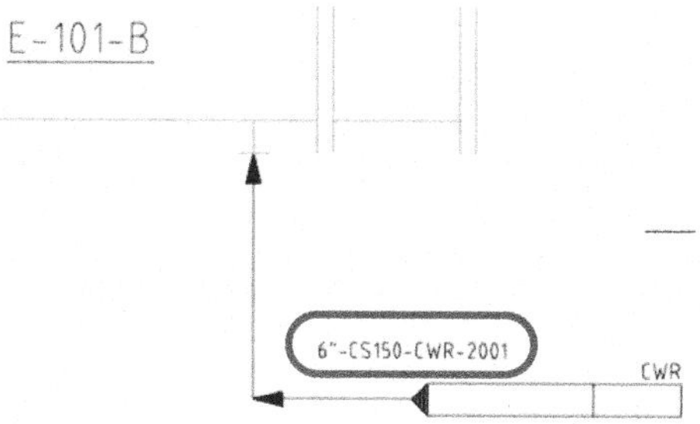

29. Switch to PID002 and note that the line data has updated to display CWR for the output pipeline from tank TK-008.

30. To assign the DWG Number property:

- Right-click on PID001 in the Project Manager and click Properties.
- In the Drawing Properties dialog box, enter **PID001** as the DWG Number property.
- Click OK.

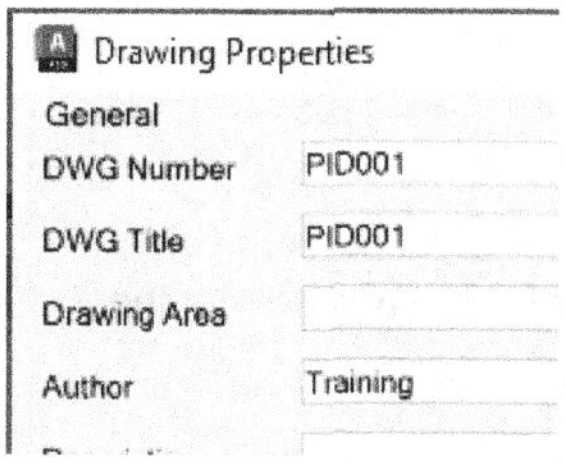

31. To assign the property values to a Offpage Connector:

- Activate PID002, if required.
- Select the Offpage Connector that is located on the pipeline leaving TK-008.
- Right-click and click Properties. The Property palette opens, if not already open.
- In the General section (below Styles at the bottom), enter **123** as the Connector Number.
- Enter **TK-008** as the Origin or Destination.

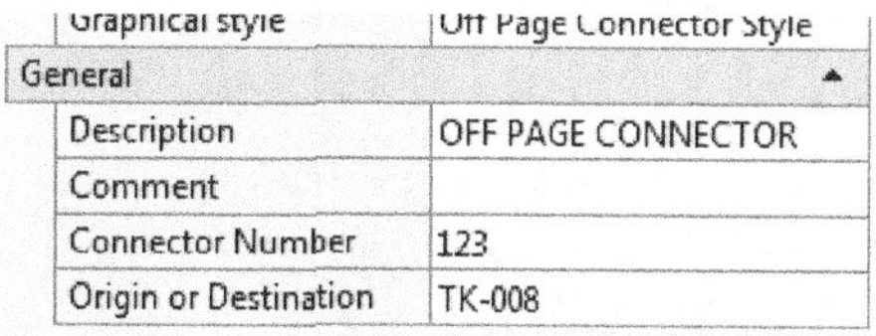

The Offpage Connector updates with all the property information.

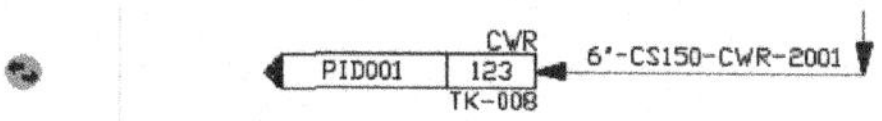

32. Save and close all drawings.

Lesson Review Questions

1. You can connect one Offpage Connector to multiple Offpage Connectors.
   a. True
   b. False
2. When placing Offpage Connectors, you must open the drawings to which you want to connect before creating the connections.
   a. True
   b. False
3. Once a connection has been made, it can be changed without deleting the Offpage Connector.
   a. True
   b. False
4. Which of the following Offpage Connector symbols indicates that a connection has been made but that there are mismatches?
   a. 
   b. 
   c. 
5. An Offpage Connector can be connected to an available connector on the same drawing.
   a. True
   b. False

Lesson: Generating Reports

Overview

This lesson describes the use of Report Creator to generate reports.

The ability to generate reports from outside the AutoCAD P&ID software enables you to create and configure reports based on project data or drawing data.

A report created early in the design process is shown in the following illustration. From this report, the engineer can begin the process of locating manufacturers.

Equipmentlist

Project: Training Project

Tag	Manufacturer	Model Number	Supplier	Material Of Construction	Weight
P-101-					
P-101-					
E-101-					
E-101-					
I-101					
V-101					

Objectives

After completing this lesson, you will be able to:

- Explain the purpose of plant design project reports and list what reports are common for a project.
- Generate different reports for a project using Report Creator.

About Project Reports

During the process of designing a plant or piping system, you need to generate a report of project items for purchasing or requisition. Throughout the project, other disciplines and managers reference the reports that you create to proceed with their assigned portion of the project. You can avoid many miscommunication errors by providing complete, updated reports from your AutoCAD Plant 3D projects. Common reports include a line list, valve takeoff, instrument takeoff, pipe components, and equipment list.

Definition of Project Reports

A project report lists items in the project with relevant information for the discipline for which it is created.

Example of Project Reports

Equipment lists typically include Tag, Description, and Drawing Name fields, etc., as shown in the following illustration. Instrument lists usually include the Tag, Description, Loop, and Drawing Name fields.

Major Equipment List

Project: Training Project

Tag	Description	Model Number	Supplier	Area	Drawing Name
P-101-	HORIZONTAL CENTRIFUGAL PUMP				PID001
P-101-	HORIZONTAL CENTRIFUGAL PUMP				PID001
E-101-	TEMA TYPE AEL EXCHANGER				PID001
E-101-	TEMA TYPE AEL EXCHANGER				PID001
T-101	VESSEL				PID001
V-101	VESSEL				PID001

Instrument List

Project: Training Project

Tag	Description	Loop	Location	Area	Drawing Name
10-PI-105	FIELD DISCRETE	105		10	PID001
10-PI-104	FIELD DISCRETE	104		10	PID001
10-LG-106	PRIMARY ACCESSIBLE DISCRETE	106		10	PID001
10-CV-106	CONTROL VALVE	106		10	PID001
10-PSV-101	PILOT OPERATED RELIEF VALVE	101		10	PID001

Generating Reports Using Report Creator

By using the Report Creator to distribute relevant reports, you can keep your project on track. The Report Creator includes a number of reference reports. You export these reports to reflect the current status of your project.

Report Creator

The Report Creator is a stand-alone application that formats reports from predefined templates and populates those reports with data from a project, as shown in the following illustration. Autodesk Report Creator for AutoCAD Plant 3D is listed on the Start menu in the expandable list for the AutoCAD Plant 3D software.

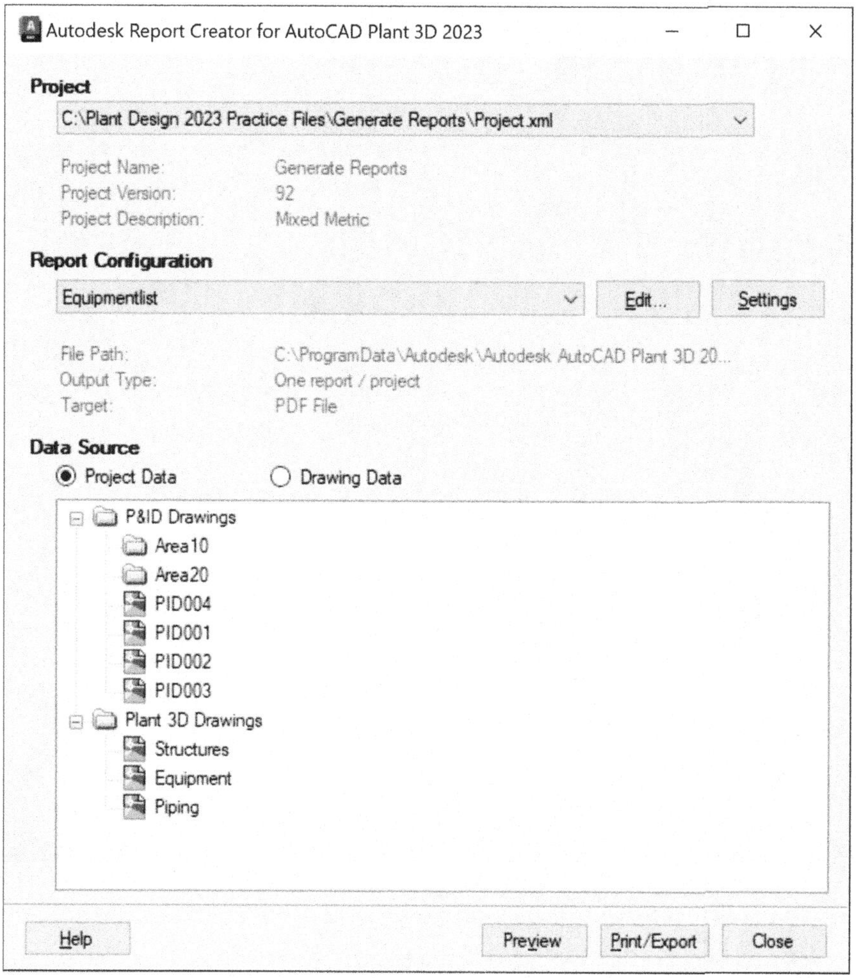

Process: Generating Reports Using Report Creator

The following steps give an overview of generating a report using Autodesk Report Creator for AutoCAD Plant 3D:

1. Start Autodesk Report Creator for AutoCAD Plant 3D by selecting it from the Start Menu.
2. Select the project for which you want to create a report.
3. Select the report configuration you want to use to generate the report.
4. Specify which drawings should be included when generating the report or whether the entire project should be used.
5. Generate the report as a print or electronic file.

Exercise: Generate Reports

In this exercise, you use Report Creator to generate an equipment list report for a project and export it as a PDF file.

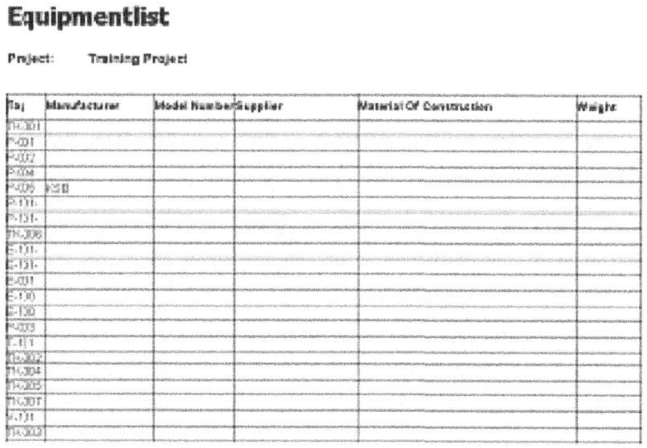

1. Start the Report Creator for AutoCAD Plant 3D application.
2. Open the project as follows:
   - If the Settings dialog box opens, click Cancel.
   - In Autodesk Report Creator for AutoCAD Plant 3D, Project list drop-down, select Open.
   - In the Open dialog box, navigate to the folder *C:\Plant Design 2024 Practice Files\Generate Reports*.
   - Select the file *Project.xml*.
   - Click Open.
   - Note that the selected path is listed in the Project list.

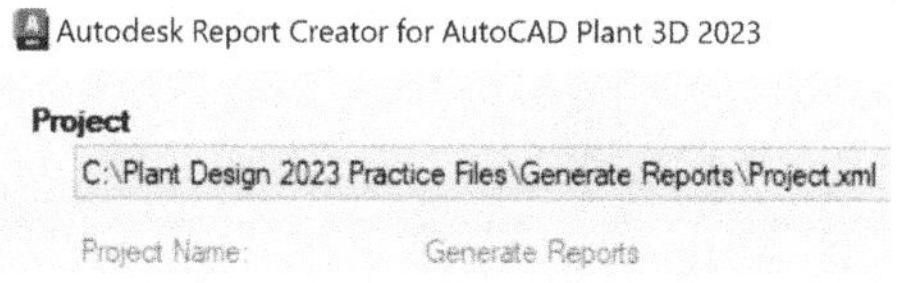

3. In the Report Configuration area, click Settings.
4. In the Settings dialog box:
   - Select the General option.
   - Click OK.
5. From the Report Configuration list, select Equipmentlist. Review the File Path, Output Type, and Target settings.

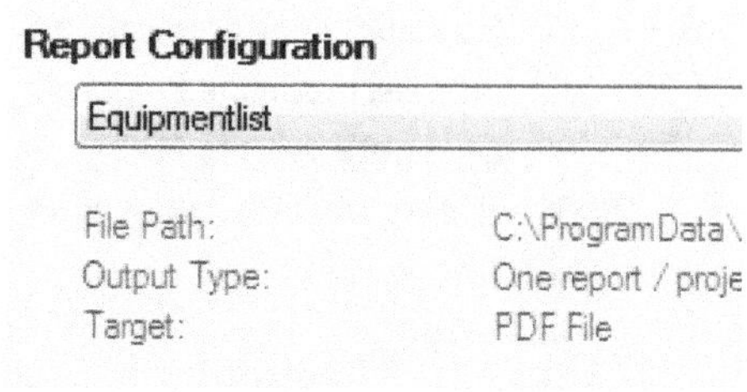

6. Click Print/Export.
7. In the PDF Export Options dialog box, click OK.
8. In the Export results dialog box, double-click on the listed PDF file to open it.

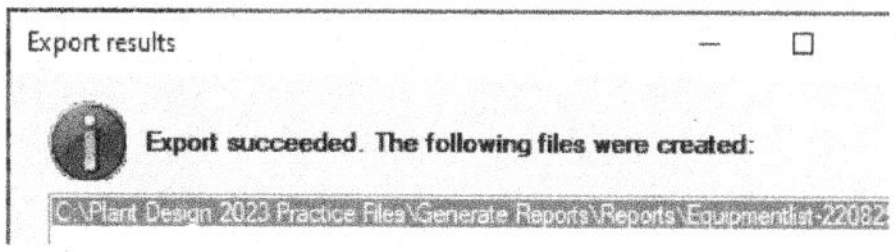

9. Review the report.

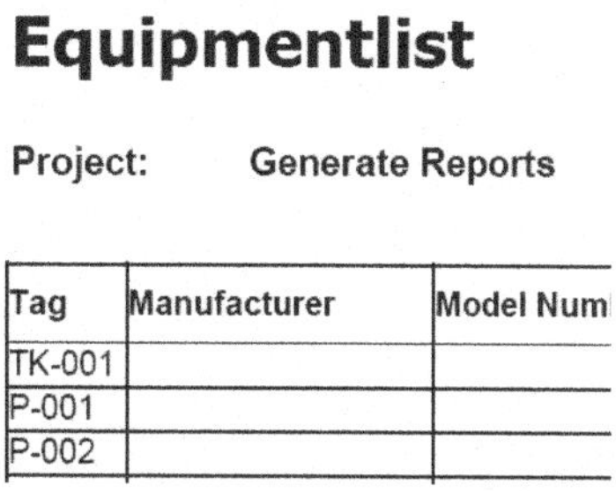
Equipmentlist

Project: Generate Reports

Tag	Manufacturer	Model Num
TK-001		
P-001		
P-002		

10. Close the PDF viewer, Export Results dialog box, and AutoCAD Plant Report Creator.

Lesson Review Questions

1. Which of the following are valid statements regarding the Report Creator? (Select all that apply.)
   a. Can be launched from the Data Manager.
   b. Is a stand-alone application.
   c. Includes predefined reports.
   d. Does not export to PDF.
2. The Report Creator enables you to create reports by project or by drawing.
   a. True
   b. False

Chapter Summary

In this chapter, you learned how to use the AutoCAD P&ID software to create, modify and manage 2D piping and instrumentation diagrams for a plant design. Some of the tasks you learned how to do included adding industry-standard symbols to the drawing, breaking and mending lines, ensuring flow direction, adding tags and annotations in industry-formats, identifying and correcting potential inconsistencies, and sharing project information.

Having completed this chapter, you can:

- Add drawings to a project by creating new drawings, linking to existing drawings, and copying them from another project.
- Place equipment, set the tag, see the predefined type, and make changes to a symbol like adding nozzles.
- Add pipelines to connect equipment, group pipe segments, assign tags and information to the line, and add and remove components to the line.
- Add general and in line instruments and set up an instrument loop.
- Describe the purpose of tags and create unique tags including a unique tag that links symbols over multiple drawings.
- Place annotations and modify the properties and data driving the annotations.
- Make changes and modifications to the generated PID using AutoCAD PID's Sline grips and substitute arrow commands and with AutoCAD's move, copy and stretch commands.
- Use the Data Manager to create reports, review information in the PID, export the data to external files (XLS, XLSX, CSV) and import that same data again after revising externally. Also adjust the columns displayed in the Data Manager.
- Create one-off symbols by converting inserted blocks of symbols to PID objects.
- Add offpage connectors and connect these with other drawings and use them to navigate between drawings.
- Use of Report Creator to generate different reports of a plant design.

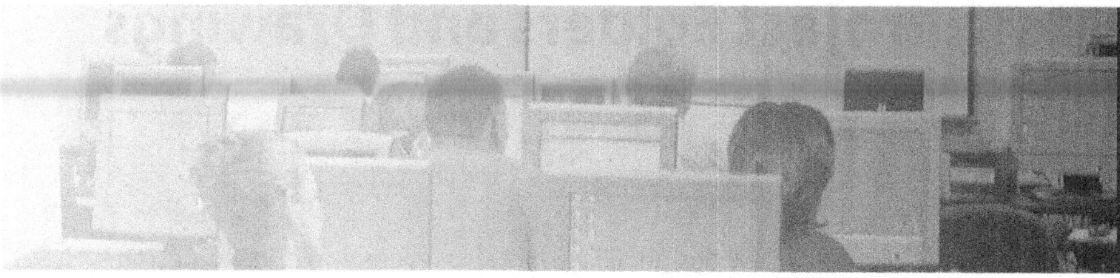

Chapter 3

AutoCAD Plant 3D

In every design field, the optimum work environment is one that enables you to spend your time and energy ensuring the design meets or exceeds the requirements of its use. When you are creating a plant design, because the plant is going to be constructed and operated in a 3D world, the optimal way of creating the design is in 3D. Using the AutoCAD® Plant 3D software to create your plant designs means you can focus on your design because the software is driven by industry specifications, it enables you to leverage existing designs and content, and it can easily generate and share isometrics, orthographics, and other construction documents. In this chapter, you learn how to use the AutoCAD Plant 3D software to create and modify a 3D plant design and 2D views of the 3D design.

Objectives

After completing this chapter, you will be able to:

- Add drawings to a project by creating them new, linking to existing drawings, and copying them from another project.
- Setup a grid, add steel members, ladders, stairs, railings, plates and footing, and modify the steel structure.
- Model and place 3D equipment.
- Create and route pipe and place pipe components.
- Create and use parts and place holder parts and change a line number, size, or spec.
- Use a P&ID to create and validate pipelines in the 3D design.
- Create and annotate orthographic views.
- Create isometric views.

Lesson: Creating Project Folders and Drawings

Overview

Projects for a plant design typically consist of new design files, while also leveraging existing design files. To have all of the required drawings correctly associated to the project, you need to know the correct way to create new drawings and incorporate the existing drawings. This lesson describes how to add drawings to the active project by creating a new AutoCAD Plant 3D drawing, linking an existing drawing to the project, and copying an existing drawing from another project to the active project. In this lesson, you also learn how to further organize the drawings in a project through the creation of folders and subfolders and how to reorganize the drawings in the folders.

Objectives

After completing this lesson, you will be able to:

- Create project folders.
- Create new drawings in a project.
- Copy existing drawings to a project.

Creating Folders

You create folders using the Project Manager to help manage where your drawings are stored, as shown in the following illustration. Folders enable you to group drawings that contain similar information. Folders can be created in one another as well.

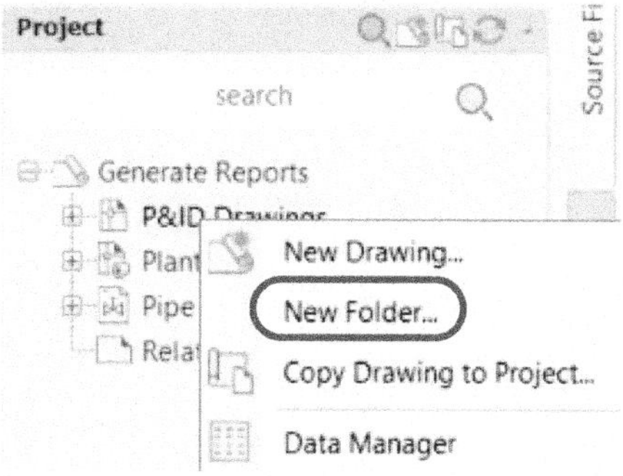

Process: Creating Folders

To create a new folder, right-click on the Plant 3D Drawings Category and click New Folder. In the New Folder dialog box, specify the folder name, as shown in the following illustration. You can also select a template that is going to be used when drawings are created in this folder.

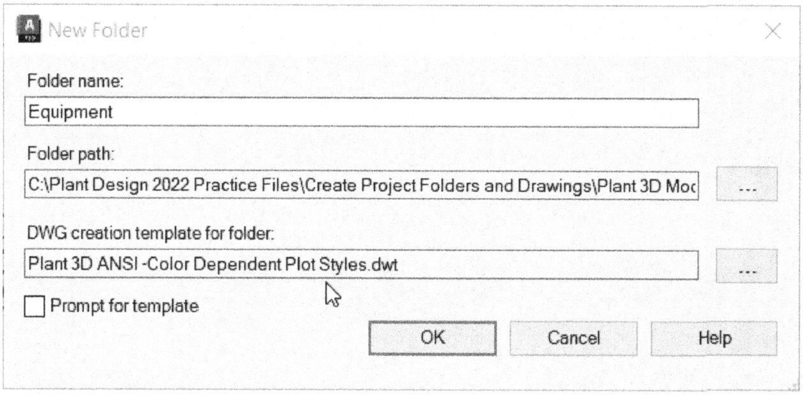

To rename folders once they have been created, right-click on their name and click Rename Folder. Renaming the folder in Windows Explorer does not reflect in the Project Manager.

Creating Drawings

You can create drawings directly in the AutoCAD Plant 3D software using the Project Manager. When added to your project, you assign a drawing number, title, and name of the designer for the drawing. A new drawing can be created at the top level of AutoCAD Plant 3D drawings or in any folder that has been created, as shown in the following illustration.

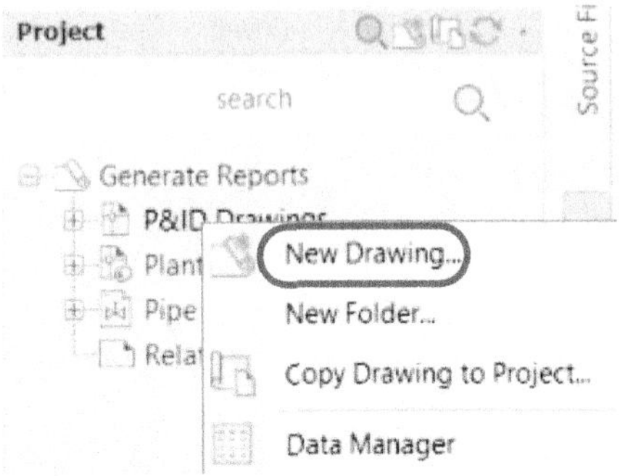

Process: Creating Drawings

To create a new drawing, right-click on the Plant 3D Drawings Category or a subfolder in the category and click New Drawing. In the New DWG dialog box, specify the File name, as shown in the following illustration. The Author property is filled in by default, but is not required. By default, the folder path and template are defined for you. Click OK.

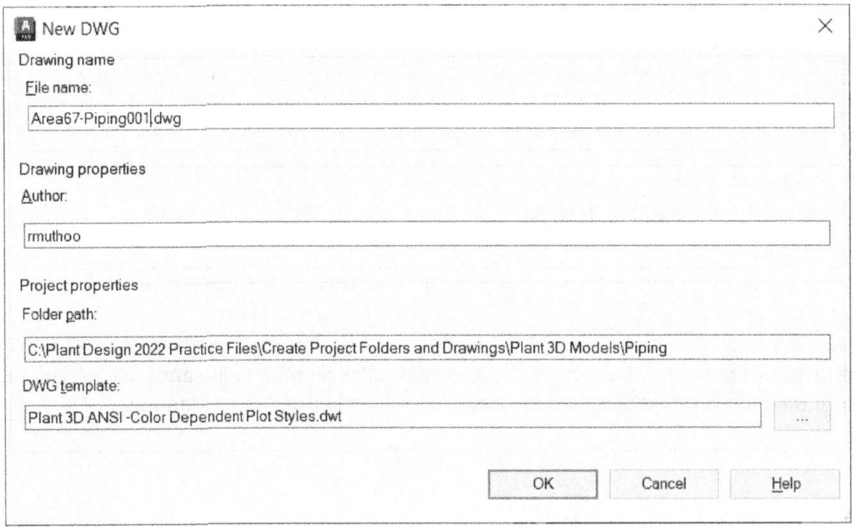

The new drawing is created in the Plant 3D Drawings or a subfolder. To specify additional drawing properties, right-click on the drawing name and click Properties. In the Drawing Properties dialog box fill in the data as required, as shown in the following illustration. Click OK.

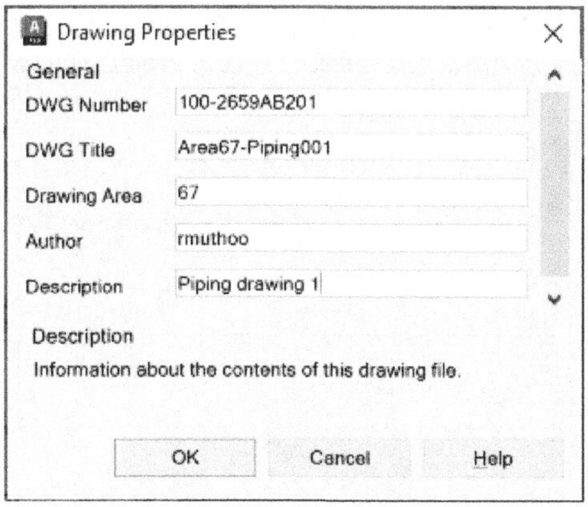

Copy Drawings to Projects

You can copy existing drawings into an AutoCAD Plant 3D project using the Project Manager, as shown in the following illustration. When added to your project, you copy it directly into your project's folder structure. If a drawing has external references to another drawing, that drawing is also copied.

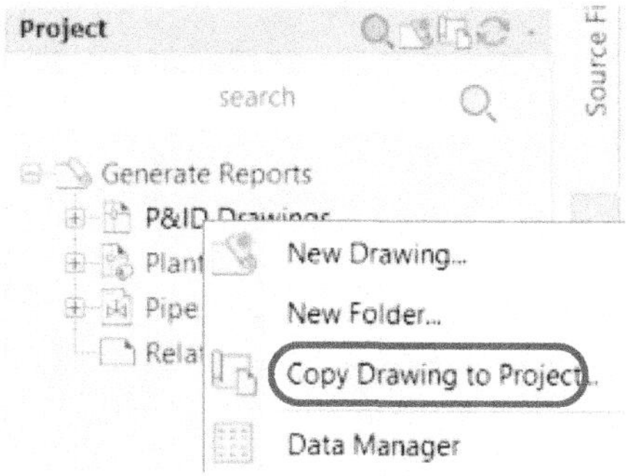

Process: Copying Drawings to Projects

To copy an existing drawing to a project, right-click on the Plant 3D Drawings Category or a subfolder with the category and click Copy Drawing to Project. In the Select Drawings to Copy to Project dialog box, navigate to the files location, select it, and click Open, as shown in the following illustration. A copy of the drawing is copied into that Project folder structure. Click OK in the Project Data Merged dialog box.

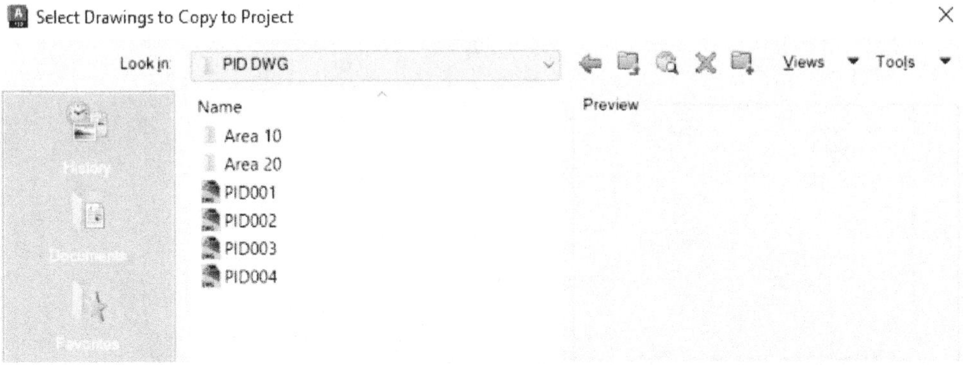

If the drawing that is being copied contains external references, you are prompted to either add external references to the project or copy external references to the project. Adding external references to the project is the recommended option.

Once drawings have been created or copied into a project, they can be moved between folders by dragging and dropping them in the Project Manager.

Exercise: Create Project Folders and Drawings

In this exercise, you create a new drawing, and copy an existing drawing to the project. You also move drawings from one location to another and locate them using the Project Manager.

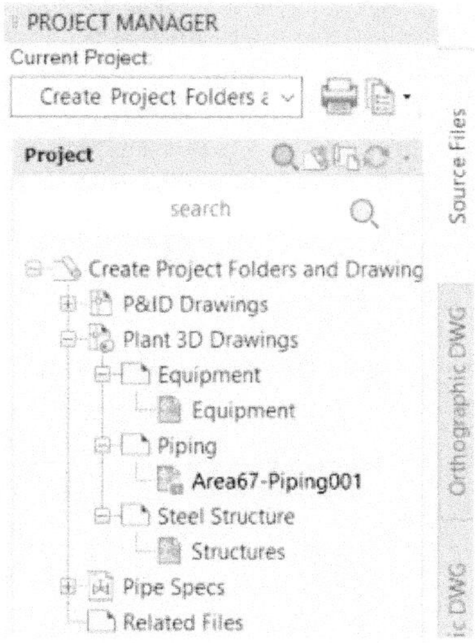

1. Start the AutoCAD Plant 3D software, if not already running.

2. Open an existing project by doing the following:
   - In the Project Manager, Current Project list, click Open.
   - In the Open dialog box, navigate to the folder *C:\Plant Design 2024 Practice Files\Create Project Folders and Drawings*.
   - Select the file *Project.xml*.
   - Click Open.

3. In the Project Manager, right-click on Plant 3D Drawings. Click New Folder.

4. In the Project Folder Properties dialog box:
   - For Folder name, enter **Equipment**.
   - Maintain the default template that is to be used.
   - Click OK.

   The folder is created and listed in the Project Manager.

5. Repeat the steps to create a *Steel Structure* and *Piping* folder.

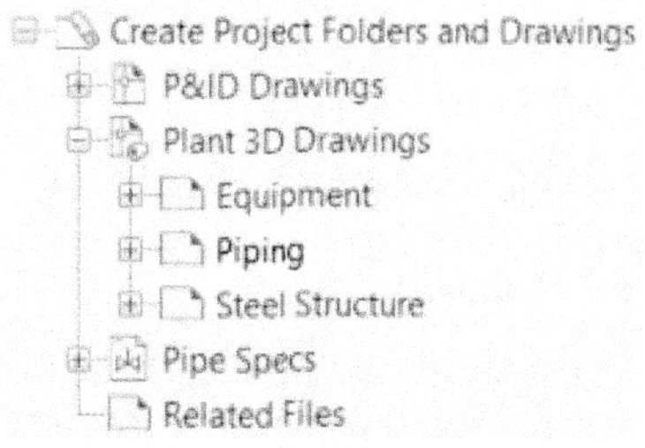

6. In the Project Manager, right-click on the Equipment folder. Click Copy Drawing to Project.

7. In the Select Drawings to Copy to Project dialog box:
   - Navigate to *C:\Plant Design 2024 Practice Files\Create Project Folders and Drawings\Drawings*.
   - Select *Equipment.dwg*.
   - Click Open.

8. In the Project Manager, verify that the Equipment drawing is listed under the Equipment folder.

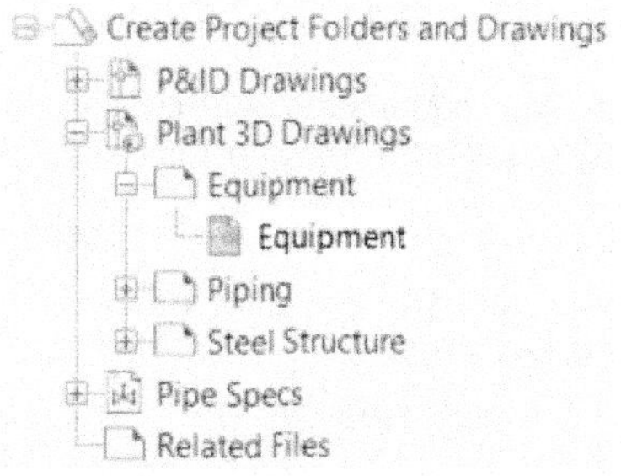

9. In the Project Manager, right-click on the Steel Structure folder. Click Copy Drawing to Project.

10. In the Select Drawings to Copy to Project dialog box:
    - Navigate to the folder C:*Plant Design 2024 Practice Files\Create Project Folders and Drawings\Drawings*.
    - Select *Structures.dwg*.
    - Click Open.
11. In the Project Manager, verify that the Structures drawing is listed under the Steel Structure folder.
12. Select the Structures drawing. In the Details area of the Project Manager verify that the drawing was copied to the *C:\Plant Design 2024 Practice Files\Create Project Folders and Drawings\Plant 3D Models\Steel Structure* folder.
13. In the Project Manager, right-click on the Piping folder. Click New Drawing.
14. In the New DWG dialog box:
    - For the File name, enter **Area67-Piping001**.
    - Under Project properties, note that the drawing will be created in the Piping folder of your practice files folder.
    - Click OK.

    The drawing is created and listed in the Project Manager. The drawing is also opened.
15. In the Project Manager, right-click on the Area67-Piping001 drawing. Click Properties.
16. In the Drawing Properties dialog box:
    - For DWG Number, enter **100-2659AB201**.
    - For Drawing Area, enter **67**.
    - For Description, enter **Piping drawing 1**.
    - Click OK.
17. Save and close all drawings.

Lesson Review Questions

1. Renaming a folder in the Project Manager also renames the folder in Windows.
   a. True
   b. False
2. How do you remove folders from the project?
   a. Open Windows Explorer, navigate to the Plant 3D Drawings folder in the working project, and delete the folder.
   b. Expand the Plant 3D Drawings node, right-click on the folder to be removed, and click Remove Folder.
   c. Either of the above.
3. You can move a drawing to a different folder in the Project Manager and the file is also moved in the Windows folder.
   a. True
   b. False

Lesson: Steel Modeling and Editing

Overview

This lesson describes how to setup a structural grid, add steel members, ladders, stairs, railings, plates and footing, and modify the steel structure.

In a plant design, the pipes and piping equipment exist relative to a building or structural framework. Because of this relationship, when creating a new 3D plant design, the place to start is to include the steel structure in your design. By having the accurate representation of the steel structure, you can accurately position the piping equipment and lines.

The same section of a plant design is shown in the following illustration. On the left, just the structural framework is shown. On the right, the design includes the structural framework and all of the piping and piping components.

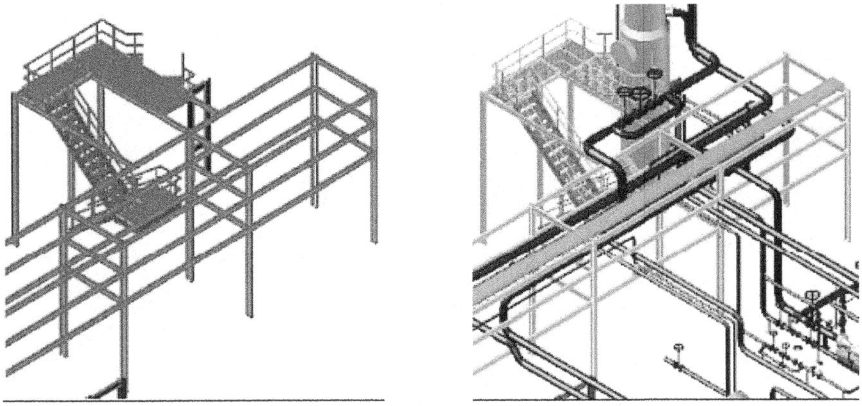

Objectives

After completing this lesson, you will be able to:

- Create a structure.
- Configure structural member settings.
- Modify structural parts.

Adding Structural Parts

When your design requires a structural framework to support the piping parts and equipment or the workers who monitor and work with the system, you should start by first modeling that structural framework.

The process of modeling a structural framework consists of defining a grid, adding and editing structural members, and adding and editing structural components like stairs, ladders, footings, and a plate or grate. The common first step in the process is to create a grid. After the grid is added, the adding and editing of structural members and structural components varies based on the requirements of your design.

Structure Tools

The Structure tab on the ribbon contains the tools for adding parts (such as members and grids) to your drawings, as shown in the following illustration. This is available when the 3D Piping workspace is active.

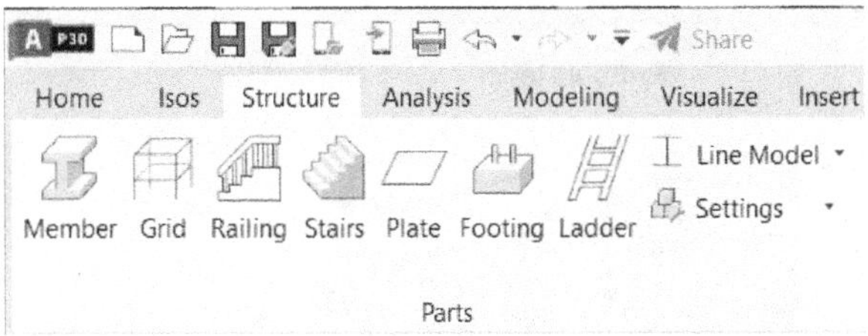

Model Display Options

You can also change the way the parts are displayed in the model. The shape of the parts can be displayed or the parts can be displayed as lines, symbols, or outlines, as shown in the following illustration.

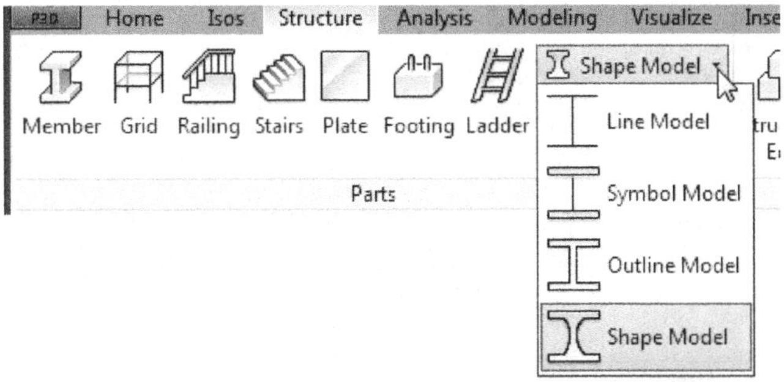

The same model using different display settings is shown in the following illustration.

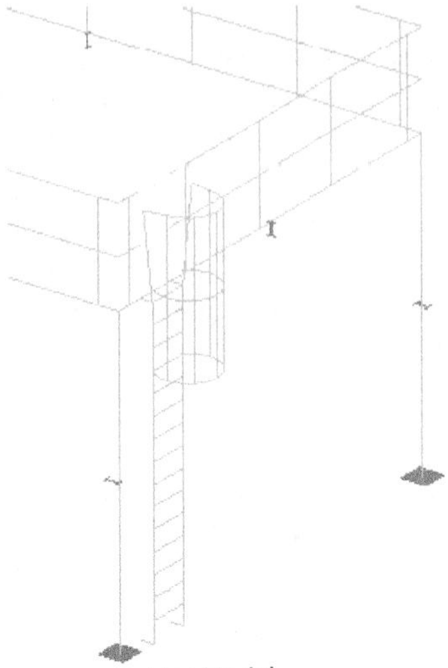

Line Model

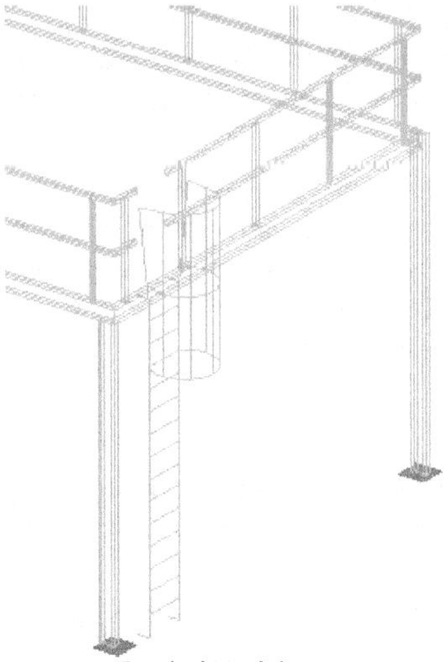

Symbol Model

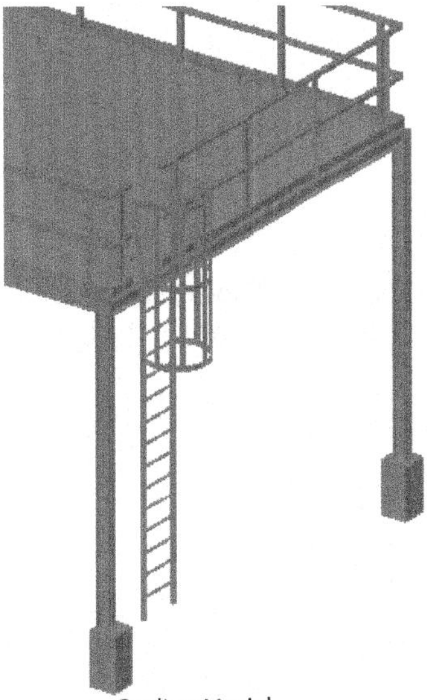

Outline Model

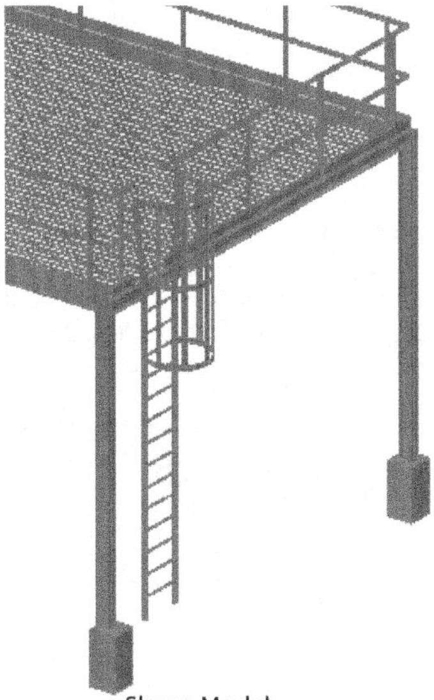

Shape Model

If your model includes mesh plate, to see through the plate you must have the option Shape Model selected. Selecting Outline Model causes the plate to display with a solid color.

Configure the Settings

When you place grids or plates, you are automatically prompted to specify their settings in their corresponding dialog boxes. When you place the other structural parts, the current settings for that object are used.

To change the settings for the other members (i.e., railing, footings, stairs, and ladders) you can use the Settings drop-down in the Parts panel (as shown in the following illustration) before starting the command or right-click on the drawing area and click Settings once the command has been initiated.

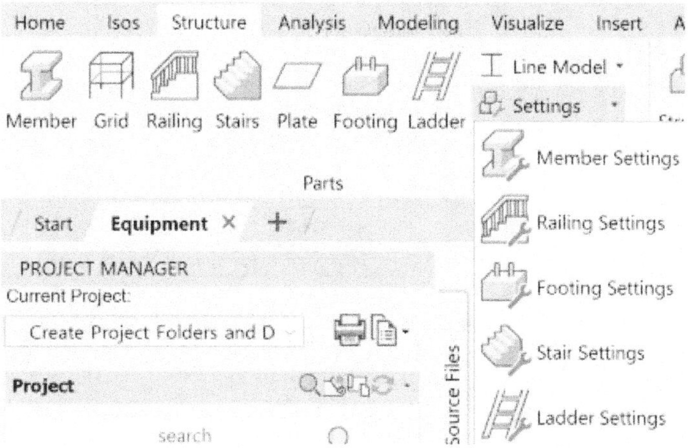

Grid Settings

When you use the Grid tool, the Create Grid dialog box opens where you can specify grid settings. The axis, row, and platform values determine the location of the grid lines in each direction from the insertion point of the grid. You use a comma to separate each grid line value.

The axis, row, and platform names are what displays in the drawing, as labels on the grid lines. The font size determines the size of the labels. When you modify the values, adding or removing the number of grid lines, you must select the update button next to the corresponding name to update the name.

You can place the grid using the WCS, the UCS, or the 3 point method.

Before you begin creating a grid, create a new layer that is going to be specific to the grid and make it the active layer.

The settings in the Create Grid dialog box that were used to create the grid are shown in the following illustration.

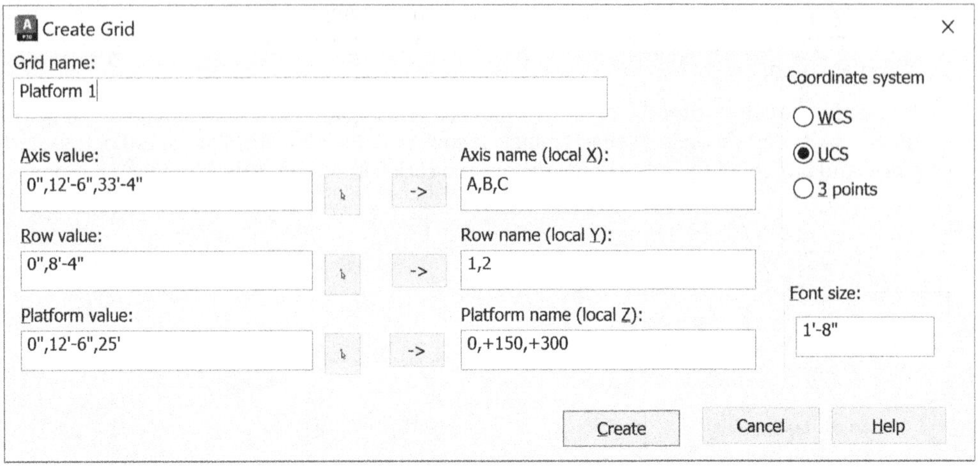

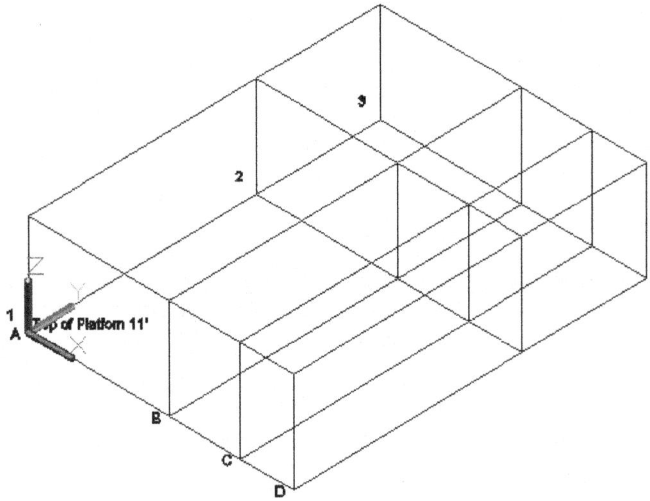

Grids are only used for reference when placing components. If changes are made to a grid the components do not immediately update. You must adjust them manually.

Member Settings

In the Member Settings dialog box, you can select from several member shape standards, types, and sizes, as shown in the following illustration. You can also specify the material standard and code, as well as the orientation point of the member.

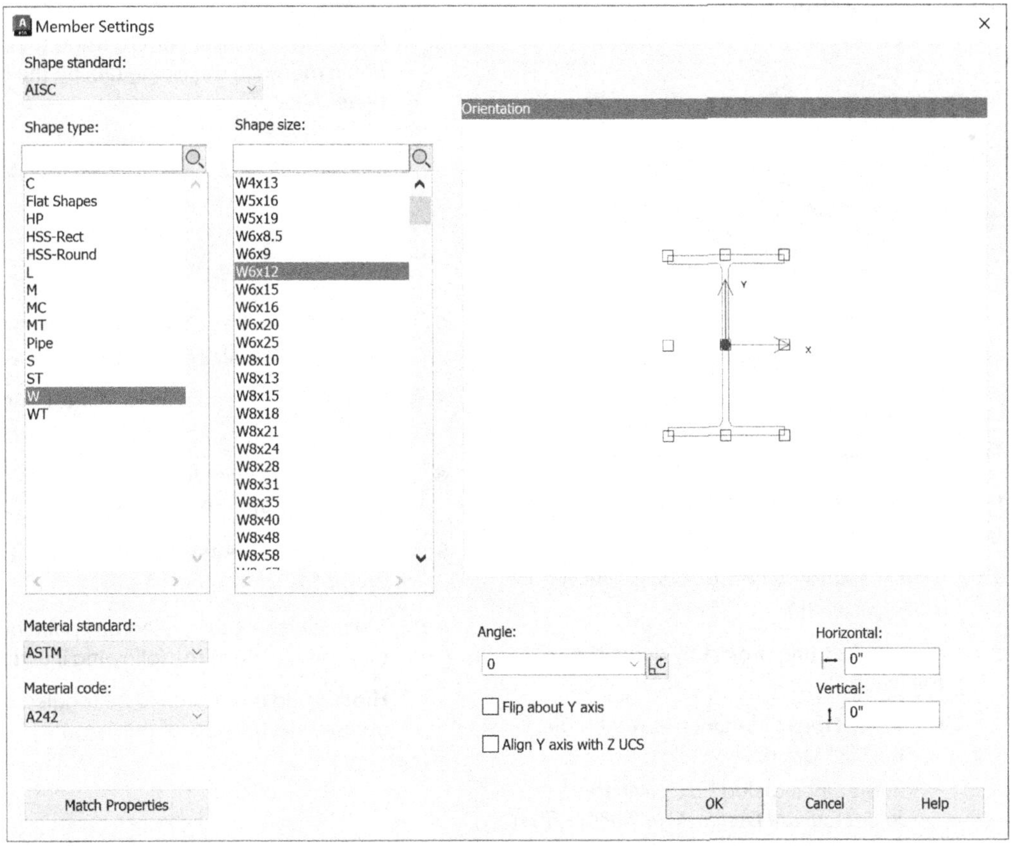

Part Modification

Modify and cutting tools are available in the Structure tab, as shown in the following illustration. You use the Structure Edit tool to modify the settings of existing parts in your drawings. When you use this tool, the corresponding dialog box for the part selected is displayed where you can modify the settings for that part. You use the cutting tools to lengthen, cut back, trim, extend, miter, or restore existing structural members.

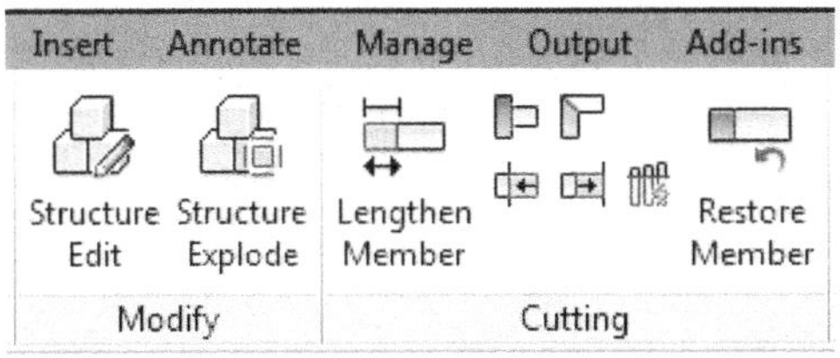

Exercise: Build a Steel Structure

In this exercise, you create a steel structure using the basic functionality of the steel structure module of the AutoCAD Plant 3D software.

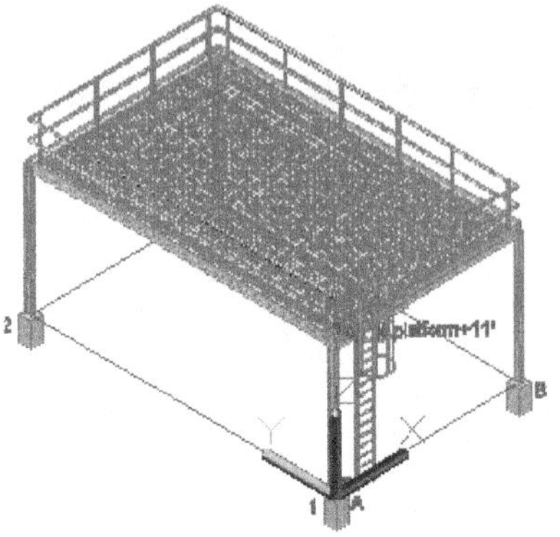

Create a Grid

In this section of the exercise, you create a structural grid.

1. Start the AutoCAD Plant 3D software, if not already running.
2. Open an existing project by doing the following:
   - In the Project Manager, Current Project list, click Open.
   - In the Open dialog box, navigate to the folder *C:\Plant Design 2024 Practice Files\Build a Steel Structure*.
   - Select the file *Project.xml*.
   - Click Open.
3. In the Project Manager, expand Plant 3D Drawings and Steel Structure. Double-click on the Structures drawing to open it.

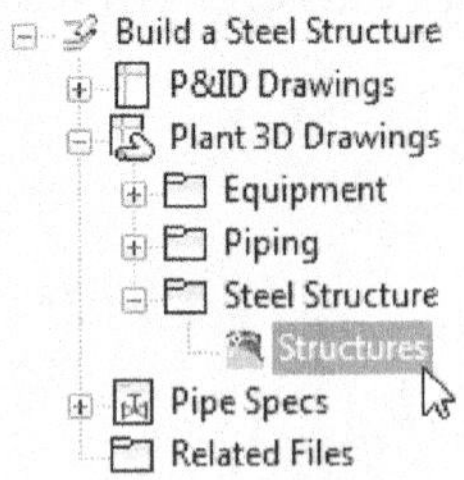

4. Activate the 3D Piping workspace and ensure that the AutoCAD Plant 3D - Piping Components Tool Palette is active.
5. Make the Grid layer current using the drop-down menu on the Home tab, on the Layers panel.

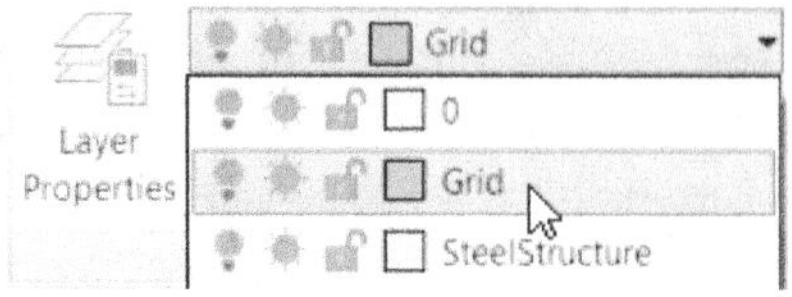

6. On the Status Bar, click Grid Display to toggle off the AutoCAD drawing grid, if it is on.
7. On the Structure tab, on the Parts panel, click Grid.
8. In the Create Grid dialog box, under Coordinate system, select 3 points.
9. For the origin, enter **0,0** at the Command Prompt.
10. To specify the X-axis, select any point on the X plane as shown in the following illustration.

    Hint: Ortho mode should be toggled on before selecting any of the axes.

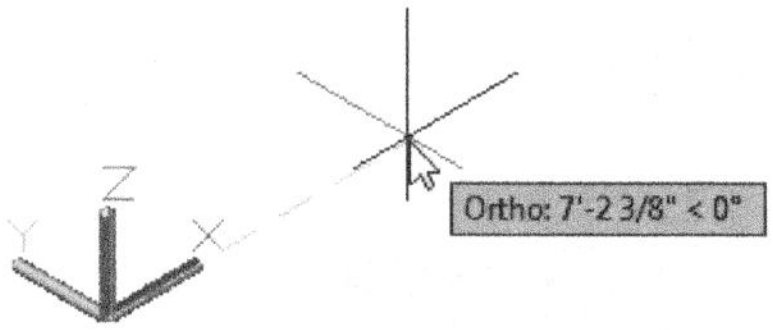

11. To specify a point on the XY plane, select any point on the Y plane as shown in the following illustration.

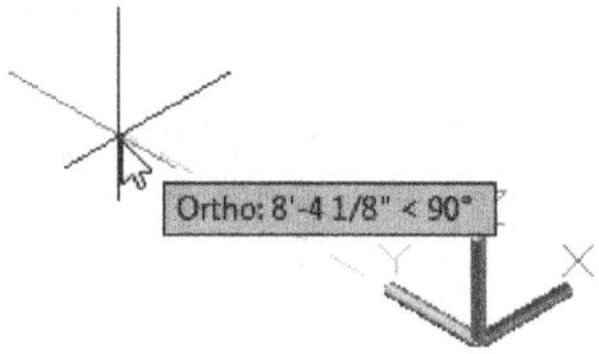

12. To specify the Z-axis, select any point on the Z plane as shown in the following illustration.

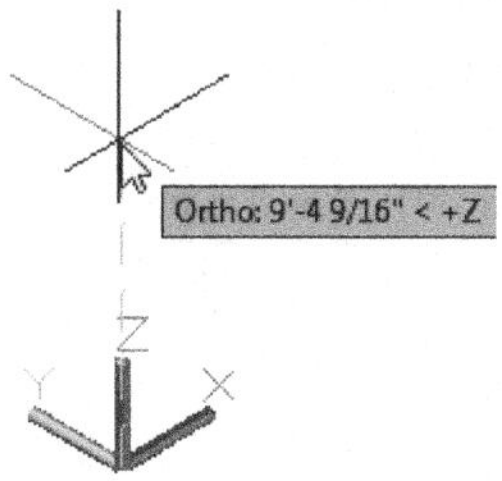

13. In the Create Grid dialog box:
   - For the Axis value, enter **0",16'**.
   - For the Row value, enter **0",26'**.
   - For the Platform value, enter **0",11'**.
   - Click the update (->) buttons next to all three values.

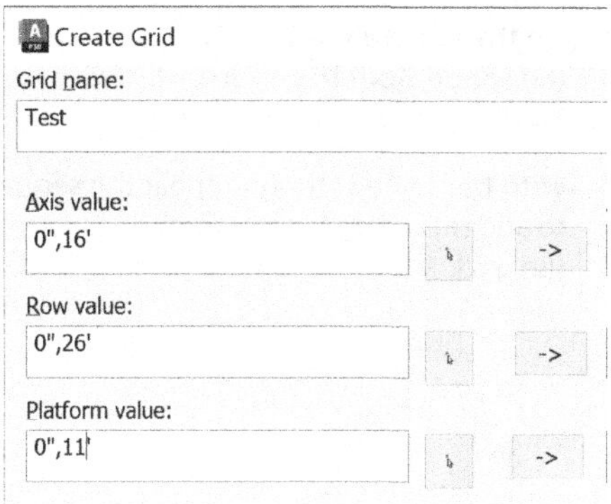

14. In the Create Grid dialog box, under Platform name (local Z), enter **Top of platform** before +11′ making it as **0",Top of platform+11′**.

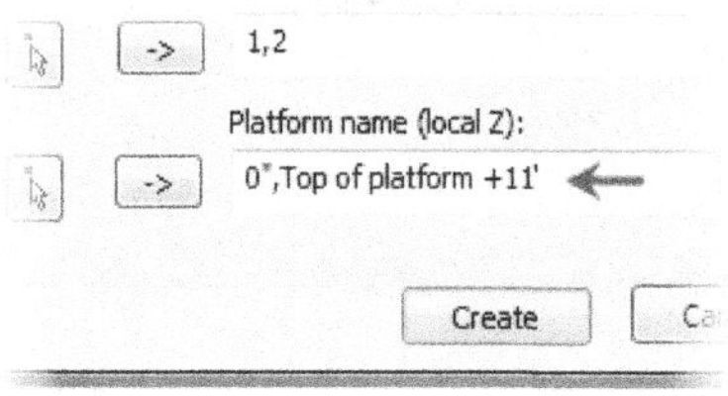

15. In the Create Grid dialog box:
   - Under Font size, enter **10.**
   - Click Create.

   The grid is created in the drawing.

   Note: The color of the layer has been changed for printing clarity.

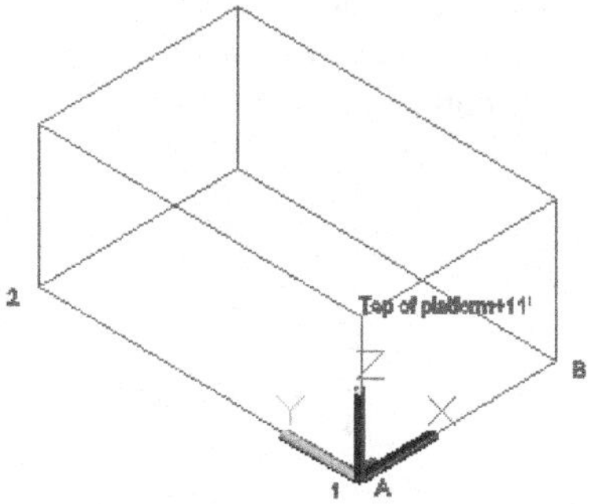

Create Structural Members

In this section of the exercise, you create structural members.

1. Make the SteelStructure layer current.
2. On the Structure tab, on the Parts panel, on the Settings drop-down, click Member Settings.

3. In the Member Settings dialog box:
   - From the Shape standard list, select **AISC**, if required.
   - From the Shape type list, select **W**.
   - From the Shape size list, select **W6x9**.
   - From the Material standard list, select **ASTM**.
   - From the Material code list, select **A242**.
   - Under Orientation, verify that the Middle orientation point is selected.

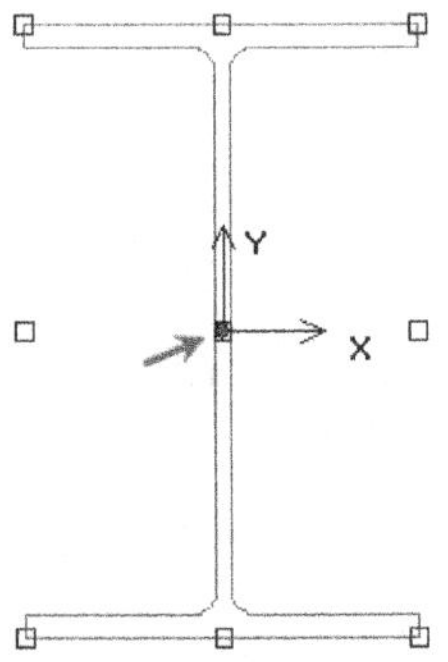

4. Click OK.
5. On the Structure tab, on the Parts panel, click Member.
6. To specify the start point of the structural member, select the bottom corner endpoint as shown in the following illustration.

   Hint: Object Snap should be toggled on before selecting the endpoint.

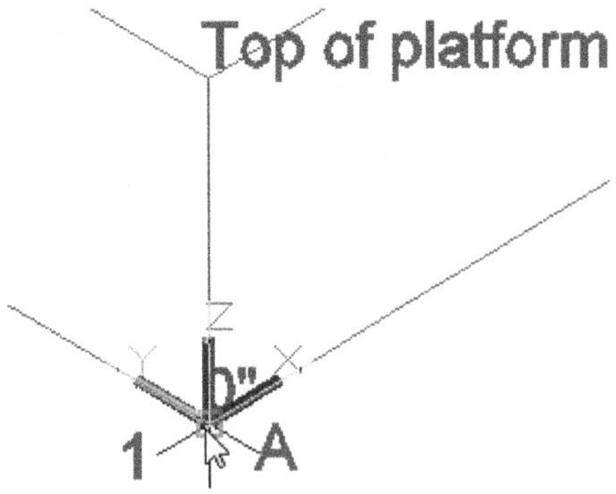

7. To specify the end point of the structural member, select the top corner of the grid box as shown in the following illustration.

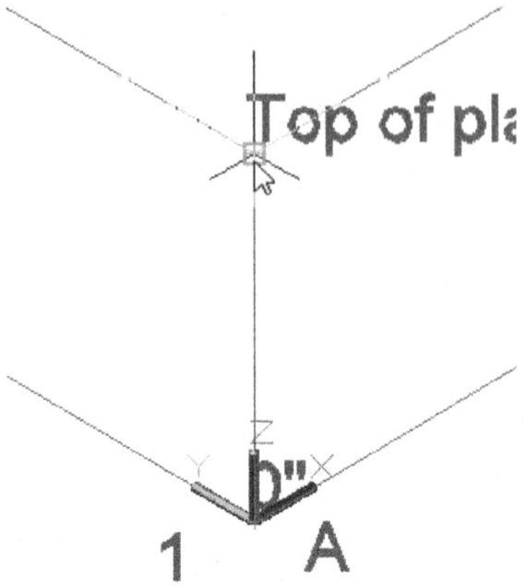

8. Press <Enter> to end the command.
9. On the Structure tab, on the Parts panel, on the Shape Model drop-down list, click Outline Model.
10. With the same settings, repeat the sequence to add members to the other three corners of the grid.

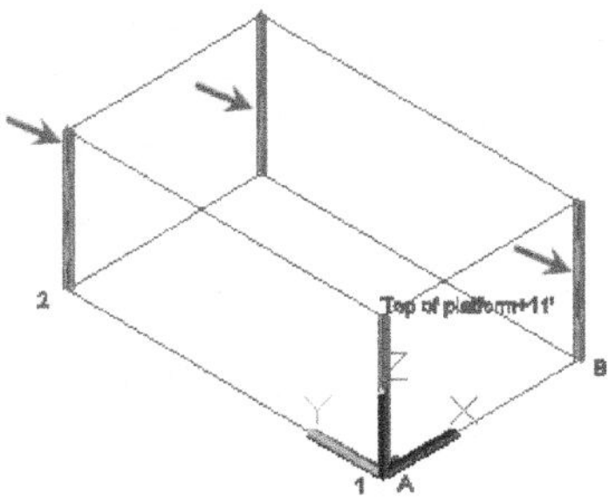

11. On the Structure tab, on the Parts panel, on the Shape Model drop-down, click Line Model. Only the outline of the members are displayed.

    Note: The color of the layer SteelStructure has been changed for printing clarity.

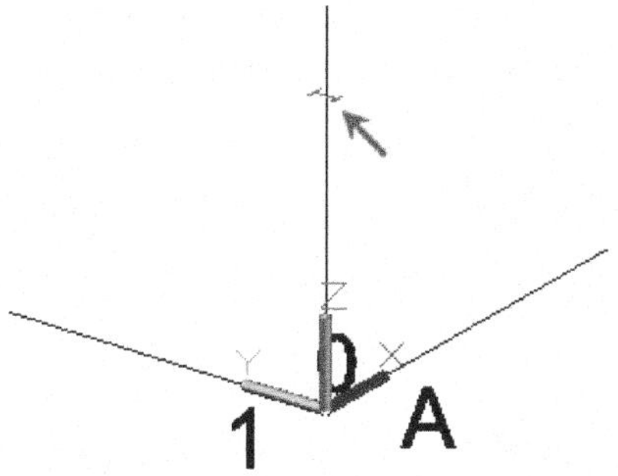

12. On the Structure tab, on the Parts panel, click Member.

13. Right-click in the drawing area. Click Settings.

14. In the Member Settings dialog box, under Orientation, select the Top Middle orientation point, as shown in the following illustration. Click OK.

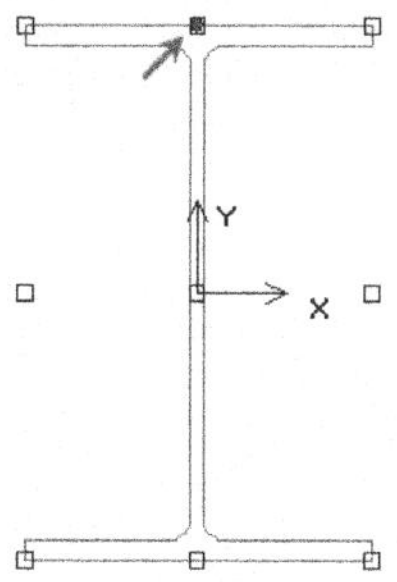

15. To specify the start point of the structural member, select the point, as shown in the following illustration.

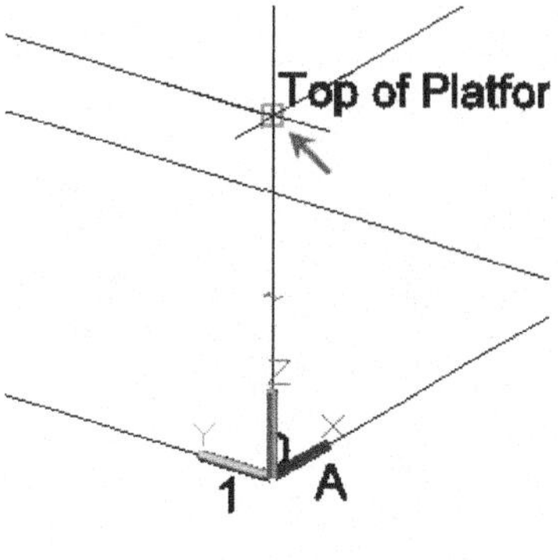

16. To specify the endpoints of the structural members, snap to the end points in a clockwise direction. Start with point 1 as shown and continue selecting the points around the top of the grid to point 4.

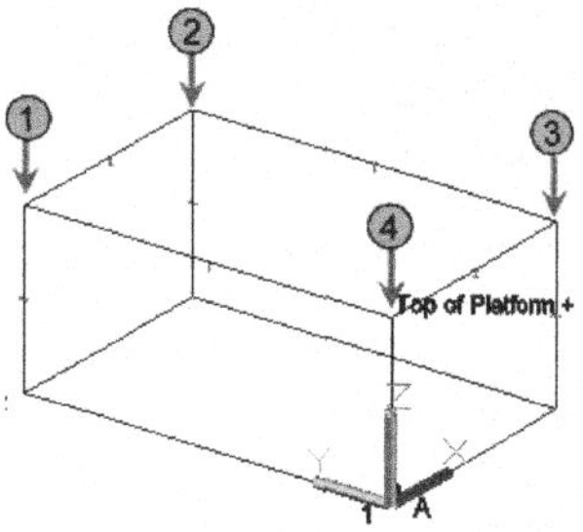

17. Press <Enter> to end the command.

18. On the Structure tab, on the Parts panel, on the Shape Model drop-down, click Shape Model.

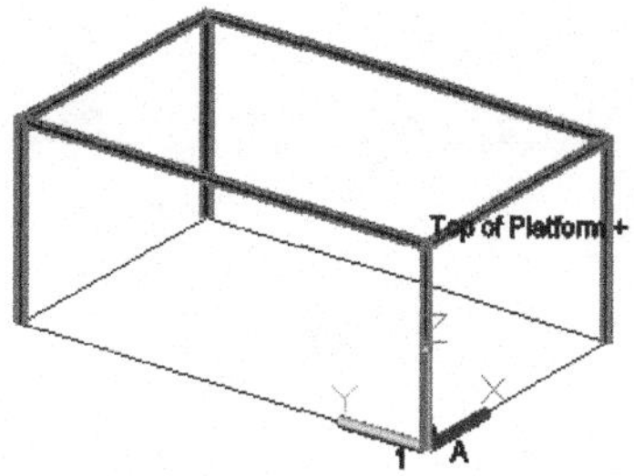

19. Save the drawing.

Edit Structural Members

In this section of the exercise, you edit structural members.

1. Zoom in on the top corner of the grid. Note that the members overlap.

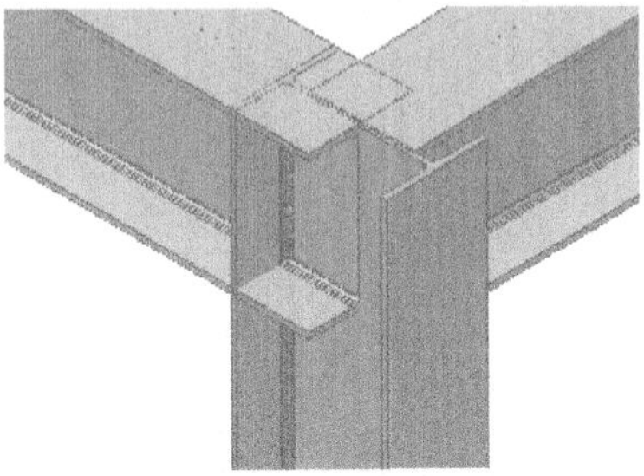

2. Select and right-click on the vertical member. Click Edit Structure.

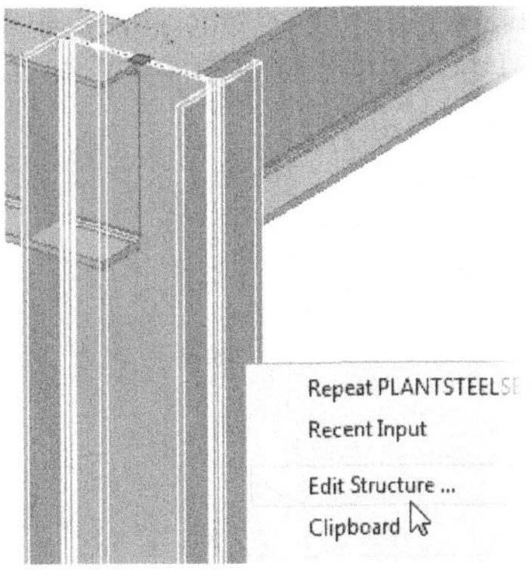

3. In the Edit Member dialog box, under Orientation, select the Bottom Middle orientation point. Click OK.

   The member is shifted so that the right edge lines up with the grid line.

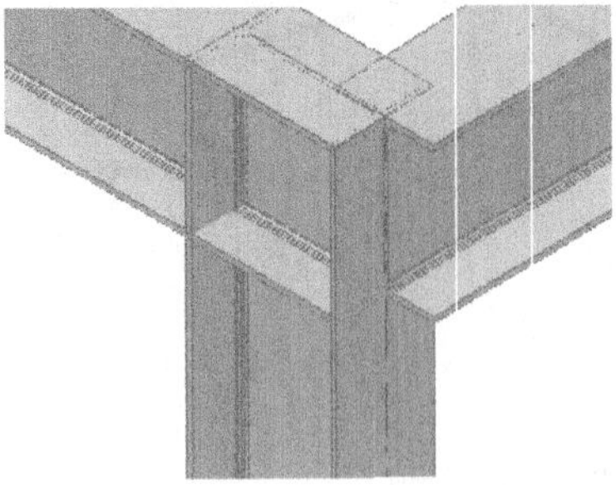

4. To trim one member to another:
   - On the Structure tab, on the Cutting panel, click Cut Back Member.
   - To specify the limiting member, select the horizontal top member on the left (1).
   - To specify the structural member to cut, select the vertical member (2).
   - Press <Enter> to end the command.

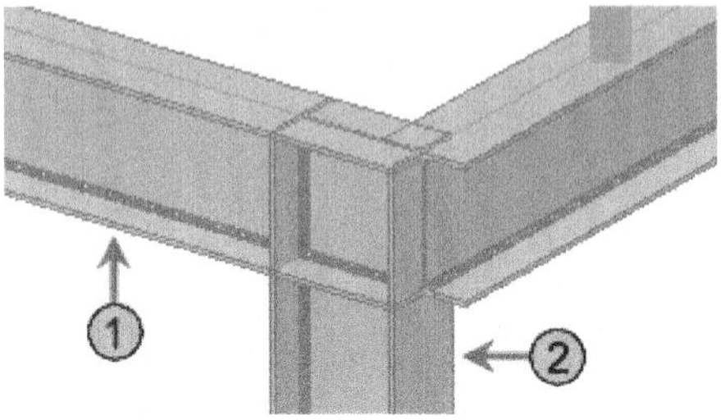

5. To miter two members:
   - On the Structure tab, on the Cutting panel, click Miter Cut Member.
   - Select the horizontal member on the left.
   - Select the horizontal member on the right.
   - Press <Enter> to end the command. The edited structural members display as shown in the following illustration.

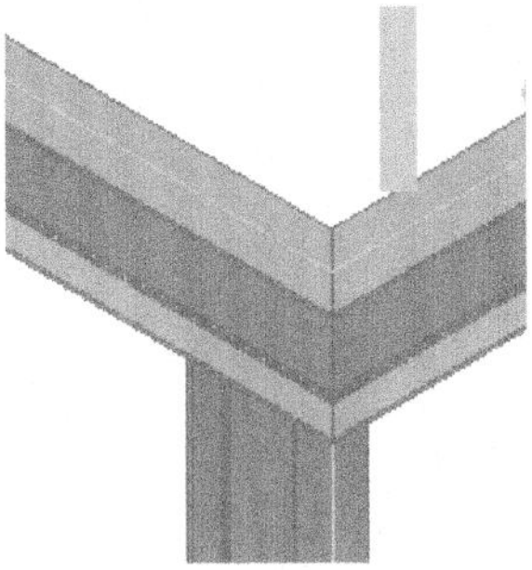

6. Save the drawing.

Place a Ladder

In this section of the exercise, you place a ladder. A ladder is oriented based on two selected points: the stand-off distance and the WCS.

1. On the Structure tab, on the Parts panel, on the Shape Model drop-down, click Line Model.

2. On the Structure tab, on the Parts panel, click Ladder.

3. Right-click in the drawing area. Click Settings.

4. In the Ladder Settings dialog box, on the Ladder tab, under Geometry, enter the following settings (18", 32", 40", 9").

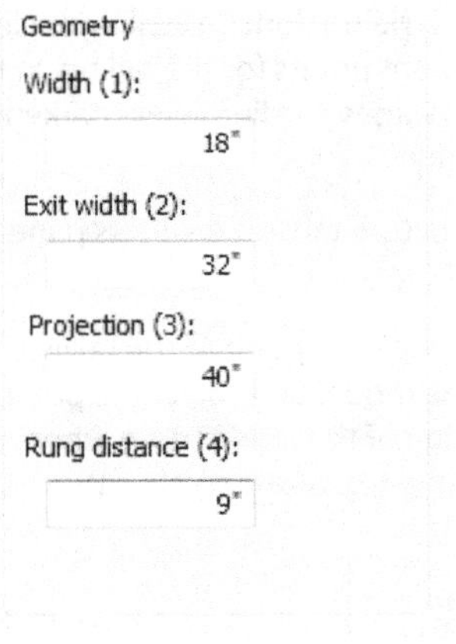

5. Open the Cage tab and enter the following settings (9', 5', 1", 1'-2", 45, 45, 2", 1/4").

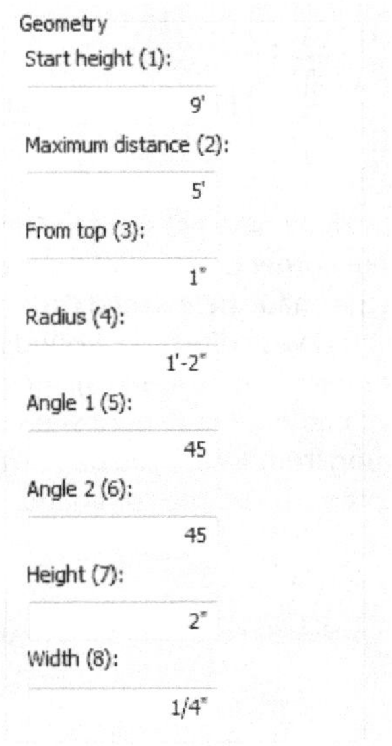

6. Click OK.

7. To specify the start point of the ladder:
   - Hold <Shift> and right-click in the drawing area.
   - Click From.
   - To specify the From Base Point, select the bottom corner of the grid (1).
   - To specify the Offset, move along the X axis and enter **2',0"**.

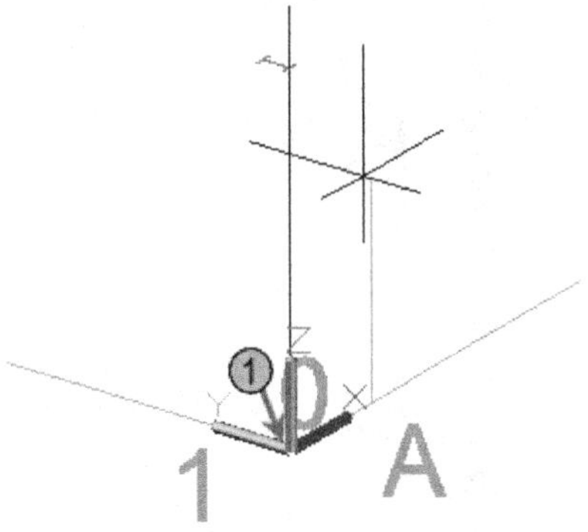

8. To specify the end point of the ladder, select the perpendicular point at the top of the platform as shown in the following illustration.

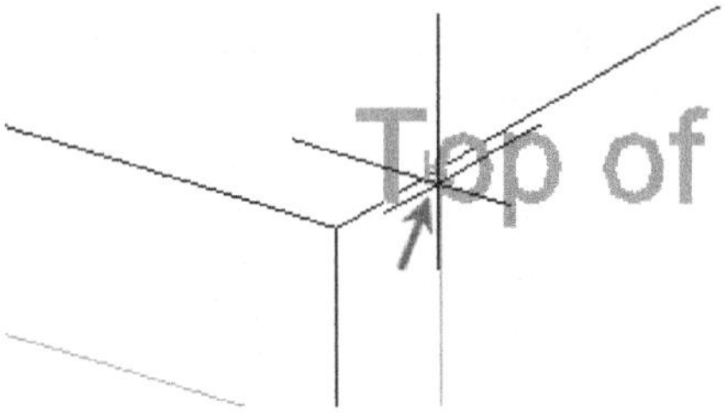

9. To specify the directional distance point:
   - From the bottom offset point, move the cursor to the front along the Y-axis.
   - Enter **6"**.
   - Press <Enter>.

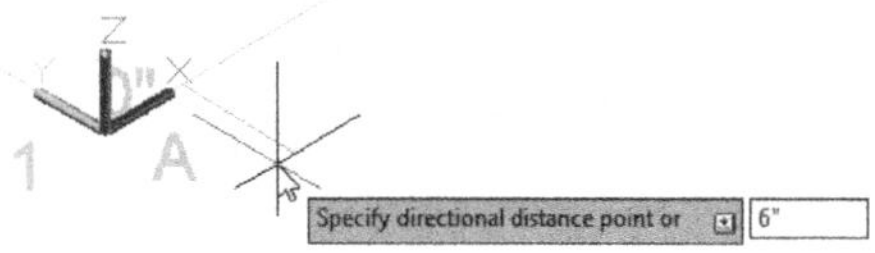

10. On the Structure tab, on the Parts panel, on the Line Model drop-down, click Shape Model.

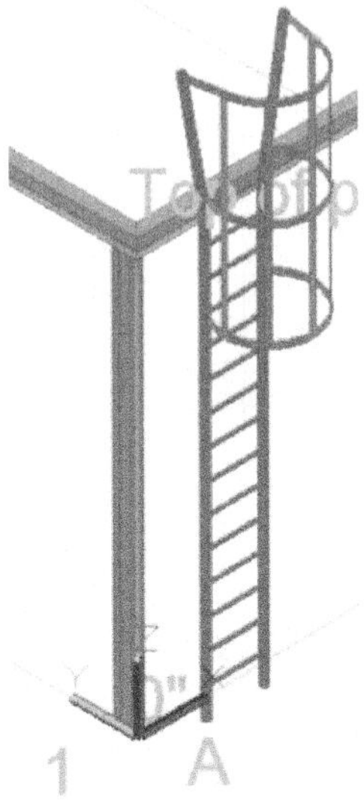

11. On the ViewCube, click Left.

12. Zoom in and note that the ladder was placed away from the grid.

    Hint: Ensure that you are looking at the Parallel view and not Perspective.

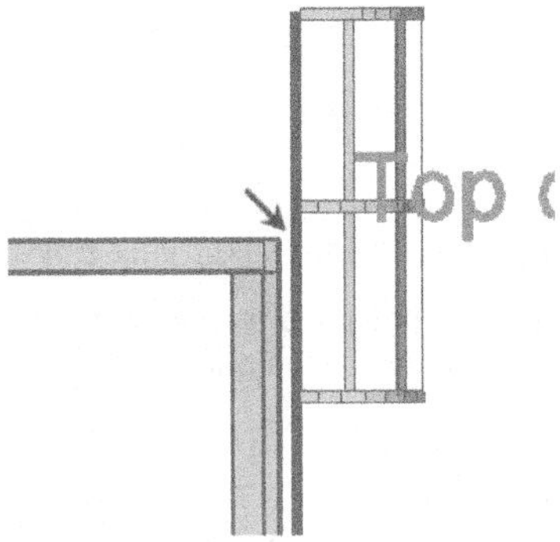

13. On the ViewCube, navigate to the SouthWest Isometric view.

14. Save the drawing.

Add Railings

In this section of the exercise, you add railings to your model.

1. On the Structure tab, on the Parts panel, on the Shape Model drop-down, click Line Model.

   Note: This is being done to facilitate selecting the placement points for the railing. In the following images, the lines were darkened for better clarity.

2. On the Structure tab, on the Parts panel, click Railing.

3. To specify the start point of the railing, reorient the model and select the point as shown (edge of the ladder rung where it intersects the top of the platform).

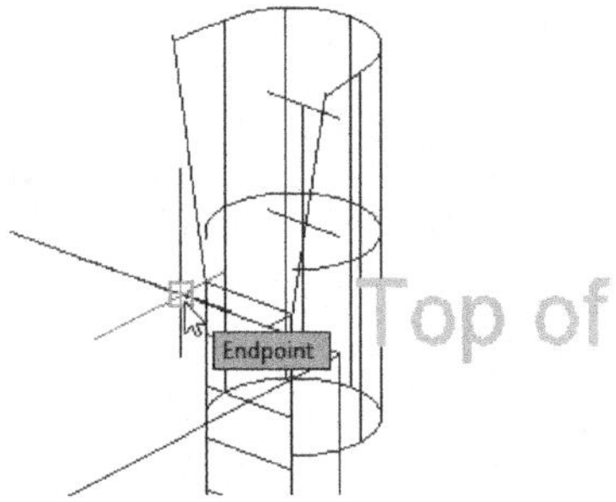

4. To define the remaining points of the railing, select the four corner points starting at point 2 (shown in the image below) and continuing in a counterclockwise direction around the top of the frame (points 3, 4, and 5), then click the last point ending on the opposite side of the ladder rung from where you began (point 6). Press <Enter> to end the command.

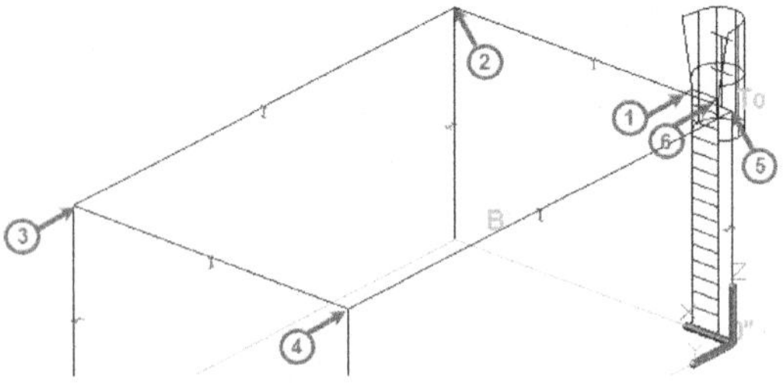

5. On the Structure tab, on the Parts panel, on the Line Model drop-down, select Shape Model. The structure displays, as shown in the following illustration.

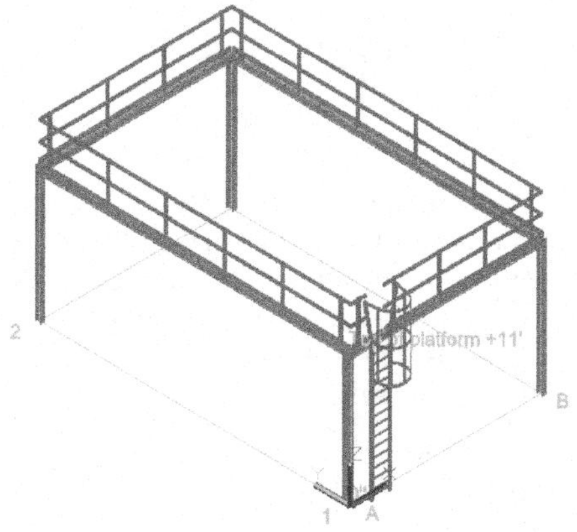

6. Save the drawing.

Create Grating

In this section of the exercise, you add grating to create a floor.

1. On the Structure tab, on the Parts panel, on the Shape Model drop-down, select Line Model.
2. On the Structure tab, on the Parts panel, click Plate.
3. In the Create Plate/Grate dialog box:
   - From the Type list, select Grating.
   - From the Material standard list, select ASTM.
   - From the Material code list, select A242.
   - From the Thickness list, select 1/2".
   - From the Hatch pattern list, select NET.
   - For Hatch scale, enter **25**.
   - Under Justification, select Bottom.
   - Under Shape, select New rectangular.
   - Click Create.
4. To specify the first corner of the grate, select the top grid corner point as shown (left corner of top of platform).

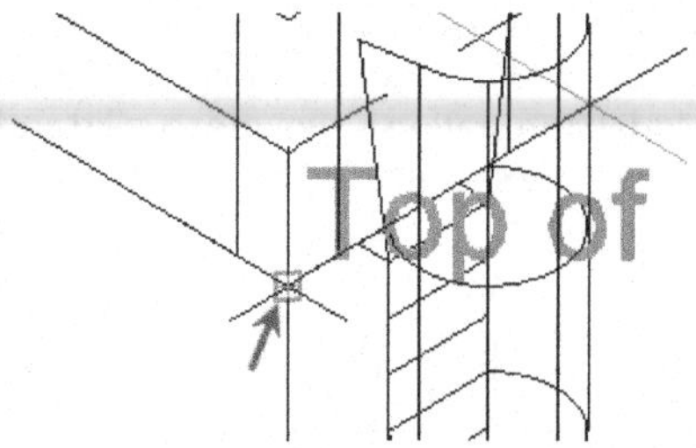

5. To specify the other corner point of the grate, select the opposite top grid corner point as shown in the following illustration.

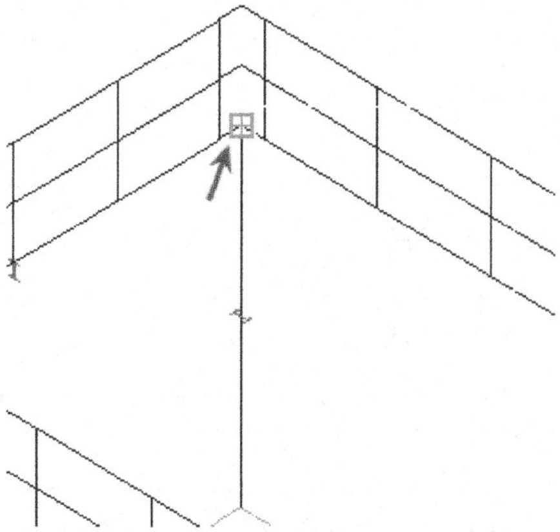

6. On the Structure tab, on the Parts panel, on the Line Model drop-down, select Shape Model.

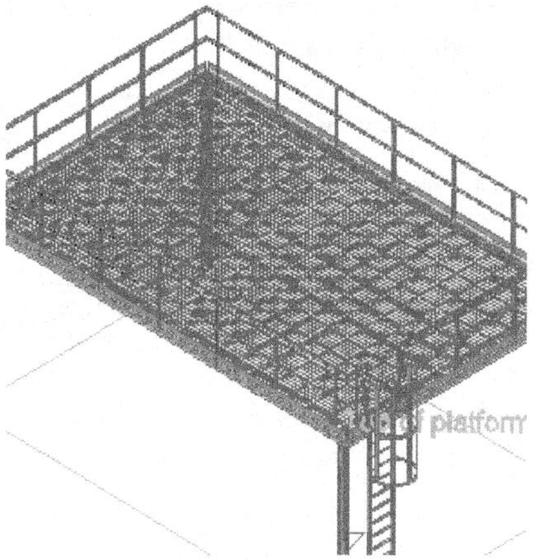

7. On the Structure tab, on the Parts panel, on the Shape Model drop-down, click Outline Model. The grating is shown as a solid and the railings are shown as square.

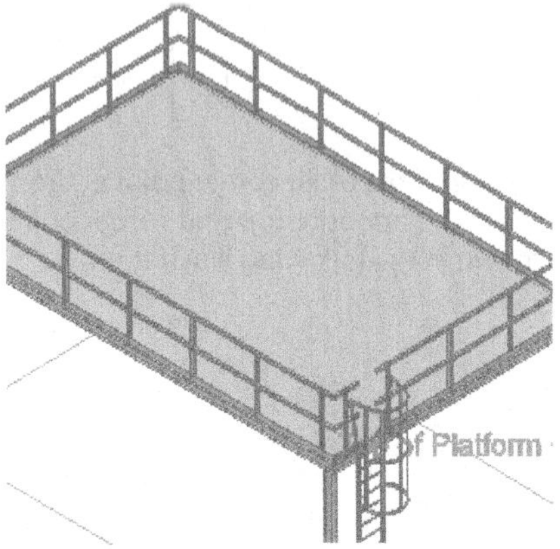

Add Footings

In this section of the exercise, you add footings below the structural members.

1. On the Structure tab, on the Parts panel, on the Shape Model drop-down, click Line Model.

2. On the Structure tab, on the Parts panel, click Footing.

3. Right-click in the drawing window. Click Settings.

4. In the Footing Settings dialog box, verify the following settings. Click OK.

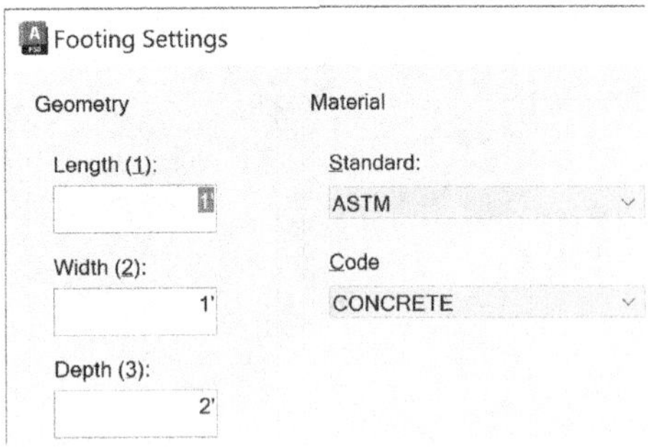

5. To specify the insert point of the footing, select the bottom grid corner point as shown in the following illustration.

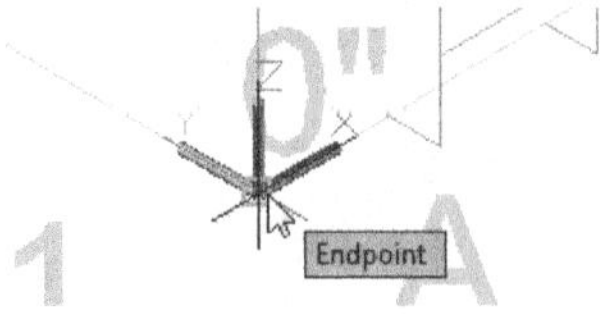

6. Press <Enter> to repeat the command to add footings at the bottom of the other three grid points. If the member located at the origin is not centered on the footing, you might need to adjust the footing placement offset from the grid vertex.

7. On the Structure tab, on the Parts panel, on the Line Model drop-down, click Shape Model.

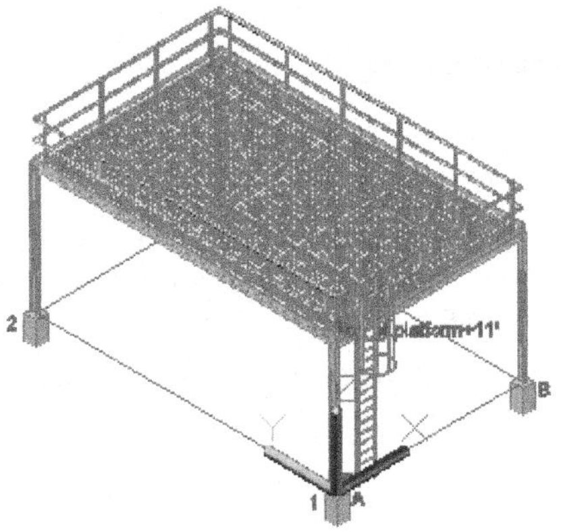

8. Save and close all drawings.

Lesson Review Questions

1. Which step should be taken before creating the grid?
   a. Save the drawing.
   b. Create and activate a layer specific to the grid.
   c. Set a different color for the active layer.
2. What happens with a placed structural member if you make changes to the grid?
   a. Nothing, members are not connected to the grid. The grid is only used for reference.
   b. The members automatically adjust to match with the grid again.
3. Which of the following workspace and tab combinations provides access to the commands for creating a structural model (e.g., Grid, Member, or Ladder)?
   a. 3D Piping workspace, on the Modeling tab
   b. 3D Piping workspace, on the Structure tab
   c. P&IP PIP workspace, on the Insert tab
   d. P&IP PIP workspace, on the Annotate tab
4. Which of the following Model display settings shows a structural model as wireframe (non-shaded) line entities?
   a. Line Model
   b. Symbol Model
   c. Outline Model
   d. Shape Model
5. Which of the following Model display settings shows grating as a solid?
   a. Line Model
   b. Symbol Model
   c. Outline Model
   d. Shape Model
6. Which of the following structural components automatically opens their settings dialog boxes when they are initiated? (Select all that apply.)
   a. Member
   b. Grid
   c. Railing
   d. Stairs
   e. Plate
   f. Footing
   g. Ladder
7. A Member setting must be set for each member that is added to an entity in the grid.
   a. True
   b. False

Lesson: Equipment Modeling and Editing

Overview

This lesson describes the modeling and placement of 3D equipment. You learn how to create equipment using the available basic shapes and how to add nozzles to that equipment. You then learn how to place the equipment in your design.

After the 3D design contains the structural steel model, your next task is to add the equipment to the design. in the field of plant design there are many types of plant and piping design requirements and the equipment that is used in those designs. The equipment can be standard or custom equipment. When the specific area you are in requires the inclusion of custom equipment, you need a way to model that equipment.

Some custom equipment, including heat exchangers, pumps, and tanks is shown in the following illustration. Each of these pieces of equipment consist of a build up of basic shapes of cylinders, cones, and spheres.

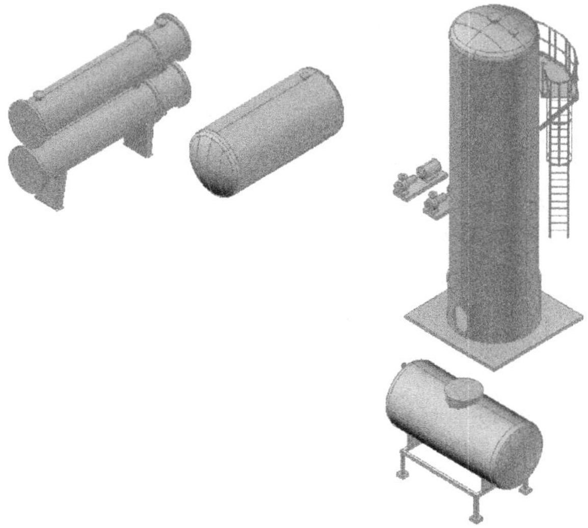

Objectives

After completing this lesson, you will be able to:

- Create equipment in a Plant 3D drawing.
- Describe the properties you can specify when you add or edit equipment nozzles.
- Describe the reason for using equipment templates.

Creating Equipment

The Equipment panel on the Home tab includes tools for creating, modifying, and attaching equipment in a Plant 3D drawing. You can also convert AutoCAD solid objects to Plant 3D equipment.

Additionally, you can import Autodesk Inventor AEC export files as Plant 3D equipment. All equipment commands are located on the Home tab, on the Equipment panel, as shown in the following illustration.

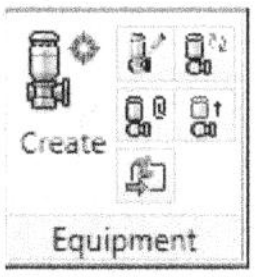

Process: Creating Equipment

To create equipment in a drawing, you use the Create Equipment tool. The Create Equipment dialog box opens. It contains several equipment types that you can place in a drawing, as shown in the following illustration. You can add or remove components of several different shapes to customize the equipment as well as specify the dimensions for each component.

To build an equipment model, use the Add Shape or Add Trim buttons to add basic shapes in sequential order. Shapes include cylinders, cones, cubes, transitions, halfsphere heads, and more. Trim includes items such as skirts, platforms, saddles, body flanges, and more. Depending on the choice of horizontal or vertical equipment, the shapes added will build the model from top to bottom or left to right, respectively.

With shapes and/or trim added to the equipment builder, their dimensions can be set in the panel on the right hand side by highlighting each shape and entering its values. The dimension fields correspond to dimensions shown in the preview image of the shape on the left. Fields with a lighting bolt indicate that they are linked to the corresponding dimension of any adjacent shapes.

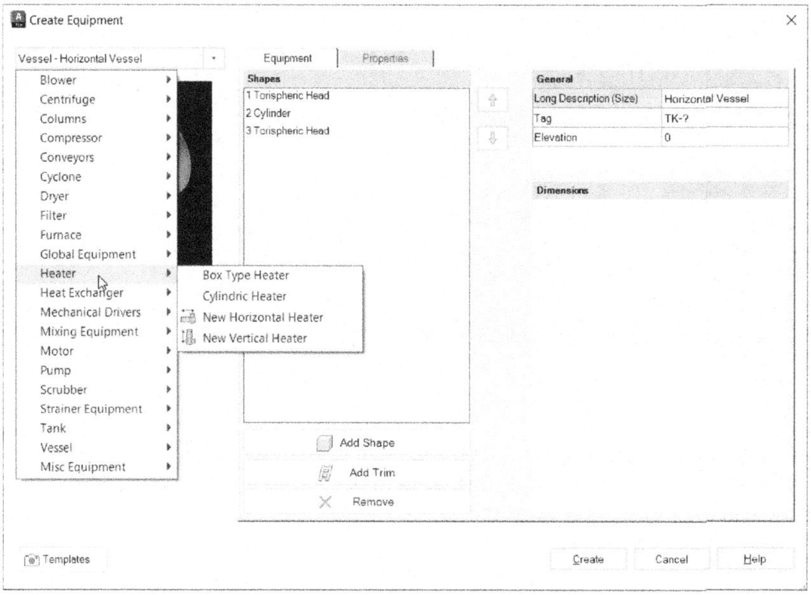

In the Properties tab, you can enter data associated with the equipment, such as material, descriptions, and type, as shown in the following illustration. You can also assign a tag to the equipment. Additionally, the nozzle information is displayed. However, you cannot edit the nozzle information from here.

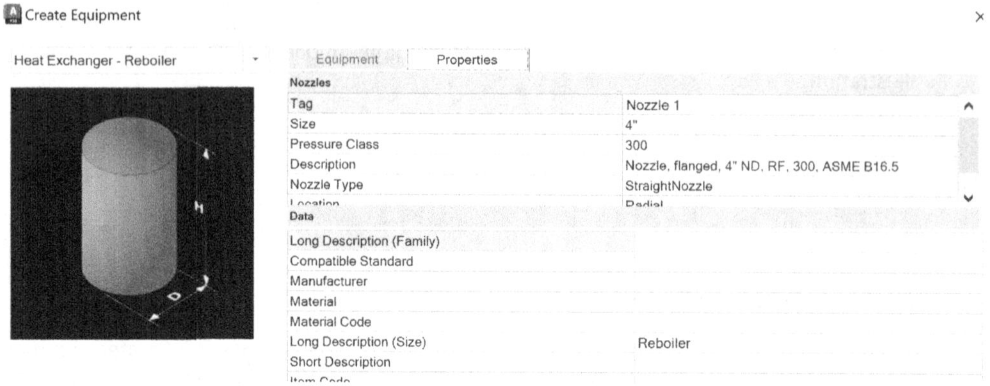

About Nozzles

By default, most equipment has at least one nozzle. You can modify its location and properties, such as the type, size, and pressure class of existing nozzles, as shown in the following illustration. New nozzles can also be added. You add or edit nozzles using the grips located on any existing piece of equipment in a drawing.

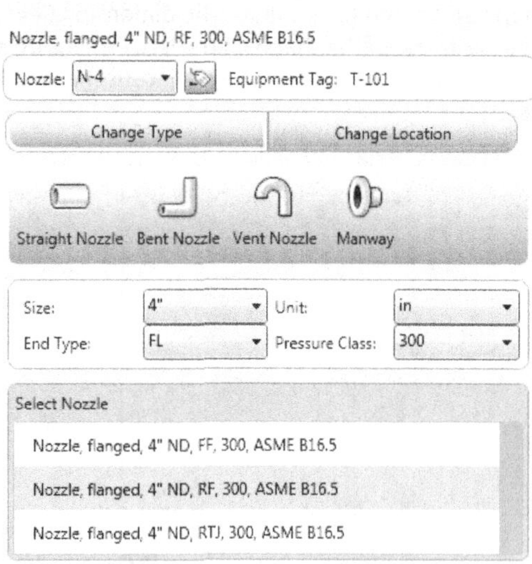

You initiate the editing of a nozzle by first selecting the nozzle. To select a nozzle, select it on the equipment. A nozzle that has been selected displays a pencil edit icon, which is used to access editing options, as shown in the following illustration.

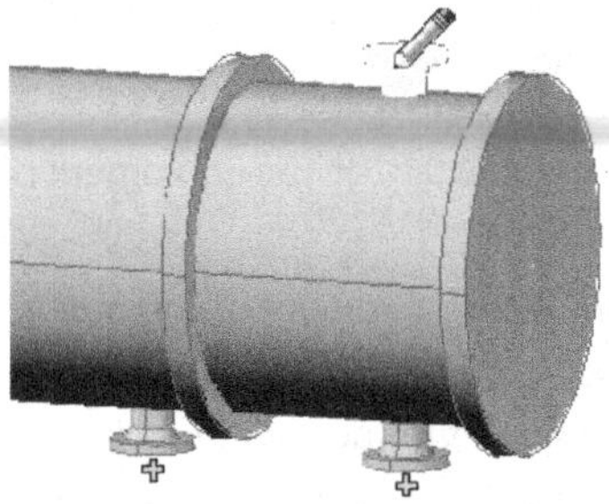

Equipment Templates

If you customize the properties of equipment in a drawing, you can save the equipment settings as an equipment template. You can load the equipment settings from the template and easily place additional equipment with the same properties.

The component shapes and dimensions are saved in an equipment template. The number of nozzles and nozzle properties are also saved in the template.

Equipment templates that are saved in the ...*Equipment Templates*\\ folder of the current project are listed in the Templates menu, as shown in the following illustration. You can also select templates from other locations. This folder can also be copied between projects to reuse templates in other projects.

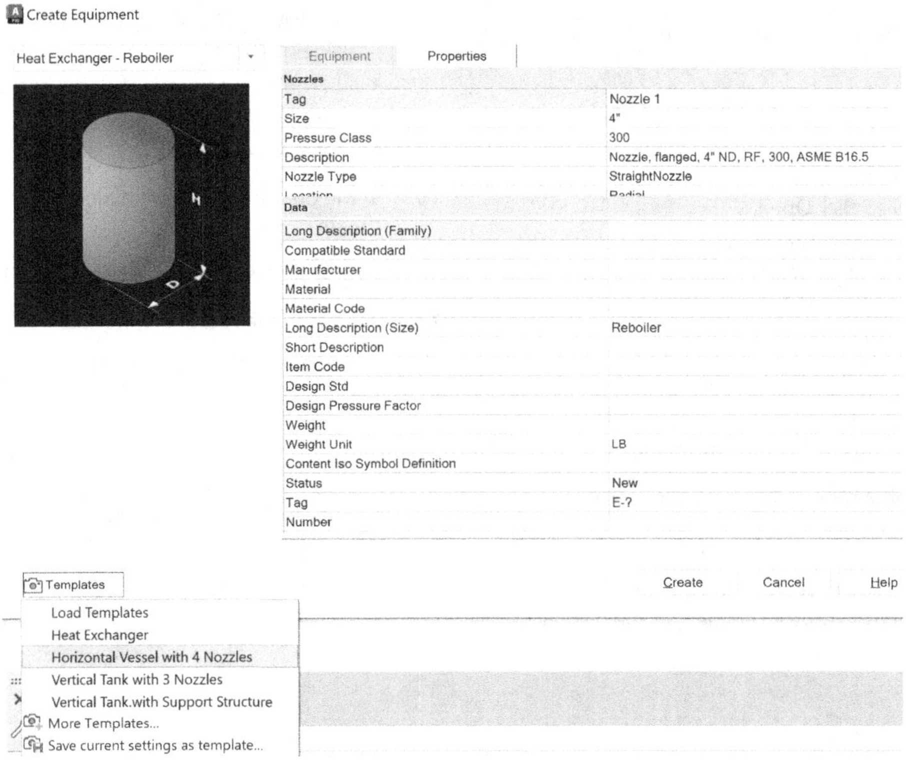

Exercise: Create Equipment

In this exercise, you will create several pieces of equipment using the standard equipment builder. You will also convert AutoCAD objects into Plant 3D equipment.

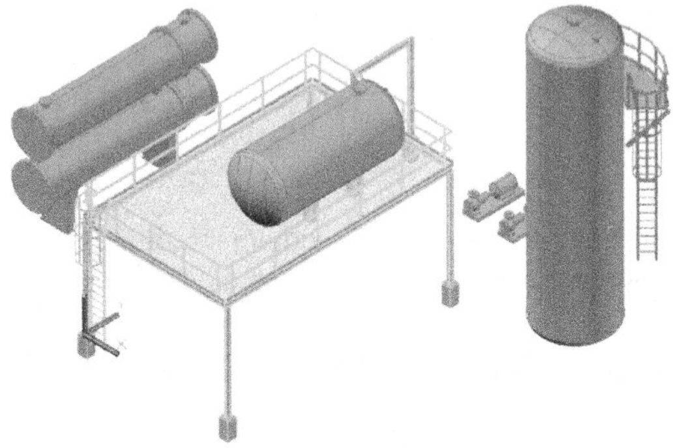

Add Pumps

In this section of the exercise, you add pumps to the drawing and tag them accordingly.

1. Start the AutoCAD Plant 3D software, if not already running.
2. Open an existing project by doing the following:
   - In the Project Manager, Current Project list, click Open.
   - In the Open dialog box, navigate to the folder *C:\Plant Design 2024 Practice Files\Create Equipment*.
   - Select the file *Project.xml*.
   - Click Open.
3. In the Project Manager, expand Plant 3D Drawings and Equipment folders.
4. Double-click on *Equipment.dwg* to open it.
5. Verify that the 3D Piping workspace is active.
6. If the steel structure is not visible, in the Structure tab, Parts panel, set the display to Shape Model.
7. On the Home tab, on the Equipment panel, click Create.
8. In the Create Equipment dialog box:
   - From the Equipment list, select Pump>Centrifugal Pump.
   - On the Equipment tab, click in the tag field.

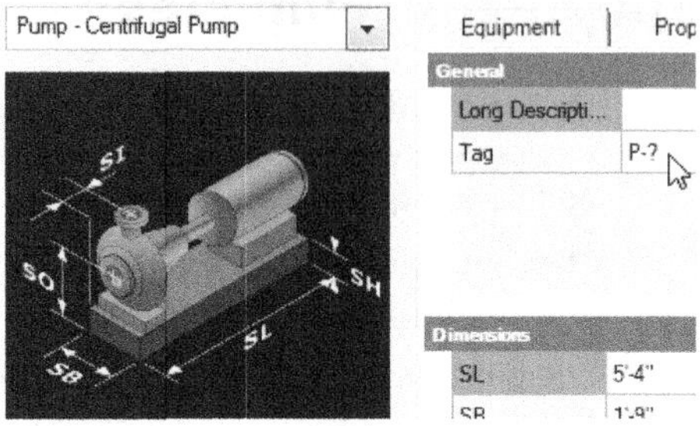

9. In the Assign Tag dialog box,
   - Click in the Number field.
   - Click Assign Number (icon along the right side of the field).
   - In the Number field, after the assigned number, enter **A**.
   - Click Assign.
10. In the Create Equipment dialog box, click Create.
11. To specify the insertion point, enter **11',33'**.
12. To specify the rotation, enter **90**.

    The pump is added to the drawing.

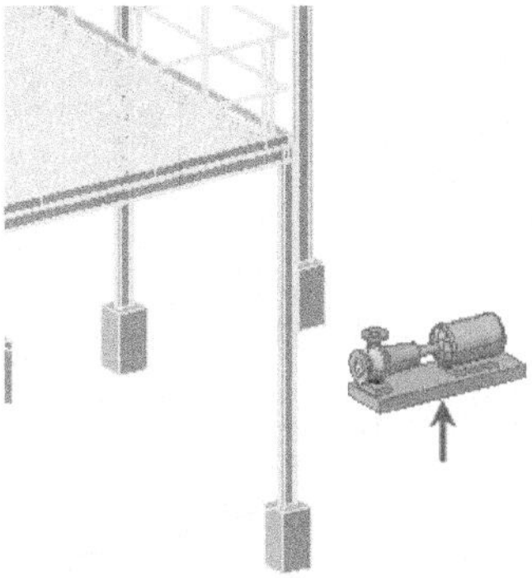

13. Hover the cursor over the nozzle on the top of the pump.

    The tooltip displays the properties of nozzle and an equipment tag of P-001A.

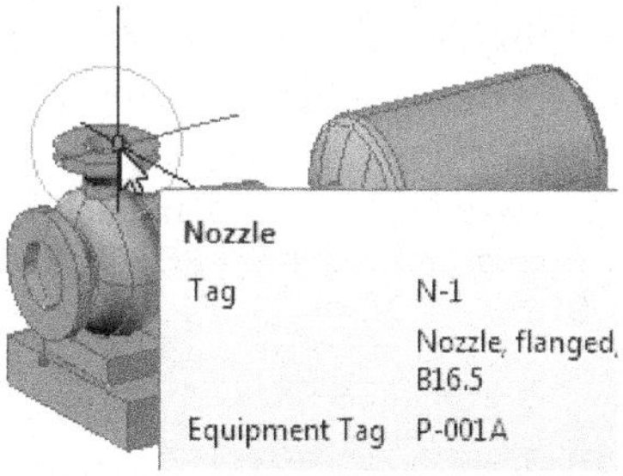

14. Hover the cursor over the nozzle on the front of the pump and note the tooltip.

15. Use the AutoCAD **Copy** command to copy the pump at a distance of **4'** along the X axis, as shown in the following illustration.

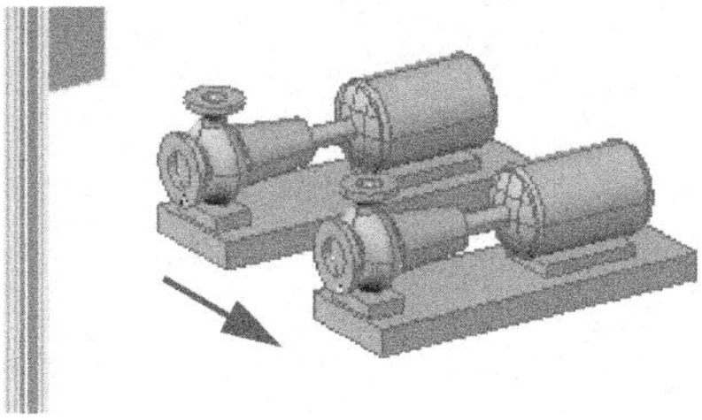

16. Hover the cursor over the second pump and note that the tooltip displays a tag of P-001A?.

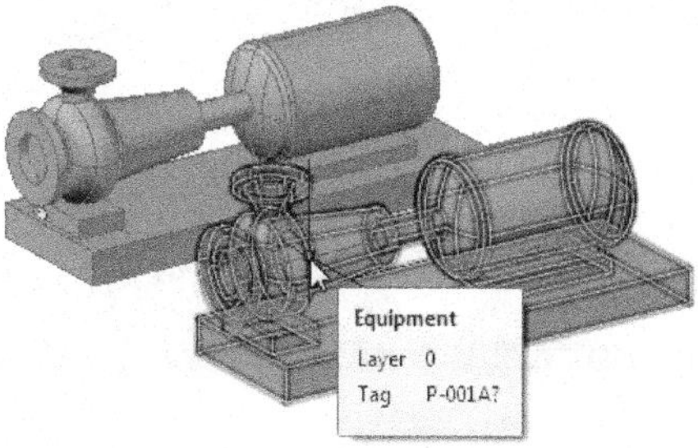

Note: If the pump is not highlighted when you hover the cursor over it, right-click in the graphics window and click Options>Selection tab>When no command is active>OK.

17. Select and right-click on the second pump. Click Assign Tag.

18. In the Assign Tag dialog box:

    - Click in the Number field.
    - Click Assign Number.
    - In the Number field, after the assigned number, enter **B**.
    - Click Assign.

Add a Tank

In this section of the exercise, you add a tank to the drawing.

1. On the Home tab, on the Equipment panel, click Create.

2. In the Create Equipment dialog box, click Templates (near the bottom left of the dialog box), and click Vertical Tank with 3 Nozzles.

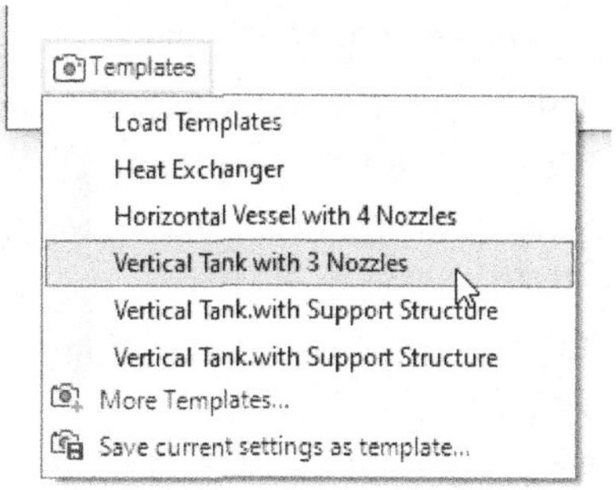

3. On the Equipment tab:

    - Under Shapes, select: 1 Torispheric Head.
    - Under Dimensions, set D to **8'**.
    - Under Shapes, select: 2 Cylinder.
    - Under Dimensions, verify D is set to **8'**.
    - For H, enter **26'**.
    - Under Shapes, select: 3 Torispheric Head.
    - Under Dimensions, verify D is set to **8'**.

4. To add a trim, on the Equipment tab:
   - In the Shapes list, select the 2 Cylinder to highlight it.
   - Below the Shapes list, click Add Trim and select Platform.
   - For Platform, under Dimensions, set H to **19'-6"**.
   - Under Ladder, set H1 to **14'-5/8"**.

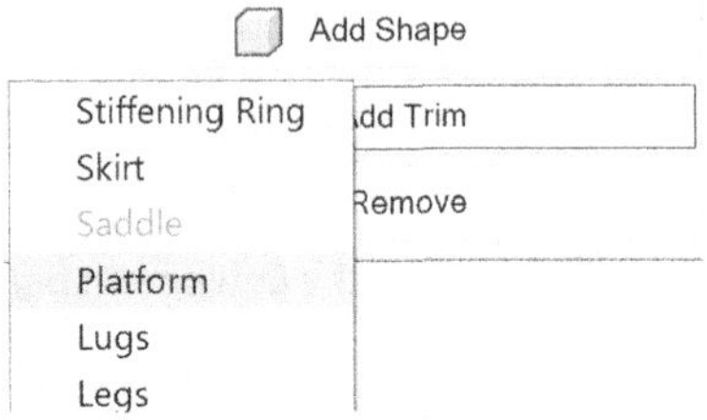

5. On the Properties tab:
   - Under Data, for Type, enter **T**.
   - For Tag, click the tag value.
6. In the Assign Tag dialog box, for Number, enter **101**. Click Assign.
7. In the Create Equipment dialog box, click Create.
8. To specify the insertion point, enter **30',26',4'**.

   Note: Initially you may only be prompted for an X and Y value. As you enter the comma after the Y value, the Z value becomes available.
9. To specify the rotation, enter **0**.
10. Select the tank you just added to the drawing. Right-click and click Add Nozzle or click the Add Nozzle icon.
11. In the Nozzle window, on the Change Location tab:
    - From the Nozzle Location list, select Top.
    - For R, enter **30"**.
    - For A, enter **0**.
    - For L, enter **6"**.
12. In the Nozzle window, on the Change Type tab:
    - Verify Straight Nozzle is selected.
    - From the Size list, select 4".
    - From the End Type list, select FL.
    - Verify "in" is selected from the Unit list.
    - Verify 300 is selected from the Pressure Class list.
    - Under Select Nozzle, double-click on Nozzle, flanged, 4"ND, RF, 300, ASME B16.5.

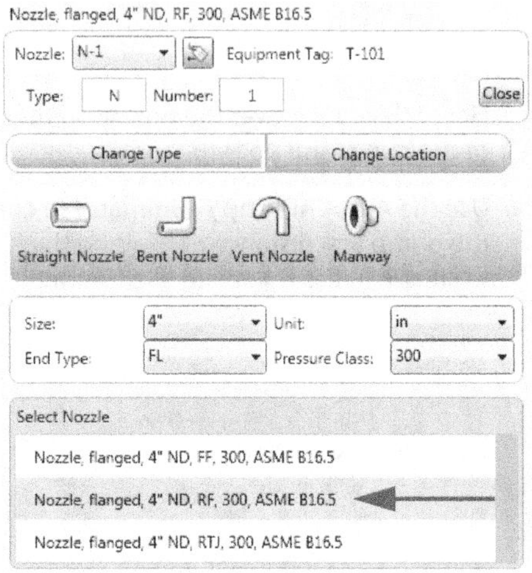

13. Click Close. The nozzle is added to the top of the tank.

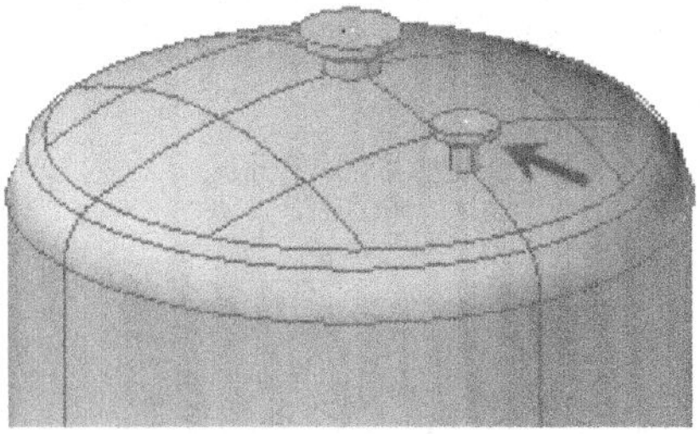

Add a Vessel

In this section of the exercise, you add a vessel to the drawing.

1. On the Home tab, on the Equipment panel, click Create.
2. In the Create Equipment dialog box, under Templates, click Horizontal Vessel with 4 Nozzles.
3. In the Create Equipment dialog box, on the Properties tab:
   - Under Data, for Type, enter **V**.
   - For Tag, click the tag value.
4. In the Assign Tag dialog box, for Number, enter **101**. Click Assign.
5. In the Create Equipment dialog box, click Create.
6. To specify the insertion point, enter **12',21',16'**.

   Note: Initially you may only be prompted for an X and Y value. As you enter the comma after the Y value, the Z value becomes available.
7. To specify the rotation, enter **270**.
8. Use the ViewCube to activate the NorthEast Isometric view. The drawing displays as shown in the following illustration.

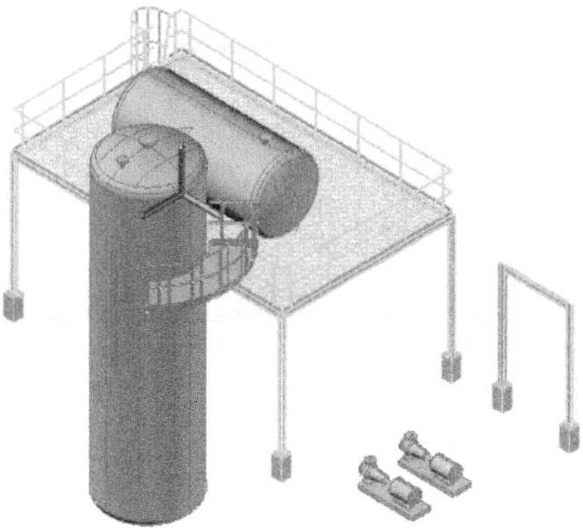

9. To hide the structural objects to make it easier to modify the vessel:
   - On the Home tab, on the Visibility panel, click Hide Selected.
   - To specify the objects to hide, select the structural railing.
   - Press <Enter> to hide the selected objects and end object selection.

   All structural objects are selected since they are all located in the referenced drawing, and are hidden.

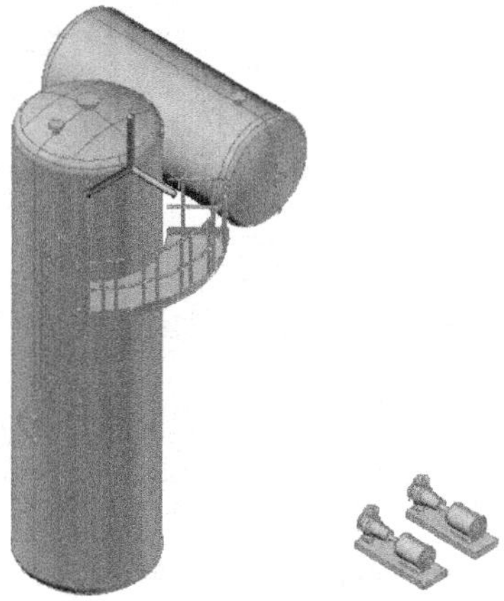

10. To edit the nozzle:
    - Zoom in to the end of the horizontal vessel that was just placed.
    - Press <Ctrl> and select the bigger nozzle on the end of the vessel.
    - Click the pencil icon to edit the nozzle.

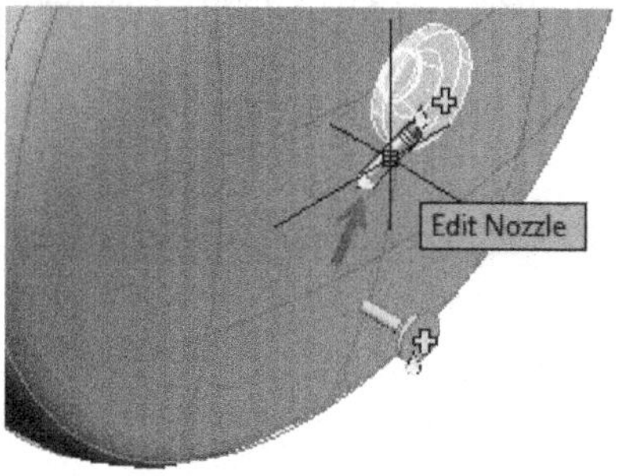

Hint: If you cannot edit the nozzle, consider changing the view to Parallel.

11. In the Nozzle window:
    - Verify that N-1 is displayed as the Nozzle.
    - Verify that you are on the Change Type tab.
    - From the Size list, select 1".
    - From the Pressure Class list, select 150.
    - Under Select Nozzle, double-click on Nozzle, flanged, 1" ND, RF, 150, ASME B16.5.

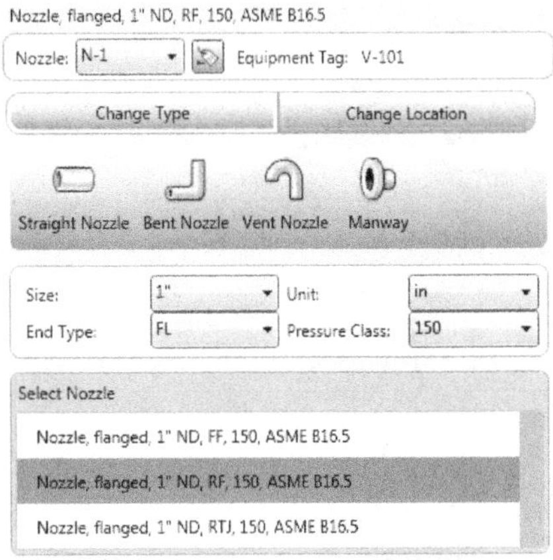

12. On the Change Location tab:
    - Verify that Bottom is selected from the Nozzle Location list.
    - For R, enter **24"**.
    - For A, enter **90**.
    - For L, enter **6"**.

13. Click Close.

    The nozzle size and location is changed.

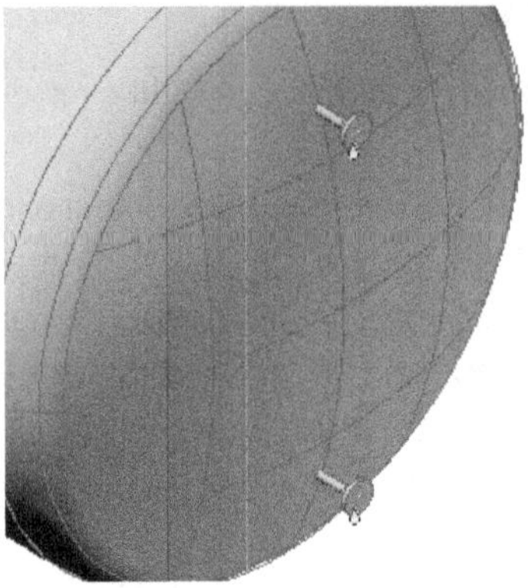

14. On the Home tab, on the Visibility panel, click Show All.

15. Perform a Zoom Extents.

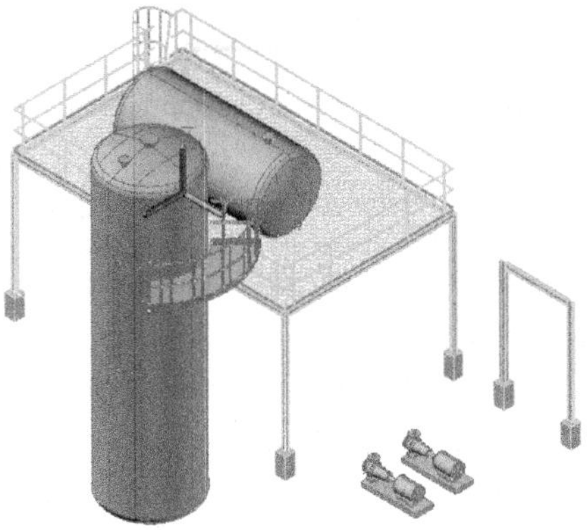

Add a Heat Exchanger

In this section of the exercise, you add a heat exchanger to the drawing.

1. Use the ViewCube to activate the SouthWest Isometric view, as shown in the following illustration.

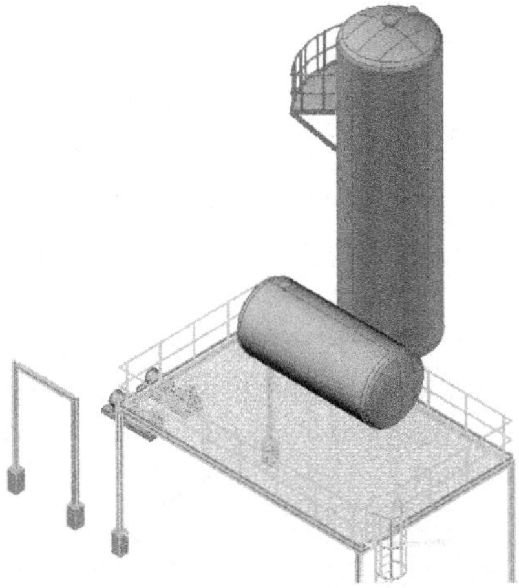

2. On the Home tab, on the Equipment panel, click Create.
3. In the Create Equipment dialog box, click Templates, and click Heat Exchanger.
4. In the Create Equipment dialog box, on the Equipment tab, under Shapes:
   - Select 1 Cylinder.
   - Click in the D value box and select the power icon and select Override mode.
   - Under Dimensions, for D, enter **4'-6"**.
   - For H, enter **4"**.

5. Select 2 Cylinder.
   - For D, select Override mode and then enter **4'**.
   - For H, enter **3'**.
6. Select 3 Cylinder.
   - For D, select Override mode and then enter **4'-6"**.
   - For H, enter **4"**.
7. Select 4 Cone. Click Remove.
8. Verify that 4 Cylinder is selected.
   - For D, select Override mode and then enter **4'**.
   - For H, enter **15'**.
9. Select 5 Torispheric Head. Click Remove.
10. Click Add Shape and click Cylinder.
11. Verify that 5 Cylinder is selected.
    - For D, select Override mode and then enter **4'-6"**.
    - For H, enter **4"**.
12. Select 4 Cylinder in the shape list.
13. Click Add Trim and select Saddle.
14. Select Saddle 1:
    - For H, enter **5'**.
    - For L, enter **2'-7 1/2"**.
    - For L3, enter **11'-6"**.
15. Under Properties tab, under Data, for Tag, click the tag value.
16. In the Assign Tag dialog box:
    - Verify that the Type is set to E.
    - For Number, enter **101A**.
    - Click Assign.
17. In the Create Equipment dialog box, click Create.
18. To specify the insertion point, enter **-12',6',5'**.

19. To specify the rotation, enter **90**.

The heat exchanger is placed, as shown in the following illustration.

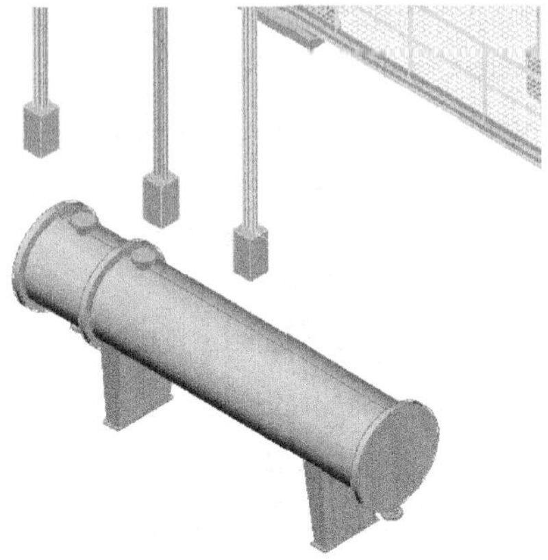

20. Use the ViewCube to change to the Left view.

21. To delete a nozzle:

- Press <Ctrl>+ select the bottom nozzle on the right side of the Heat Exchanger.
- Press <Delete>.

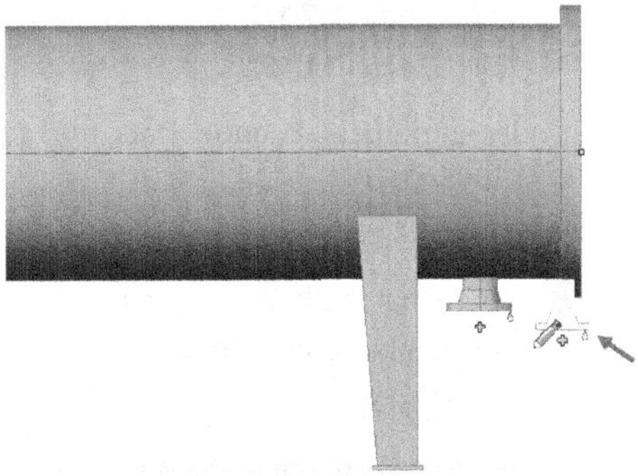

22. On the Home tab, on the Equipment panel, click Create.

23. In the Equipment tab, under Shapes, select Saddle 1 and click Remove.

24. As the values for heat exchanger are already saved, provide the new tag and insertion point. In the Create Equipment dialog box:

- Under Properties, under Data, for Tag, click the tag value.
- In the Assign Tag dialog box, for Number, enter **101B**.
- Click Assign.
- Click Create.

25. To specify the insertion point, enter **-12',6',10'**.

26. To specify the rotation, enter **90**.

Note that another heat exchanger without a saddle is placed above the first heat exchanger.

27. Repeat the steps to delete the same nozzle on the right end of the second heat exchanger.

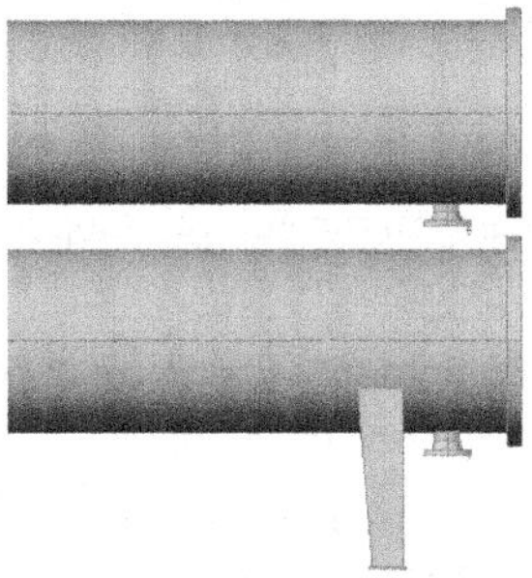

28. Press <Ctrl>+select the nozzle on the right side of top heat exchanger, as shown in the following illustration. Click Edit Nozzle.

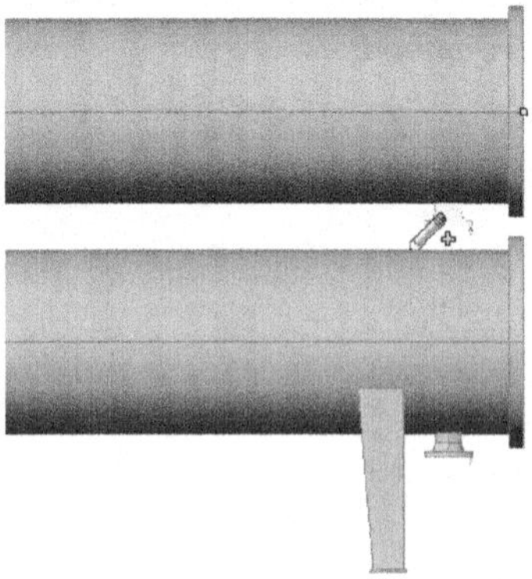

29. In the Nozzle window:

- Verify that N-3 is selected from the Nozzle list.
- Click the Change Location tab.
- For A, enter **90**.
- From the Nozzle list, select N-5.
- For A, enter **270**.
- Click Close.

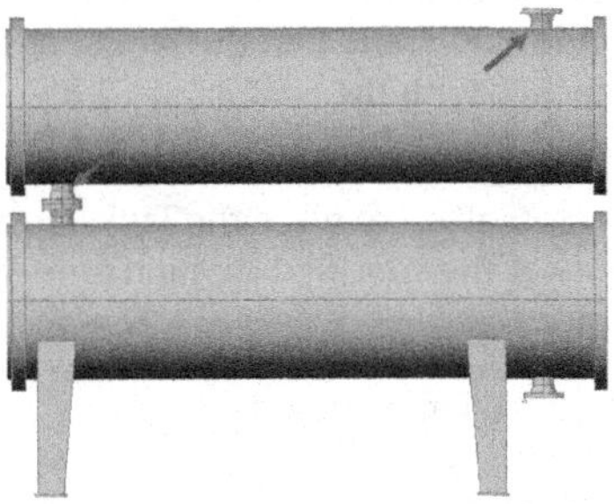

30. Zoom to the extents of the drawing.

31. Use the ViewCube to activate the Southeast Isometric view.

32. Save and close the drawing.

Exercise: Convert Equipment and Attach AutoCAD Objects

In this exercise, you will convert AutoCAD objects into Plant 3D equipment.

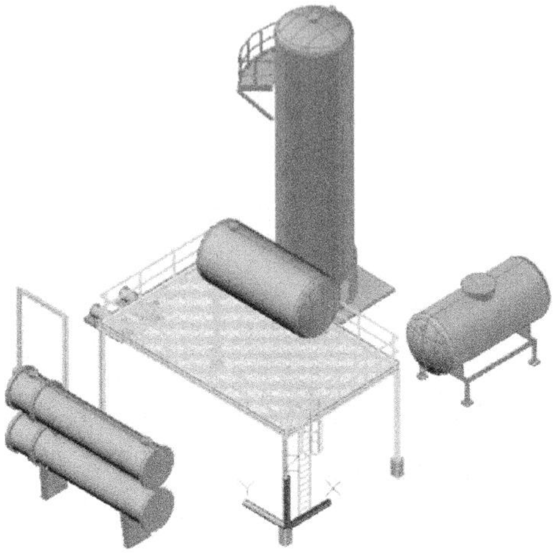

Attach AutoCAD Objects to Equipment

In this section of the exercise, you insert a block made of AutoCAD solids that represents a support for the tank. You attach the support to the tank.

1. Start the AutoCAD Plant 3D software, if not already running.
2. Open an existing project by doing the following:
   - In the Project Manager, Current Project list, click Open.
   - In the Open dialog box, navigate to the folder *C:\Plant Design 2024 Practice Files\Convert Equipment*.
   - Select the file *Project.xml*.
   - Click Open.
3. In the Project Manager, expand Plant 3D Drawings and Equipment folders.
4. Double-click on *Equipment.dwg* to open it.
5. Verify that the 3D Piping workspace is active.
6. On the Insert tab, on the Block panel, click Insert to open the Insert gallery. Click Recent Blocks to open the Blocks palette.
7. In the Blocks palette:
   - Switch to the Current Drawing tab.
   - Scroll down in the Current Drawing Blocks list and select Tank Support.
   - Under Insertion Options, clear Insertion Point.
   - Move the cursor over the Drawing window and note that the Tank support is attached with the cursor.
   - For Insertion point, enter **30', 26'**.
   - Press <Enter> to place the Tank Support block at the specified location (under the tank).
   - Close the Blocks palette.

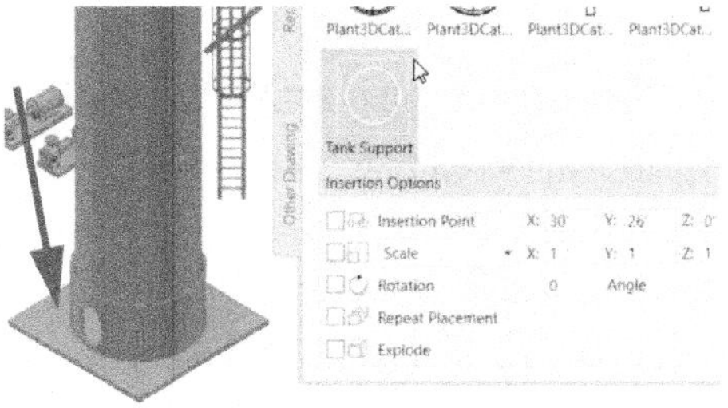

8. To attach the tank support to the tank:
   - On the Home tab, on the Equipment panel, click Attach Equipment.
   - To specify the equipment item, select the tank.
   - To specify the other objects, select the tank support.
   - Press <Enter> to end object selection.
9. Select the tank. Verify that both the tank and support are selected.
10. Right-click on the tank. Click Save Selected Equipment as Template.

11. In the Save Template To dialog box,

- For File name, enter **Vertical Tank with Support Structure**.
- Click Save.
- Press <Esc> to clear selection.

The tank with the support structure is now saved in the Equipment Templates folder of the current project.

Convert AutoCAD Objects to Equipment

In this section of the exercise, you insert a block that is made up of AutoCAD solids to represent a vessel with nozzles. You convert the solids to a Plant 3D piece of equipment and specify where the nozzles are located.

1. On the Insert tab, on the Block panel, click the Insert arrow to open the Insert gallery. Click Blocks from Libraries.
2. In the Select a folder or file for Block Library dialog box:
   - Navigate to the *C:\Plant Design 2024 Practice Files\Convert Equipment\Related Files* folder.
   - Select *AutoCAD Horizontal Vessel.dwg*.
   - Click Open.
3. In the Blocks palette:
   - Verify that the Libraries tab is open and the horizontal vessel is displayed.
   - Click Insertion Point to select it.
   - Clear Explode, if required.
4. Click on the horizontal vessel in the palette. Select an insertion point anywhere in the drawing. Close the Blocks palette.
5. On the Home tab, on the Equipment panel, click Convert Equipment.
6. To specify the AutoCAD objects to convert, select the vessel block that you just inserted. Press <Enter>.
7. In the Convert to Equipment dialog box, select Vessel. Click Select.
8. Use the Midpoint object snap on the lower bar to select the insertion point of the block.

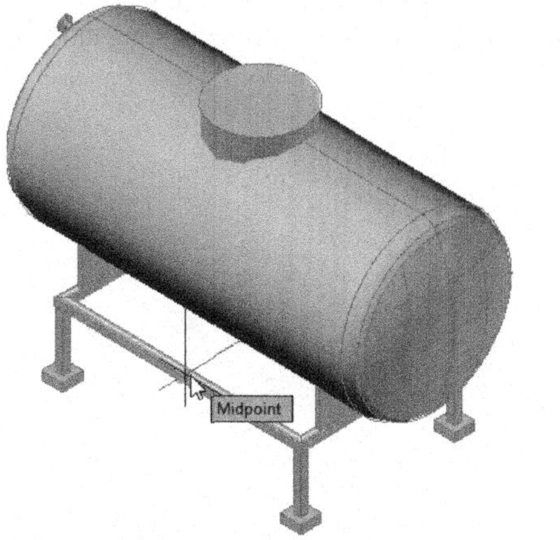

9. In the Modify Equipment dialog box, for Tag, click tag value.
10. In the Assign Tag dialog box:
    - For Type, enter **V**.
    - For Number, enter **102**.
    - Click Assign.
11. Click OK to exit the Modify Equipment dialog box.
12. Change to the Southwest Isometric view and zoom in to see the geometry that represents the nozzles on the end of the vessel.

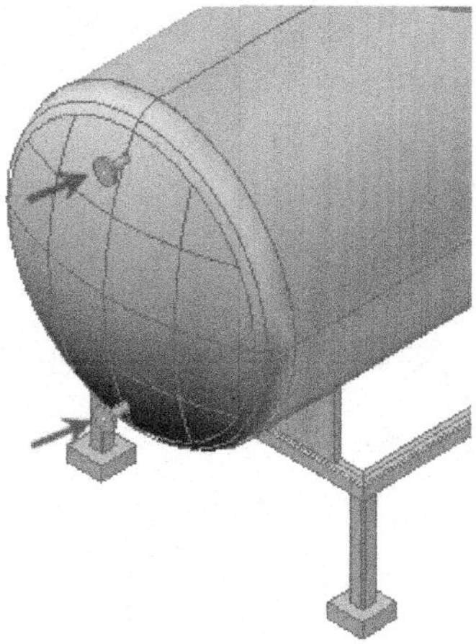

13. In the drawing, select the vessel. Right-click and select Add Nozzle.

14. Use object snaps to select the center of the nozzle as shown in the following illustration.

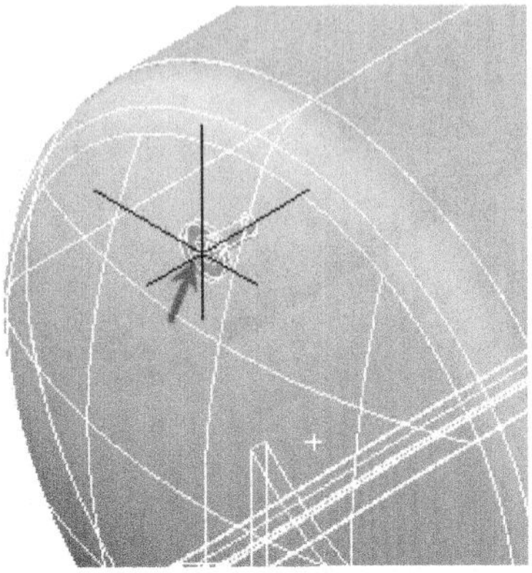

15. To specify the direction, enter **180**.

16. In the Nozzle window, on the Change Type tab:

- From the Size list, select 2".
- From the Pressure Class list, select 150.
- Under Select Nozzle, double-click on Nozzle, flanged, 2" ND, RF, 150, ASME B16.5.
- Click Close.

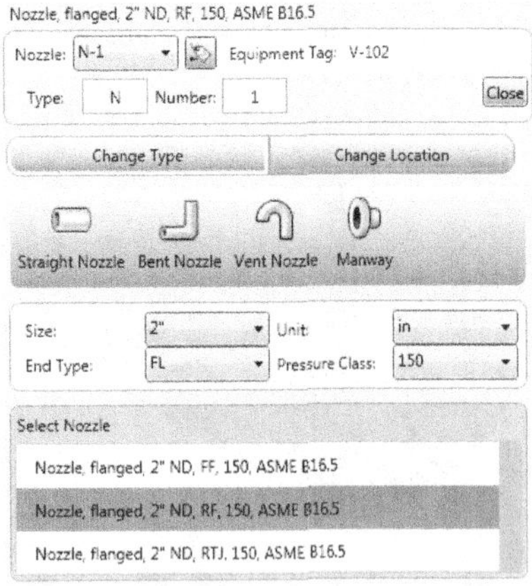

17. Repeat the steps to add the lower nozzle with the same properties.

18. Repeat the steps to add a 6" nozzle with a pressure class of 300 on the bottom of the tank pointing down.

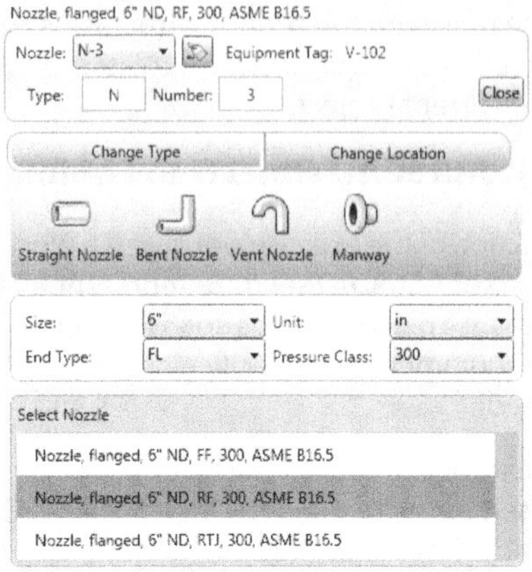

Tip: Use the ViewCube to get a better view of the bottom of the nozzle.

19. Save and close all drawings.

Lesson Review Questions

1. Where are templates of equipment stored, and can you use them on other projects as well?
   a. Templates are stored in the projectsymbstyle.dwg and cannot be used with other projects.
   b. Templates are stored in the equipment template folder in your active project. To use them on a different project, copy the contents of this folder to the equipment template folder of another project.
   c. It is not possible to store any templates of equipment, you only have the original templates in the equipment creation dialog box.
2. You can attach a converted AutoCAD solid to a piece of equipment so that it moves with the equipment when moved.
   a. True
   b. False
3. Which symbol is selected to edit a nozzle?
   a. Plus sign
   b. Pencil
4. Which of the following are included in a saved equipment template? (Select all that apply.)
   a. Equipment Tag
   b. Nozzle Types and Locations
   c. Attached AutoCAD Geometry
   d. Steel Structure and Trim

Lesson: Piping Basics

Overview

This lesson describes the creation and routing of pipe and the placement of inline components.

The design of the plant shown on the left in the following illustration is further defined with the inclusion of the pipelines and inline equipment, as shown on the right.

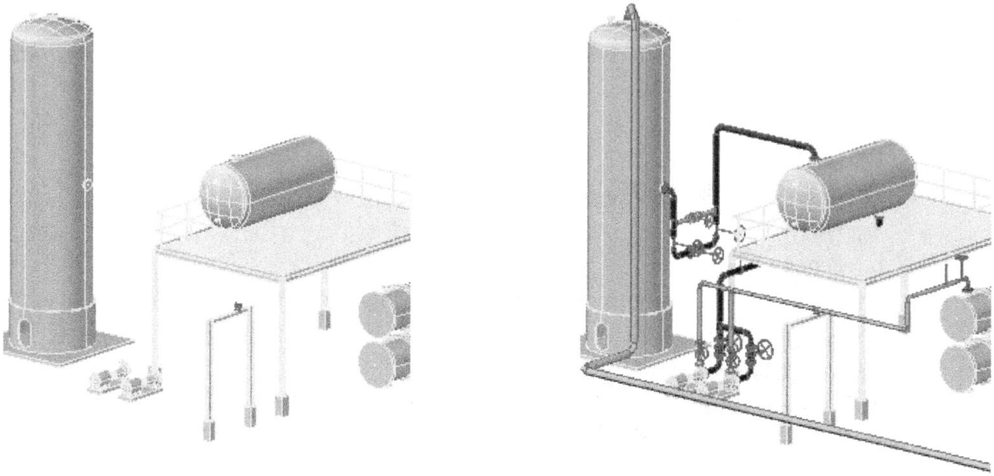

Objectives

After completing this lesson, you will be able to:

- Route pipe in a 3D model.
- Identify the grips you can use to modify pipe.
- List the tools available for adding valves and fittings.
- List the pipe support tools and types available.

Routing Pipe

The Part Insertion panel on the Home tab includes tools you can use to route pipe, convert AutoCAD lines to pipe, and assign tags to pipe, as shown in the following illustration. It is useful to assign tags for the purposes of identifying material associated to a particular run (using Data manager) and also is required for creating isometric drawings. You can specify pipe settings, such as pipe size, pipe spec, and pipe number before placing pipe in a drawing. You can also connect custom and placeholder parts to a pipeline that are not in the pipe spec. Additionally, you use the P&ID Line List tool if you have a P&ID object you want to place in a Plant 3D model.

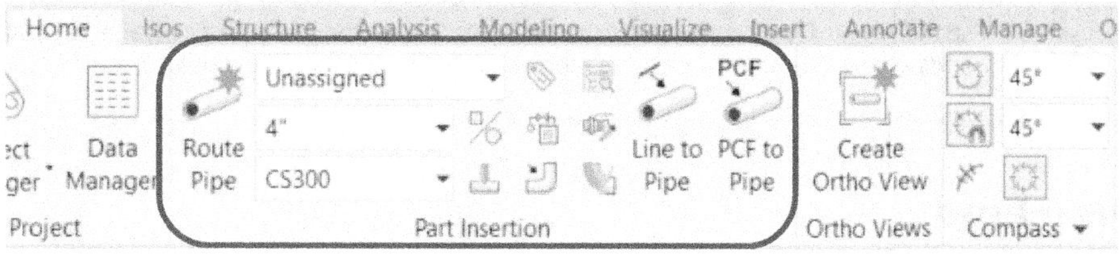

Process: Route Pipe

You use the Route Pipe tool to draw a pipeline in the drawing. To connect a pipe to a nozzle on an existing piece of equipment, use the Node object snap when prompted for a start or next point, as shown in the following illustration.

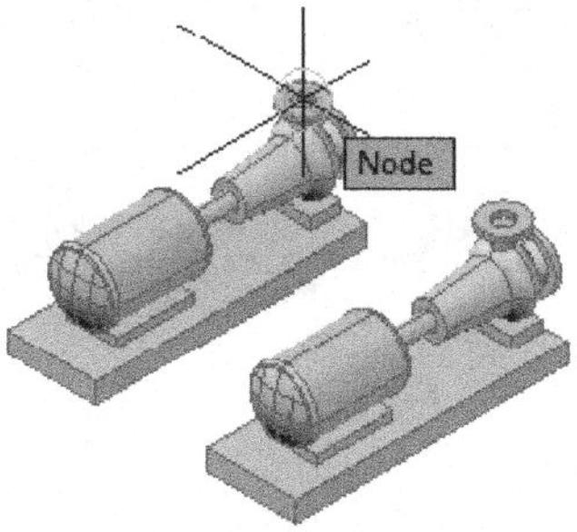

While routing pipe, the compass is displayed so you can accurately place pipelines at precise angles. Press <Ctrl>+right-click to cycle the compass rotation between the different axes. You can also click Plane from the context menu to cycle the compass or enter **P** and press <Enter>.

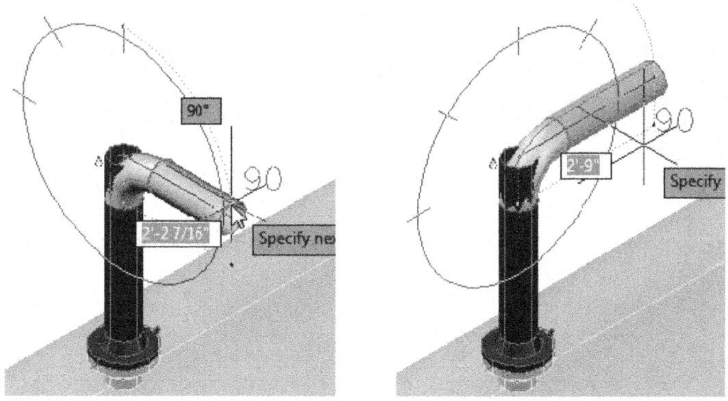

As you select the points for the pipe run, the required fittings are automatically inserted.

If the points you select in a pipe run make a connection to existing equipment or another pipe run, the auto-routing feature routes pipe and add the required fittings to complete the connection. If multiple paths are available, you can select from multiple solutions.

> You can make connections with existing equipment or pipe runs that are located in externally referenced drawings.

> Use the Toggle Pipe Bends option on the Home tab, on the Part Insertion panel to create pipe bends as an alternative to creating elbows as you are creating pipelines.

Modifying Pipe

The grips that are activated when you select a pipe enable you to add pipe branches, change the elevation of existing pipe, and substitute parts in the piping run, as shown in the following illustration.

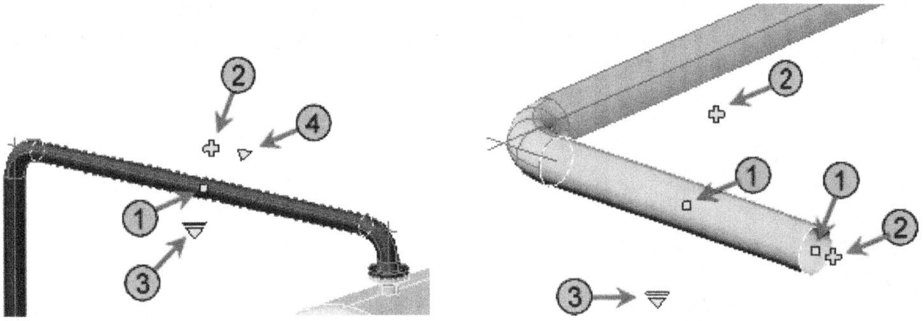

1. Standard grip
2. Continue Pipe Routing
3. Substitute Part
4. Change Pipe Elevation

Valves and Fittings

Valves and fittings can be added to an existing pipe run using the tools on the Tool Palettes, as shown in the following illustration. You can select from tools that correspond to the valves and fittings listed in the project spec sheets.

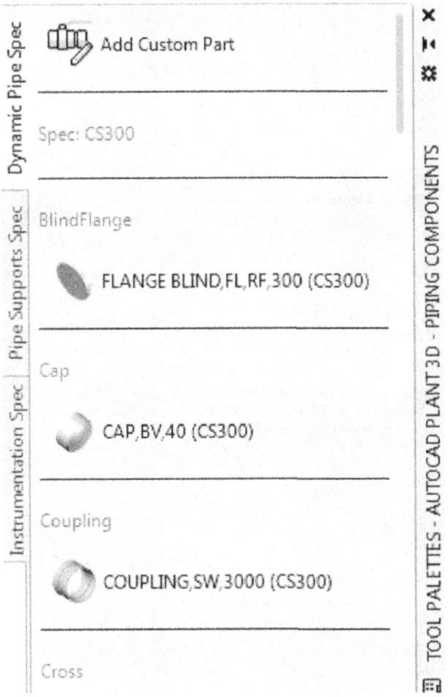

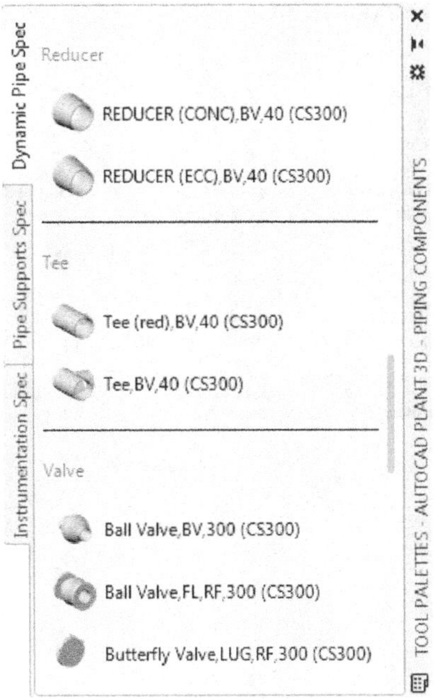

About Pipe Supports

You can create and connect pipe supports to pipes in a 3D model. The Pipe Supports panel on the Home tab contains tools that you can use when creating, modifying, converting, and attaching pipe supports, as shown in the following illustration. Alternatively, pipe supports in AutoCAD Plant 3D are also contained in a spec and can be placed using the Pipe Supports Spec tab of the Tool Palette. Support type and sizes can be edited using the Spec Editor in a similar manner used to edit a piping spec.

You can use the Create tool to add pipe supports to a 3D model. A variety of pipe support types are available in the Add Pipe Support dialog box, as shown in the following illustration. By default, the dialog box shows all supports. Select the type option buttons at the top left to refine the list and select a support type. Click OK once selected to place the support in a drawing. To change the properties of the support use the Properties palette. Additionally, you can select the support after you place it and select the Change Support Elevation grip to set the elevation. AutoCAD objects can also be converted and used as supports.

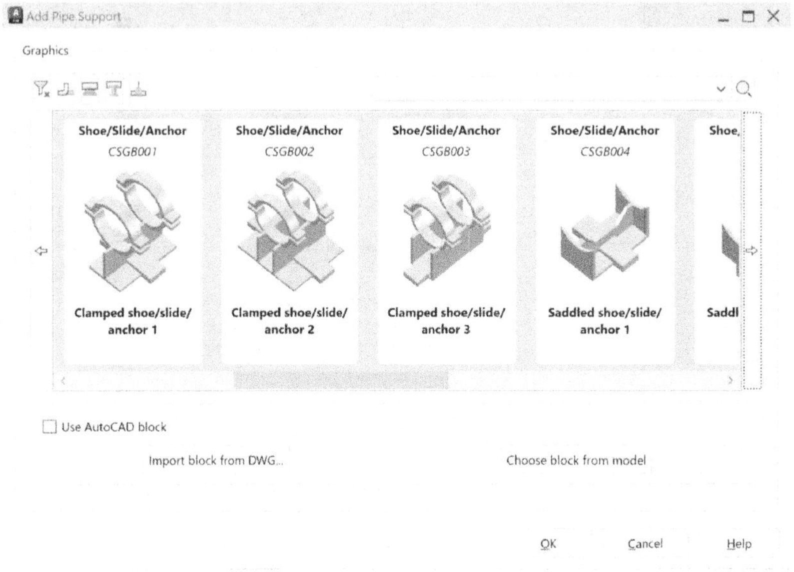

About Instrumentation

AutoCAD Plant 3D also includes an Instrumentation Spec tab in the Tool Palette that can be used to place instruments in your piping model. Similar to pipe specs and support specs, the Instrument Spec tab in the Tool Palette is dynamically populated by the instruments defined in the instrument spec. 3D instruments can be placed from the palette or as custom objects using the custom part tool.

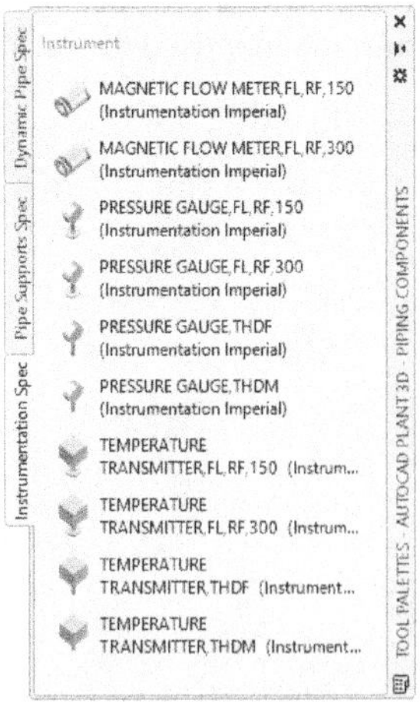

Exercise: Route Pipe and Add Fittings, Branch Connections, and Pipe Supports

In this exercise, you create a new piping run with fittings, branch connections, and pipe supports that are all positioned relative to the referenced drawing containing the structural steel and equipment design.

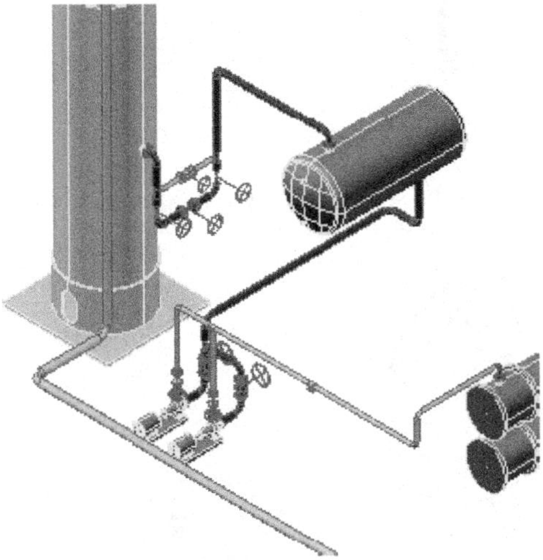

Route Pipe

In this section of the exercise, you route pipe from a nozzle on the tank to a nozzle on the vessel. You also add a loop to the pipe.

1. Start the AutoCAD Plant 3D software, if not already running.
2. Open an existing project by doing the following:
    - In the Project Manager, Current Project list, click Open.
    - In the Open dialog box, navigate to the folder *C:\Plant Design 2024 Practice Files\Route Pipe and Add Fittings, Branch Connections, and Pipe Supports*.
    - Select the file *Project.xml*.
    - Click Open.
3. In the Project Manager, expand Plant 3D Drawings and Piping folders.
4. Double-click on *Piping.dwg* to open it.
5. Hover the cursor over the nozzle that is located halfway up the vertical tank. Note that it is a flanged 6" ND, RF, 300, ASME B16.5 nozzle.

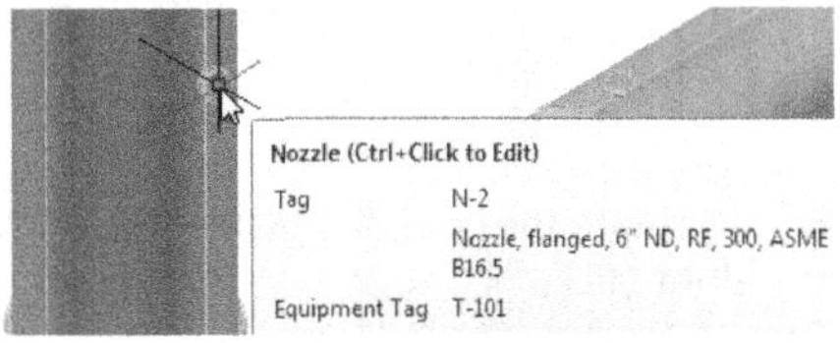

6. On the Home tab, on the Part Insertion panel:
    - From the Pipe Size Selector list, select 6".
    - From the Spec Selector list, select CS300.

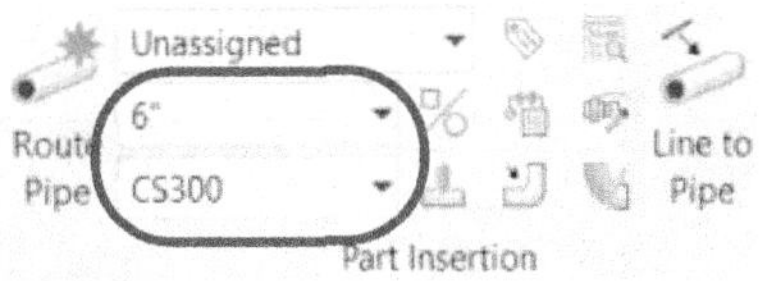

7. On the Home tab, on the Part Insertion panel, click Route Pipe.
8. To specify a start point, select the node on the tank nozzle as shown in the following illustration.

    Note: You might need to use Snap Overrides and enable Node to be able to select the node.

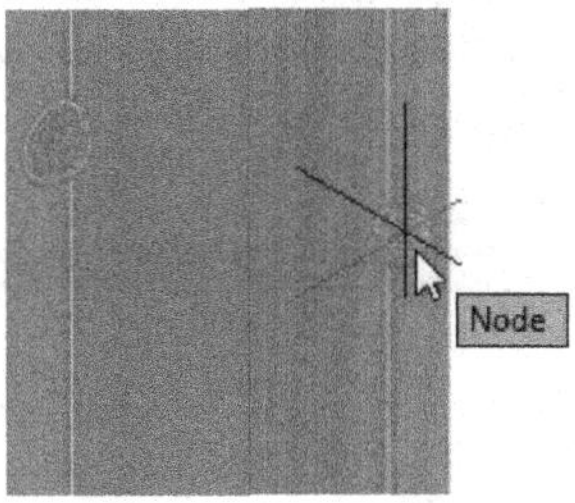

9. To rotate the compass plane to display vertically, press <Ctrl>+ right-click.

10. Move the cursor vertically down and verify that 90° is displayed as the angle. Enter **6'** and press <Enter>.

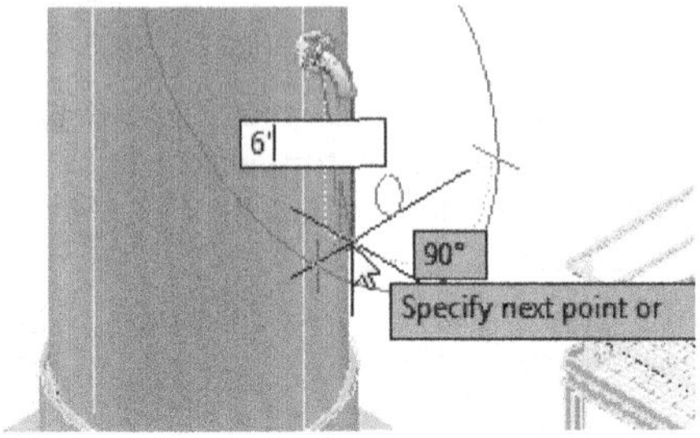

11. To rotate the compass plane, press <Ctrl>+ right-click.

12. Move the cursor to the right and verify that 90° is displayed as the angle. Enter **6'** and press <Enter>.

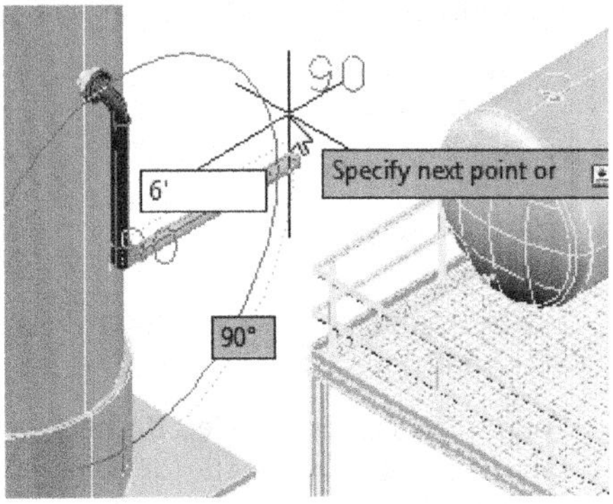

13. To specify the next point, select the node on the nozzle of the horizontal vessel as shown in the following illustration.

Note: You might need to use Snap Overrides and enable Node to be able to select the node.

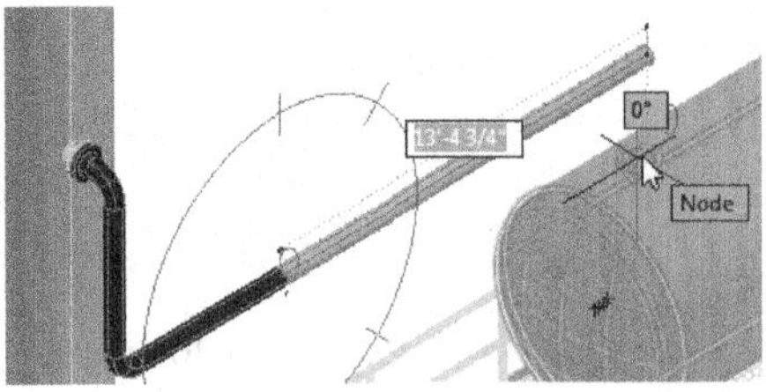

14. In the Command display list in the drawing area, click Next.

15. In the Command display list in the drawing area, click Accept.

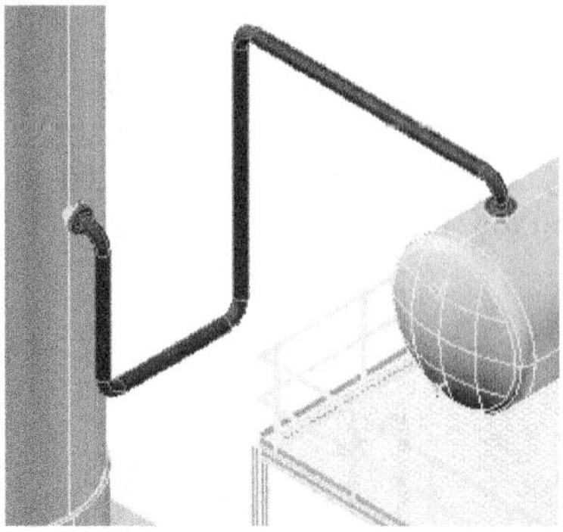

16. Select the short vertical pipe segment. Click Continue Pipe Routing.

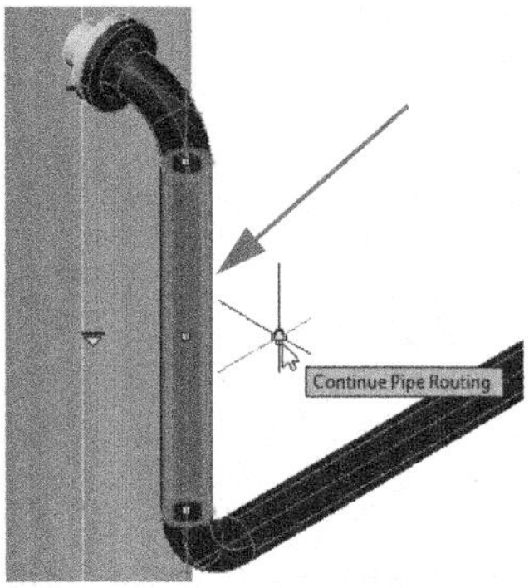

17. To specify the next point, select the perpendicular point on the long vertical pipe as shown in the following illustration.

Note: You might need to use Snap Overrides and enable Perpendicular to be able to select a point on the long vertical pipe.

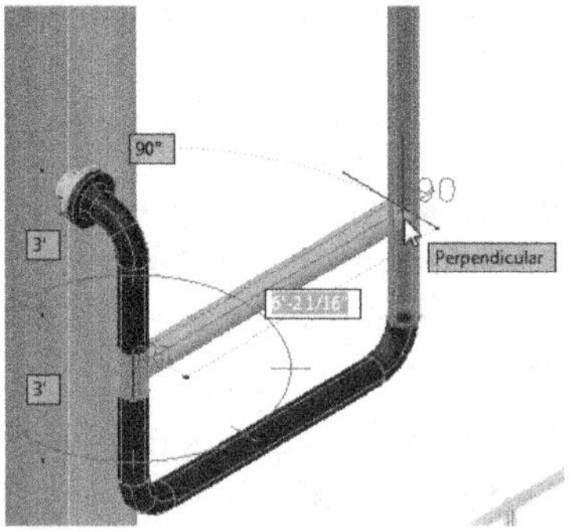

18. To change the size of the pipe:

- Double-click on the pipe segment that you just added.
- On the Properties palette, from the Size list, select 4".

Once you move your cursor anywhere in the drawing area, the pipe is changed to a 4" pipe. Reducers are automatically added.

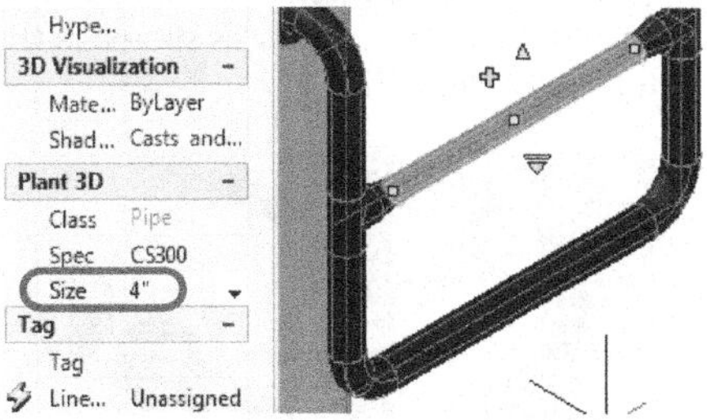

19. Press <Esc> to clear selection.

20. To specify that the tee does not use a reducer:

- Select the tee on the right.
- Click the Substitute Part grip.
- Click 6"x4" TEE (RED).

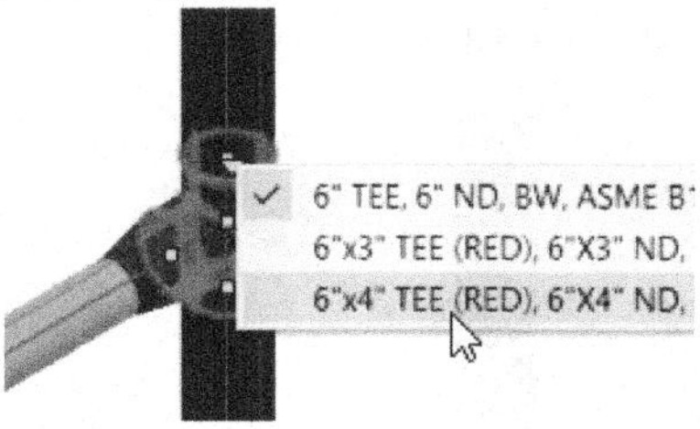

The tee without a reducer is used.

21. Repeat the steps to substitute the tee on the left side.

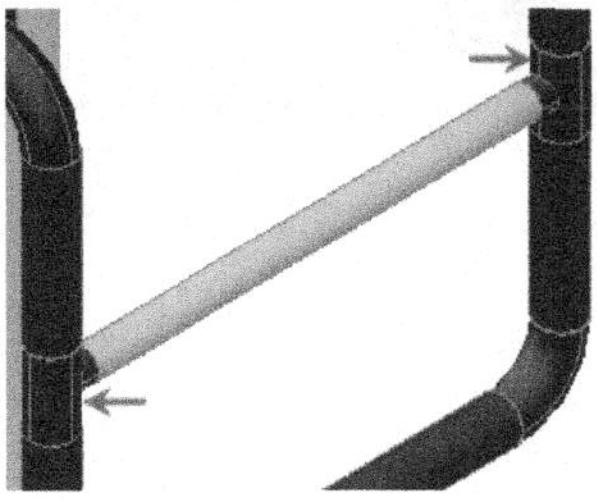

Add Valves

In this section of the exercise, you add different valves to the pipe in your drawing.

1. On the Tool Palette, on the Dynamic Pipe Spec tab, under Valve, click Globe Valve, FL, RF, 300.

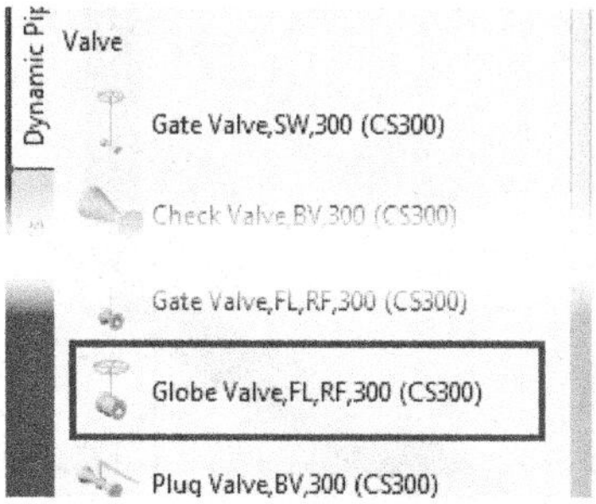

2. To specify the insertion point:

- On the status bar, verify that Dynamic Input is toggled on.
- Verify that Object Snaps is toggled on and Midpoint osnap is selected.
- To change the basepoint on the valve, press <Ctrl>. This toggles the basepoint between the two ends.
- Change the basepoint to the left end. Move the cursor over the 4" horizontal pipe.
- With the left dynamic dimension highlighted, enter **2'-11"**.

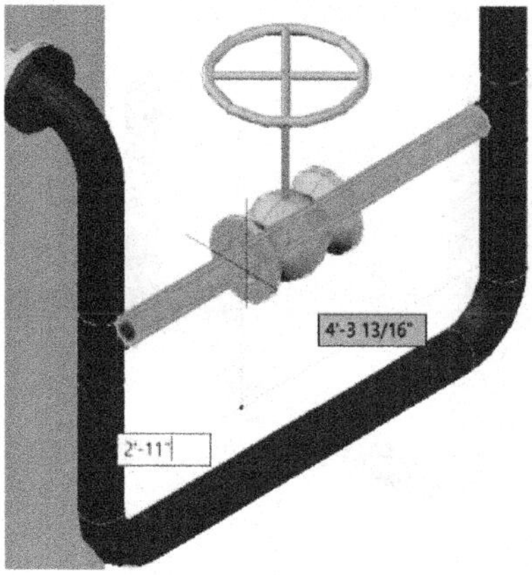

3. To specify a rotation, select a point to the front as shown in the following illustration.

   Press <Esc> to exit the command.

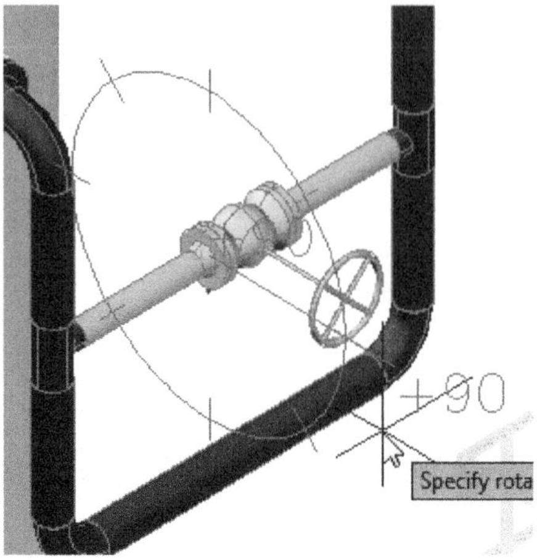

4. On the Tool Palettes, click Gate Valve, FL, RF, 300.

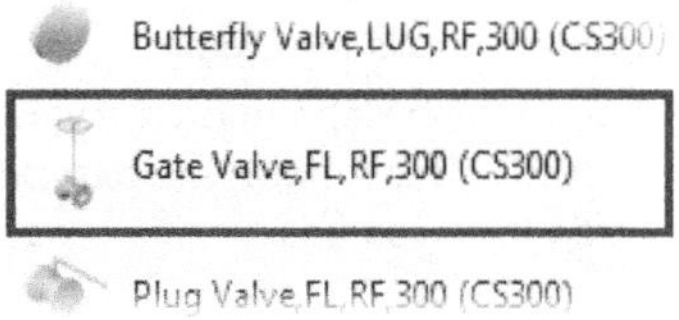

5. Repeat the steps to place the gate valve in the 6" pipe directly below the globe valve using the left dynamic dimension of **2'-11"**. You can also use the Midpoint snap. Press <Esc> to exit the command.

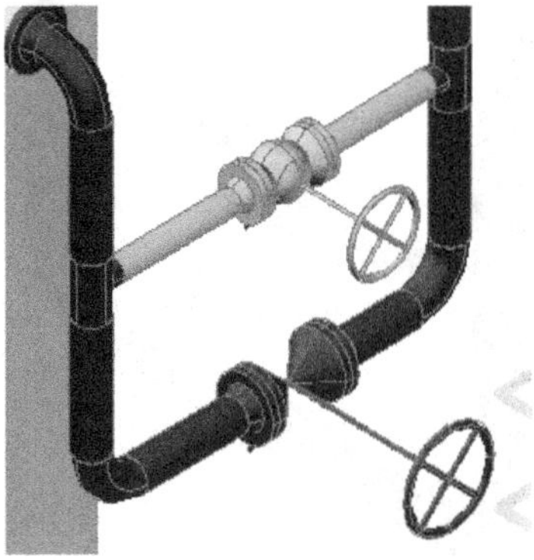

6. On the Tool Palettes, click Gate Valve, BV, 300.

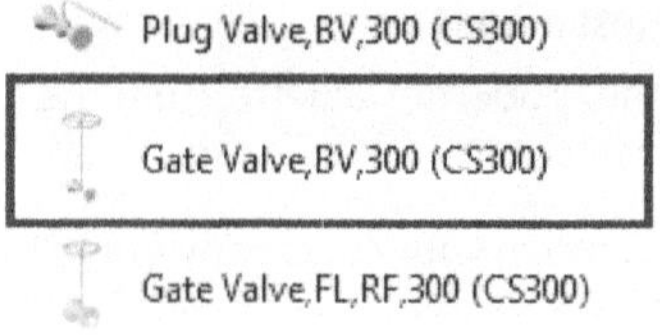

7. To specify the insertion point, select the node or endpoint of the elbow as shown in the following illustration.

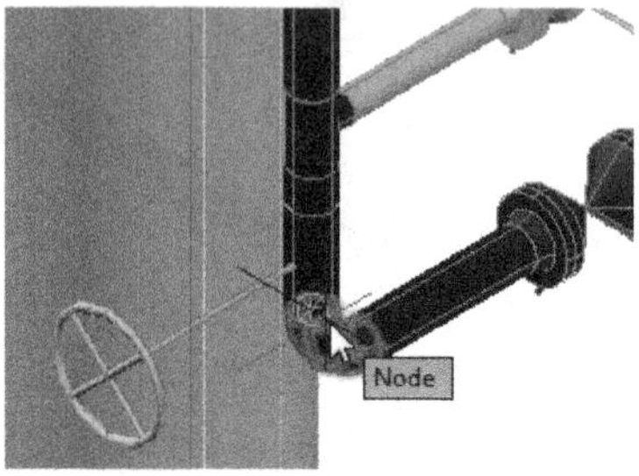

8. To specify the rotation, select a point to the front as shown in the following illustration. If the valve does not face the right direction, you can select the valve and use the Rotate grip to rotate it.

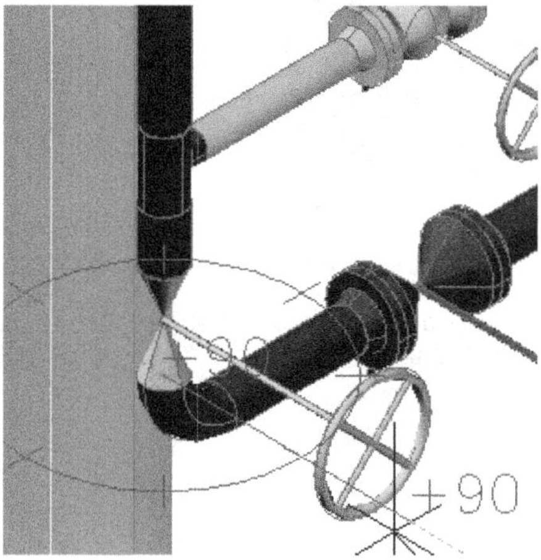

9. Repeat the steps to place another butt-welded gate valve in the opposite pipe segment as shown in the following illustration. Press <Esc> after placing the valve.

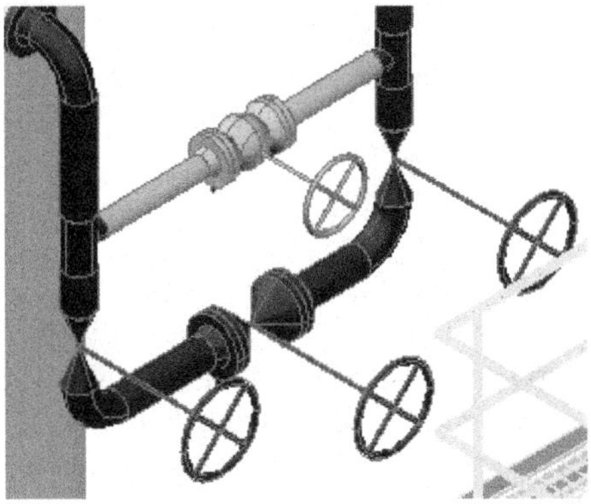

10. To add a line number to the existing pipe run:

- Select one of the pipes. Right-click.
- Click Add To Selection, and click Connected Line Number.
- On the Properties palette, under Tag, from the Line Number Tag list, select New.
- In the Assign Tag dialog box, for Number, enter **1001**.
- Click Assign.

11. Press <Esc> to clear selection.

12. Hold the cursor over several pipe segments and valves. Note that the tooltip displays their Layer and Line Number Tag as 1001.

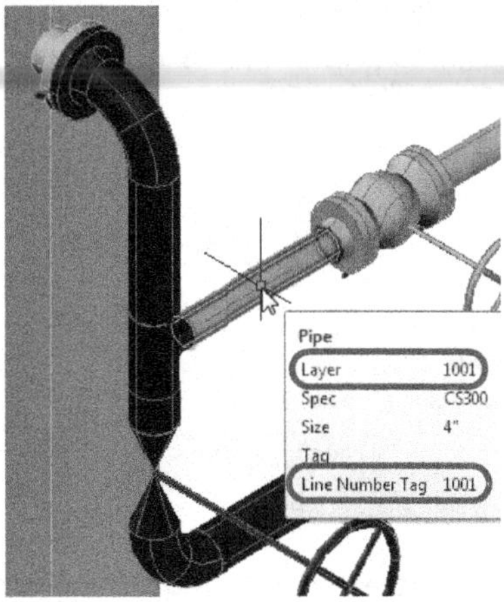

Add Additional Pipe and Valves

In this section of the exercise, you add pipes from the pumps to a heat exchanger.

1. Hold the cursor over the nozzle on top of one of the pumps. Verify that it is a flanged 4" ND, RF, 300, ASME B16.5 nozzle.

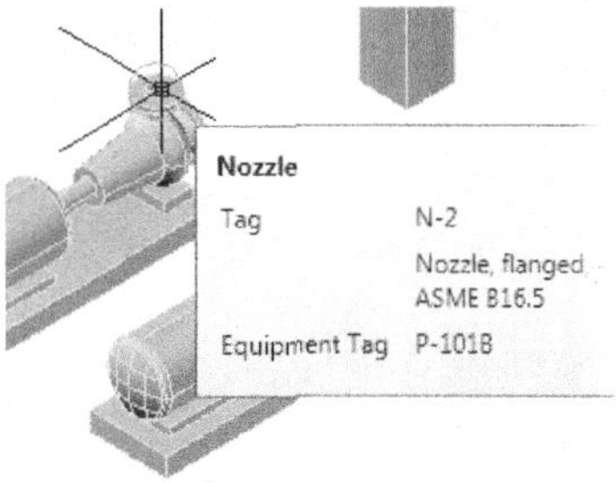

2. On the Home tab, on the Part Insertion panel:

- From the Pipe Size Selector list, select 4".
- From the Spec Selector list, select CS300.
- From the Line Number Selector list, select Route New Line.

3. In the Assign Tag dialog box, for Number, enter **1002**. Click Assign.

4. To specify the start point, select the node of the top nozzle on the pump as shown in the following illustration.

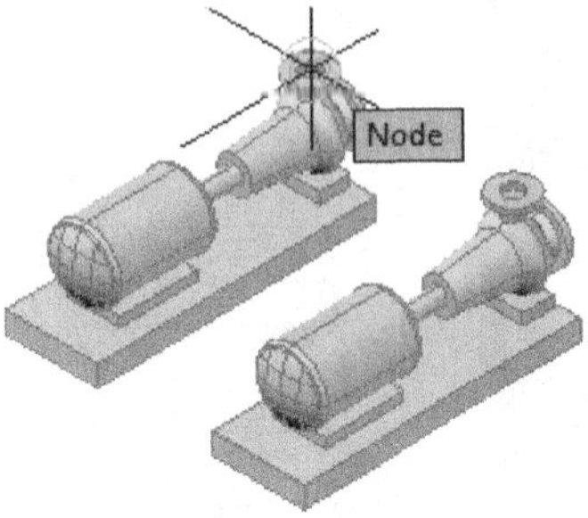

5. To specify the next point, move the cursor up. Enter **6'**. Verify that the angle displays as 0. If not, use <Ctrl>+right-click to have the rotation as shown.

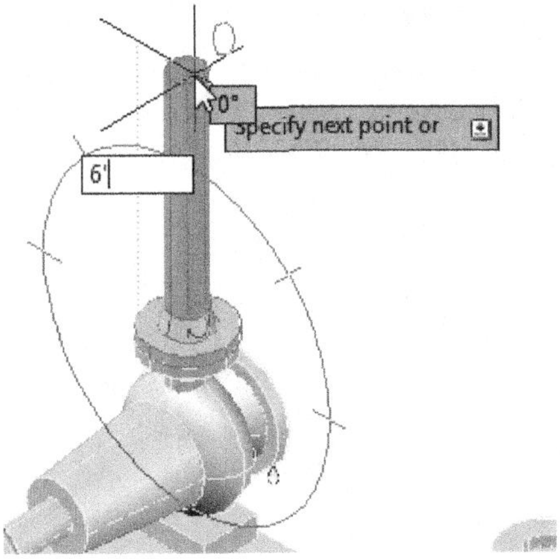

6. To specify the next point, select the node of the nozzle on top of the heat exchanger as shown in the following illustration.

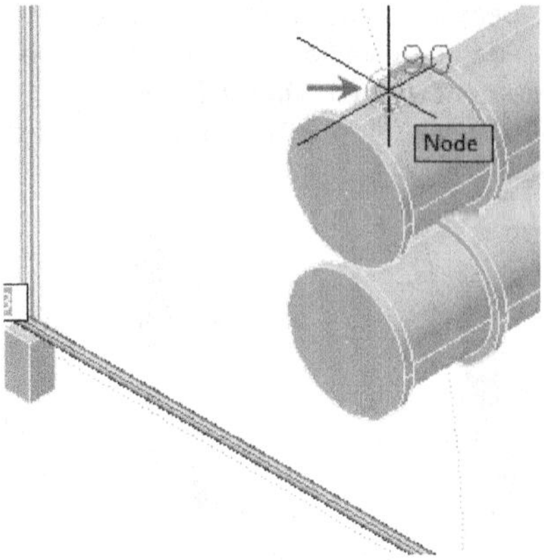

7. Press <Enter> to accept the first pipe configuration. Click Accept in the menu.

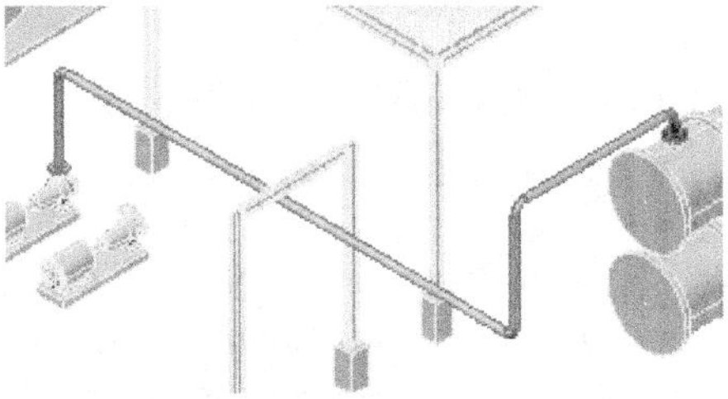

8. On the Tool Palette, click Check Valve, FL, RF, 300.

9. To specify the insertion point, select the node on the top nozzle of the other pump.

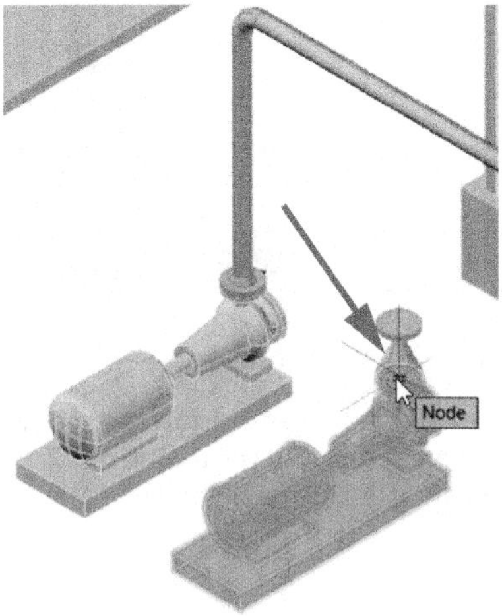

10. To specify the rotation, enter **180**.

11. Press <Esc> to complete the command.

12. Select the check valve that you just placed. Click Continue Pipe Routing.

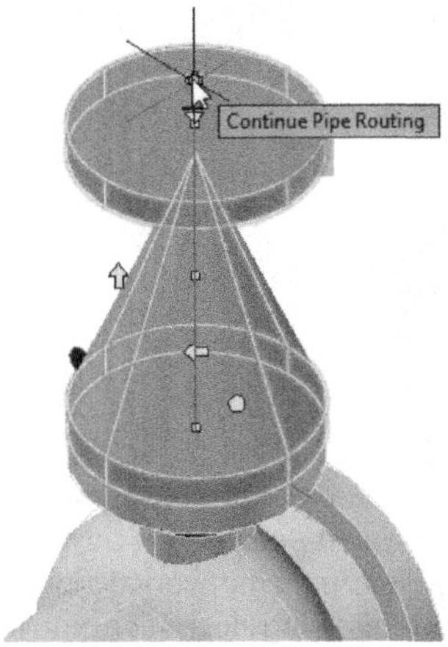

13. Right-click in the drawing area. Click pipeFitting.

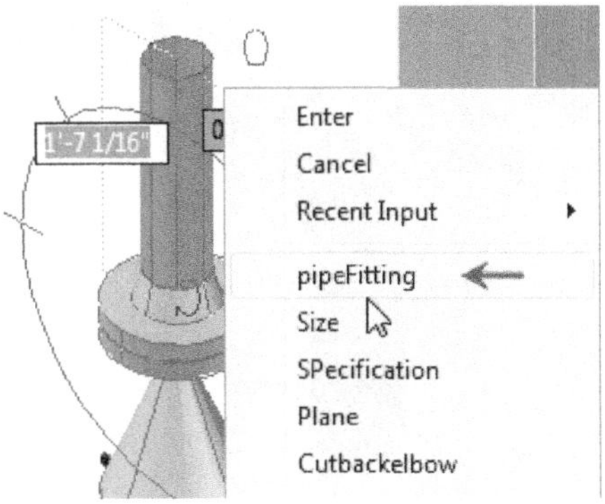

14. In the Fitting panel:

    - Select Valves.
    - From the Class Types list, select Gate Valve.
    - Under Available Piping Components, select 4" Gate Valve, Double Disc, 300 LB, RF.
    - Click Place.

15. Move the cursor vertically up and right-click in the drawing. Click Fitting-to-fitting.

16. To finish placing the fitting:

    - To specify the next point, enter **0**.
    - To specify the rotation, enter **45**.

17. To specify the next point, select the perpendicular point as shown in the following illustration.

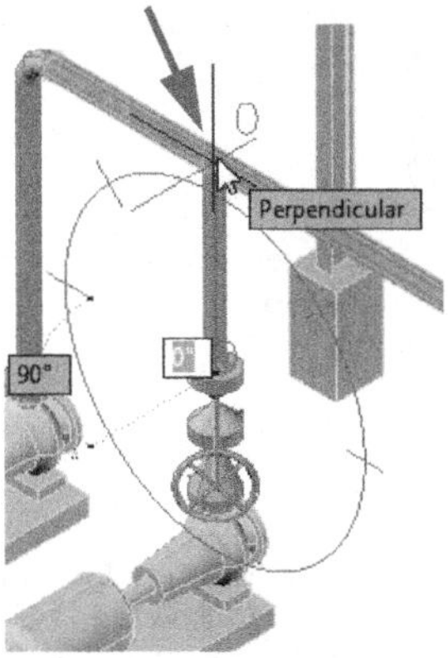

18. Use the ViewCube to activate the Northeast Isometric view. Zoom in on the pumps and the pipe fittings as shown in the following illustration. If the valve is not facing the correct direction, use the Rotate Part grip.

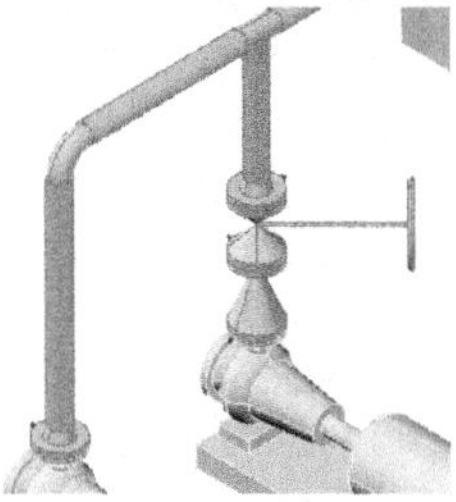

19. Select the elbow, pipe, and flange connected to the pump on the left. Press <Delete>.

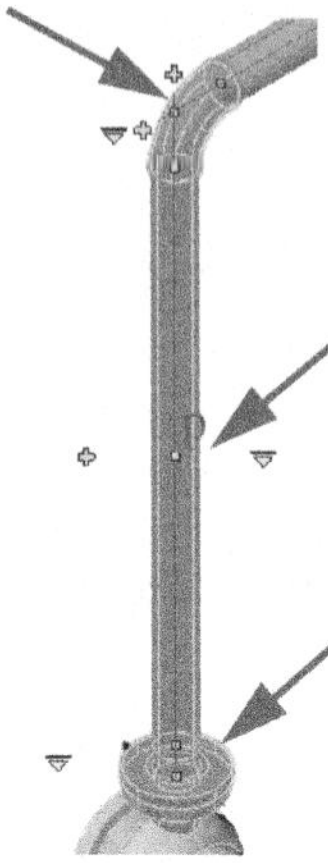

20. Use a crossing window as shown to select the objects that make the configuration from the pump (right side) to the horizontal pipe.

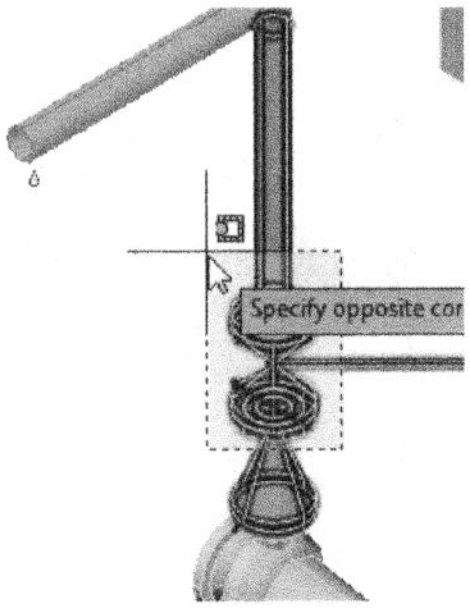

21. Use the AutoCAD **Copy** command to copy the objects to the other pump whose piping was deleted. Use the Node or the Center object snap as the base point.

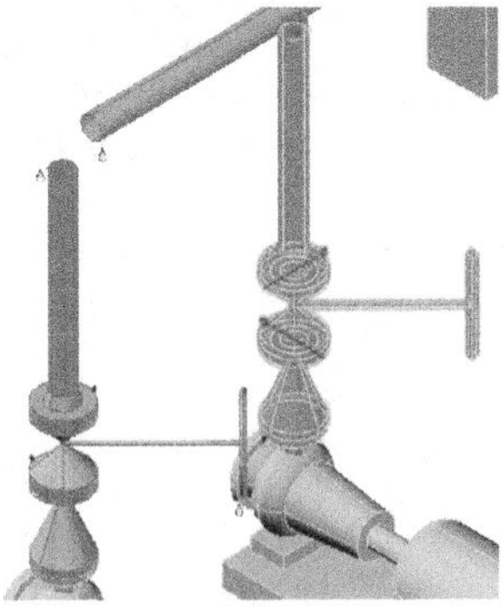

22. Select the vertical pipe of the copied objects. Click Continue Pipe Routing.

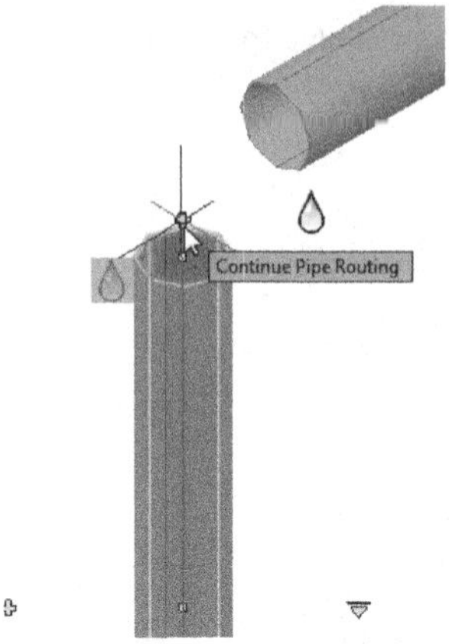

23. To specify the next point, select the node/endpoint on the horizontal pipe as shown in the following illustration. You might have to use <Ctrl>+right-click for the rotation angle.

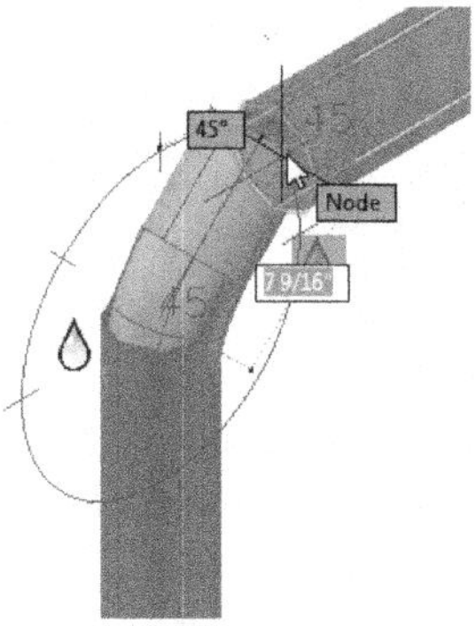

24. Press <Enter> to accept.

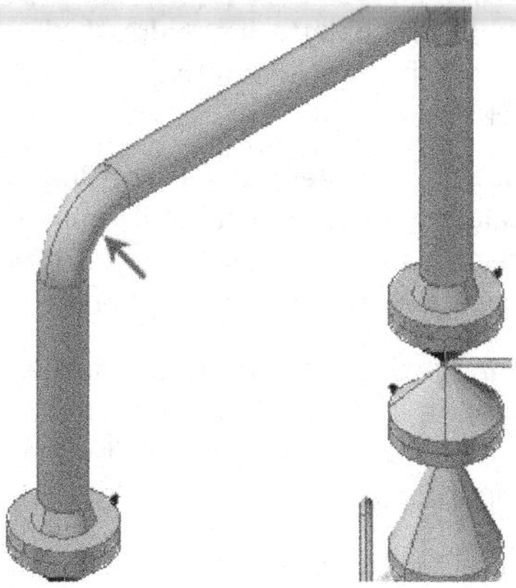

Change Pipe Elevation

In this section of the exercise, you use grips to change the elevation of a pipe.

1. Zoom out so you can see the entire section of 4" pipe.

2. Select the long horizontal section of pipe.

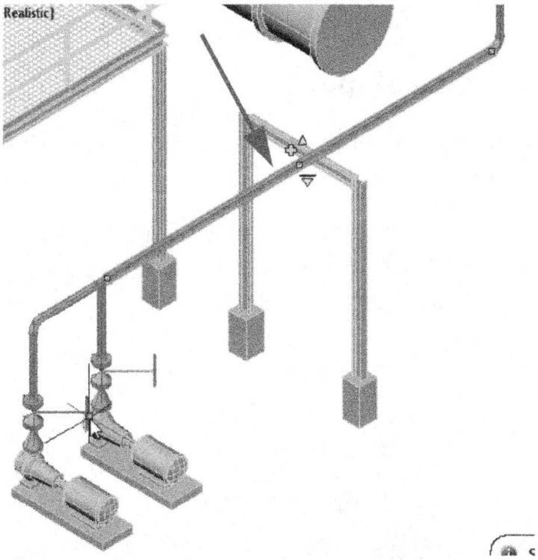

3. Click Change Pipe Elevation.

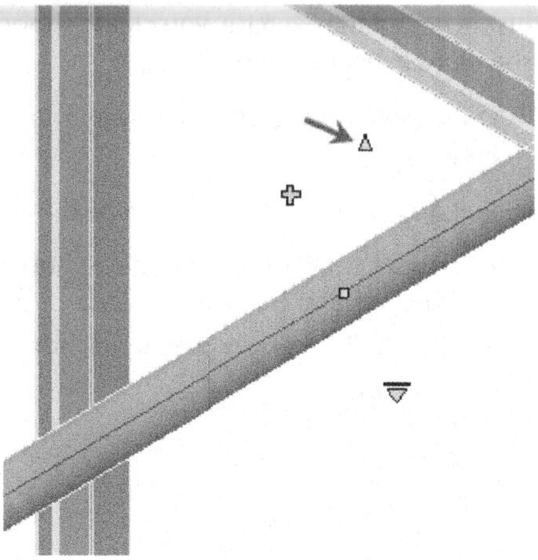

4. Press TAB repeatedly until BOP:8′ (the left most edit box) is highlighted.

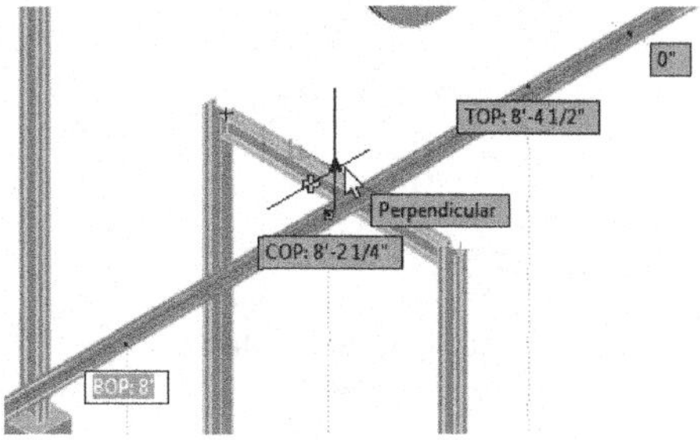

5. Enter **10'** and press <Enter> to accept the values. Press <Esc> to end the selection.

   The horizontal pipe run is moved above the steel structure. All connected pipes are stretched accordingly.

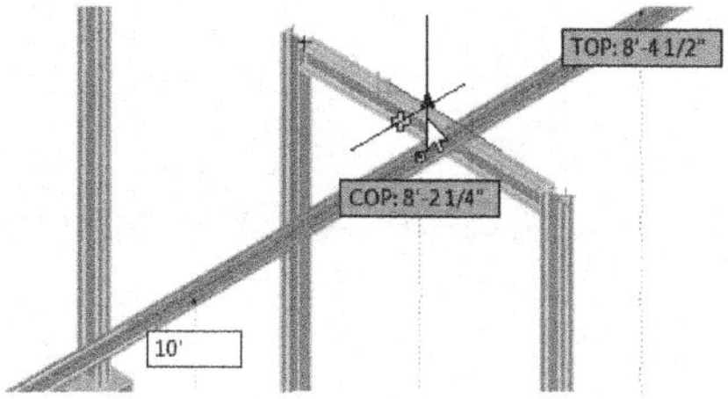

Create Pipe Supports

In this section of the exercise, you create supports for the pipes in your drawing.

1. On the Home tab, on the Pipe Supports panel, click Create.
2. In the Add Pipe Support dialog box:
   - From the filter buttons, select Shoes, Anchors and Guides.
   - Select Clamped shoe/slide/anchor 1.
   - Click OK.

3. To specify the insertion point, use the Nearest object snap to select a point on the pipe above the steel structure as shown (the long horizontal 4" pipe).

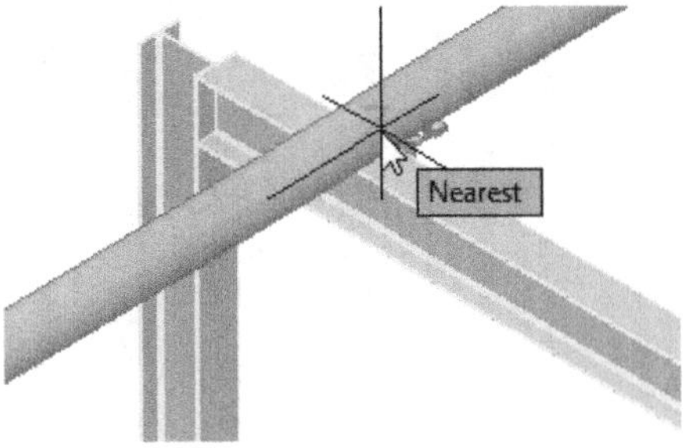

4. Press <Enter> to end the command.

   The support is added to the pipe.

5. If it is not sitting correctly on the steel structure, select the support and open the Properties palette, if not already displayed. Under the Part Geometry>Dimensions, for SH, enter **7 1/4"**.

   Note: As an alternative to the Properties palette you can select the support after you place it and select the Change Support Elevation grip to set the elevation.

6. Change the view so you can see that the pipe support is sitting on the steel structure. Move the support, if required, to be located over the support structure.

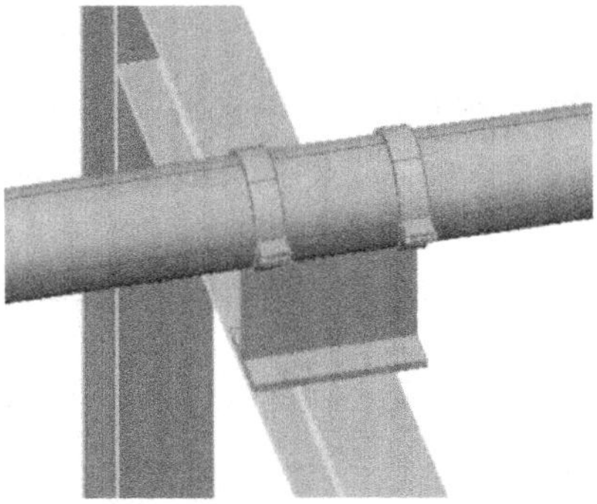

Edit Pipe Slope

In this section of the exercise, you edit the slope of the pipe.

1. Use the ViewCube to activate the Northwest Isometric view. On the Home tab, on the Visibility Panel, click Show All.

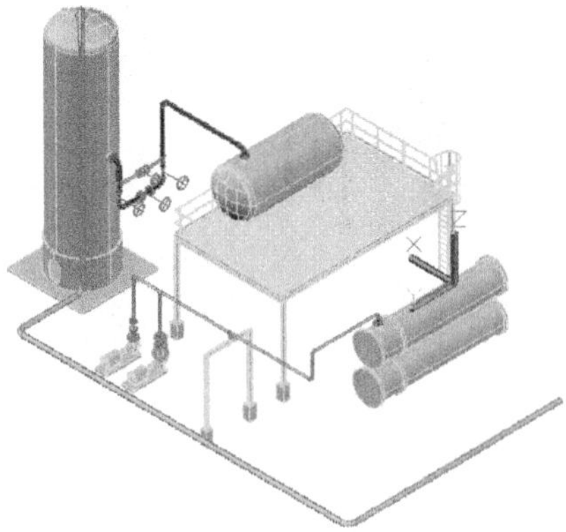

2. Select the long horizontal segment of 8" pipe. Right-click. Click Pipe Slope Editing.

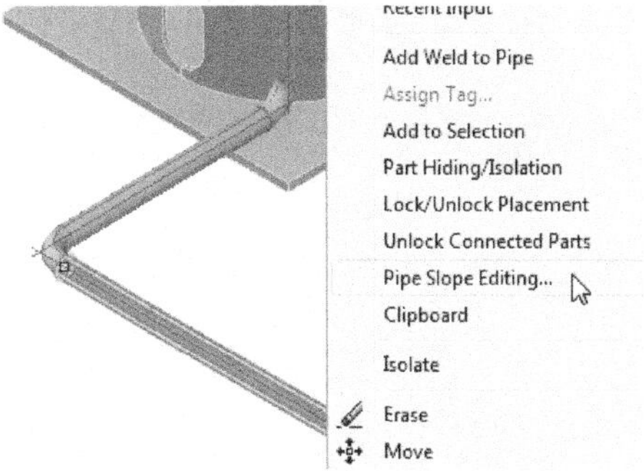

3. In the Edit Slope dialog box, click Start Point.

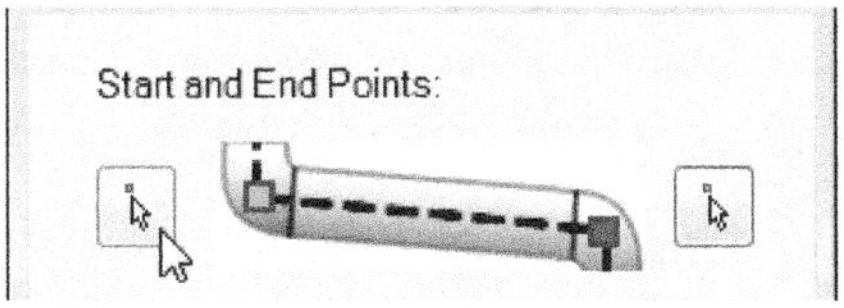

4. To specify the start point for the slope, select a point near the red dot on the pipe as shown in the following illustration.

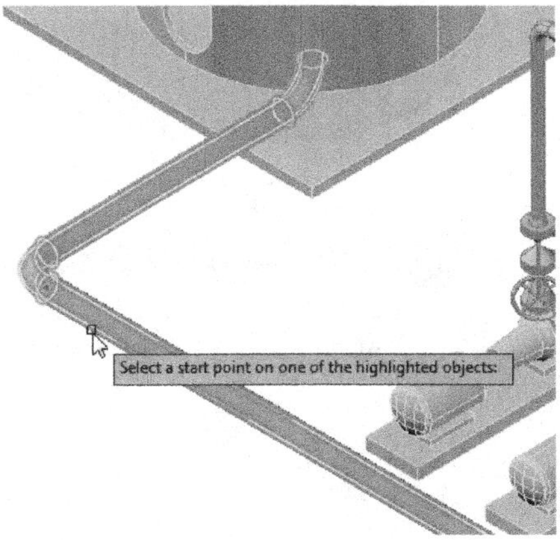

5. In the Edit Slope dialog box, click End Point.

6. To specify the end point for the slope, select a point near the end of the pipe run as shown in the following illustration.

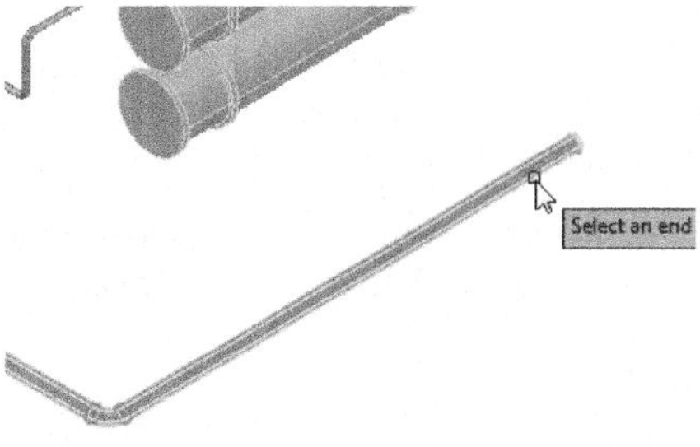

7. In the Edit Slope dialog box:

- From the Calculation list, select Slope.
- For End Elevation, enter **4"**.
- Click OK.

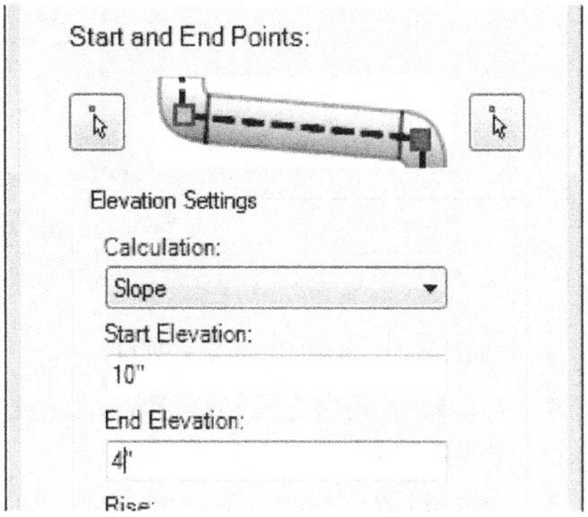

8. Use the ViewCube to activate the Back view. Note that the blue 8" pipe slopes downward to the right.

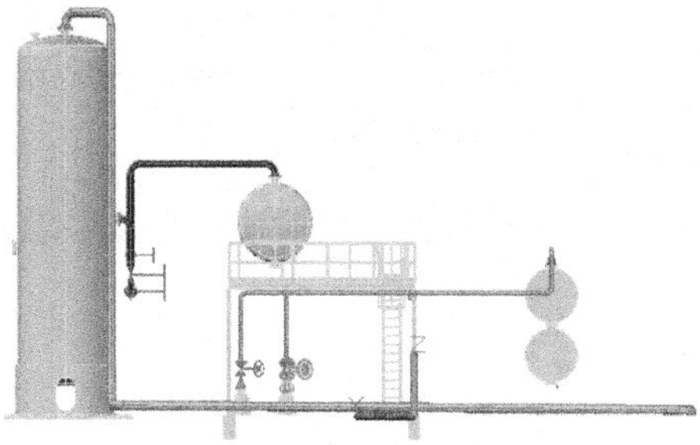

Create Pipes from AutoCAD Lines

In this section of the exercise, you create pipes from AutoCAD lines.

1. Use the Hide Selected tool on the Home tab, on the Visibility panel, to hide the steel structures and the sloped pipe.
2. Activate the Front view and then use the ViewCube Orbit to get a view similar to the one shown.

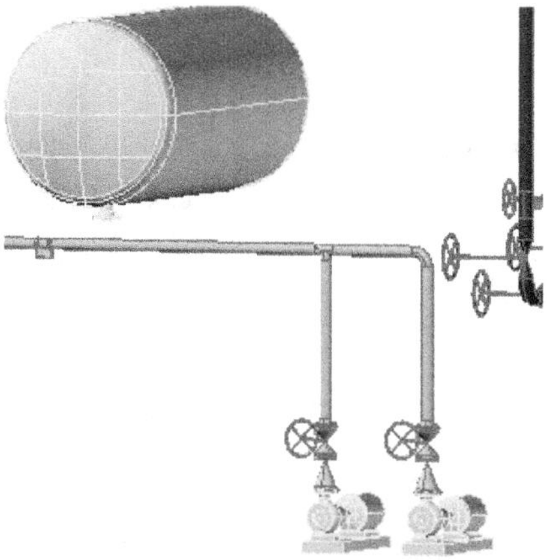

3. To insert a block with AutoCAD lines:
   - On the Insert tab, on the Block panel, click the Insert drop-down list.
   - Select Recent Blocks at the bottom of the drop-down list.
   - In the Blocks palette, switch to Current Drawing tab, and from the gallery, select Pipe Lines.
   - Verify that Insertion point is checked.
   - In the Scale list, for X, enter **1**, if required.
   - Select Explode.

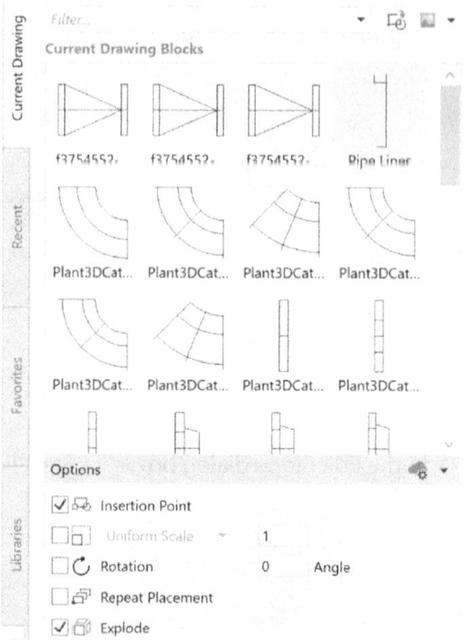

4. Double-click on Pipe Lines and then specify an insertion point by selecting the Node osnap on the bottom nozzle of the vessel. Close the Blocks palette.

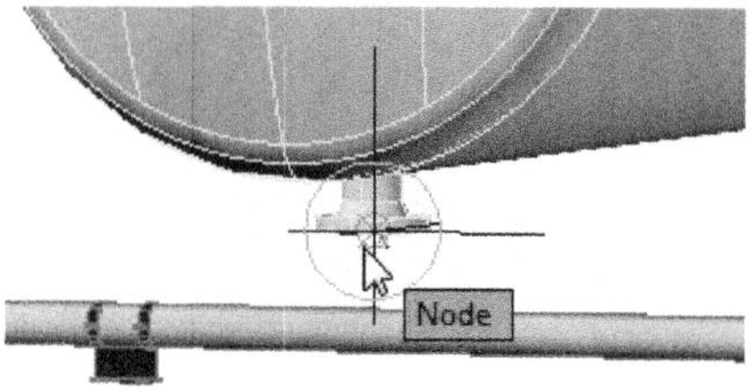

The AutoCAD lines are added to the drawing.

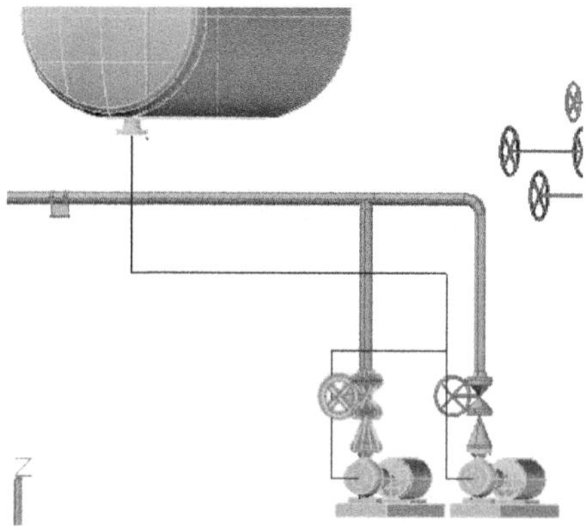

5. On the Home tab, on the Part Insertion panel:
   - From the Pipe Size list, select 6".
   - Click Line to Pipe.
6. To specify the AutoCAD lines to convert, drag a window around all the AutoCAD lines inserted from the block and press <Enter>.

   The lines are converted to pipes with the required fittings and elbows.

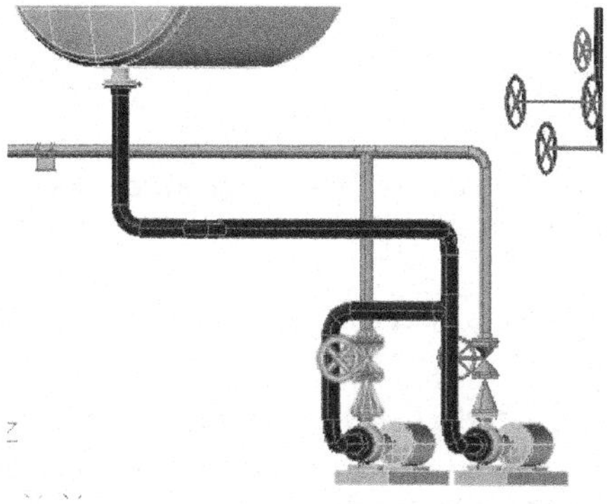

7. Place a globe valve in each short pipe segment as shown in the following illustration. Use the Globe Valve, FL, RF, 300 on the Tool Palettes.

8. Save and close all drawings.

Lesson Review Questions

1. To change a pipe diameter from the size originally set in the Part Insertion panel, you can access the Properties palette and change the Size parameter value.
   a. True
   b. False
2. How do you change the direction of the compass that is used while routing pipe to determine its direction? (Select all that apply.)
   a. Press <Ctrl>+right-click.
   b. Click Plane in the context menu.
   c. Select the correct elbows and bends in the specification.
3. When placing a fitting or a valve, multiple dimension scenarios display, enabling you to select the dimensioning type to use to locate the component along the pipe. How can you toggle between the dimensioning types?
   a. Dimension types cannot be changed; a valve is always placed in the same way.
   b. Press <Tab> to toggle between values.
   c. You can only change the basepoint of the valve, not which dimension you want to use.
4. Which of the following best describe actions that can be performed in the AutoCAD Plant 3D software when working with supports? (Select all that apply.)
   a. Pipe supports are placed using the Tool Palette.
   b. Existing supports can be modified by editing their properties.
   c. Support types and sizes are automatically applied where required in a drawing.
   d. Converting AutoCAD objects for use as supports.
   e. Pipe supports can be created from predefined parametric shapes.
   f. Pipe supports automatically resize to the pipe they are attached to.

Lesson: Piping Editing and Advanced Topics

Overview

In this lesson, you learn to reuse parts and models in the drawing and between drawings. You also learn about creating custom parts and placing placeholder parts. To help you change a line number, size, or spec, you learn how to make selections correctly and how to lock or isolate objects.

Objectives

After completing this lesson, you will be able to:

- Copy parts and pipeline sections in a single drawing or from one drawing to another.
- Setup Xrefs for best use in Plant3D.
- Understand what placeholders are and how to place custom parts.
- Select entire pipe runs.
- Isolate, lock, and unlock pipes and components.

Copying Parts and Pipeline Sections

You can copy parts and sections of a pipeline in a single drawing or from one drawing to another. You use the AutoCAD Copy command to duplicate parts or sections of a pipeline in a single drawing. You use the traditional Copy/Paste features located on the Clipboard section of the context menu to duplicate them from one drawing to another, as shown in the following illustration. The Copy/Paste Clipboard features can also be used in a single drawing. You can also use the keyboard shortcuts <Ctrl>+<X>, <Ctrl>+<C>, <Ctrl>+<Shift>+<C>, <Ctrl>+<V>, and <Ctrl>+<Shift>+<V> to copy parts or pipeline from one drawing to another. Access to the Clipboard options can also be found in the right-click context menu.

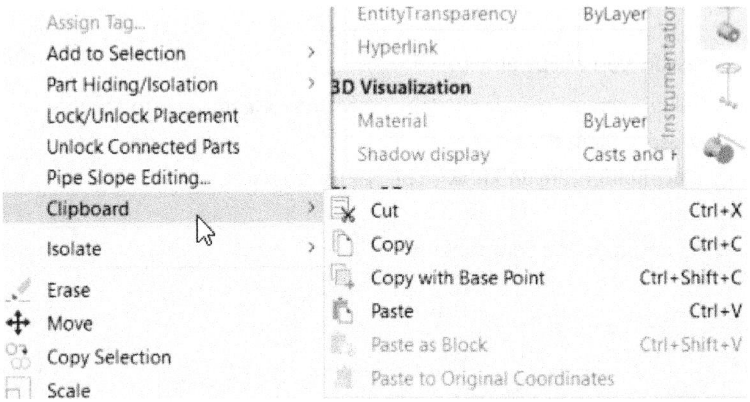

When you copy parts and/or pipelines, the tags might need to be reassigned. Line numbers tags also need to be assigned to copied pipelines, as shown in the following illustration.

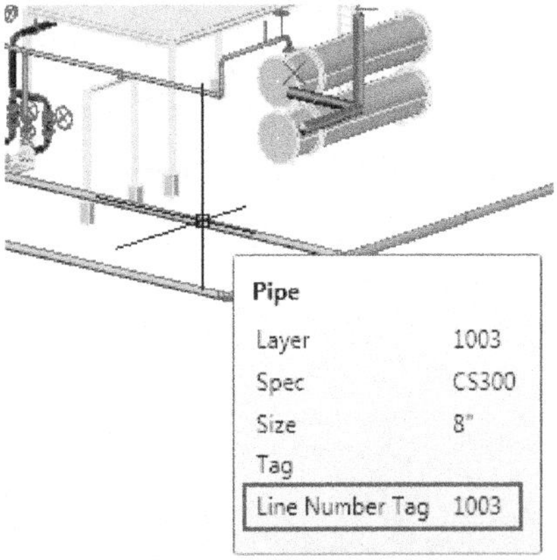

Line number tag of 1003 applied to original pipeline

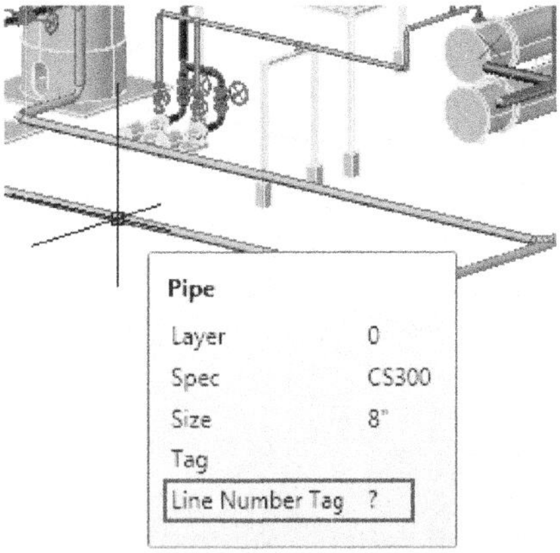

Copied pipeline without a line number tag assigned

Managing Changes in Xref files

When working with project files in the AutoCAD Plant 3D software, it is recommended that you reference the files (using Xrefs) with relative paths, as shown in the following illustration. This enables the project files to be moved or shared with others without the links to the referenced files being lost.

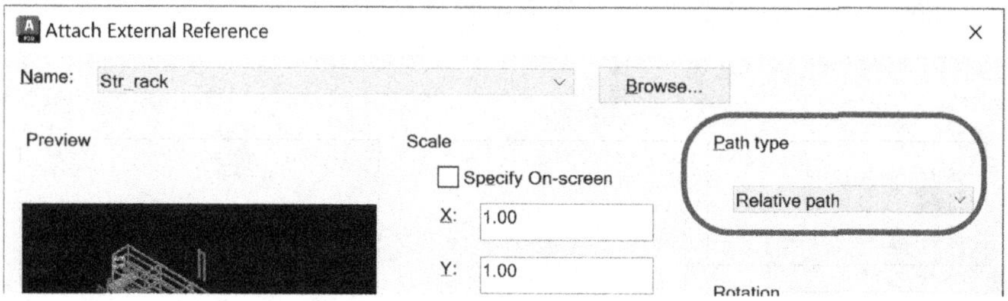

Adding External References

Before adding an external reference to a Plant 3D drawing, ensure that the file you are going to attach is already copied to the project and listed in the Project Manager. All external references attached to project drawings also need to be project drawings. External references can be added using traditional AutoCAD commands or by using the shortcut menu in the Project Manager, as shown in the following illustration.

To add an external reference to a drawing in Plant 3D, you must first open the host drawing. With the host drawing active, right-click on the drawing to be attached in the Project Manager and select Xref into current DWG. This opens the traditional Attach External Reference dialog box, where you can specify the placement options and click OK to attach the Xref.

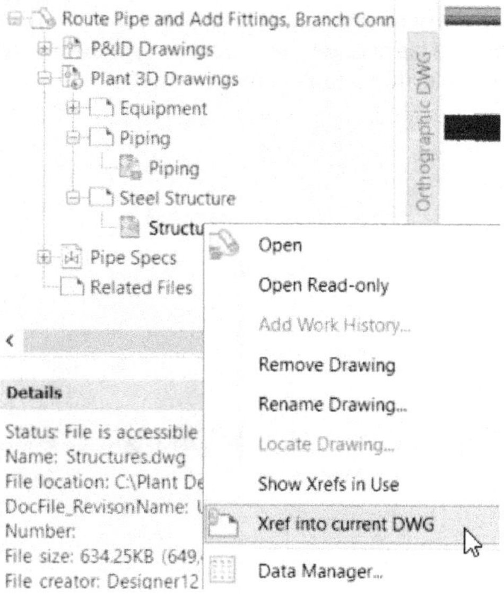

Viewing External References

To view which files are attached to a project drawing, you can right-click on a drawing in the Project Manager and select Show Xrefs in Use (or Refresh Xref List). This loads a list of the Xrefs without the need to open the host drawing. All attached files are listed beneath the drawing in the Project Manager, as shown in the following illustration. The view of this listing is only temporary and when the Project Manager is refreshed, all attachments listed are hidden.

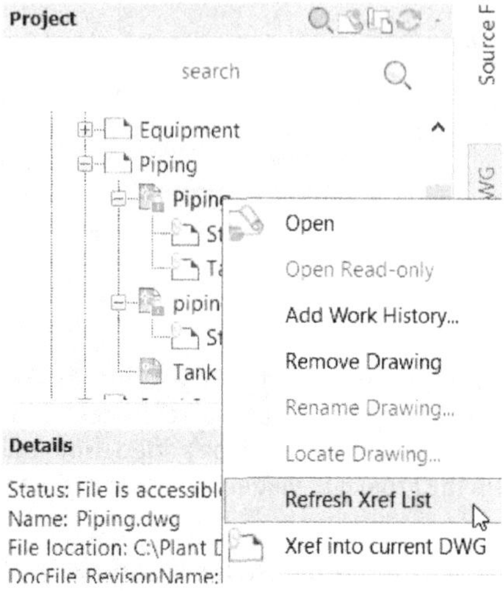

External References Palette

The AutoCAD External References palette can be used to view and manage any attached files. If the path of a referenced file is lost, you use the External References palette to locate the file, as shown in the following illustration. You can browse to find the file or enter the correct path of the file. You enter **.** or **..** at the beginning of the path to manually indicate that the path is relative to a project folder. For example, .*Tanks.dwg*.

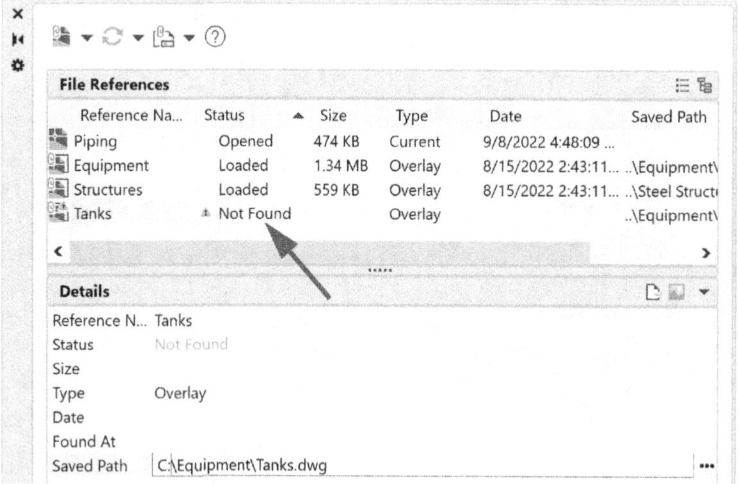

Custom Parts: Permanent and Placeholder

Custom parts are parts that you place in a specific drawing that are not listed in the project specification sheets. They are independent of a project specification and are representative of the overall dimensions. Custom parts can be defined as Permanent or Placeholder. Placeholder parts are placed in anticipation of an equivalent part being created in the project specification. When the equivalent part is created, the placeholder part is replaced using the Substitute option with a valid part from the project specification. Permanent and Placeholder parts look the same in the piping system. However, when selected a placeholder part is identified with a yellow exclamation mark symbol, as shown in the following illustration.

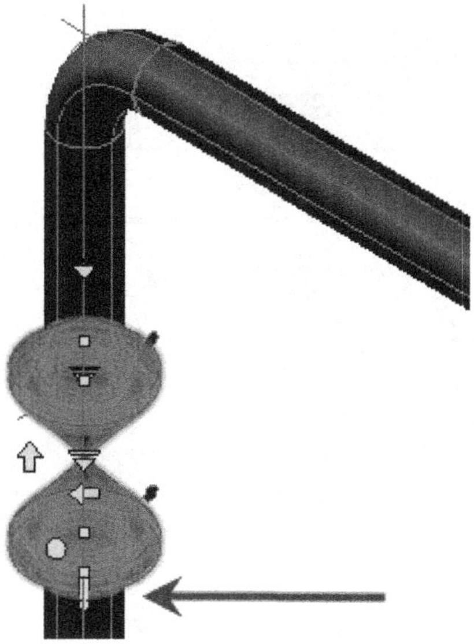

To create custom parts you use the Custom Parts Builder Palette, as shown in the following illustration. To open the Palette, select the Custom Parts tool in the Home tab, on the Part Insertion panel. To begin, select the Part Type from list and then select whether the custom part is based on Plant 3D shapes or AutoCAD Blocks. Using Plant 3D, you can select from the Shape Browser to select a shape for the selected part type. Once selected, its default dimensions and custom properties appear on the right side of the Palette for you to edit as required to customize your part. If creating the part based on AutoCAD Blocks, you can select the block from a model or import it from a DWG. Once you have defined the properties for the custom part, click Insert in Model and place the component.

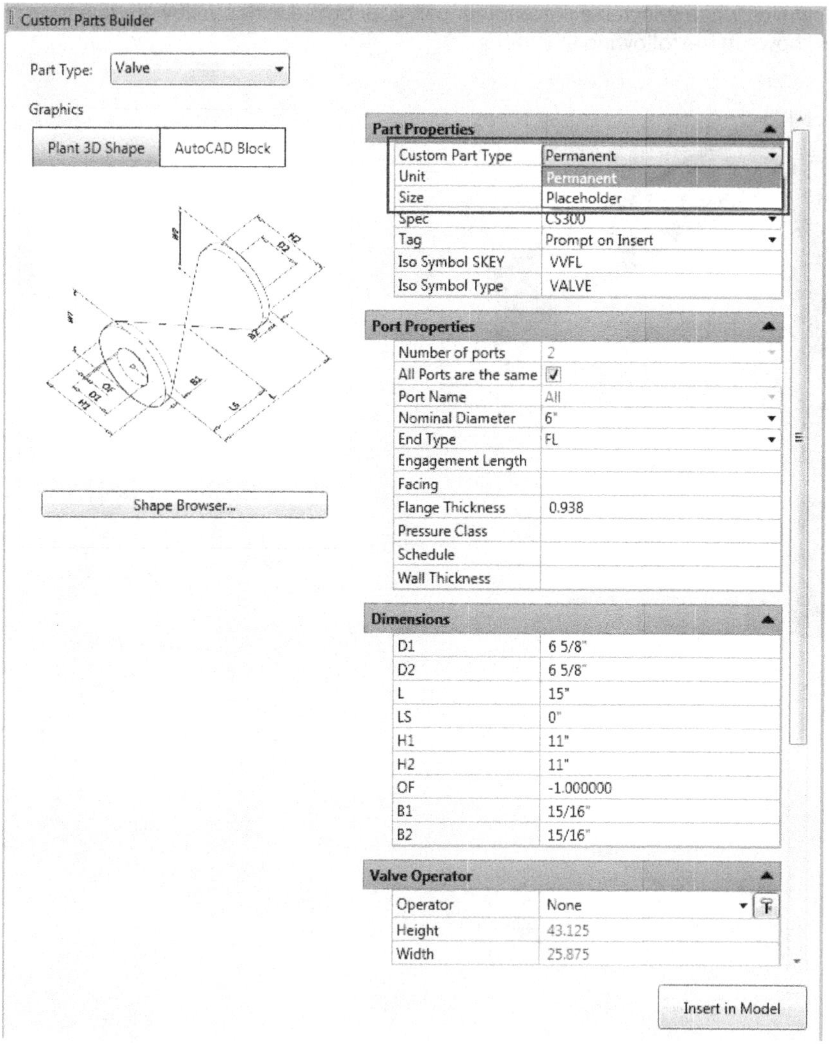

Selecting an Entire Pipe Run

Tools for selecting an entire pipe run are available when you select and right-click on any object that is part of a pipe run, as shown in the following illustration. On the shortcut menu, under Add to Selection, you can specify to select all objects in the drawing that connect to the current selection, share a connected path between the current selection, connected and share the same line number, or you can select the all parts with same line or spool number.

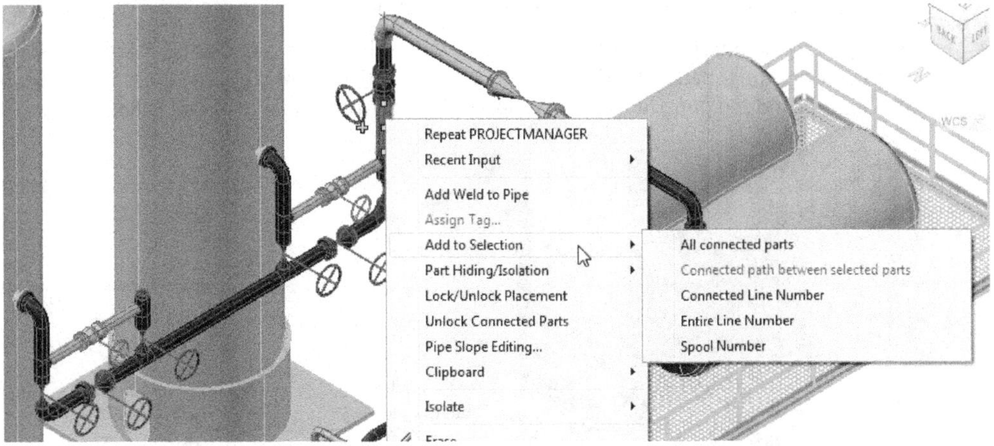

Connected objects selected by line number are shown in the following illustration.

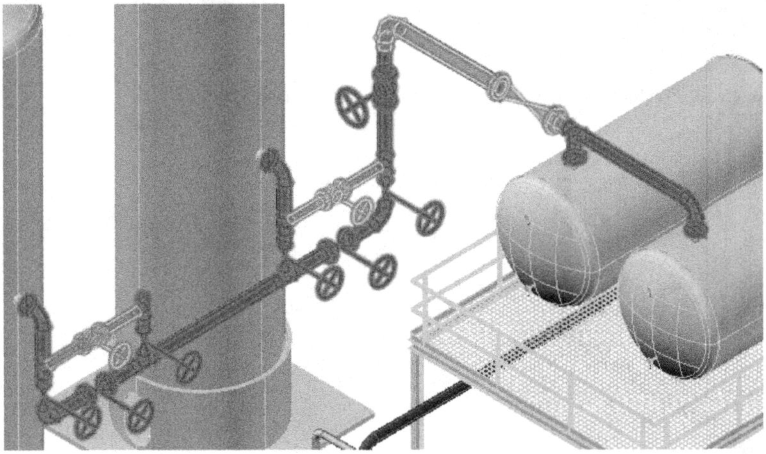

Isolate, Hide, and Lock Pipe Runs

You use the Part Hiding/Isolation option on the shortcut menu of selected objects to hide or isolate them. When you hide selected objects, they no longer display. When you isolate them, all other objects in the drawing are hidden and only the selected objects display. This enables you to more clearly view the objects you need to work on in a drawing.

You can end the hiding/isolation of parts when you no longer need the objects hidden or isolated. When you end the hiding/isolation of parts, all objects in the drawing are again displayed.

Note: Object isolation/hiding does not affect the layers the objects are placed on, and the status of the layer overrides the isolation/hidden status, as shown in the following illustration. For example, if an object is on a hidden or frozen layer, it is not displayed when you end object isolation.

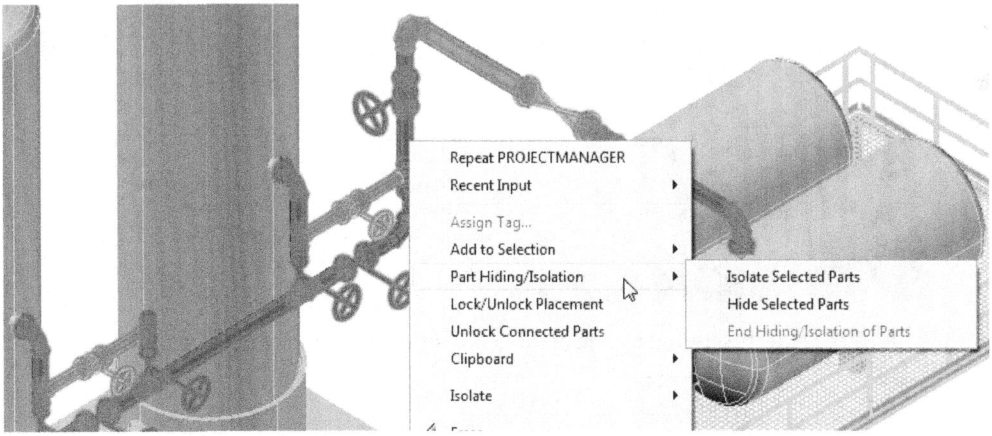

Once isolated, the drawing displays as shown in the following illustration.

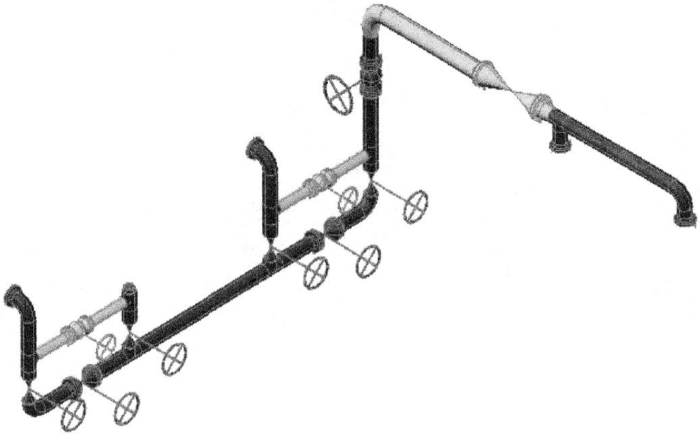

Lock and Unlock Pipes

You can lock the placement of one or more pipes and parts so that they cannot be moved. Modifications to component properties can still be made and it can also be deleted. To lock placement, use the Lock/Unlock Placement option on the shortcut menu when the components are selected, as shown in the following illustration. You also use the Lock/Unlock Placement option on the shortcut menu to unlock selected object(s). Or you unlock an entire pipe run using the Unlock Connected Parts option.

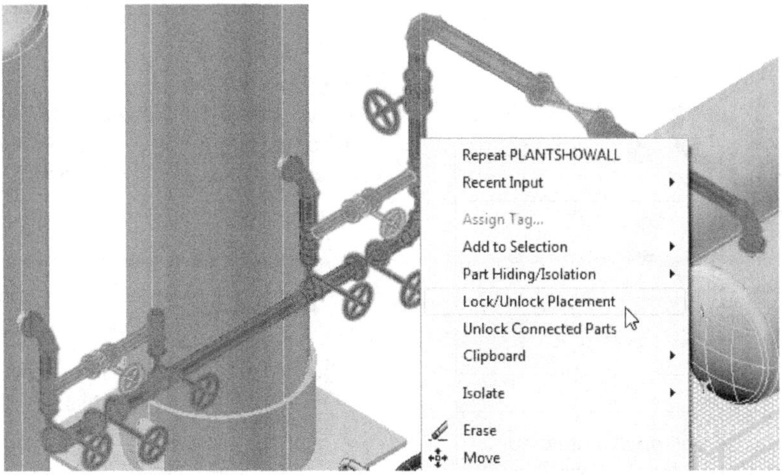

Once a pipe has been locked, selecting it displays a locked symbol as a visual indication that the pipe cannot be moved, as shown in the following illustration.

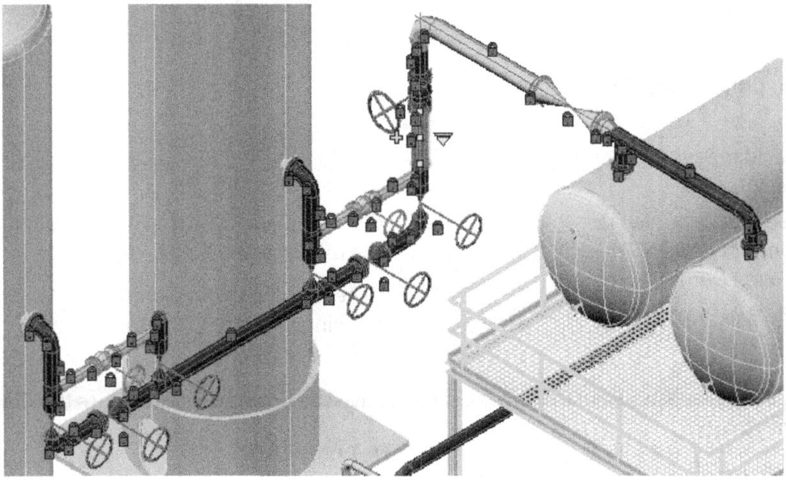

Exercise: Modify and Reuse Data

In this exercise, you reuse sections of pipeline in a single drawing and between multiple drawings. You also use auto connect to connect the pipes and make necessary modifications to the pipelines.

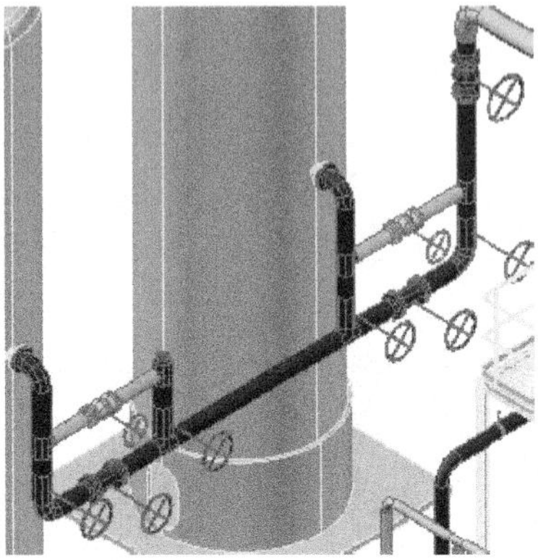

Correct Xref Path

In this section of the exercise, you open a drawing that contains an error due to the location of an Xref file. You correct the path by setting the drawing up to use a relative path.

1. Start the AutoCAD Plant 3D software, if not already running.
2. Open an existing project by doing the following:
   - In the Project Manager, Current Project list, click Open.
   - In the Open dialog box, navigate to the folder *C:\Plant Design 2024 Practice Files\Modify and Reuse Data*.
   - Select the file *Project.xml*.
   - Click Open.
3. In the Project Manager, expand Plant 3D Drawings > Piping folders.
4. Double-click on *Piping.dwg*.

   The External References palette is displayed. Under File References, note that the Tanks drawing is not found. This is because the Tanks drawing was referenced using the Full Path setting and the path has changed.
5. On the External References palette:
   - Under File References, select Tanks.
   - Under Details, for Saved Path, click on the path (which is a full path) and replace it by entering **..\Equipment\Tanks.dwg**.
   - Press <Enter> to accept the new relative path.

   This sets the drawing reference so that it uses a relative path and the drawing is found in the folder of the current project. The Found At field resolves to display the full path.

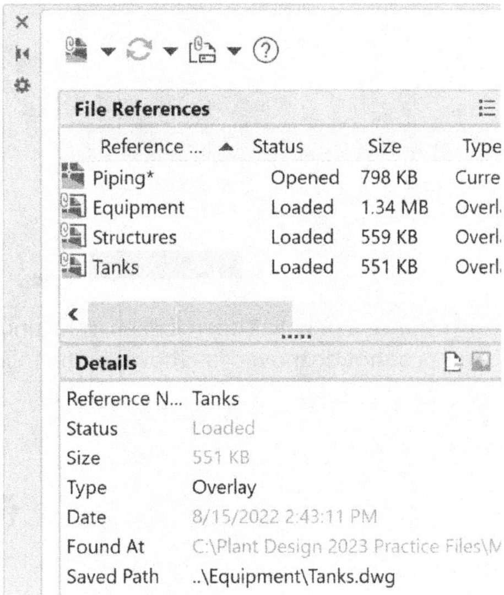

6. Click the Refresh button in the Xref palette if the drawing needs to be reloaded.

   Note that the two tanks are displayed in the drawing window. Close the External References palette.
7. Save the drawing. Do not close the drawing.

Insert a New Xref

1. Open piping_002.dwg.
2. In the Project Manager, expand the Steel Structure folder. Right-click on Str_rack and select Xref into current DWG.

3. In the Attach External Reference dialog box, set the following settings:
   - Reference Type: Overlay
   - Scale: Verify Specify- On-screen is cleared.
   - Insertion Point: Clear specify On-screen and verify X,Y,Z display 0,0,0
   - Path type: Relative path
   - Rotation Angle: 0

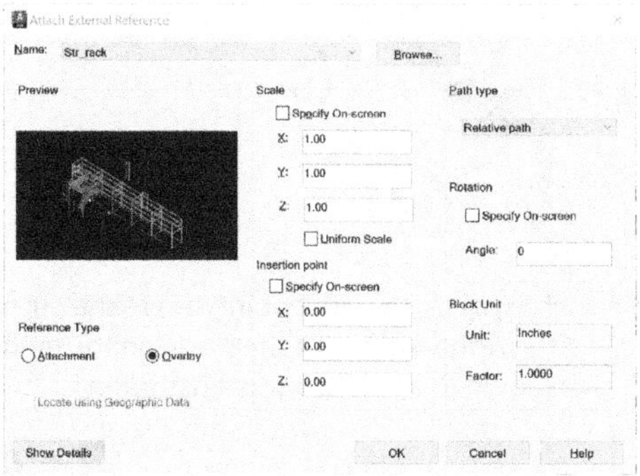

4. Click OK to place the Xref.
5. In the Project Manager, right-click on piping_002 and select Refresh Xref List. Note that the Str_Rack node displays.
6. Repeat Step 5 in the Project Manager for Piping.dwg.

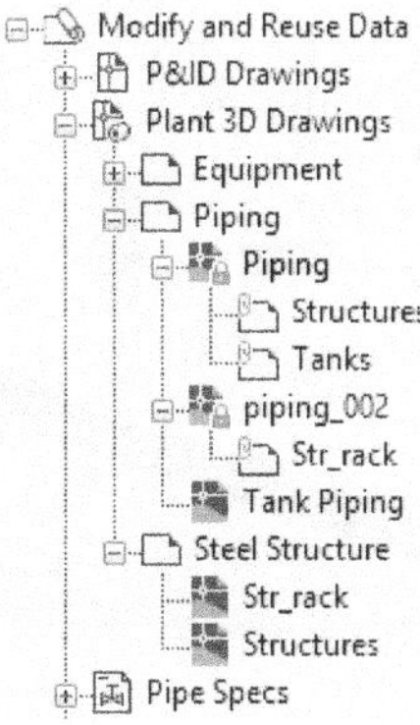

7. Save and close piping_002.

Copy and Connect a Pipe Run

In this section of the exercise, you copy a pipe run with all of its components in a single drawing. You connect the new pipe run to the old one and assign a line number tag to the copied objects.

1. Verify that the Piping drawing is open. Use the AutoCAD **Select** command and the window option to select the pipes, connectors, and valves as shown in the following illustration. Forty-three objects are selected.

   Note: Use the ViewCube to display the Back view. Then, using the Select command and a selection window, select the objects (42 objects are selected). Select the remaining object (flange) individually in the North West isometric view. Do not select the nozzle. Verify that forty-three objects are selected. If required, press <Shift> and click to deselect any extra object from the group.

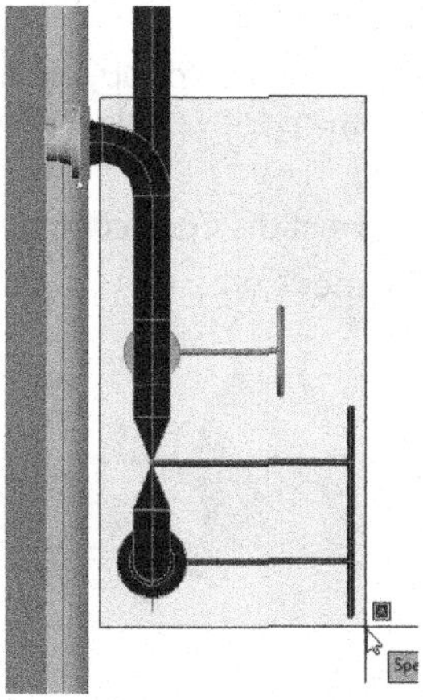

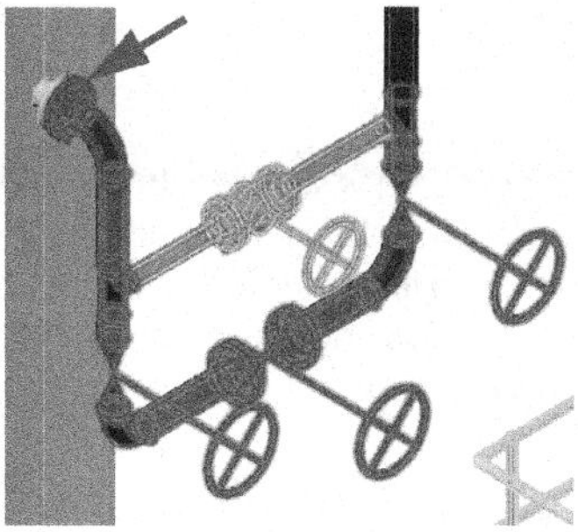

2. Right-click on the selected objects. Click Part Hiding/Isolation, and click Isolate Selected Parts.

   Only the selected objects are visible in the drawing. All others are hidden.

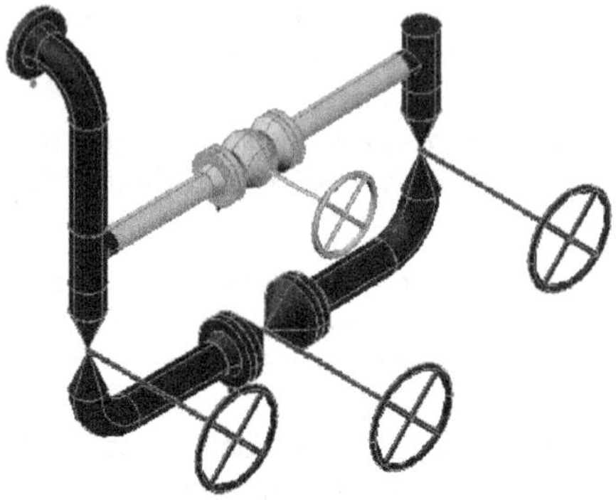

3. Select all visible parts.

4. To copy the objects:
   - Toggle Ortho mode on.
   - Use the **Copy** command to copy all visible objects **16'** in the positive Y-direction (towards left).
   - Press <Esc> to exit the Copy command.
   - Toggle Ortho mode off.

5. Verify that nothing is selected. In the copied objects, select the elbow (right side) as shown in the following illustration. Select the Continue Pipe Routing grip as shown in the following illustration.

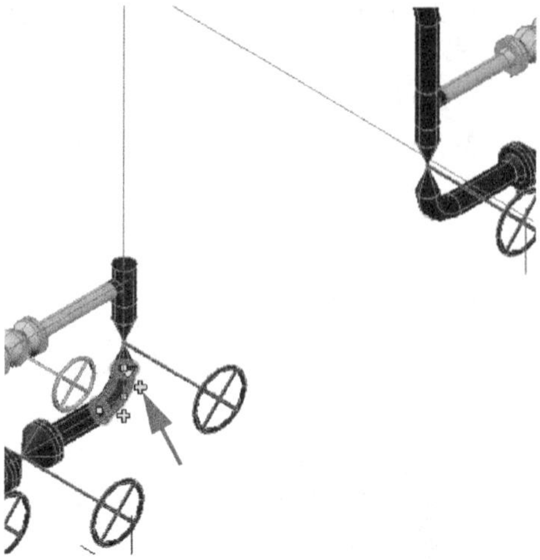

6. To specify the next point, move the cursor to the right and select the Node on the elbow as shown in the following illustration.

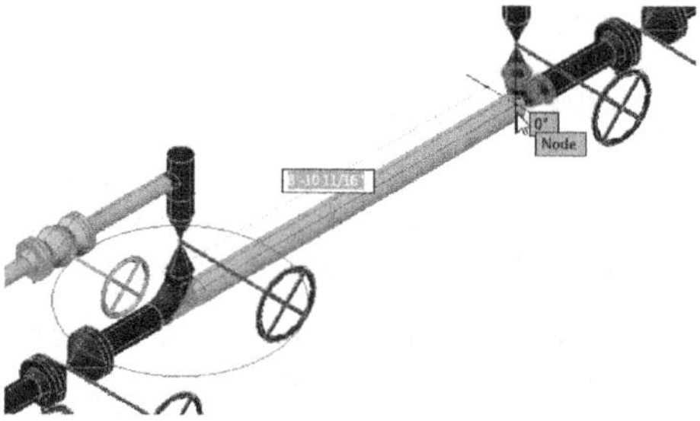

7. Note that the pipes are connected and both elbows are replaced with tees.

8. On the Tool Palettes, on the Dynamic Pipe Spec tab, under Cap, click CAP,BV,40.

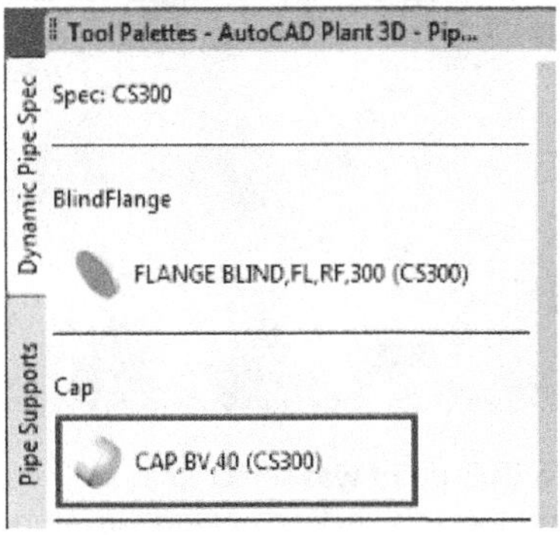

9. To specify the insertion point, select the top Node on the open pipe (copied pipes) as shown in the following illustration.

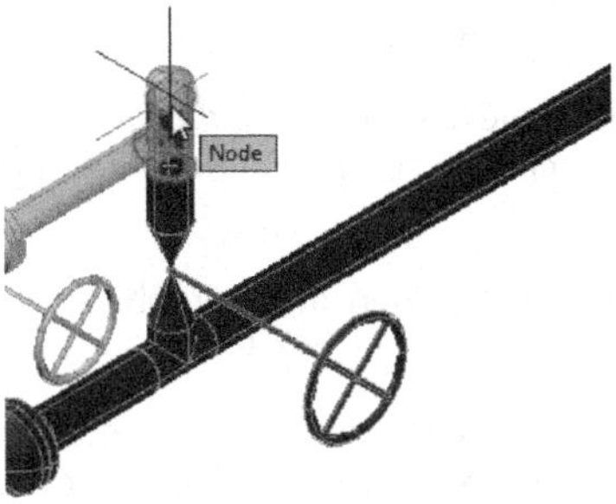

10. To specify the rotation, enter **0**.

11. Press <Enter> to end the command. The cap is added to close off the pipe.

12. Hold the cursor over any of the copied pipes. Note that there are no line number tags assigned to the objects that were copied.

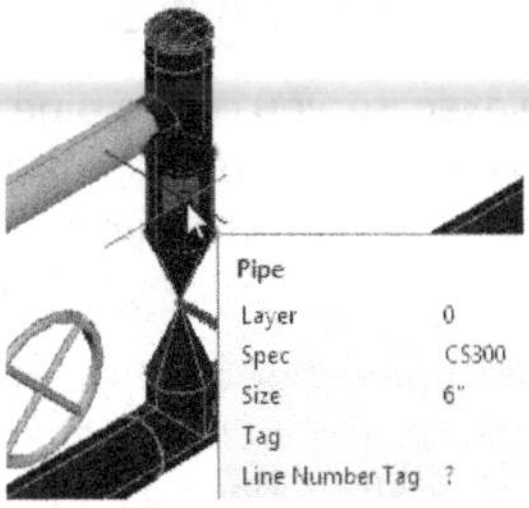

13. To assign a line number tag to the objects:
    - Open the Properties palette, if not already displayed.
    - Select all the copied objects, by first selecting the newly drawn connection and then using the Add To Selection> Connected Line Number shortcut menu option.
    - On the Properties palette, under Tag, click VARIES, from the Line Number Tag list, and select 1001 in the drop-down list.

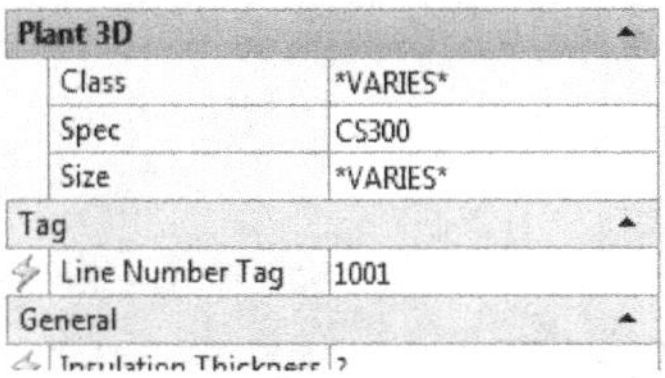

14. Press <Esc> to clear the selection.

15. Right-click anywhere in the model space. Click Plant3D>End Hiding/Isolation.

    The equipment is again displayed. The copied pipes should line up with the nozzle on the second tank.

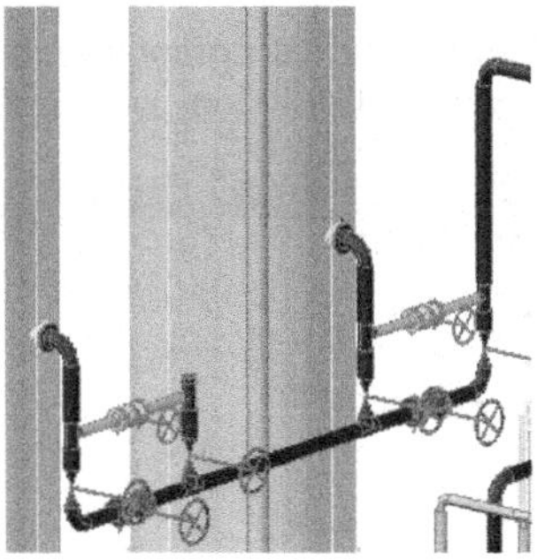

16. Save the drawing.

Copy Piping to Another Drawing

In this section of the exercise, you copy a pipe run from one drawing to another and reassign the line number tag. You also copy pipes and make the necessary connections.

1. Select the cyan colored pipe as shown in the following illustration. Right-click. Click Add to Selection, and click All connected parts.

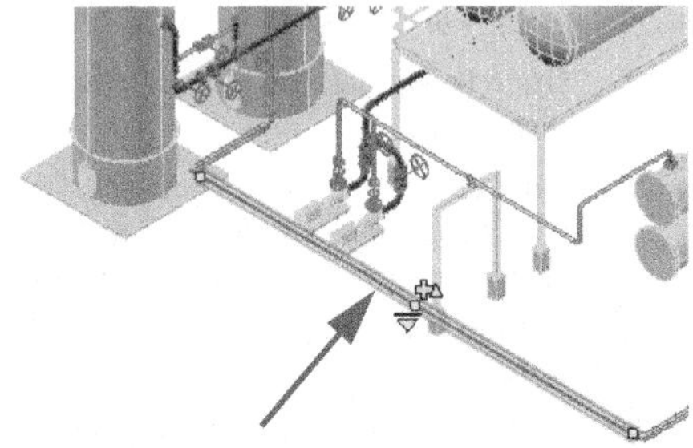

2. All connected pipes are selected.

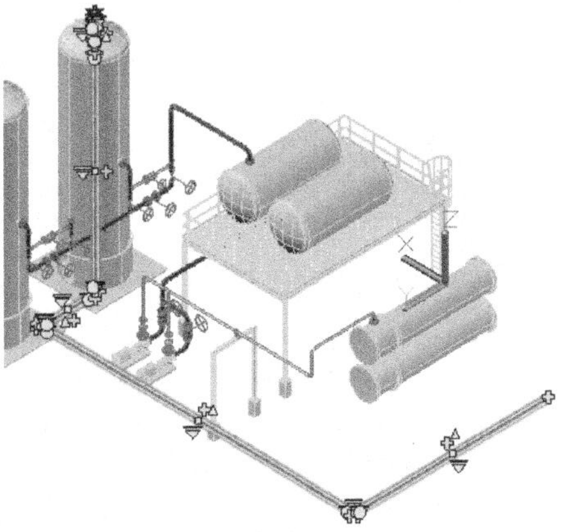

3. Right-click anywhere in the graphics window. Click Clipboard, and click Copy with Base Point.

4. Select the connection point Node on the smaller nozzle on the tank T-101 (closest to the structure) as the Base Point, as shown in the following illustration.

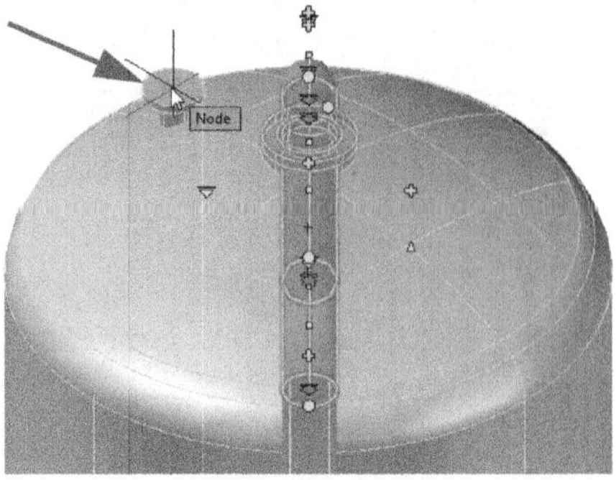

Note: This point was selected as an alternative to selecting one on the flange itself to ensure correct placement on an identical tank in another drawing.

5. Press <Delete> to remove the selected pipeline.

6. Save the drawing.

7. On the Project Manager, under Piping, double-click on the Tank Piping drawing to open it.

8. Right-click anywhere in the graphics window. Click Clipboard, and click Paste.

9. Select the smaller nozzle on the tank T-101 (closest to the structure) to locate the copied pipe as shown in the following illustration.

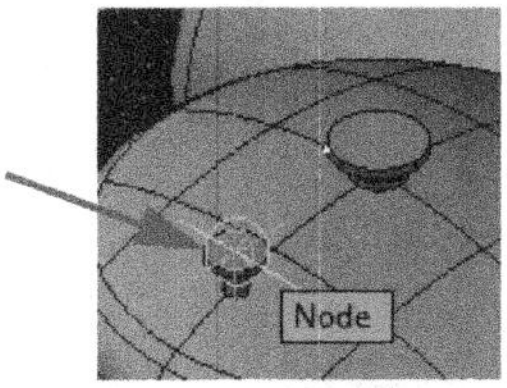

Note: There are additional copy/paste options that can be used to accomplish the same thing.

10. With the copied pipeline still on the clipboard, right-click anywhere in the graphics window, click Clipboard, and click Paste.

Note: If the Paste operation does not display the pipeline, reselect and copy it again. Use the small nozzle as the Base Point.

11. Select the smaller nozzle on the tank T-102 (farther from the structure) to place the copied pipeline.

12. Select and delete the pipe (horizontal piece on the ground, between the elbow and the end piece) as shown in the following illustration.

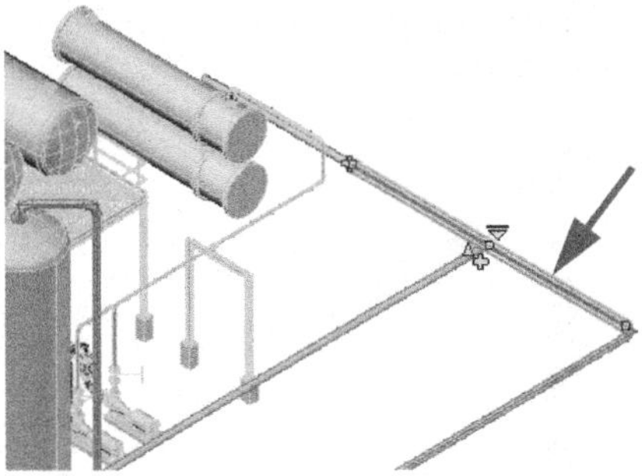

13. Select the open elbow. Click Continue Pipe Routing.

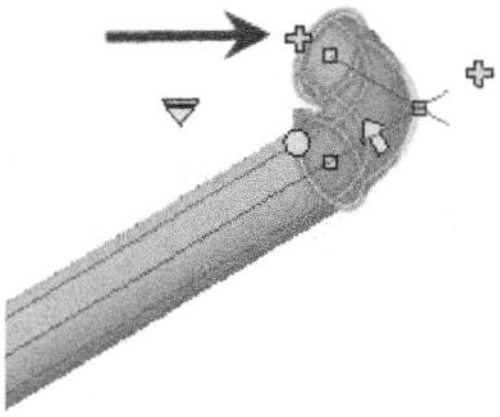

14. To specify the next point, use the Midpoint/Node object snap to select a point on the elbow, as shown in the following illustration.

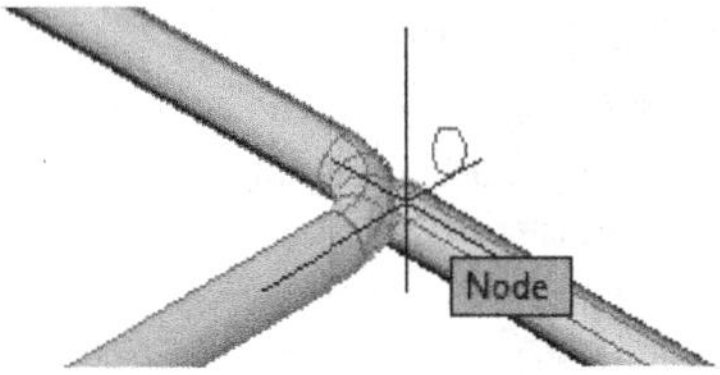

15. Review the results. The pipes are now connected, as shown in the following illustration.

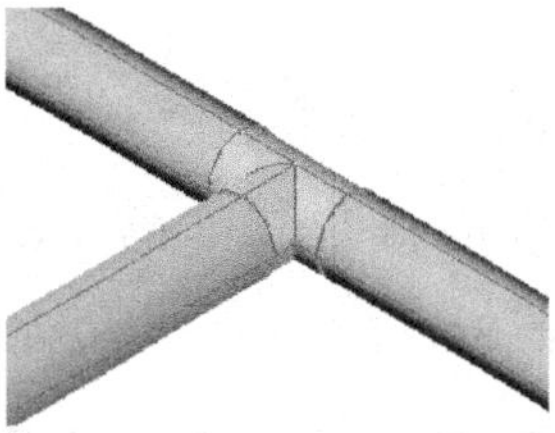

16. Hold the cursor over one of the cyan pipes. Note that the tooltip indicates that the pipe run does not have a tag assigned to it.

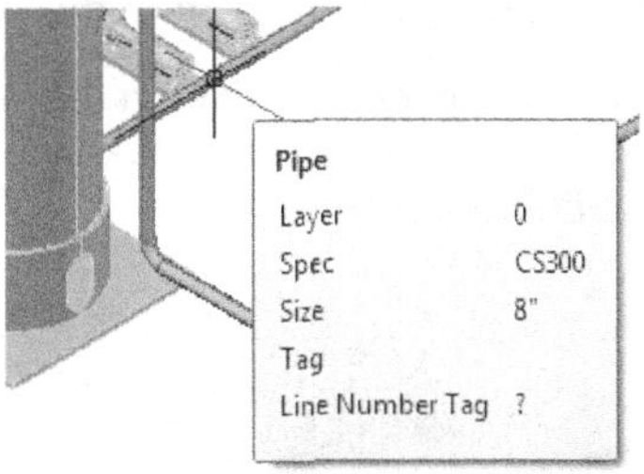

17. Select any portion of the cyan pipe. Right-click. Click Add to Selection, and click All connected parts.

18. To assign a new line number tag:

- On the Properties palette, under Tag, click VARIES. In the drop-down list, select New.
- In the Assign Tag dialog box, Number field, enter **1003**.
- Click Assign.
- Hover the cursor over any pipe and note the tag is added.

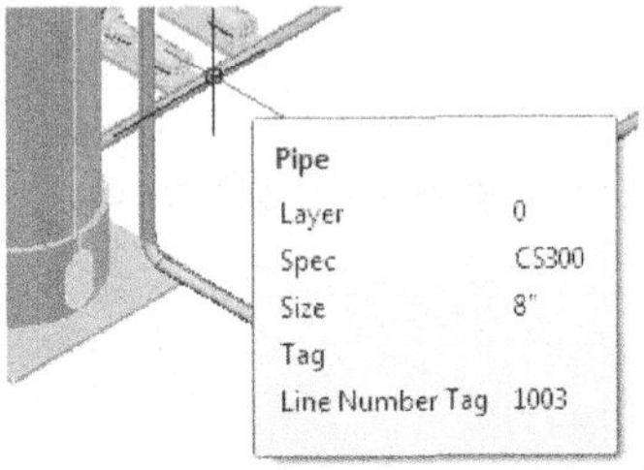

19. Save and close the Tank Piping drawing.

Create a Custom Part

In this section of the exercise, you create a custom part that does not currently exist in a project spec sheet.

1. Open the *Piping.dwg*, if not already open. Zoom to the pipe that connects to the vessel.

2. Verify that Orthomode is off. Select the elbow that connects to the vessel and click Continue Pipe Routing.

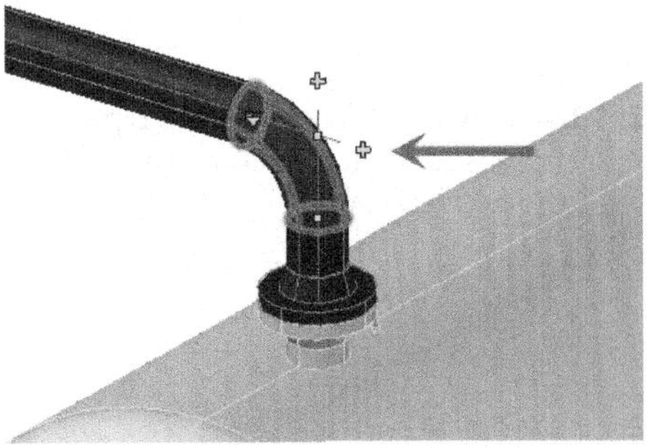

3. To specify the second point, select the Node on the top nozzle of the other vessel and click at the same point again to place it. Press <Enter>.

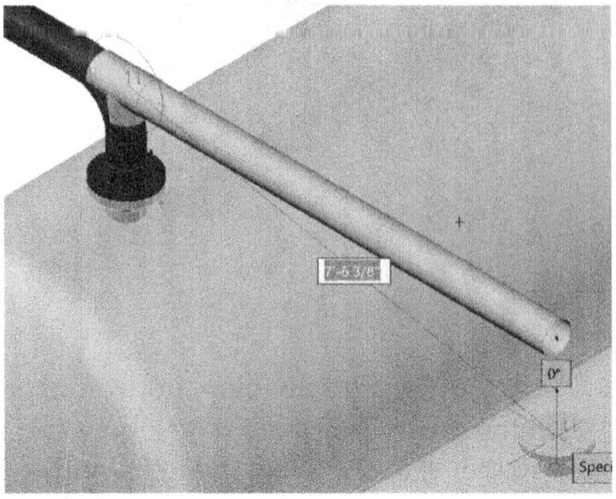

4. Select the elbow and pipe connecting to the first vessel as shown in the following illustration.

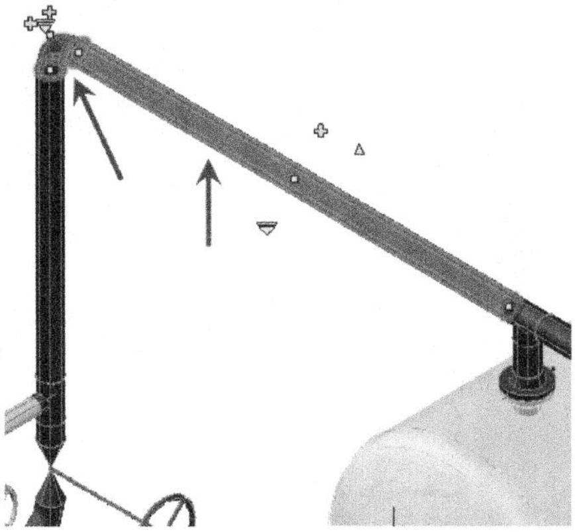

5. On the Properties palette, under Plant 3D, from the Size list, select 8".

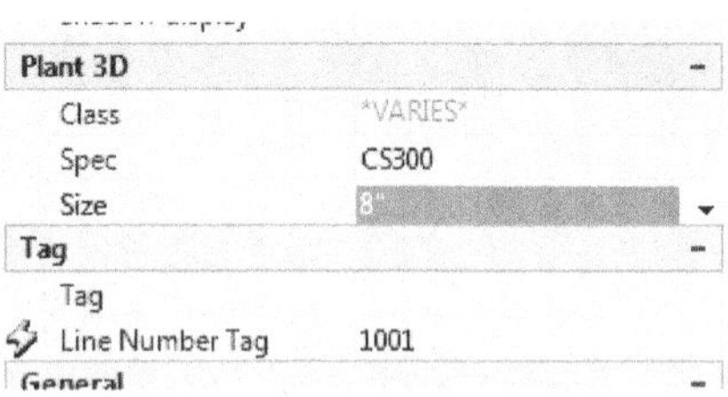

6. Press <Esc> to clear the selection.

7. On the Home tab, on the Part Insertion panel, click Custom Part.

8. In the Custom Parts Builder Palette:
   - From the Part Type list, select Valve.
   - Expand the palette to display the Part Properties section. From the Unit list, select Imperial.
   - From the Size list, select 8".

Part Properties	
Custom Part Type	Permanent
Unit	Imperial
Size	8"
Spec	Adopt spec when placed
Tag	Prompt on Insert
Iso Symbol SKEY	VVFL
Iso Symbol Type	VALVE

Note: You can click Shape Browser to select a valve shape to use. In this exercise you will just use the default shape.

9. In the Port Properties area, for the first port:
   - Ensure that All Ports are the same is selected (check mark).
   - From the End Type list, select FL.
   - For Facing, enter **RF**.
   - For Pressure Class, enter **300**.
   - Verify that Nominal Diameter is 8".

Port Properties	
Number of ports	2
All Ports are the same	☑
Port Name	All
Nominal Diameter	8"
End Type	FL
Engagement Length	
Facing	RF
Flange Thickness	
Pressure Class	300
Schedule	
Wall Thickness	

10. Click Insert in Model.

11. Select a point and rotation to place the part on the 8" pipe as shown in the following illustration. Click Cancel when prompted to assign the tag for the valve.

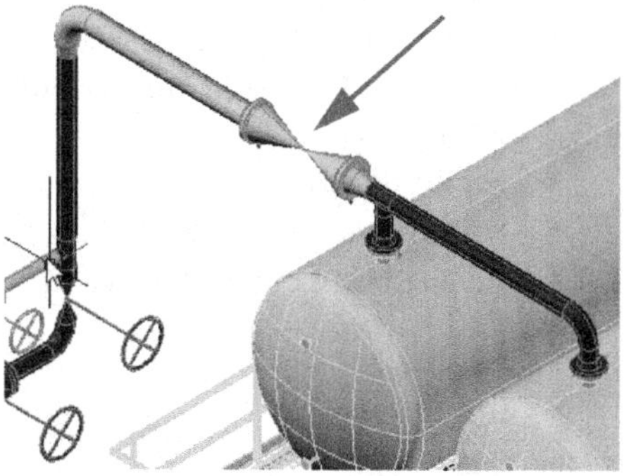

12. Press <Enter> to end the insertion.

13. Press <Esc> to cancel placement of additional valves.

Create a Placeholder Part

In this section of the exercise, you create, place, and edit a placeholder part.

1. Open the Custom Parts Builder palette, if not already opened. (Custom Part in the Part Insertion panel, or Add Custom Part in the Dynamic Pipe Spec tab in the Properties palette.)

2. In the Custom Parts Builder Palette:
   - From the Part Type list, select Valve.
   - Under Part Properties, from the Custom Part Type list, select Placeholder.
   - From the Unit list, select Imperial.
   - From the Size list, select 6".
   - From the Spec list, select CS300.
   - Under Port Properties, from the End Type list, select FL.
   - For Facing, enter **RF**.
   - For Pressure Class, enter **300**.
   - Under Dimensions, for L, enter **15"**.

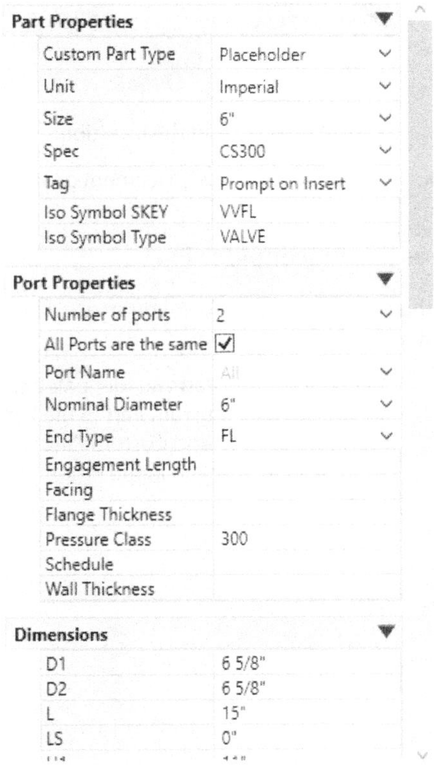

3. Click Insert in Model.

4. Specify the insertion point to place the valve as shown in the following illustration. Click Cancel when prompted to assign the tag for the valve.

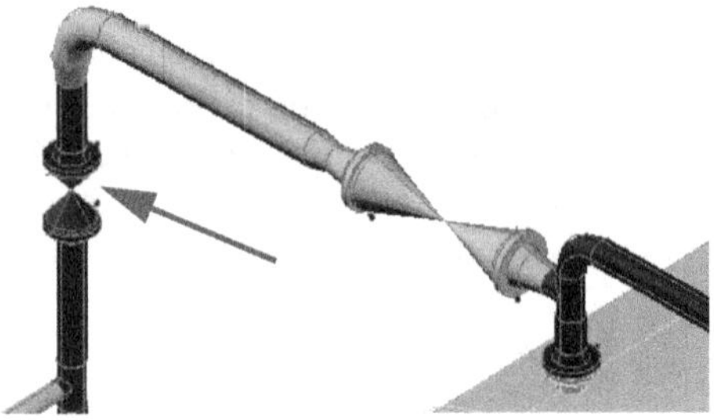

5. Press <Enter> to end the insertion.

6. Press <Esc> to cancel placement of additional valves.

7. Close the Custom Parts Builder.

8. To change the placeholder part to permanent:
   - Select the new valve. (You do not have to select its flanges). The exclamation symbol that displays when selected indicates that it is a placeholder.
   - Select the Substitute Part grip.
   - From the Part list, select the 6" Globe Valve.
   - Note that all the valves in the list come from the CS300 spec sheet.

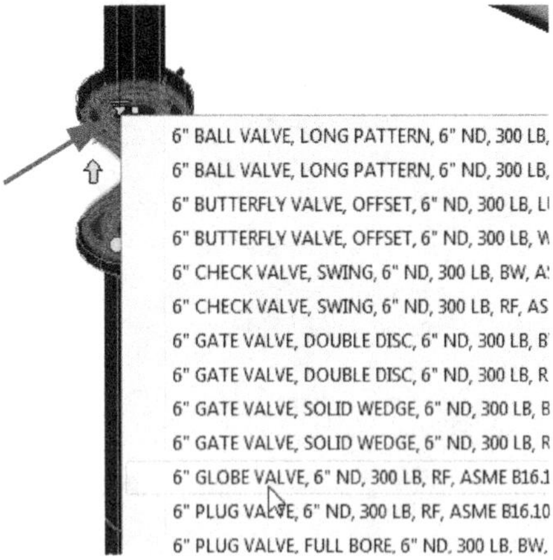

The valve changes to a globe valve. Its orientation might differ from the one shown, depending on the rotation that you selected in the previous step when you placed the placeholder valve.

Lock a Pipe Run

In this section of the exercise, you lock and unlock a section of pipe.

1. Select any part in run 1001. Right-click. Click Add to Selection, and click Connected Line Number.
2. With the pipe run selected, right-click in the drawing area. Click Lock/Unlock Placement.
3. Select a piece of the pipe run. Note that the lock symbols are displayed to indicate that the pipe run is locked.

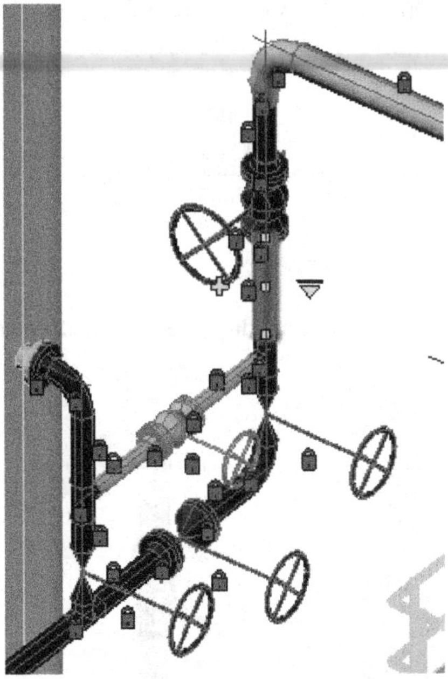

4. To unlock the pipe run, right-click and click Unlock Connected Parts with all connected parts selected.

Add Insulation to Piping

In this section of the exercise, you add insulation to a section of piping.

1. Select any part in run 1001. Right-click. Click Add to Selection, and click Entire Line Number.
2. On the Properties palette, under Process Line:
   - From the Insulation Thickness list, select 1 - 1".
   - From the Insulation Type list, select PP - Personal Protection.

Unit	
Shop/Field	*VARIES*
Process Line	-
Service	
Insulation Thickness	1 - 1"
Insulation Type	PP - Personal Protecti...
PnPGuid	6a058428-b81f-47f6-a4e...

3. Press <Esc> to clear the selection.

4. On the Home tab, on the Visibility panel, click Toggle Insulation Display.

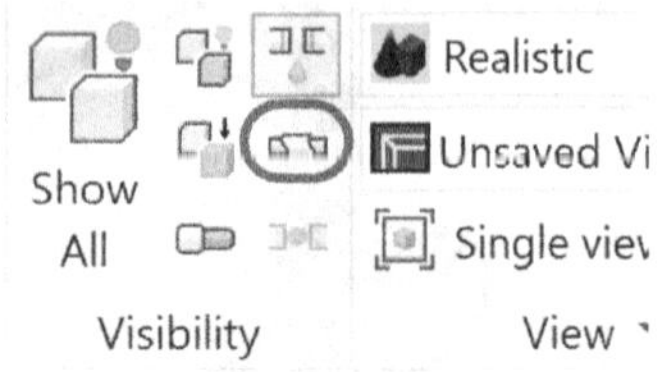

The insulation is displayed on the objects in the pipe run.

5. Save and close all drawings.

Lesson Review Questions

1. Can you copy a pipe route or sections of pipe routes from one drawing to another?
   a. Yes, using the Clipboard copy options.
   b. Yes, using the AutoCAD copy option.
   c. It is not possible to copy objects between drawings in AutoCAD Plant 3D.
2. A single pipe in a pipeline is untagged. It will be added to the selection set if the Add to Selection>All connected parts option is selected.
   a. True
   b. False
3. Can you hide a single pipeline segment?
   a. No, all connected lines of the same number hide at the same time.
   b. Yes, selecting the line using the selection options and then clicking the Hide option hides the selected line.
4. In the AutoCAD Plant 3D software, pipelines can be locked. Which of the following actions cannot be done once a pipeline is locked?
   a. The pipeline cannot be moved.
   b. The size and specification cannot be altered.
   c. Pipe components cannot be deleted.
5. When a pipeline has been hidden or isolated, how do you reverse the hiding or isolating?
   a. Switch the layer containing the pipeline so that it is toggled on.
   b. Right-click and select End Hiding/Isolation of Parts.
   c. Close the drawing and reopen it from the Project Manager.

Lesson: Working with P&ID Data in Plant 3D

Overview

In this lesson you learn to use the P&ID Line List to place P&ID components in the 3D design and then validate the 3D pipeline against the P&ID design. You also learn to link a 3D piping spec to the P&ID portion of your project.

Plant designs often start with the creation of a piping and instrument diagram because they are schematic in nature and do not require exact size and position. The system design is being engineered and design issues are being resolved. When you have created an AutoCAD P&ID drawing for the project, you can use these drawings to minimize data entry when creating a 3D model.

By linking a piping spec to your P&ID drawings, you can be aware of which components placed in your P&ID drawings are available when 3D modeling. Schematic lines and in-line components display whether they are in or out of a selected piping spec. AutoCAD Plant 3D Spec files only include inline components, so Equipment and other P&ID symbols retain their standard behavior.

A portion of the P&ID drawing is shown on the left in the following illustration and the corresponding 3D plant design of the piping run is shown on the right. Design information already created and captured in the P&ID drawing was used to create the appropriate pipelines and place the correct inline components.

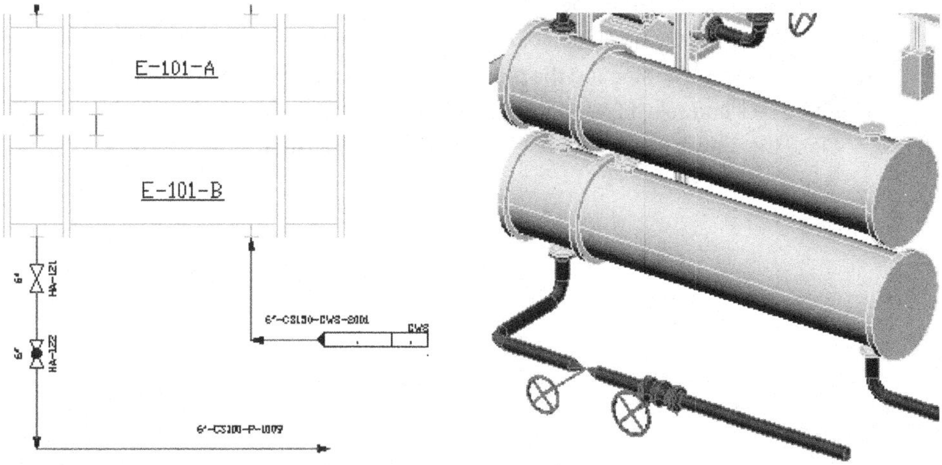

Objectives

After completing this lesson, you will be able to:

- Describe how data from a P&ID drawing can be used to create the 3D plant design.
- Place lines using the P&ID list.
- Validate the project using various settings.

About Working with P&ID Data in Plant 3D

Because plant designs start with the creation of a P&ID drawing and all of the information is captured in that drawing, it only makes sense to directly reuse what exists during the creation of the 3D model. When you work with P&ID data in a 3D design, you leverage what exists to assist in the creation and placement of equivalent 3D pipelines and inline equipment. The tag information in the 3D object reflects the tag information from the P&ID drawing. The actual information added to the 3D objects depends on the property values in the P&ID tags and the current mapping of the properties.

When you assign tags to the lines you create in P&ID, you can make several entries, including (as shown in the following illustration):

- Size
- Spec
- Pipe Line Group.Service
- Pipe Line Group.Line Number

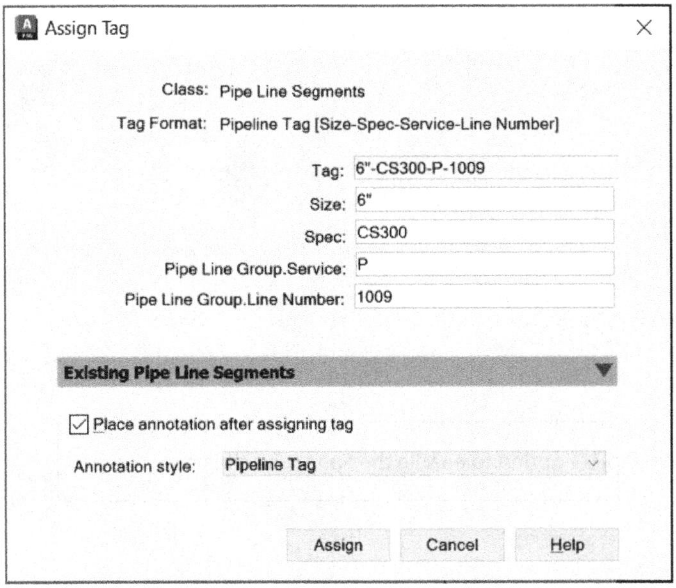

The specifications that are listed in the Assign Line Number Tag dialog box are only selections. They do not necessarily represent the specifications that are used in the AutoCAD Plant 3D software. P&ID is not spec driven. Any specification that you enter in this dialog box must be available in the AutoCAD Plant 3D software.

While the 3D models that you create can have the same information as what is in the P&ID drawing, the information is not linked between the drawings. This means that if a design change occurs, changing the information in one location does not automatically update the other location. To ensure everything is in sync between the drawings, you run a validation.

Create a Spec Driven Project

To gain visibility on the spec components available when drawing lines in a P&ID, you must enable the spec driven P&ID option from the project setup. By default, this option is off for new and existing migrated projects. Once a P&ID project becomes a spec driven project, the Schematic Line panel on the ribbon and the P&ID Tool Palette display which lines and inline components are in or out of the current piping spec.

Process: Enable a Spec Driven Project

The following steps describe how to toggle on the spec driven P&ID feature.

1. In the Project Manager, right-click on the top level node and click Project Setup to open the Project Setup dialog box.
2. In the Project Setup, expand P&ID DWG Settings and select Pipe Specs in P&ID, as shown in the following illustration.

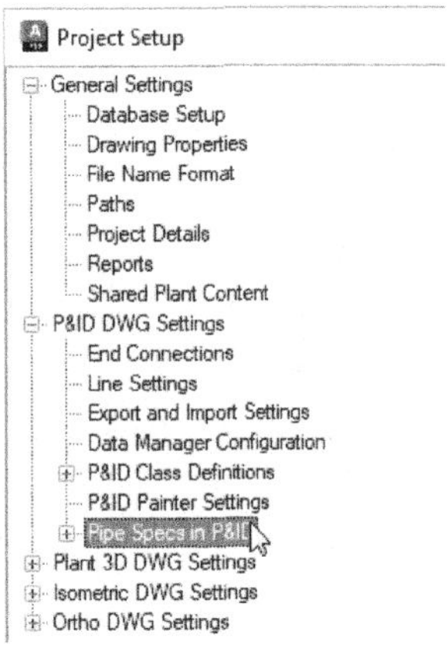

3. Select the Spec Driven Project option to enable the Spec driven feature.

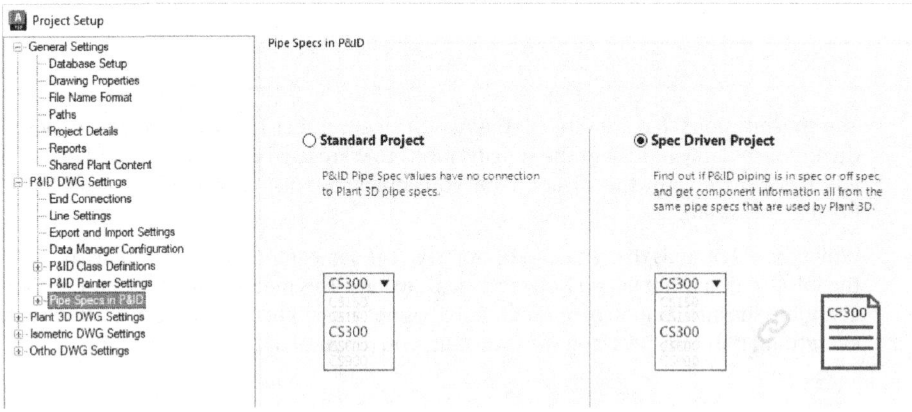

4. Click OK to close the Project Setup.

Set a Spec for Use in P&ID

Once a P&ID Project becomes a spec driven project, you must preselect the piping spec from the drop-down list before drawing spec components. In the Home tab in the Schematic Line panel, in the P&ID workspace, select the spec drop-down to view a list of the specs available for selection.

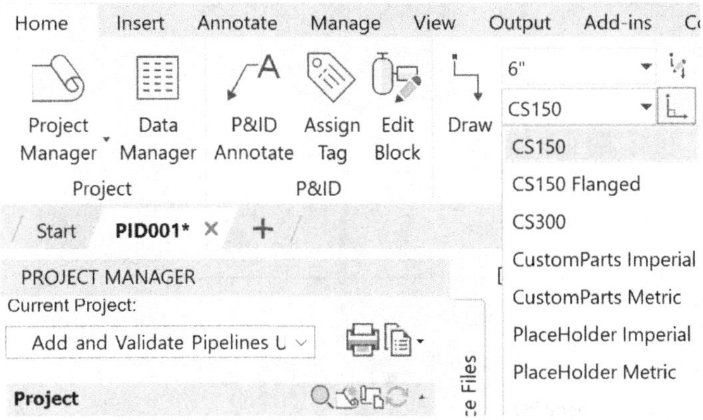

The piping spec drop-down list is populated from the Spec list property in your P&ID project and might not match the list of 3D piping specs shown in the Project Manager. Spec names in the drop-down list that do not match a 3D piping spec display with a gray cross-hatch, indicating they do not have a 3D equivalent.

Place Lines and In-line Components

After selecting the spec from the Schematic Line panel, select the size of the line or the inline component for placement using the drop-down list above the list of specs. This list contains the listing of available pipeline sizes from another P&ID list property. A cross-hatched size means that the size is not available in the 3D piping spec selected.

Similarly, once a size and spec are selected, the P&ID Tool Palette dynamically updates the thumbnail images of the symbols to be placed. Lines and inline components display a gray cross-hatch if they are out of spec, when compared to the 3D piping spec.

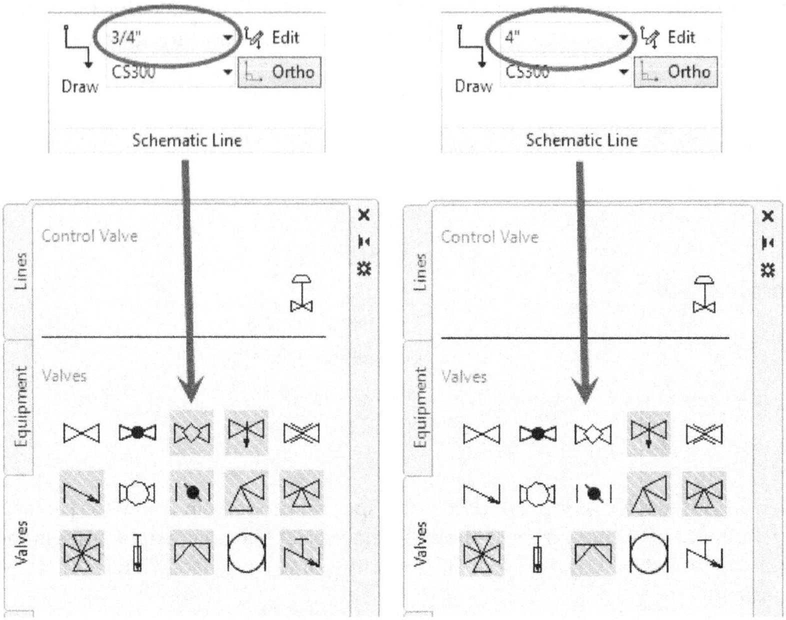

Components that are out-of-spec can still be placed in the P&ID drawing. The spec driven P&ID feature only visually indicates which parts are out-of-spec prior to placing them. As you change the pipe size property in the Schematic Line panel from one size to another, is a component becomes available at the new size, its thumbnail image changes and the cross-hatch is removed.

Map Properties from P&ID to 3D

Symbols in project P&ID drawings can also be used to set property values for the corresponding components in the 3D piping model. Some of these properties from the P&ID class definition are mapped to the 3D objects by default and additional property mappings can be set if required by overriding the current settings. Overrides are set on the Pipe Spec Object Mapping node of the Project Setup when working with Pipe Specs in P&ID.

Process: Applying Property Mappings and Overrides

1. Select the type of inline component to work with using the selections at the bottom of the list and then browse to the component.
2. Select the component to set the mappings for.
3. Select the Property Mapping tab.

4. In the P&ID column, if the acquired property is acceptable, no further action needs to be done. To override the property mapping, select the lightning bolt and in the drop-down, select Override Mode.
5. In the Pipe Specs column, select the 3D property to apply the value from the P&ID property listed in the P&ID column.

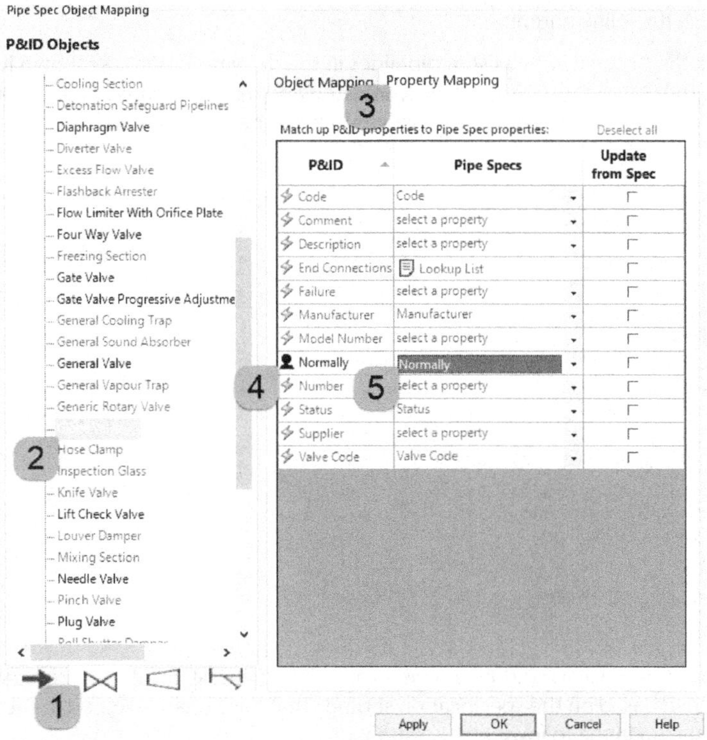

In the example above, the Normally state property applied to a valve in the P&ID populates the Normally property of the same valve in the 3D model. In order for property mappings to be applied to the 3D objects, components must be placed and routed using the P&ID line list.

Using the P&ID Line List to Place Lines and Inline Equipment

You use the P&ID Line List palette when you want to add 3D pipelines or inline equipment to your 3D design when the line has already been created in a P&ID drawing. On the Home tab, on the Part Insertion panel, click P&ID Line List to display the P&ID Line List palette, as shown in the following illustration.

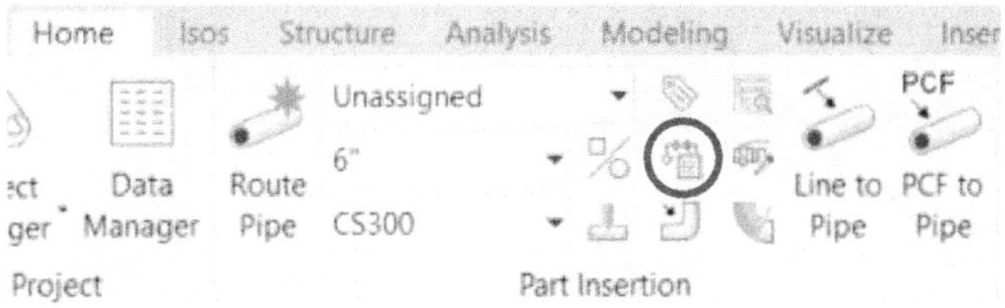

After displaying the P&ID Line List palette, the process of placing 3D pipelines and inline equipment into a Plant 3D drawing is very straight forward. The first thing you do is select from the drop-down list the P&ID drawing that you want to use. The next thing to do is select the line or inline equipment you want to add. For ease of creation, you want to place the pipelines before placing the inline equipment. By having the line exist first, placing the inline equipment is easier and quicker. After selecting what to place, you either click Place on the palette or click Place Item from the shortcut menu. You then create the 3D pipeline or place the inline equipment.

The P&ID Line List palette is shown with a list of pipelines in the drawing PID001, as shown in the following illustration. The 6" line for 1009 is currently selected and being prepared to be added to the design. The 1009 line also consists of two types of valves that can be easily placed.

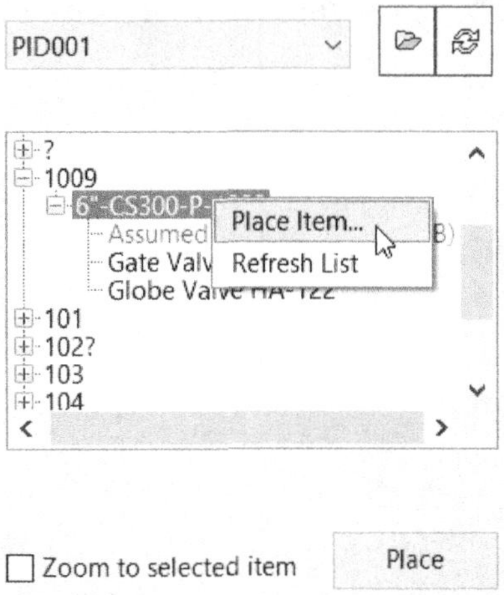

When you start a connection, such as starting a pipe on an existing nozzle, the correct connectors are automatically established based on the specification settings that have been assigned to the items in the P&ID drawing, as shown in the following illustration.

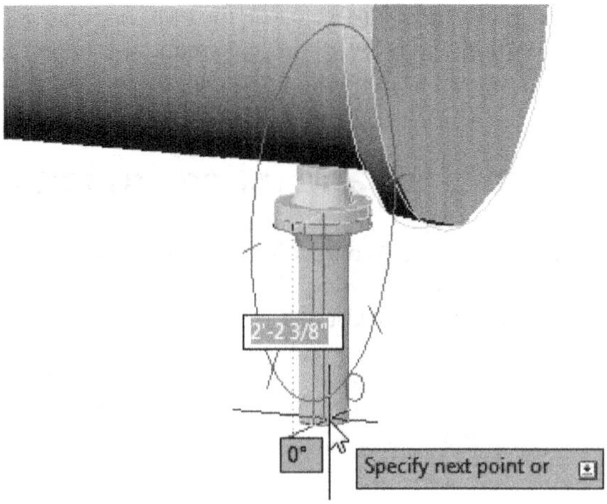

Validating the P&ID and Plant 3D Designs

As you are creating a design, you have the option of checking individual P&ID drawings or all the drawings in a project to validate that they adhere to company and industry standards. When you create Plant 3D drawings based on P&ID drawings, the information used and added to the model is not linked to the P&ID drawing. To ensure the P&ID and Plant 3D design and data are in sync, you need to validate the project. While you can run a validation on individual P&ID drawings, when you want to validate a model against a P&ID drawing, you need to run the validation for the entire project.

The validation between the P&ID drawings and Plant 3D drawings is bi-directional. In other words, mismatches that have been introduced in the P&ID drawing that conflict with data in the 3D model are identified, and so are mismatches that have been introduced in the 3D drawing that do not comply with the P&ID drawings.

After the validation is run on the entire project, any issues that exist between the Plant 3D drawings and the P&ID drawings are listed in the Validation Summary palette. To focus the results on what you are most interested in, you should configure the validation settings before running a validation.

In the example shown in the following illustration, Item line mismatches were found in the Equipment drawing. When you select any of these errors, the details panel displays information about the error.

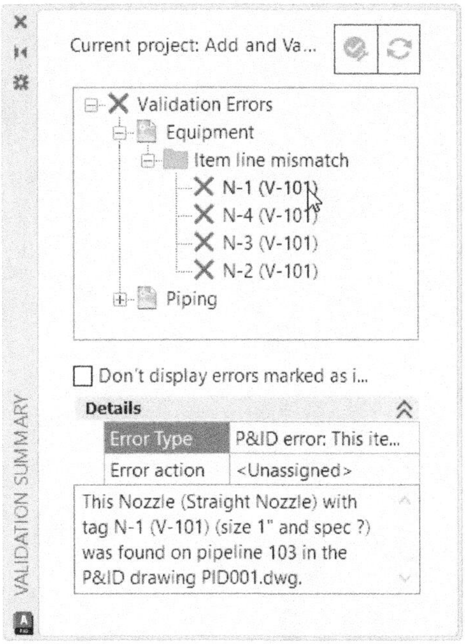

Process: Validating the P&ID and Plant 3D Designs

The following steps describe the overall process of validating a project to ensure the P&ID drawings and the Plant 3D drawings correspond with each other.

1. Configure the validation settings to have the validation results list the type of issues or potential issues you are interested in having identified.
2. Run Validate Project to have the validation check run against all of the drawings in the project.
3. Review the validation results and correct or flag any identified issue.

Access Validate Project and Validation Settings

You can access the validation settings or run the validation on the entire project from the shortcut menu after right-clicking on the project name, as shown in the following illustration.

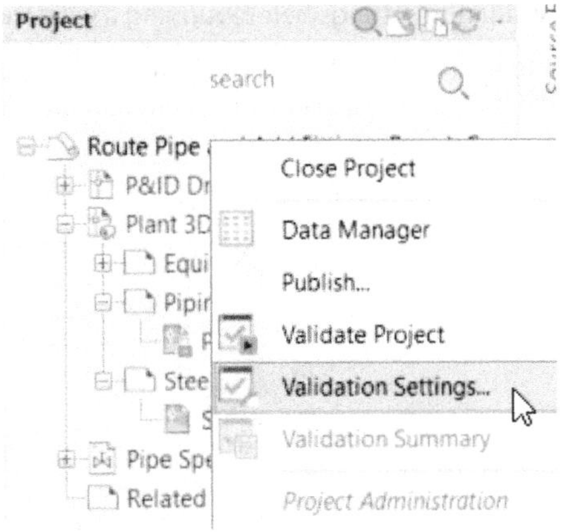

Validation Settings

Several types of validations can be set. The high-level organization of these is in the P&ID Validation Settings dialog box, as shown in the following illustration:

- P&ID objects
- 3D Piping
- Base AutoCAD objects
- 3D Model to P&ID checks

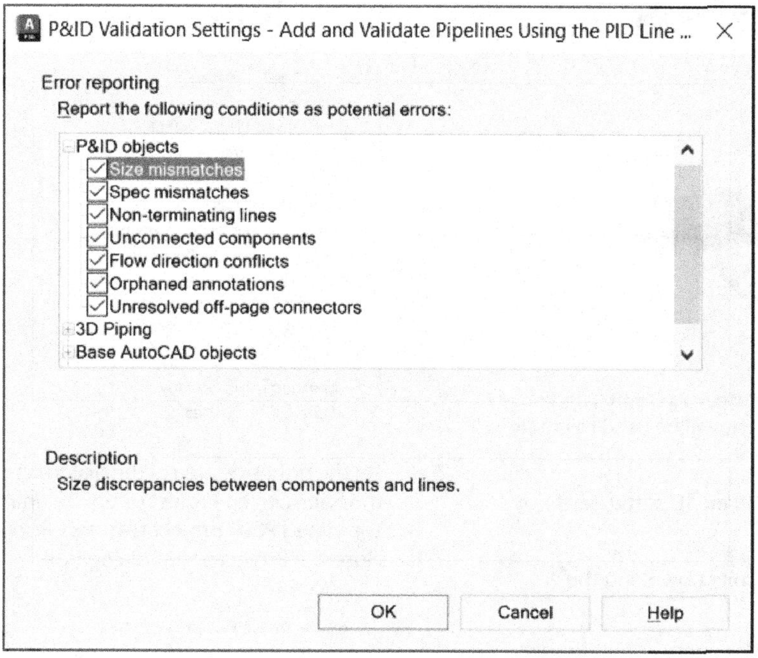

Refer to the help system topics "About Validating the 3D Model" and "P&ID Validation Settings Dialog Box" for more information and details on design validation.

Exercise: Add and Validate Pipelines Using the P&ID Line List

In this exercise, you create a line with inline items using P&ID. You assign a line number and specifications to the new line. You then use this line to create the line in Plant 3D. Once this is complete, you set validation settings and run a validation on the project.

Add a P&ID Line

In this section of the exercise, you create a new line and assign tags in P&ID that will be used to create the line in Plant 3D.

1. Start the AutoCAD Plant 3D software, if not already running.
2. Open an existing project by doing the following:
   - In the Project Manager, Current Project list, click Open.
   - In the Open dialog box, navigate to the folder *C:\Plant Design 2024 Practice Files\Add and Validate Pipelines Using the PID Line List*.
   - Select the file *Project.xml*.
   - Click Open.
3. In the Project Manager, right-click on Add and Validate Pipelines Using the PID List and select Project Setup.
4. In the Project Setup dialog box, expand P&ID DWG Settings and select Pipe Specs in P&ID.

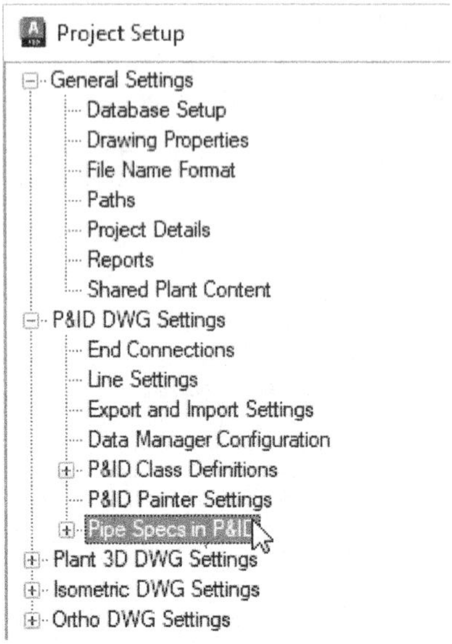

5. On the right side area of the dialog box, select the Spec Driven Project option to enable a spec lined P&ID project feature. Click OK to close the Project Setup dialog box.

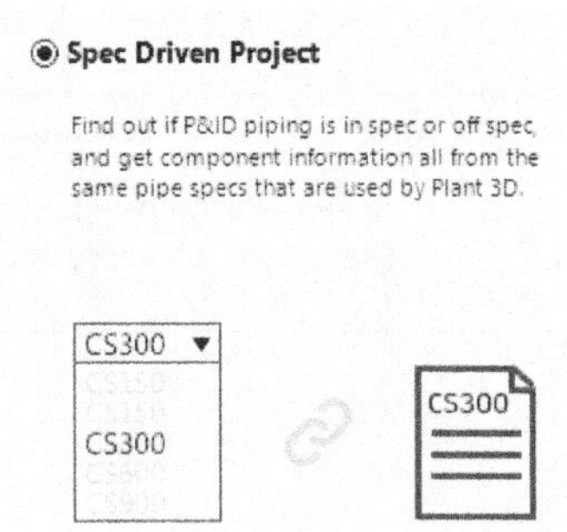

6. In the Project Manager, expand P&ID Drawings. Open the PID001 drawing.
7. Switch to PID PIP workspace.

8. Zoom in to the heat exchanger E-101-B.

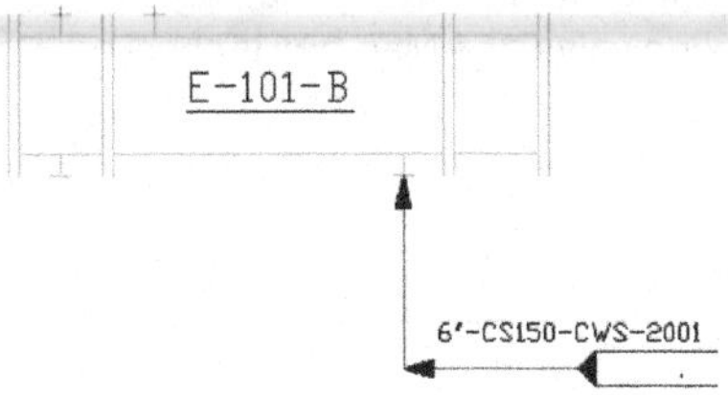

9. In the Home tab, in the Schematic Line panel, select CS300 from the Spec drop-down list and select 6" from the Size drop-down list.

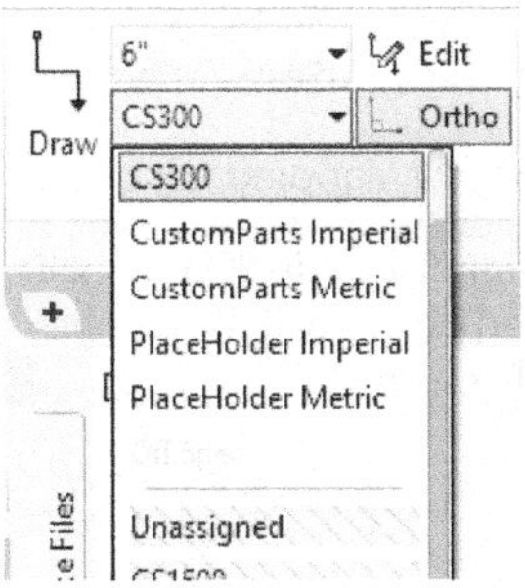

10. On the Lines tab of the Tool Palettes, click Primary Line Segment.

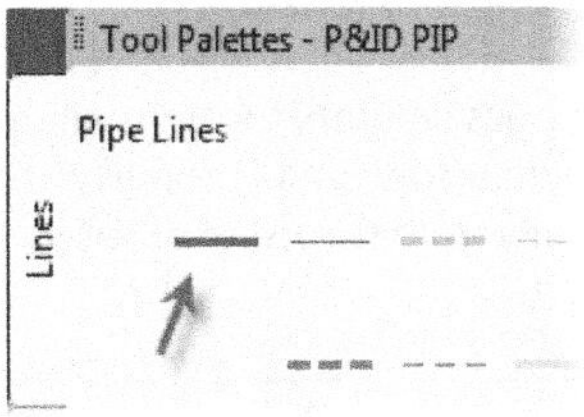

11. To begin drawing the line, click the node on the open nozzle along the bottom left of E-101-B heat exchanger.

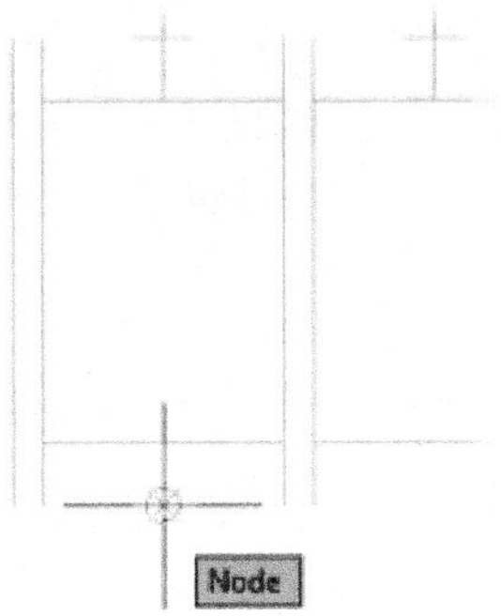

12. Draw the line, down and right, similar to that shown in the following illustration.

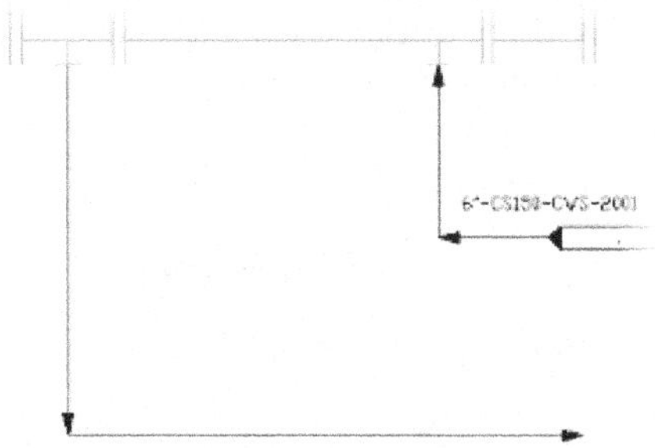

13. Right-click on the new pipeline. Click Assign Tag. Note that the Size and Spec are already set.

14. In the Assign dialog box:

- For Pipe Line Group.Service, select P-GENERAL PROCESS.
- For the Pipe Line Group.Line Number, enter **1009**.
- Click the Place annotation after assigning tag.
- Click Assign.

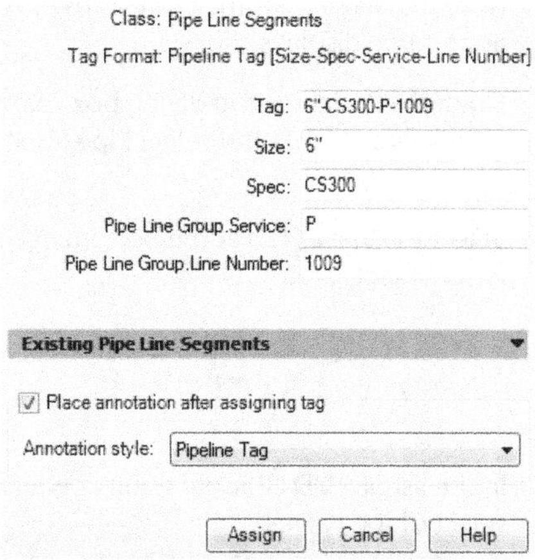

15. Place the tag above the line.

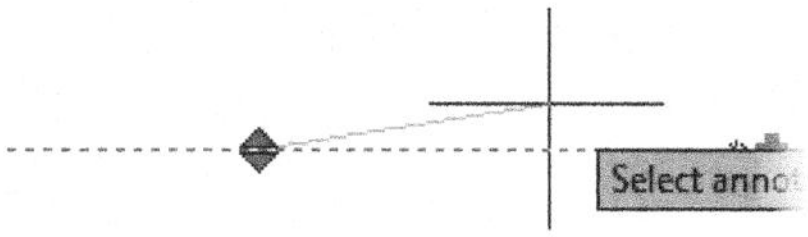

16. On the Tool palette, on the Valves tab, select a Gate valve. Note that the Needle valve and Angle valves are hatched, indicating that they are out of spec for the 6" - CS 300 combination.

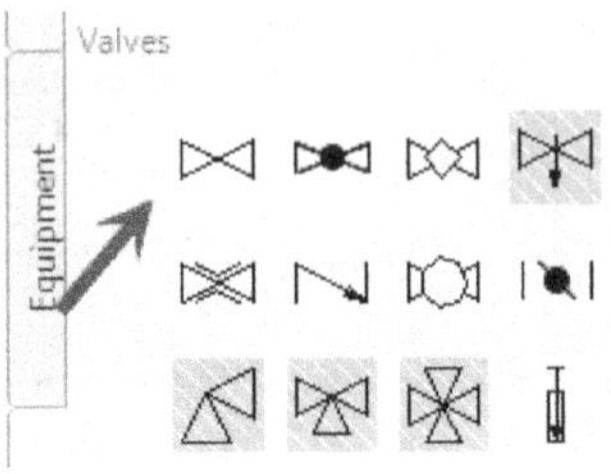

17. Place the Gate valve on the vertical portion of the line as shown in the following illustration.

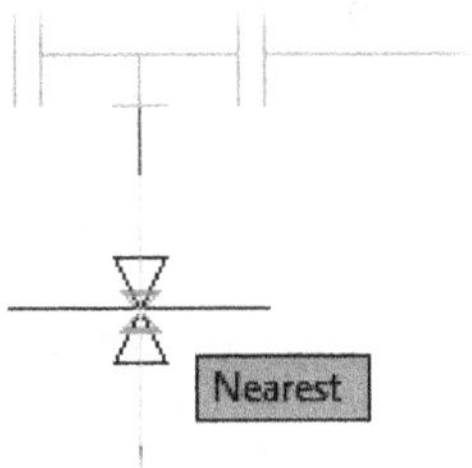

Note that as soon as the valve is inserted the annotation displays.

18. Open the Project Setup dialog box. Expand Pipe Specs in P&ID and select Pipe Spec Object Mapping.

19. Select the Valves tab at the bottom of the P&ID Objects area.

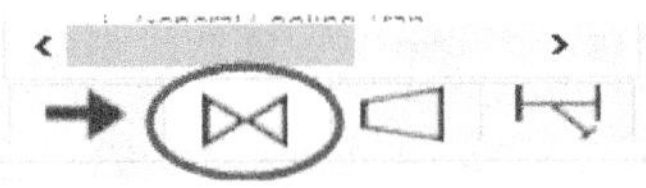

20. In the list of P&ID Objects, scroll down and select Globe Valve.

21. On the right side, in the Object Mapping tab, scroll down and verify that, for the Globe-Inline valve, the Map box is checked.

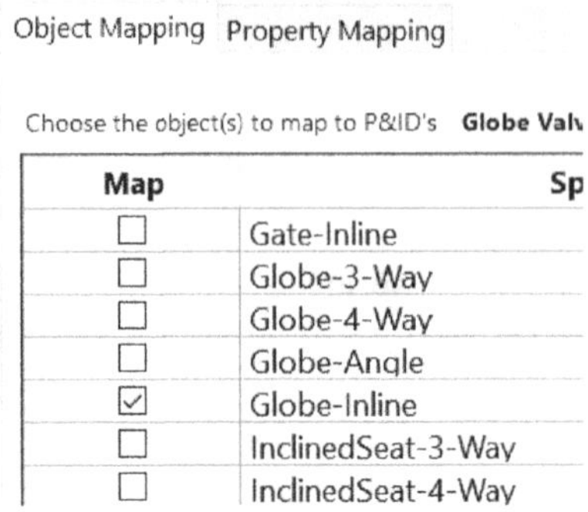

22. Select the Property Mapping tab.

23. In the P&ID column, beside the Normally, click on the acquired property lightning bolt and select Override mode.

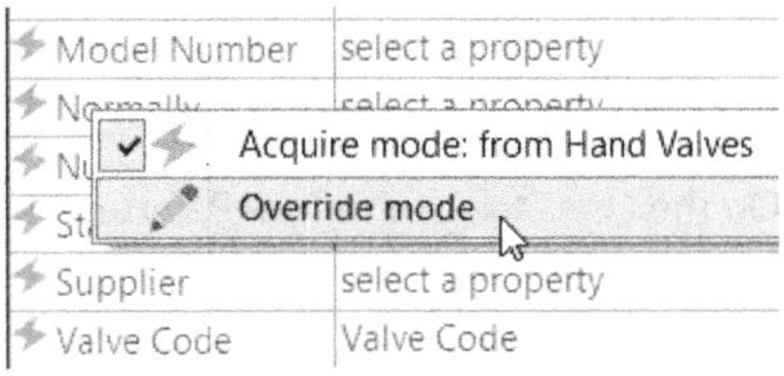

24. In the Pipe Specs column, for Normally, click the drop-down arrow for its property and select Normally from the list of 3D object properties.

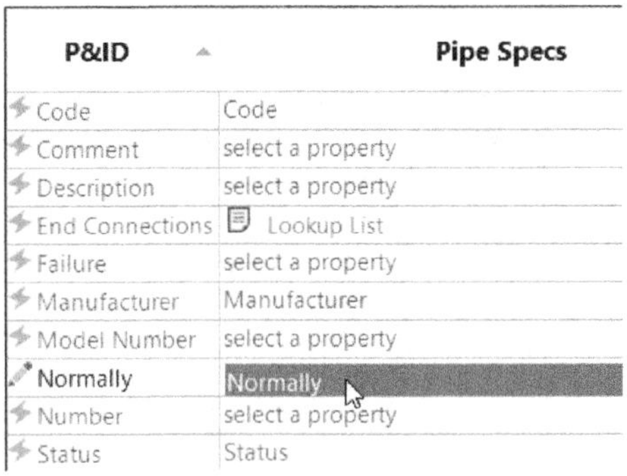

25. Click OK to close the Project Setup dialog box.

26. On the Tool palette, on the Valves tab, select a Globe valve.

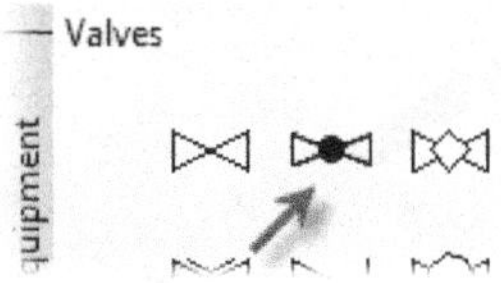

27. Place the Globe valve below the Gate valve on the vertical portion of the line as shown in the following illustration.

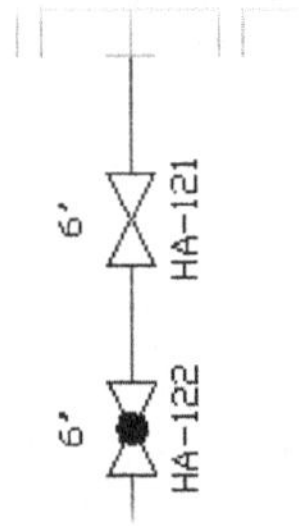

28. Right-click on the newly placed Globe Valve and select Set Open Closed State>Normally Closed. Note that the Globe Valve changes to Normally closed.

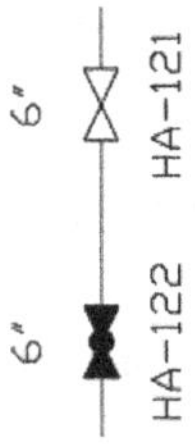

29. Save the drawing and leave it open.

Create the P&ID Line in the Model

In this section of the exercise, you use the P&ID Line List to create the line in the AutoCAD Plant 3D software.

1. In the Project Manager, expand Plant 3D Drawings and Piping folders. Open the Piping drawing.

2. Change the workspace to 3D Piping. Also change the Tool Palette to the AutoCAD Plant 3D - Piping Components Tool Palette, if required.

3. Zoom and position the model to the open nozzle on the left side of the heat exchangers.

4. On the Home tab, on the Part Insertion panel, click P&ID Line List.

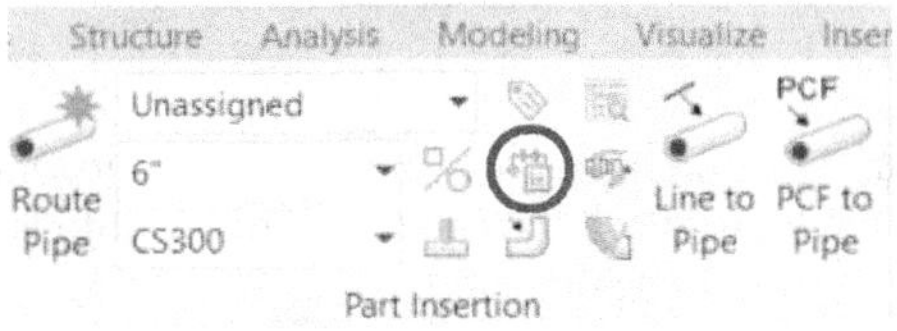

5. On the P&ID Line List Palette, expand the 1009 line to examine the components.

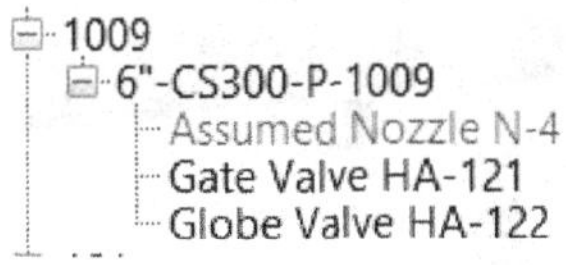

6. Right-click on 6"-CS300-P-1009. Click Place Item.

7. Select the node on the open nozzle.

8. Extend the pipe vertically down. For Distance, enter **24"**. Use <Ctrl>+right-click for appropriate direction.

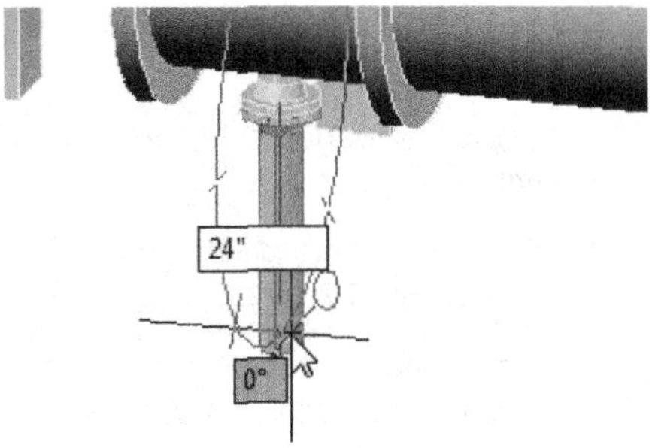

9. Extend the pipe as shown in the following illustration. For Distance, enter **6'**.

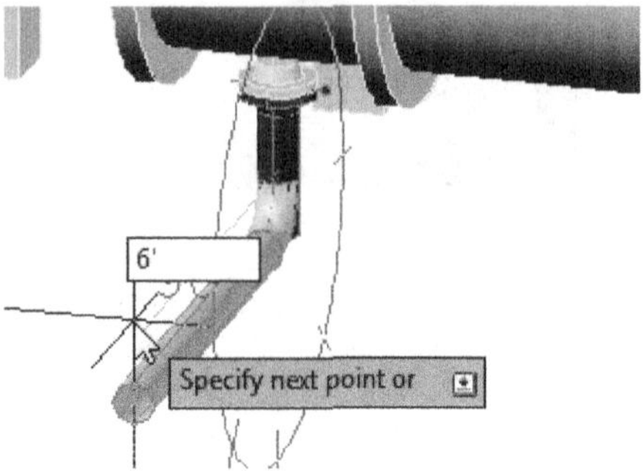

10. Extend the pipe as shown in the following illustration. You can use <Ctrl>+right-click to rotate the direction.

   - For Distance, enter **18'**.
   - Press <Enter> to end the command.

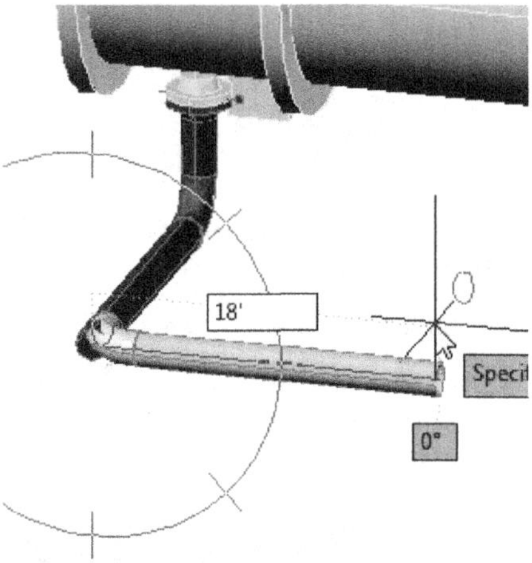

11. Using the ViewCube, change to South West isometric view.

12. On the P&ID Line List palette, right-click on the Globe Valve HA-122. Click Place Item.

13. Place the Globe valve on the new line, as shown in the following illustration.

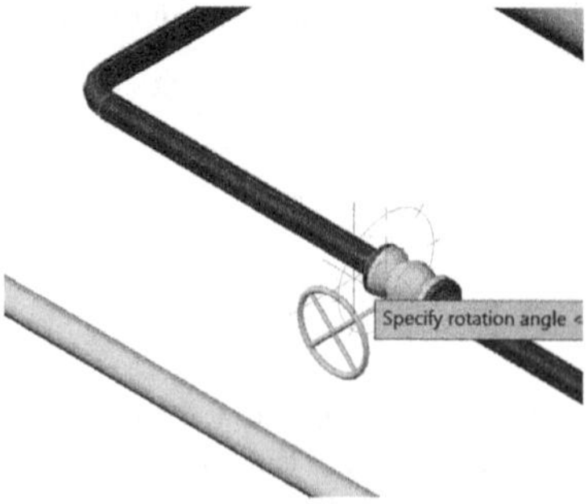

14. Hover the cursor over the line and valve to confirm the information on these components.

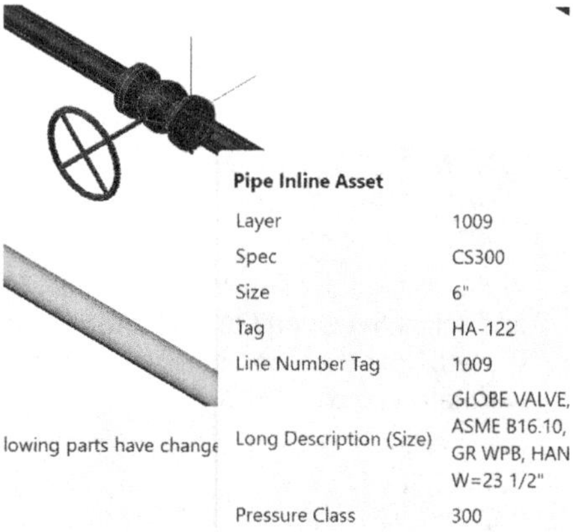

15. Select the Globe Valve tagged HA-122 and access the Properties palette.

16. Scroll in the Properties palette to locate the Normally property and verify that NC is entered as its value.

Valve Code	
Normally	NC
Failure	
End Connections	Unspecified
Number	122
Code	HA

17. Close the P&ID Line List palette.

18. Save the drawing and leave it open.

Validate Line Tags and Fix

In this section of the exercise, you deliberately place a valve on a wrong line, then run a validation of the project.

1. Using the Move grip, move the existing globe valve from the new line to the cyan line that was already in the model. These two lines do not have the same line number tags, and the valve is a mismatch on the line it has been moved to.

2. To review validation settings:
   - Right-click on the Project in the Project Manager.
   - Click Validation Settings.

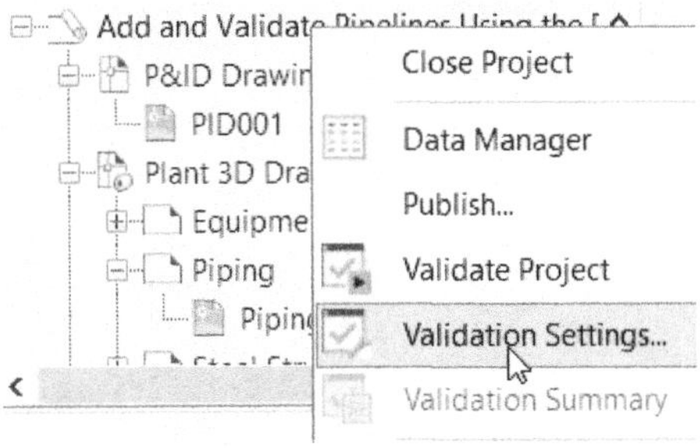

3. In the P&ID Validation Settings dialog box:
   - Expand P&ID objects. Clear all the options.
   - Expand 3D Piping objects. Clear all the options.
   - Expand Base AutoCAD objects. Clear all the options.
   - Expand 3D Model to P&ID checks. Clear all the options, except Inline items are on different lines in P&ID drawings and 3D models.
   - Click OK.

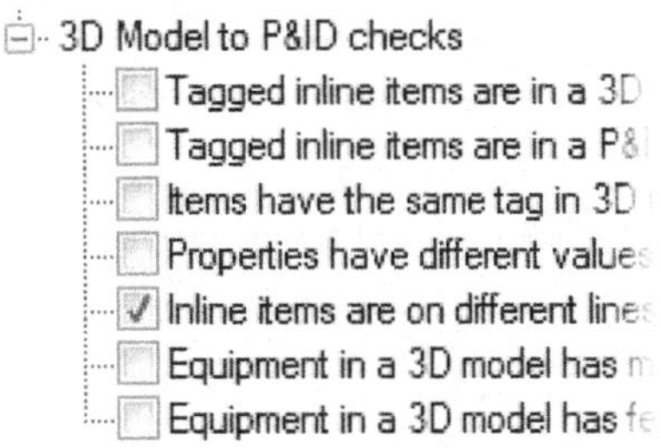

4. To validate the model, in the Project Manager:
   - Right-click on the Project.
   - Click Validate Project.

5. On the Validation Summary palette, there are several errors found, including errors in the Equipment drawing.
   - Collapse the errors on the Equipment drawing.
   - Expand the Piping drawing.
   - Examine the results. The misplaced valve is listed as an error.

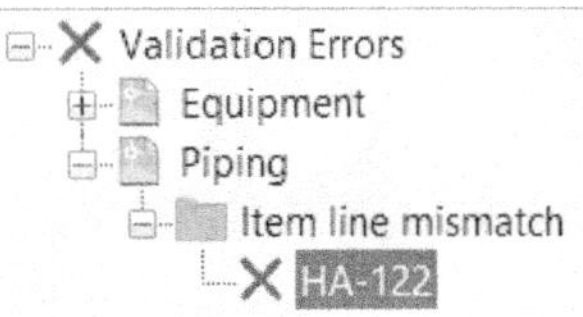

6. On the Validation Summary palette, click the HA-122 item.

7. In the Details section, examine the details of the error.

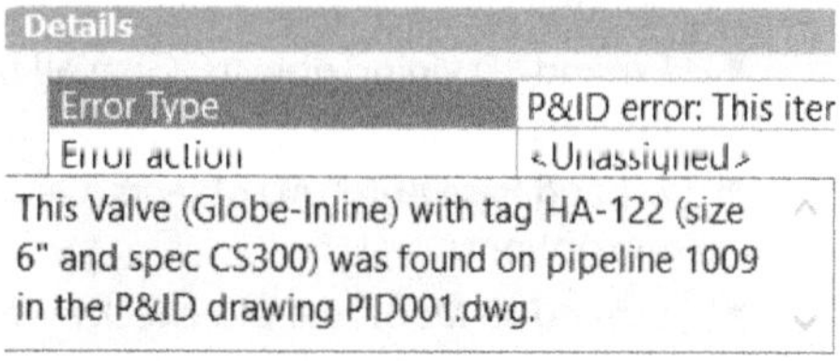

8. In the drawing, using grips, move the Globe valve back on line 1009.

9. On the Validation Summary palette:

   - Select the Piping drawing.
   - Click Revalidate Selected Node.

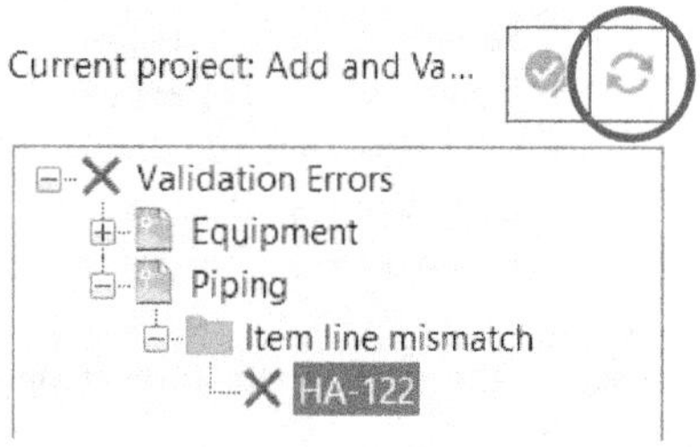

10. Examine the results on the Validation Summary palette. The Piping drawing has been removed from the summary. The Equipment drawing remains with errors.

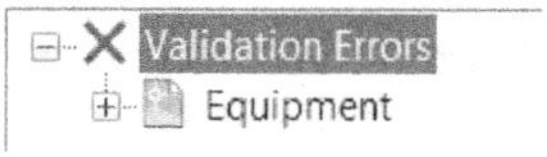

11. Save and close all drawings.

Lesson Review Questions

1. When a line is created in P&ID, you add a piping spec property to the tag. Does the specification used in P&ID need to be available in 3D as well?
   a. Yes, otherwise the P&ID list cannot generate the correct pipe route.
   b. No, the specifications in the AutoCAD P&ID software and the AutoCAD Plant 3D software are not referenced to each other.
   c. The P&ID spec property is not important, you only need to select which specification you want to use in Plant 3D.
2. Validating can be done at the P&ID level and also between the P&ID and 3D model. What type of validations are used between the P&ID and 3D model? (Select all that apply.)
   a. Pipeline size, specification, line number, and service.
   b. Tag of the inline components.
   c. Number of nozzles on Equipment in 3D and on the P&ID.
   d. If the inline components have been placed on the correct pipe route.
3. Can the validation tool determine whether a valve is placed on the wrong pipe route?
   a. No, validation does not check if components are placed on the correct line.
   b. Yes, but only one pipe route at a time.
   c. Yes, a validation can check all pipe routes to see if components are on the right line.

Lesson: Creating and Annotating Orthographic Views

Overview

This lesson describes the creation and annotation of 2D views from the 3D model. In this lesson, you learn how to create orthographic and sectional drawing views and update them when changes have been made in the 3D model. You also learn how to place, modify, and update dimensions and annotations.

After a plant design has been created and finalized, you need to communicate the design to others. To build and install the piping lines and equipment, you must create and supply construction documents. From the 3D model, you can easily generate the construction documents. Information is directly exchanged with the 3D model, producing more accurate, consistent, and up to date construction documents.

Objectives

After completing this lesson, you will be able to:

- Understand what orthographic drawings are in AutoCAD Plant 3D-P&ID.
- Explain how orthographic drawings are created.
- Identify the annotation and dimensioning tools.
- Explain how orthographic drawings are updated to represent changes in the 3D model.

About Orthographic Drawings

Orthographic drawings are 2D representations of a Plant 3D model. Rather than drawing them, you can generate them from the model using general layouts, which are then used as views in the orthographic drawing, as shown in the following illustration.

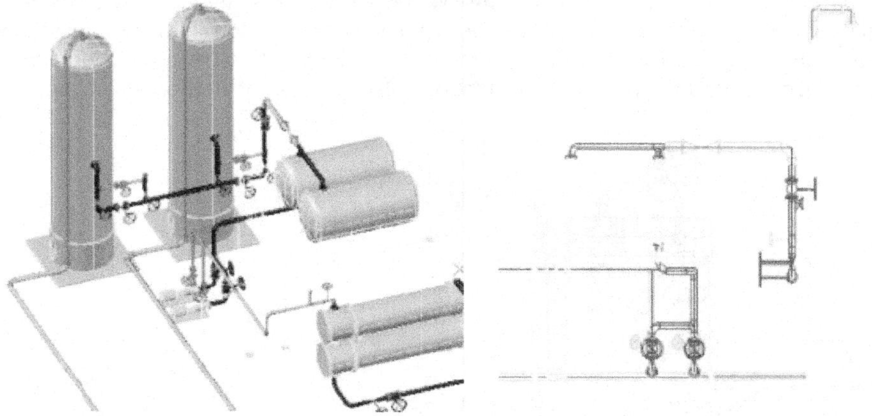

Creating and Editing Orthographic Views

To create an Ortho View from a 3D Piping drawing, on the Home tab, on the Ortho Views panel, click Create Ortho View. The Select Orthographic Drawing dialog box opens enabling you to select an existing orthographic drawing to which to add or to create a new one. Alternatively, you can select the Orthographic DWG tab in the Project Manager to open an existing orthographic drawing.

When you create a new orthographic drawing, the Ortho Editor tab displays and a bounding box is displayed to define the geometric extents of the resulting orthographic drawing, as shown in the following illustration. The options on the Ortho Editor tab can be used to define the following:

- View orientation and extents.
- Models to be included.
- Output Appearance and Size.

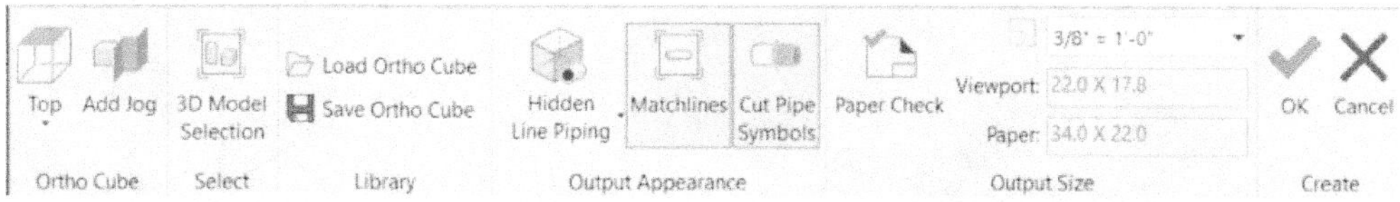

View Orientation and Extents

The Ortho Cube panel enables you to define the orientation of the view. This is done by selecting a default view in the drop-down. The options include: Top, Bottom, Right, and Left views, as well as NW, NE, SW, and SE Isometric views. The physical orientation of the model does not change on screen when a view option is selected. The current view of the layout is indicated by brown highlighting which indicates the viewing direction. For the NW, NE, SW, and SE Isometric views, two sides and the top of the cube are highlighted brown to indicate the viewing direction. In the example shown in following illustration, the Top view was selected and is highlighted. To create a orthographic view showing the currently displayed model orientation, select the Current View option on the drop-down.

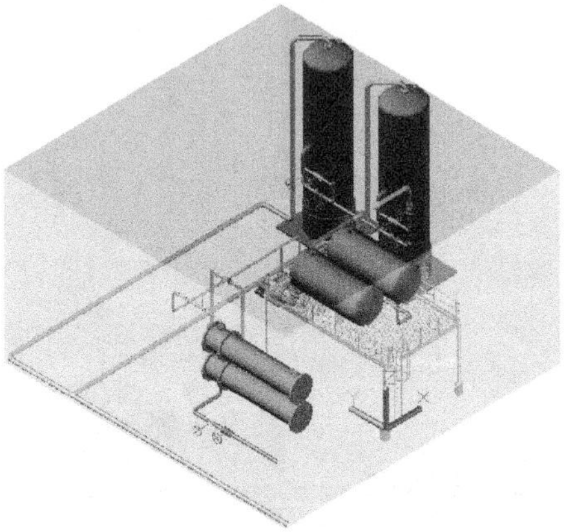

To modify the geometric extents of the view, select the bounding box that displays around the model to activate its grips, as shown in the illustration on the left. Select any of the grips and drag them to resize the extents of the view, as shown in the illustration on the right. Once selected, you can enter values at the prompt, using dynamic input to define the size of the box.

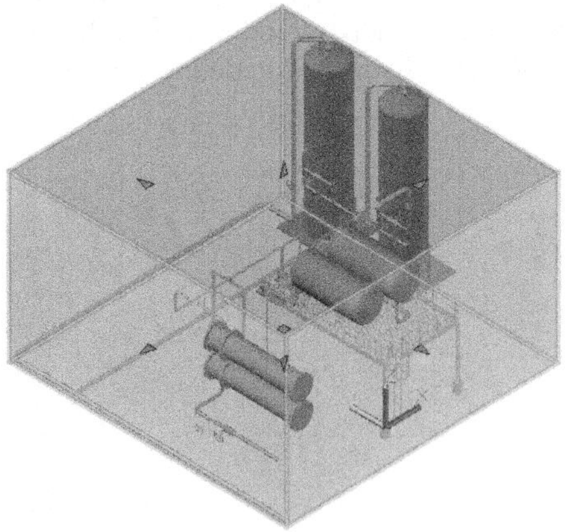

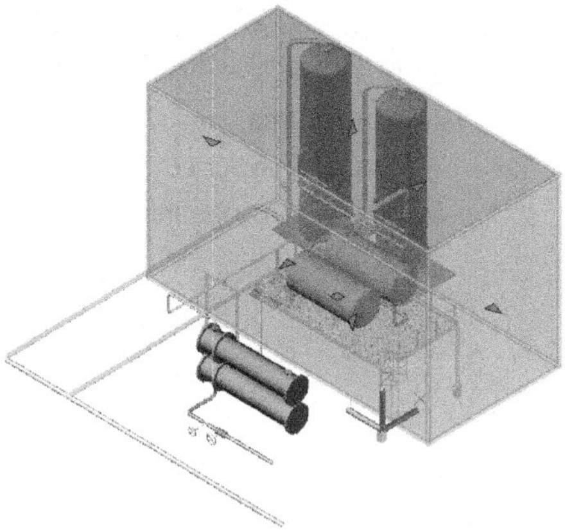

Use the Add Jog option on the Ortho Cube tab to create irregular shaped (jogged) views. Once active, select a top or bottom edge on the Orthocube to create a vertical jog (as shown on the left in the following illustration) or select a vertical edge to create a box shaped jog (as shown on the right). Modify the size of a jog by selecting the Orthocube and using the grips or entering values at the prompt. Multiple jogs can be added to a model to create the required ortho view. To remove a jog, select a grip associated with the jog and select the parallel edge associated with the original bounding box.

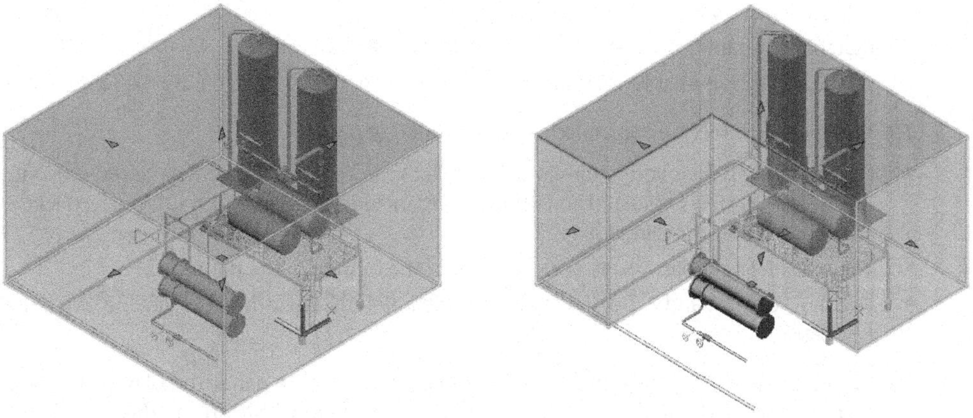

Models to Be Included

The 3D Model Selection command on the Ortho Editor ribbon enables you to toggle the inclusion of drawings for the ortho view. Using the Select Reference Models dialog box, select the 3D models that are to be included in the view, as shown in the following illustration. Once a view has been created, the models included or excluded can be modified by selecting the Edit View option on the Ortho View tab and then selecting the 3D Model Selection option to modify which drawings are included.

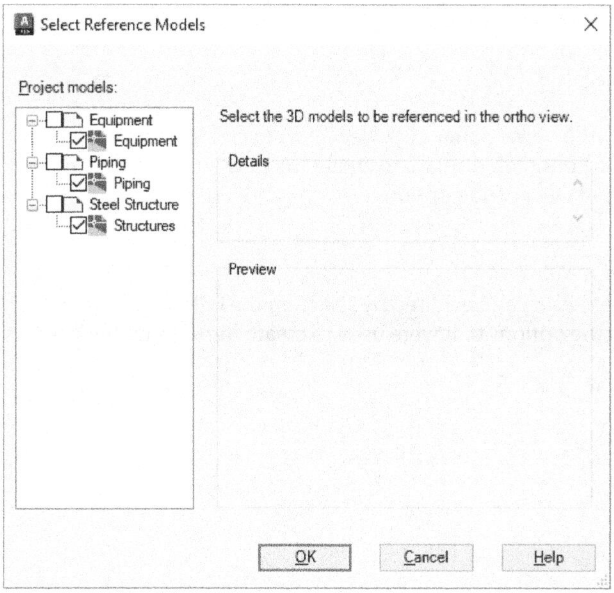

Output Appearance and Size

The Output Appearance and Output Size panels on the Ortho Editor enable you to refine how the view displays in the ortho view.

The following controls are controlled in the Output Appearance panel:

- Hidden Line Piping enables you to control how the lines display in the view. You can hide all hidden lines (pipes behind pipes do not show), show only hidden piping (pipes behind other pipes show), or you can show everything.
- Matchlines enable you to display the perimeter of a plant area.
- Cut Pipe Symbols enable you to identify the pipes that have been cut by the OrthoCube.

The following controls are controlled in the Output size panel:

- Paper Check enables you to preview the scale of the cube in relationship to the drawing. This is done once you have adjusted an OrthoCube to include the area you want. Once checked, you can adjust the scale accordingly.
- The scale field enables you to scale the size of the model for the paper.
- Use the Viewport and Paper fields to enter the height and width of the viewport or paper, respectively.

Once an Ortho view has been customized, click OK on the Create panel and place the view on the sheet. In the Ortho Editor tab, you can also save the view to the library using the Save Ortho Cube option. The options on the Library panel enable you to save and reuse views in other ortho views.

Once the first Ortho view has been placed or if you have opened the Orthographic drawing using the Project Manager, the Ortho View tab is active, as shown in the following illustration. It provides options for editing the view, creating new or adjacent views, deleting views, or updating them. Additionally, there are tools for annotating the views.

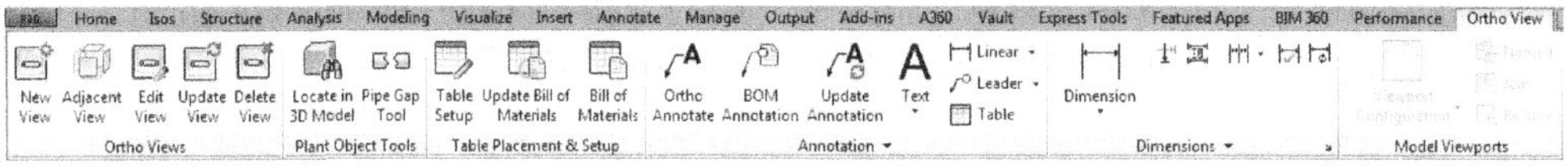

Creating New Views

On the Ortho View tab, on the Ortho Views panel, click New View to create new views in an orthographic drawing. The Ortho Editor tab displays to create the new view or you can open an existing saved view using the Load Ortho Cube option.

Modifying Views

Once an ortho view has been created, it can be edited by selecting the Edit View option on the Ortho Views panel. Edit the view using the options that were used to create the view in the Ortho Editor tab.

Creating Adjacent Views

On the Ortho View tab, on the Ortho Views panel, click Adjacent View, to easily create and name adjacent views in an orthographic drawing. Using the Create an Adjacent View dialog box, as shown on the left in the following illustration. An adjacent view can be created based on any existing view. All views created are listed on the Orthographic tab of the Project Manager, as shown on the right.

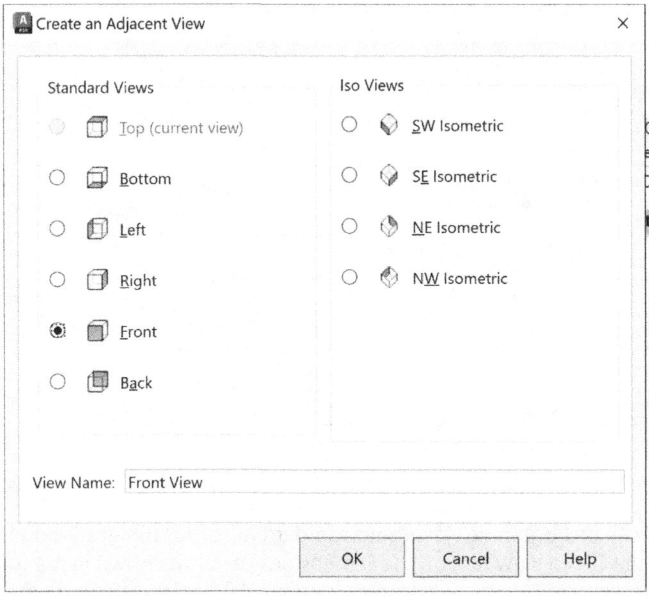

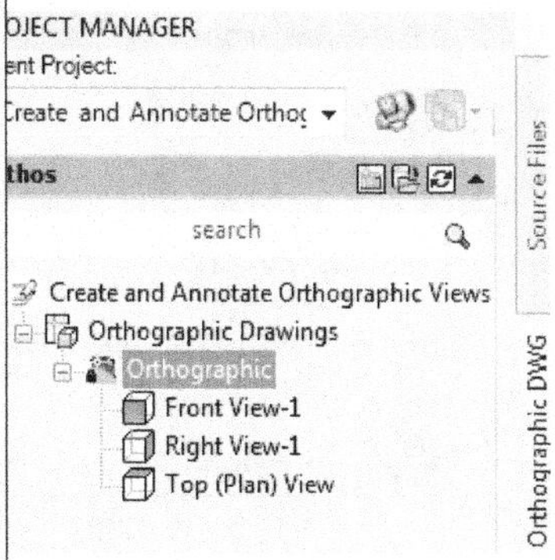

Annotations and Dimensions

Annotations

In an orthographic drawing, you can create annotations that include data from the objects in the 3D model or by adding information in the form of text, a leader, or a table. Annotations are added using the options on the Ortho View tab, on the Annotation panel, as shown in the following illustration.

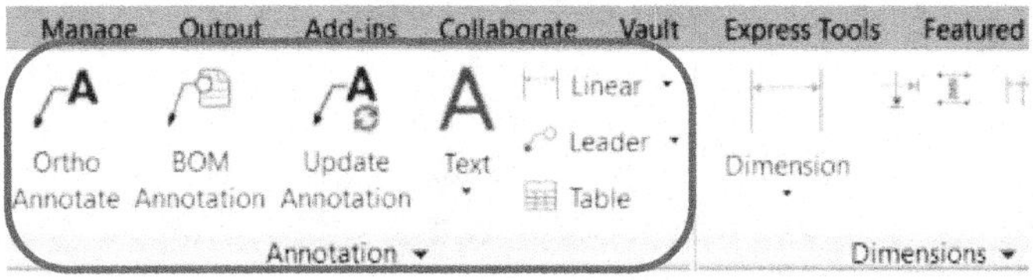

Orthographic annotations can also be accessed on the shortcut menu by clicking Ortho Annotate and selecting from any of the annotation styles, as shown in the following illustration. Once the style has been selected, make the appropriate selection in the drawing to add the annotation. This is the recommended method of assigning annotations.

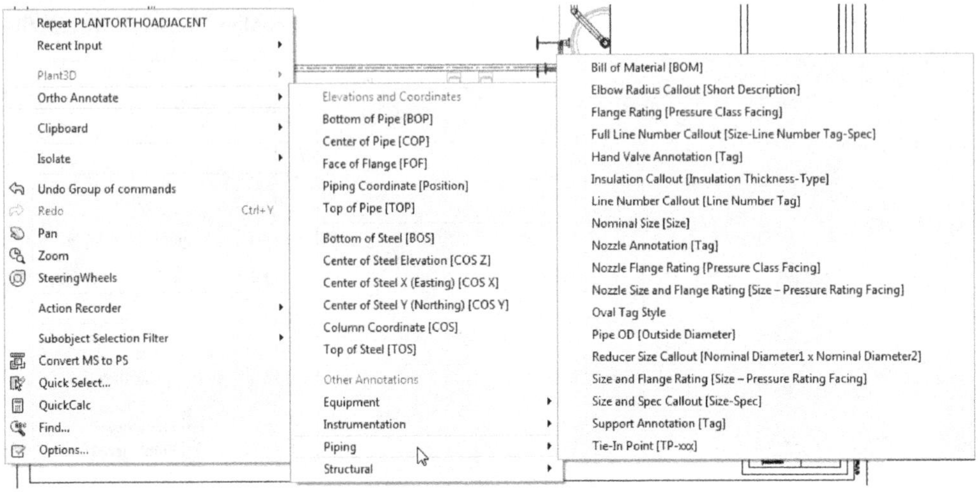

Dimensions

You can create dimensions in an orthographic view using standard AutoCAD dimensioning tools. These tools are available on the Ortho View tab, on the Dimensions panel, as shown in the following illustration. Expand the Dimension drop-down to select from the available dimensioning types. These include: Linear, Aligned, Angular, Arc Length, Radius, Diameter, Jogged, and Ordinate.

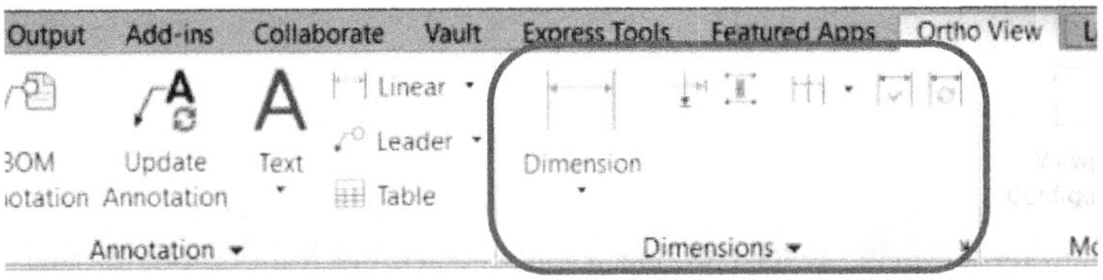

In the example shown on the left in the following illustration, an annotation was added to the ortho view using the Full Line Number Callout [Size-Line Number Tag-Spec] annotation style to annotate a pipeline with its line number from the model. In the example shown on the right, a linear dimension was added to the ortho view using the Linear Dimension option and by selecting pipelines.

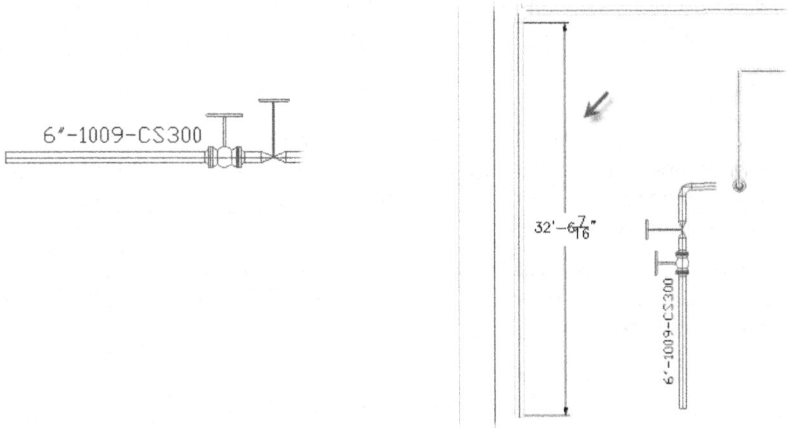

Ortho Bill of Materials

You can insert a Bill of Materials (BOM) table into an Ortho drawing. The BOM table lists items that are in the Ortho view. Use Table Setup to specify grouping and properties (columns), as well as specify whether to include cut-lists. The commands for setting up the table, and creating and updating the Bill of Materials, is shown in the following illustration.

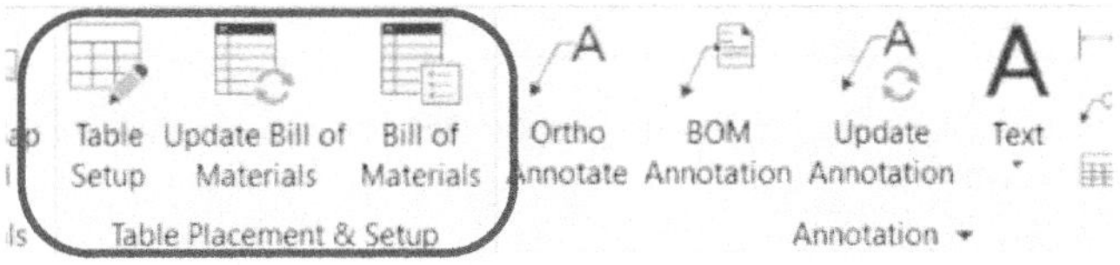

Ortho BOM setup is similar to isometric BOM for table columns and grouping. Like an Iso BOM, table setup can be saved with the title block. Unlike Iso BOMs, draw and table areas are not supported. Refer to About Ortho Bill of Material in the help documentation for more information on Ortho BOMs.

> Ortho settings (including new BOM table settings) are stored in the project Orthos\Styles folder. You can share them by copying the style folder to another project.
>
> Administrators can set the default BOM table for a project in the Ortho title block using Project Setup. If set up in the title block, new Ortho drawings do not prompt for location or size.

Updating Orthographic Drawings

Once an orthographic drawing has been created, you can regenerate it if changes are made to the model. You can regenerate a single view or all views in the orthographic drawing. Most of the characteristics of the model are dynamic and are updated during the regeneration. These include line tags, annotations, physical characteristics of objects, such as length, etc.

Updating Dimensions

While annotations and underlying data are dynamic and update along with objects when you regenerate an orthographic drawing, dimensions do not. If the physical characteristics of an object that is dimensioned in the orthographic drawing changes, for example in length, the dimensions are no longer correct representations.

In the example shown in the following illustration, a pipe was shortened in the model. When the orthographic drawing was updated, the dimension still represents the original length. To correct this, you manually update the dimension.

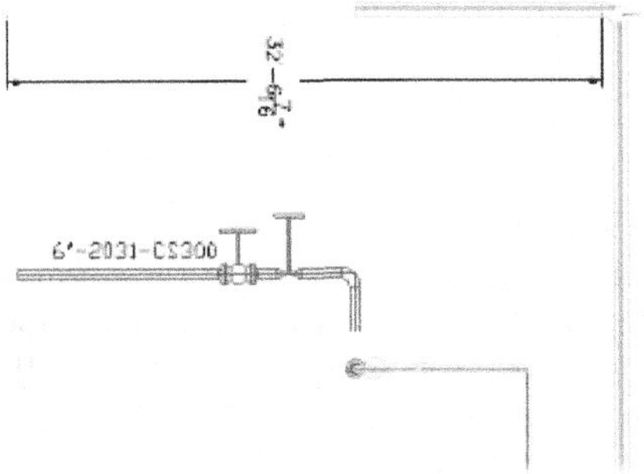

> If you are going to dimension objects in an orthographic view, it is recommended that you do so after the model is complete.

Exercise: Create and Annotate Orthographic Views

In this exercise, you create a general layout of the 3D model that consists of a number of views including a sectional view. You further enhance the views by adding dimensions and annotations. You also update the views and annotations after making changes to the 3D model.

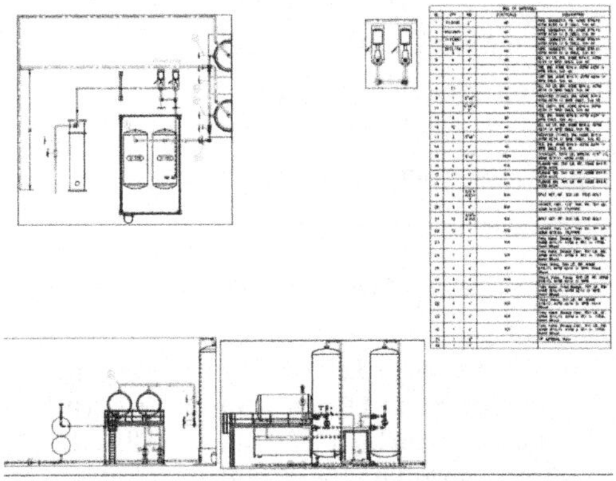

Set Up and Create an Orthographic Drawing

In this section of the exercise, you set up an orthographic view by selecting the models to include, setting the scale settings, and then creating the view.

1. Start the AutoCAD Plant 3D software, if not already running.
2. Open an existing project by doing the following:
   - In the Project Manager, Current Project list, click Open.
   - In the Open dialog box, navigate to the folder *C:\Plant Design 2024 Practice Files\Create and Annotate Orthographic Views*.
   - Select the file *Project.xml*.
   - Click Open.
3. In the Project Manager, expand the Plant 3D Drawings and Piping folders. Open the Piping drawing.
4. Verify that you are in the 3D Piping workspace. On the Home tab, on the Ortho Views panel, click Create Ortho View.

5. In the Select Orthographic Drawing dialog box, click Create New.
6. In the New DWG dialog box:
   - Under Drawing name, for File name, enter **Orthographic**.
   - For the DWG template, click Browse and navigate to *C:\Plant Design 2024 Practice Files\Create and Annotate Orthographic Views\Drawing Templates*, select *CompanyCustom.dwt* and click Open.
   - Click OK.
7. Examine the new orthographic representation in the drawing screen. Note that one side (top) is red. The red face represents the current orthographic view.

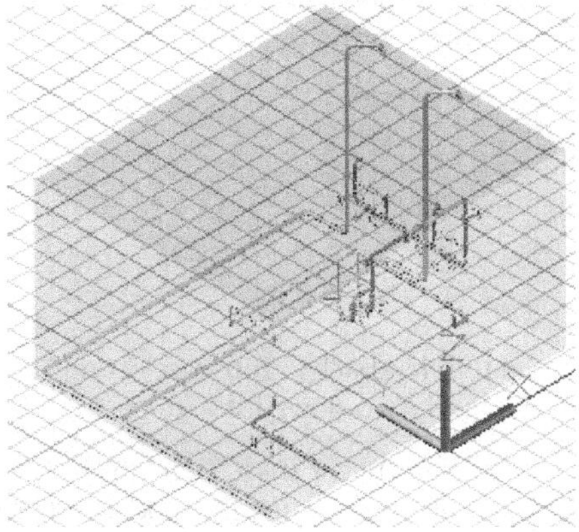

8. To add models to the orthographic drawing, on the Ortho Editor contextual tab, on the Select panel, click 3D Model Selection.

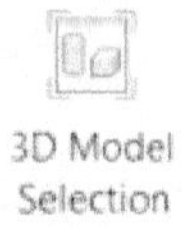

9. In the Select Reference Models dialog box:
   - Select the Equipment, Piping, and Structures drawings by selecting the check boxes in front of the drawing names.
   - Click OK.

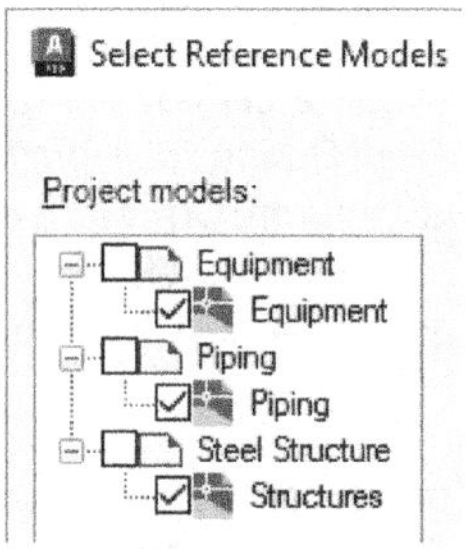

10. To change the view, on the Ortho Editor tab, on the Ortho Cube panel, click Front in the View drop-down list. Note that the front view of the ortho is now red.

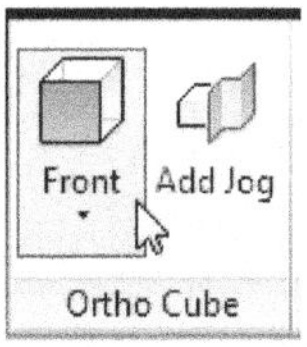

11. Set the view back to Top by selecting Top in the View drop-down list.

12. Toggle off Object Snap. Select the ViewCube box around the model and use the displayed grips to expand the cube, so that the entire model is fully constrained within it. Press <Esc> to clear the ViewCube selection.

13. In the Output Size panel:
   - Set the Scale to 1:50.

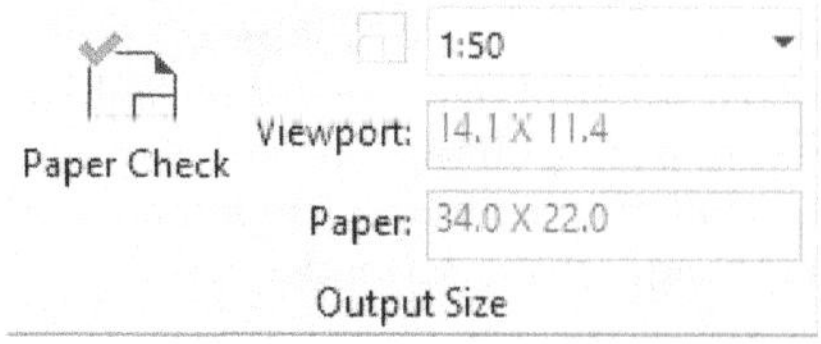

14. In the Library panel:
   - Click Save Ortho Cube.

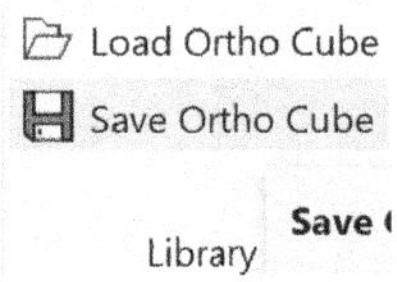

15. In the Save View dialog box, for View Name, enter **Top View-1 Scale 1-50**. Click OK. This saved view can be reloaded using all of the settings including the boundary geometry using the Load Ortho Cube option on the Library panel.

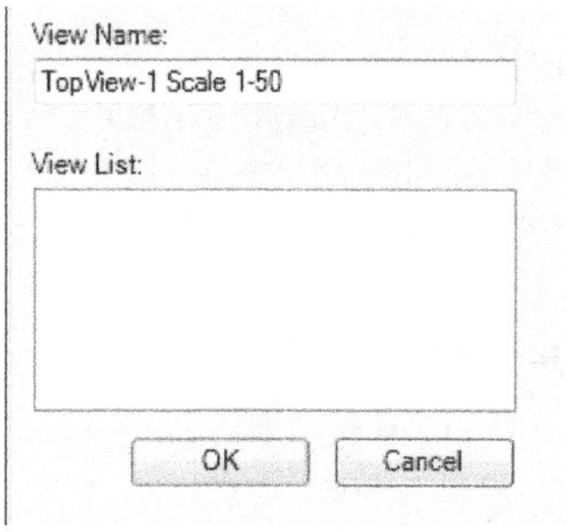

16. Click Paper Check to toggle it on. Verify that the entire red face of the ViewCube box fits within the representation of the title block. Click it again to toggle it off.

17. To create the ortho view, on Ortho Editor tab, on the Create panel, click OK.

18. To place the new viewport:
    - Drop the new view anywhere into the layout.
    - The Ortho Generation dialog box opens with the progress of the generation.
    - The new viewport is created in the layout.

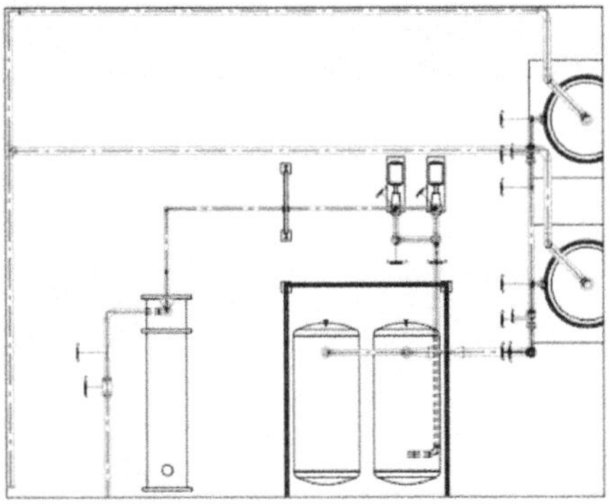

19. Save the drawing and leave it open.

Edit View Scale

In this section of the exercise, you use Edit View to change the scale of the view.

1. To edit the scale of a view, on the Ortho View contextual tab, on the Ortho Views panel, click Edit View.

2. Select the view frame in the layout, as shown in the illustration.

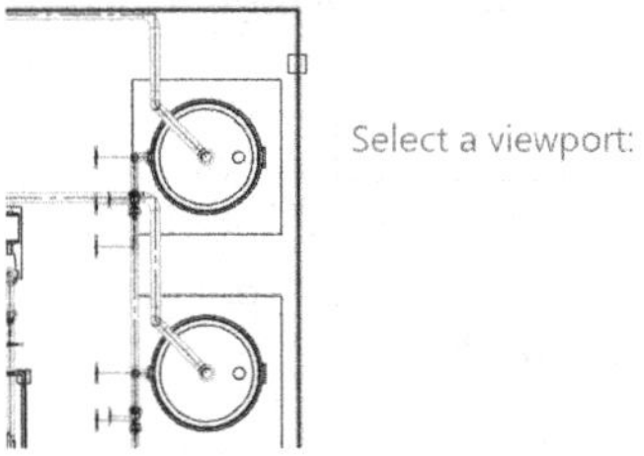

3. On the Ortho Editor tab, on the Output Size panel, for scale, enter **0.01333** and press <Enter>.

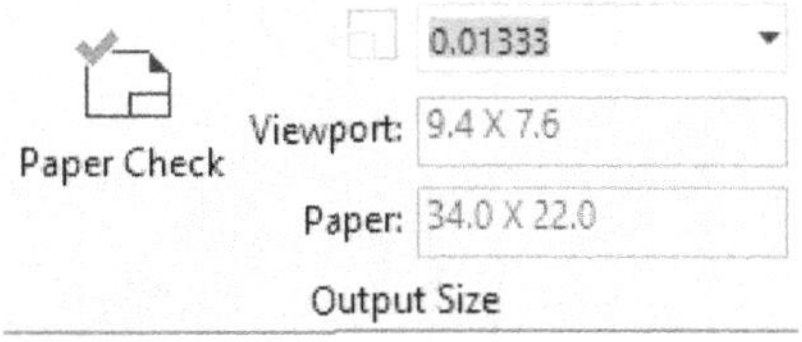

4. To complete the editing:
    - In the Ortho Editor tab, in the Create panel, click OK.
    - The Ortho Generation dialog box opens with the progress of the generation.
    - The edited viewport is updated in the layout with the new scale.

5. Select the view frame to display its grips. Using the middle square grip, reposition the view in the layout to the upper left corner. Press <Esc> to clear the selection.

Create Adjacent Views

In this section of the exercise, you create front and right views of the model.

1. To create a front view, on the Ortho View tab, on the Ortho Views panel, click Adjacent View.

2. In the layout, select the view frame of the view already there (Top View-1).

3. In the Create an Adjacent View dialog box:
    - Select Front in the dialog box.
    - For View Name, enter **Front View-1**.
    - Click OK.

4. Place the front view in the layout below the top view.

5. Repeat steps 1 to 3 using the following settings:

   - Right view.
   - Name the view **Right View-1**.
   - Place the view in the layout to the right of the front view.

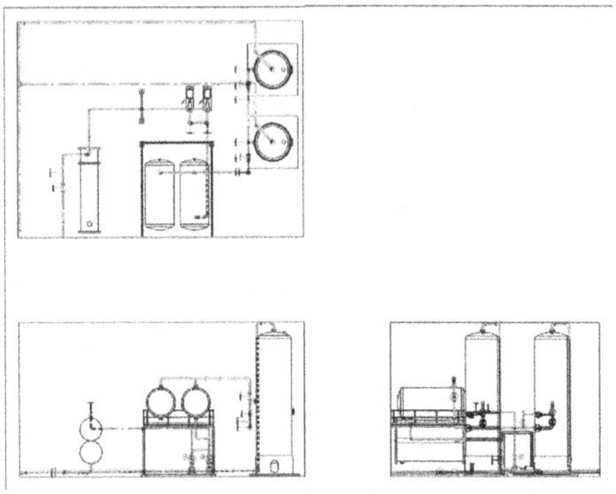

6. Save the drawing and leave it open.

Create a Sectional View

In this section of the exercise, you create a sectional view of the pumps in the model.

1. On the Ortho View tab, on the Ortho Views panel, click New View.

2. In the Select Reference Models dialog box, ensure that the Equipment, Piping, and Structures drawings are selected (checked). Click OK.

3. On the Ortho Editor tab:

   - On the Ortho Cube panel, set the view to Top.
   - On the Output Size panel, set the scale to 1:40.

4. In the drawing screen, select the box to display grips.

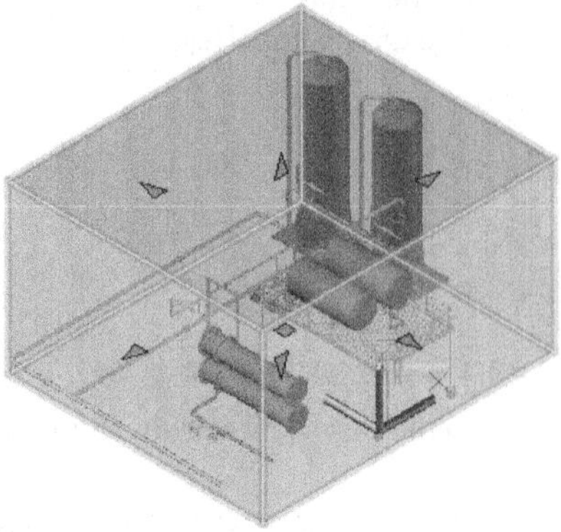

5. In the drawing window, using the ViewCube, change the view to Top.

6. Using the grips, drag the box to enclose only the pumps in the model similar to that shown in the following illustration.

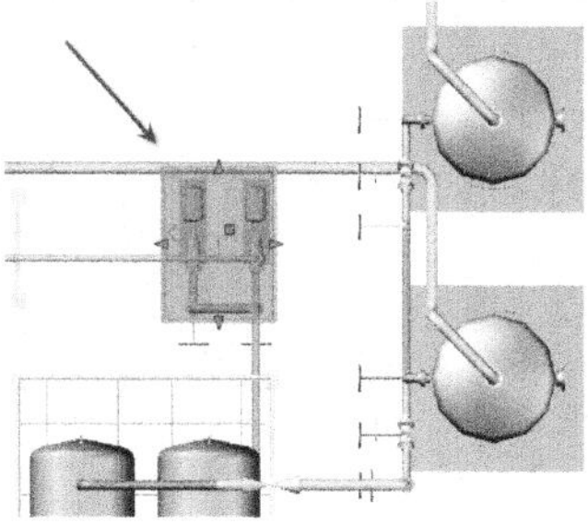

7. In the drawing window, using the ViewCube, change the view to Front.

8. Drag the box to enclose only the pumps in the model similar to that shown in the following illustration.

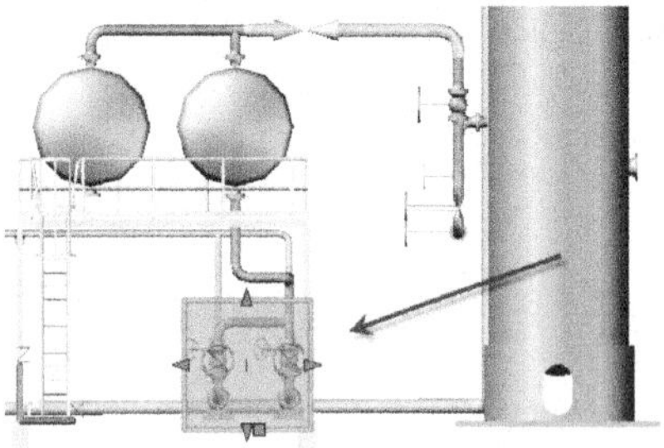

9. On the Ortho Editor tab, on the Create panel, click OK.

10. Place the view in the drawing to the right of the top view.

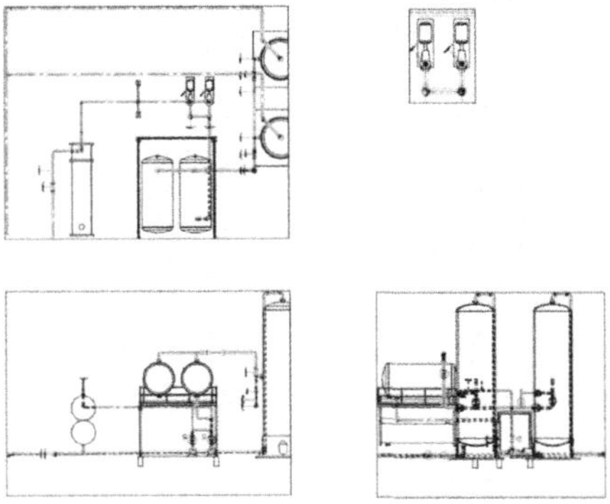

11. Save the drawing and leave it open.

Add Annotation

In this section of the exercise, you annotate the top orthographic view by retrieving and placing tags and adding dimensions.

1. Zoom in to the Top View-1 view and select it (double-click inside it).

   Note: Top View-1 should have a thick outline indicating it is in Model space. The Model button displays in the Status Bar.

2. To add annotation to the vessels on the platform, select the left vessel, right-click and select Ortho Annotate>Oval Tag Style.

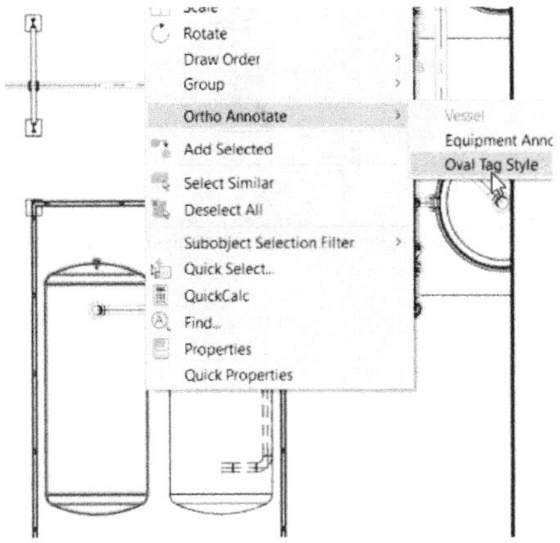

3.
   - Click to place the annotation in the center of the vessel.
   - Select the right vessel as another component to tag.
   - Press <Enter> to select the Oval Tag Style.
   - Click to place the annotation in the center of the right vessel.
   - Press <Esc> to exit the command.

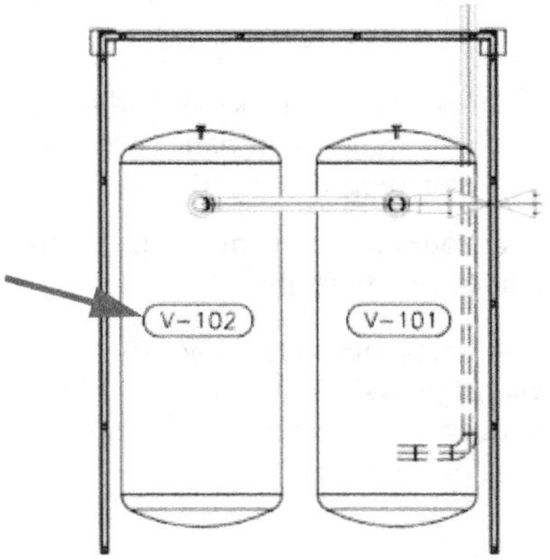

4. To annotate a pipe:
   - Select the pipe as shown in the following illustration.
   - Right-click on it and click Ortho Annotate>Full Line Number Callout [Size-Line Number Tag-Spec].
   - Click to place the annotation at the top of the pipe, as shown in the illustration. Note that the line tag is 1003.

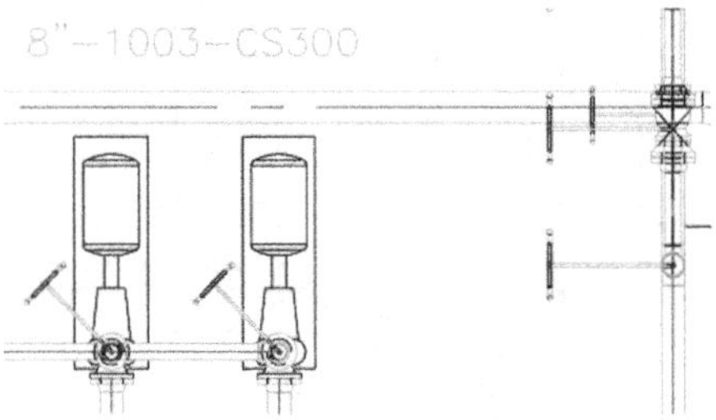

Note: Using the shortcut menu is the preferred method for annotating ortho views. When using the Ortho Annotate command on the Ribbon you do not have easy access to the extended list of annotation styles. To access the other styles, press the down arrow key twice and then press <Enter> twice. Press F2 to open the AutoCAD Text Window and copy the annotation style. Paste it into the command line at the bottom of the window and press <Enter> to activate this style.

5. To place a dimension, on the Ortho View tab, on the Dimensions panel, expand the Dimension drop-down and select Linear.

   Note: You will be switched to paper space to dimension the pipe.

6. Using endpoint osnaps, place the dimension as shown in the following illustration. Depending on your selection, the value might vary.

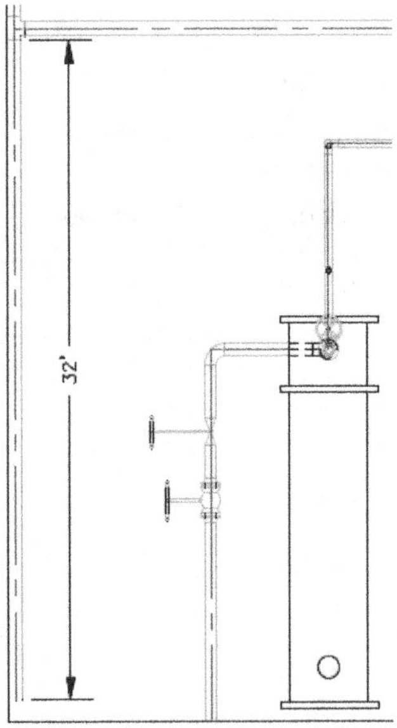

7. Save the drawing and leave it open.

Add Annotations from BOM

1. On the Ortho View tab, on the Table Placement & Setup panel, click Bill of Materials.

2. Select the Top viewport.

3. Along the right side of the smallest view of the pumps, click two opposite points of a window (shown in the illustration) to place the Bill of Materials.

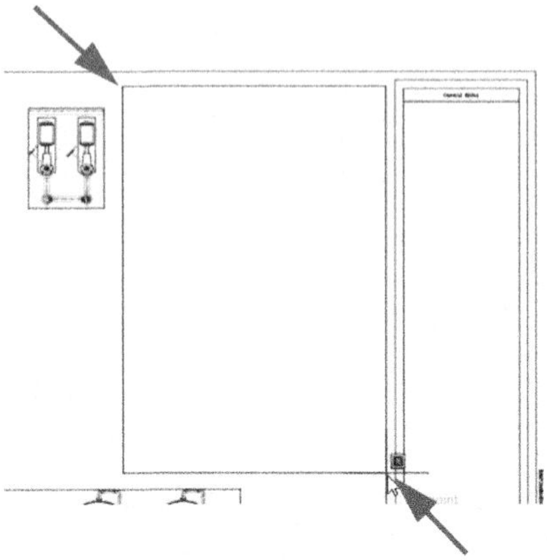

4. The Bill of Materials is placed.

   Note that the items that are cropped out of the viewport are not included in the Bill of Materials.

   If the BOM is overlapping any of the viewport, select the viewport, and using grips, move it.

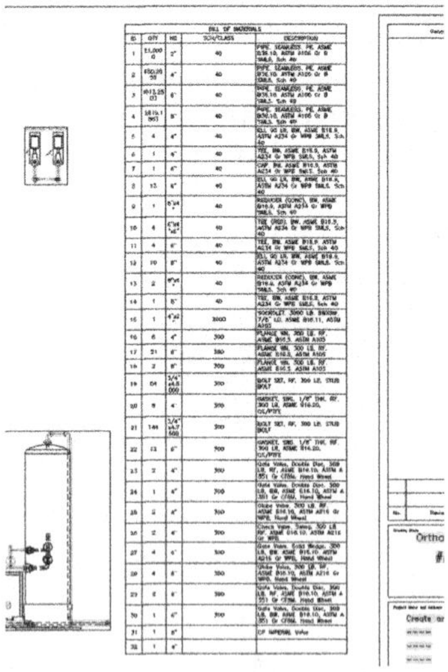

5. To annotate the view:

- Zoom into the top right side portion of the Top view.
- On the Ortho View tab, on the Annotation panel, click BOM Annotation.
- Select the row for ID 27 in the table. The cursor snaps to one of the valves.
- Click to place the bubble near the valve.
- The cursor snaps to another valve.
- Click to place 4 bubbles for the 4 instances of valves as shown in the illustration.

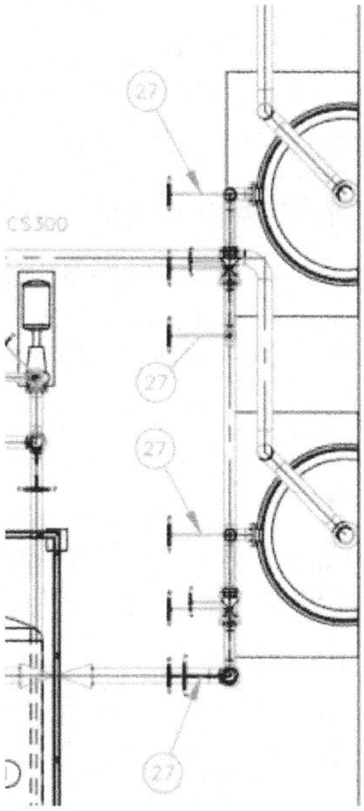

6. In the Front and Right views, note that the annotations are not applied. Using the Ribbon tool, the annotations are only applied to the view from which the BOM is created from.

7. To apply BOM annotations using the right-click menu:

- In the Top view, right-click on the elbow coming out of the left vessel.
- In the right-click menu, select Ortho Annotate>Bill of Material (BOM).
- Click to place the item bubble. A bubble with ID 8 is placed.

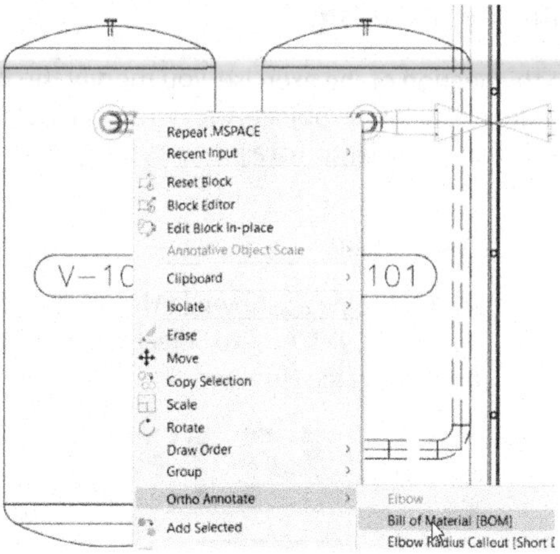

8. To apply BOM annotations using the right-click menu:

- Double-click inside the Front view to activate it.
- In the Front view, locate the same elbow which comes out of the left vessel, as shown in the illustration.
- Right-click on it and select Ortho Annotate>Bill of Material (BOM).
- Click to place the item bubble. A bubble with the same ID 8 is placed, as shown in the illustration.

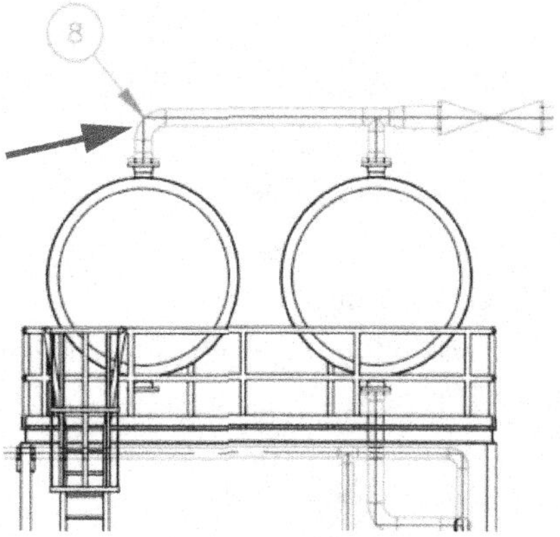

9. Save the drawing and leave it open.

Modify the Design

In this section of the exercise, you modify the tag value for one of the objects previously annotated and change the length of a pipe segment that was dimensioned.

1. Activate the Piping drawing.
2. Select the pipe as shown in the illustration. Right-click, click Add to Selection, and click Connected Line Number.

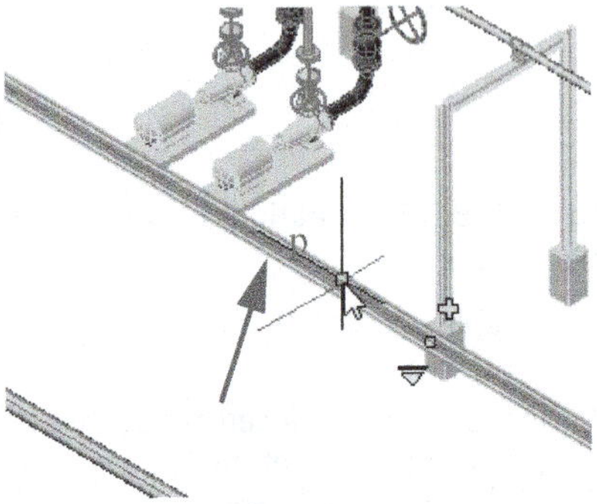

3. On the Properties palette, under Tag, for Line Number Tag, select New.

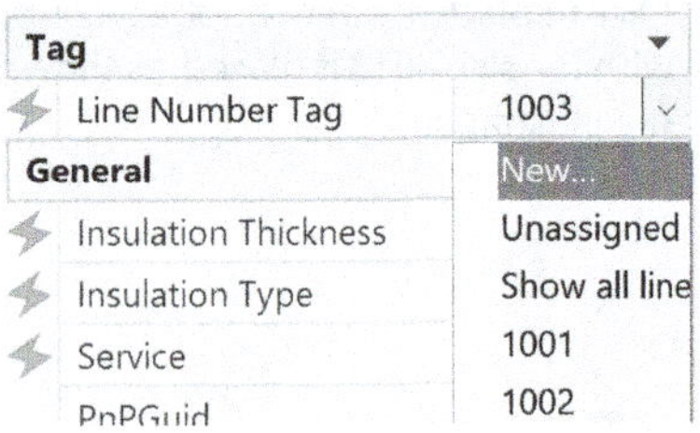

4. In the Assign Tag dialog box:
   - For Number, enter **2031**.
   - Click Assign.
   - Press <Esc> to clear the selection of the line.

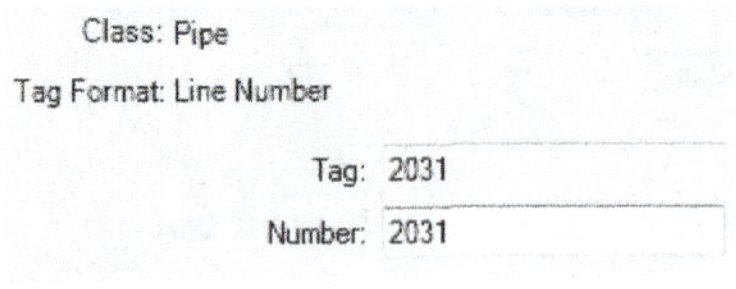

5. Using the ViewCube, change to South-West isometric view.
6. Select the cyan pipe near the open end as shown:
   - Select the Move Part grip at the end.
   - For Length, enter **13'**. Note that the pipe is shortened.
   - Press <Esc> to exit selection.

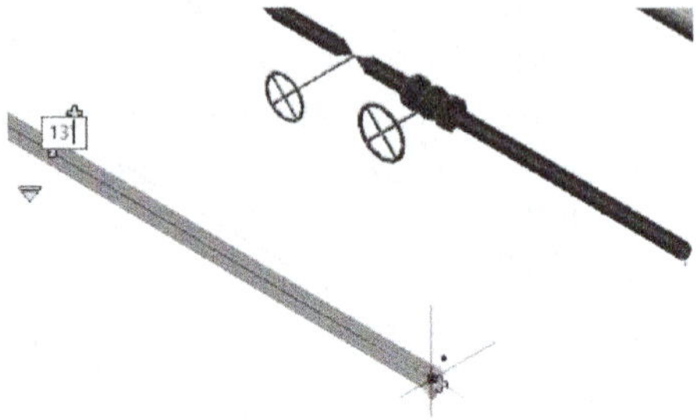

7. Save the drawing and leave it open.

Update Orthographic Drawings

In this section of the exercise, you validate and update the orthographic drawings to represent the changes made in the last section of the exercise.

1. In the Project Manager, click the Orthographic DWG tab.
2. Expand Orthographic Drawings and right-click on Orthographic. Click Validate Views.

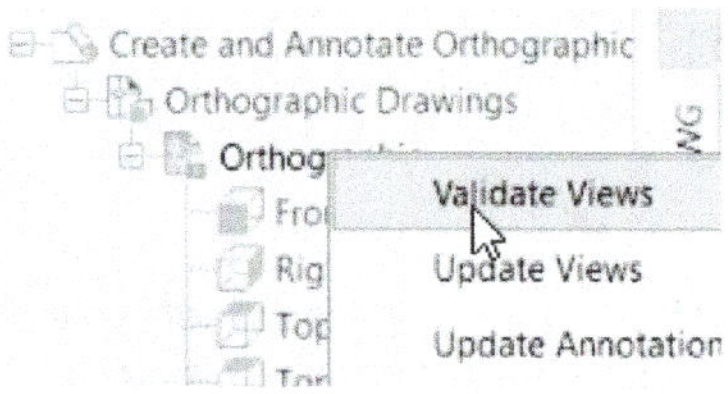

3. Examine the results of the validation. The view icons turn red, indicating that they no longer represent the latest version of the model.

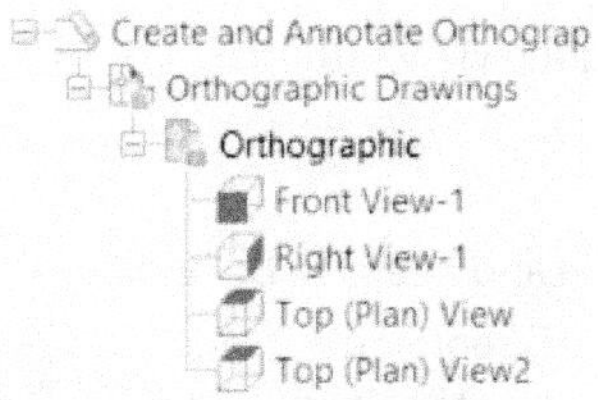

4. Right-click on Orthographic again. Click Update Views. If one of the views was already up-to-date, you can validate it again.

5. Examine the results of the update:

   - In the Project Manager, all the view icons turn to regular color (not red).
   - The annotation on the line is updated to reflect the new line number.
   - The pipe that was shortened is represented in orthographic view, as shown in the following illustration.
   - The dimension did not update, as shown in the following illustration. Dimensions in orthographic views must be adjusted manually.

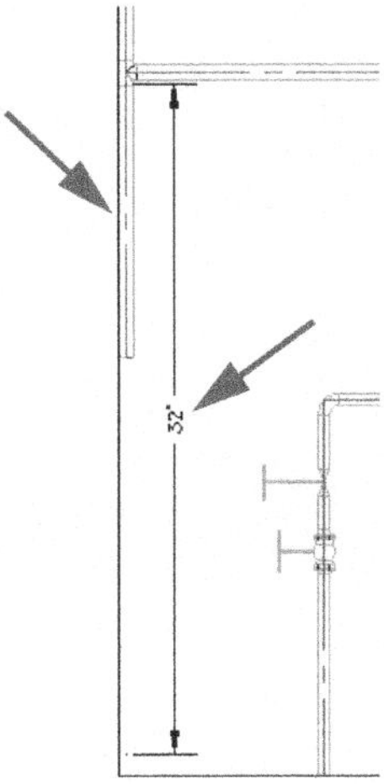

6. Select the dimension. Using an endpoint osnap, place the dimension on the new endpoint of the shortened pipe. Note that it is updated to display 13'.

7. Save and close all drawings.

Lesson Review Questions

1. Can you store the settings of an orthographic ViewCube?
   a. Yes, you can save the ortho cube while creating or editing the view settings.
   b. This has to be done in your orthographic drawing template.
   c. Saving orthographic view settings is not possible.
2. How do you know whether an orthographic view is out of date and needs to be updated?
   a. Select the update view button to show whether an update is required.
   b. Right-click on the drawing name in the Project Manager and click the Validate Views option to show which views need to be updated.
   c. Views are not linked to the 3D model and must be recreated if they are out of date.
3. Is it possible to create an adjacent orthographic view from any existing orthographic view?
   a. No, only the first view placed can be used to create adjacent views.
   b. Yes, each view you create can be used to create adjacent views.
   c. Yes, but there is a maximum number of adjacent views that can be created.
4. When properties have changed in the 3D model (such as the tag), how do you update any corresponding annotation in the orthographic drawing?
   a. On the Ortho View tab, on the Annotation panel, click Update Annotate. This checks the value of the annotation in the 3D model and updates it if required.
   b. Annotations cannot be updated and need to be replaced if they are out of date.
   c. Annotations update automatically as properties change in the 3D model.

Lesson: Creating Isometric Drawings

Overview

This lesson describes the creation and modification of an isometric drawing. Along with learning how to create an Iso, you learn how to add Iso-specific information, such as insulation, flow arrows, and floor penetration. You also learn how to change the components and connectors from shop to field and how to show the 3D insulation.

A single pipe run is rarely all in the same plane. Because a pipe run typically changes direction multiple times, trying to visualize the pipelines can be challenging when viewing the design in orthographic views. To make it easier to view and visualize pipelines, you need to create isometric drawings. Isometrics are also used to fabricate the pipelines.

Objectives

After completing this lesson, you will be able to:

- Describe what isometric drawings are in the project.
- Identify the tools used to add data to an isometric drawing.
- State the high-level process to create an isometric drawing.

About Creating Isometric Drawings

Isometric drawings are representations of the model that include additional data in the form of symbols, labels, and drawing objects that describe model components, connections, and requirements for either the entire model, or specific lines only, as shown in the following illustration. Isometric information, symbols, and labels are represented in the model by points, or small globes. The data itself is not visible in the model. Rather, the data is mapped through specifications to generate the symbols and additional information in the isometric drawing once it is created.

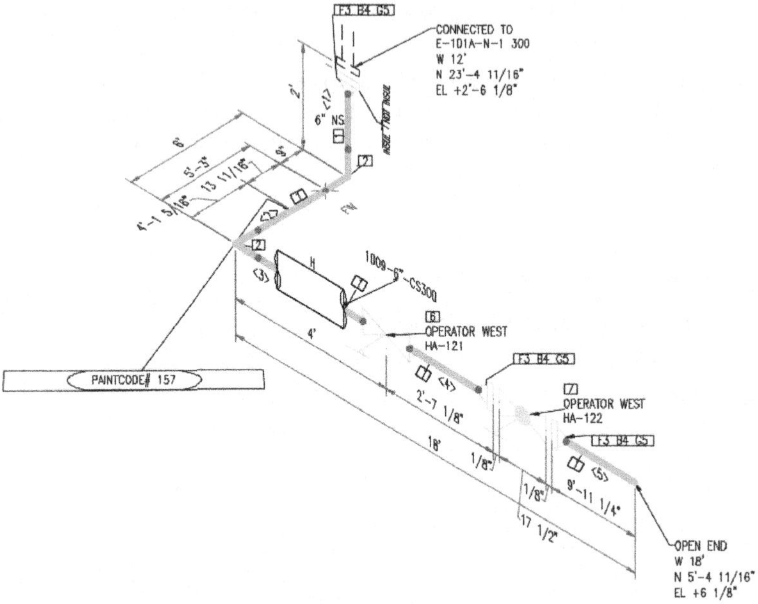

Creating and Adding Data to Isometric Drawings

There are three main tasks in documenting a 3D plant design:

- Annotating the 3D model geometry with information so that the isometric drawings are annotated as required.
- Producing the isometric drawings of the 3D design.
- Locking the line so that changes are not made by mistake.

Iso Annotations

You add Iso information to the 3D design by using the tools on the Isos tab, on the Iso Annotations panel, as shown in the following illustration. The annotation information you add to the model is then automatically included in isometric drawings of that line.

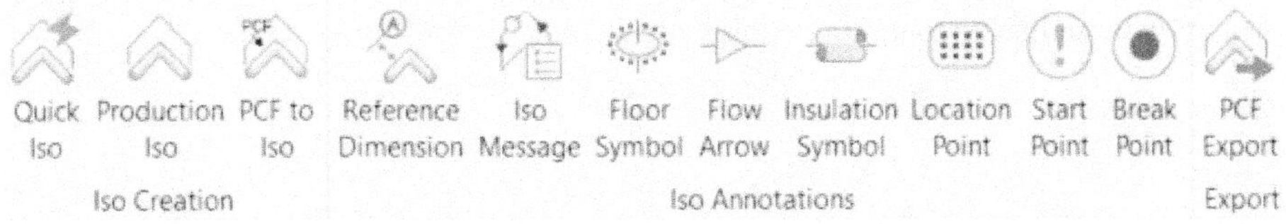

You add Iso messages to the isometric drawing using the Create Iso Message dialog box, as shown in the following illustration. There are several additional enclosure types that can be selected in the drop-down.

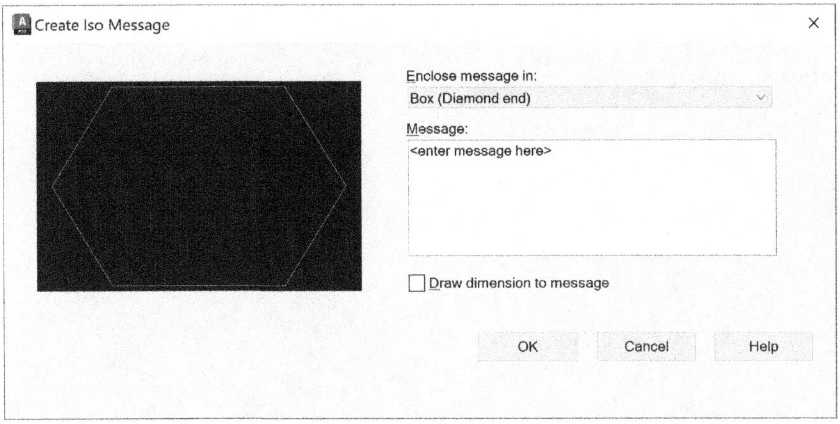

Other isometric references can be added to the model (e.g. insulation symbols, Location points, the iso Start Point, Break points etc.). Reference dimensions can be added in addition to dimensions that are automatically applied during isometric creation. Dimensions applied here can reference adjacent pipelines, structure, equipment etc. from the model.

Production ISO

When you create a Production Iso, you select the lines from which to create it in the Create Production Iso dialog box, as shown in the following illustration. Select the Overwrite if existing check box to prevent creating multiple isometric versions of the same line. By selecting the Create DWF check box, DWF files are created of the Isos generated. This enables you to create DWF files of the isometric drawings without having to use the Publish command.

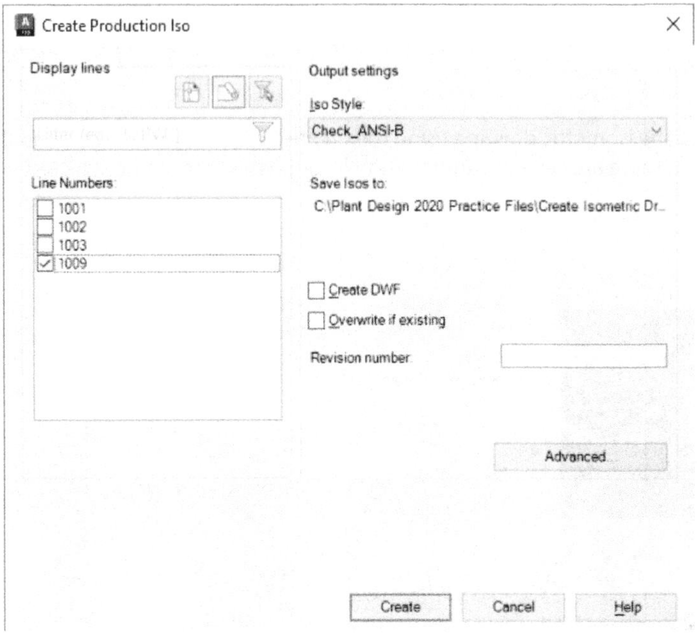

Line Lock and Issue

You can lock a line in a project, including the model, directly from the line number in the Isometric DWG tab of the Project Manager.

Once locked, a lock symbol displays on the item when you hover over it, as shown in the following illustration. Additionally, a line of text is added to the top of the tooltip. To review when the item was locked and by whom, you can review the Lock Change By and Lock Change At options in the Properties palette.

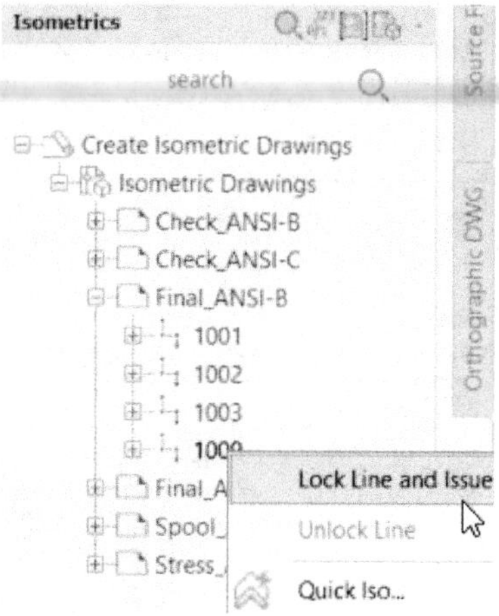

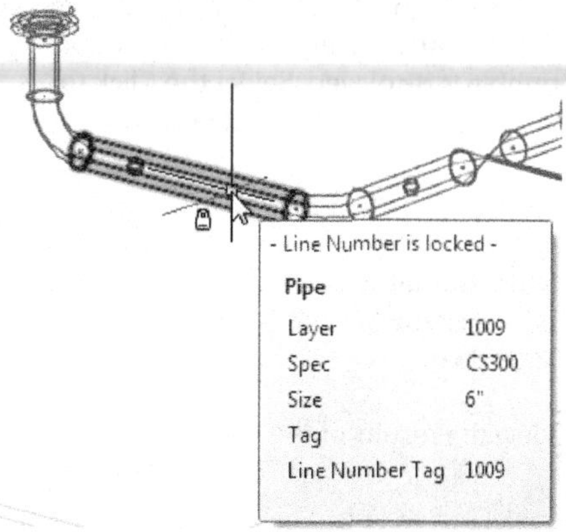

Refer to the help system to learn more about additional tools and options for creating and troubleshooting isometric drawings.

Process to Create Isometric Drawings

Creating isometric drawings can be an iterative process that might require changes to be made to the model if there are missing components, or changes to be made to existing components. The basic process is as follows:

1. Start the Production Iso command.
2. Select the line from which you want to create the isometric drawing. Click Create.

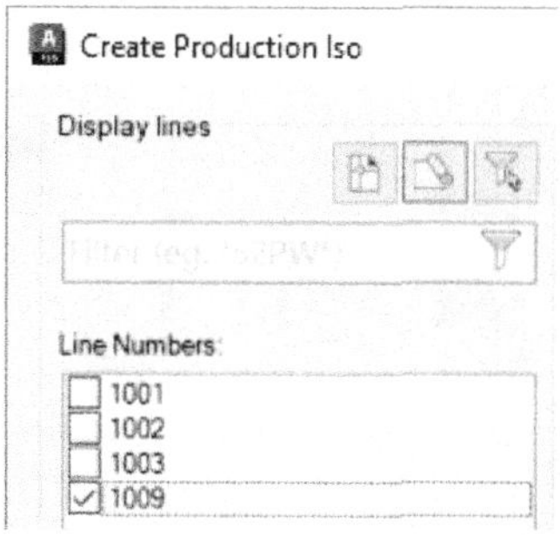

3. In the Create Production Iso dialog box, under Output settings, select an Iso Style from the drop-down. Select any additional options and click Create.

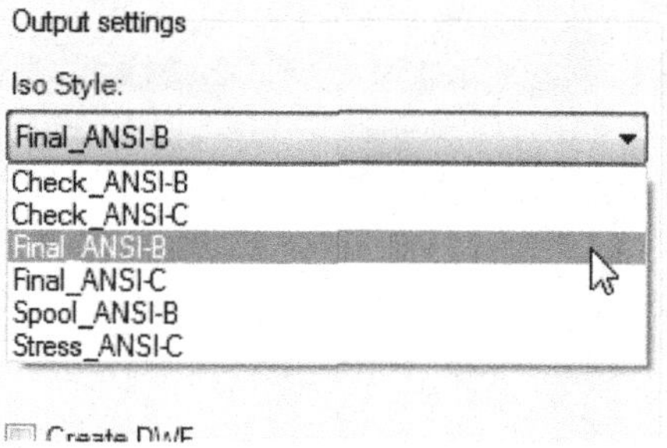

4. When the Isometric creation is complete, in the Status Bar, an Isometric Creation bubble is displayed. Select the Click to view isometric creation details link.

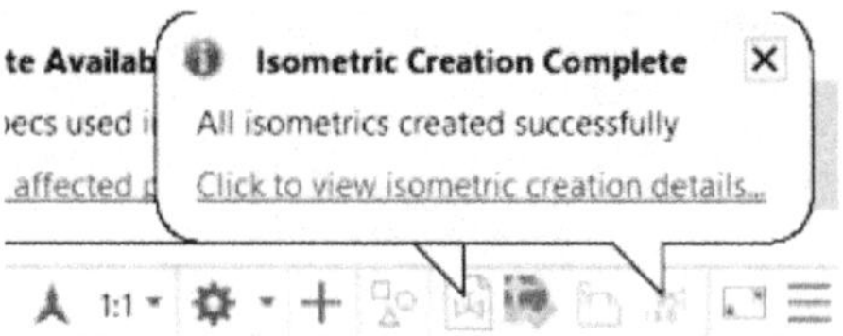

5. In the Isometric Creation Results dialog box, click the link for the file. (e.g., 1009.dwg).

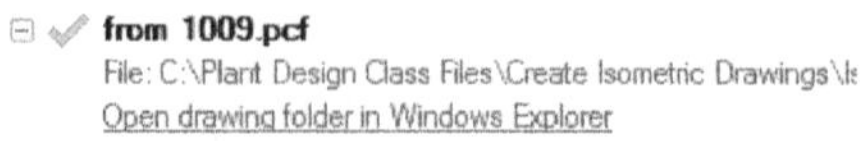

6. View the results of the creation.

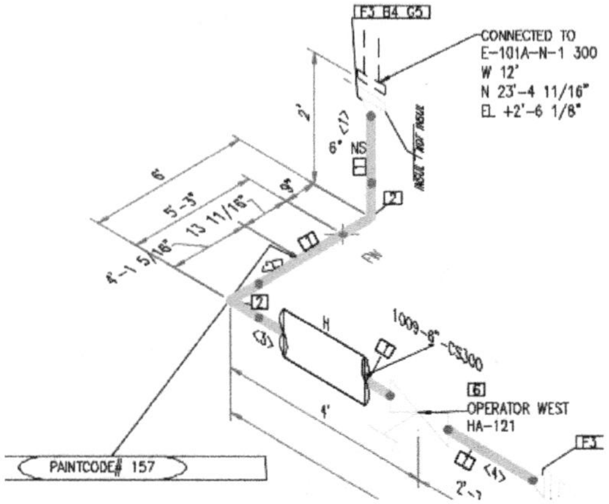

Exercise: Create Isometric Drawings

In this exercise, you create an isometric drawing based on a line number. You then make changes in the model, such as adding information and messages, changing shop and field values, adding insulation, and locking layers. After each change, you recreate the isometric drawing to examine the result of your changes.

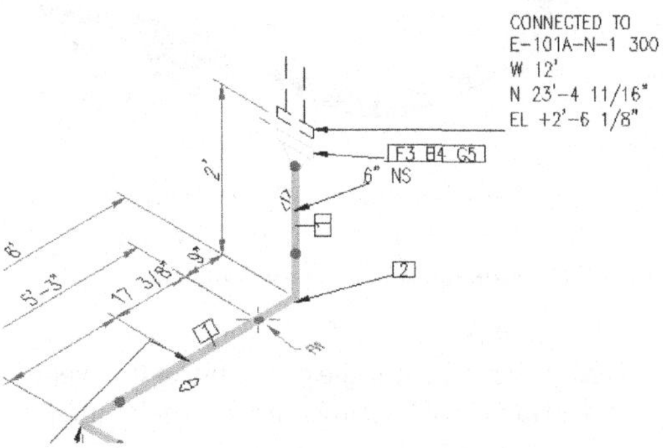

Create an Isometric Drawing

In this section of the exercise, you create an isometric drawing based on a single line section.

1. Start the AutoCAD Plant 3D software, if not already running.
2. Open an existing project by doing the following:
   - In the Project Manager, Current Project list, click Open.
   - In the Open dialog box, navigate to the folder *C:\Plant Design 2024 Practice Files\Create Isometric Drawings*.
   - Select the file *Project.xml*.
   - Click Open.
3. In the Project Manager, expand Plant 3D Drawings and Piping folders. Open the *Piping* drawing.
4. To identify the line from which you will create the Iso, in the drawing screen, hover the cursor over the line coming out from the bottom of the heat exchangers. Note that the line number is 1009.

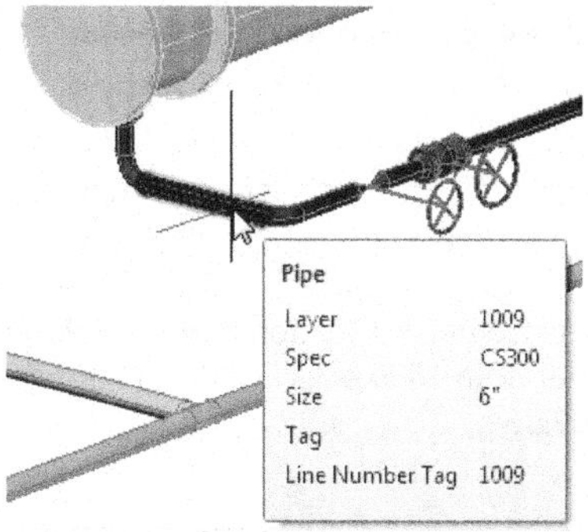

5. Activate the 3D Piping workspace, if not already active.
6. On the Isos tab, on the Iso Creation panel, click Production Iso.
7. In the Create Production Iso dialog box, under Line Numbers, select the 1009 check box.

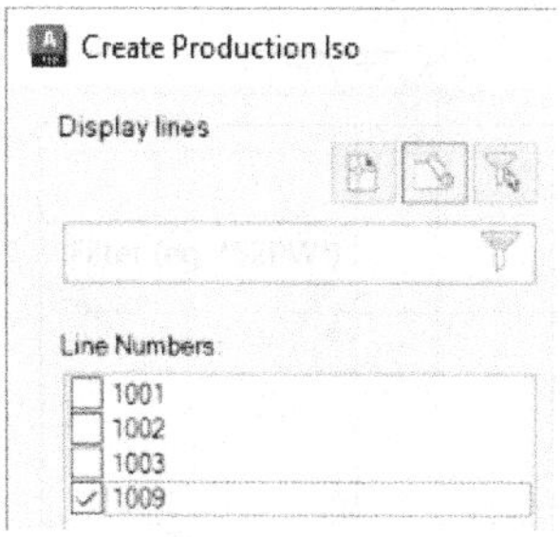

8. In the Create Production Iso dialog box, under Output settings:
   - From the Iso Style list, select Final_ANSI-B.
   - Click Create.

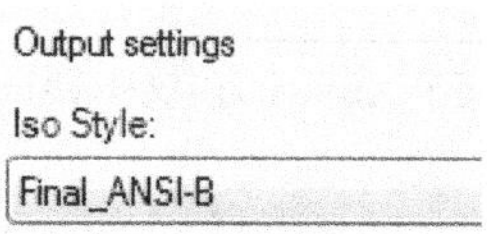

9. Note that in the status bar, the Isometric Creation icon is red, indicating the isometric creation process is in progress. When the Isometric creation is complete, the Isometric Creation icon turns blue and an information bubble is displayed. Click the Click to view isometric creation details link.

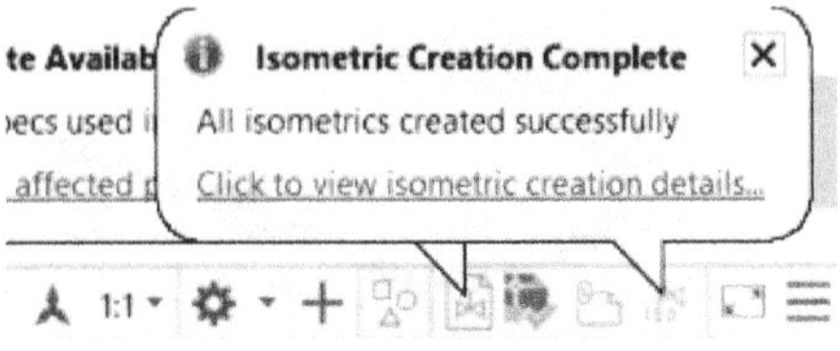

10. In the Isometric Creation Results dialog box, under from 1009.pcf, click the link for the file 1009.dwg.

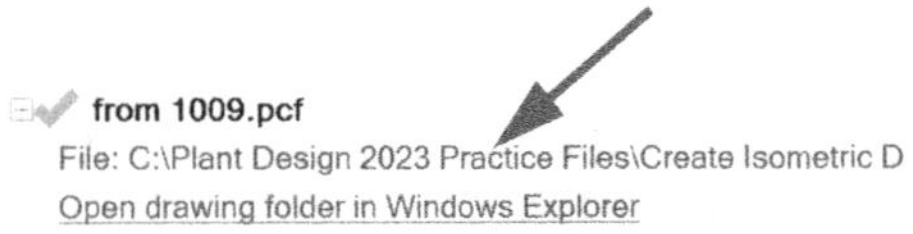

11. In the 1009 drawing that opens, review the symbols and labels in the new Iso drawing.

12. Review the Bill of Materials and Cut Piece list tables.

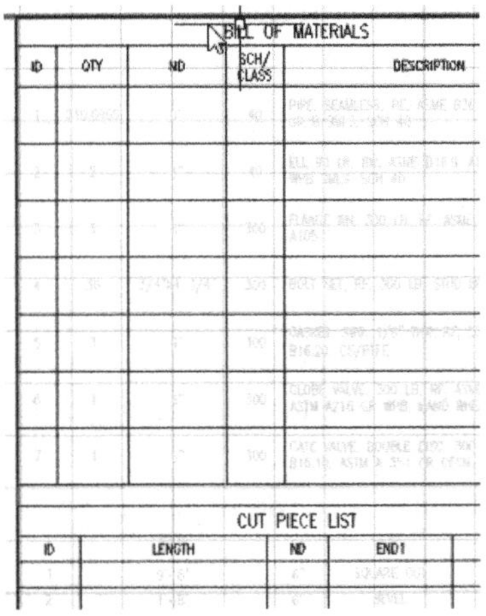

13. Close the isometric drawing 1009 without saving.

Change a Shop Weld to a Field Weld

In this section of the exercise, you change shop welds to field welds in the model, and regenerate the isometric drawing to view the results.

1. Return to the Piping drawing, if required.

2. To change the view to 2D Wireframe, on the Home tab, on the View panel, click 2d Wireframe from the Visual style list.

3. In the Home tab, in the Visibility panel, click Weld Symbols (toggle on) to make the weld symbols visible. Type REGEN in the Command line to update the screen.

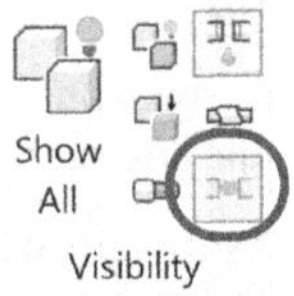

4. Connectors in the 3D wireframe view are represented by points. Using a window (not a crossing window), select the connector as shown in the following illustration.

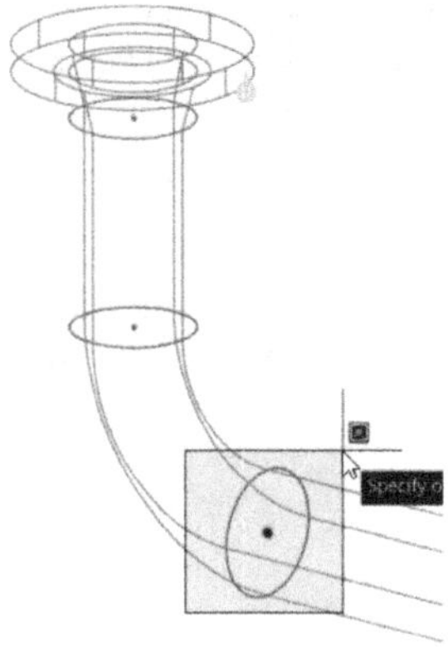

5. With the grip displayed on the connector, right-click and click Properties, if the Properties palette is not displayed.

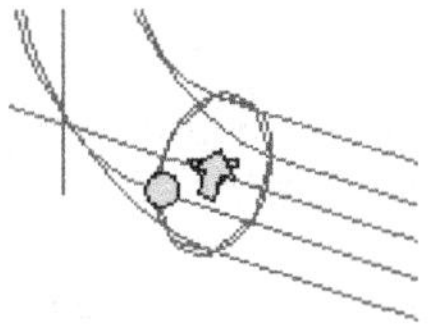

6. On the Properties palette:
   - Verify that you have selected the connector.
   - In the lower General section, change Shop/Field to FIELD.

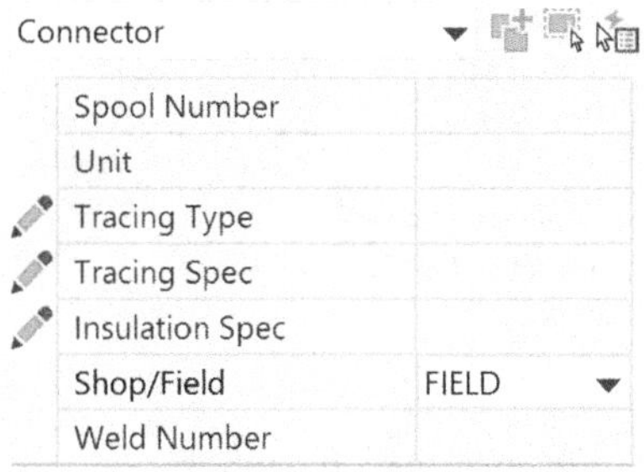

7. Close Properties and press <Esc> to clear the selection. Note that the drawing marker updates to the FIELD WELD symbol (cross).

   Type REGEN in the Command line to update the view and display the new weld symbols.

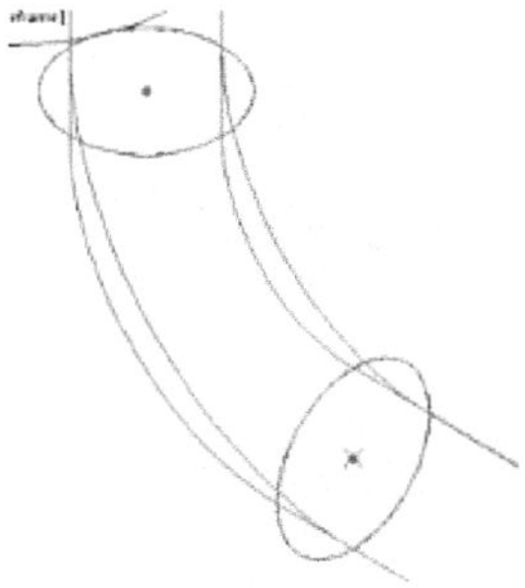

8. Save the drawing.

9. To regenerate the isometric drawing, on the Isos tab, on the Iso Creation panel, click Production Iso.

10. Recreate the 1009 line by selecting 1009 in the dialog box. Also select Overwrite if existing. This prevents the creation of multiple isometric versions. Click Create.

11. When the creation is complete, click on the link in the Isometric Creation Complete bubble and then in the Isometric Creation Results dialog box to view the isometric creation details. Note that your weld is now indicated by an FW symbol.

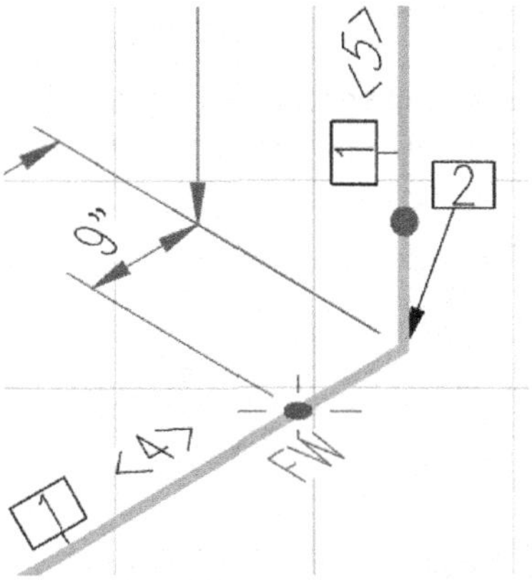

12. Close the isometric drawing without saving.

Adding Messages

In this section of the exercise, you add an isometric message to the drawing.

1. With the Piping drawing open, select the pipe, as shown in the following illustration, to display the pipeline.

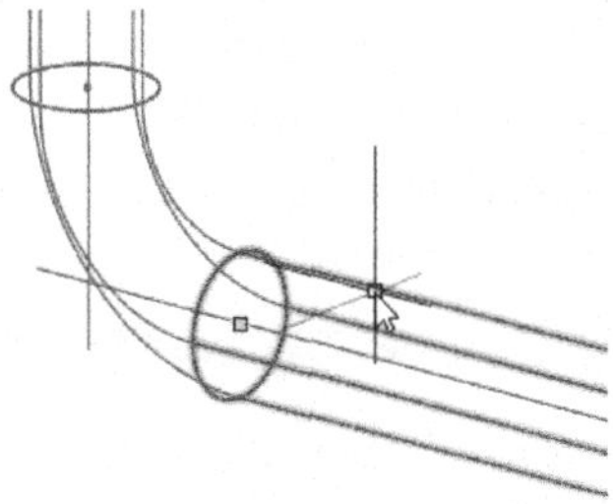

2. On the Isos tab, on the Iso Annotations panel, click Iso Message.

3. In the Create Iso Message dialog box:
   - Under Enclose message in, select Box (Round end).
   - In the Message window, enter **Paintcode# 157**.
   - Click OK.

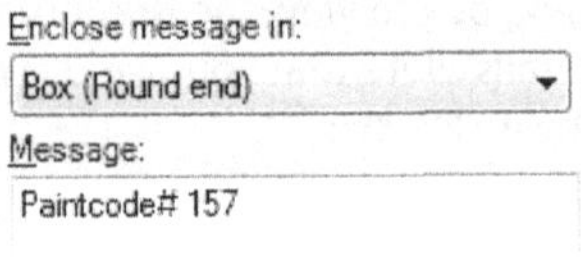

4. When prompted for location, select the pipe as shown in the following illustration.

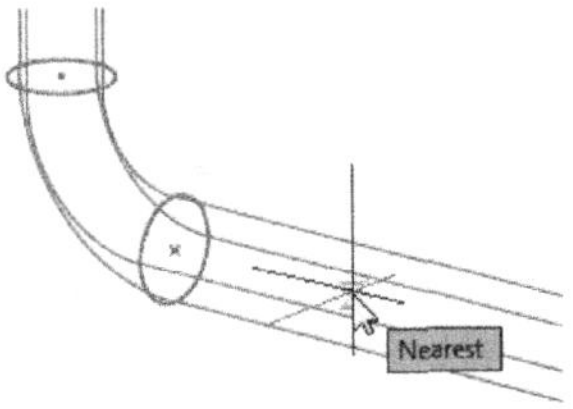

5. Note the glyph that is inserted.

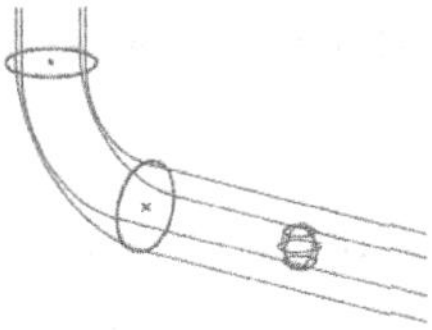

6. Save the drawing.
7. Recreate the isometric drawing for line 1009. In the Create Production Iso dialog box, select Overwrite if existing to prevent the creation of multiple isometric versions.
8. Examine the results of the isometric message in the isometric drawing.

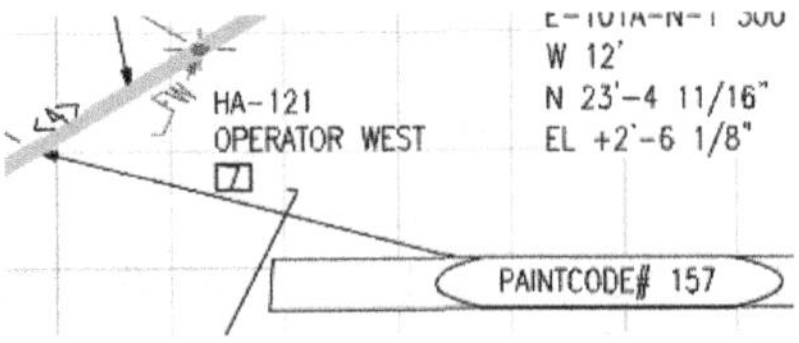

9. Close the isometric drawing without saving.

Create Isometric Information

In this section of the exercise, you add insulation to a line and specify where to show the insulation symbol on the line.

1. To select the entire line number that you want to add insulation to, select the flange that connects to the bottom of the heat exchanger and select the pipe segment with the open end along the right side.

   Right-click and in the shortcut menu, select Add to Selection> Connected path between selected parts.

2. On the Properties palette, under Process Line:
   - For Insulation Type, select **H - Hot**.

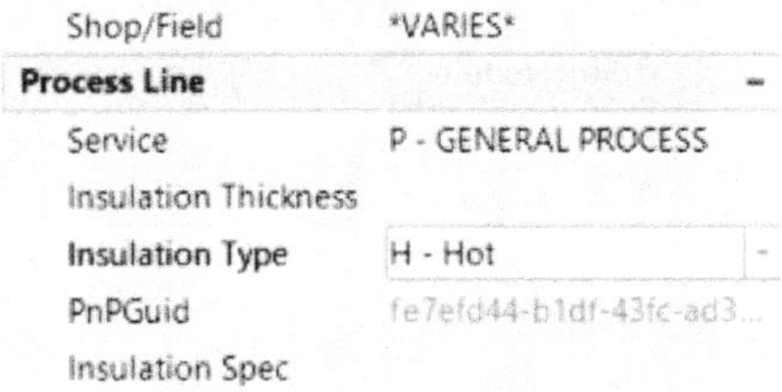

3. To add an insulation symbol:
   - On the Isos tab, on the Iso Annotations panel, click Insulation Symbol.
   - Click to position the insulation symbol on the pipe where identified. Note the glyph that is inserted in the line.

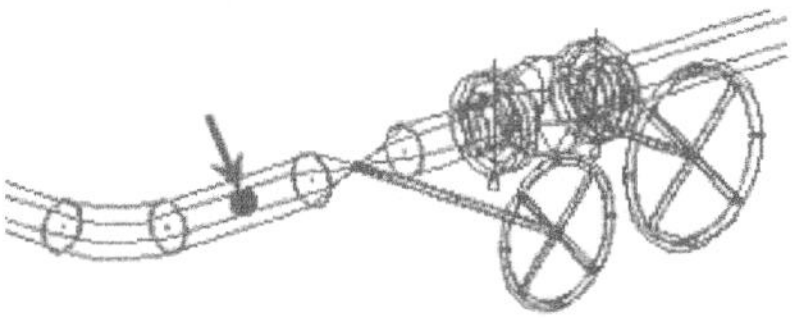

4. To add a Reference Dimension to the pipeline 1003:

   - On the Isos tab, on the Iso Annotations panel, click Reference Dimension.
   - Click to position the dimension location by the elbow on line 1009 as shown below.
   - Click to select a perpendicular point on line 1003.

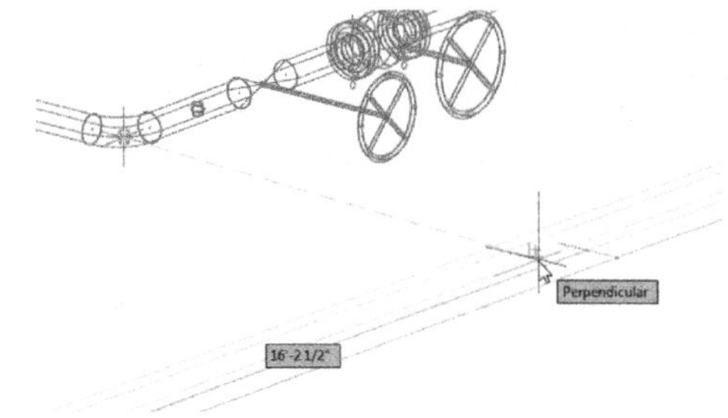

5. On the Properties palette, under Reference Dimensions, for Y Dimension, select Hide from the pull-down list.

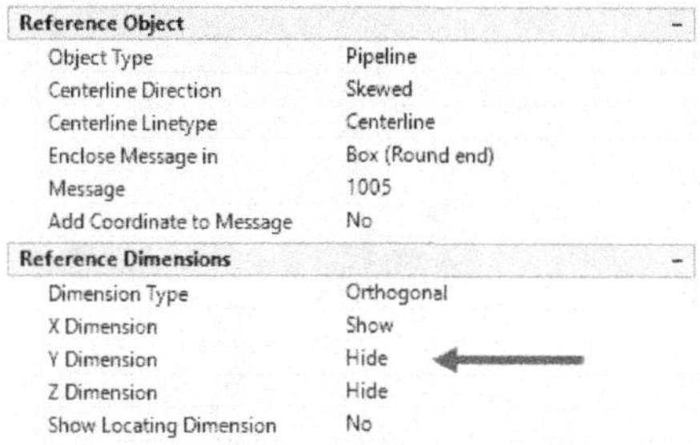

Reference Object	-
Object Type	Pipeline
Centerline Direction	Skewed
Centerline Linetype	Centerline
Enclose Message in	Box (Round end)
Message	1005
Add Coordinate to Message	No
Reference Dimensions	-
Dimension Type	Orthogonal
X Dimension	Show
Y Dimension	Hide
Z Dimension	Hide
Show Locating Dimension	No

6. Recreate the isometric for line 1009 with Overwrite if existing.

7. When the creation is complete, click to view the isometric creation details.

8. Examine the results in the isometric drawing. The insulation symbol is now added and a reference dimension to line 1003 is added.

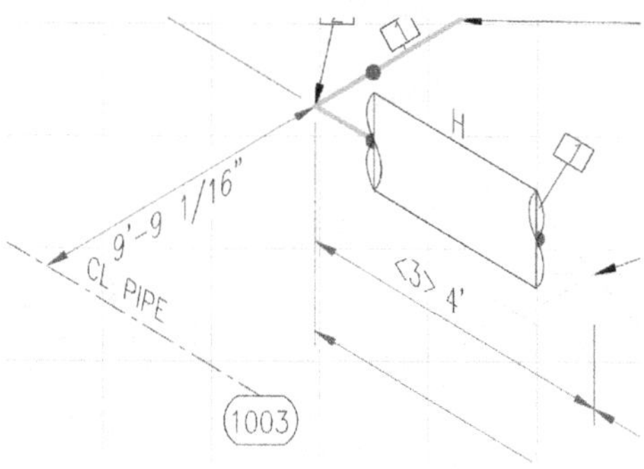

9. Close the isometric drawing without saving.

Line Lock and Issue

In this section of the exercise, you lock a line so that it cannot be edited.

1. With the Piping drawing open, in the Project Manager, click the Isometric DWG tab.

2. Under Final ANSI-B, right-click on the 1009 line. Click Lock Line and Issue.

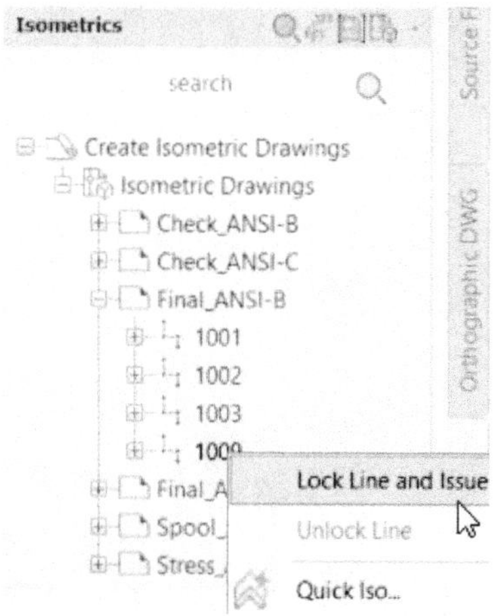

3. In the drawing screen, hover the cursor over line 1009 in the model. Note the lock symbol and the Line Number is locked text in the tooltip.

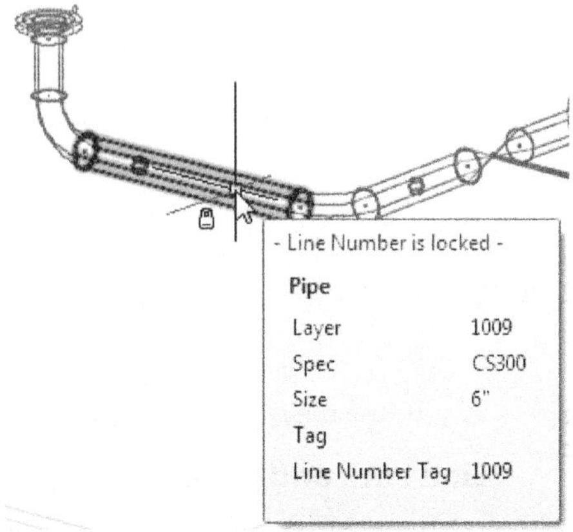

4. Save and close all drawings.

Lesson Review Questions

1. In the Project Manager, you can lock lines on the Isometric Drawing tab. Is it possible for others to see when this line was locked and who locked it?
   a. Yes, the properties of the 3D pipe show who locked the pipe and when it was locked.
   b. No, only the information that it is locked is available.
2. Often an Iso is created multiple times. How do you prevent creating multiple Isos of the same line?
   a. Manually remove the Iso from the Project Manager and delete the file using Windows Explorer.
   b. Change the line number.
   c. Select Overwrite if existing in the Create Production Iso dialog box.
3. Can you create DWF files of the generated Isos without using the Publish command?
   a. In the Create Production Iso dialog box, an option can be found to automatically create a DWF file of each Iso that is generated.
   b. The only way to create DWF files is by using the Publish command.
   c. You can create DWF files from the Command Line.

Chapter Summary

In this chapter, you learned how to use the AutoCAD Plant 3D software to create and modify a 3D plant design and 2D views of the 3D design.

Having completed this chapter, you can:

- Add drawings to a project by creating them new, linking to existing drawings, and copying them from another project.
- Setup a grid, add steel members, ladders, stairs, railings, plates and footing, and modify the steel structure.
- Model and place 3D equipment.
- Create and route pipe and place pipe components.
- Create and use parts and place holder parts and change a line number, size, or spec.
- Use a P&ID to create and validate pipelines in the 3D design.
- Create and annotate orthographic views.
- Create isometric views.

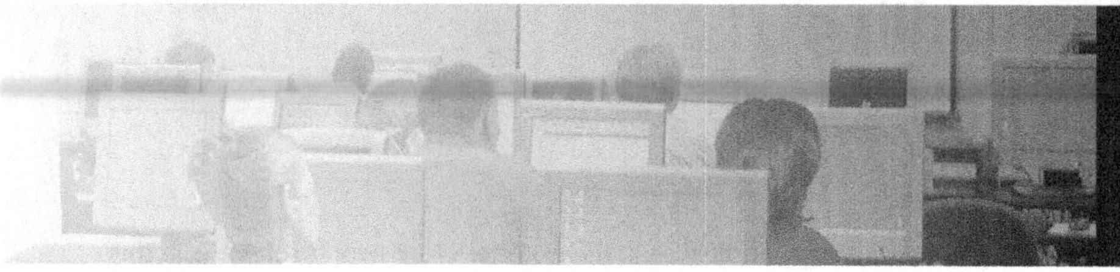

Chapter 4

Autodesk Navisworks

Design review, visualization, and error identification are tasks and benefits of creating 3D plant designs. Being able to do these tasks project-wide when design data is created in a variety of design and engineering applications can be a daunting task. By using the Autodesk® Navisworks® software, you can combine design files into a single integrated project model for efficient whole-project review. In this chapter, you learn how to use the Autodesk Navisworks software to view, review, and analyze a plant design.

Objectives

After completing this chapter, you will be able to:

- Work with and handle files in the Autodesk Navisworks software.
- Navigate and walk through a design in the Autodesk Navisworks software.
- Conduct clash tests and work with clash detection results.
- Create rendered images and animations and use TimeLiner to link to an external scheduling project file and to create a simulation.

Lesson: File Handling

Overview

This lesson describes how to work with and handle files in the Autodesk Navisworks software. In this lesson you learn how to open existing NWD files, import 3D data from DWG files, save NWF files, and publish NWD files for sharing with others. You also learn how to set file units, merge 3D design information, refresh files, and send and receive files by email.

It has become common practice that design projects are created in separate parts by different people using different design software. These separate files need to be reviewed at the same time to permit correct collaboration. One of the important capabilities in the Autodesk Navisworks software is the ability to open and combine different files for review.

Objectives

After completing this lesson, you will be able to:

- Recognize when to use NWD versus NWF files.
- Set the units in an Autodesk Navisworks file.
- Publish NWD files.

File Formats

Autodesk Navisworks File Formats

The Autodesk Navisworks software can create and open the following formats of files:

- **NWD -** This type of file contains all the graphics and data from one or more DWG files that make up an AutoCAD Plant 3D project. When you save the NWD file, all the information from the DWG files is contained within the NWD file. External files are not attached.
- **NWF -** This type of file is a dynamic view of a project. When you use a NWF, you link the various DWG files together. The Autodesk Navisworks software automatically makes NWC (cache) files for each DWG to improve performance. When you open a NWF file, the Autodesk Navisworks software automatically checks to see if a DWG file has been changed since it was last cached and makes a new cache if it is out of date. An NWF file is much smaller than an NWD file.
- **NWC -** Autodesk Navisworks cache files are used to load NWF files.

If you are going to send someone a project, you should use an NWD file. It is preferred because it is all inclusive and contains the required information in the single file. This makes it easier to manage. With the compression, it is not as large a file, which makes sharing more manageable. NWF files are less attractive because of its lack of compression and requirement for all attachments. The disadvantage to using the NWD versus the NWF is that it is a snapshot in time and does not automatically update.

Working with Files

Appending Files

To add models to an existing scene, you can append model files. When appending files, multiple file formats can be opened. These file formats include Autodesk Navisworks files, AutoCAD files, Microstation files, 3D Point Clouds that come in from scanned data, SketchUp files, etc. The file formats that can be appended are shown in the following illustration.

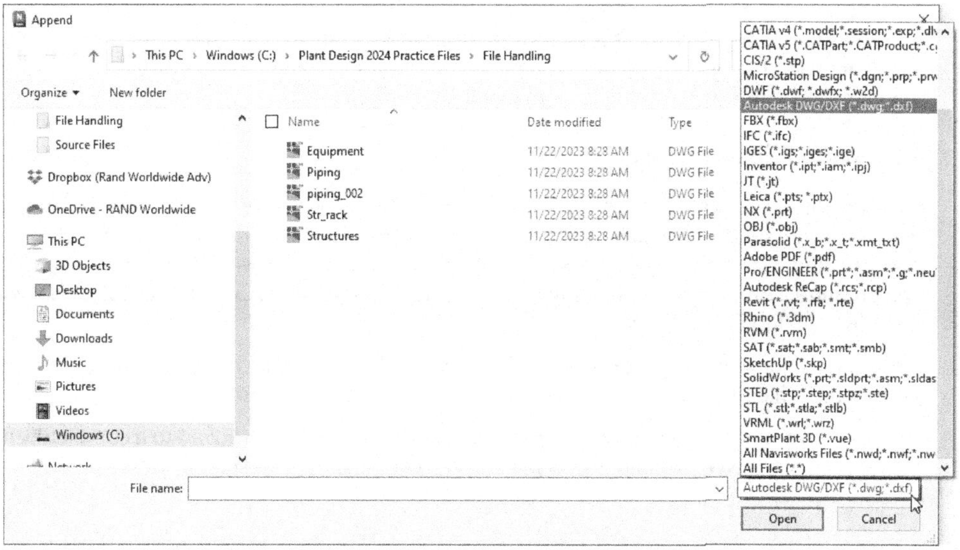

Another option is to make a master model in the AutoCAD software and Xref all the parts into it before you create a NWD in the Autodesk Navisworks software. If all the parts of the model are in DWG files and already Xref'd together, this would be easier than appending each file in the Autodesk Navisworks software. The advantage of doing it this way is that you would only have a single NWD file to work with. The disadvantage is that you would have to recreate the NWD file any time one of the Xrefs changes.

Merging Files

An NWD file might be sent by a project coordinator to multiple parties for review. Each party adds review markups and data to the model, which can include any combination of viewpoints, comments, redlines, Clash Detective results, etc.

Each party can save their review session as an NWF file that references the original NWD file. The project coordinator can then merge all of the NWF files into a single file, duplicating neither the NWD file (referenced by all NWFs) nor any other review markup that is common to all NWFs.

Refreshing Files

When working on files in the Autodesk Navisworks software, others might be working on the linked CAD files. To ensure that the data being reviewed is current, the Autodesk Navisworks software has a refresh function, enabling you to reload any files that have been modified since commencing the review session. This feature does not reload all files that were previously loaded, only those modified since they were last opened.

To refresh the data, on the Home tab, on the Project panel, or in the Quick Access Toolbar, click Refresh.

Emailing Files

The Autodesk Navisworks software is also a communication tool. The Send by Email command makes it easy to send the current model along with its viewpoints by email. It uses the available mail exchange service. Sending a file as mail saves the current working file to ensure that the latest review is sent.

To send a file by email from in the Autodesk Navisworks software, click Application Menu>Send by Email or on the Output tab, on the Send panel, click Send by Email. This accesses the available email software and sends the current file as an email attachment.

Receiving Files by Email

If an NWF file is received, the application searches for the appended files first using the absolute path with which the sender originally saved the file. This is useful if a team is on a local network and the files can be found using the Universal Naming Convention (UNC). Otherwise, a team not sharing a server can organize a project using the same file hierarchy and drive letter, and the Autodesk Navisworks software can find the files this way.

If the application cannot find the files, the recipient can save the attached NWF in a directory in which all appended files are located. The NWF can then look for these files relative to its own location.

This way, an entire sub-directory from the project's directory can be moved to a completely new location. Save the NWF file in this new place and it can search for the files from there.

Setting File Units

When you measure lengths in the Autodesk Navisworks software, the value is displayed using the unit specified in the Options Editor, as shown in the following illustration. When you change the units, any measurement you have placed in the file is automatically updated to the new units you select. These units are independent of and do not affect the units set in the individual DWG files to an Autodesk Navisworks file.

To open the Options Editor dialog box, select Options in the Application menu.

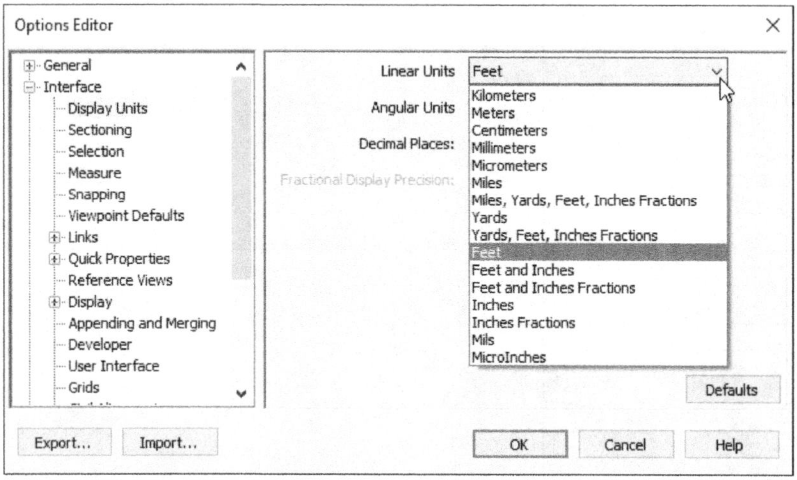

For more information on the other settings in the Options Editor, see the Autodesk Navisworks Help documentation.

Sharing

You use the Publish command to share information about a project with other Autodesk Navisworks users. When you publish an NWF file that has attached files, an NWD file is created that contains all the information from the attached files inside a single compressed file.

You can specify the information you want to share and password-protect the file if required, as shown in the following illustration.

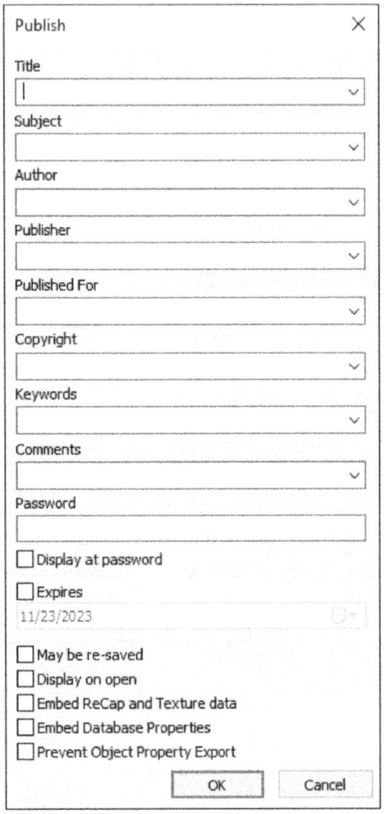

Troubleshooting

Autodesk offers free downloadable enablers that you can use to access, display, and manipulate object data in applications different from their native environment. This provides essential data accessibility for design teams who create or receive files using Autodesk software. In particular, the AutoCAD Plant 3D object enabler enables Autodesk Navisworks users to directly retrieve property data while reviewing AutoCAD Plant 3D models. Object enablers exist for many AutoCAD-based products.

If you open a drawing in the Autodesk Navisworks software that contains external references, properties for AutoCAD Plant 3D objects in external reference drawings might not display. To solve this, delete the NWC file for the external reference, load the Autodesk Navisworks software, and open the external reference DWG before opening up the master drawing.

Exercise: Work with Autodesk Navisworks Files

In this exercise, you open an NWD file, measure distances and establish file units. You start a new file and append a DWG file with associated Xrefs, and save it as an NWF file. You then publish a NWD file after reviewing the publish options.

Verify that the appropriate Plant 3D Object enabler is installed on the system before proceeding with the practices.

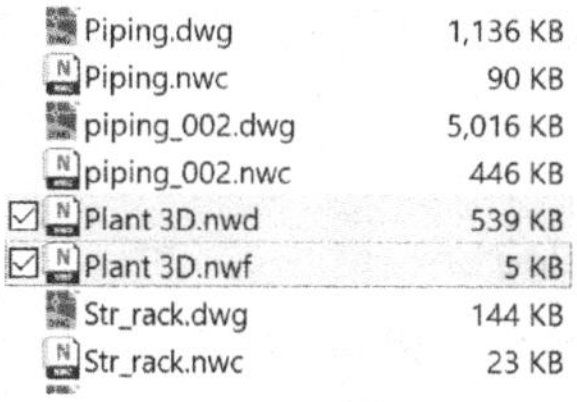

1. Start the Autodesk Navisworks software, if necessary.
2. Open an existing file by doing the following:
   - On the Quick Access Toolbar, click Open.
   - In the Open dialog box, navigate to the folder *C:\Plant Design 2024 Practice Files\File Handling*.
   - Set the Files of type to Navisworks (*.nwd).
   - Select the file *Equipment.nwd*.
   - Click Open.
3. To measure a distance:
   - Zoom and pan to select the points shown.
   - On the Review tab, on the Measure panel, on the Measure list, click Point to Point.
   - Select point 1.
   - Select point 2.

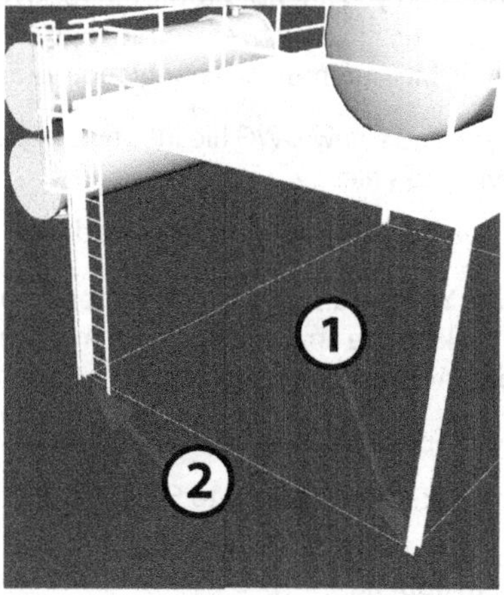

4. To change the display units, if required:
   - On the Application menu, click Options.
   - In the Options Editor dialog box, left pane, expand Interface.
   - Click Display Units.
   - In the right pane, from the Linear Units list, select Feet and Inches, if not already selected.
   - Change the Decimal Places to **2,** if not already selected.
   - Click OK.

The measured units now display as feet and inches. The measurement in the image may be different than yours depending on the points selected in your model.

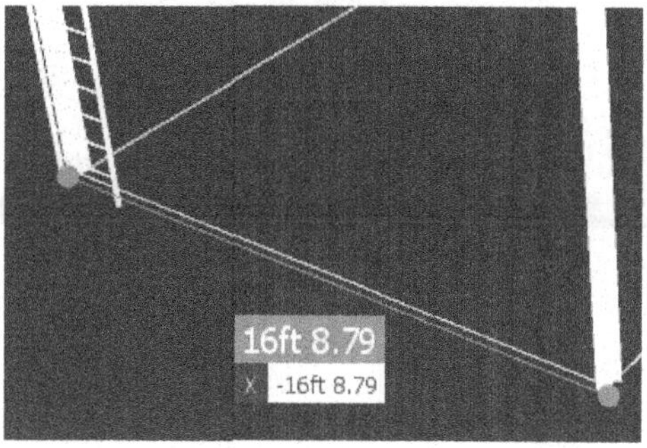

5. To start a new Navisworks file, in the Quick Access Toolbar, click New. The current file is closed and you are not prompted to save because no changes were made to the model. Measurements are only temporary.

6. To append a new DWG file into the Navisworks file:

   - On the Home tab, click Append.

   Note: You can also access the Append option by clicking the arrow next to Open in the Quick Access Toolbar and clicking Append.

7. In the Append dialog box:

   - Click the arrow next to Files of Type.
   - Note all the different file formats available to append.
   - Select Autodesk DWG\DXF (*.dwg; *.dxf).
   - Navigate to the *C:\Plant Design 2024 Practice Files\File Handling* folder if not already active.
   - Select *Piping.dwg*.
   - Click Open.

8. The Piping drawing is a parent drawing and references the other drawings in this folder (piping_002.dwg, Structures.dwg, Str_rack.dwg, and Eqipment.dwg). If these associated externally referenced files cannot be found, you will be prompted to resolve. If so, complete the following:

   - In the Resolve dialog box, click Browse.
   - Navigate to the *C:\Plant Design 2024 Practice Files\File Handling* folder.
   - Select *Equipment.dwg*.
   - Click Open.
   - Click OK.
   - Repeat the steps to select all additional files that cannot resolve their external references.

9. To save the file:

   - On the Quick Access Toolbar, click Save.
   - In the Save As dialog box, for File Name, enter **Plant 3D**.
   - Verify that Navisworks File Set (*.nwf) is selected from the Save As Type list.
   - Click Save.

10. On the Application menu, click Publish.

11. In the Publish dialog box:

    - For Title, enter **Plant3D**.
    - For Author, enter **Autodesk**.
    - Click OK.

12. In the Save As dialog box:

    - For File Name, enter **Plant 3D**.
    - Verify that Navisworks (*.nwd) is selected from the Save As Type list.
    - Click Save.

13. Open a Windows Explorer window. Navigate to the folder in which your files are saved. Note the file sizes of the different file formats.

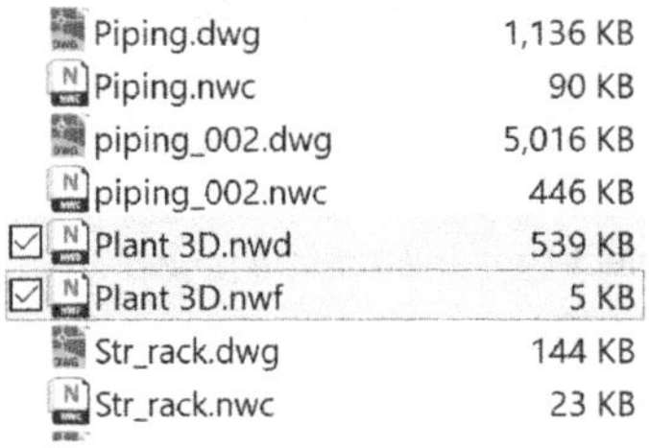

14. The Navisworks NWF file remains open. Save the file.

Lesson Review Questions

1. Autodesk Navisworks NWD files contain all required related files and do not require external files links.
    a. True
    b. False
2. After missing Xref files are located in the NWF file and it is saved, you need to relocate the files each time you open the NWF file.
    a. True
    b. False
3. Navisworks Manage can directly append or merge AutoCAD files.
    a. True
    b. False

Lesson: Basic Navigation and Walkthroughs

Overview

This lesson describes basic navigation and walkthroughs in Navisworks. You learn to work with objects by selecting them, viewing them, and displaying their properties.

When reviewing designs, you might need to select objects in the design to inspect. Large projects can make selecting objects a difficult process. The Autodesk Navisworks software enables you to simplify this task by providing a range of tools to help you quickly select interactively, manually, and automatically.

The Autodesk Navisworks software provides numerous ways to navigate and walk through a design. Viewpoints are an important tool to save time and return to important model views.

Objectives:

After completing this lesson, you will be able to:

- Describe the different ways of viewing a model.
- Select objects in a model.
- View object properties.

Viewing a Model

There are several different ways to view models in the Autodesk Navisworks software including the ViewCube, tools on the Navigation Bar, and using viewpoints.

ViewCube

You use the ViewCube to change the view of the 3D model by clicking on one of the surfaces, corners, or edges of the cube, as shown in the following illustration. Dragging the position of the ViewCube also rotates the 3D model. Selecting the Home icon at the upper left of the ViewCube reorients the model to its default isometric orientation.

Additionally, you use the wheel on the mouse to zoom and pan the view of the 3D model.

Navigation Bar

The Navigation Bar includes five navigation modes and six Steering Wheels for interactive navigation around your 3D models. Most navigation modes have further options accessed by selecting the down arrow beneath the icon.

The tools on the Navigation Bar are shown in the following illustration. Press and hold the left mouse button and use the appropriate command to navigate.

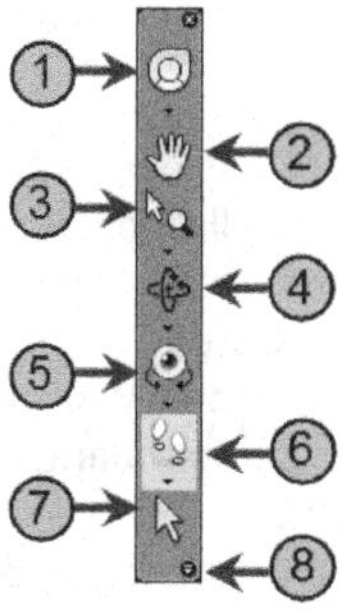

(1)	Steering Wheels	Steering wheels are task-based floating tool palettes that travel with the cursor to minimize tool access time. There are three standard wheels, and three mini wheels. These provide access to eight different navigation tools (Orbit, Zoom, Rewind, Pan, Center, Walk, Look, and Up/Down). Various combinations of these tools are available in the different versions of the Steering wheel. In the Autodesk Navisworks software, the Full Navigation Wheel (or mini version of this) is likely the most useful for navigating the 3D model scene.

2	Pan	Press and hold the left mouse button to drag the cursor in any direction to pan the model by moving the camera.
3	Zoom	The Zoom mode includes the following tools: **Zoom Window** - Enables you to draw a box and zoom into that area. **Zoom** - Click a point in the scene view then drag the cursor up or down to zoom the camera in and out. **Zoom Selected** - Zooms in/out of the selected geometry. **Zoom All** - Zooms out to show the whole scene.
4	Orbit	The Orbit Mode includes the following tools: **Orbit** - Moves the camera around the focal point of the model. The up direction is always maintained, and no camera rolling is possible. **Free Orbit** - Rotates the model around the focal point in any direction. **Constrained Orbit** - Spins the model around the up vector as though the model is sitting on a turntable. The up direction is always maintained.
5	Look	The Look Mode includes the following tools: **Look Around** - Looks around the scene from the current camera location. **Look At** - Looks at a particular point in the scene. The camera moves to align with that point. **Focus** - Centers a particular point in the scene. The camera stays where it is.
6	Walk and Fly	The Walk and Fly Modes include the following tools: **Fly Mode** - Enables you to fly the camera through the scene. Hold the left mouse button and drag the mouse up or down to ascend or descend and left or right to move correspondingly. **Note:** Holding <Shift> speeds up this movement and holding <Ctrl> rotates the camera around its viewing axis, while still moving forward. **Walk Mode** - Enables you to walk around and through the model scene. Walk mode resets the model to an upright position. Press <Shift> to increase walking speed or press <Ctrl> to temporarily switch to Pan to adjust the camera position. Press <Spacebar> to temporarily crouch under an obstacle. The Walk and Fly Modes also include the following options: **Collision** - Select this check box to define a viewer as a collision volume in Walk and Fly modes. As a result, a viewer acquires some mass, and cannot pass through other objects, points, or lines in the Scene View. **Gravity** - Select this check box to give a viewer some weight in Walk mode. This option is useful when walking up or down stairs, ramps, changing levels, etc. and also works in conjunction with Collision. **Crouch** - Select this check box to enable a viewer to crouch under objects that are too low to pass under in Walk mode. This option works in conjunction with Collision. **Third Person** - This function enables you to navigate the scene from a third person's perspective. When activated you can see an avatar, which is a representation of yourself in the 3D model. Using the third person in connection with collision and gravity, enables you to visualize exactly how a person would interact with the intended design. You can customize settings, such as avatar selection, dimension, and positioning, for the current viewpoint or as a global option.

(7)	Select	The Select button provides an alternative method to activate Selection Mode in Navisworks.
(8)	Navigation Bar Customize	The Navigation Bar Customize arrow enables you to: ▪ Activate or deactivate navigation modes currently on the navigation bar. ▪ Dock the Navigation bar in a different position. ▪ Select Navigation Bar Options to change Orbit and Walk options. ▪ Access the Navisworks Help documentation.

> In Walk and Fly modes, you can set a speed that is suitable for the model size. Select a viewpoint from where you wish to navigate, then click Application Menu>Options to open the Options Editor. In the Options Editor, under Interface, click Viewpoint Defaults. In the right pane of the Options Editor, select the Override Linear Speed checkbox and set the speed as required.

Viewpoints

Viewpoints are used to save specific views of a 3D model. Creating viewpoints of frequently used views can save you time. Once viewpoints are created, you select the viewpoint in the Saved Viewpoints palette to change to that view. To create a viewpoint, navigate to the required location, right-click in the Saved Viewpoints palette and click Save Viewpoint. You can also create folders in the Saved Viewpoints palette for organizing multiple viewpoints, as shown in the following illustration. To create a folder, right-click in the Saved Viewpoints palette and click New Folder. You can drag and drop viewpoints in a folder to organize the viewpoints in the file.

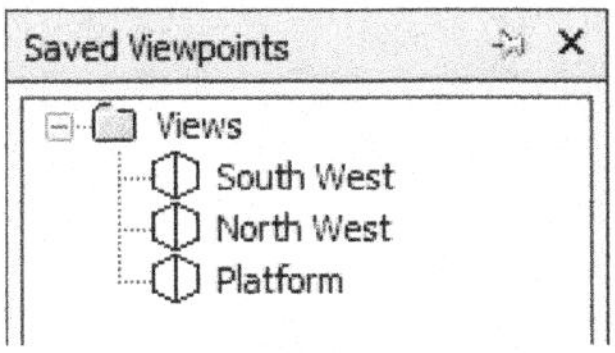

Animations

You can create animations from the viewpoints you create. An animation enables you to see your model transition from one viewpoint to another. To create an animation, right-click on the Saved Viewpoints palette and click New Animation. Drag and drop viewpoints into the animation to create it. The order in which they are listed in the animation determines how the viewpoints are played back. Use the controls on the Viewpoint tab, on the Save, Load & Playback panel to select the animation to play and to control its playback, as shown in the following illustration. Once you have created an animation you can export it as an external file that can be viewed independent of the Autodesk Navisworks software and shared with others using the Animation option on the Output tab.

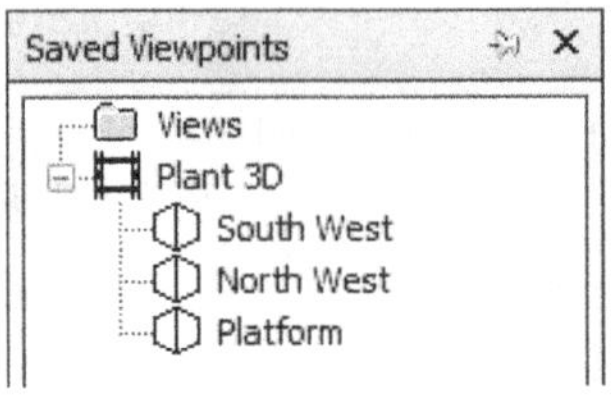

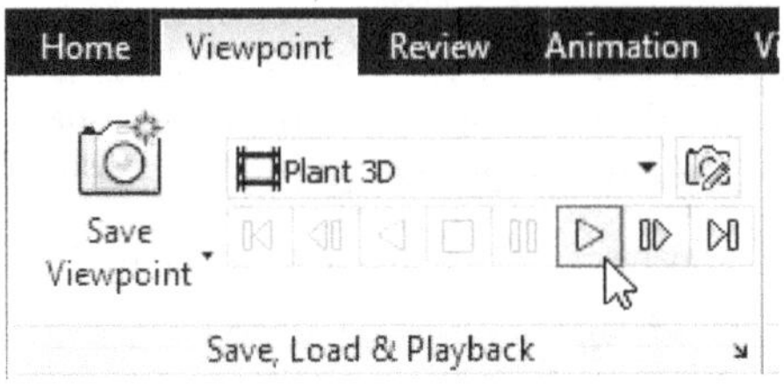

Markups

Markups and comments can also be added to an active viewpoint. Select the Review tab and use the tools in the Markup panel to add text or draw revision notes (clouds, lines, etc.), as shown in the following illustration. The markups are stored in a viewpoint that gets automatically created. You can also erase or change the color and size of redlines.

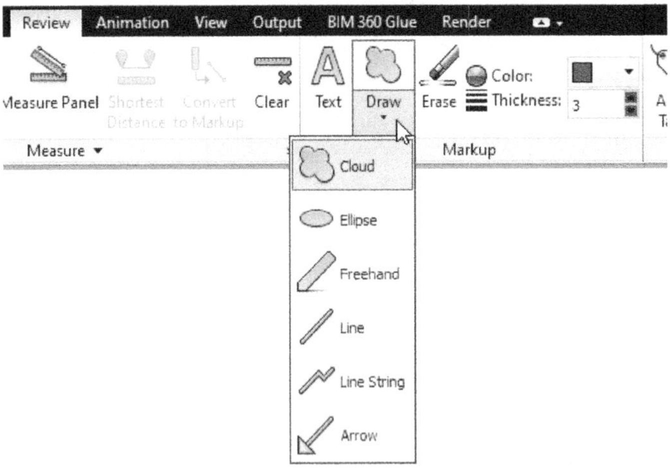

Selecting Objects in a Model

With large models, it can be time-consuming to select items of interest. In the Autodesk Navisworks software, there are several tools available, including the Selection Tree and Selection Sets, that give you flexibility in selecting the required items in your model.

Selection Tree

When you select one or more items in the Selection Tree, the corresponding objects are selected in the viewing window. You can also select objects in the model, and in turn, the corresponding items in the Selection Tree are highlighted.

Additionally, you can use the Zoom Selected option on the Zoom Window drop-down of the Navigation toolbar to zoom in on selected objects, as shown in the following illustration.

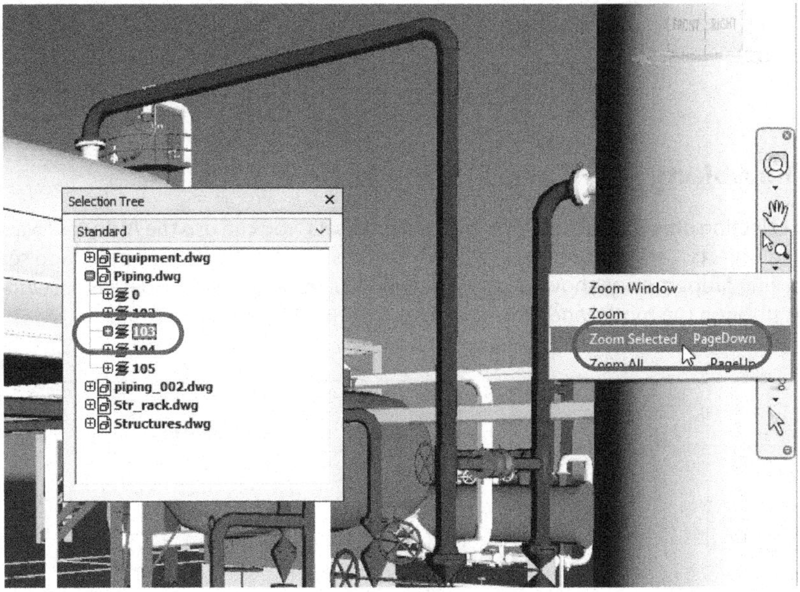

The selection tree hierarchy starts with the DWG file at the top level. The next level lists the layers in the drawing followed by the objects on the layers. If the object contains other objects, such as blocks, they are listed in the next level. The levels continue to the lowest level primitive.

Selection Resolution

When you select an item in your model, you can specify whether additional associated items are also selected. For example, if you change the Selection Resolution to layer (as shown in the following illustration), when you select an item, all the items on the same layer are also selected.

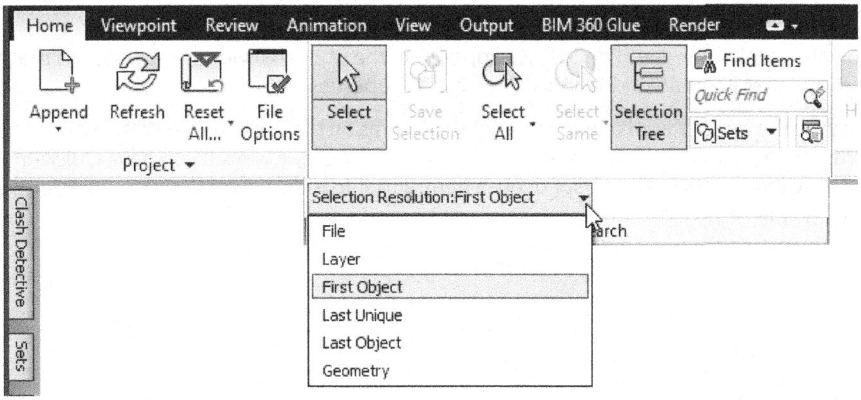

Selection Sets

Using Selection Sets, you can select multiple objects and group them together. You can select the objects in the viewer or use the Selection Tree to select the required objects. Once you have selected the objects, you add the current selection to the Sets palette using the Save Selection option in the Sets palette, as shown in the following illustration.

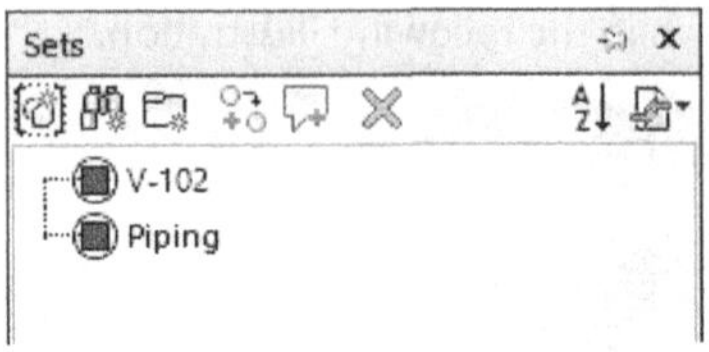

Searching for Objects

In addition to selecting objects and then putting them into sets, you can use the Autodesk Navisworks software to find objects. On the Home tab, select Find Items. Use the Find Items palette to search for items with specific properties, as shown in the following illustration. The Autodesk Navisworks software goes through the model and finds the items that fit the specified criteria.

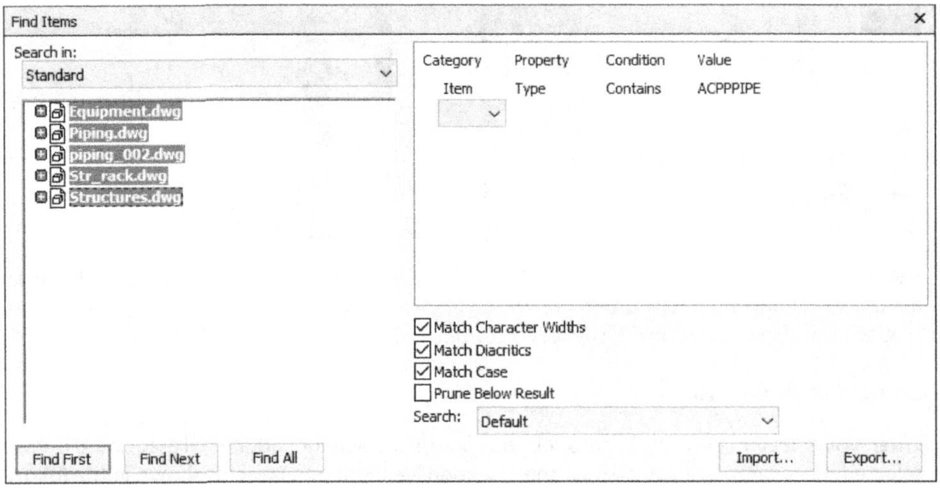

You can also add the current search as a selection set. This creates a dynamic search that updates as the design progresses.

Additionally, you can use the Hide Selected option on the ribbon to view only the items that are selected. All other items are hidden.Viewing Object Properties

You can view the properties of one or more selected items on the Properties palette. You can also view Quick Properties, or information specific to an object in the scene view. If you have Quick Properties toggled on, when you hold the cursor over an item, a tooltip is displayed showing the information, as shown in the following illustration.

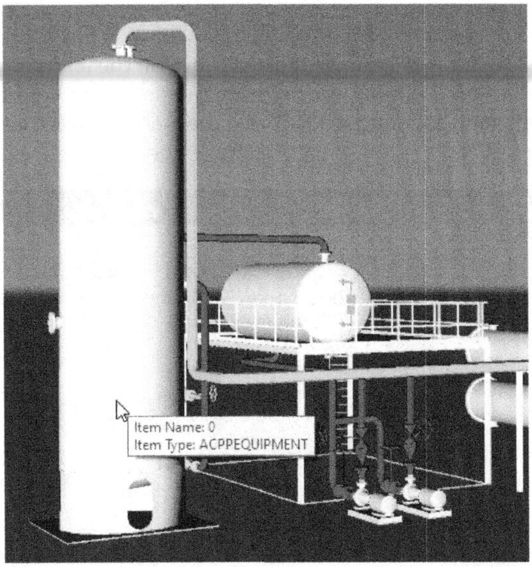

You can customize the information that is displayed in the tooltip using the Options command in the Application Menu. In the Options Editor, expand Interface>Quick Properties and select Definitions. Manipulate the elements in the list to display what is required in the Quick Properties tooltip, as shown in the following illustration.

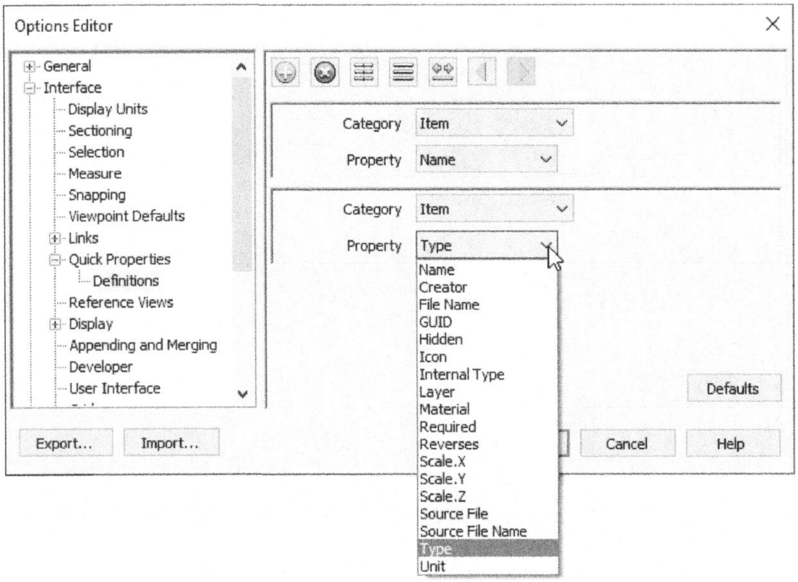

> If the Plant3D attributes do not display, you need to load the Object Enablers. Using the Object Enablers provides access to AutoCAD Plant 3D attributes, including size, specification, long description, etc.

Tags

You use the Tags panel on the Review tab to add and manage tags, as shown in the following illustration. Tags combine the features of redlining, viewpoints, and comments into a single, easy to use review tool. This enables you to tag anything you want to identify in the model scene. A viewpoint is automatically created for you, and you can add a comment and status to the tag.

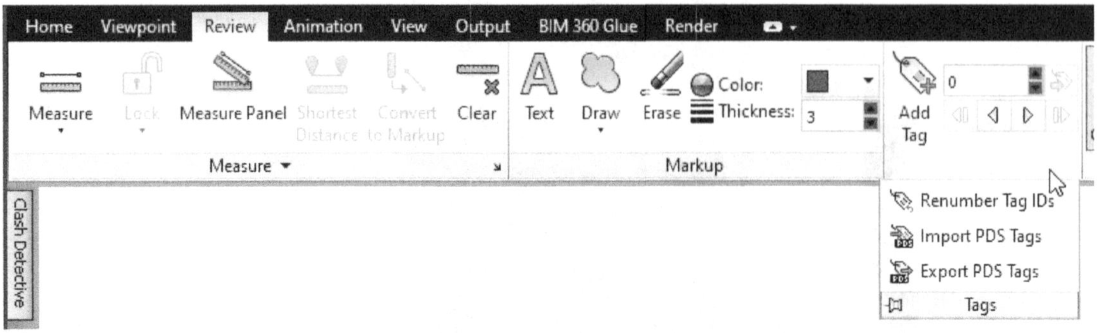

For example, during a review session, you locate an item in the scene that is incorrectly sized or positioned. You can tag this item, stating the problem, save your review results as an NWF file, and pass the file to the design team. The design team can search the file, for any tags of status 'new' and locate your review comments. Once any necessary modification are made to the drawing files, these can be reloaded into the NWF file, and the tag status can be changed accordingly. You can review this latest version of the NWF file, ensure all tags have been resolved, and finally 'approve' them.

Exercise: Navigate Your Way Through a Design

In this exercise, you practice navigating a model, selecting objects, using selection sets, and searching.

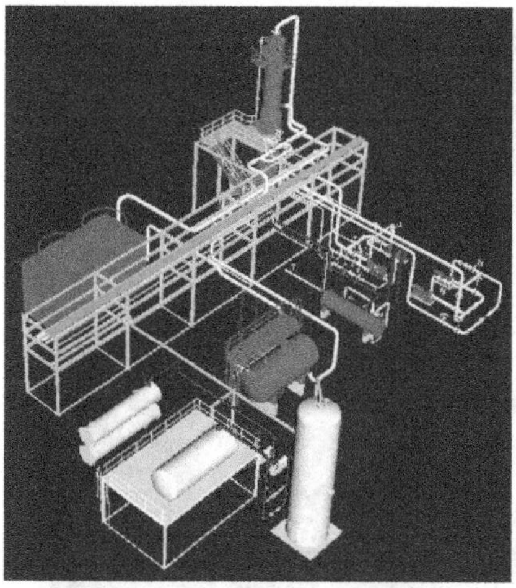

Open a File and Control Lights

In this section of the exercise, you open a model and manipulate the lights displayed in the model.

1. Start the Autodesk Navisworks software, if not already running.
2. Open an existing file by doing the following:
   - On the Quick Access Toolbar or in the Application Menu, click Open.
   - In the Open dialog box, navigate to the folder *C:\Plant Design 2024 Practice Files\Basic Navigation and Selection*.
   - Select the file *Plant 3D.nwf.*
   - Click Open.

   Note: Change the file of type if the .nwf files are not displaying.
3. Use your mouse wheel to zoom in, then click the wheel and move your mouse to pan to change your vantage point.
4. On the ViewCube, click Home to return the model to its default orientation.

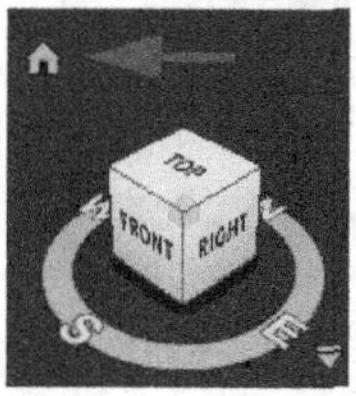

5. On the Viewpoint tab, on the Render Style panel, on the Lighting list, click No Lights. The background turns black.

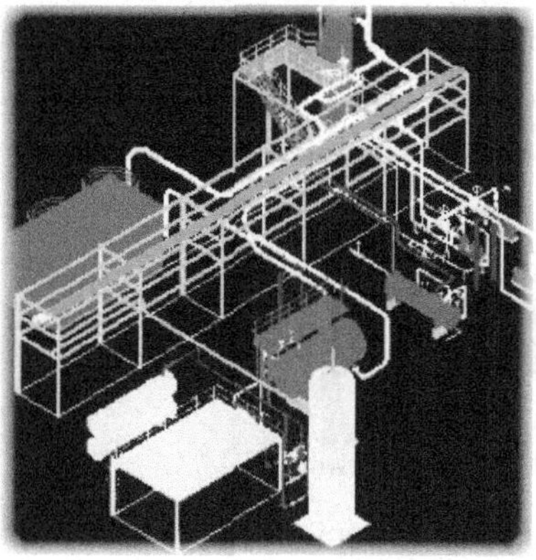

6. On the Viewpoint tab, on the Render Style panel, on the Lighting list, click Head Light.
7. On the Viewpoint tab, on the Render Style panel, on the Lighting list, click Full Lights.
8. Return to the Head Light lighting setting.
9. On the Viewpoint tab, on the Camera panel, on the Orthographic list, click Perspective, if not already set.
10. On the ViewCube, click the Northeast Isometric view.

11. Review the new orientation of the model.

12. On the ViewCube, click Top.

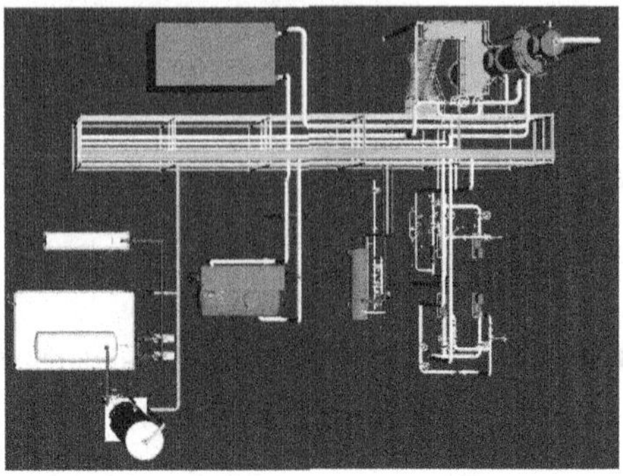

13. On the ViewCube, click several other views.

14. On the ViewCube, click Home to return to the Home view.

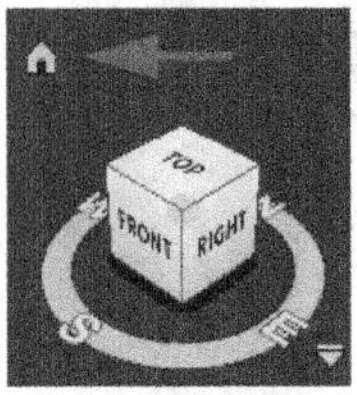

15. Click and hold anywhere on the ViewCube. Move around while you continue to hold the left mouse button down. Note that the model orbits.

16. Use the wheel on the mouse to zoom in and out. To pan, hold the mouse wheel. To rotate, hold <Shift> and the mouse wheel.

17. On the ViewCube, click Home.

Save Viewpoints

In this section of the exercise, you save different views of the model as viewpoints

1. On the ViewCube, click the Southwest isometric view.

2. On the Viewpoint tab, on the Save, Load & Playback panel, click Save Viewpoint. The Saved Viewpoints palette opens.

3. Enter **South West** to rename the viewpoint.

4. On the ViewCube, click the Northwest isometric view.

5. On the Viewpoint tab, on the Save, Load & Playback panel, click Save Viewpoint.

6. Rename the new viewpoint **North West**.

7. Use the mouse wheel and ViewCube to zoom, pan, and orbit in on the green platform.

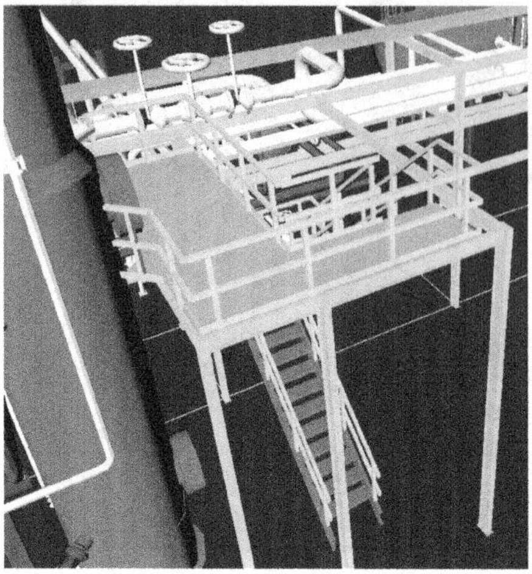

8. Create a new viewpoint named **Platform**.

9. Select the Saved Viewpoint palette title to expand the window, if compressed. On the Saved Viewpoints palette, click the South West and North West viewpoints. Note the view change.

10. Select the Platform viewpoint. Notice that viewpoints store the orientation and zoom level of the view.

11. On the Saved Viewpoints palette, right-click in a blank area. Click New Folder. For Name, enter **Views**.

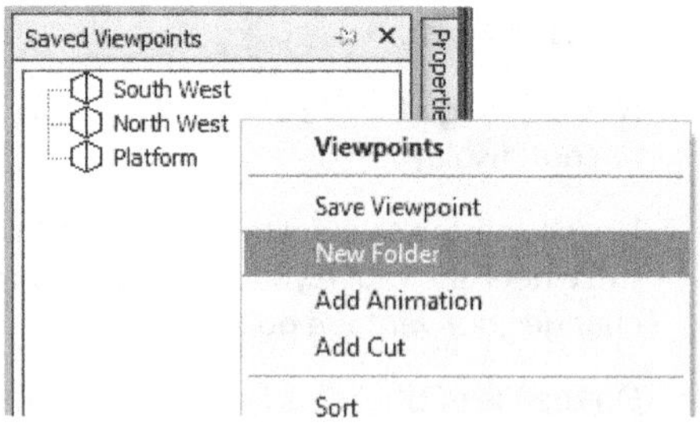

12. Drag each viewpoint into the Views folder.

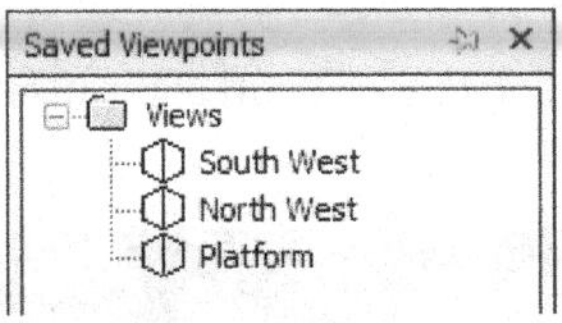

Create Animations

1. To create an animation:
   - On the Saved Viewpoints palette, right-click in a blank area.
   - Click Add Animation.
   - For the Name, enter **Plant 3D**.

2. On the Saved Viewpoints palette, drag the South West viewpoint to the AutoCAD Plant 3D animation. Repeat the steps for the North West and Platform viewpoints.

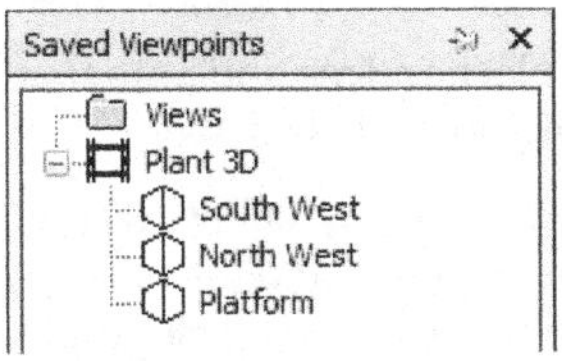

3. Return to the Home view.

4. On the Viewpoint tab, on the Save, Load, & Playback panel, click Plant 3D from the animation list. Click Play.

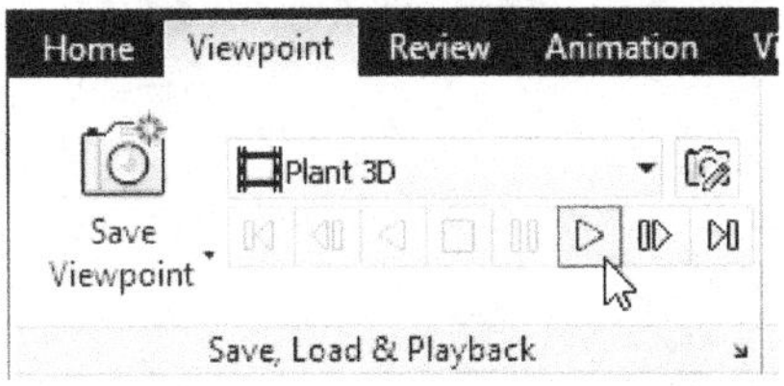

5. Use the other controls on the Save, Load & Playback panel to step forward, step back, and play different parts of the animation.

   Note: The order in which the viewpoints are listed in the animation determines the animation sequence.

6. To export the animation:
   - On the Output tab, on the Visuals panel, click Animation.
   - In the Animation Export dialog box, set the following settings as shown in the illustration below:
     - Source: Current Animation
     - Renderer: Viewpoint
     - Output: Windows AVI
     - Size - Type: Use Aspect Ratio
     - FPS: 6
     - Anti-aliasing: None
   - Click OK.
   - The height size may differ from the value as shown due to the Aspect Ratio.

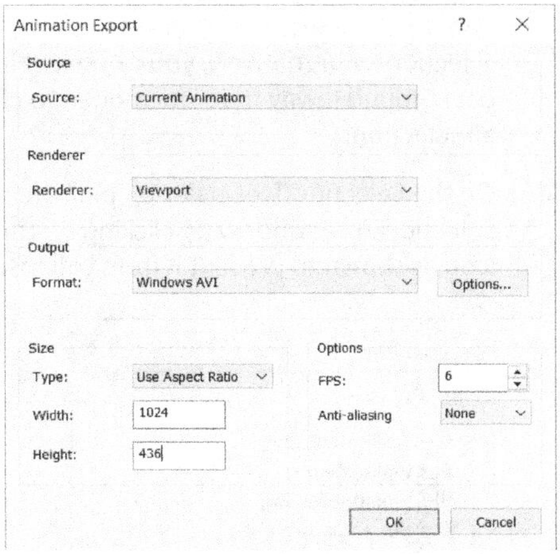

   - In the Save As dialog box, provide a filename and save the file to the *C:\Plant Design 2024 Practice Files\Basic Navigation and Selection* folder.
   - Click Save.

7. Use Windows Explorer to locate the animation file and play the file.

8. When you are finished reviewing the animation, select the Saved Viewpoint South West.

9. Save the file.

Selection Properties

In this section of the exercise, you select items in the selection tree and view their properties.

1. On the Home tab, on the Select & Search panel, click Selection Tree. If it is already enabled, you can select the Selection Tree title bar where it is compressed.

2. In the scene view, different components have been assigned colors to help identify them. In this exercise, when you select items, they will display dark blue, which is the selection color.

3. On the Selection Tree palette, select each of the five drawings individually to identify which items are associated with each drawing.

4. On the Home tab, on the Select & Search panel, click Select None. This clears all selections. Alternatively, you can select in the background (away from the model) to clear all selections.

5. On the Selection Tree palette, "pin" the Selection Tree window by clicking on the Pin icon as shown to prevent it from collapsing.

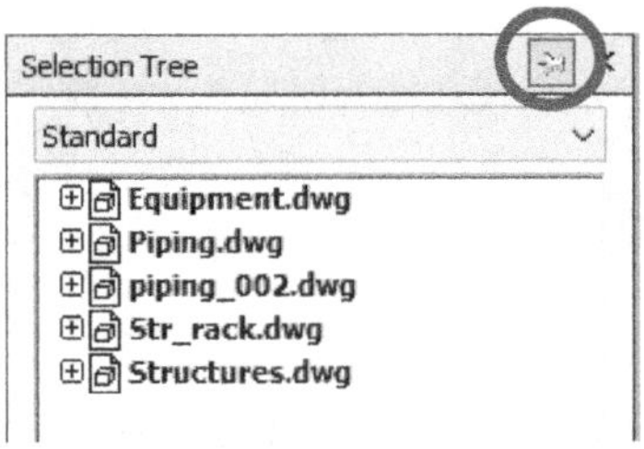

6. On the Selection Tree palette, expand *piping_002.dwg* and select T-100. Note the objects that are selected.

7. On the Selection Tree palette, under *piping_002.dwg*, select Layer V-102. Note the objects that are selected.

8. On the Navigation toolbar, expand the Zoom Window list, and click Zoom Selected. Alternatively, you can press <Page Down> on the keyboard.

9. To clear the selection, click in a blank area of the screen.

10. Select the railing that was part of the previous selection.

11. Review the Selection Tree and note that the corresponding object is selected.

    Note: If the entire piping_002|V-102 item was selected when you selected the railing, you must change the selection resolution.

    - On the Home tab, expand the Select & Search panel.
    - Expand the Selection Resolution and click First Object.

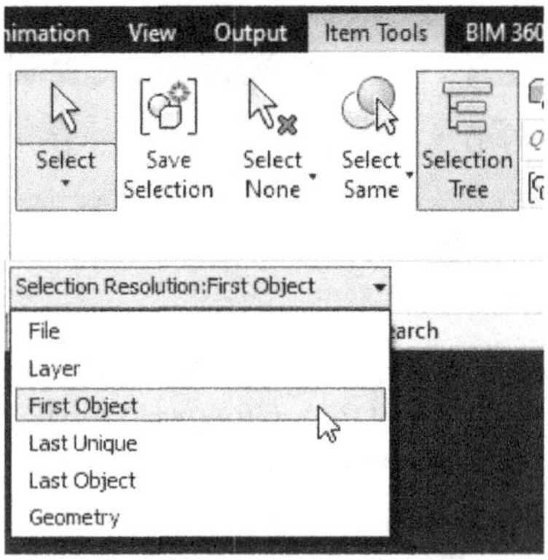

The ACPPSTRUCTURERAILING is highlighted in the model and in the Selection Tree.

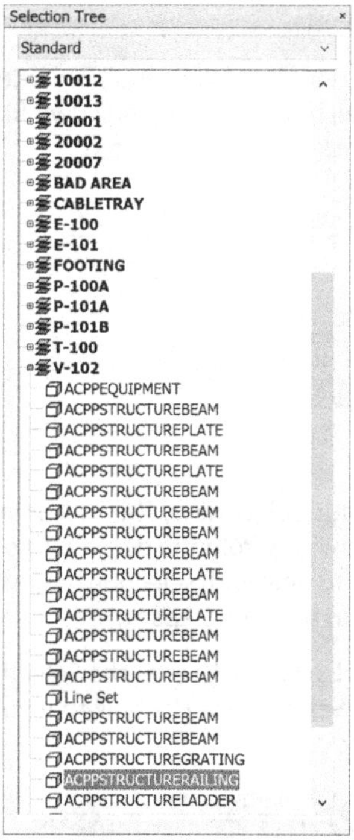

12. To clear the selection, click in a blank area of the screen.

13. Select the platform as shown in the following illustration. The corresponding object is selected on the Selection Tree palette (ACPPSTRUCTUREGRATING).

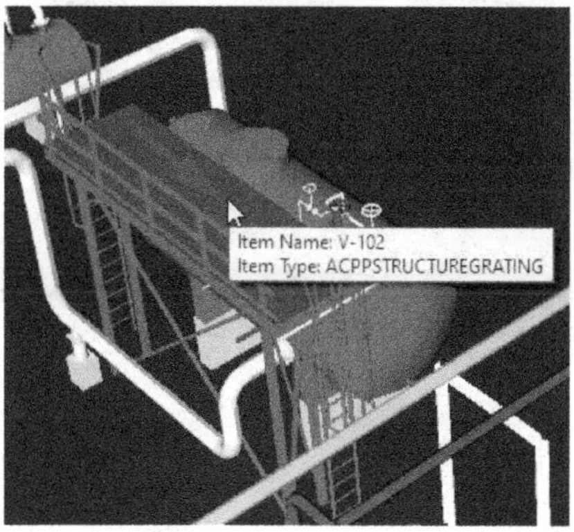

14. To clear the selection, click in a blank area of the screen.

15. On the Home tab, on the Select & Search expanded panel, on the Selection Resolution list, click Layer.

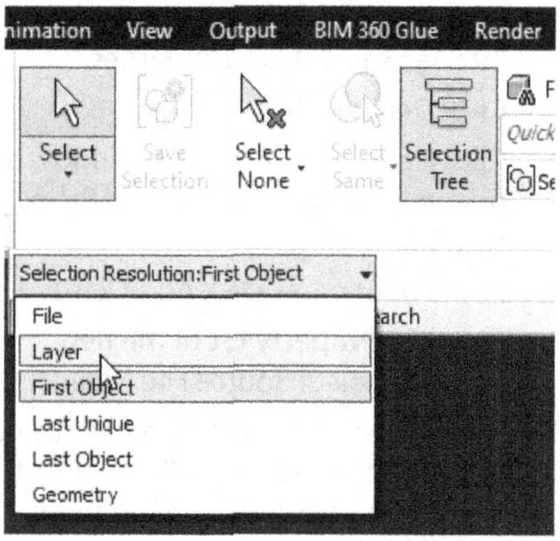

16. Select the same platform as before. Note that all the objects on the same V-102 layer are automatically selected.

17. On the Home tab, on the Display panel, click Properties if the Properties palette is not already displayed and compressed on the right-hand side of your screen. Examine the properties displayed on the Properties palette. These are the properties for the V-102 layer.

18. On the Home tab, on the Display panel, click Quick Properties to ensure that it is enabled. Move the mouse and hold it over the highlighted objects. Examine the quick properties displayed as a tooltip.

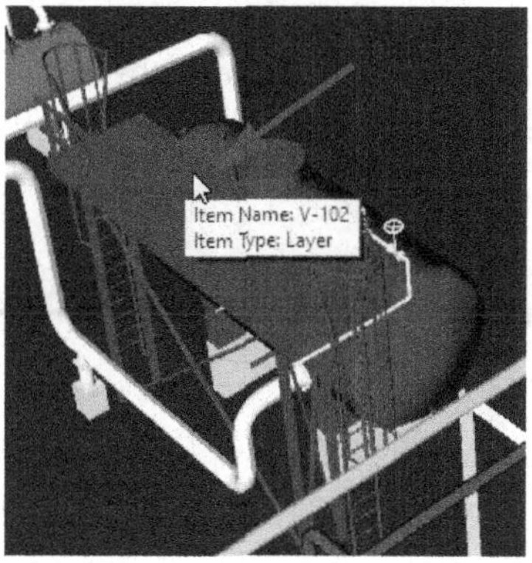

19. To change what is displayed in the Quick Properties tooltip:
   - On the Application menu, click Options.
   - In the Options Editor, left pane, expand Interface and Quick Properties.
   - Click Definitions.
   - Click Defaults to return the window to the original default Category and Property settings. Click Yes.
   - In the right pane, click Add Element.
   - From the Property list of the new element, select Source File Name.
   - Ensure that all three properties appear as shown in the following illustration. If not, change the properties as required.
   - Click OK.

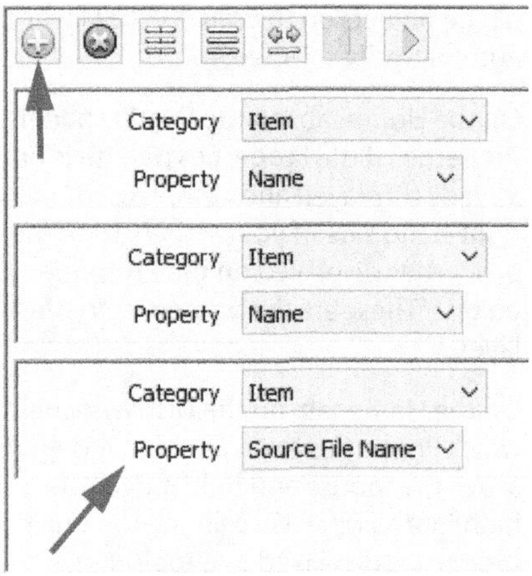

20. Move the mouse and hold it over the highlighted objects. Examine the quick properties displayed as a tooltip. Note that the source filename is now displayed in the tooltip.

21. Select the Pin icon again on the Selection Tree to unpin it. It compresses back to the side.

Manage Sets

In this section of the exercise, you save groups of items as selection sets.

1. In the Selection Tree, press and hold <Ctrl> and select all but the piping_002.dwg file. Four drawings should be selected.

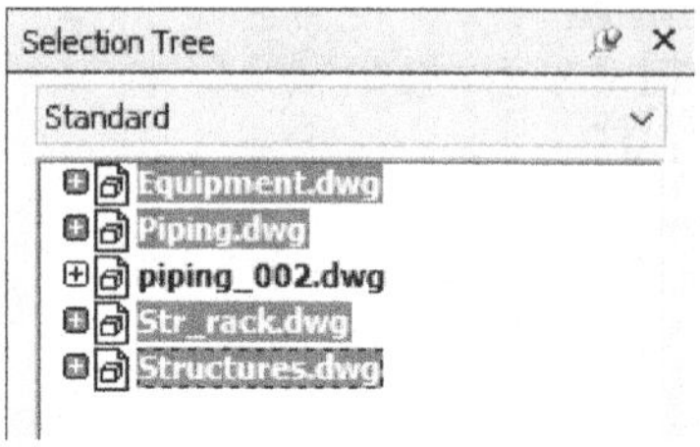

2. Right-click and select Hide. This hides the selected drawings from the display. This is being done to help with selection that will be completed in the next steps.

3. Ensure that Layer is still set as the Selection Resolution. Select the V-102 tank that you previously located.

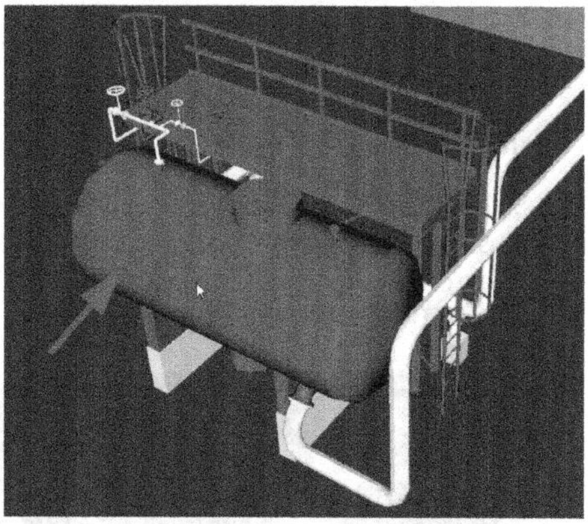

4. Press and hold <Ctrl> and select the the five pipes that attach to the vessel.

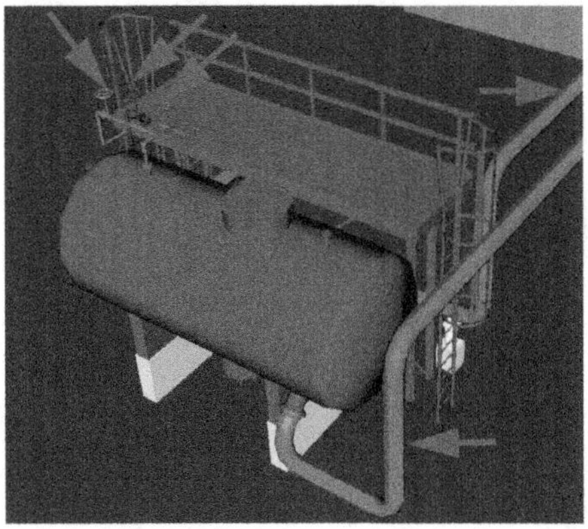

5. Reset the Selection Resolution back to First Object as follows:
   - On the Home tab, expand the Select & Search panel.
   - Expand the Selection Resolution and click First Object.

6. Select the footings and supports for the vessel. You were required to change the Selection Resolution so that you could pick these individually.

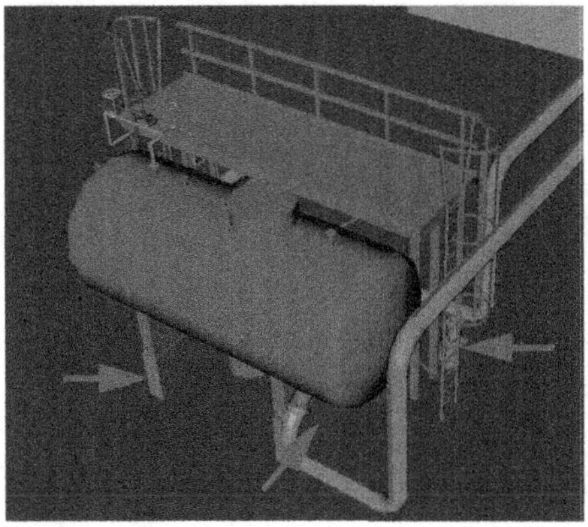

7. On the Home tab, on the Select & Search panel, on the Sets drop-down, click Manage Sets.

8. You may want to "Pin" the Sets window by clicking on the Pin icon as you did previously, to prevent it from collapsing.

9. To create a selection set:
   - On the Sets palette, click Save Selection.
   - For the Name, enter **V-102**.

10. To add a comment:
    - On the Sets palette, right-click on the V-102 selection set.
    - Click Add Comment.
    - In the Add Comment dialog box, enter **V-102 related pipes and tank**.
    - Click OK.

11. Select away from the vessel to clear the selection set.

12. In the Selection Tree, press and hold <Ctrl> and select all but the piping_002.dwg file again. Right-click and select Hide to clear its selection. The drawings are returned to the scene view.

13. Return the model to the Home view, and in the Sets window, select V-102. Notice that the vessel and all related pipes are selected. Selection sets enable you to create sets of items so that you do not have to select them individually if you need the set selected again.

14. To find specific items:
    - On the Home tab, on the Select & Search panel, click Find Items.
    - In the Find Items palette, right pane, from the Category list, select Item.
    - From the Property list, select Type.
    - From the Condition list, select Contains.
    - From the Value list, select ACPPPIPE.
    - Click Find All.

    The Autodesk Navisworks software goes through the model and finds all the items that meet that specific criteria. The items are highlighted in the Selection Tree.

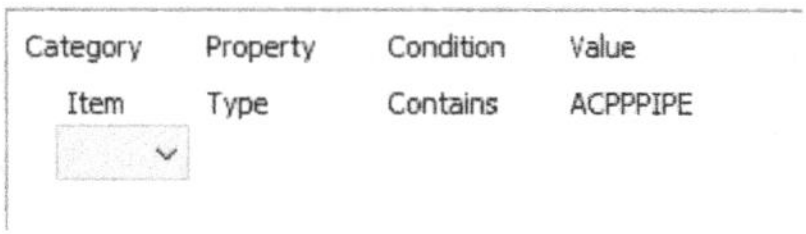

15. Close the Find Items palette.

16. On the Home tab, on the Display panel, click Properties if the Properties palette is not already displayed on the right-hand side.

    The Properties palette displays the number of items selected. In this case, 648 items are selected.

17. On the Home tab, on the Visibility panel, click Hide Unselected. The Autodesk Navisworks software hides everything except what met the search criteria.

    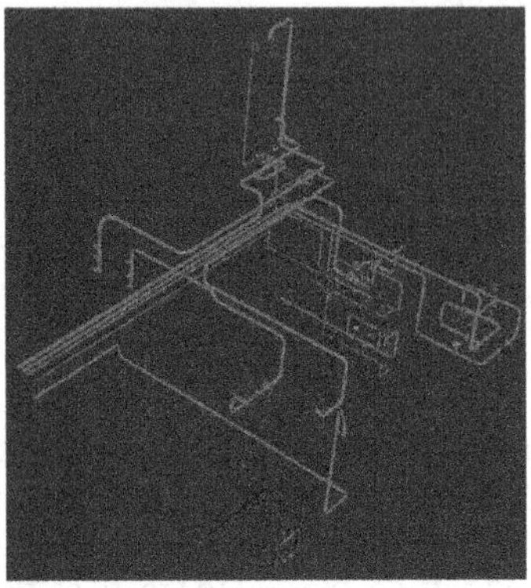

18. To save the items as a selection set:

    - On the Sets palette, click Save Selection.
    - For the name, enter **Piping**.

19. On the Home tab, on the Visibility panel, click Unhide All.

20. Unpin the Sets and the Selection Tree windows so that they compress back to the side of the interface.

21. Save the file.

Lesson Review Questions

1. Viewpoints that are listed in the Saved Viewpoints palette can be combined to create an animation.
   a. True
   b. False
2. Which of the following best describes a Selection Set?
   a. Selecting the Selection Set immediately zooms to the selection group.
   b. Lists all files and their structure in a tree-type structure.
   c. Groups selected items into a group.
   d. Enables you to refine whether additional associated items are selected when a selection is made.
3. When using the Find Items palette, all found items are selected in the Selection Tree and must be reselected in the tree to display them in the graphics window on the model.
   a. True
   b. False
4. Which of the following options are available for selection in the Resolution list? (Select all that apply.)
   a. File
   b. Layer
   c. First Layer
   d. Last Object
   e. View

Lesson: Clash Detection

Overview

This lesson describes how to conduct clash tests and work with clash test results.

Bringing multiple 3D designs together from multiple sources into the Autodesk Navisworks software enables the design review process to check for possible geometry interferences. Being able to locate these interferences in the 3D prototype means that you can attempt to eliminate the conflicts before they become an actual problem in the field.

The Clash Detective is only available in Autodesk Navisworks Manage.

Objectives

After completing this lesson, you will be able to:

- Describe the process for conducting a clash test in the Autodesk Navisworks software.
- Describe how to select geometry and view the results of a clash test.

Conducting a Clash Test

You use the Clash Detective tool in the Autodesk Navisworks software to effectively identify, inspect, and report interferences (clashes) in a 3D project model. Using Clash Detective can help you to reduce the incidents of error during model inspections. To conduct a clash test, you perform the following steps.

1. On the Home tab, on the Tools panel, click Clash Detective.
2. Use the Rules tab to select any rules to ignore, as shown in the following illustration. Using the Ignore Clashes Between options reduces the number of clash results by ignoring combinations of clashing items.

3. Use the Select tab to select the geometry to test. A selection must be made in both the Selection A and Selection B panes, as shown in the following illustration. The geometry you select in the Selection A pane is checked against the geometry selected in the Selection B pane. You can hold <Shift> or <Ctrl> to select multiple items in the list. Additionally, you can select directly from the scene view or use predetermined selection sets or searches. Once all selections are made you can define the Clash Settings to determine whether you want to find hard interferences or specify clearances. Click Run Test to run the clash test.

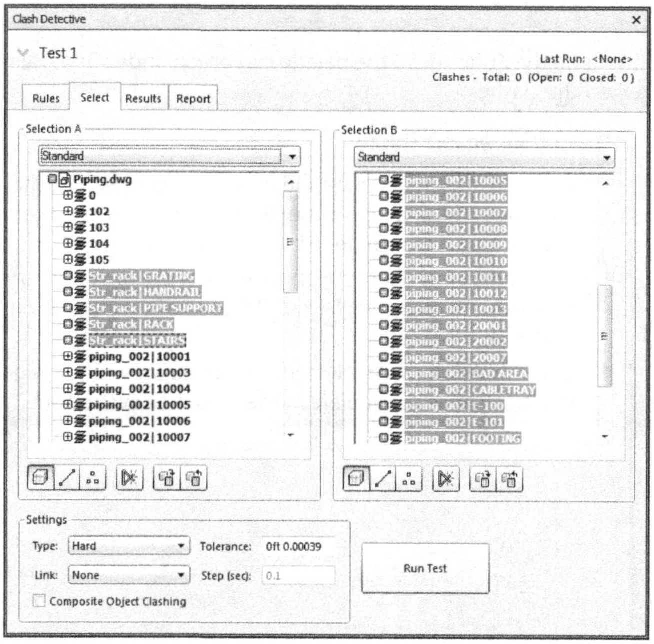

4. Use the Results tab to view the results. Selecting each clash zooms to the affected geometry and highlights it to help you identify the clashing geometry. The corresponding items are also highlighted in the tree views at the bottom of the Clash Detective, as shown in the following illustration. Expand the Items list if not displayed by default.

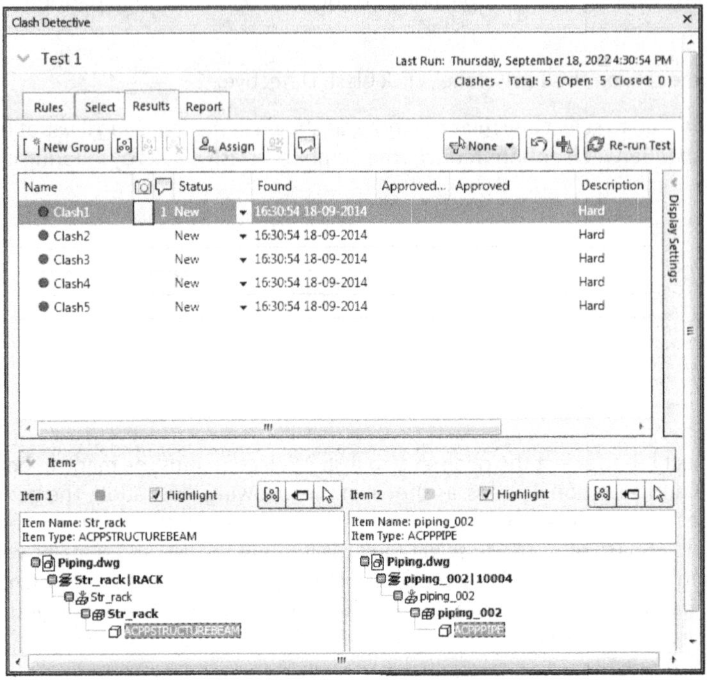

The Display Settings options on the right side of the palette can be expanded and used to refine how you see the model to review the clashes.

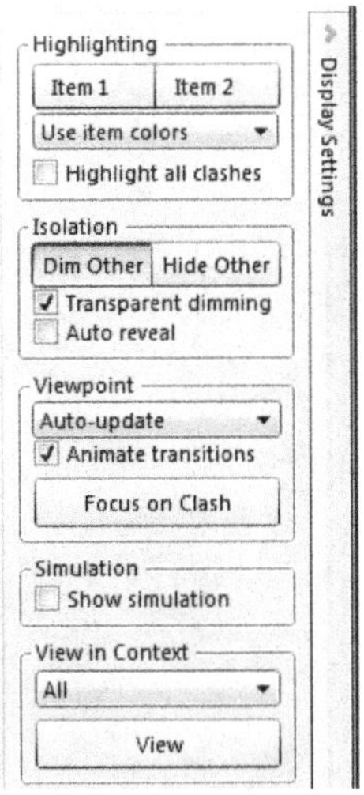

The options enable you to:

- Animate transitions to set the transitions between clashes as animated. This makes it easier to see where you are when you move between clashes. (Animate transitions)
- Dim to gray out geometry that does not clash, clarifying where the clashes are in the model. (Dim Other and Transparent Dimming buttons)
- Zoom in and out on a selected clash to regain your vantage point if you lose track of where you are in the model. (View button)

You can also rename clashes, change their status, and add comments to a clash by right-clicking on the clash name or selecting from the Status list. Changing the status of a clash result also changes the color of the geometry in the scene view when it is selected.

5. Use the Report tab to generate a report to send to other members of the design/construction team. Select options in the Contents area to determine the information that will populate the report, as shown in the following illustration. Define the Output Settings to determine the file format for the report (XML, HTML, HTML (Tabular), Text, and As viewpoints) and click Write Report.

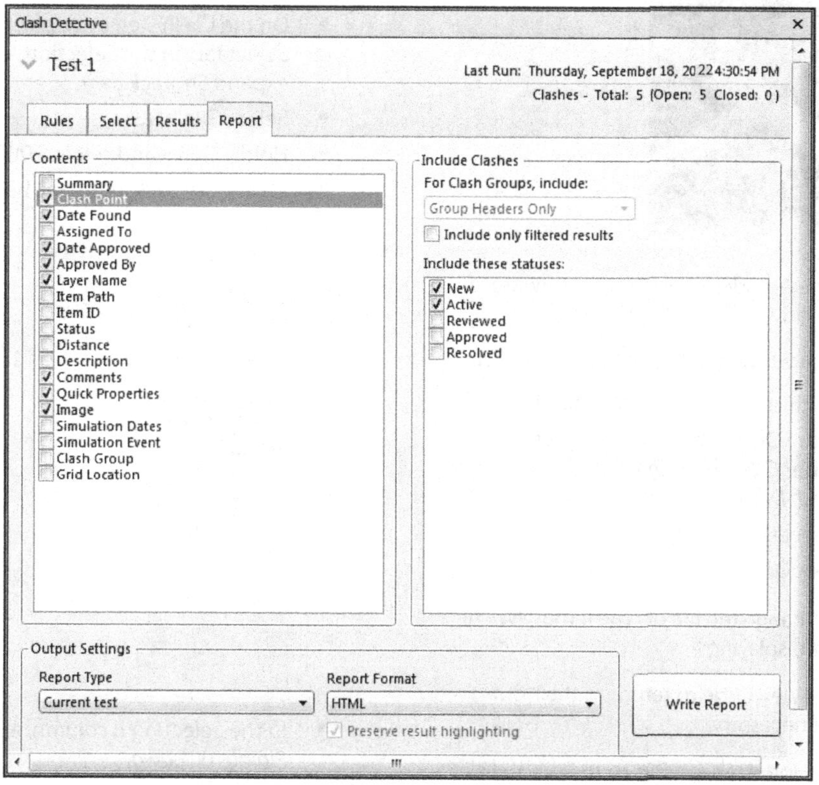

SwitchBack

You can use the SwitchBack functionality to send the current view back to the original software (AutoCAD, Plant 3D, Autodesk Revit, Autodesk Inventor, or MicroStation-based CAD products). This makes locating the clash easier for correcting the clash. The Switchback command can be found at the bottom of the Results tab in the Items panel in the Clash Detective palette.

> The native CAD package must be installed on the same machine as the Autodesk Navisworks software for SwitchBack to work.

Exercise: Conduct Clash Tests

In this exercise, you conduct clash tests and work with clash test results. The Clash Detective works best in a dual screen system.

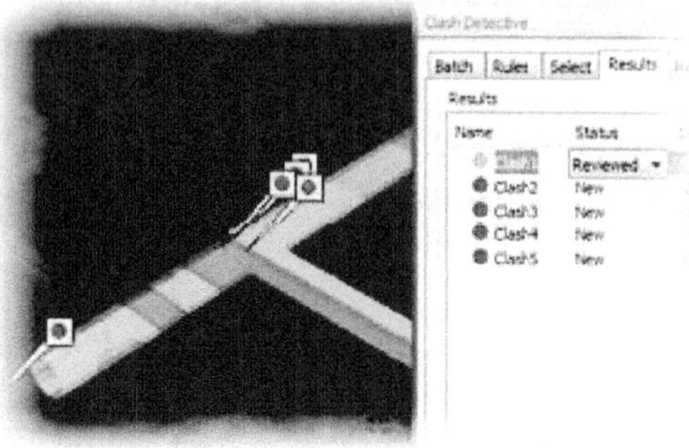

1. Start the Autodesk Navisworks software, if not already running.

2. Open an existing file by doing the following:
   - On the Quick Access Toolbar, click Open.
   - In the Open dialog box, navigate to the folder *C:\Plant Design 2024 Practice Files\Clash Detection*.
   - Select the file *Plant 3D.nwf*.
   - Click Open.

   Note: Change the file of type if the .NWF files are not displaying.

3. Use the ViewCube to return to the Home view, if necessary.

4. On the Home tab, on the Tools panel, click Clash Detective, if not already enabled.

5. You may want to "Pin" the Clash Detective window by clicking on the Pin Icon as you did previously, to prevent it from collapsing. You may also need to widen it by hovering over the right edge of the window and clicking and dragging it.

6. To select the items to run the clash detection on:
   - Expand the top portion of the palette by selecting the down arrow.
   - In the Clash Detective palette, click Add Test in the upper-right corner.
   - On the Clash Detective palette, on the Select tab, in the Selection A column, expand *Str_rack.dwg*.
   - Select GRATING.
   - Hold <Shift> and select STAIRS.
   - All five Str_rack items will be selected.

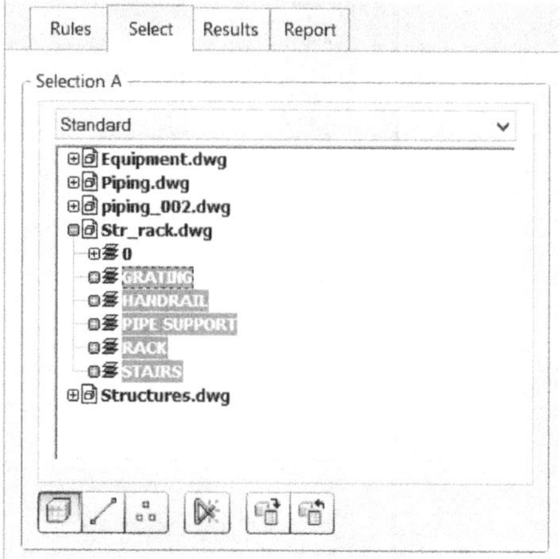

   - In the Selection B column, expand *Piping_002.dwg*.
   - Select 10001.
   - Scroll down and use <Shift> to select V-102. All piping_002 items are selected.

7. In the Settings panel, verify that the Type is set to Hard. Click Run Test.

   The Results tab is displayed with the list of clashes.

8. Clash1 is selected by default and the model is zoomed to the items that clash.

   Note that items that clash can also be reviewed in the Items panel at the bottom of the Clash Detective. By default, the Items portion is collapsed and needs to be expanded by clicking on the Items titlebar.

   The items are highlighted in the Item Trees.

9. Expand the Display Settings options on the right edge of the Clash Detective palette, if not already expanded. If you don't see the options on the right-hand side, you may have to widen the Clash Detective window.

10. Select Animate transitions.

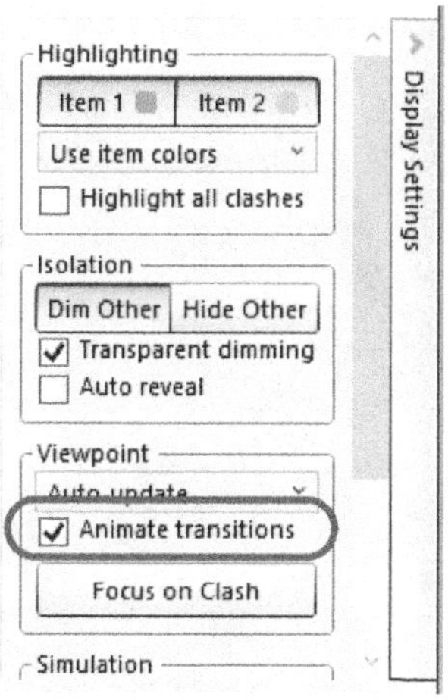

11. In the Results tab, select Clash2, select Clash3, and then select Clash4. Note that the window makes a smooth transition from each clash.

12. In the Display Settings, toggle Dim Other on and off in the Isolation list. When enabled, all items that do not clash turn gray making it easier to identify the clash. Leave the Dim Other option selected. This option is enabled by default.

13. In the Display Settings, toggle the Transparent dimming option on and off. When enabled, all items that do not clash are made transparent. Leave the Transparent dimming option enabled. This option is enabled by default.

14. In the Display Setting, select All in the View in Context list. Click View and watch as you are zoomed out to view all items and then zoomed back in to the clashed items.

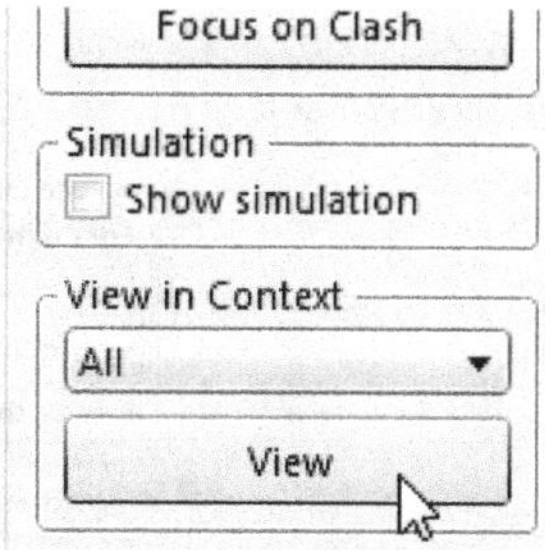

15. Collapse the Display Settings panel.

16. To rename the clashes:
    - On the Results tab, select and right-click on Clash1.
    - Click Rename.
    - For the name, enter **Pipe and Rack Clash**.

17. From the Status list for the Pipe and Rack Clash, select Reviewed. Note that the bubble next to the name changes color.

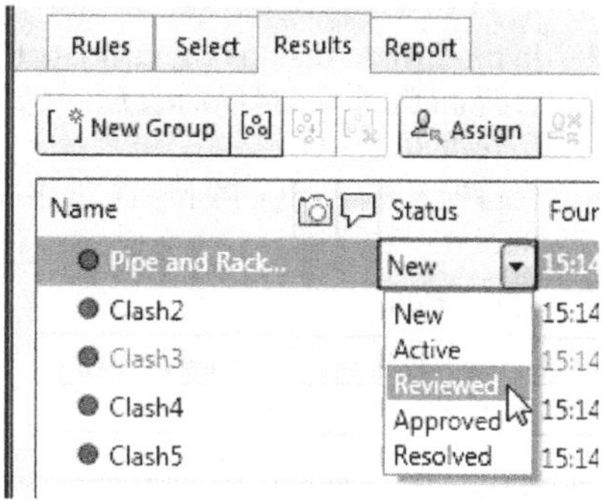

18. To add a comment to a clash:
    - Right-click on Pipe and Rack Clash.
    - Click Add Comment.
    - In the Add Comment dialog box, enter **This needs to be checked**.
    - At the bottom of the Add Comment dialog box, from the Status list, verify that New is selected.
    - Click OK.

19. To create a clash report:

- Select the Report tab.
- Under Contents, select the options as shown in the following illustration.

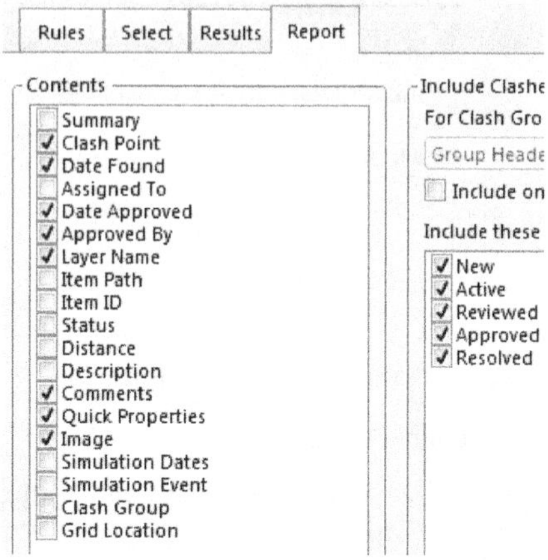

- In the Output Settings, verify that Current test is selected from the Report Type list.
- From the Report Format list, select HTML.
- Click Write Report.

20. To save the file:

- In the Save As dialog box, navigate to the *C:\Plant Design2024 Practice Files\Clash Detection* folder.
- For File Name, enter Plant 3D Clash Test Report.
- Click Save.

21. Open the HTML file just created from Windows Explorer and review it.

22. Close the Clash Detective palette and save the file.

Lesson Review Questions

1. Object selection for clash testing can only be made from the Select tab in the Clash Detective palette by selecting items in the Selection A and Selection B panes.
   a. True
   b. False
2. The Autodesk Navisworks software can detect which of the following object clashes? (Select all that apply.)
   a. Clearance
   b. Piping
   c. Hard
   d. Soft
   e. Duplicates
3. Which of the following Report Formats are available for exporting Clash Detection? (Select all that apply.)
   a. XLS
   b. HTML
   c. XML
   d. TEXT
   e. VIEWPOINTS
4. Which of the following are Display Setting options to help you review the results of a clash? (Select all that apply.)
   a. Transparent dimming
   b. Hard
   c. View
   d. Hide Other
   e. Dim Other
   f. Items in the same layer

Lesson: Highlights of Scheduling and Rendering

Overview

This lesson describes the use of TimeLiner to link to an external scheduling project file and to create a simulation. In this lesson you also learn how to create rendered images.

The Navisworks TimeLiner enables you to create 4D simulations of 3D designs that you use to create real-time walkthroughs and to review complex 3D design projects. 4D simulation enables better planning and helps to identify scheduling risks at an early stage, which can significantly reduce waste.

The Autodesk Navisworks software enables you to create high resolution renderings and save them.

Objectives

After completing this lesson, you will be able to:

- Describe using timeliner for visual 4D planning.
- Describe how to use Autodesk Rendering to add materials and lighting to your scene.

TimeLiner

The TimeLiner tool (shown in the following illustration) enables you to link your 3D model to an external schedule, such as a construction schedule or maintenance process, for visual 4D planning. This enables you to see the effects of the schedule on the model, and compare planned dates against actual dates. You can combine the functionality of TimeLiner with other Autodesk Navisworks tools, such as Clash Detective and Animator.

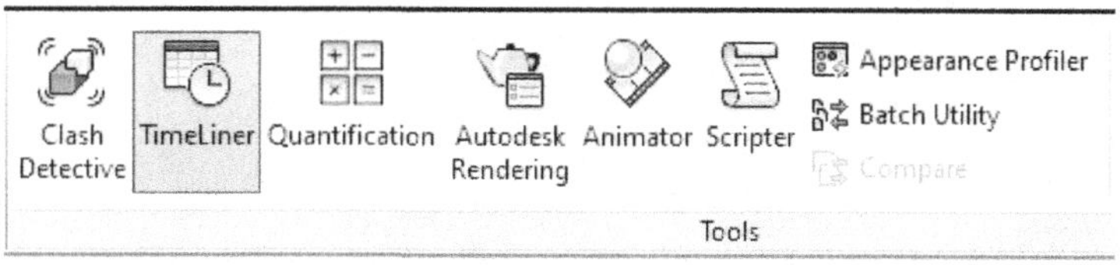

TimeLiner Tasks

You use the Tasks tab to create and edit tasks, to attach tasks to geometry items, and to validate your project schedule, as shown in the following illustration.

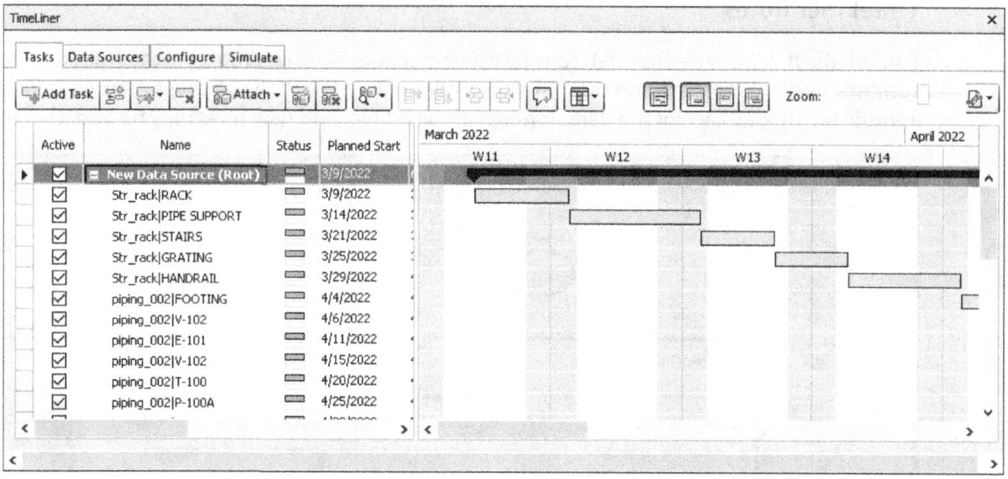

TimeLiner Links

You use the Data Sources tab to link external schedule information, as shown in the following illustration. You can import a list of tasks from a project file directly into TimeLiner, including start dates, end dates, and times.

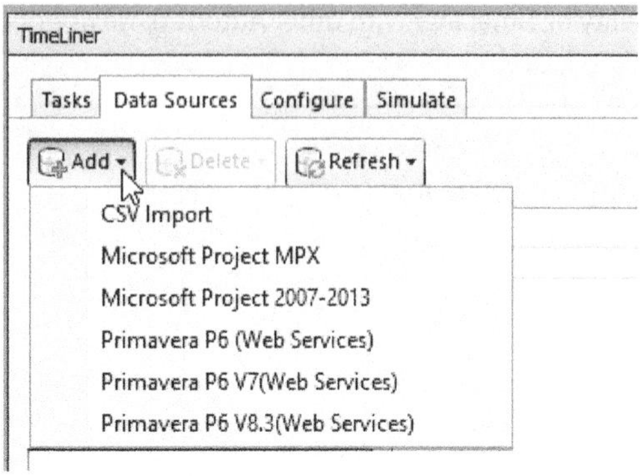

TimeLiner Rules

You use the Rules on the Tasks tab to create and manage TimeLiner rules. All the rules that are currently available are listed on the TimeLiner Rules dialog box. You use these rules to map tasks to items in the model. Each of the default rules can be edited, and new rules may be added as required.

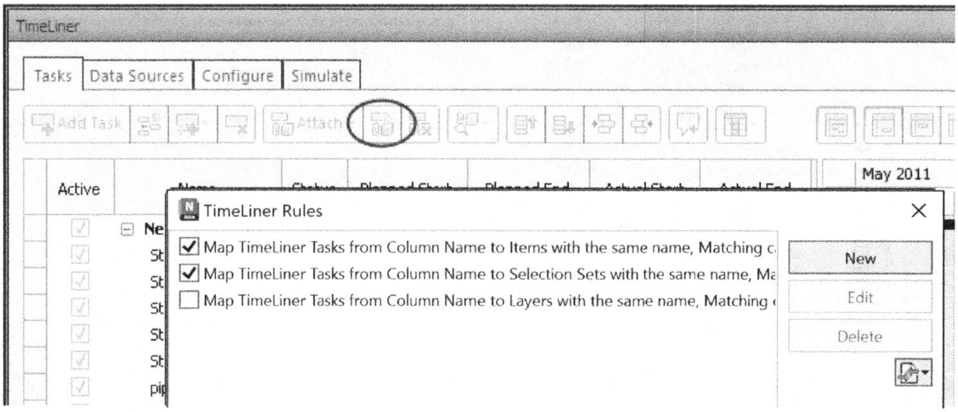

TimeLiner Simulate

You use the Simulate tab to simulate your TimeLiner sequence throughout the duration of the project schedule, as shown in the following illustration. You use the playback buttons to play through and optionally reverse the simulation as well as rewind and forward it. You can also position the slider to quickly move through the simulation.

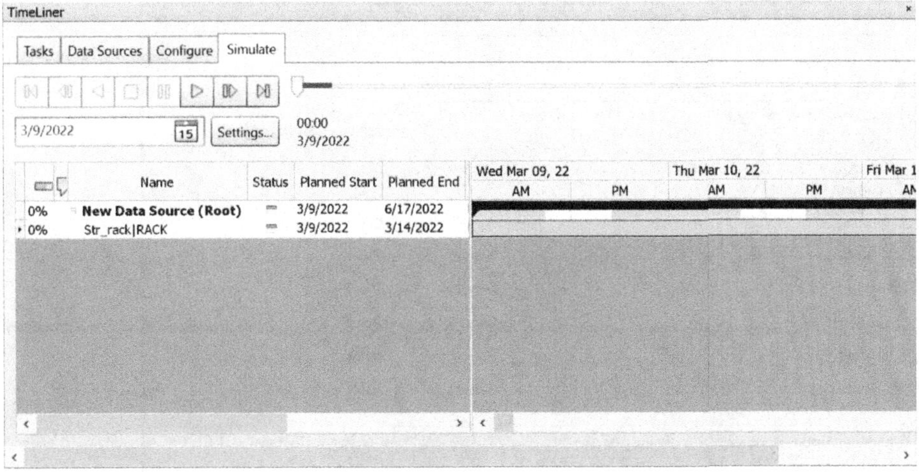

Autodesk Rendering

You use the Autodesk Rendering tool to add materials and lighting to your scene to incorporate realism and effects for rendering. To access this tool, on the Home tab, on the Tools panel, click Autodesk Rendering, as shown in the following illustration.

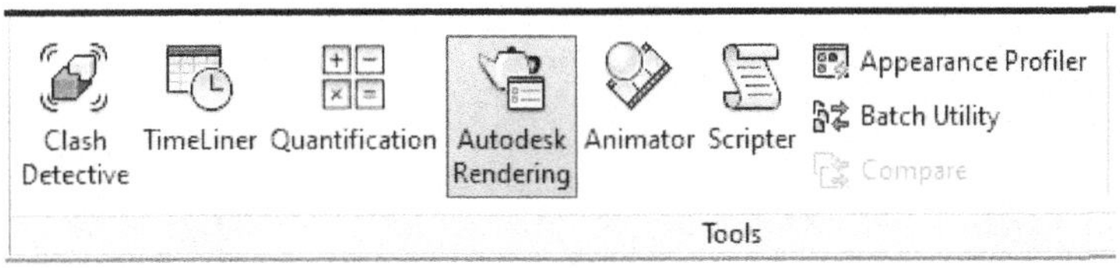

Default materials for the elements in a model are based on the colors they were in the application in which they were created, such as the AutoCAD software. In some applications (like Revit), the materials assigned in the application come across into Navisworks. You can assign predefined Autodesk materials to the elements using the Materials tab in the Autodesk Rendering palette, as shown in the following illustration. You can also use this tab to create new materials, or customize existing materials. You can also select and apply different lighting options using the Lighting tab.

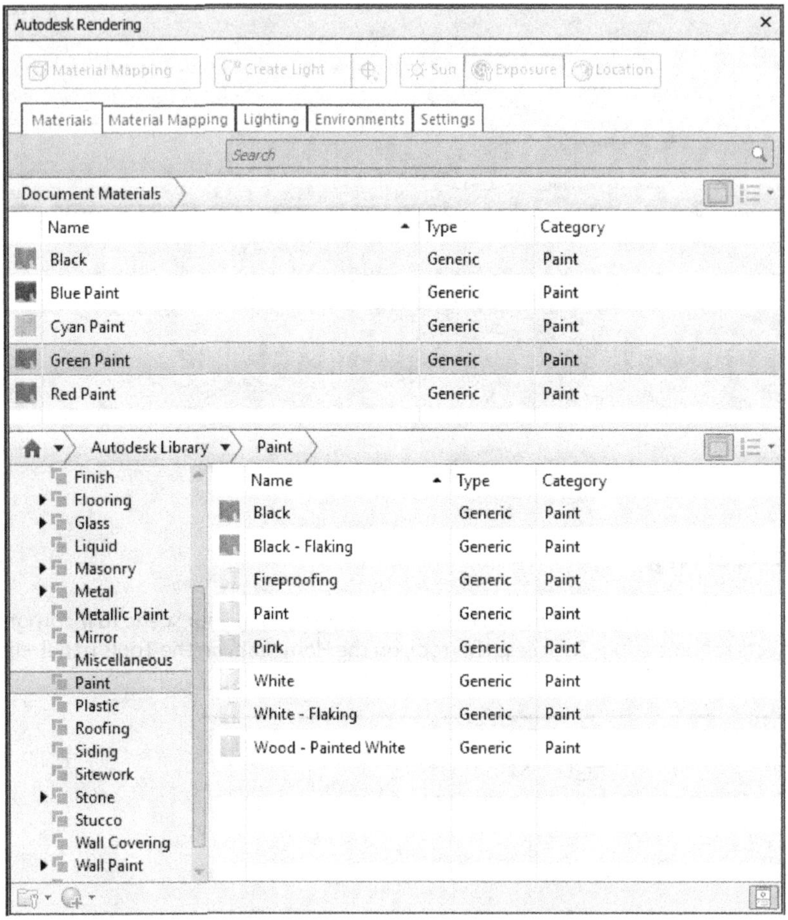

Exercise: Working with the Fourth Dimension

In this exercise, you work with Navisworks TimeLiner to create a 4D simulation. You create, play, and export an animation. You also add materials to the elements in your model and export a rendered image

1. Start the Autodesk Navisworks software, if not already running.
2. Open an existing file by doing the following:
   - On the Quick Access Toolbar, click Open.
   - In the Open dialog box, navigate to the folder *C:\Plant Design 2024 Practice Files\Work with the Fourth Dimension*.
   - Select the file *Plant 3D.nwf.*
   - Click Open.

   Note: Change the file of type if the .nwf files are not displaying. Additionally, if the Resolve dialog box appears, resolve the external reference by clicking Browse. Then navigate to *C:\Plant Design 2024 Practice Files\Work with the Fourth Dimension* and select the file Equipment.dwg. Do the same for any other externally referenced files that cannot be found.
3. On the Viewpoint tab, on the Render Style panel, on the Lighting list, click Full Lights.
4. On the Home tab, on the Tools panel, click TimeLiner.
5. You may want to "Pin" the TimeLiner window by clicking on the Pin Icon as you did previously, to prevent it from collapsing.
6. On the TimeLiner palette, click the Tasks tab, if not already active. Note that there are no tasks listed.
7. On the Data Sources tab, expand Add and click CSV Import.
8. In the Open dialog box, navigate to the *C:\Plant Design 2024 Practice Files\Work with the Fourth Dimension* folder and select *Plant 3D-2022-23.csv.*
9. Click Open.
10. In the Field Selector dialog box:
    - Select the Row 1 contains headings option.
    - Define the External Field Names column with the following values, as shown in the illustration below:
      - Task Name: Name
      - Display ID: 1001
      - Task Type: Task
      - Synchronization ID: 1001
      - Planned Start Date: Start_Date
      - Planned End Date: Finish_Date
    - Click OK.

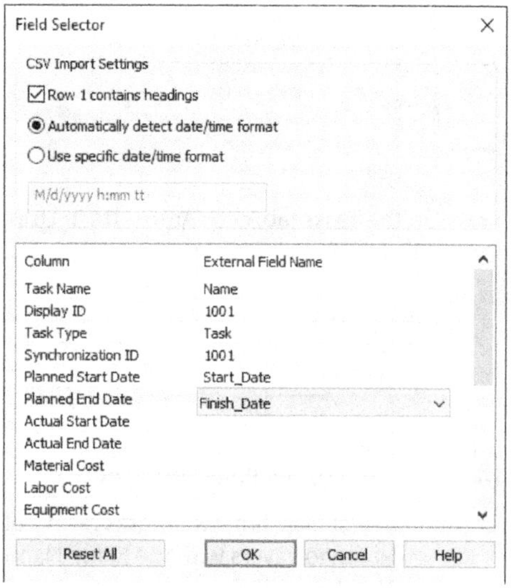

11. On the Data Sources tab, right-click on the new link. Click Rebuild Task Hierarchy.

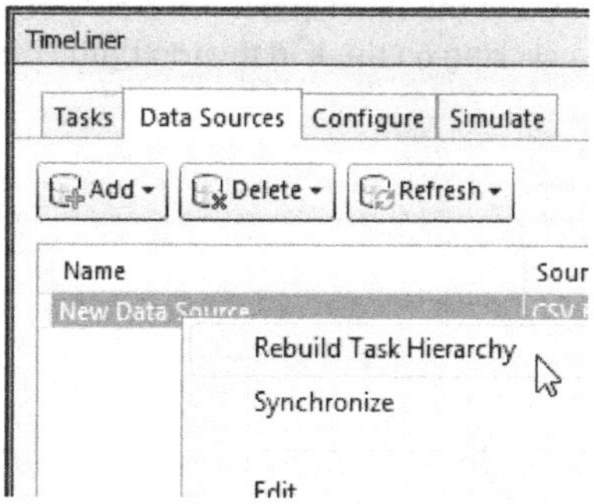

12. On the Tasks tab, verify that there is a list of tasks.

    Note that the Attached column for each task does not have a value. If this is the first time TimeLiner has been run, the Attached column might not be visible. To expand, click and drag the left side divider between the Gantt view and the task list. Alternatively, you can scroll to see it.

13. On the Tasks tab, click Auto-Attach Using Rules.

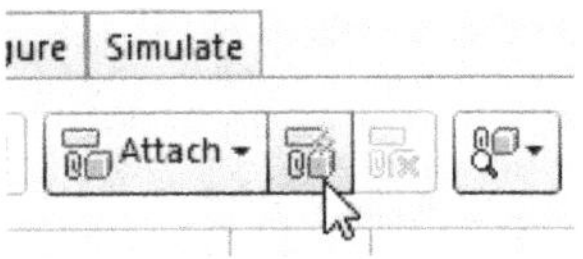

14. In the TimeLiner Rules dialog box:

    - Select Map TimeLiner Tasks from Column Name to Layers with the Same Name, Matching Case.
    - Uncheck the other two choices.
    - Click Apply Rules.
    - Close the TimeLiner Rules dialog box by clicking on the **X** in the top right corner.

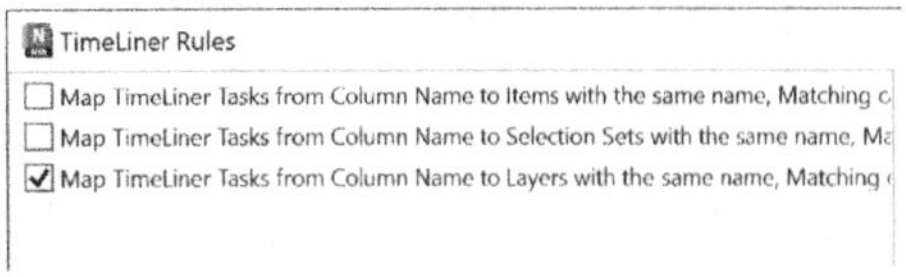

15. On the Tasks tab, verify that in the Attached field for each task, the value is Explicit Selection.

16. On the Tasks tab, for the first task, set the Task Type column value to Construct.

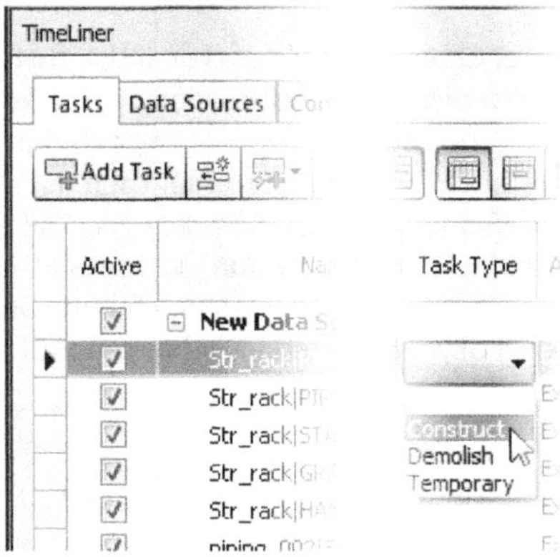

17. Many of the task types were imported, but not all. Go to the second and third tasks and set them to Construct.

18. On the TimeLiner palette, click the Simulate tab.

19. To display the task:

- On the Simulate tab, click Settings.
- In the Simulation Settings dialog box, under View, click Planned.
- Click OK.

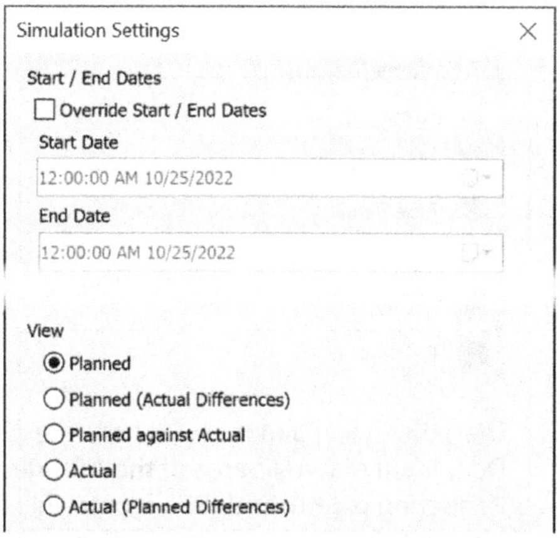

20. On the Simulate tab, click Play. Watch the objects added to the model per the task schedule.

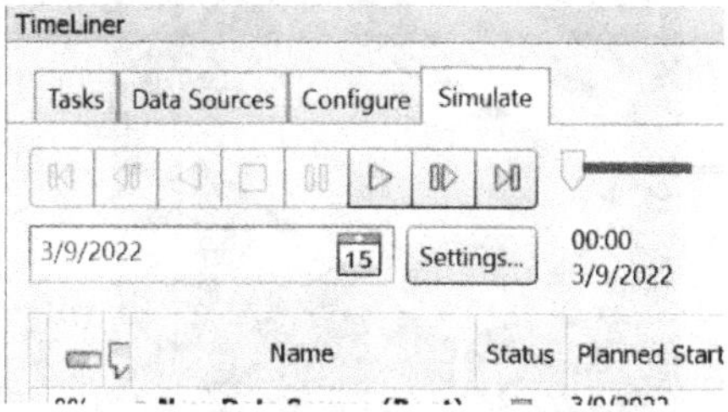

21. Use the other buttons, such as Back, Forward, and Pause to step through the animation.

22. Close the TimeLiner window.

Use Autodesk Material Library and Rendering

In this section of the exercise, you assign materials to elements and export a rendered image.

1. Orient the model to its Home view using the ViewCube, if not already set.

2. On the Render tab, click Ray Trace.

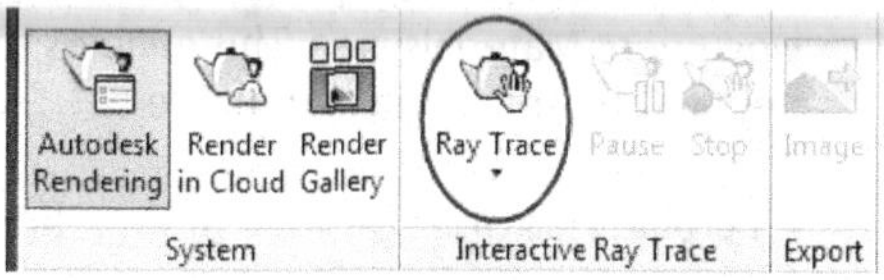

Note that the rendering is completed with the default Low Quality setting. To change this, Stop the rendering and expand and select a new option in the Ray Trace drop-down list.

3. The model is rendered with the elements displaying in their currently assigned colors.

4. On the Interactive Ray Trace panel, click Stop. The rendering is no longer displayed. The display is returned to its shaded display.

5. On the Home tab, on the Tools panel, click Autodesk Rendering.

6. You may want to "Pin" the Autodesk Rendering window by clicking on the Pin Icon as you did previously, to prevent it from collapsing.

7. On the Autodesk Rendering palette, on the Materials tab, on the left pane, expand the Autodesk Library category and select Paint.

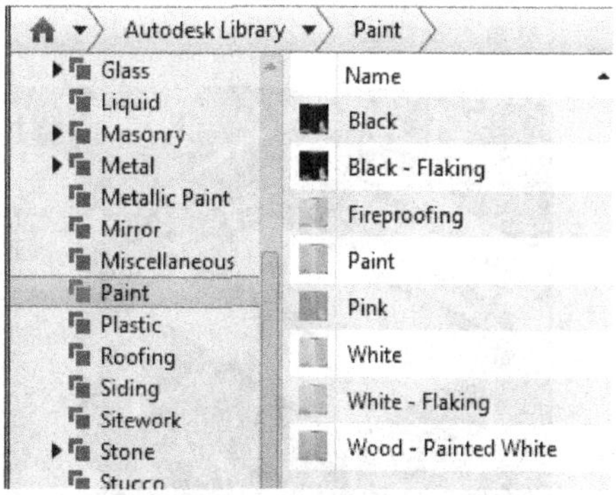

8. In the column on the right, select and drag the Black item to the top of the palette in the Document Materials area. This enables the item to be used in the current file.

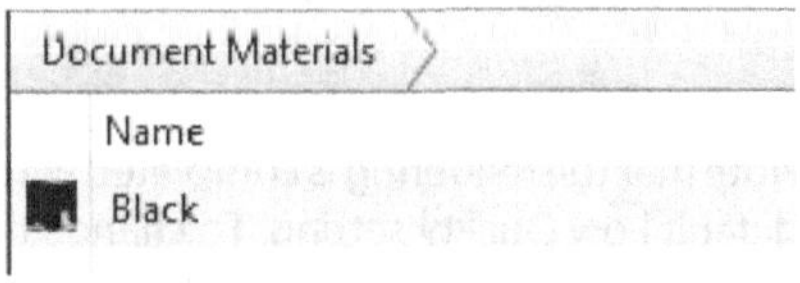

9. Right-click on the Black material from the Document Materials area and select Duplicate.

10. Right-click on the Black(1) material and select Edit.

11. In the Material Editor, select the Color field and change the color to Blue using the Color dialog box. Close the Material Editor.

12. Right-click on Black(1) and select Rename. Enter Blue Paint as the new name.

13. Drag the Blue Paint material from the Document Materials area of the Autodesk Rendering palette and drop it onto the element as shown in the following illustration.

    Note: Ensure that the Selection Resolution: Layer is active.

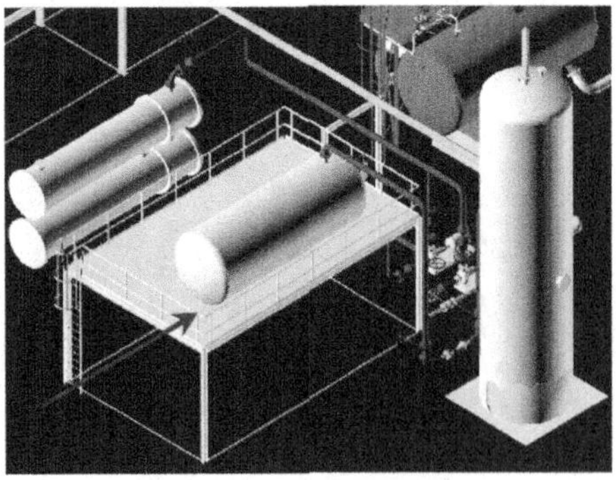

14. Duplicate the Blue Paint item three additional times. Edit and rename the materials to obtain the following paint colors:
    - Cyan Paint
    - Green Paint
    - Red Paint

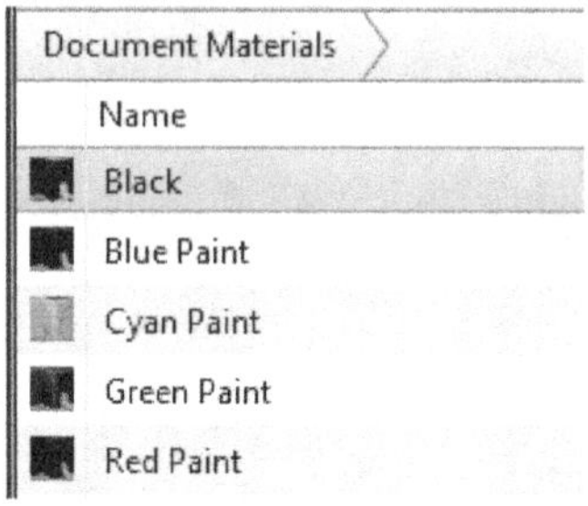

15. Drag the Cyan Paint material from the Document Materials area of the Autodesk Rendering palette and drop it onto the elements (pressure vessels), as shown in the following illustration.

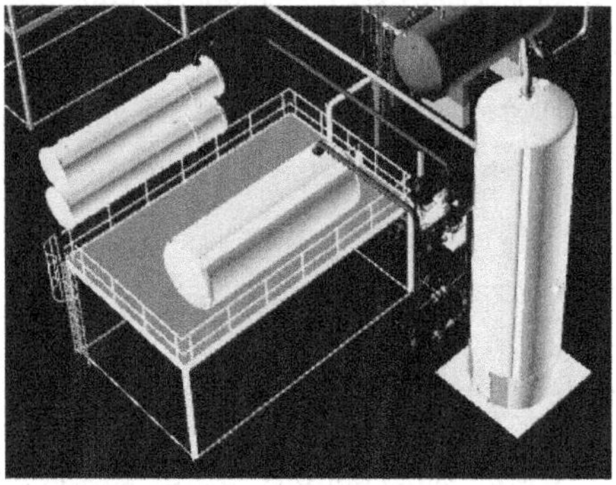

16. Drag the other paint materials from the Document Materials area of the Autodesk Rendering palette and drop it onto the elements in the model, as desired.

17. On the Render tab, click Ray Trace. The model is rendered with the elements displaying in their assigned colors.

18. To export the rendered image:
    - On the Render tab, on the Export panel, click Image.
    - From the Type list, verify that JPEG is selected.
    - Click Browse and navigate to the *C:\Plant Design 2024 Practice Files\Work with the Fourth Dimension* folder.
    - Give it an appropriate file name.
    - Click Save.
19. Use Windows Explorer to locate the image file and review it.

    Note that the Plant 3D_High_Res.jpg has been provided for review.
20. Unpin the Autodesk Rendering window so it collapses back to the side of the interface.
21. Save the file and close Navisworks.

Lesson Review Questions

1. Which file formats can be linked to an Autodesk Navisworks file in the TimeLiner module? (Select all that apply.)
   a. Microsoft Word
   b. Primavera
   c. AutoCAD
   d. Microsoft Excel using a CSV file
2. Microsoft Project must be installed to be able to link Microsoft Project MPP files in the TimeLiner.
   a. True
   b. False
3. To which of the following formats can the Autodesk Navisworks software export rendered images?
   a. PNG
   b. QuickTime
   c. Flash
   d. TIFF
4. Which of the following can be applied to a model using Autodesk Rendering? (Select all that apply.)
   a. Materials
   b. Lighting
   c. RPC
   d. Visibility Settings

Chapter Summary

In this chapter, you learned how to use the Autodesk Navisworks software to view, review, and analyze a plant design. This included learning how to combine design files from a variety of design and engineering applications into a single integrated project model for efficient whole-project review.

Having completed this chapter, you can:

- Work with and handle files in the Autodesk Navisworks software.
- Navigate and walk through a design in the Autodesk Navisworks software.
- Conduct clash tests and work with clash detection results.
- Create rendered images and use TimeLiner to link to an external scheduling project file and to create a simulation.

Chapter

5

Setting Up and Administering a Plant Project

In this chapter, you learn the skills and knowledge for setting up and administering a plant project. This includes tasks like setting up the project file for large projects, controlling the project structure and file location, customizing the data manager, and creating and editing drawing borders to name just a few.

Objectives

After completing this chapter, you will be able to:

- Create a new project and structure it to your needs.
- Explain how projects are structured in the AutoCAD Plant 3D software and the AutoCAD P&ID software and identify where the project files are located.
- Set up and maintain a project that can be used for larger projects with multiple users.
- Set up the tagging scheme and place symbols on the correct layer with the required color.
- Set up any report or view in the Data Manager and use that set up to export data from the project.
- Create drawing templates and use data from the project and the drawing in your title block.
- Create, modify, and convert a spec and create and duplicate components to build your own components.
- Create a custom isometric set up and add additional information to your drawing when generating the Iso.
- Troubleshoot issues by recovering drawings and solving error messages.
- Create and manage the report configuration files that are used to generate reports.
- Set up SQL Express for the AutoCAD Plant 3D software.

Lesson: Overview of Project Setup

Overview

This lesson describes how to create a new project and structure it to your needs.

The number of drawings required to document and communicate a process piping design depends on the complexity of that design. Being able to create and set up a project is important to ensure correct management and access to the drawing files and data associated with the project.

Objectives

After completing this lesson, you will be able to:

- Open an existing project and explain where the project name is derived from.
- Create a new project.
- Identify where and how the default drawing templates are configured for a project.
- Explain the purpose of project folders and how they can be configured.

Opening an Existing Project

Opening an existing AutoCAD P&ID or AutoCAD Plant 3D project is a straightforward process. There are two key things you need to know about opening an existing project. First, you initiate the opening of a project from the Project Manager by clicking Open in the Current Project list or from the Project panel on the Home tab, as shown in the following illustration. Second, the file you select to open is always titled *Project.xml*.

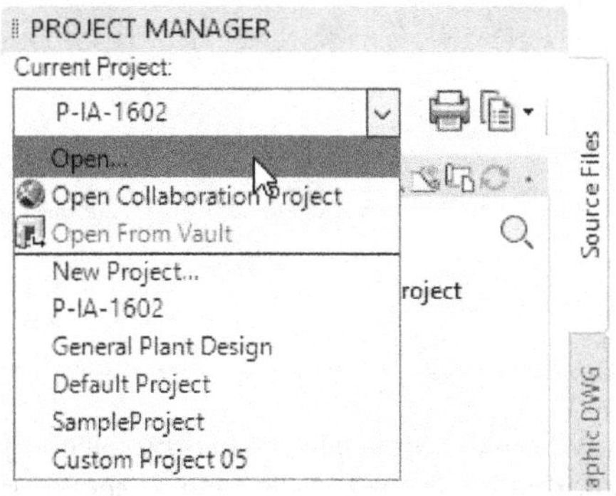

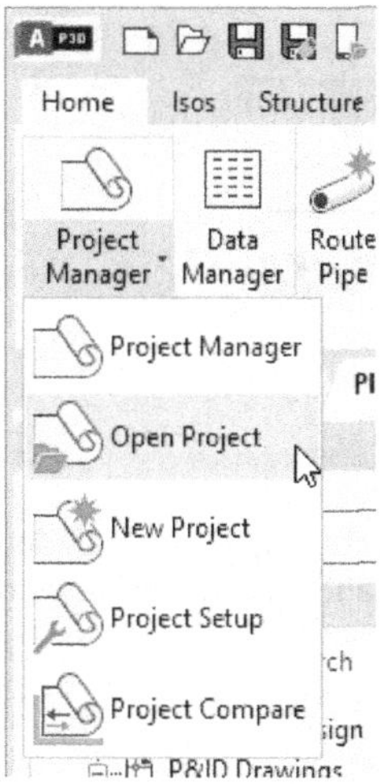

Project Names

After opening a project, a name for the project displays in the Current Project list. The name that displays in the Project Manager's Current Project list is the folder name where the '*Project.xml*' file resides. The name of the top node in the Project pane might or might not match the name of the current project. The name of the top node in the Project pane is the name of the project that was entered when the project was initially created.

The Project Manager with an active project and a representation of the relationship between the project file and project folder are shown in the following illustration. Based on the Project Manager, the current project is P-IA-1602 and the top node is titled Set Up and Structure Your Project. This indicates that when the project was initially created, it was called Set Up and Structure Your Project. At some point after the project was created, the folder in which the *Project.xml* resides was renamed from Training Project to P-IA-1602.

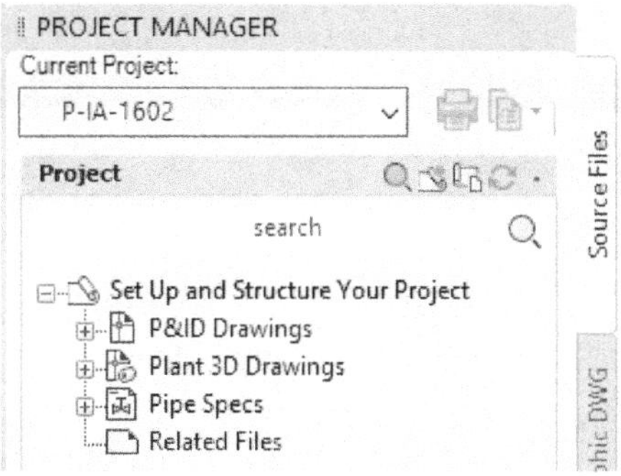

Location of Projects

To make switching between projects easy and quick, the most recent projects you opened are listed in the Current Project list. By hovering the cursor over a listed project name, the full path to the *Project.xml* file displays in a tooltip, as shown in the following illustration. This helps you determine whether this is truly the project you want to open.

After you have opened a project, you can determine where the project file resides by selecting the top node in the Project pane and then reviewing the information in the Details pane, as shown in the following illustration.

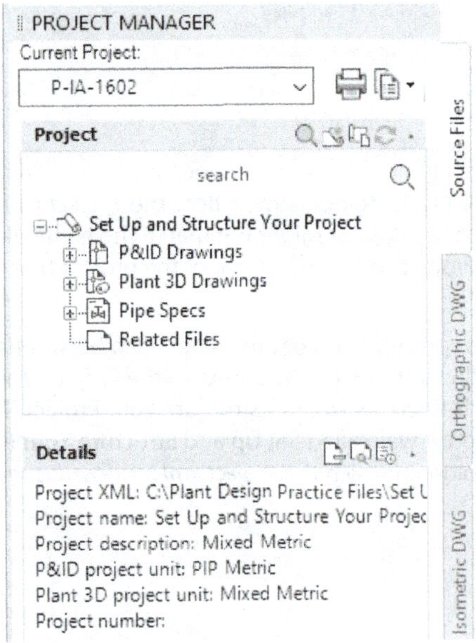

Creating a New Project

The AutoCAD P&ID software and the AutoCAD Plant 3D software use a project environment to help in the creation and management of drawings, models, and other related files. The project also helps ensure that you are working with the correct data and templates.

When you need to create an all new design and you want the design files to be separate from any past designs, you create a new project. The new project defines the new project environment.

There are a number of locations where you can start the wizard to create a new project. The most likely access location is the Project Manager, as shown in the following illustration.

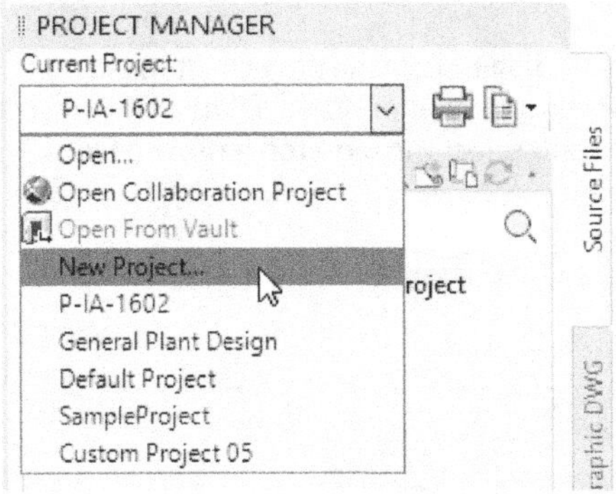

Process: Creating a New Project

When you create a new project, a wizard guides you through the steps. The key tasks the wizard undertakes are:

- Set the name for the project.
- Set the initial project folder name and path.
- Specify the base units for the project.
- Select the standard to be used for P&ID tool palette content.
- Specify the storage location for created drawings.
- Create the corresponding folders and files on the specified drive.
- Specify the database settings and configuration.

To make it easier and quicker to configure a new project, the project wizard has an option that enables you to copy the settings from an existing project. When you do this, although some of the options in the wizard are automatically set, you can still modify some things like the storage locations for the created drawings.

Default Drawing Templates

Every time you create a new drawing, its initial settings and content are based on a drawing template file. You configure the default drawing template file that should be used for the creation of a new AutoCAD P&ID, AutoCAD Plant 3D, or Ortho drawing in the overall project setup. You select the settings for the overall project in the Project Setup dialog box and save them in conjunction with the projSymbolStyle.dwg file. An easy was to access the project settings is in the Project Manager. You right-click on the project name in the Project pane and then click Project Setup.

To set the drawing template file for P&ID drawings, in the Project Setup dialog box under General Settings, you first select Paths. Then, in the P&ID section, for the Drawing template file (DWT) field, click browse and select the required template file.

To set the drawing template file for AutoCAD Plant 3D drawings, in the Project Setup dialog box under General Settings, select Paths, as shown in the following illustration. Then, in the Plant 3D section, for the Drawing template file (DWT) field, click browse and select the required template file.

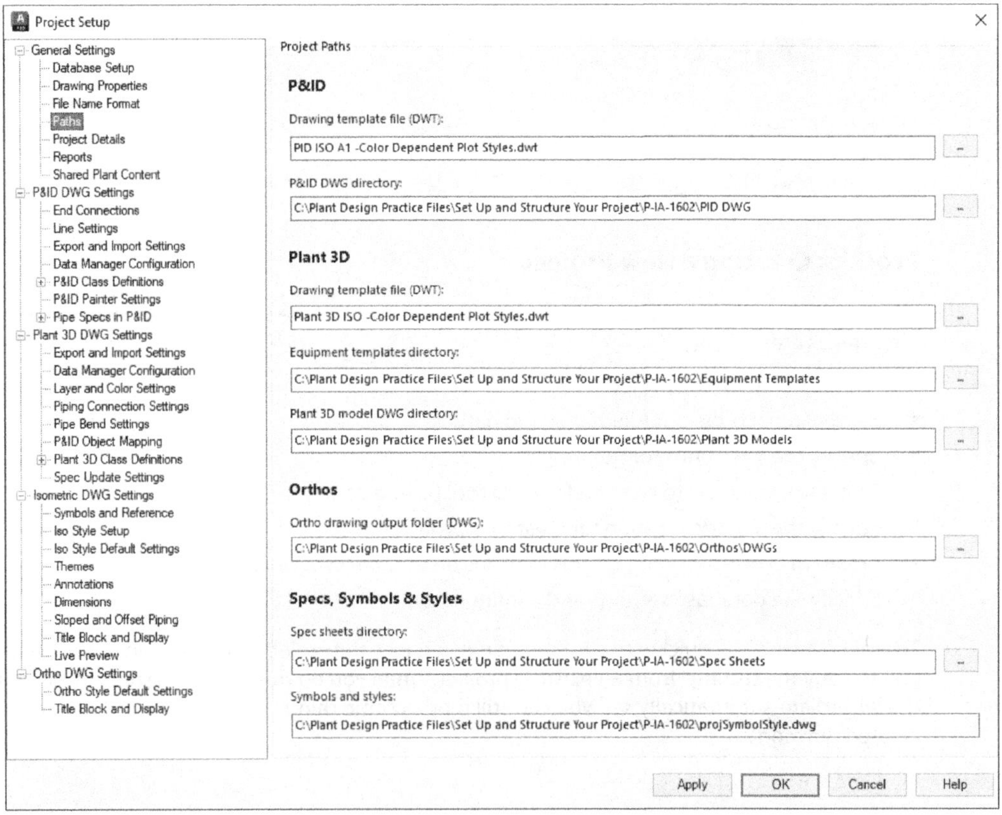

To set the drawing template file for orthographic drawings, in the Project Setup dialog box under Ortho DWG Settings, select Title Block and Display and select a template in the Ortho drawing template (DWT) field.

Project Folders

You add folders to a project to visually organize drawings and related files in the Project Manager. You also add them to assist in controlling the creation of new drawings. The folder adds control because all project folders are configured with a location where new drawings are saved and with the drawing template that should be used when new drawings are created. By default, all drawings are stored relative to the parent folder storage location.

A project that has project folders added under Plant 3D Drawings is shown in the following illustration. The New Folder dialog box is used when you create and modify a project folder.

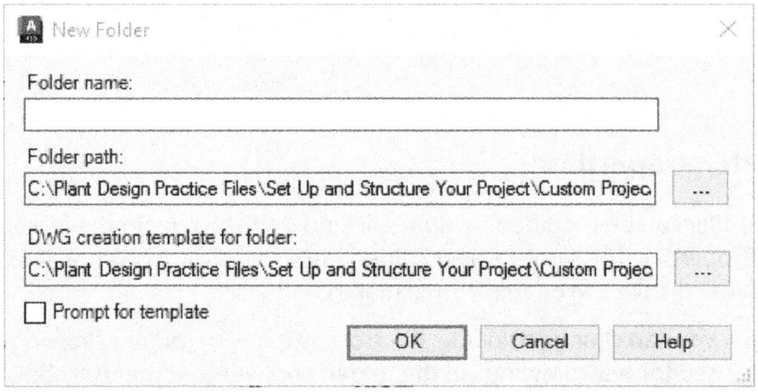

The template specified for a project folder is used by default when a new drawing is being created in that folder. A new drawing is created directly in a folder when you right-click on the folder and then click New Drawing. The new drawing automatically uses the specified settings as the initial settings in the New DWG dialog box. While a different template can be selected during the creation of the new drawing, you should have the required template set as the default template. If you want to force the selection of a drawing template each time a new drawing is created in the folder, select the Prompt For Template option when configuring the project folder.

> Configure the required default template files in the project before you create folders in the project. The template file set in the Project Setup dialog box is the template drawing that is configured for a new folder by default. If you change the default template in the overall project after creating the folders and you want the folders to use that other template, you need to modify each folder's properties accordingly.

Project Folder Order and Location

When a project folder is created, the order in which it displays in the Project Manager is based on standard alphanumeric rules. While you cannot change the order in which project folders display, you can adjust their position by nesting them in other folders. Bars or arrows display as you drag the folder to indicate where the folder is going to be nested.

The position of the Equipment folder being modified is shown in the following illustration. The modification process is shown on the left and the results of the modification are shown on the right.

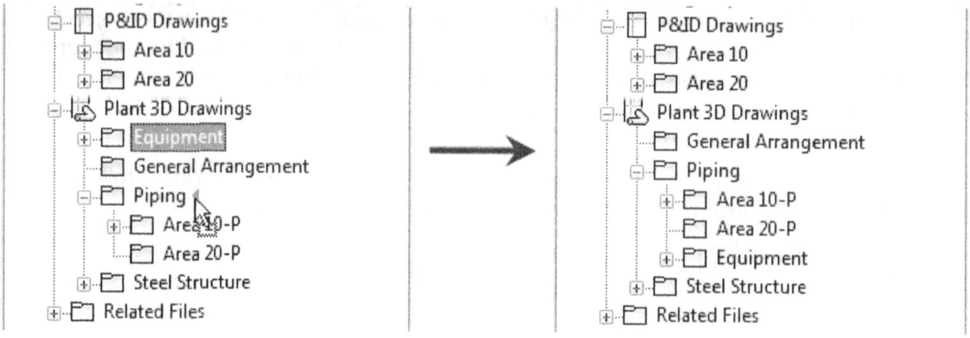

Modifying Project Folder Properties

The properties of a project folder can be modified by right-clicking on the folder in the Project Manager and then clicking Properties. The same Project Folder Properties dialog box that was used to initially create the project folder displays to enable you to make changes.

When you edit a project folder you can change its name, the storage location for new drawings, which drawing template should be used for new drawings in the folder, and whether the user should be prompted to select a drawing template for each newly created drawing.

> Renaming a project folder does not automatically change the name of the folder on the drive where new drawings are going to be created. If the drive folder needs to be updated, you need to modify the name of that folder and then select that modified drive folder as the storage location.

Exercise: Set Up and Structure Your Project

In this exercise, you create your own project, add folders to set up a structure, and change the necessary paths to locate template files.

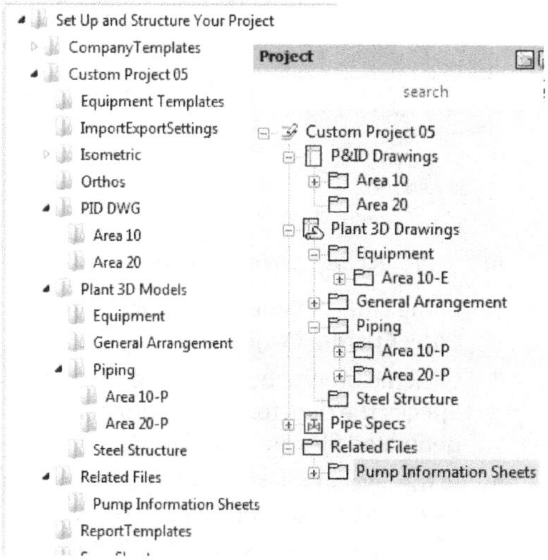

Open, Close, and Create a New Project

In this section of the exercise, you open an existing project to review its structure and associated files. You then close the project and begin creating a new project.

1. Start the AutoCAD Plant 3D software, if not already running.
2. Open an existing project by doing the following:
   - In the Project Manager, Current Project list, click Open.
   - In the Open dialog box, navigate to the folder *C:\Plant Design 2024 Practice Files\Set Up and Structure Your Project\P-IA-1602.*
   - Select the file *Project.xml.*
   - Click Open.
3. Review the contents of this active project as seen in the Project Manager.
   - On the Source Files tab, expand the tree structure to see the folders and source files.
   - Click the Orthographic DWG tab to view the drawing files that contain orthographic views for the project.
   - Click the Isometric DWG tab. Each pipeline is listed under the Check, Final, Spool, and Stress folders. Each folder is suffixed by a page size designation. Because no drawing files are listed under any of the pipelines, no isometric drawings have been created at this time.

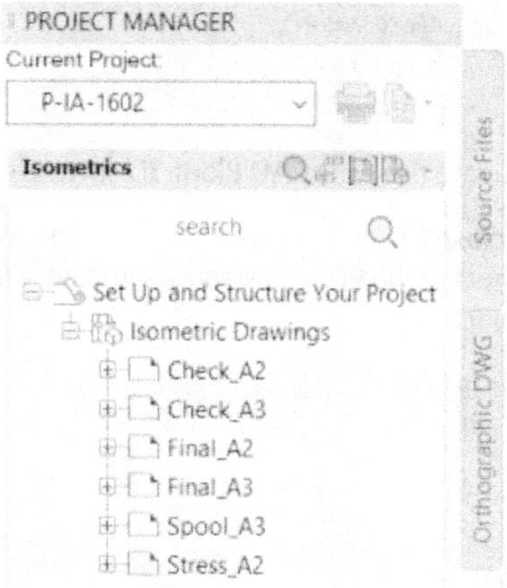

4. Review the folder and files structure for the project in Windows Explorer.
   - Open Windows Explorer.
   - Navigate to and select the *C:\Plant Design 2024 Practice Files\Set Up and Structure Your Project\P-IA-1602* folder.
   - Open the subfolders Isometric, Orthos, PID DWG, and Plant 3D Models to see the actual files and file storage location for the files listed in the project.

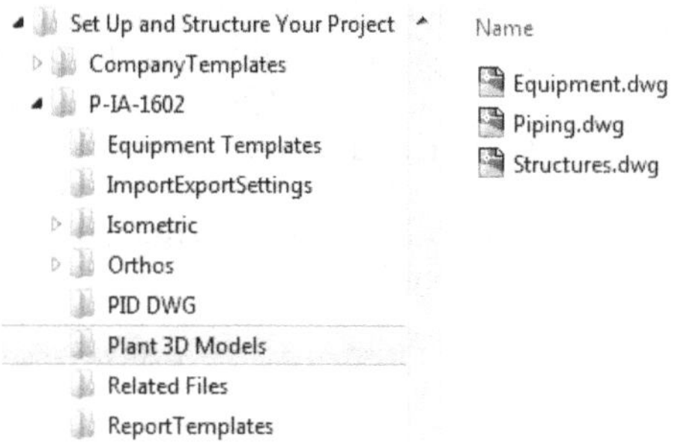

5. Activate the AutoCAD Plant 3D software.
6. To close the active project, right-click on the Project in the Project Manager and click Close Project.

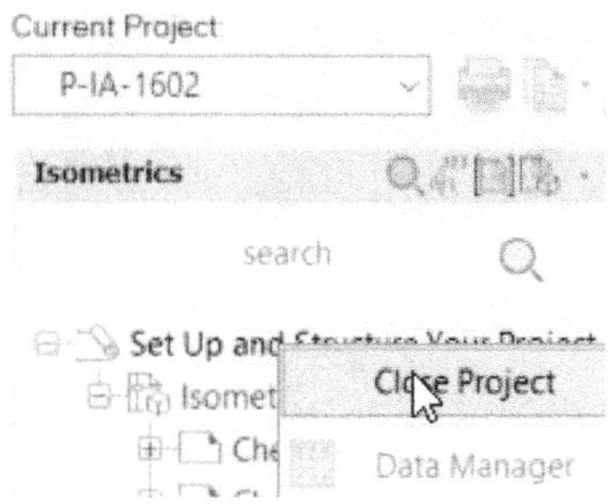

7. To begin creating a new project, in the Project Manager, Current Project list, click New Project.

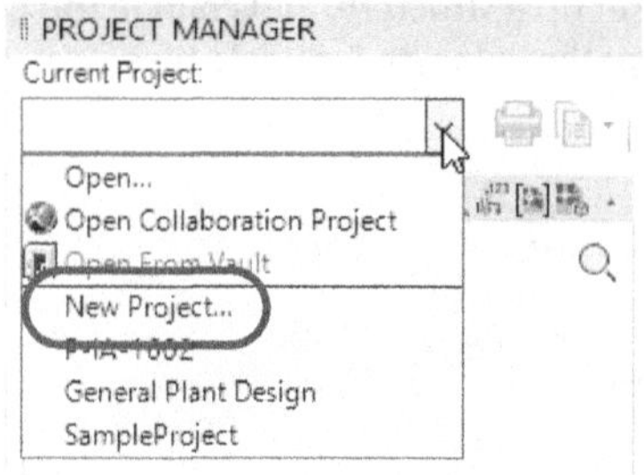

8. In the Project Setup Wizard, Page 1:
   - In the Enter a name for this project field, enter **Custom Project 05**.
   - Click the browse button to the right of Specify the directory where program-generated files are stored field.
   - In the Select Project Directory dialog box, navigate to and select the *C:\Plant Design 2024 Practice Files\Set Up and Structure Your Project* folder.
   - Click Open.
   - Click Next>>.

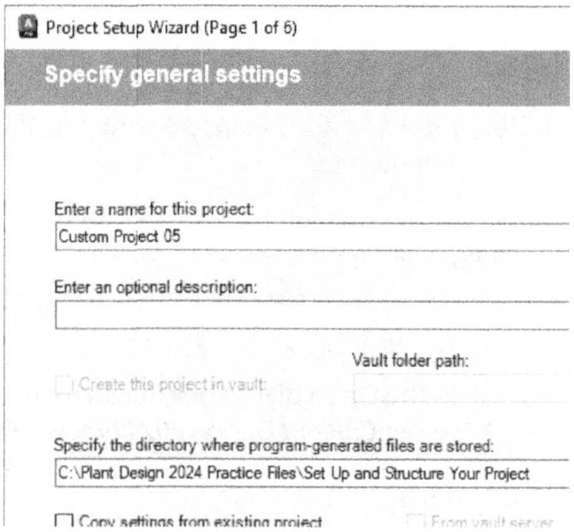

9. On Page 2 of the wizard, for the base units for the project:
   - Ensure Imperial is selected.
   - Click Next>>.

10. On Page 3 of the wizard:

- Review the folder location where the P&ID drawings will be stored.
- Ensure that the PIP standard is selected so that it is used for the palette content.
- Click Next>>.

11. On Page 4 of the wizard:

- Review the paths specific to the AutoCAD Plant 3D software that can be set during project creation.
- Click Next>>.

12. On Page 5 of the wizard, ensure that Single User - SQLite local database is selected. Click Next>>.

13. On Page 6 of the wizard, click Finish. The Project Manager now displays as shown in the following illustration.

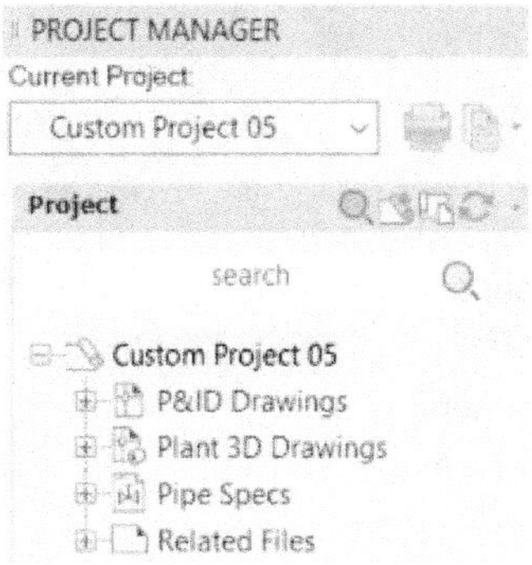

14. To review the files and folders that were automatically created for the new project:

- Switch to Windows Explorer.
- Navigate to the *C:\Plant Design 2024 Practice Files\Set Up and Structure Your Project\Custom Project 05* folder.
- Quickly review the files and subfolders in the project folder.

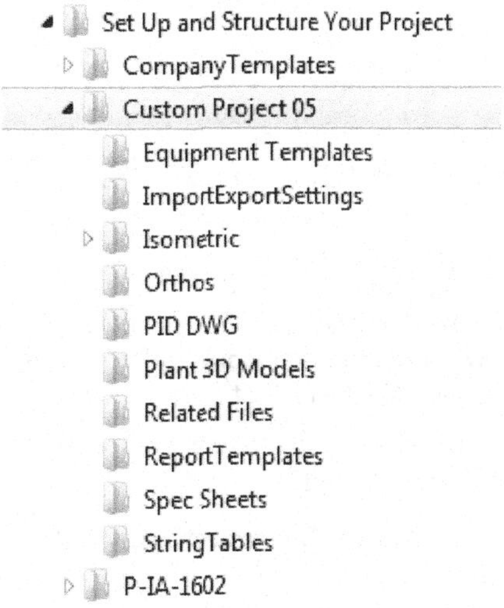

Work with Folders in a Project

In this section of the exercise, you create folders for the project and modify their properties.

1. To create a new project folder under P&ID Drawings and have a corresponding folder created on the drive with the project:

- In the Project Manager, Project panel, right-click on P&ID Drawings. Click New Folder.
- In the New Folder dialog box, for Folder name, enter **Area 10**.
- In the Folder path field, review the listed folder path.
- Click OK.

2. In the Project Manager and in Windows Explorer, review what was created. The resulting project folder and drive folder are created as shown in the following illustration.

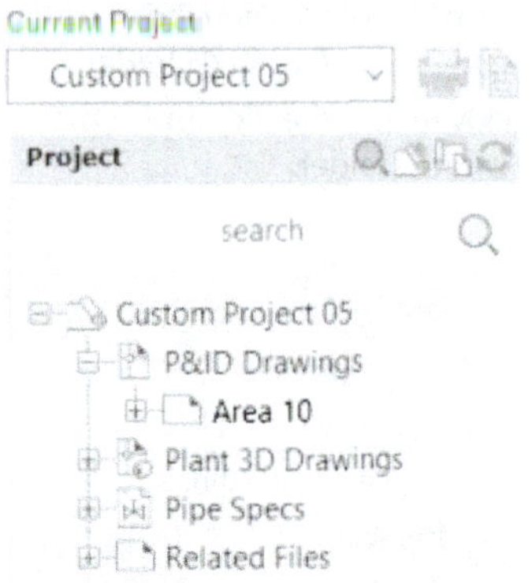

Note: By default, a folder is created in Windows Explorer along with a new folder created in the Project.

The following steps show how to create and reassign folders.

3. To create another project folder in P&ID Drawings:
   - Right-click on P&ID Drawings. Click New Folder.
   - In the New Folder dialog box, for Folder name, enter **Ar 20**.
   - Click OK. Note that the Folder (Ar 20) is automatically created in the PID DWG folder.

4. In the Project Manager and in Windows Explorer, ensure that the resulting project folder was created. In the Project Manager, select Ar 20. The details for the project folder shows that it is set to the PID DWG folder.

5. To rename the folder in the project:
   - Right-click on Ar 20. Click Rename Folder.
   - Enter **Area 20**.
   - Press <Enter> or click in the panel to accept the change.

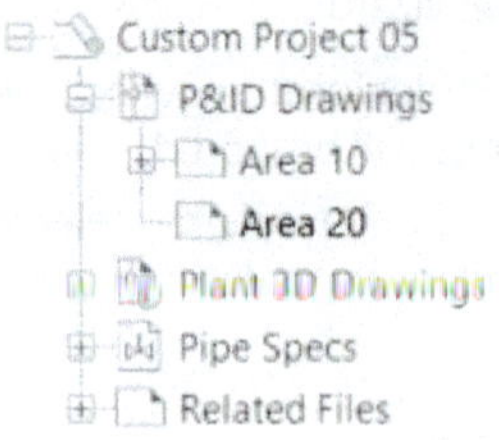

6. Although the folder name is changed here, the path location cannot be changed and remains as Ar 20. You can check this in Details area of the Project Manager and in the PID DWG folder in the Windows Explorer.

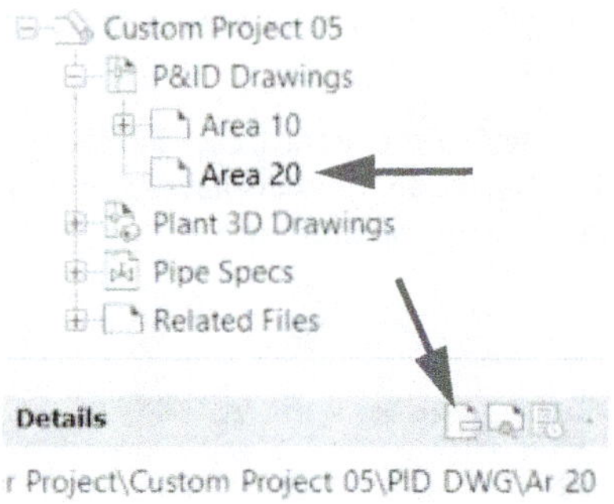

7. Create four new project folders under Plant 3D Drawings.
   - Equipment
   - Steel Structure
   - Piping
   - General Arrangement

Note: Regardless of the order in which you create the folders, they display alphabetically in the list.

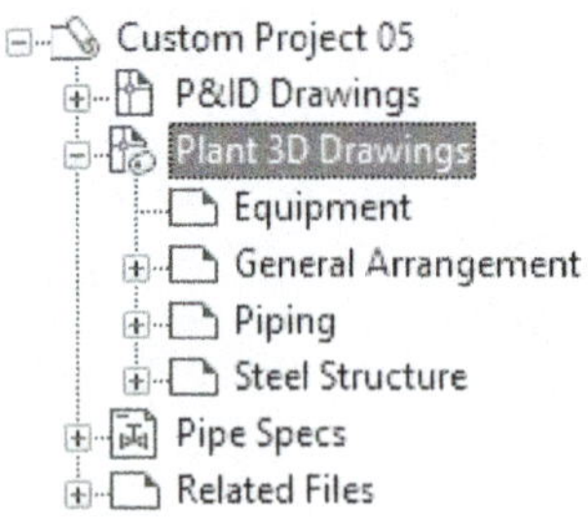

8. To set up the Piping folder so that it has additional organization with subfolders that correspond to the P&ID folder structure:
   - Right-click on Piping. Click New Folder.
   - In the Project Folder Properties dialog box, for Folder name, enter **Area 10-P**.
   - In the Folder path field, review the listed folder path. The folder is nested in the Piping folder.
   - Click OK.

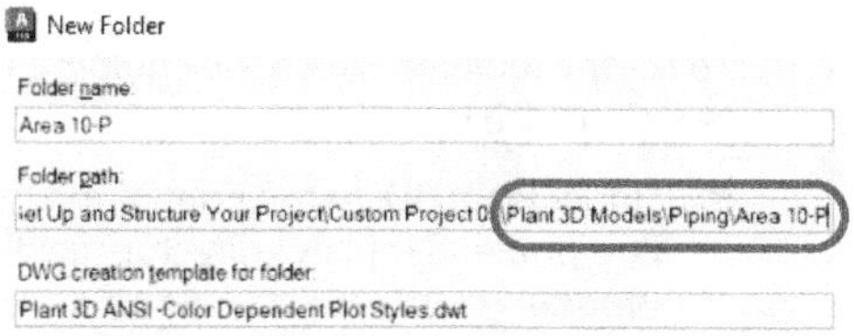

9. Repeat the process to create an Area 20-P subfolder to create the results as shown in the following illustration.

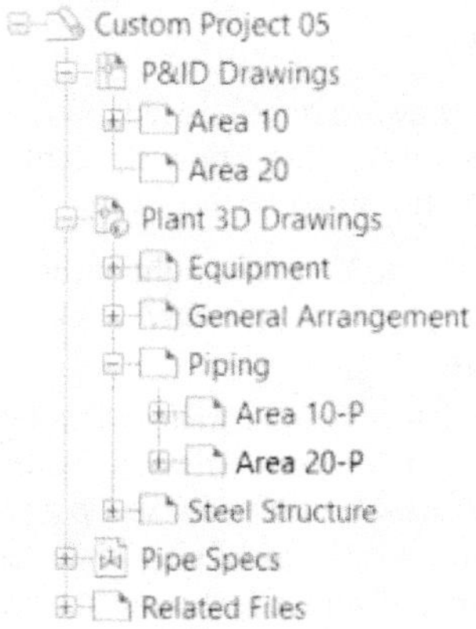

10. To set up the Equipment folder so that it also has additional organization with subfolders:
    - Right-click on Equipment. Click New Folder.
    - In the New Folder dialog box, for Folder name, enter **Area 10-E**.
    - In the Folder path field, review the listed folder path.
    - Click OK.

11. To add a folder under Related Files:
    - Right-click on Related Files. Click New Folder.
    - In the New Folder dialog box, for Folder name, enter **Pump Information Sheets**.
    - Click OK.

12. Review the folder structure created for this project. At this time the project folders and subfolders are configured to save their new files to specific drive folders and to use the same template drawing that is set for the project for new drawing files.

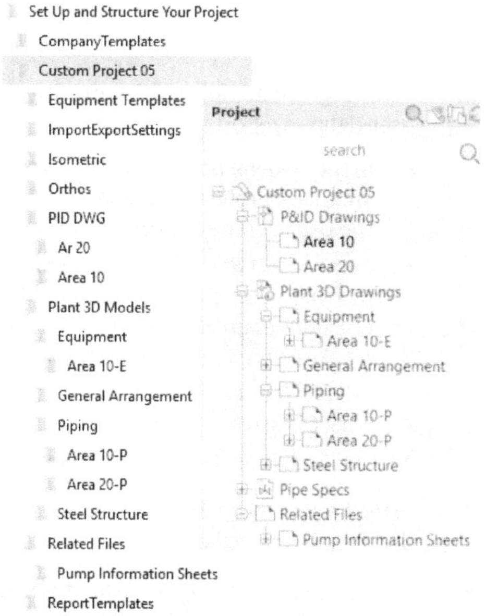

Modify Project Properties

In this section of the exercise, you modify the project properties to specify where templates are retrieved, what drawing templates should be used, and where the spec sheets for the AutoCAD Plant 3D software are located.

1. In the Project panel, right-click on Custom Project 05. Click Project Setup.

2. In the Project Setup dialog box, under General Settings, select Project Details.

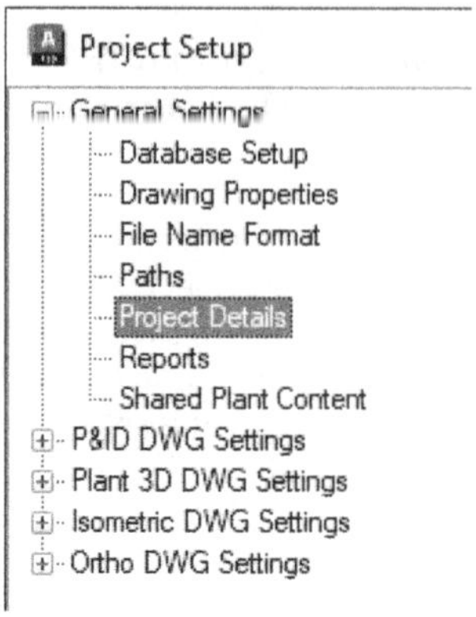

3. To change the template directory for user-defined reports:
   - In the General paths and file locations area, click Browse, located to the right of the User-defined reports directory field.
   - In the Select Reports Directory dialog box, navigate to and open the folder *C:\Plant Design 2024 Practice Files\Set Up and Structure Your Project\Company Templates\Reports* folder.
   - Click Open.
   - The path now displays the updated path.
4. In the Project Setup dialog box, in the General Settings, select Paths.
5. To change the drawing template to be used when creating a new P&ID drawing in this project:
   - In the Project Paths area, under P&ID, click Browse, located to the right of the Drawing template file (DWT) field.
   - In the Select Template File dialog box, navigate to and open the file *C:\Plant Design 2024 Practice Files\Set Up and Structure Your Project\CompanyTemplates\Drawings\ PID_CompanyD_common.dwt.*
   - Click Open.
6. To have the spec sheets referenced from a common location:
   - Under Specs, Symbols & Styles, to the right of the Spec sheets directory field, click Browse.
   - In the Select Spec Sheets Directory dialog box, navigate to and open the *C:\Plant Design 2024 Practice Files\Set Up and Structure Your Project\CompanyTemplates\Spec Sheets* folder.
   - Click Open.
7. To set the folder in which the equipment templates are located:
   - Under Plant 3D, to the right of the Equipment templates directory field, click Browse.
   - In the Select Equipment Templates Directory dialog box, navigate to and open the *C:\Plant Design 2024 Practice Files\Set Up and Structure Your Project\CompanyTemplates\Equipment* folder.
   - Click Open.
8. To set the drawing template file that should be used when creating a new 3D plant drawing in this project:
   - Under Plant 3D, to the right of the Drawing template file (DWT) field, click Browse.
   - In the Select Template File dialog box, navigate to and open the file *C:\Plant Design 2024 Practice Files\Set Up and Structure Your Project\CompanyTemplates\Drawings\Plant3D_Company_common.dwt.*
   - Click Open.

9. In the Project Setup dialog box, expand Isometric DWG Settings. Click Iso Style Setup.

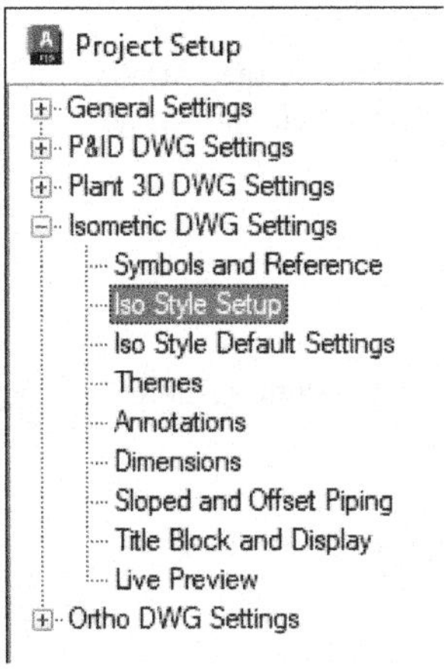

10. To configure the template directory for Final Iso type drawings, in the Iso Style list (at the top of the window), select Final_ANSI-B.

11. In the Project Setup dialog box, expand Ortho DWG Settings. Click Title Block and Display.

12. 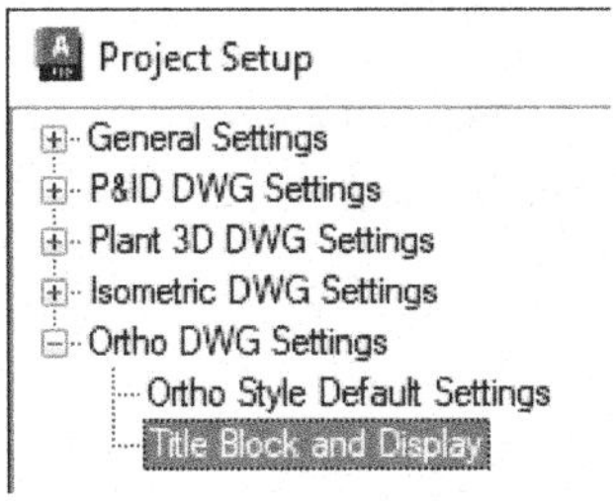

13. To set the file to be used for orthographic drawings:
    - To the right of the Ortho drawing template (DWT) field, click Browse.
    - In the Select Template File dialog box, navigate to and open the file *C:\Plant Design 2024 Practice Files\Set Up and Structure Your Project\CompanyTemplates\Drawings\Ortho_CompanyD_common.dwt*.
    - Click Open.

14. Click OK in the Project Setup dialog box. The paths and templates for this project are now configured.

Lesson Review Questions

1. There are several templates (DWT) that you can set up to be used in the AutoCAD Plant 3D software. Which of the following templates can be configured? (Select all that apply.)
   a. P&ID template
   b. Orthographic drawing template
   c. Isometric drawing template
   d. 3D piping template
2. Once you have created a project, how can you modify the settings that define where drawings and templates are stored?
   a. Windows Explorer
   b. Right-click on the project name in the Project Manager and click Properties.
   c. These can only be set up when creating a project.
   d. Changing these settings is not possible.
3. Is it possible to create a structure on your hard drive or network before you have created a project and then use that structure as the project's structure?
   a. No, you can only create a structure using the Project Manager.
   b. Yes, you can use the Project Manager after that to point to the already created structure.
   c. Yes, but it cannot be used to store drawing locations.
4. Can you use multiple templates for the same type of drawings in a project?
   a. Yes, the number of templates that you can use is unlimited.
   b. No, by default you can only use one type of template for each type of drawing.
   c. Yes, you can have multiple templates if you set them per subfolder in the Project Manager.
5. Can you set multiple locations in which drawings must be stored?
   a. Yes, the number of locations that you can use is unlimited. There are no restrictions.
   b. Yes, you can have multiple locations if you set them per subfolder in the Project Manager.
   c. No, by default you can only use one location for each type of drawing.

Lesson: Overview of Project Structure and Files

Overview

This lesson describes how AutoCAD Plant 3D projects are structured and where the project files can be found.

If you are responsible for setting up and administering a plant project, along with knowing how to create a new project, you need to understand what a project consists of and how it can be edited. This is especially important if you need to move a project to a different location.

Objectives

After completing this lesson, you will be able to:

- Describe the two types of data and files that are in a project.
- State where to configure the DWG creation directory.
- Manage the files and folders in a moved or copied project.
- Explain how Plant 3D and P&ID drawing data can be used in the standard AutoCAD software.

Prerequisites

Before taking this lesson, you should be able to:

- Create a new project and access the properties of the project.
- Set the default drawing templates for the project.
- Create and configure project folders.

About the Data and Files in a Project

The data and files that make up a design project can be grouped into one of two categories: either the data and files that support the project or those that contain the design and design information. Files that support the design include spec sheets, equipment templates, and configuration files, such as the *projSymbolStyle* drawing and the XML files. The files that contain the design and design information include the DWG drawings and the DCF and DCFX files.

Two different techniques for structuring the folders and files in a project are shown in the following illustration. The structure that is set up by default when a new project is created is shown on the left. A custom structure in which the drawing files and some common project files have been separated is shown on the right. The configuration of a project is flexible, enabling you to set up your projects the way that you need to.

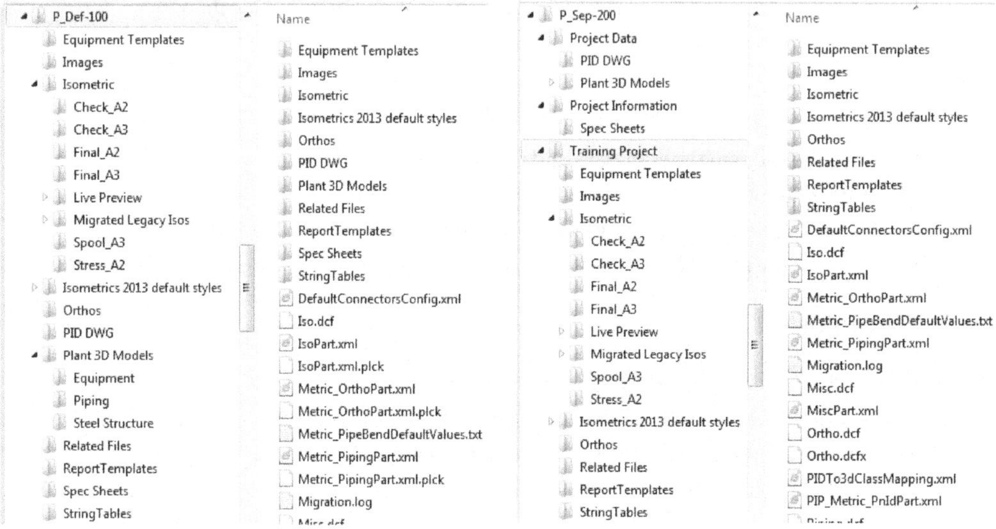

New Drawing Creation Locations

When a new project is created using the project creation wizard, the folders where the drawings are created are set based on what was set in the wizard. If you want to change the location where new drawings are created after a project has been created, you need to be able to edit the project properties to specify the required directory.

This type of edit is common when you want to change the location where drawing files are created and stored. Because in this scenario the project and folders would already exist, you would start making the change by moving the drawing folders and files to their new location. Then you would set the project settings so all new drawings are created in that location.

The creation of a new P&ID drawing is shown in the following illustration. The default location for the new drawing is based on the path defined in the project setup.

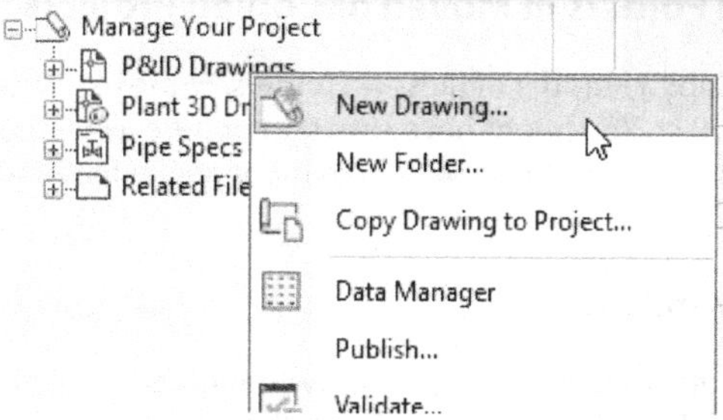

In the Project Setup dialog box, you can edit the paths that specify where all new P&ID, Plant 3D, Isometric, and Ortho drawings are created. In the Project Setup dialog box, in the General Settings, select Paths. You configure the path by selecting the Paths entry that corresponds to what you want to configure. After selecting Paths, you then enter or navigate to the folder of your choice, as shown in the following illustration. The paths for the Iso and Ortho drawings are located in the Iso Style Setup and Title Block and Display tree entries, respectively.

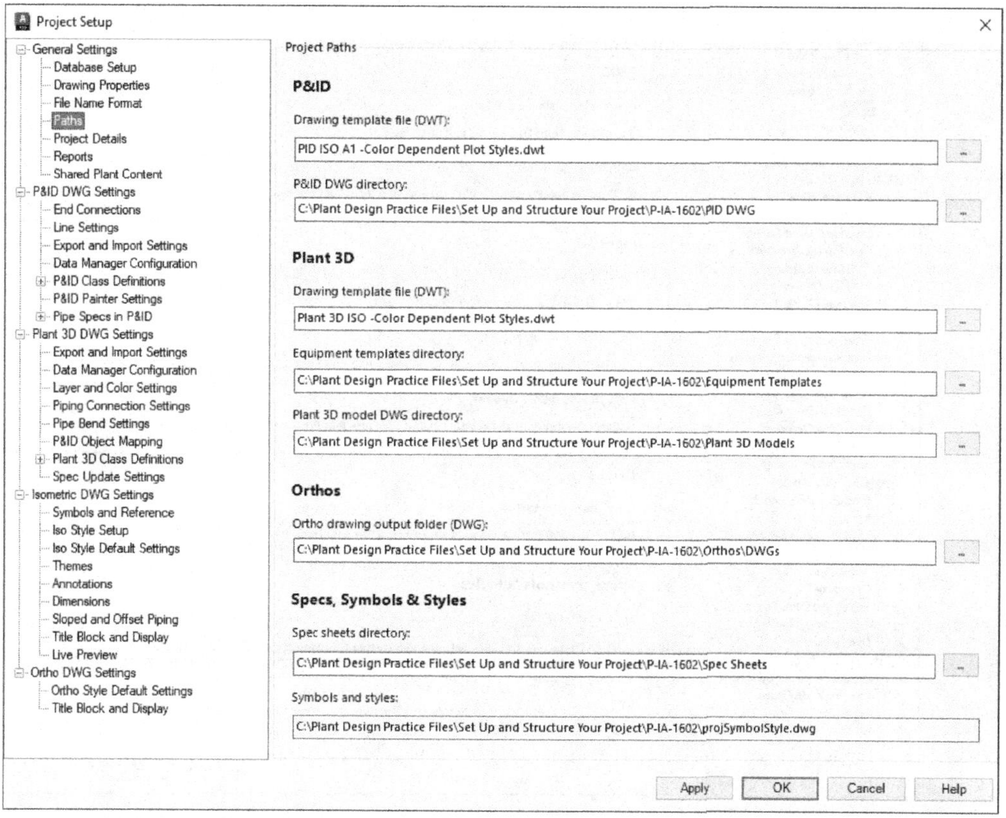

Changing the DWG creation directory for P&ID Drawings or Plant 3D Drawings in the Project Setup only affects the drawings and project folders that are created at that category's root level, going forward.

Managing Files and Folders in Moved or Copied Projects

Introduction to Managing Files and Folders in Moved or Copied Projects

As you are aware at this point, a project contains a number of files and folders. Some files support the project and others are the product of the project. You might have situations where a created project needs to be moved or copied. In those cases, you need to know how to manage the files and folders in the moved or copied projects.

Correcting Paths and Locating Drawings

When project files and folders are moved around after a project is initially configured, you might need to correct some paths and locate drawings. If the path is associated with the P&ID Drawings or Plant 3D Drawings directory, you make the path changes in the Project Setup.

The drawing areas of the project and their corresponding path configuration areas in the Project Setup dialog box are shown in the following illustration. If you move the PID DWG or Plant 3D Models folders to a location outside the project, you need to modify the directory paths so that they match their current location.

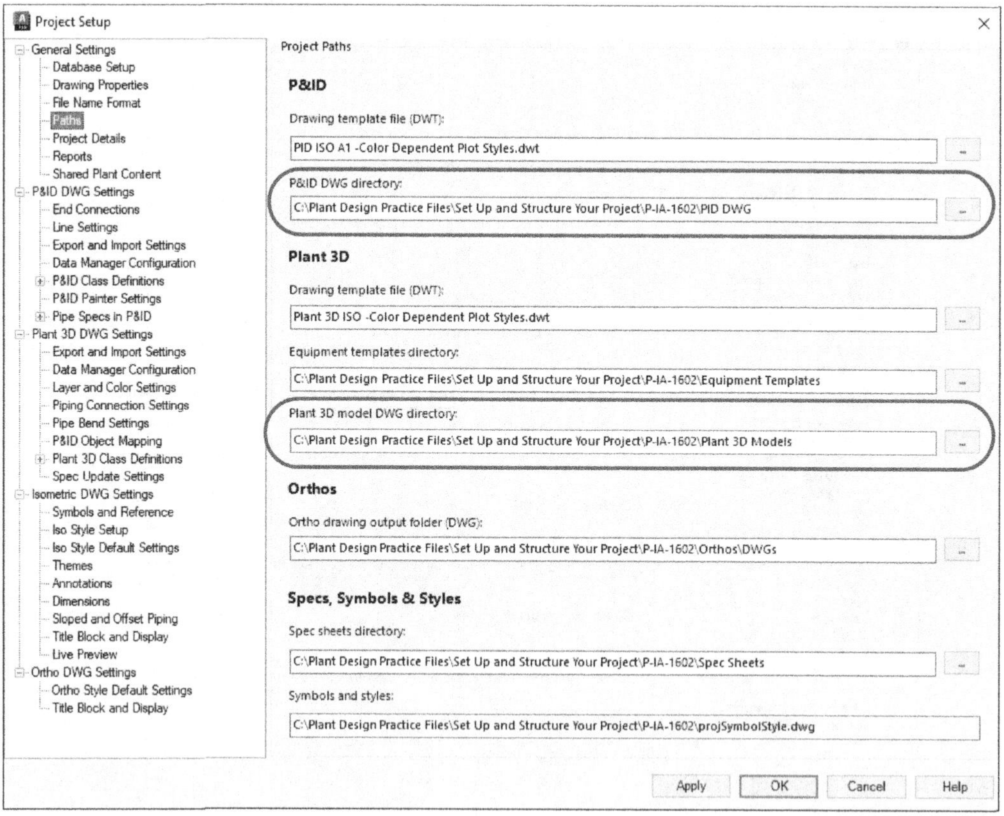

Backing Up a Project

Another method of copying a project is to create a project backup. Instead of manually copying a project folder or any external files and collecting any hosted databases, AutoCAD Plant 3D provides a backup command that duplicates a project setup, its drawings and databases and stores them inside a single folder for archiving or backup purposes.

The backup command can archive any type of project whether using SQLite databases, SQL Server database system, or Autodesk Vault or BIM 360 Team to host your project. Once run, the backup tool collects the project setup, drawings and databases together, converts the databases to SQLite and stores everything in a folder with the project name followed by a time and date stamp. This folder can then be easily moved or compressed without losing any data.

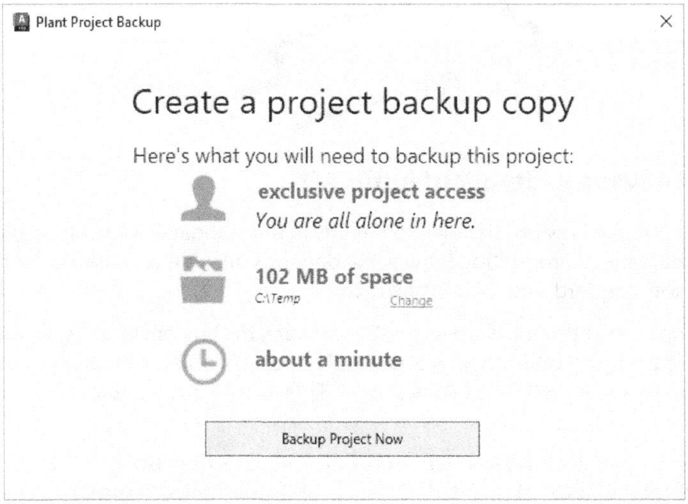

Process: Creating a Project Backup

1. Open the Project in AutoCAD Plant 3D and ensure that no other person has the project loaded.
2. Select **Create Project Backup** from the project node shortcut menu.
3. Set the location and create the project backup.

Working with Plant 3D and P&ID Drawings in AutoCAD

When you create a design in AutoCAD P&ID or Plant 3D, you often add objects that are unique to these applications. For some design projects, you might be required to supply a final drawing file that only contains native AutoCAD objects. Other individuals who just have the standard AutoCAD software might need to review your drawings. To supply a drawing with what they require, you need to know how Plant 3D and P&ID drawing data can be used in the standard AutoCAD software.

A P&ID and a Plant 3D design are shown in the following illustration. While it appears as though the pipelines consist of just lines or 3D cylinders, the objects in the drawings are actually custom objects with data and behavior that are focused on the needs of process piping. In P&ID, the pipeline lists as an SLINE object and the exchanger equipments lists as an ACCPASSET object. In Plant 3D, the pipeline lists as a PIPE object and the exchanger equipment lists as an EQUIPMENT object.

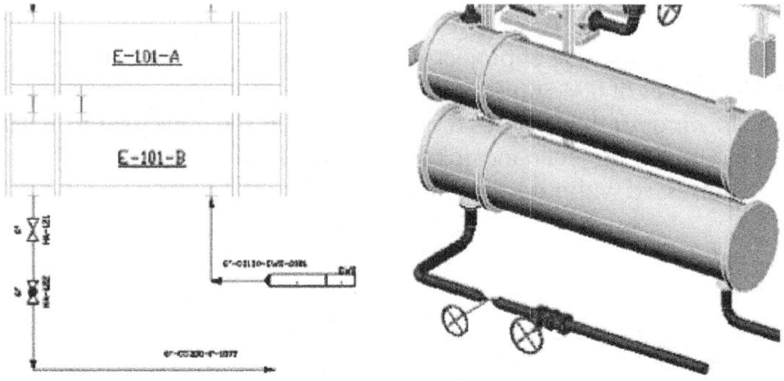

Directly Opening a Drawing in Standard AutoCAD

AutoCAD P&ID and Plant 3D drawings can be opened directly in the standard AutoCAD software. What is displayed and what object information is available depends on what was opened and the current configuration of the standard AutoCAD installation.

When a P&ID drawing is opened in the standard AutoCAD software, the custom objects display in the drawing if the option to show proxy graphics was enabled. The custom objects showing as proxy objects cannot be edited in the standard AutoCAD software. Their display just enables the drawing to be visually reviewed.

When a Plant 3D drawing is opened in the standard AutoCAD software, the display of the custom objects depends on whether the AutoCAD Plant 3D Object Enabler is installed. If the Object Enabler is not installed, then the custom objects display as proxy objects. If the Object Enabler is installed, then the AutoCAD software can display the geometry and its properties as if the objects were native. A major benefit of having the Object Enabler installed is that the properties of the objects can be reviewed in the Properties palette.

> You can download the AutoCAD Plant 3D 2024 Object Enabler from the *Plug-ins* tab of your Autodesk Account>Products and Services.

Exporting to Native AutoCAD Objects

When you need to supply a drawing file that contains only objects that are native to the standard AutoCAD software, you need to export the P&ID or Plant 3D drawing. When you do this, the custom objects become native objects like blocks, lines, circles, arcs, and text.

Process: Exporting to Native AutoCAD Objects

The following steps describe how to export a P&ID or Plant 3D drawing to a drawing that contains only objects that are native to the standard AutoCAD software.

1. Open the P&ID or Plant 3D drawing.
2. In the Project Manager, Project pane, right-click on the opened drawing to export. Click Export to AutoCAD.
3. Save the drawing file after specifying the location and a new filename.

Exercise: Manage Your Project

In this exercise, you conduct various project management tasks and create a backup for archiving purposes.

Drawings in a Default Project Structure

In this section of the exercise, you review the project settings and file structure in a default structured project. You then copy that project and see where this new project resolves the copied drawings.

1. Start the AutoCAD Plant 3D software, if not already open.
2. Open an existing project by doing the following:
   - In the Project Manager, Current Project list, click Open.
   - In the Open dialog box, navigate to the folder *C:\Plant Design 2024 Practice Files\Manage Your Project\P_Def-100.*
   - Select the file *Project.xml.*
   - Click Open.
3. In the Project Manager, in both P&ID Drawings and Plant 3D Drawings, review the linked drawings and their location using the Details panel in the Project Manager. All four linked files have been located and thus resolved. Note the prefix folder location for the files. The default path is *C:\Plant Design 2024 Practice Files\Manage Your Project\P_Def-100.*
4. Open the Project Setup dialog box for this project and review the P&ID DWG directory path:
   - In the Project Manager, right-click on the Project node and click Project Setup.
   - In the Project Setup dialog box, under General Settings, click Paths.
   - In the Project Paths area, under P&ID, review the path information in the P&ID DWG directory field.
   - Similarly, review the path information under Plant 3D, in the Plant 3D model DWG directory field
   - Click Cancel.
5. To close the active project:
   - In the Project Manager, right-click on the Project node.
   - Click Close Project.

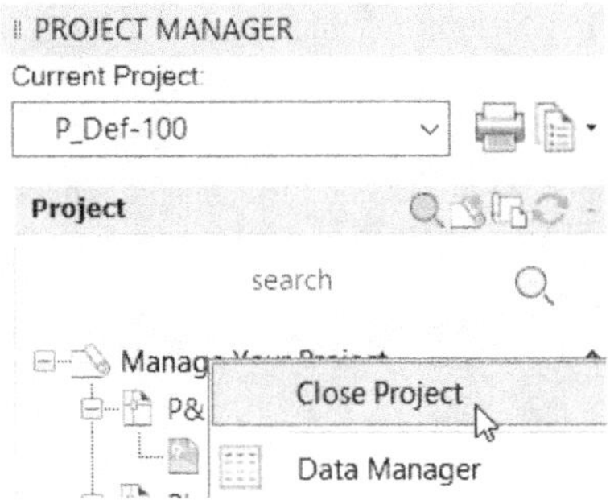

6. Review the folder and file structure for the project in Windows Explorer as follows:
   - Open Windows Explorer.
   - Navigate to and open the folder *P_Def-100* in *C:\Plant Design 2024 Practice Files\Manage Your Project.*
   - Select the folder PID DWG and expand the subfolders in Plant 3D Models to see the actual files and file storage location for the files listed in the project.

7. In Windows Explorer, copy and paste the folder P_Def-100 and its contents. Rename the copy as **P_Def-101**.

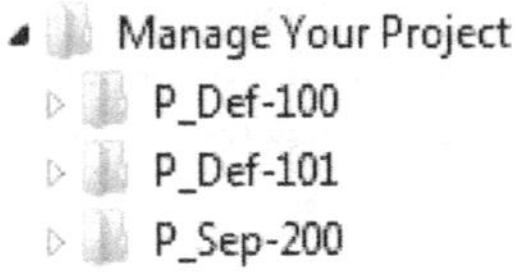

8. To set P_Def-101 as the current project:
   - In the software, in the Project Manager, Current Project list, click Open.
   - In the Open dialog box, navigate to the folder *C:\Plant Design 2024 Practice Files\Manage Your Project\P_Def-101*.
   - Select the file *Project.xml*.
   - Click Open.

9. In the Project Manager, review the linked drawings and their location. All four linked files have been located and thus resolved. Note the prefix folder location for the files. The drawings are now being resolved from the folder in the path of the *\P_Def-101* folder.

10. To open the Project Setup dialog box for this project and review the directory paths:
    - In the Project Manager, right-click on the Project node and click Project Setup.
    - In the Project Setup dialog box, under General Settings, click Paths.
    - In the Project Paths area, under P&ID, review the path information in the P&ID DWG directory field. Note that the path in the project setting automatically updated to the subfolder that is in the path of the active project.
    - Similarly, review the path information under Plant 3D, in the Plant 3D model DWG directory field. The project setting automatically updates to the subfolder that is in the path of the active project.
    - Click Cancel.

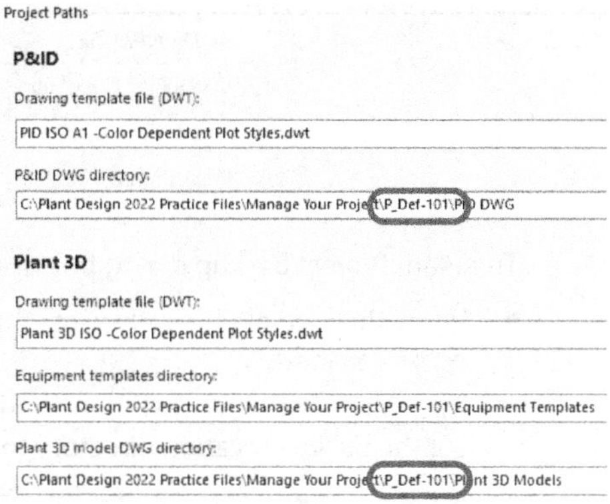

Back Up Your Project

In this section of the exercise, you use the Backup tool to create an archived copy of the project.

1. In AutoCAD Plant 3D, open and activate the project P_Def-100.

2. In the Project Manager, right-click on the project node and select Create Project Backup.

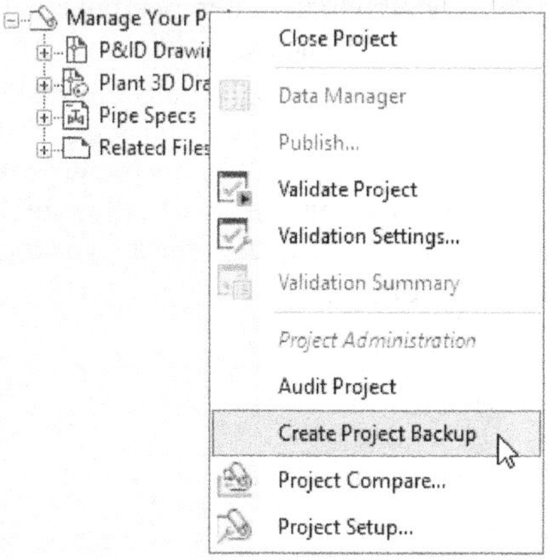

3. The Plant Project Backup dialog box displays.
   - Verify that you are the only user with the project loaded.
   - Click on Change link next to the path and set the backup location directory to *C:\Plant Design 2024 Practice Files\Manage Your Project*. Click OK.
   - The Plant Project Backup dialog box also displays the final size of the backup and how long the backup might take.

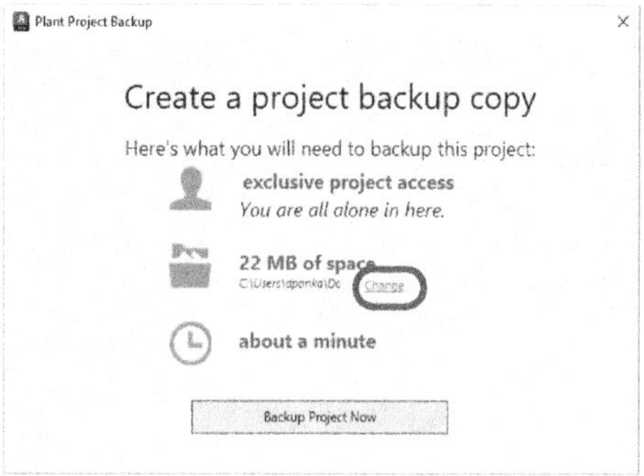

4. Click Backup Project Now to perform the backup.

5. Once the dialog box indicates that the backup is complete, click Open backup folder... You can also open the folder through the Windows Explorer directly if the window closes.

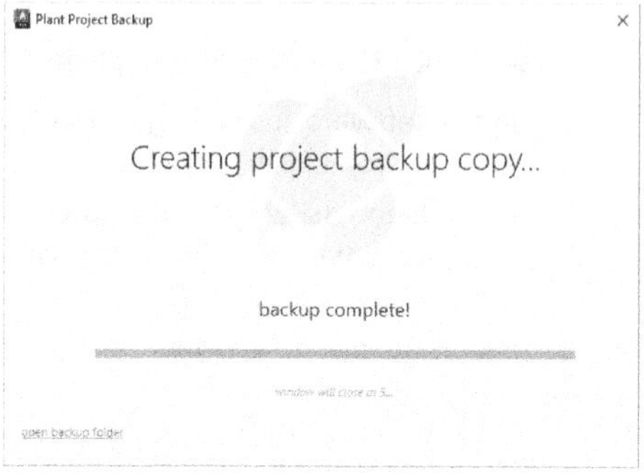

6. You should see a project folder with a time and date stamp that can be archived.

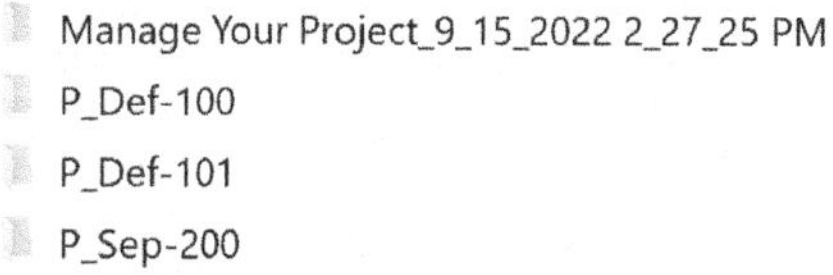

P&ID and Plant 3D Drawings in Standard AutoCAD

In this section of the exercise, you learn how P&ID and Plant 3D drawings can be used or converted for use in the standard AutoCAD software.

1. In the Project Manager, verify that P_Def-100 is the current project.

2. To export PID001 as a standard AutoCAD drawing file:
   - Open *PID001.dwg*.
   - In the Project Manager, right-click on PID001. Click Export to AutoCAD.
   - Save the file in the PID DWG folder with the name **PID001-ACAD.dwg**.

3. Close *PID001.dwg*.

4. Follow the same process to export the Piping drawing as a standard AutoCAD drawing file. Save the file in the *Plant 3D Models\Piping* folder with the name **Piping-ACAD.dwg**. Close *Piping.dwg*. In the Windows Explorer, verify the newly created drawings.

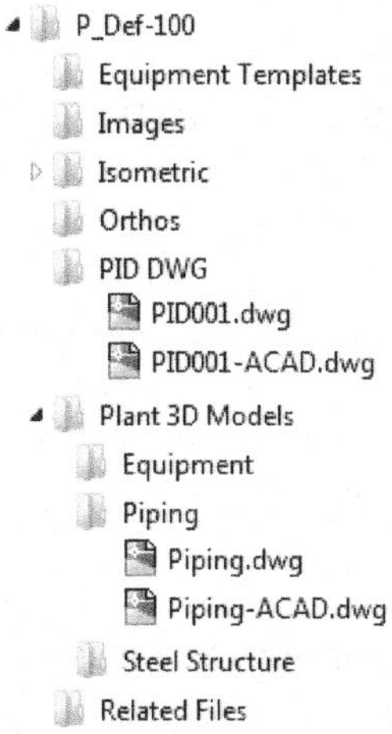

5. Close the active project.

6. Start the AutoCAD software.

7. Open *PID001.dwg* from the *Manage Your Project\P_Def-100\PID DWG* folder. If the Proxy Information dialog box opens, you do not have the Plant 3D Object Enabler installed or configured to work with your AutoCAD installation. Select Show proxy graphics and click OK.

8. List the properties of one of the pipelines. Note that it is ACAD_PROXY_ENTITY. These objects cannot be edited in the AutoCAD software.

9. Open *PID001-ACAD.dwg*.

10. List the properties of one of the pipelines. Note that it is a standard AutoCAD entity (line).

11. Open *Piping.dwg*.
    - If the Proxy Information dialog box opens, select Show proxy graphics and click OK.

12. To review the properties of a pipeline:
    - Select a pipeline.
    - Right-click in an open area. Click Properties.
    - On the Properties palette, review the type of object and the Plant 3D properties that are included. The objects and properties displayed are dependent on whether the Object Enabler is installed.

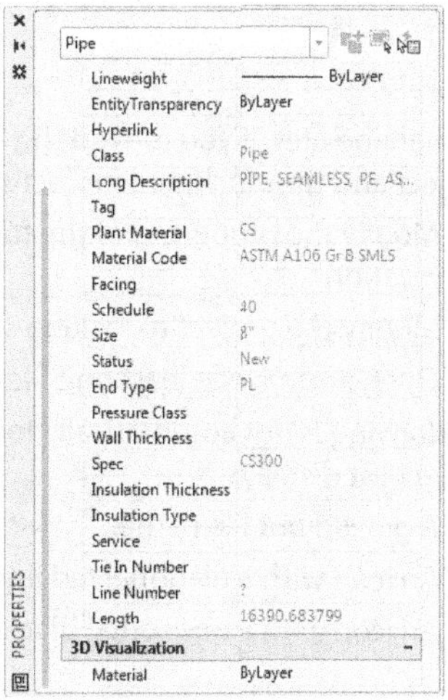

With the Object Enabler Installed

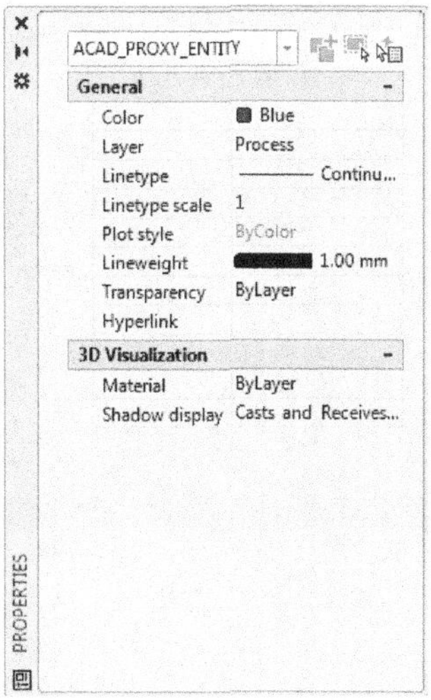

Without the Object Enabler Installed

13. Close all files and exit the AutoCAD software.

Lesson Review Questions

1. Is it possible to have the drawing in a different location than the project file?
   a. Yes
   b. No
   c. Only if you use a Document Control System
2. To specify the path for new drawings that are being created in the top-level P&ID Drawing node you must modify the properties for that folder.
   a. True
   b. False
3. To manage files, if you moved the PID DWG or Plant 3D Models folders to a location outside the project and they included project subfolder, you need to...
   a. Modify the properties of the folders in the project to point to the drive folders at their new location.
   b. Modify the project to include subfolders.
   c. Open and save at least one file in each subfolder.
4. If a drawing is not automatically located, the drawing icon that displays for that drawing in the Project list displays:
   a. A grayed out file name.
   b. An icon with a diagonal red line through the icon.
   c. An icon with a horizontal black line through the icon.

Lesson: Setting Up Larger Projects

Overview

This lesson describes how to set up a project that is going to be used by multiple users and contains a large numbers of objects and drawings. After completing this lesson, you can set up and maintain a project that can be used for larger projects with multiple users.

Large or complex plant designs are rarely completed by a single person. Therefore, when you set up a project, you need to know how to set it up so that multiple users can simultaneously work on the same project. You should also know what you can do to help ensure consistency and adherence to company standards regardless of who creates the drawing.

Objectives

After completing this lesson, you will be able to:

- State the guidelines for setting up a project for multiple user access.
- Configure the project so it uses a custom file naming format for new drawings.
- Lock the project settings by setting the projSymbolStyle.dwg file for the project to read-only.
- Set the external reference options so that someone else can edit a referenced drawing.

Setting Up a Project for Multiple User Access

When you set up a project for use by multiple people, you need to create the project in a location that all of the users can access.

Follow these guidelines when setting up a project that is going to be accessed by multiple users.

- Create a new project that is located at a shared network location.
- Configure the project so it uses shared files that are common between projects.
- If a file naming scheme is required for the drawing files in the project, configure the file naming format in the project.
- Lock the project properties so they cannot be inadvertently modified by someone.
- Have each project team member open the *Project.xml*.
- Ensure that everyone working on the project has their AutoCAD external reference demand loading setting set to Enable with Copy.

As a variation in the setup of the project, when the project is worked on by multiple users you can set the project up to use SQL Server instead of the default SQLite.

There are different techniques that can be used to access shared network files and folders. To ensure that every person utilizing the same project file can access the network location configured in the project, you need to keep the following things in mind:

- If the path uses mapped drive letters, you need to ensure that every user has that same drive letter and path to that location.
- Instead of using mapped network drives, use the UNC path instead.
- To make the paths a little more dynamic, edit the XML files to ensure that the relative path information is valid.

The pipe design projects are created and saved on a shared network, as shown in the following illustration. In this situation, if everyone has a K-drive mapped to the EngDesigns share on CRWARE-IA10, then the paths in the project can use the *K:* drive letter in the paths. If the mapped drive varies between computers, then the paths should use *\\CRWARE-IA10\EngDrive* in place of *K:*.

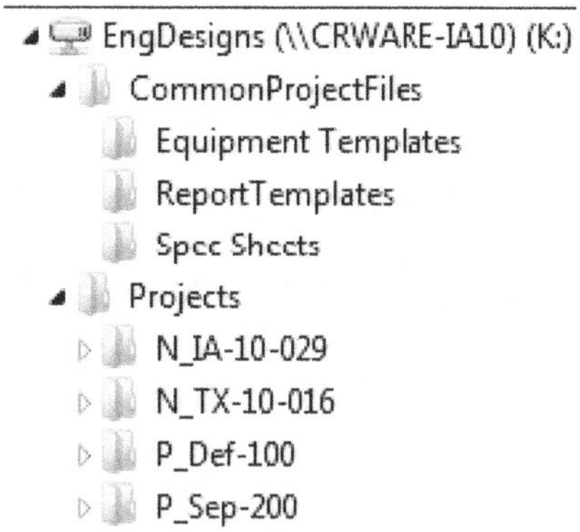

Configuring the File Name Format

Many companies have a standardized format for naming their drawing files. This format is often a set schema consisting of specific field length and use of defined nomenclature. If your company has a defined format for drawing filenames, then you should configure the project so it uses a custom file naming format for all new drawings.

The New DWG dialog box is shown in its default format on the top of the following illustration and in a custom format on the bottom. The custom format uses a combination of list fields and text fields to guide the creation of the drawing name. The resulting filename is shown in the File Name field. If you need to enter a filename that does not follow the custom filename format, selecting the Override check box enables you to enter any valid filename.

Default format

Custom format

Process: Configuring the File Name Format

You configure the filename format as part of the project setup. You start the process of configuring the filename format by opening the Project Setup dialog box. With File Name Format selected under General Settings, you can click to add fields to the filename or modify any fields already added, as shown in the following illustration. When you are defining a field, you enter the name of the field, its data type, whether there is a limit to the number of characters in the field, and whether a delimiter should be added at the end of the field.

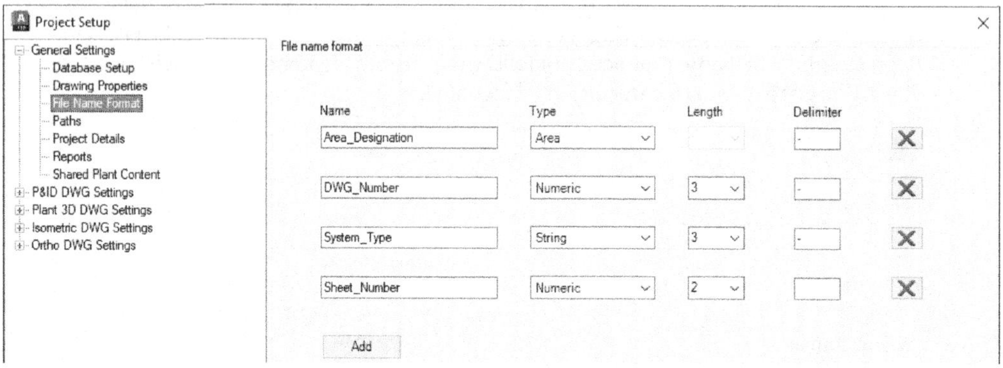

The types of data can be string, numeric, or custom property. If you want to use a custom property in the filename format, you should create that custom property before adding the custom File name field.

Locking the Project Properties

Having multiple people able to work on the same project is good practice. However, having multiple people able to modify the settings for a project is not. After you have configured the project and you are ready to roll it out to all the designers tasked to work on the project, you need to lock the project settings. You do this to ensure someone does not inadvertently change a setting that is going to have a negative impact on the project.

You lock the properties of a project by setting the *projSymbolStyle.dwg* file for the project to read-only. When that file is set to read-only, the option to access the project properties is not available. The *projSymbolStyle.dwg* file is in the same folder as the *project.xml* file and you set the drawing file to read-only in the operation system.

The Read-Only attribute is selected in the projSymbolStyle.dwg Properties dialog box, as shown in the following illustration. This dialog box was opened by right-clicking on the drawing file in Windows Explorer and then clicking Properties.

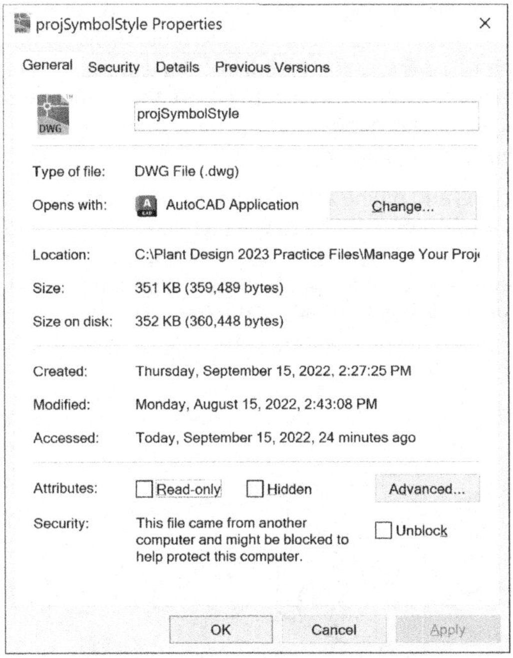

The Project Setup option, accessed when the file is not locked and when it is locked, is shown in the following illustration. When the file is set to read-only, the Project Setup option is grayed out and is not available, as shown on the right.

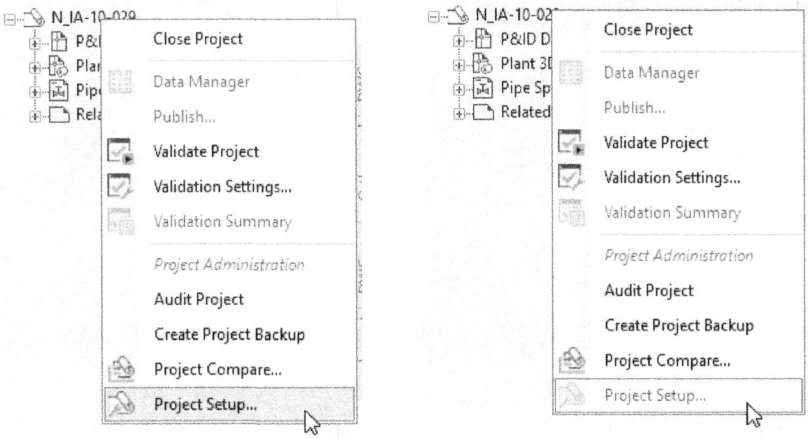

Xref Demand Load

You use external references to separate the design geometry so multiple people can work on the same overall design at the same time. While everyone is working on the overall design, only one person is actively editing any one drawing. Therefore by separating the design into multiple files, multiple people can work on the same project. Different aspects of the design from an external file are viewed in another drawing by referencing the data from that external file. To ensure that someone else has the ability to edit a drawing currently being externally referenced, you need to ensure that the demand loading setting for external references is set correctly.

The drawing for the equipment, steel structure, and piping are all separate files, as shown in the following illustration. To correctly position the equipment, the steel structure was externally referenced into the equipment drawing. To create the piping design, the equipment and steel structure drawing files were externally referenced into the piping drawing. With the external references set to demand load, three different people could work on this overall design all at the same time. One person could be editing the equipment drawing, another updating the steel structure, and a third completing the piping drawing.

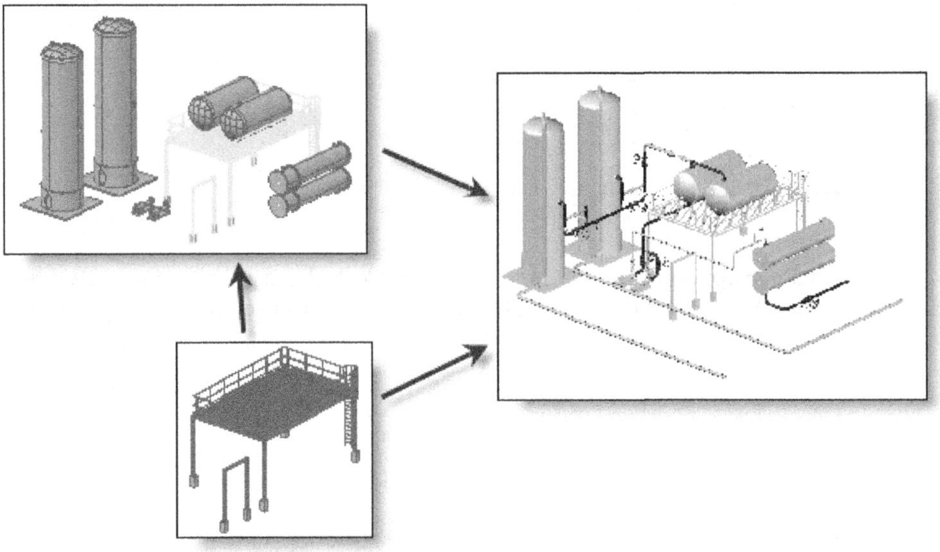

XLOADCTL System Variable

The XLOADCTL system variable toggles Xref demand-loading on and off. The variable also determines whether the Xref or a copy of the Xref is opened.

If you or someone on your network attempts to open a file that is currently referenced by an open drawing, depending on the setting of the XLOADCTL system variable, you might be given read-only access to the drawing.

The XLOADCTL system variable has the following settings:

- **XLOADCTL = 0 -** Demand-loading is toggled off and the entire drawing is loaded.
- **XLOADCTL = 1 -** Demand-loading is toggled on and reference drawings are kept open and locked.
- **Note:** The software can display a read-only message if the referenced drawing is opened by you or someone on your network and the host drawing is currently open.
- **XLOADCTL = 2 -** Demand-loading is on and copies of referenced drawings are opened and locked. The original reference drawing is not locked. This is the default setting of the XLOADCTL variable.

> You can also change the XLOADCTL settings on the Open and Save tab of the Options dialog box, in the External References (Xrefs) area. The three options listed for the Demand Load Xrefs option specify the XLOADCTL setting as follows:
>
> - Disabled = 0
> - Enabled = 1
> - Enabled with Copy = 2

Exercise: Optimizing a Project for Multiple Users

In this exercise, you create and set up a new project that can be used by multiple users.

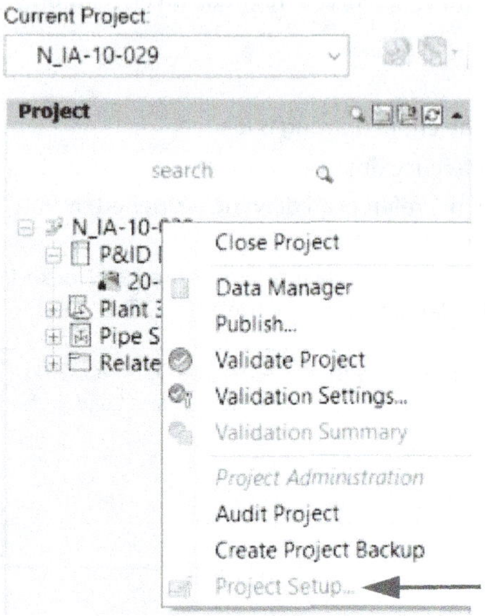

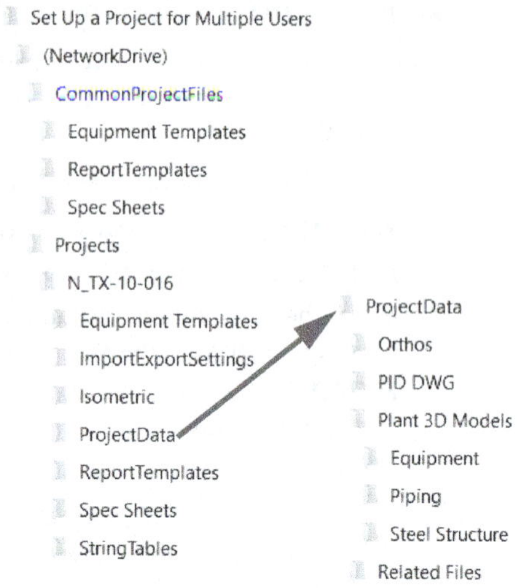

Create a New Multi-User Project

In this section of the exercise, you create a new project that can be used by multiple users. You modify the paths for the project to use files that are common to multiple projects.

1. In Windows Explorer, review the folder and files structure set up in the *C:\Plant Design 2024 Practice Files\Set Up a Project for Multiple Users* folder.

   Note: Because the network configuration and user rights vary between training site and work site, this exercise simulates the use of a network drive. The structure in the (Network Drive) folder is an implementation where multiple users are accessing the project. The project information common to multiple projects is separate and resides in the *CommonProjectFiles* folder. The individual projects are created and stored under the *Projects* folder.

2. Start Plant 3D software, if not already running.

3. To begin to create a new project configured to be used by multiple users and accessible from a network drive, in the Project Manager, Current Project list, click New Project.

4. In the Project Setup Wizard, Page 1:
   - In the Enter a name for this project field, enter **N_IA-10-029**.
   - In the Enter an optional description field, enter **Project for multiple user access**.
   - In Specify the directory where program-generated files are stored, browse to *C:\Plant Design 2024 Practice Files\Set Up a Project for Multiple Users\(Network Drive)\Projects* folder.
   - Click Open.
   - Click Next in Project Setup Wizard.

5. On Page 2 of the wizard:
   - Select Imperial, if required.
   - Click Next.

6. On Page 3 of the wizard:
   - In the Specify the directory where P&ID drawings are stored field, enter **Project Data** before the PID DWG folder as shown in the following illustration.
   - Click Next.

7. On Page 4 of the wizard:
   - In the directory paths for the Plant 3D model DWG file and Orthographic output directory, enter **Project Data** before the folders Plant 3D Models and Orthos respectively, as shown in the following illustration.
   - For the Spec sheets directory, browse to and select the folder *C:\Plant Design 2024 Practice Files\Set Up a Project for Multiple Users\(Network Drive)\ CommonProjectFiles\Spec Sheets*.
   - Click Open.
   - Click Next.

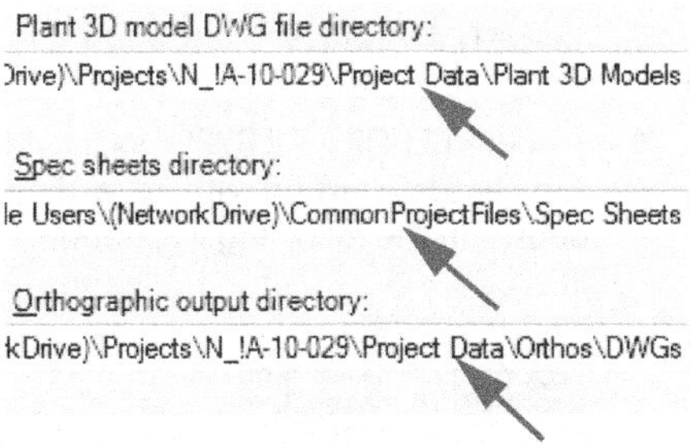

8. On Page 5 of the wizard, verify Single User-SQLite local database is selected. Click Next.

9. On Page 6 of the wizard:
   - Click the Edit additional project settings after creating project check box.
   - Click Finish.

10. In the Project Setup dialog box, to set the directory paths for user-defined reports and related files, do the following:
    - Under General Settings, click Project Details. Under General Paths and file locations area, for User-defined reports directory, browse to and select the folder *C:\Plant Design 2024 Practice Files\Set Up a Project for Multiple Users\(Network Drive)\ CommonProjectFiles\ReportTemplates* as shown in the following illustration.
    - For the Related files directory, browse to the *C:\Plant Design 2024 Practice Files\Set Up a Project for Multiple Users\ (NetworkDrive)\ Projects\N_IA-10-029\ Project Data* folder. In this new project, create a new folder titled **Related Files**.
    - Select and open that new folder. The new paths are shown in the following illustration.
    - Click Apply.

11. Set the directory path for the Plant 3D equipment templates. Do the following:
    - In the Project Setup dialog box, in General Settings, click Paths.
    - Under Plant 3D, for the Equipment templates directory, browse to and select the folder *C:\Plant Design 2024 Practice Files\Set Up a Project for Multiple Users\(NetworkDrive)\ CommonProjectFiles\Equipment Templates.*
    - Click Open.

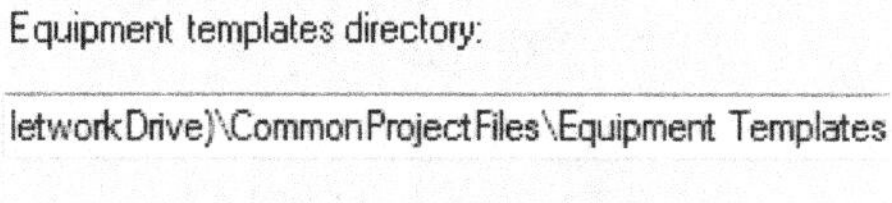

12. In the Project Setup dialog box, click OK.

13. Close the project.

14. In Windows Explorer, review the folder and files structure set up for the newly created project. Note that the folders Equipment Templates, Related Files, and ReportTemplates are listed in two different locations. The folders in the main project folder identified with the arrows were automatically created by the wizard. The second set of folders are what the project is now configured to use.

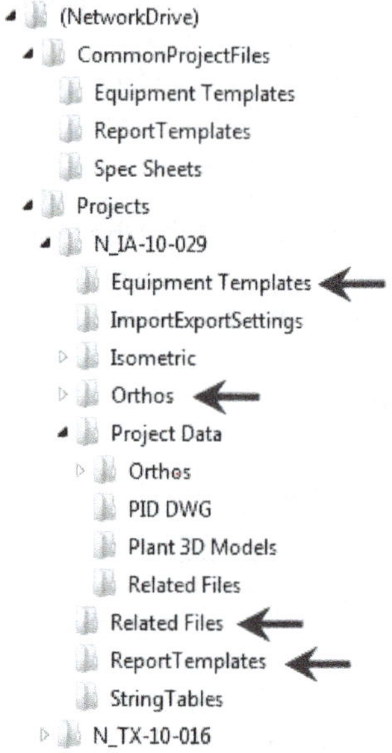

15. Delete the four previously identified folders (Equipment Templates, Orthos, Related Files, and ReportTemplates in N_IA-10-029 folder). The project folder structure now displays as shown in the following illustration.

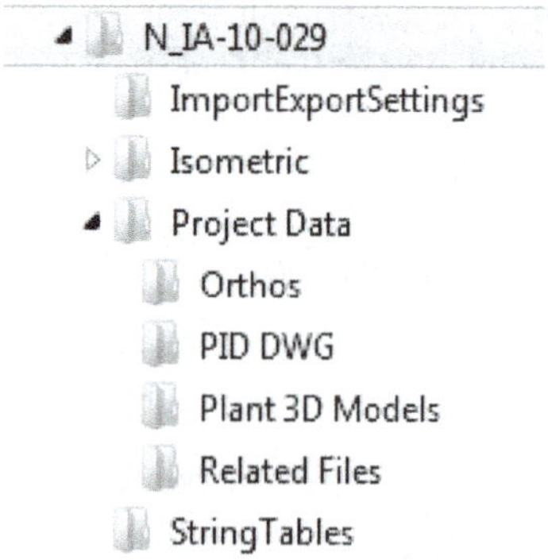

16. To begin to update the relative directory for report queries:

- In the N_IA-10-029 folder, open *PipingPart.xml*. (Open with Notepad).
- Under <PROJECTDIRECTORIES>, locate the entry ReportQueriesDirectory as shown in the following illustration.

17. Follow that line of text until you get to the text starting with relativeDirectoryName=". Change the text "ReportTemplates" to **"..\..\CommonProjectFiles\ReportTemplates"** by adding **..\..\CommonProjectFiles** in the beginning of the text.

18. Save and close the file.

19. To begin to update the relative paths for individual report query files:

- In the N_IA-10-029 folder, open *PnIdPart.xml*. (Open with Notepad).
- Under <REPORTQUERYFILES>, locate the nine entries starting with ReportFile as shown in the following illustration.

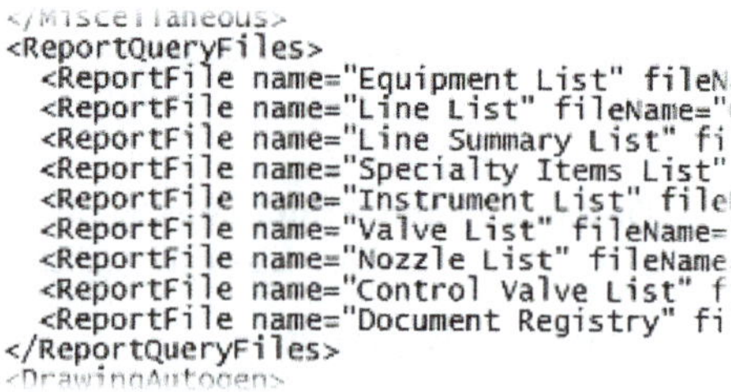

20. Follow each line of text until you get to the text starting with relativeFileName=". Change the beginning of each of the nine relative filename paths to **"..\..\CommonProject Files\ReportTemplates\"**.

    For example, the text for the "Valve List" entry becomes **relativeFileName= "..\..\Common ProjectFiles\ReportTemplates\ ValveList.xml"**.

    Tip: To quickly change all nine entries, copy and paste the text ..\..*CommonProjectFiles* before Report Templates.

21. After changing the relativeFileName paths for the nine report files, save and close the file.

22. Switch to Plant 3D software.

23. In Plant 3D software, open the project N_IA-10-029.

24. In the Project list, right-click on N_IA-10-029. Click Project Setup.

25. In the Project Setup dialog box, under General Settings, click Reports. The list of nine defined reports displays under Project reports as shown in the following illustration. If you get an error message, then either all of the stated changes were not made or a mistake was made in one or more of the relative paths. You might have to open the XML file and correct the file.

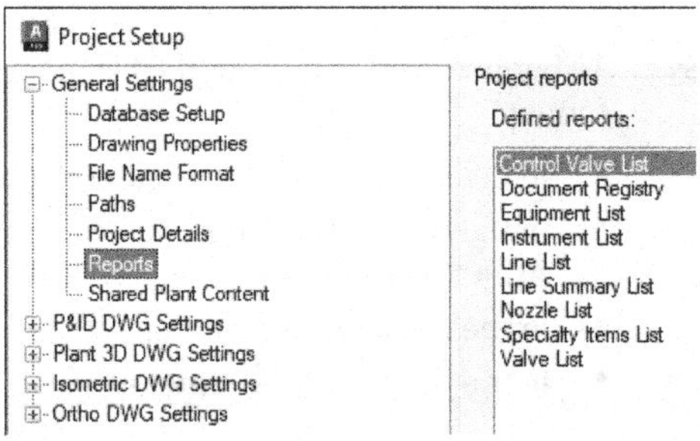

Configure the Filename Format

In this section of the exercise, you configure a required filename format that users will use when creating new drawings.

1. In the Project Setup dialog box, expand P&ID DWG Settings and P&ID Class Definitions. Select Engineering Items.

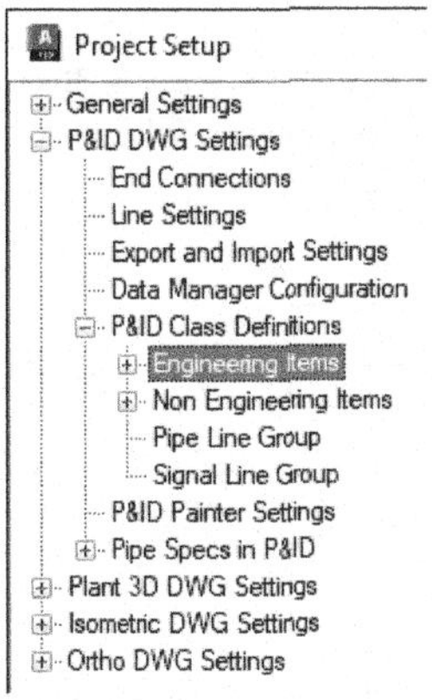

2. To begin to add a new property for use in the filename, in the Properties area, click Add.

3. In the Add Property dialog box:
   - In the Property name field, enter **Area_Designation**.
   - In the Choose a type area, click Selection List.
   - Click OK.

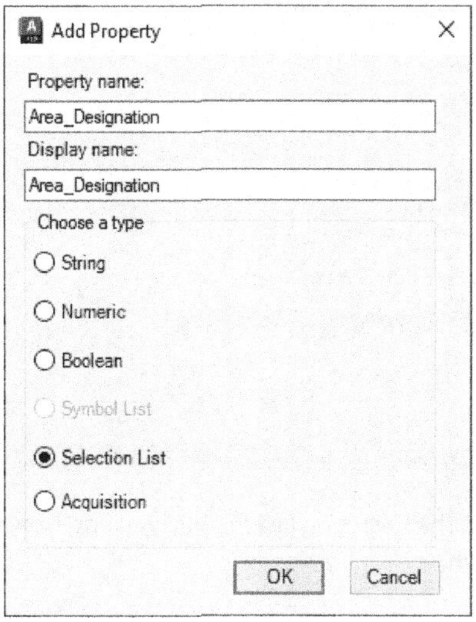

4. In the Selection List Property dialog box:
   - Click Add List.
   - In the Add Selection List dialog box, enter **Area**.
   - Click OK. The new Area name is displayed in the list as shown in the following illustration.

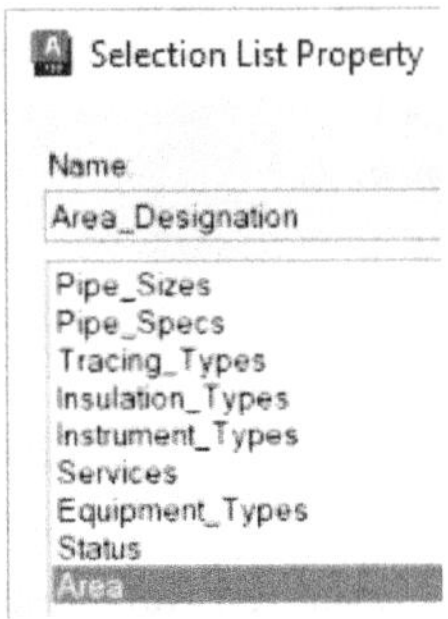

5. To add values for the Area selection list:
   - Verify that Area is selected, click Add Row.
   - In the Add Row dialog box, Value field, enter **10**.
   - Click OK.
   - Add rows until you have the values 10 through 90 added as shown in the following illustration.

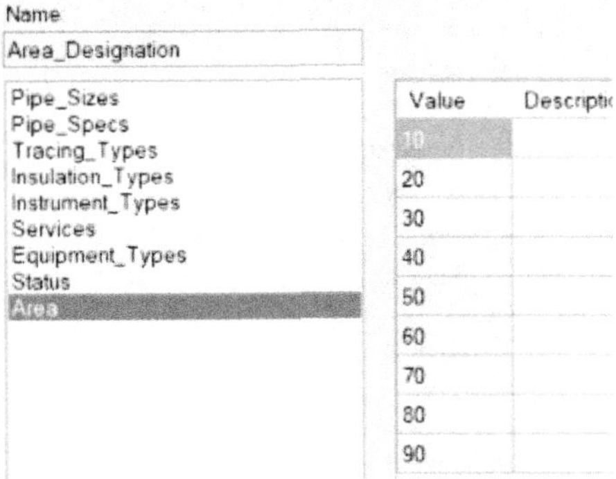

6. In the Selection List Property dialog box, click OK.

7. To set the default list value for this new list, in the Default Value column, for the Area_Designation row, select the top empty row in the list of values as shown in the following illustration.

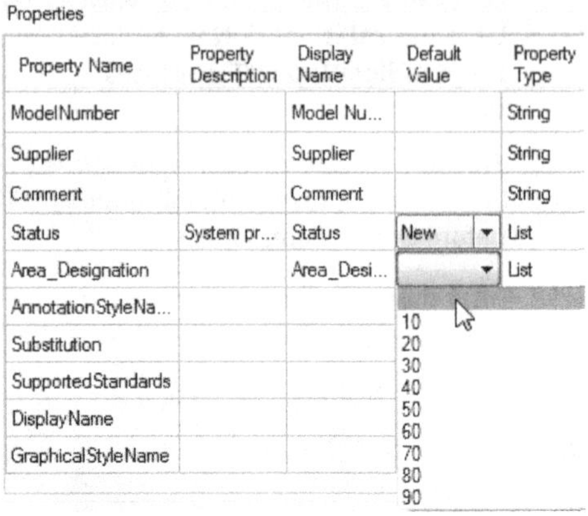

8. Under General Settings, in the tree list, select File Name Format.

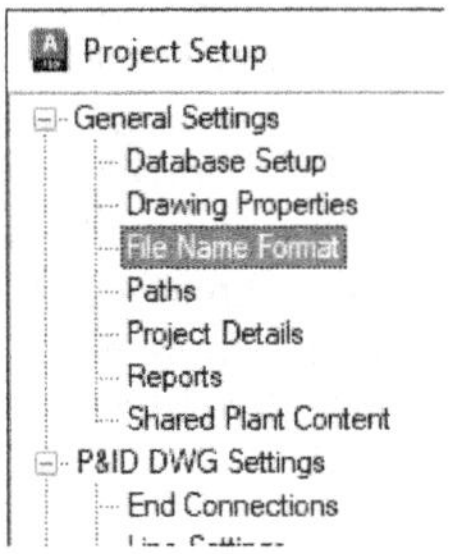

9. To begin to add a value for the filename format:
   - In the File name format area, click Add.
   - In the Name field, enter **Area_Designation**.
   - In the Type list, select Area.
   - In the Delimiter field, enter -.

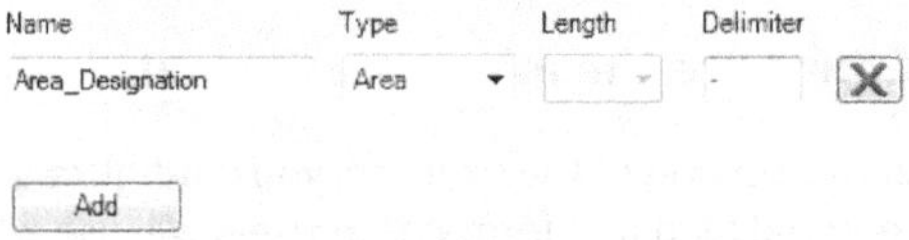

10. Add a second tag to the filename. Do the following:

- Click Add.
- In the Name field, enter **DWG_Number**.
- In the Type list, select Numeric.
- In the Length list, select 3.
- In the Delimiter field, enter -.

11. Add a third tag to the filename. Do the following:

- Click Add.
- In the Name field, enter **System_Type**.
- In the Type list, select String.
- In the Length list, select 3.
- In the Delimiter field, enter -.

12. Add the fourth and last tag to the filename. Do the following:

- Click Add.
- In the Name field, enter **Sheet_Number**.
- In the Type list, select Numeric.
- In the Length list, select 2.

13. With the filename format now displaying as shown, click OK.

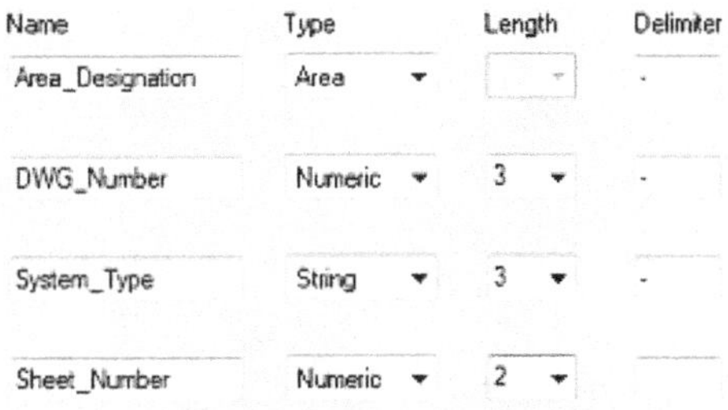

14. To begin to test the file naming configuration, right-click on P&ID Drawings. Click New Drawing.

15. In the New DWG dialog box:

- For Area_Designation, select 20.
- For DWG_Number, first attempt to enter **1010**. Note you are limited to three characters. Enter **001**.
- For System_Type, enter **Oil**.
- For Sheet_Number, enter **01**.
- Review the File name field for the name of the drawing that will be created.

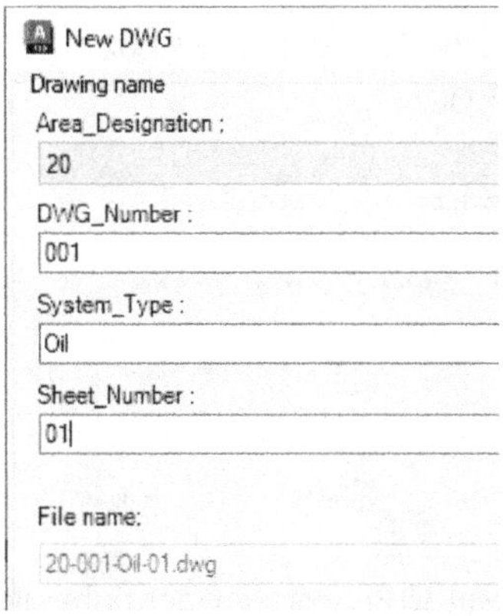

16. In the New DWG dialog box, click OK. The new drawing is added to the project as shown in the following illustration.

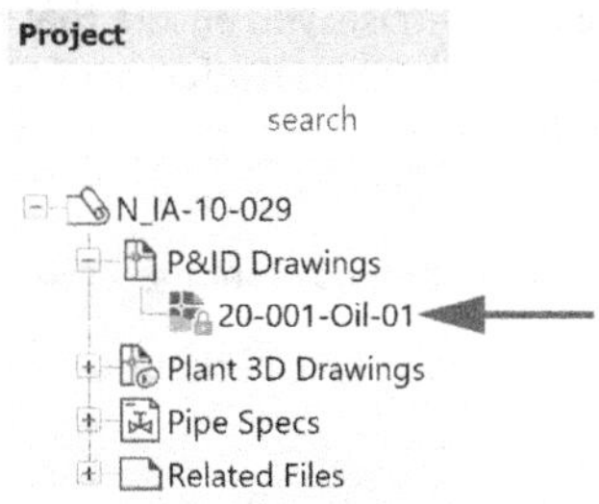

Lock Project Properties

In this section of the exercise, you lock the properties for a project so others cannot easily go in and modify the settings.

1. In Windows Explorer, N_IA-10-029 folder, right-click on *projSymbolStyle.dwg*. Click Properties.
2. In the Properties dialog box, on the General tab:
   - Click the Read-only check box.
   - Click OK.

3. In the Plant 3D Project Manager, right-click on N_IA-10-029. Note that the Project Setup option is now unavailable.

Set External References Demand Load

In this section of the exercise, you ensure that the demand load setting for external references is set correctly to enable multiple users to work with the drawings

1. Click Application menu>Options.
2. In the Options dialog box, click the Open and Save tab.
3. In the External References (Xrefs) area, Demand load Xrefs list, ensure the option Enabled with copy is selected.

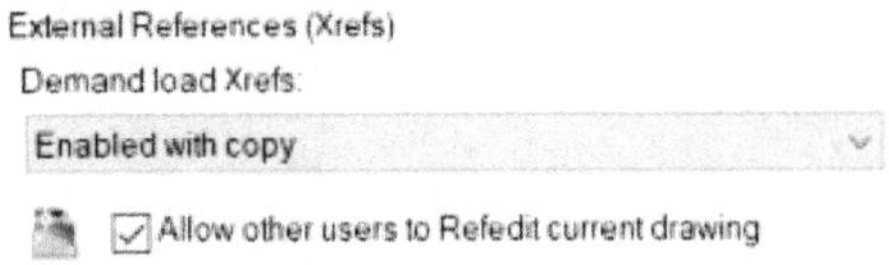

4. In the Options dialog box, click OK.
5. Save and close all drawings.

Lesson Review Questions

1. External Reference functionality can be used to work with multiple users on a project so that various drawings can be open at one time by multiple users.
   a. True
   b. False
2. Which of the following fields can be used to customize the default naming scheme for a drawing? (Select all that apply.)
   a. Name
   b. Length
   c. Type
   d. Properties
3. When working in a network environment, all users must have access to the same networked driver letter (e.g., F) to be able to access a common project.
   a. True
   b. False
4. How do you keep users from being able to modify the settings for a project?
   a. In the Project Setup dialog box, select the Password Protect option and enter a password.
   b. In the operating system, set the *projSymbolStyle.dwg* file for the project to read-only.
   c. In the operating system, set the *project.xml* file for the project to read-only.
   d. In the Project Manager, right-click on the project name. In the shortcut menu, click Lock Project Settings.
5. For a project that is set up to be accessed by multiple users, each project team member opens the same *project.xml* file from the project's shared network location.
   a. True
   b. False

Lesson: Defining New Objects and Properties

Overview

This lesson describes how to set up the tagging scheme in combination with the Acquire functionality and how symbols are defined and what settings are required before placing them. After this lesson you can create P&ID Symbols, define new properties, define various tags, and ensure that the symbols perform as correct P&ID symbols.

Objectives

After completing this lesson, you will be able to:

- Create a custom symbol and assign properties.
- Create a selection list for properties.
- Create a tag format for a class.
- Create a custom annotation style that displays specified properties.

Creating Symbols and Setting Color and Layer

When creating a custom symbol, you can apply specific settings to automate the insertion of the symbol in your design. After creating the geometry for the symbol, you enter the Project Setup dialog box, and click P&ID Class Definitions and locate the class that best fits the new symbol. If required, you can create a new class.

As the symbol is added to the class, the Symbol Setting dialog box opens. This dialog box is divided into three sections. In the first section, Symbol Properties, you name the symbol and select the block to be used. When you select the block, regardless of the drawing where it resides, it is copied into the *projSymbolStyle.dwg* drawing.

In the General Style Properties section, you can set properties, such as Layer, Color, Linetype, and Lineweight. The Other Properties section can vary slightly depending on the type of symbol being created. You use this section to set the behavior upon insertion. You set standard AutoCAD functions, such as Scale, Mirror and Rotate here, as well as symbol-specific behavior, such as Tagging, Join Type, Nozzles, and Nozzle style.

The Symbol Settings dialog box is shown in the following illustration.

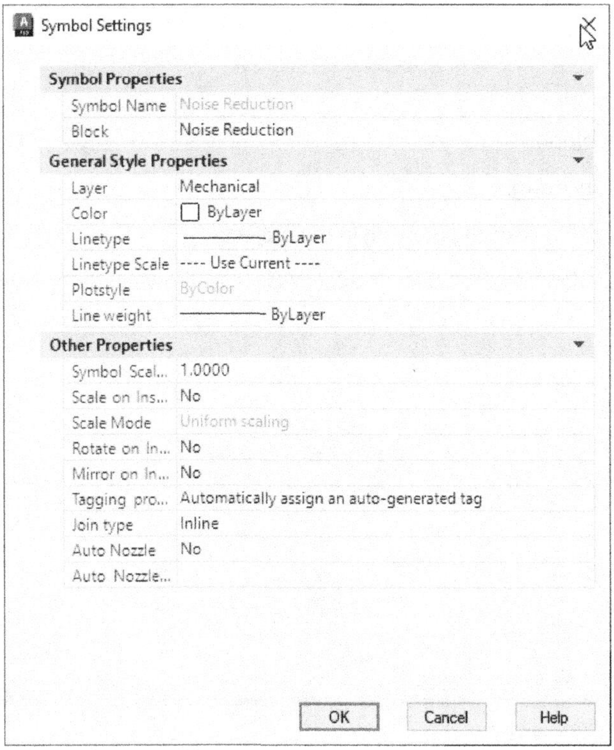

Process: Creating Symbols and Setting Color and Layer

The following steps describe setting color and layer properties for a custom symbol.

1. Open *projSymbolStyle.dwg*.
2. Create new geometry or explode an existing symbol and modify to create the symbol, as shown in the following illustration.

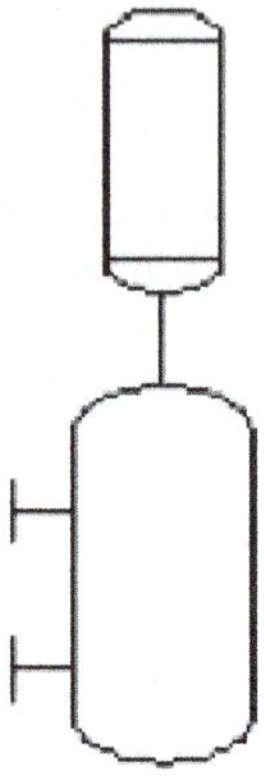

3. Convert the geometry to a block.
4. Save and close *projSymbolStyle.dwg*.
5. Create a new drawing or open an existing drawing in the project.
6. Display the Project Setup dialog box and select or create a class, as shown in the following illustration.

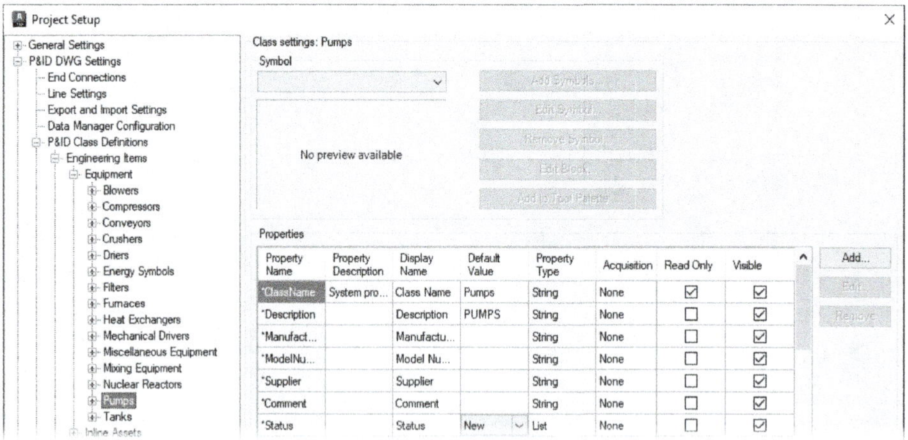

7. In the Project Setup dialog box, under Symbol, click Add Symbol. The Add Symbols - Select Symbols dialog box opens, as shown in the following illustration.

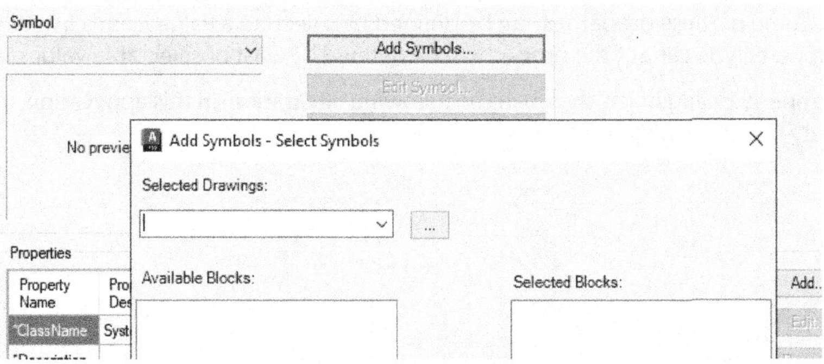

8. Browse to the drawing in which the Block resides. Select the Block and click Add, as shown in the following illustration. Click Next.

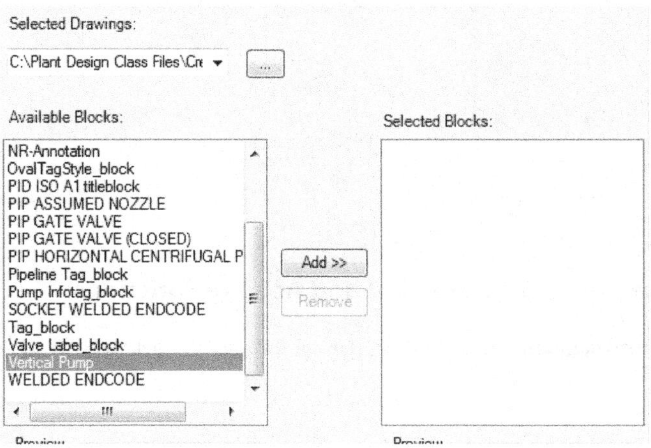

9. Add a Symbol Name, and set any of the required custom properties, as shown in the following illustration.

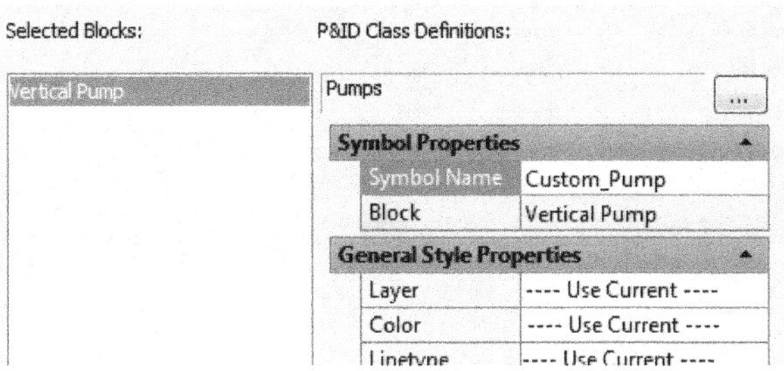

10. Click Finish.

Add Properties as Selection List and Acquire Functions

The Properties section of the Project Setup dialog box contains a table of properties for each class definition. Some of these properties can be defined by selecting a value from a list. When adding a custom property, you can set the property to be defined by a list of selectable values.

The Add Property dialog box is shown in the following illustration. In this application, a new Selection List property is being added to the project.

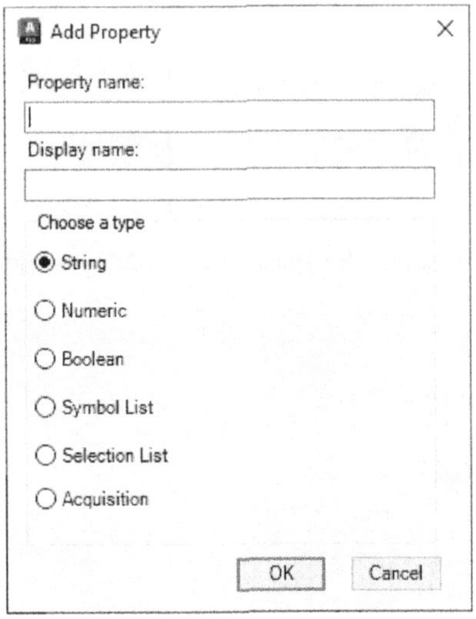

Process: Add Properties as Selection List and Acquire Functions

1. In the Project Setup dialog box, select a class. Under Properties, click Add, as shown in the following illustration.

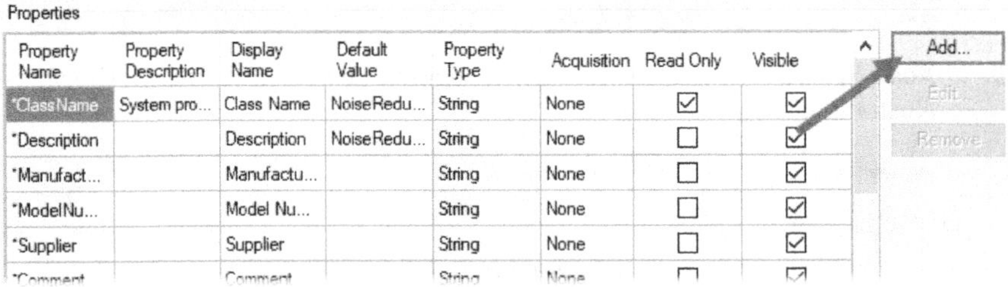

2. In the Add Property dialog box, enter a name for the property and under Choose a Type, click Selection List, as shown in the following illustration.

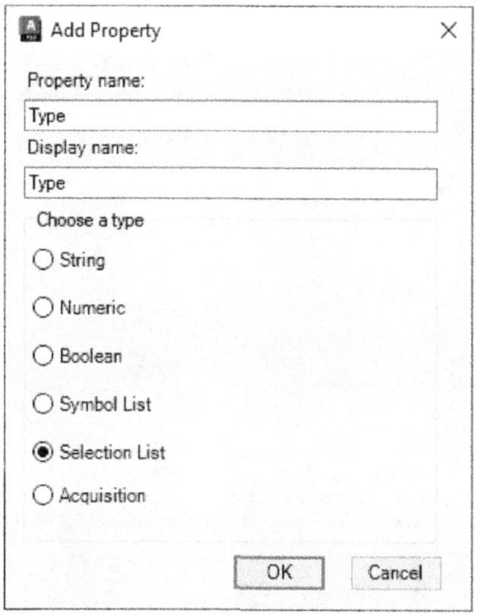

3. In the Selection List dialog box, select from the list of available selection lists or create a new one by clicking Add List.

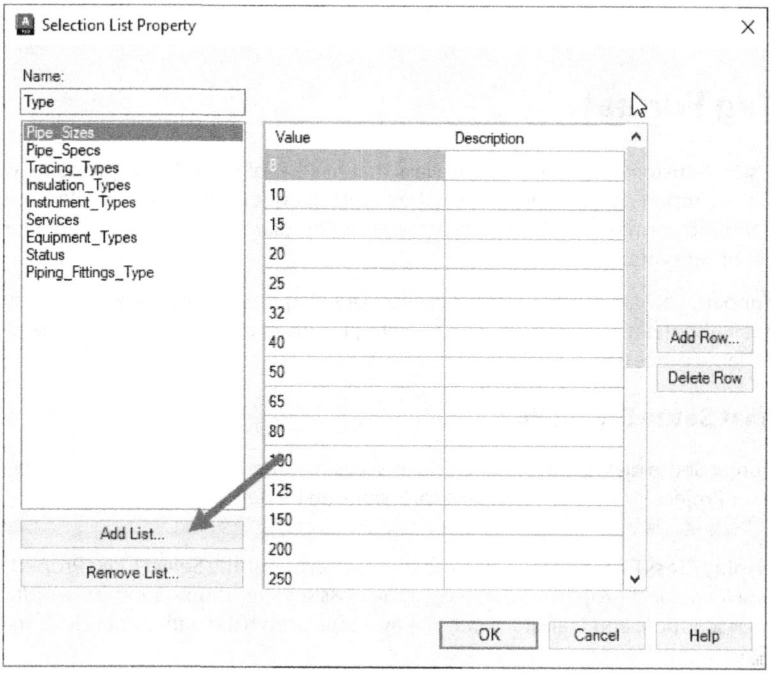

4. If creating a new list, name the list, as shown in the following illustration.

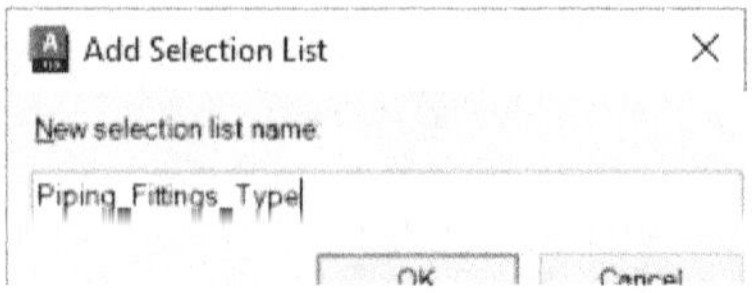

5. Click Add Row. Enter a Value and Description, as shown in the following illustration.

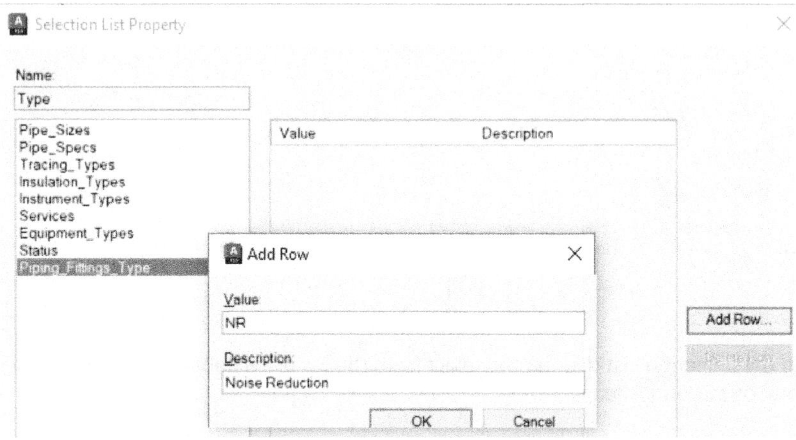

Setting a Tag Format

You can assign a custom tag format to any class that has a TagFormatName property assigned to it. If a class has this property, when selected, the New button under Tag Format is selectable. When you click New, the Tag Format Setup dialog box opens. In this dialog box, you assign a name and specify the number of subparts.

For each subpart, you can assign Class Properties, Drawing Properties, and Project Properties to the class. You can also define Expressions. Once the tag format is complete, you can assign to the TagFormatName property.

Tag Format Setup Dialog Box

The Tag Format Setup dialog box enables you to access properties based on Class Properties, Drawing Properties, or Project Properties. Also, an expression can be defined.

- **Display Class Properties -** Selecting this button opens the Select Class Properties dialog box. Here, you can select properties defined for the class selected. Some examples might include Class Name, Description, and Manufacturer. The available properties vary depending on the class selected.

- **Display Drawing Properties** - Selecting this button opens the Select Drawing Property dialog box. Here, you can select properties defined for the drawing. Some examples might include DWG Number, DWG Title, and Description. The available properties can vary depending on the category selected.

- **Display Project Properties** - Selecting this button opens the Select Project Property dialog box. Here, you can select properties defined for the project. Some examples might include Project Name, Project Description, and Company Name. The available properties can vary depending on the category selected.

- **Define Expression** - Selecting this button opens the Define Expression dialog box. Here, you can define tagging format expressions.

Process: Setting a Tag Format

The following steps outline the process to assign a tag format to a property.

1. In the Project Setup dialog box, select a Class Definition with a tag property. Under Tag Format, click New, as shown in the following illustration.

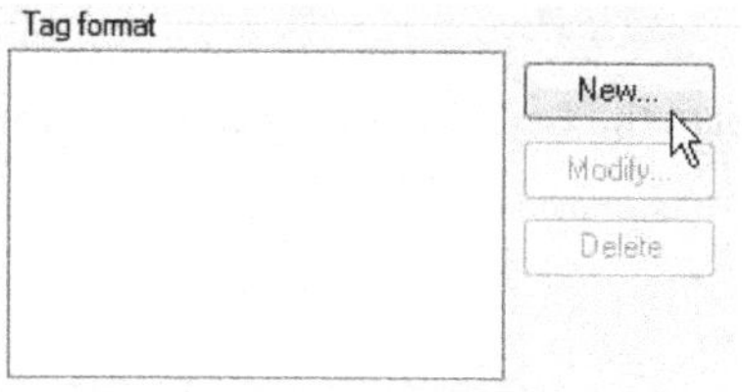

2. In the Tag Format Setup dialog box, enter a Format Name and the number of subparts, as shown in the following illustration.

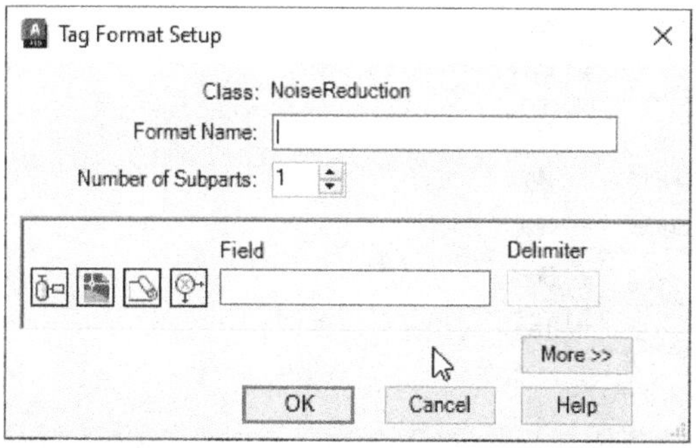

3. Define the Class Properties, Drawing Properties, Project Properties, or Expression to define the fields of the subparts, as shown in the following illustration. Click OK.

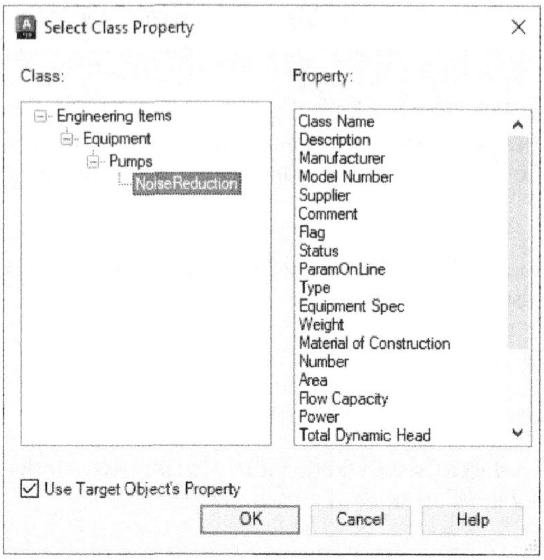

4. In the Properties table, assign the tag format to the TagFormatName property, as shown in the following illustration.

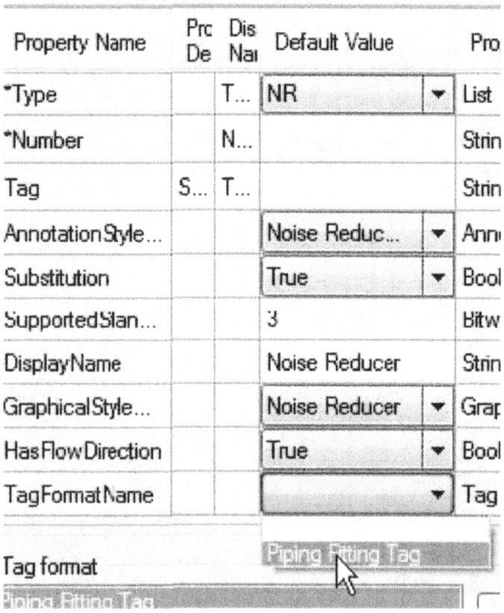

Creating a Custom Annotation Style

A custom annotation style enables you to add annotation to symbols that correspond to your company or customer specifications.

It is important to understand the difference between a tag and an annotation. In Plant 3D, the tag is a property which is defined in the properties, while an annotation is what is actually displayed on the drawing. Both tags and annotations can be formatted to reflect combinations of properties.

Two different annotation styles are shown with the same symbol in the following illustration. The configured annotation style as it is configured in the project setup is shown below each example. The difference between these styles is the inclusion of an oval around the value and the automatic offset distance from the symbol.

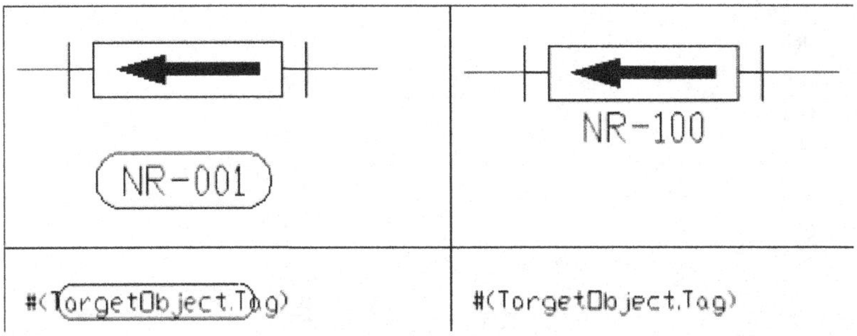

You create custom annotation styles in the project. Custom annotation styles are available for use at and below the level they are created. So for example, if a custom annotation style is created at the Engineering Items level under P&ID Class Settings, every class under that can use that annotation style. If you create an annotation style at an individual a class level, then only that class has access to that annotation style.

If you set a custom annotation style as the default annotation for a class, then that annotation style is used when a symbol from that class is added to the drawing.

Annotation Styles

An annotation style consists of overall properties and a block definition with a formatted attribute definition. The formatted attribute definition is configured to be dynamic based on specified properties or expressions.

When working with annotation styles, your main tasks are to add, edit, or remove the annotation for a selected class or edit the block definition used by the annotation style.

The Annotation area of the Project Setup dialog box is shown in the following illustration.

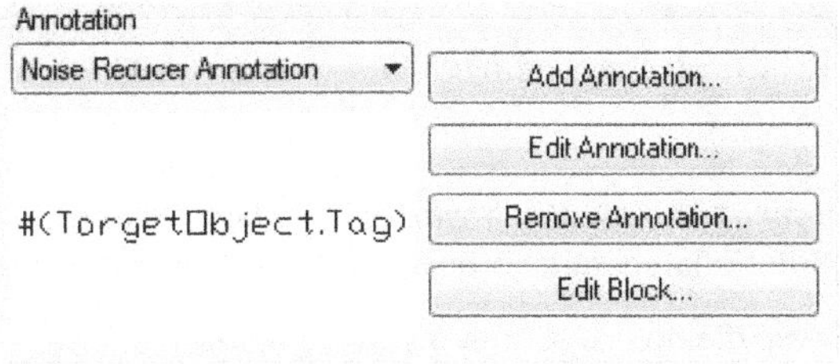

When you are first creating a new annotation style, you select a block definition from a drawing to base it on. That block definition is then added to the projSymbolStyle drawing file in the active project. The name of the added block is the name of the annotation style with a _block suffix. So when you edit the block for an annotation style, you edit the unique block definition in the projSymbolStyle drawing file.

The display and placement for the annotation is based on the properties configured in the Symbol Settings dialog box, as shown in the following illustration. You configure how the annotation should display by adjusting the settings under General Style Properties. You change the different settings under Other Properties to things like the symbol size, if it is automatically inserted when the symbol is added, where the block is inserted relative to the symbol insertion point, if a leader line should be included, and the text orientation.

Symbol Properties	
Symbol Name	Noise Reducer Annotation
Block	Noise Reducer Annotation_block
General Style Properties	
Layer	Text
Color	■ ByLayer
Linetype	———— ByLayer
Linetype Scale	---- Use Current ----
Plotstyle	ByColor
Line weight	———— ByLayer
Other Properties	
Symbol Scale ...	25.0000
Use target pr...	No
Linked	Yes
Auto insert?	Auto Insert
Offset X	0.0000
Offset Y	-5.0000
Use leader	No
Orientation	Orthogonal

Process: Creating a Custom Annotation Style

The following steps describe the overall process for creating a custom annotation style.

1. Create a custom block for the annotation and save it in a drawing file.
2. Define a new annotation style.
3. Edit the annotation block and replace the placeholder geometry with an attribute and any other required geometry.
4. Configure the attribute definition to have an annotation format.
5. Save the changes to the block.
6. If you want this custom annotation style to be used by a symbol by default, assign the new custom annotation style to the AnnotationStyleName property at the required level.
7. Apply the changes in the Project Setup dialog box so they are saved in the projSymbolStyle.dwg file. The newly configured annotation style is now available for use in any drawing when the current project is active.

Create a Custom Block for the Annotation

The block that you create in the first step of the process can consist of any type of geometry as a placeholder, as shown in the following illustration. You just need a block definition saved in a drawing that you can select later in the process.

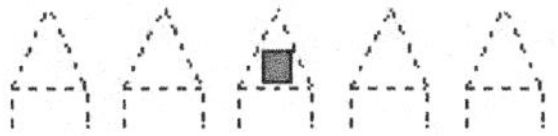

Define a New Annotation Style

The creating and defining of a new annotation style is done in the Project Setup dialog box, as shown in the following illustration. Because the annotation style is associated with a class definition, the first thing you need to do is select the level where you want to create a new custom annotation style. After selecting the level, you click Add Annotation in the Annotation area to begin creating the new annotation style. You then enter a name for the annotation style and select the custom annotation block from the drawing file you saved it in. After entering the name and selecting the block, you then set the properties for the annotation block. Properties like layer, layer properties, auto insertion, the text insertion position, and the use of a leader.

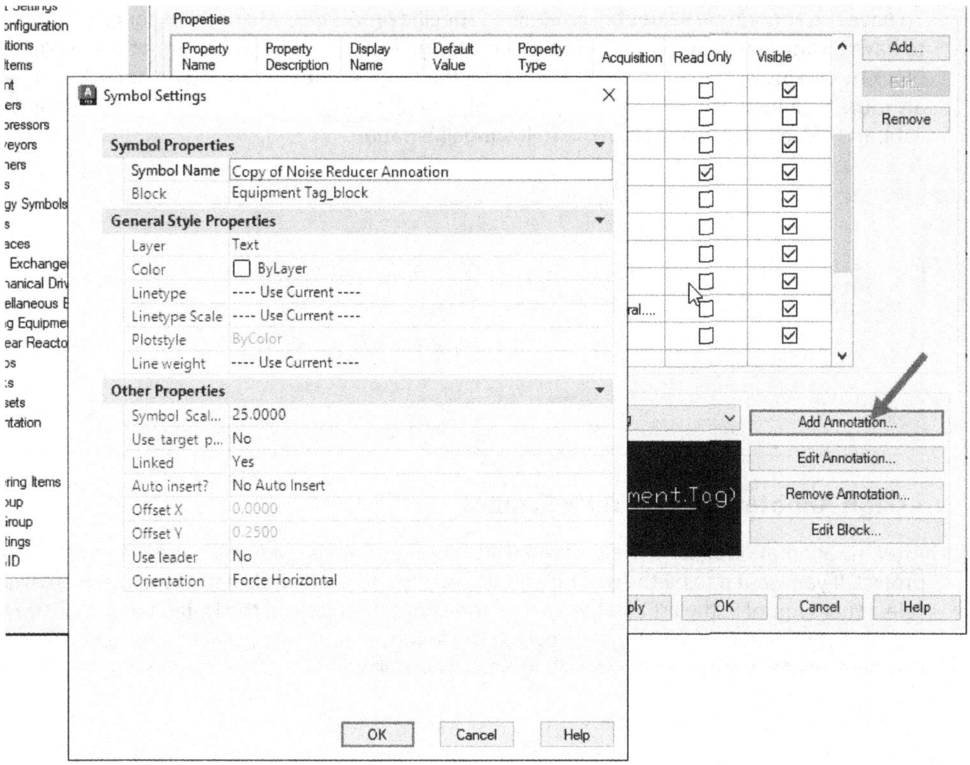

Edit the Block - Add an Attribute

After the new annotation style has been added, your next task is to edit the block associated with the annotation style, as shown in the following illustration. In the Block Editor you delete the placeholder geometry and create an attribute and specify its insertion point to coincide with the insertion point of the block. This would be the logical point on the placeholder geometry your object snapped to during the creation of the block. In the Block Editor environment, it should also be the 0,0 point.

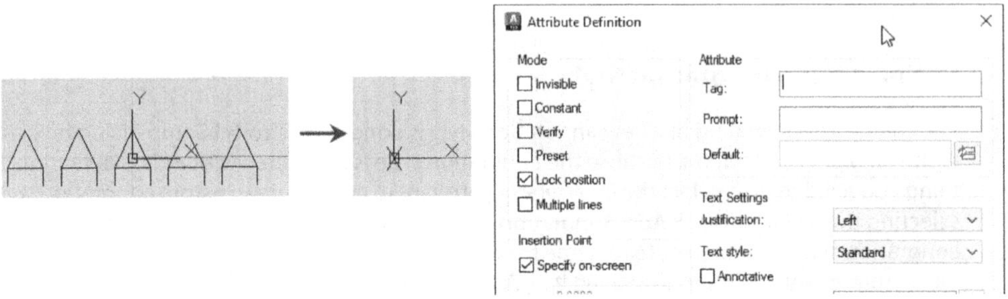

Configure the Attribute to Have an Annotation Format

To have the annotation values be dynamic to specific properties, you need to configure the attribute to have an annotation format. You initiate the assigning of an annotation format while editing the block by clicking Assign Annotation Format on the PnID Annotation toolbar. After selecting the attribute definition, you specify the number of subparts and where the property values for those subparts come from, as shown in the following illustration.

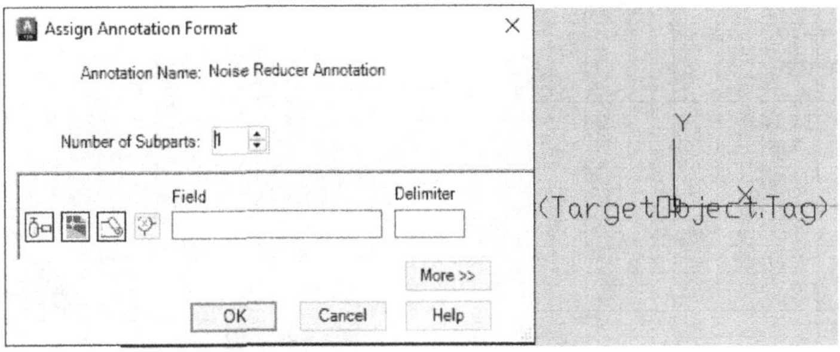

Assign Annotation Style for a Symbol

After the annotation style has been created and configured, it is ready to be used in any drawing in the project. If you want it to be the default annotation style for a symbol, in the Project Setup dialog box, select that symbol in the list and then select the annotation style in the Default Value cell for the AnnotationStyleName property, as shown in the following illustration. Refer to the help system topic Set Up Annotations to learn more about creating annotation styles.

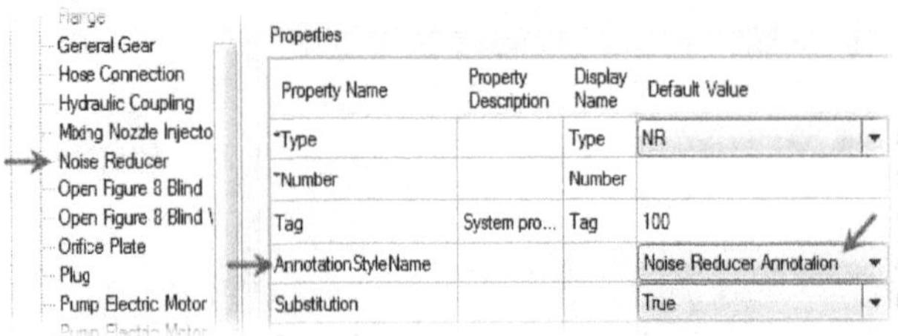

Property Name	Property Description	Display Name	Default Value
*Type		Type	NR
*Number		Number	
Tag	System pro...	Tag	100
AnnotationStyleName			Noise Reducer Annotation
Substitution			True

Exercise: Create Symbols and Set Up the Tagging Scheme

In this exercise, you will learn how to create symbols, set the layer and colors, set up the tag, and create annotations.

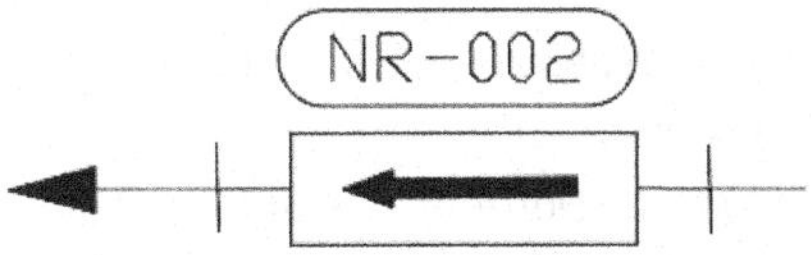

Creating New Symbols

In this section of the exercise, you create a new inline symbol, and modify a standard symbol to create a new endline symbol. It is recommended you use both snap and grid during this exercise. The grid will be toggled on and off throughout the exercise for clarity purposes.

1. Start the AutoCAD Plant 3D software, if not already running.

2. Open an existing project by doing the following:
   - In the Project Manager, Current Project list, click Open.
   - In the Open dialog box, navigate to the folder *C:\Plant Design 2024 Practice Files\Create Symbols and Set Up the Tagging Scheme.*
   - Select the file *Project.xml.*
   - Click Open.

3. To create a new P&ID drawing:
   - In the Project Manager, right-click on P&ID Drawings. Click New Drawing.
   - In the New DWG dialog box, for File name, enter **New_Symbols**.
   - Click OK.

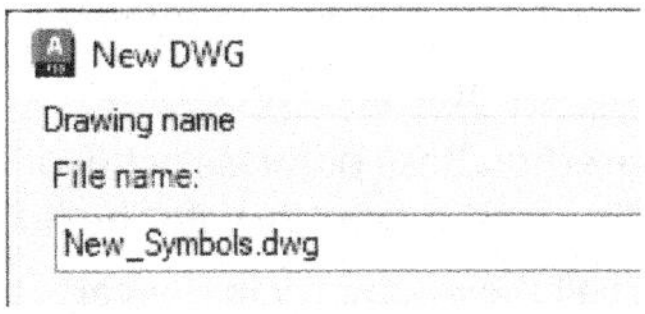

4. To prepare the drawing file:
   - Activate the PID PIP workspace, if required.
   - Switch to the Model Environment, if required.
   - Make the P&ID PIP tool palette current.

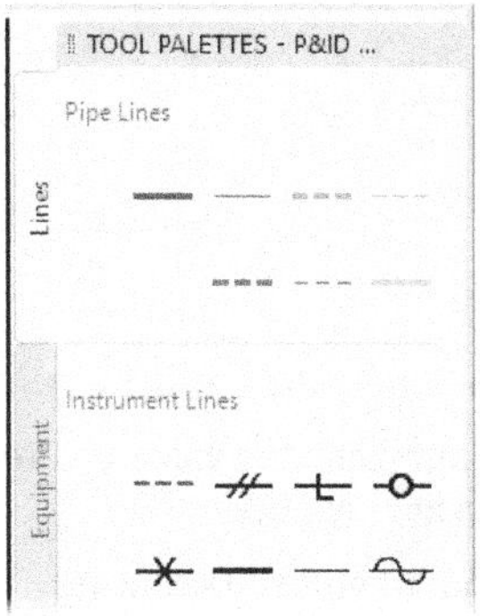

5. To insert a symbol:
   - On the P&ID PIP tool palette, click the Equipment tab.
   - Under Pumps, click Horizontal Centrifugal Pump.
   - Place the pump anywhere in the drawing as shown in the following illustration.
   - When the Assign Tag dialog box opens, click Cancel.

Note: The standard symbol will provide a size reference for the creation of new symbols.

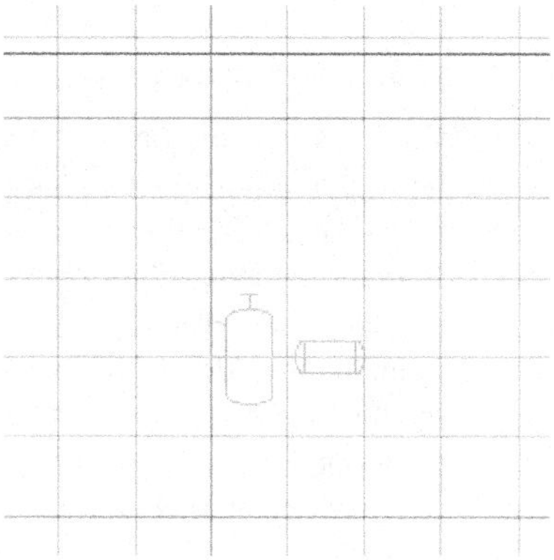

6. From the Valves tab, place a Gate Valve as shown in the following illustration.

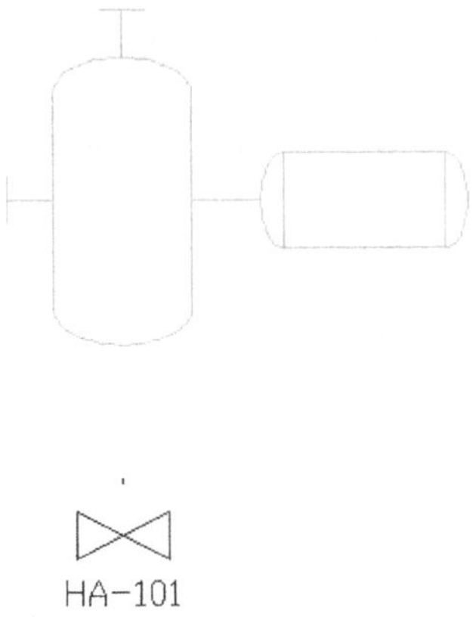

7. Between the pump and the valve, create the geometry for a new symbol:
   - Using standard AutoCAD drawing commands, create geometry that closely resembles the drawing shown.
   - Use a Polyline for the arrow.

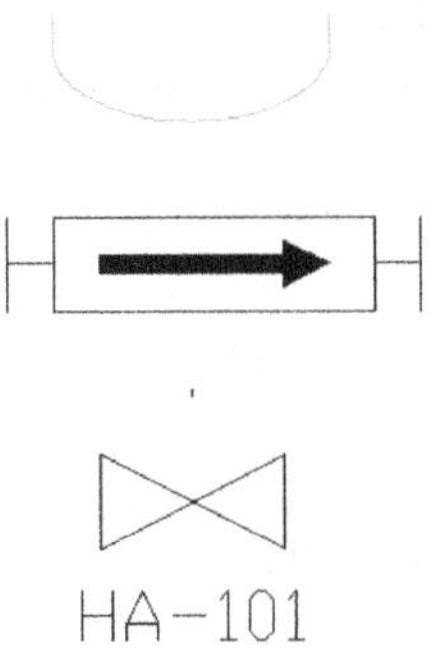

8. To create a block of the geometry:
   - On the ribbon, on the Insert tab, on the Block Definition panel, click Create Block.
   - In the Block Definition dialog box, for Name, enter **Noise Reduction**.
   - For Base point, click Pick point. Select a point in the middle of the newly created geometry (use tracking points).
   - Under Objects, click Select objects. Select the newly created geometry.
   - Click OK.

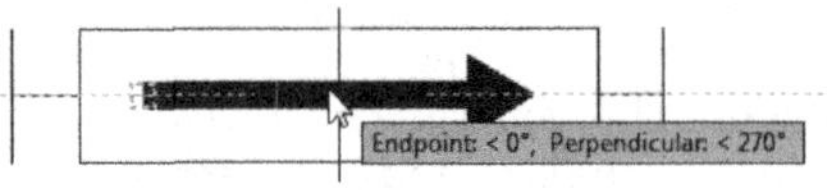

9. Save the drawing.
10. To begin to create a new symbol from an existing symbol:
    - Explode the Horizontal Centrifugal Pump.
    - Explode the same geometry again. This reverts the geometry to lines and arcs.
11. To edit the geometry:
    - Delete the top nozzle.
    - Move the side nozzle lower. Copy or mirror as shown (1).
    - Move and rotate the geometry on the right to the top as shown (2). You can use grips to move and rotate.

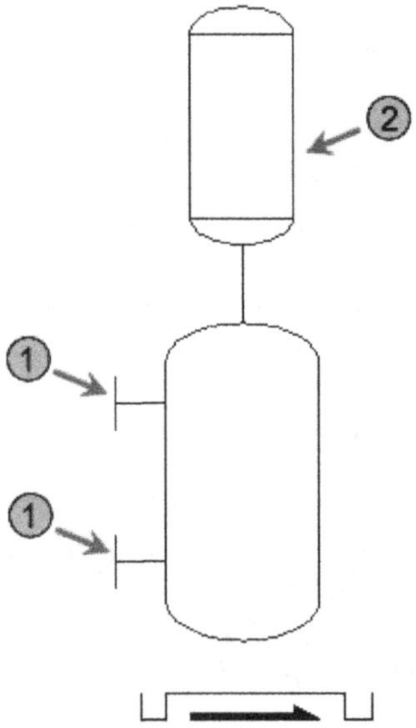

12. Create a block of the edited geometry:
    - For Name, enter **Vertical Pump**.
    - For Insertion base point, select near the middle of the geometry with the nozzles.
    - Select all the geometry in the vertical pump.
13. Save the drawing.

14. To create a new tool palette:

- Right-click on any tab on the tool palette.
- Click New Palette.
- For name, enter **New_Symbols**.
- Move the palette to the bottom of the existing palettes by right-clicking on the new tab and clicking Move Down.

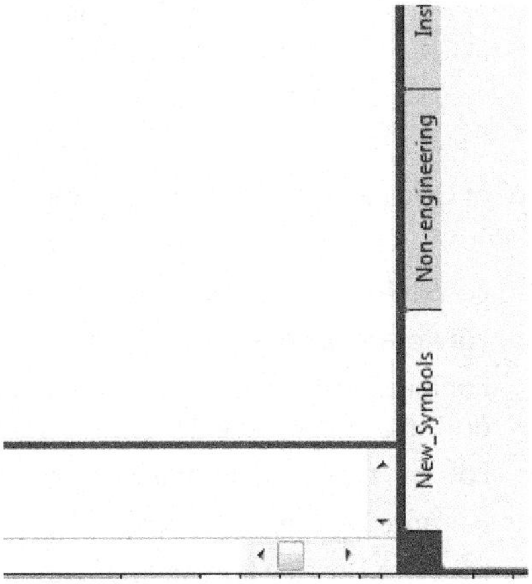

Assign Properties to New Symbols

In this section of the exercise, you assign properties to the new symbols

1. To access the Project Properties, in the Project Manager, right-click on the project. Click Project Setup.

2. To begin to add the pump symbol:

- In the Project Setup dialog box, expand P&ID DWG Settings>P&ID Class Definitions>Engineering Items> Equipment.
- Click Pumps.

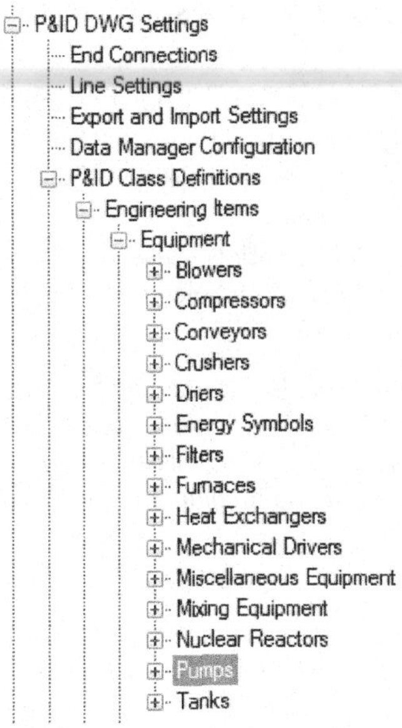

3. To create a new class:

- Right-click on Pumps.
- Click New.
- In the Create Class dialog box, for Class Name, enter **VerticalPump**.
- For Display Name of the Class, add a space between the two words as **Vertical Pump**.
- Click OK.

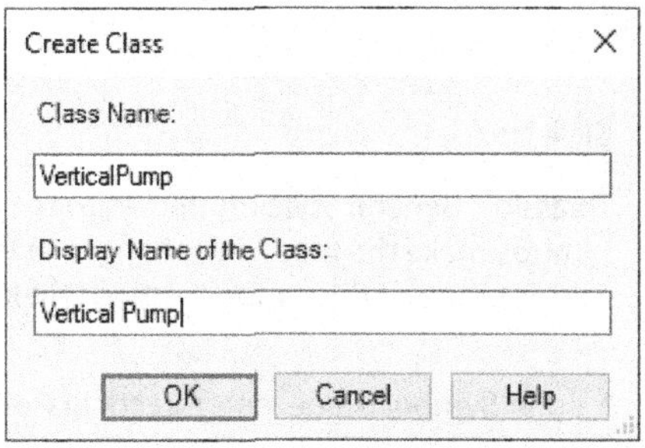

4. To begin to add the new symbol to the new class:
   - In the Project Setup dialog box, in the list, verify that Vertical Pump is selected. Under Class settings: Vertical Pump, click Add Symbols.
   - In the Add Symbols - Select Symbols dialog box, under Selected Drawings, click Browse.
   - In the Select Block Drawing dialog box, navigate to the Training Project, *C:\Plant Design 2024 Practice Files\Create Symbols and Set Up the Tagging Scheme\PID DWG* folder.
   - Select *New_Symbols.dwg*.
   - Click Open.
   - Under Available Blocks, click Vertical Pump.
   - Click Add.

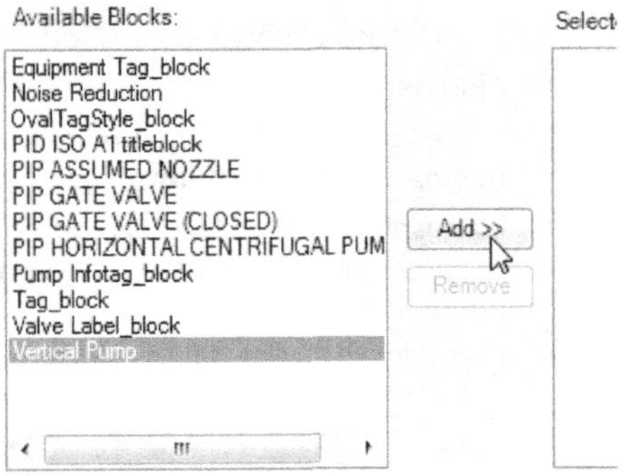

5. Click Next.

6. To assign General Style Properties to the symbol, make the following changes in the Add Symbols - Edit Symbol Settings dialog box:
   - For Symbol Name, enter **Vertical Pump**.
   - For Layer, select Equipment.
   - For Color, select ByLayer.
   - For Linetype, select ByLayer.
   - For Line weight, select ByLayer.

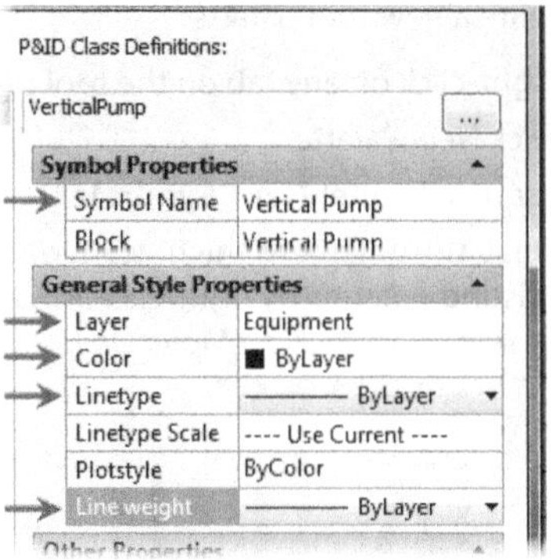

7. To set Other Properties, make the following changes:
   - For Scale on Insert, select Yes.
   - For Rotate on Insert, select Yes.
   - For Tagging prompt, select Prompt for tag during component creation.
   - For Join type, select Endline.
   - For Auto Nozzle, select Yes.
   - For Auto Nozzle Style, select Assumed Nozzle Style.

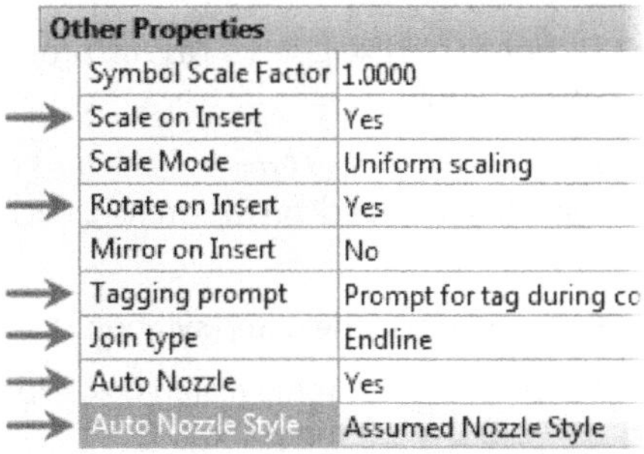

8. Click Finish. Note the symbol preview is displayed under Class settings: Vertical Pump.

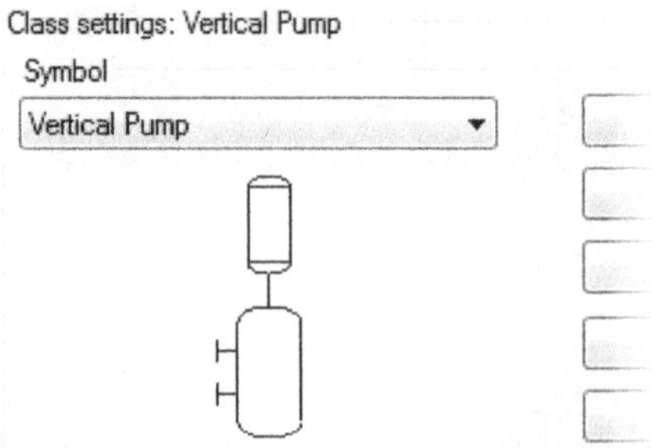

9. To add attachment points to the symbol:

- Under Symbol, click Edit Block to open the geometry in the Block Editor.
- On the Block Authoring Palettes> Parameters tab, click Point.
- Use an Endpoint or Midpoint object snap to locate the point on the top nozzle and place Position 1 as shown in the following illustration.
- Add a second point (Position 2) to the bottom nozzle, as shown in the following illustration.

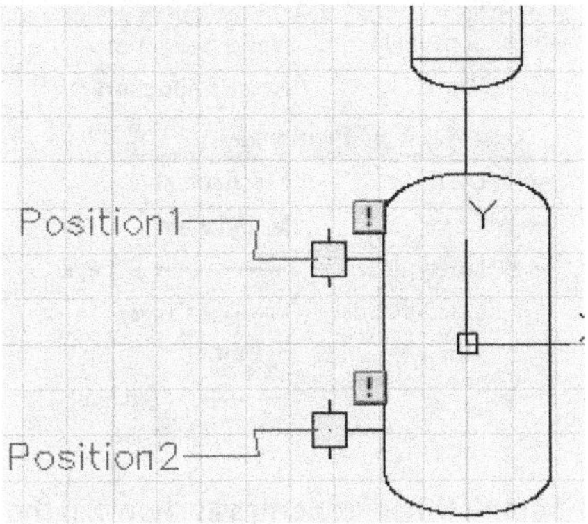

10. To edit the Point parameters:

- Right-click on the Position1 parameter.
- Click Rename Parameter.
- Enter **AttachmentPoint1**.
- Rename Position 2 to **AttachmentPoint2**.

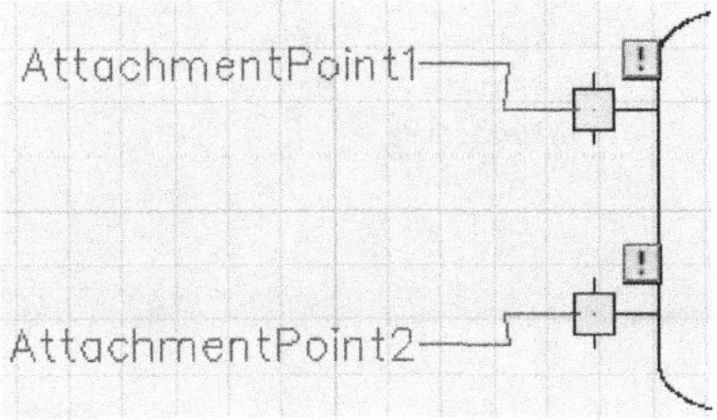

11. Close the Block Editor. Click Save the changes to Vertical Pump.

12. In the Project Setup dialog box, click Apply. Click OK.

13. To add the symbol to the P&ID PIP tool palette:

- In the P&ID PIP tool palette, verify that the New_Symbols is currently the active tab.
- Reopen the Project Setup dialog box and select Vertical Pump (P&ID Class Definitions>Engineering Items> Equipment>Pumps).
- With Vertical Pump displayed under Class settings: Vertical Pump, click Add to Tool Palette.
- In the Create Tool dialog box, click OK.
- In the Project Setup dialog box, click OK.

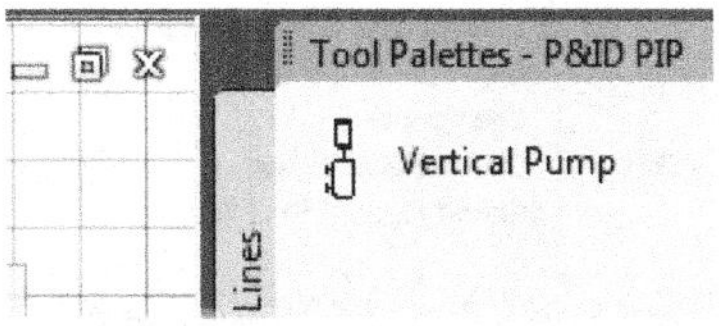

14. To test the symbol:

- On the New_Symbols tool palette, click Vertical Pump.
- Click a location next to the existing block.
- An information dialog box might display. Click Don't show me this again. Click OK.
- Accept the default values for scale and rotation angle.
- In the Assign Tag dialog box, for Type, verify that P is displayed.
- For Number, click Next Available.
- Click Place annotation after assigning tag.
- Click Assign.
- Locate the tag below the new symbol.

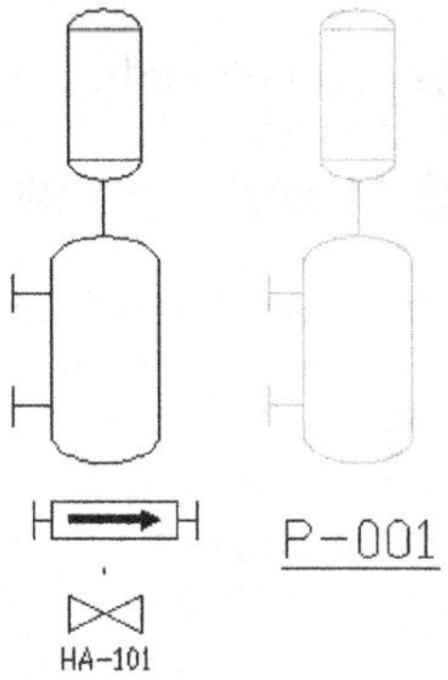

15. To begin to add the Noise Reducer symbol:
   - Open the Project Setup dialog box.
   - Expand to the P&ID Class Definitions> Engineering Items>Inline Assets>Piping Fittings.

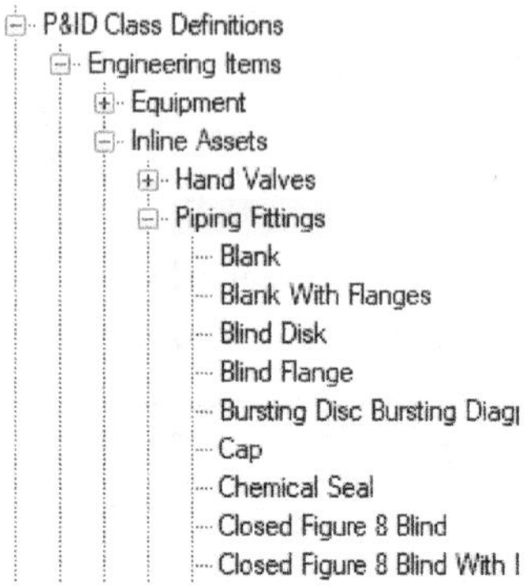

16. To create a new Piping Fittings class:
   - Right-click on Piping Fittings. Click New.
   - For Class Name, enter **NoiseReducer**.
   - For Display Name, add a space between the two words **Noise Reducer**.
   - Click OK.

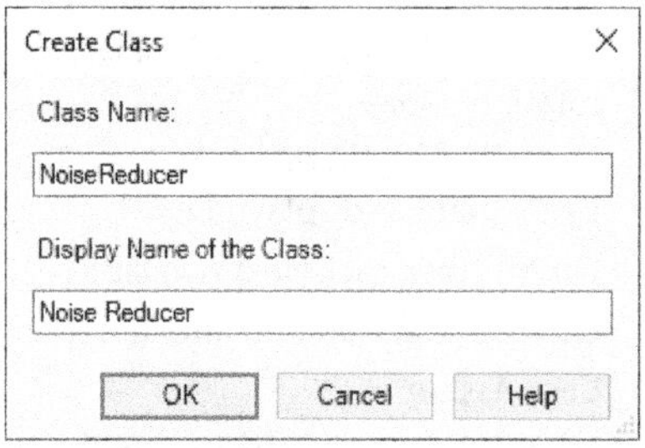

17. To add the symbol:
   - In the Project Setup dialog box, verify that Noise Reducer is selected and under Class settings: Noise Reducer, click Add Symbols.
   - In the Add Symbols - Select Symbols dialog box, under Selected Drawings, click Browse.
   - Navigate to the Training Project, *C:\Plant Design 2024 Practice Files\Create Symbols and Set Up the Tagging Scheme\PID DWG* folder.
   - Select New_Symbols.dwg.
   - Click Open.
   - Under Available Blocks, click Noise Reduction.
   - Click Add.

18. Click Next.

19. In the Add Symbols dialog box, Set the Symbol Properties and General Style Properties as shown in the following illustration.

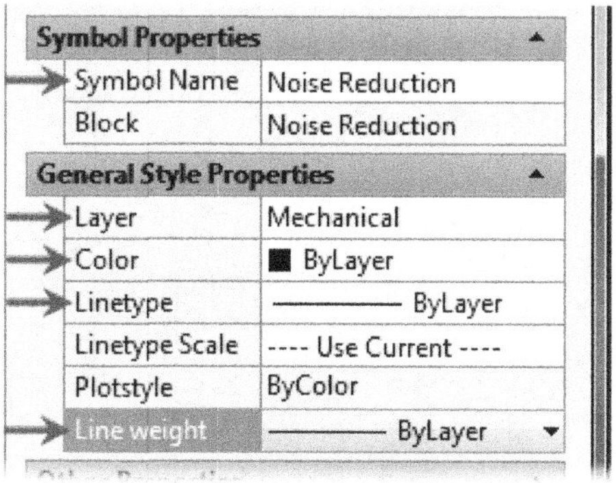

20. Set the Other Properties as shown in the following illustration. Click Finish.

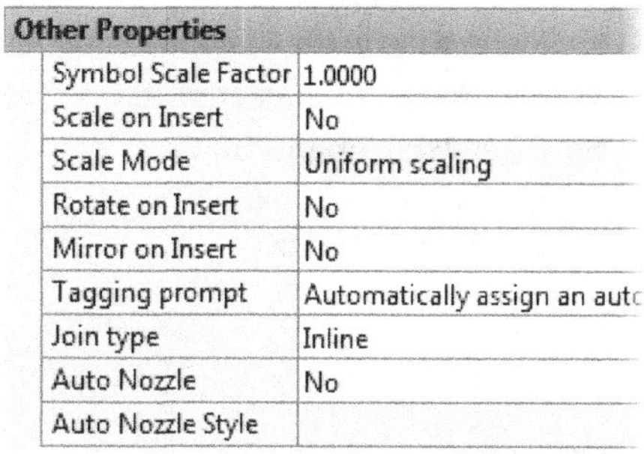

21. In the Project Setup dialog box, under Symbol, click Edit Block.
    - Edit the block and add two points on either side as shown:
    - Rename the left point to **AttachmentPoint1**.
    - Rename the right point to **AttachmentPoint2**.
    - Close the Block Editor. Save changes to Noise Reduction.

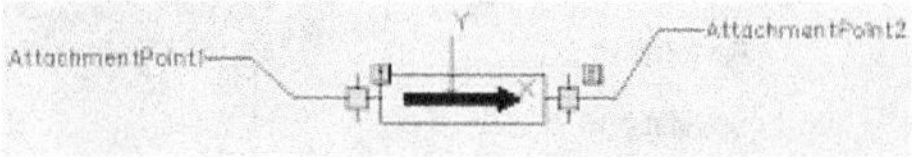

Creating Selection Lists and Setting Tag Information

In this section of the exercise, you add properties to both the symbol and the class to enable you to apply properties and tags to the symbol

1. To create a tag format:
    - In the Project Setup dialog box, under Properties, click Add.
    - In the Add Property dialog box, for Property name, enter **Tag**.
    - Click OK.

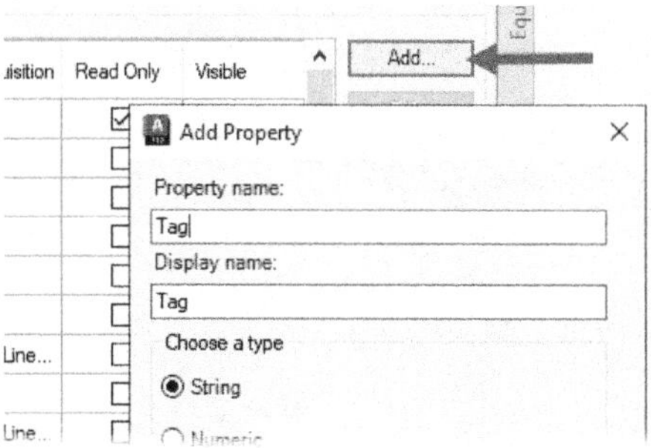

2. In the Properties table, locate Tag. Note that in Tag format area, the New button is now selectable.

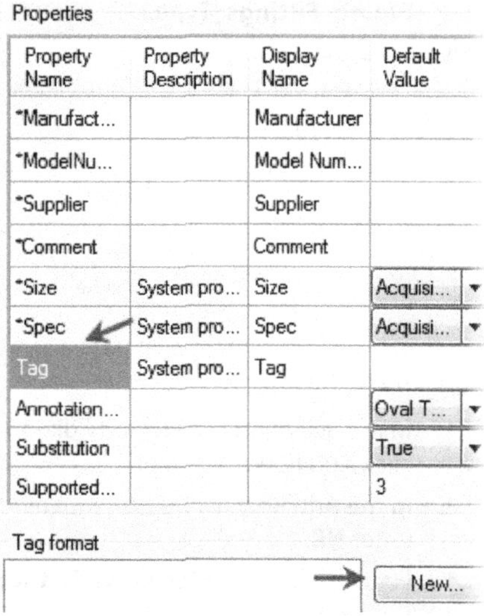

Property Name	Property Description	Display Name	Default Value
*Manufact...		Manufacturer	
*ModelNu...		Model Num...	
*Supplier		Supplier	
*Comment		Comment	
*Size	System pro...	Size	Acquisi...
*Spec	System pro...	Spec	Acquisi...
Tag	System pro...	Tag	
Annotation...			Oval T...
Substitution			True
Supported...			3

3. To enter a Tag Format, a Type must exist. To add a Type:
    - From the Project Setup's P&ID Class Definitions list, select Piping Fittings.
    - Under Properties, click Add.
    - In the Add Property dialog box, for Property name, enter **Type**.
    - Under Choose a type, select Selection List.
    - Click OK.

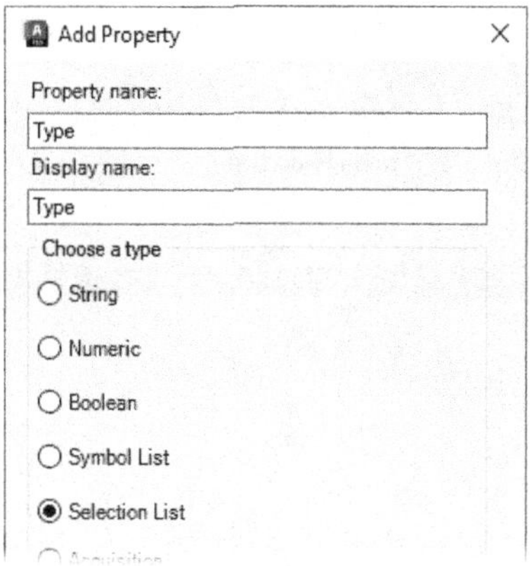

4. In the Selection List Property dialog box:
   - Click Add List.
   - In the Add Selection List dialog box, enter **Piping_Fittings_Type**.
   - Click OK.

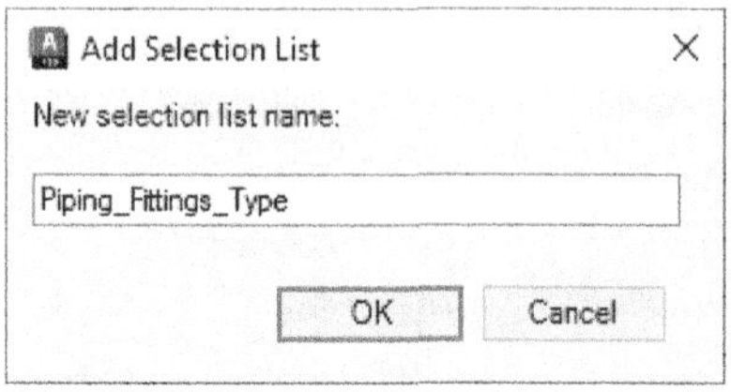

5. To create the list:
   - In the Selection List Property dialog box, click Add Row.
   - In the Add Row dialog box, for Value, enter **NR**.
   - For Description, enter **Noise Reduction**.
   - Click OK.

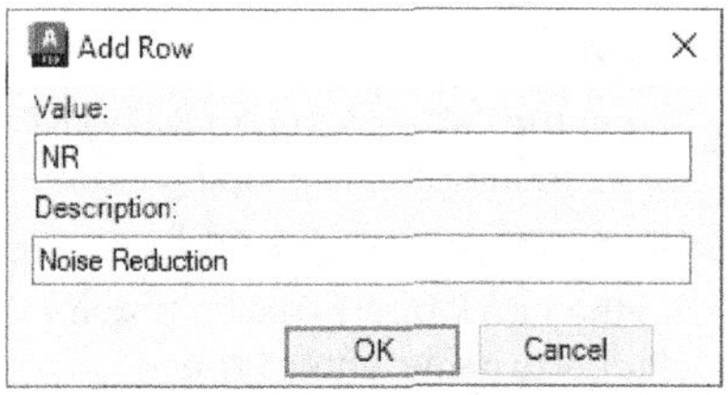

6. Add two additional rows as shown in the following illustration. Click OK.

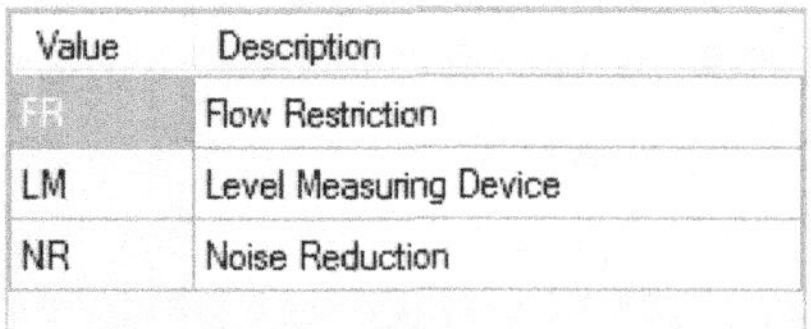

7. In the Properties table, for the Property Name: Type, verify that the selection list is valid. Select the Blank option.

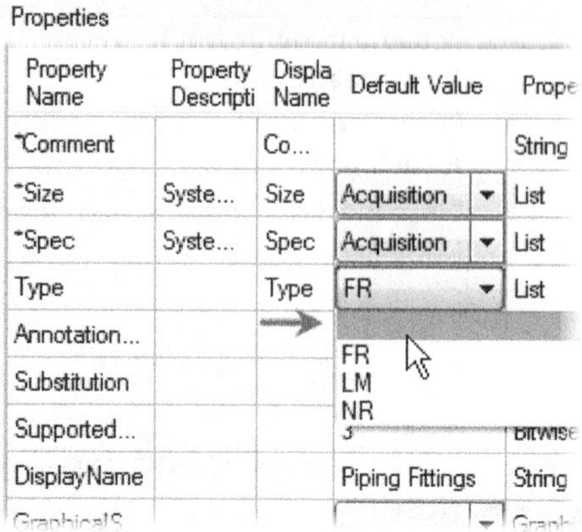

8. To create an additional property for a number:
   - Click Add.
   - In the Add Property dialog box, for Property name, enter **Number**.
   - Verify that the Type is String.
   - Click OK.

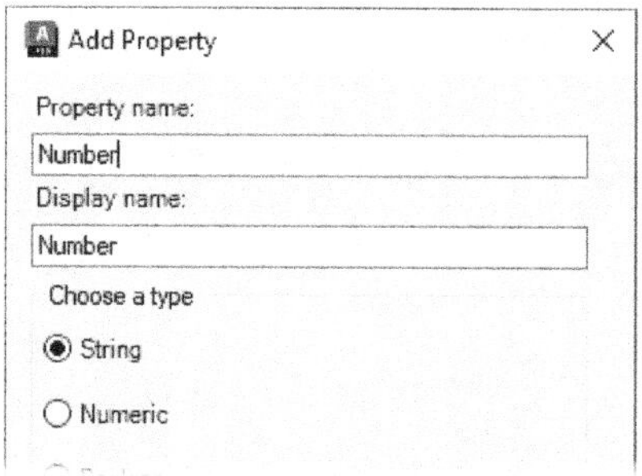

9. In the P&ID Class Definitions List, select Noise Reducer.

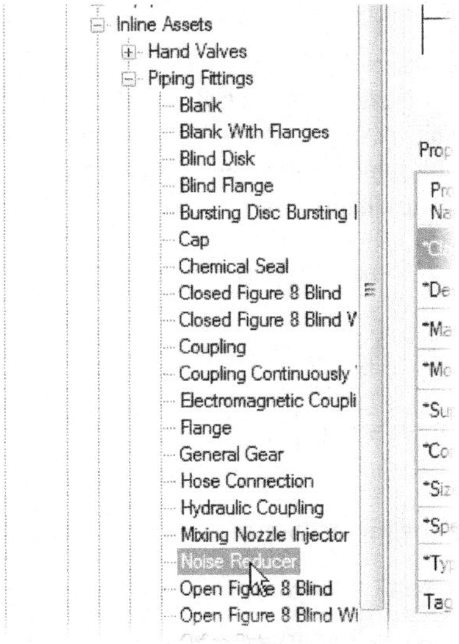

10. With Noise Reducer selected, under Properties, set the Type to NR.

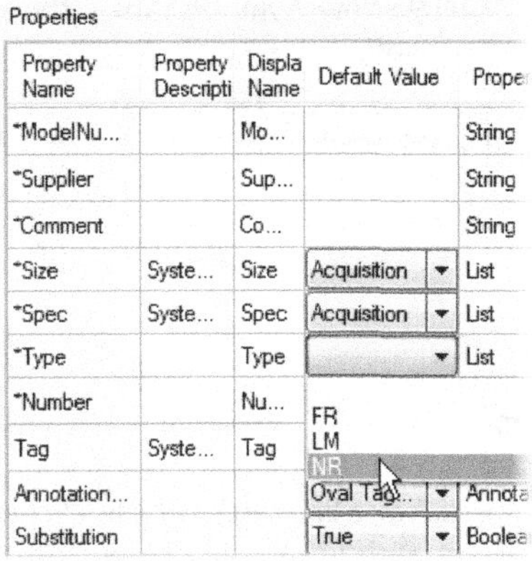

11. To set up a new tag format:

- In Tag format area, click New.
- In the Tag Format Setup dialog box, for Format Name, enter **Piping Fitting Tag**.
- For Number of Subparts, select 2.
- For the first field, click Select Class Properties.

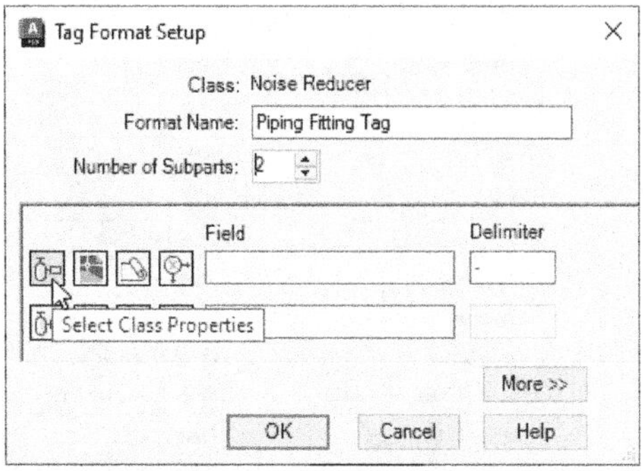

12. To set the Class Properties:

- In the Select Class Property dialog box, with the Noise Reducer class selected, under Property, click Type.
- Click OK.
- For the second subpart, click Select Class Properties.
- Under Property, click Number.
- Click OK. The fields now display as shown in the following illustration.

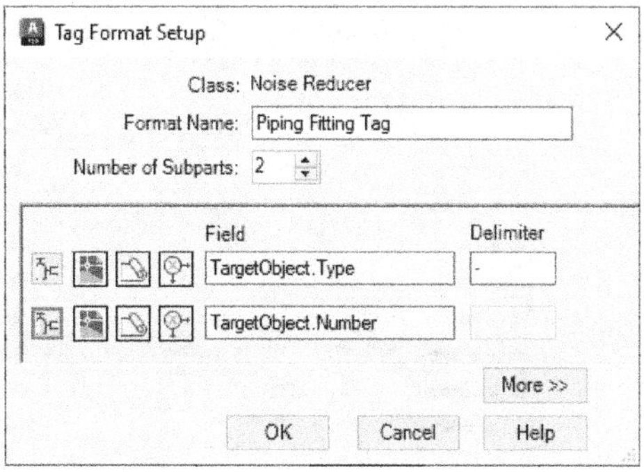

13. In the Tag Format Setup dialog box, click OK.

Note that in the Project Setup dialog box, under Tag format, Piping Fitting Tag is displayed. Also note that in the Properties table, under Property Name, TagFormatName is listed, and the Default Value is set to Piping Fitting Tag.

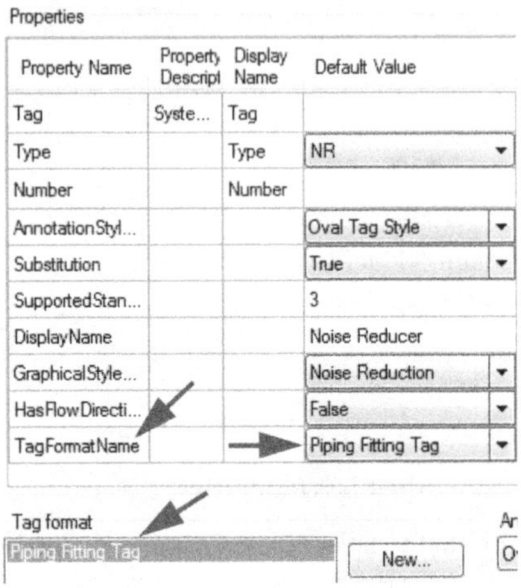

14. To set the Flow Direction property for the symbol:

- In the Properties table, locate the HasFlowDirection property.
- Note that the Property Type is Boolean.
- Under Default Value, set to True.

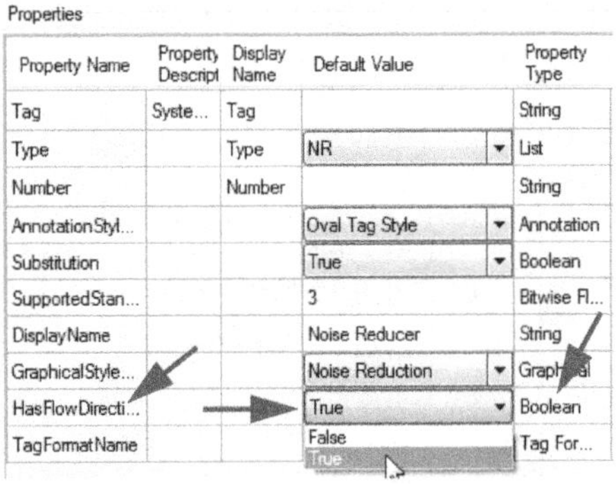

15. In the Project Setup dialog box, click Apply.

16. To place the symbol on the tool palette, under Symbol, click Add to Tool Palette.

In the Create Tool dialog box, click OK.

Note: Verify that the New_Symbols tool palette is current. If not, exit the Project Setup dialog box, make the New_Symbols (P&IP PIP) palette active, and return to the Project Setup dialog box.

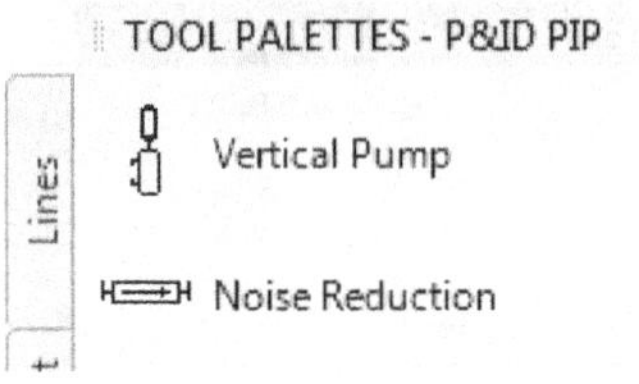

17. In the Project Setup dialog box, click OK.

18. To test the new symbol functionality:

- Add Primary Line Segment lines (Tool Palette>Lines tab) in various directions to the drawing.
- Add the Noise Reducer symbol (Tool Palette>New_Symbols tab) to the pipelines.

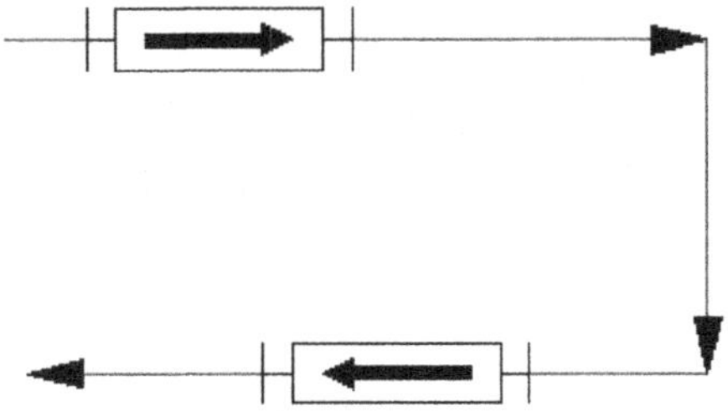

19. Right-click on a line segment. Click Schematic Line Edit, and click Reverse Flow. Note that the flow direction automatically updates for the Noise Reducer.

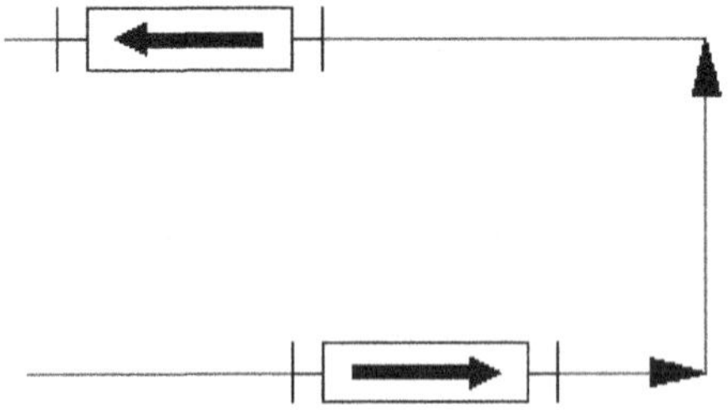

20. To change the flow direction of the symbol:

- Select one of the symbols.
- Click the directional arrow.

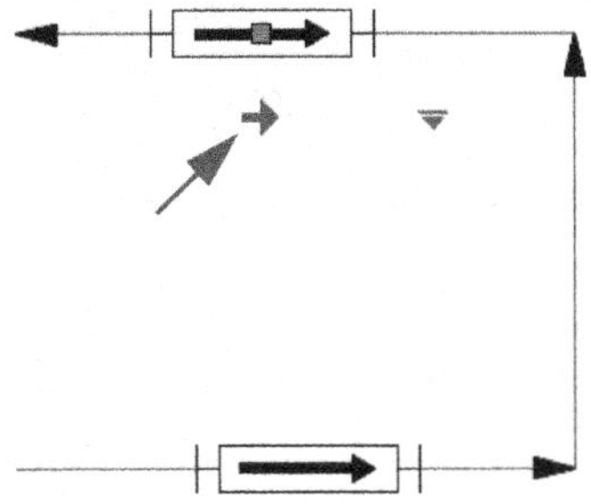

21. To assign a tag:

- Right-click on one of the symbols.
- Click Assign Tag.
- In the Assign Tag dialog box, for Number, enter **001**.
- Verify that Place annotation after assigning tag is selected.
- Click Assign.

22. Place the tag below the Noise Reducer.

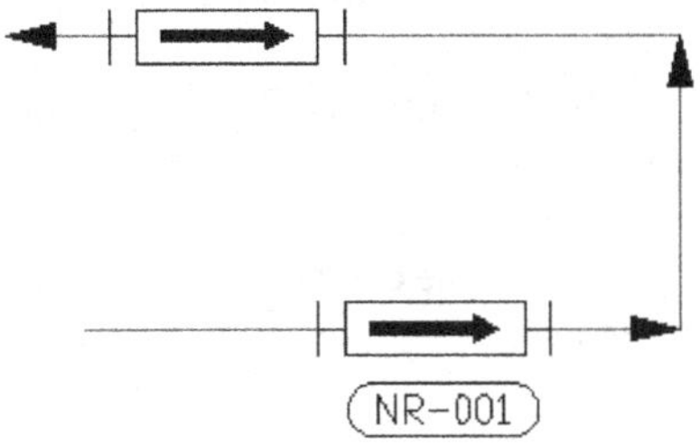

Create a Custom Annotation

In this section of the exercise, you create a custom annotation and use it in combination with a custom symbol.

1. To begin to create the custom annotation for the symbol:

- Start the text command.
- Set the Justification to Middle Center.
- In the drawing, click a centered point below a Noise Reducer symbol.
- Accept the default values for Height and Rotation.
- Enter any line of text.

2. Make a block of the new text:

- For Block Name, enter **NR-Annotation**.
- For insertion Base point, select the insertion point of the text.
- For object, select the text that you just created.
- Click OK.

3. Save the drawing file.

4. Open the Project Setup dialog box. Verify that the Noise Reducer is selected.

5. To begin to create a custom annotation, in the Annotation area, click Add Annotation.

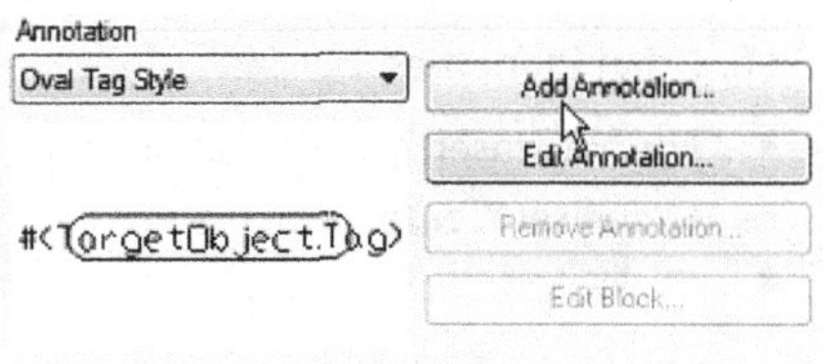

6. In the Symbol Settings dialog box, under Symbol Properties:
   - For Symbol Name, enter **Noise Reducer Annotation**.
   - Click in the Block field. Click More.
   - In the Select Block Drawing dialog box, browse to the *C:\Plant Design 2024 Practice Files\Create Symbols and Set Up the Tagging Scheme\PID DWG* folder.
   - Select and open *New_Symbols.dwg*.
   - In the Select Block dialog box, under Available Blocks, select NR-Annotation.
   - Click OK.

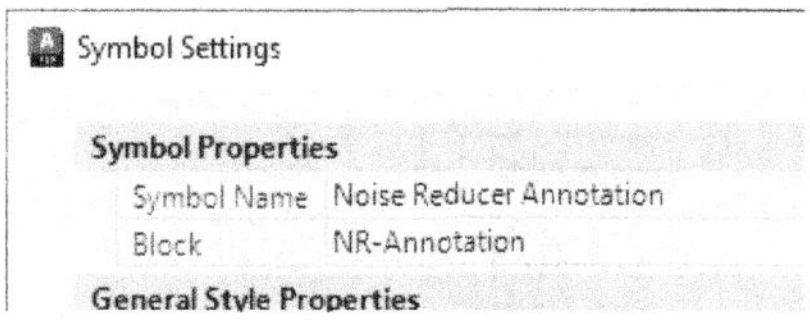

7. To set General Style Properties:
   - For Linetype, select ByLayer.
   - For Line weight, select ByLayer.

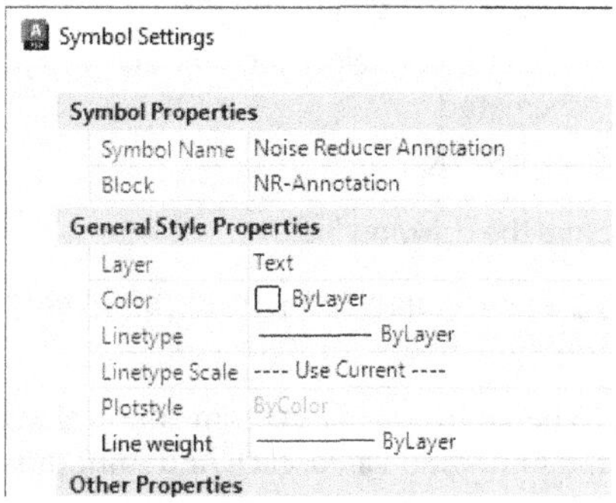

8. For Other Properties:
   - For Auto insert?, select Auto Insert.
   - For Offset Y, enter **-5**.
   - Click OK.

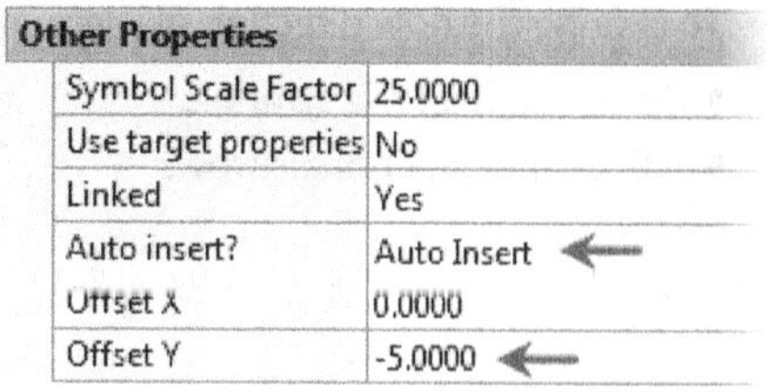

9. Note that the annotation style is added.

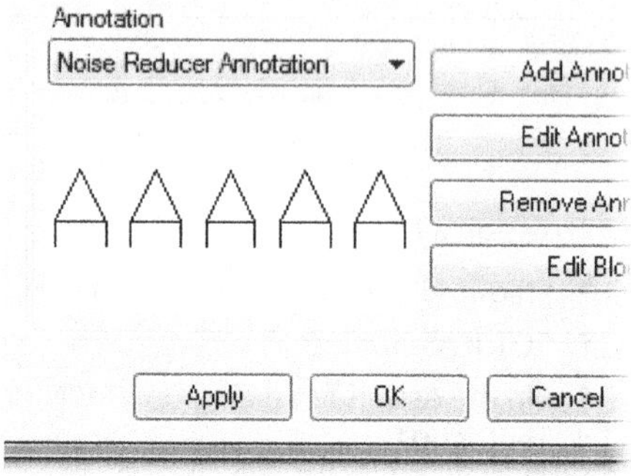

10. To edit the annotation:
    - Under Annotation, click Edit Block.
    - In the Block Editor, on the ribbon, in Action Parameters panel, click Attribute Definition.
    - In the Attribute Definition dialog box, under Attribute, for Tag, enter **X**.
    - Under Text Settings, for Justification, select Middle center.
    - Click OK.

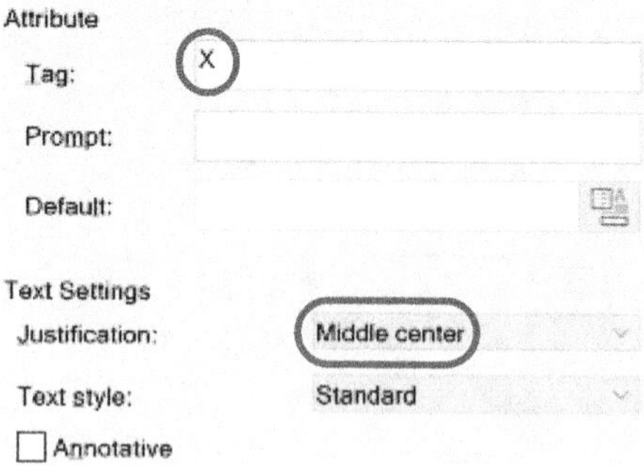

11. Use the Insertion object snap and select the existing text to place the X.

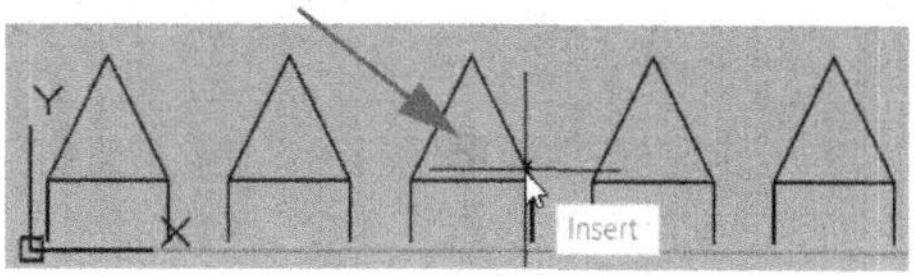

12. Delete the original text. Note only the X remains.

13. To begin to configure the attribute to have an annotation format:

   - Select the X attribute.
   - On the PnID Annotation toolbar, click Assign Format.

14. To set the annotation format:

   - In the Assign Annotation Format dialog box, under Delimiter, delete the X.
   - Click Select Class Properties.
   - Under Class, expand Engineering Items> Inline Assets>Piping Fittings.
   - Select Noise Reducer.
   - Under Property, click Tag.
   - Click OK.

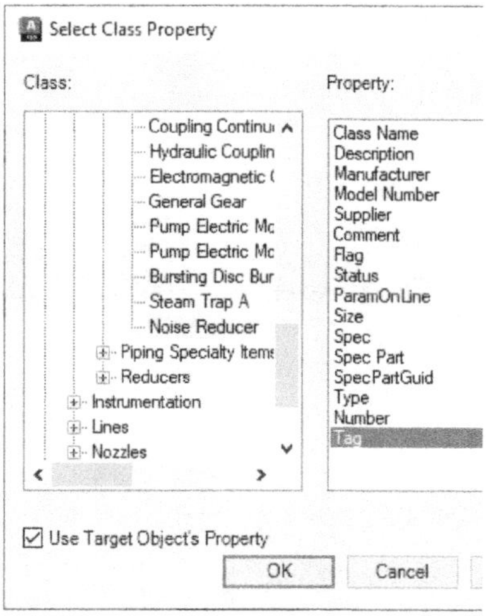

15. In the Assign Annotation Format dialog box, click OK.

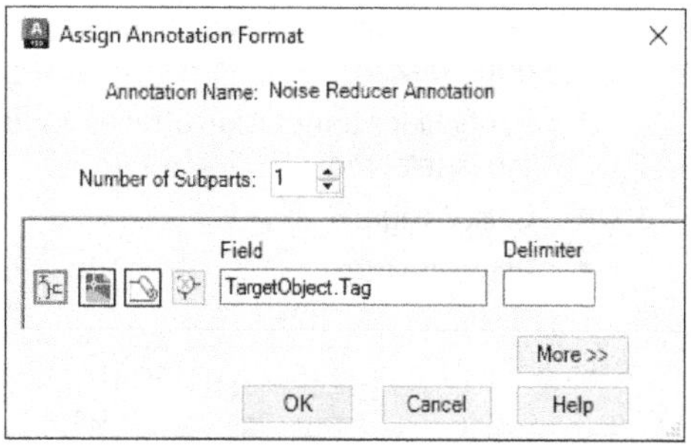

16. Close the Block Editor. Click Save the changes to Noise Reducer Annotation_block.

17. In the Project Setup dialog box, in the Properties table, locate AnnotationStyleName. Set the Default Value to Noise Reducer Annotation.

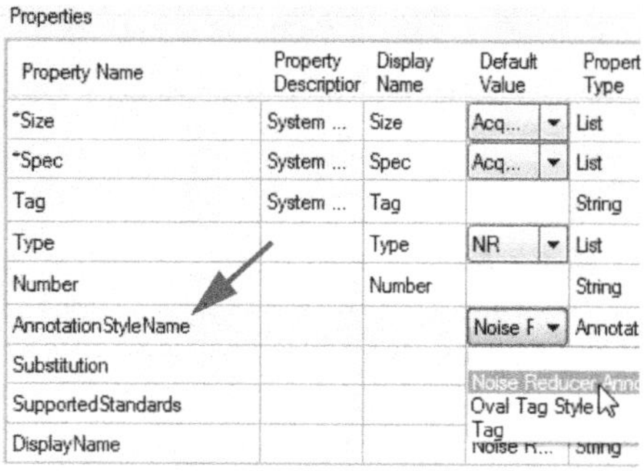

18. In the Project Setup dialog box, click Apply. Click OK.

19. In the drawing, delete one of the Noise Reducer symbols and also its pertaining tag.

20. Place another Noise Reducer symbol.

21. To add the tag information:
    - Right-click and select Assign Tag.
    - In the Assign Tag dialog box, for Number, enter **002**.
    - Verify Place annotation after assigning tag is selected
    - Click Assign.
    - Place the tag.

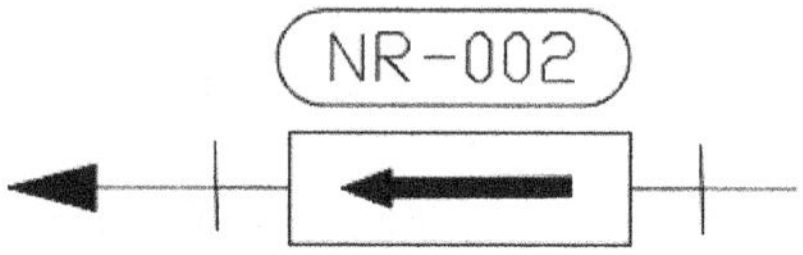

22. Close all files. Do not save.

Lesson Review Questions

1. Which of the following best describes the file in which a new symbol is stored?
   a. A drawing called *symbols.dwg* must be created in all projects to store symbols.
   b. First drawing created in the project.
   c. The Project symbol drawing *projSymbolStyle.dwg*.
2. In P&ID and Plant 3D, there are multiple classes. What is the purpose of these classes?
   a. They provide a structure so you can easily find the required symbol.
   b. Each class can carry its own settings and properties, and it divides the specific symbols into easy-to-understand groups.
   c. Classes have no specific use, they just help organize your project's setup.
3. You can combine multiple properties in one annotation.
   a. True
   b. False
4. When configuring a project, you can use the Symbol List property type for changing the symbol from one symbol (for instance from NO to NC) to another. Is it possible to create more than one symbol list per class?
   a. Yes, the number of symbol lists in one class is unlimited.
   b. Yes, but each symbol list should be defined with different properties.
   c. No, each class is limited to one symbol list.

Lesson: Customizing Data Manager

Overview

This lesson describes how to manipulate views in the Data Manager and how to edit or create your own project reports. After this lesson you can set up any report or view in the Data Manager that could then be used to export data from the project.

Objectives

After completing this lesson, you will be able to:

- Access and view the default reports in the Data Manager.
- Modify the default reports in the Data Manager.
- View project data in the Data Manager.
- Configure a report to display custom data.
- Change export and import settings for project data.

Default Reports and Views in the Data Manager

Included in AutoCAD P&ID and Plant 3D Data Manager are many default reports that enable you to access data at the drawing or project level. To open the Data Manager, click Data Manager on the Home tab. Alternatively, you can open it through the Project Manager.

Data Manager access to drawing and project data and project reports is shown in the following illustration.

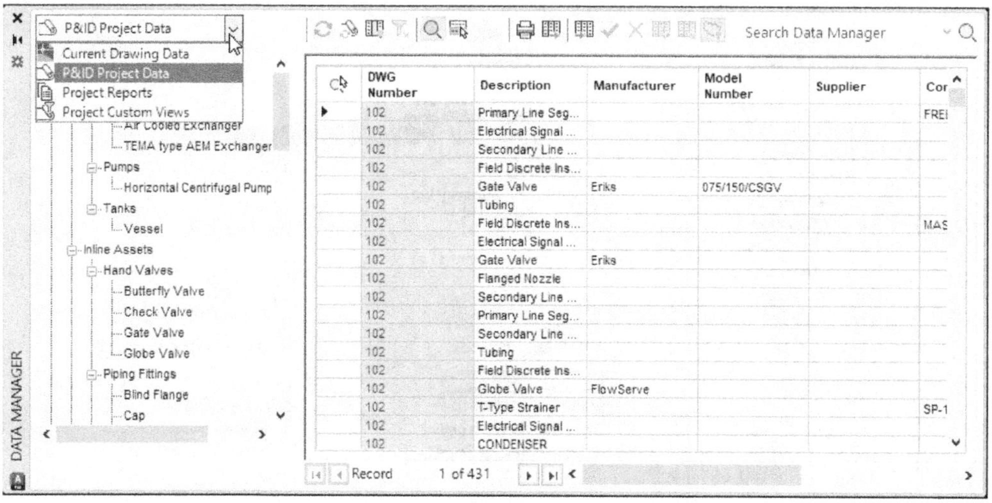

Process: Viewing Default Reports in the Data Manager

There are a multitude of reports available in the Data Manager. The following steps give an overview of accessing default reports. To access these reports, you start the Data Manager and select Project Reports. Under Project Reports, you then select a specific report from the list, as shown in the following illustration.

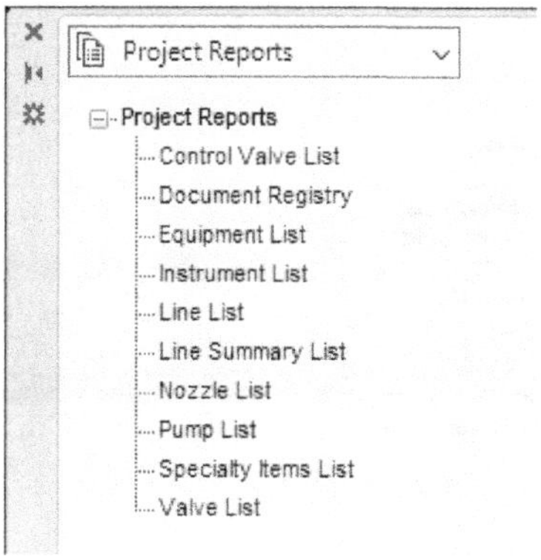

Modifying Existing Reports

The default reports that are included can be modified to fit your needs.

The modification of an existing report is shown in the following illustration. After accessing the default reports in the Project Setup dialog box, a specific report is selected and properties are defined to include or remove from the report.

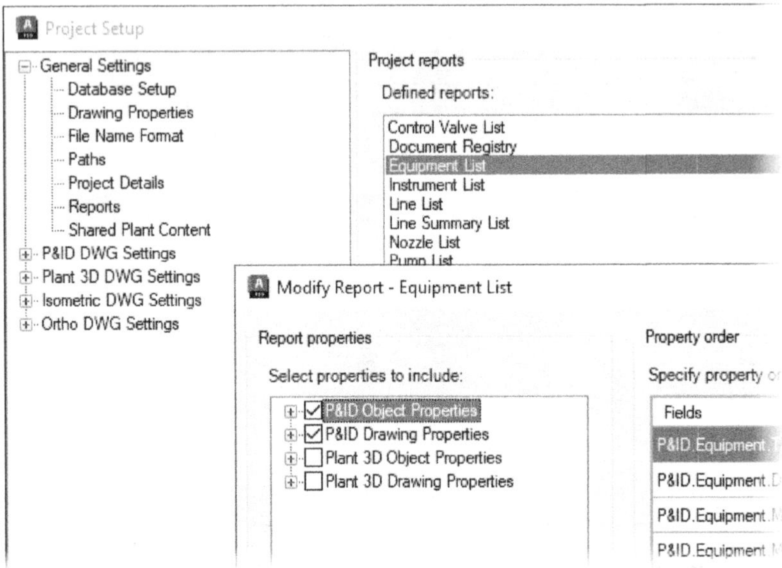

Process: Modify Existing Reports

The following steps give an overview of modifying an existing report.

1. In the Project Setup dialog box, expand General Settings and select Reports.
2. In the Project Setup dialog box, select a defined report. Click Modify.

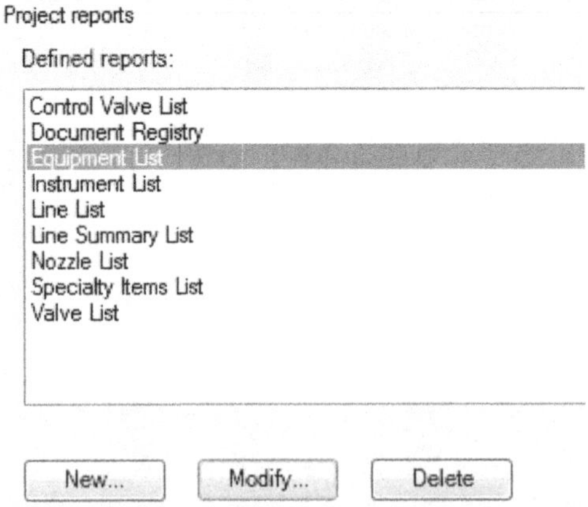

3. Under Report Properties, select a class and add or remove properties as required.

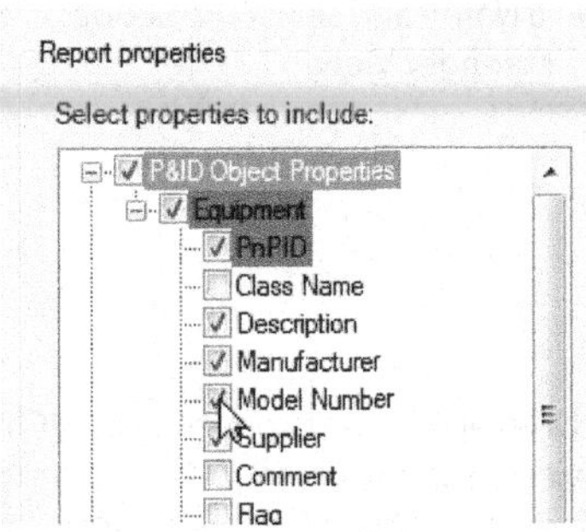

4. Order the properties as required.

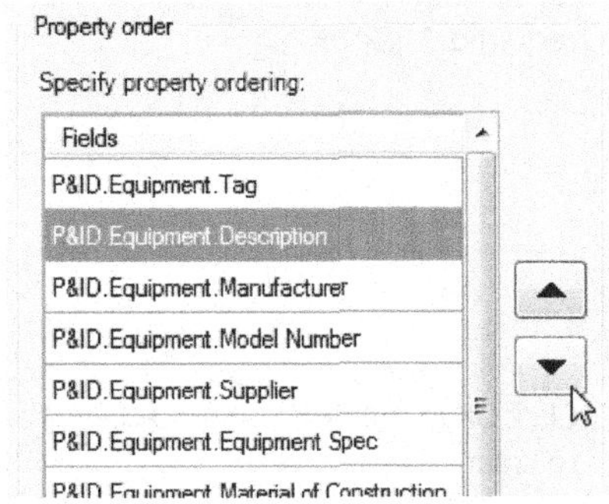

Setting Up Data Manager Views Used in the Project

You can create views in the Data Manager to reflect specific data. To set up views in the Data Manager, you open the Project Setup dialog box and click the Data Manager Configuration in either the P&ID DWG Settings or Plant 3D DWG Settings.

Process: Setting Up Data Manager Views

The following steps describe setting up views in the Data Manager.

1. In the Project Setup dialog box, select Data Manager Configuration in the P&ID DWG Settings or the Plant 3D DWG Settings.

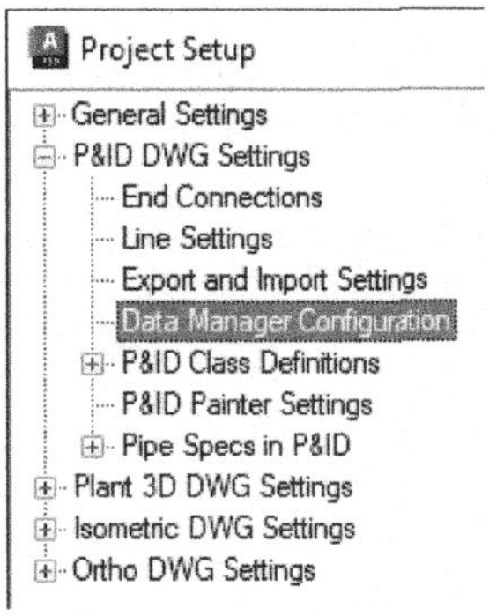

2. Click Create View.

3. Enter a Name and select the Scope of the Data Manager View.

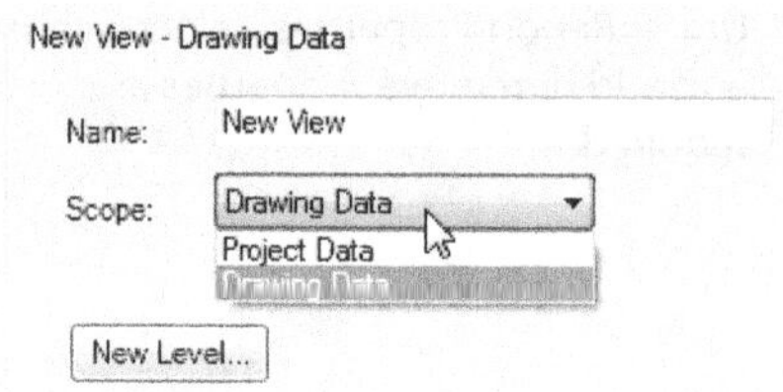

4. Add a level to the customized view. Click New Level. In the Select Class Property dialog box, select a Class and Property for the view. Continue to add levels, as required. Click OK.

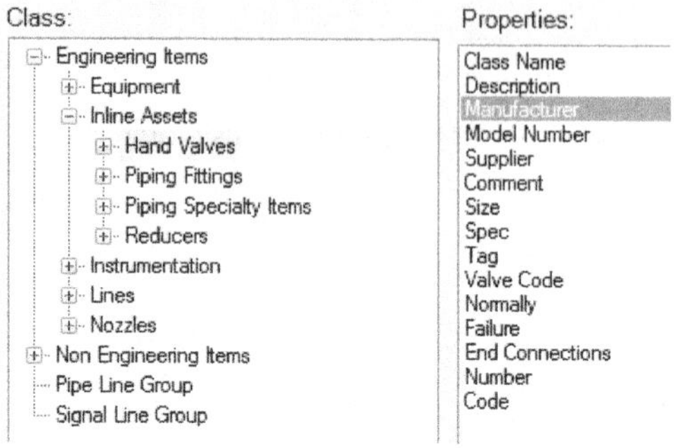

5. Click OK in the Project Setup dialog box to create the new View.

Configuring a Custom Report

Creating a custom report enables you to report on specific components in your design. To create a custom report, you start with one of the default reports supplied and adjust to fit your needs.

Process: Configuring a Custom Report

The following steps give an overview of configuring a custom report based on a default report.

1. In the Project Setup dialog box, expand General Settings and select Reports.

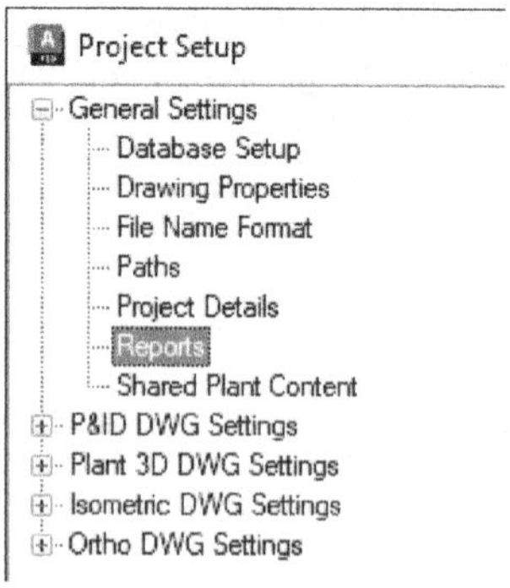

2. Select the default report that best fits your needs.

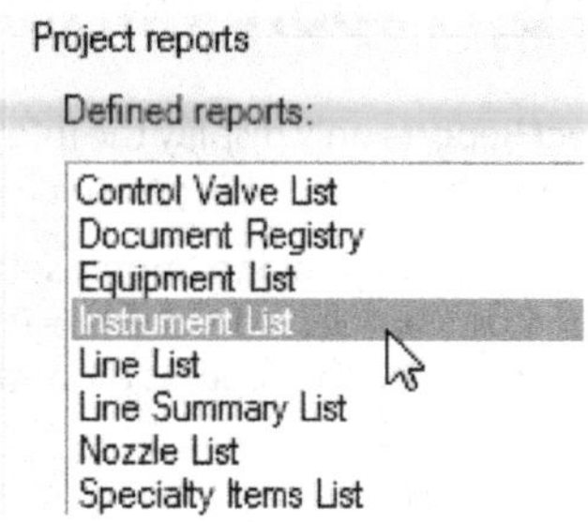

3. Click New. Enter a Name and replace the default tables. Click Continue.

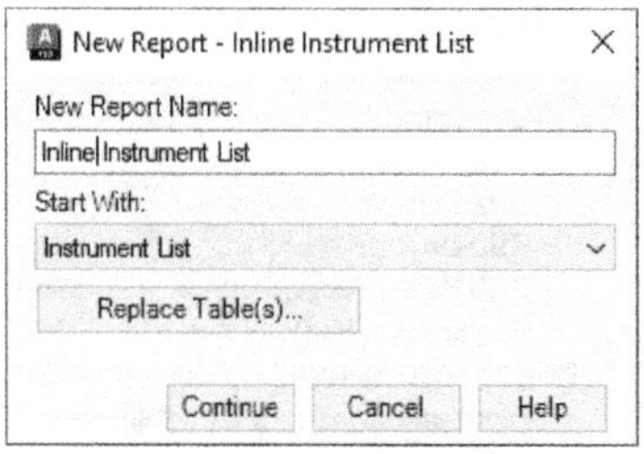

4. Add or remove properties as required.

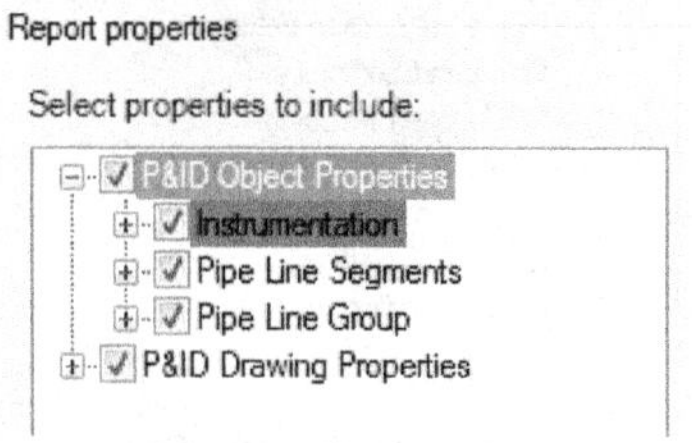

5. Order the properties as required. Click OK.

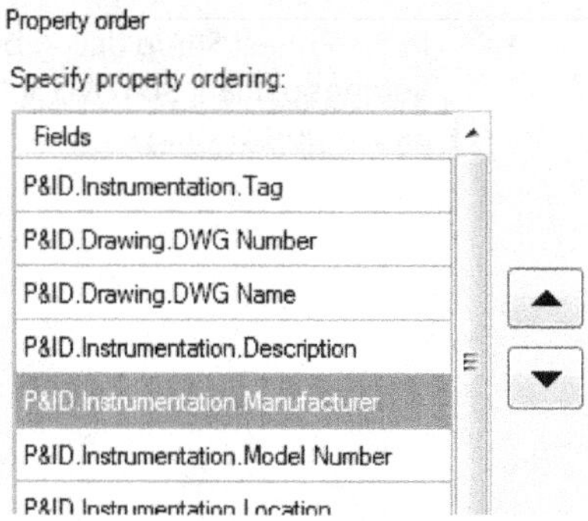

Setting Up Export and Import Settings

Project Reports only display the information based on the class selected. You must use the export and import settings to enable you to create a report based on all the components inside your drawing.

Access to the export and import settings is shown in the following illustration. In the Project Setup dialog box, you expand either the P&ID DWG Settings or Plant 3D DWG Settings to access export and import settings. The process for both products is the same.

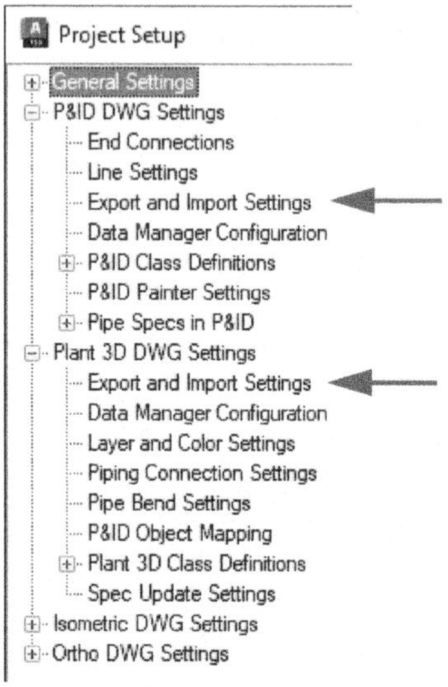

Process: Setting Up Export and Import Settings

1. In the Project Setup dialog box, expand P&ID DWG Settings or Plant 3D DWG Settings and select Export and Import Settings.

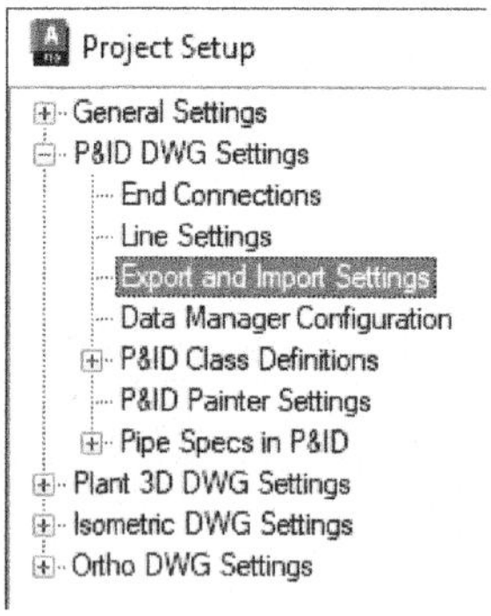

2. Click New.

3. Enter a name and description.

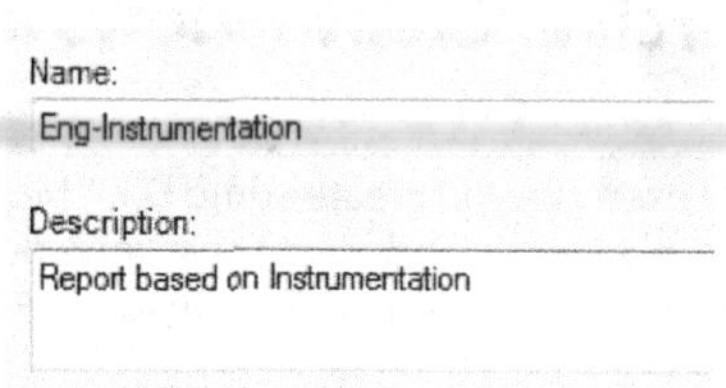

4. Select class(es).

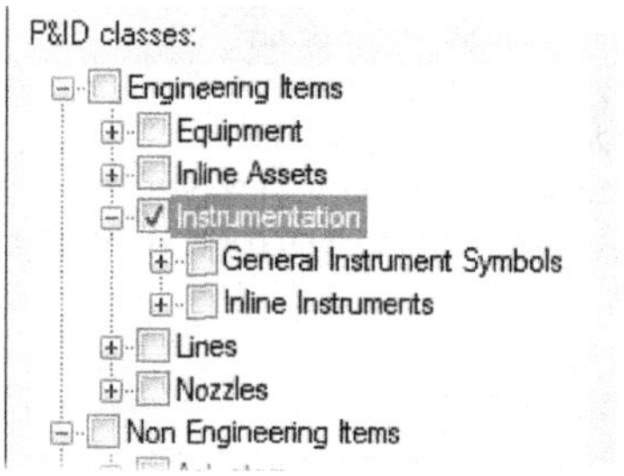

5. Adjust properties as required. Click OK.

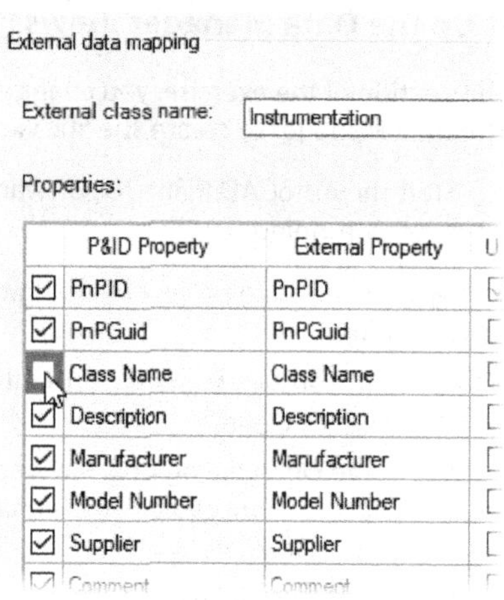

Exercise: Create Views and Manage Reports

In this exercise, you create some Data Manager views and modify and create custom reports, all to be used to export and import Microsoft Excel data.

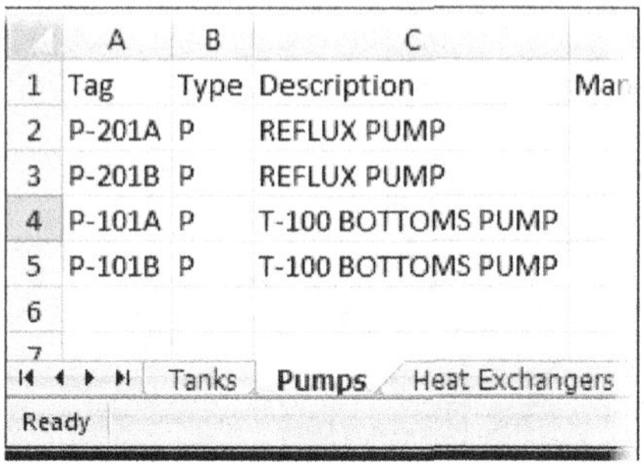

Set Up the Data Manager Views

In this section of the exercise, you change settings in the Data Manager to create specific views.

1. Start the AutoCAD Plant 3D software, if not already running.
2. Open an existing project by doing the following:
   - In the Project Manager, Current Project list, click Open.
   - In the Open dialog box, navigate to the folder *C:\Plant Design 2024 Practice Files\Create Views and Manage Reports.*
   - Select the file *Project.xml.*
   - Click Open.
3. Open an empty AutoCAD drawing by clicking + in the File Tabs bar. Close any of the project drawings if they are open.
4. To open the Data Manager, on the Home tab, Project panel, click Data Manager.
5. Select Project Reports in the drop-down list.

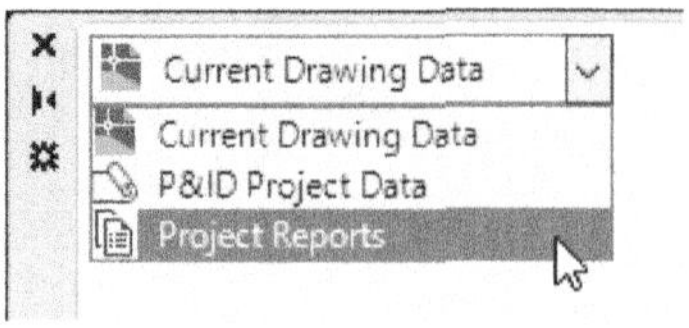

6. In the Project Reports list, click Control Valve List.

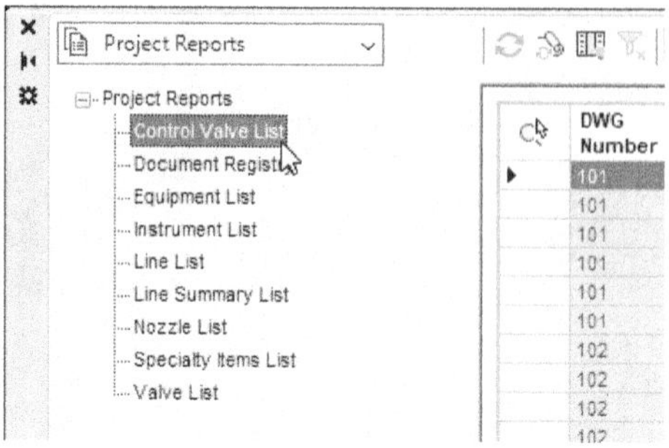

7. Take time to view the standard default report data for this and other Project Reports.

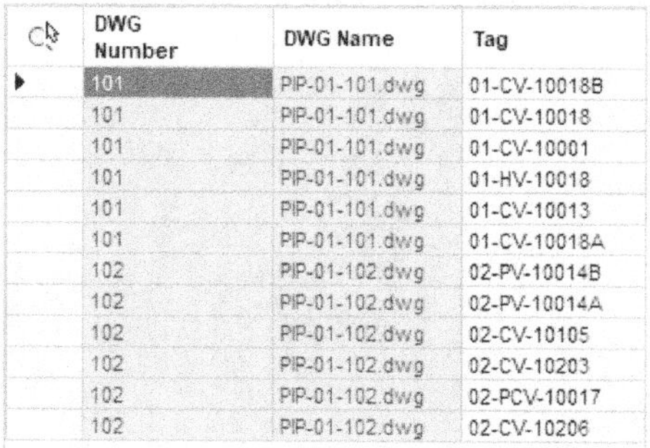

8. From the drop-down list, select P&ID Project Data.

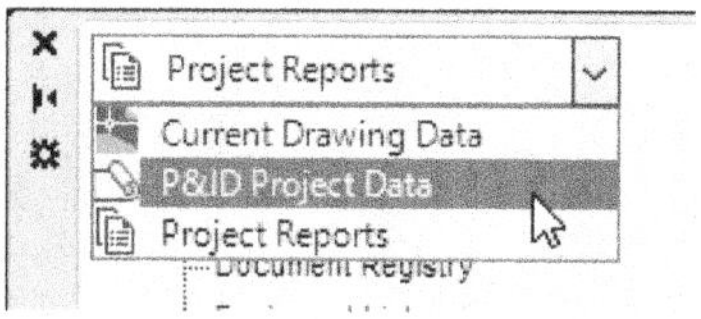

9. To view more detailed information:
   - Click Engineering Items, and click Equipment.
   - Note the rows and columns of data.
   - Expand Equipment, and click Pumps.
   - Note the increased number of columns.

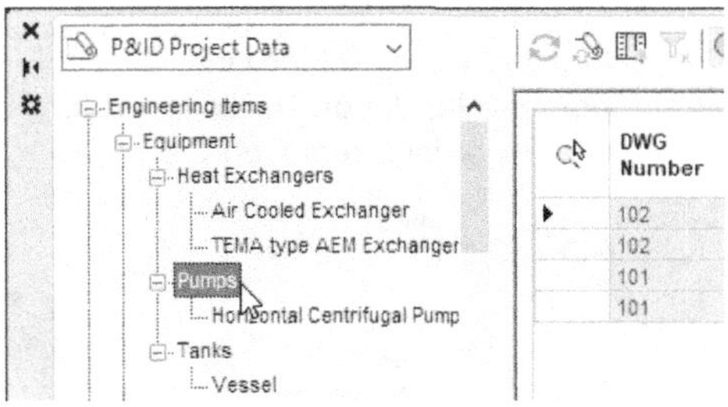

10. Close the Data Manager.

11. Display the Project Setup dialog box:
   - In the Project Manager, right-click on the current project and click Project Setup.
   - Click General Settings, and click Reports.

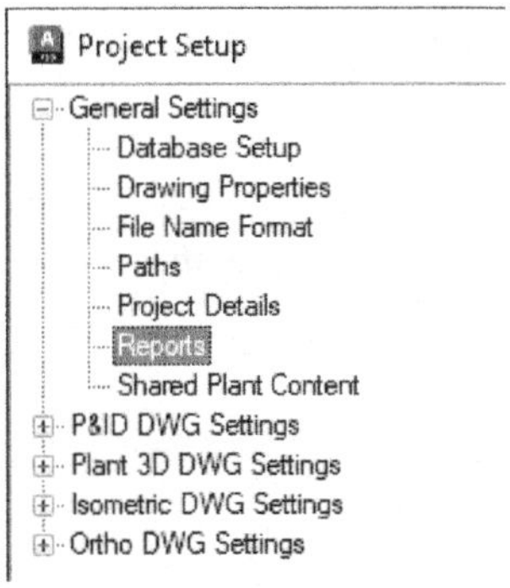

12. Under Project reports>Defined reports, note the list. It is the same list that was displayed in the Data Manager.

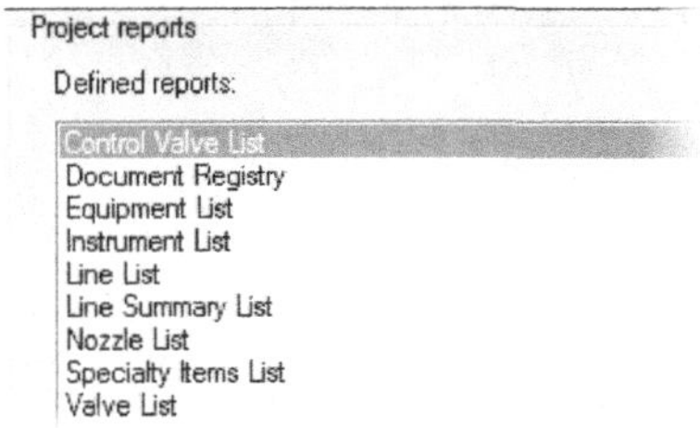

13. To begin to modify a report:
   - In the Defined reports list, click Valve List.
   - Click Modify.

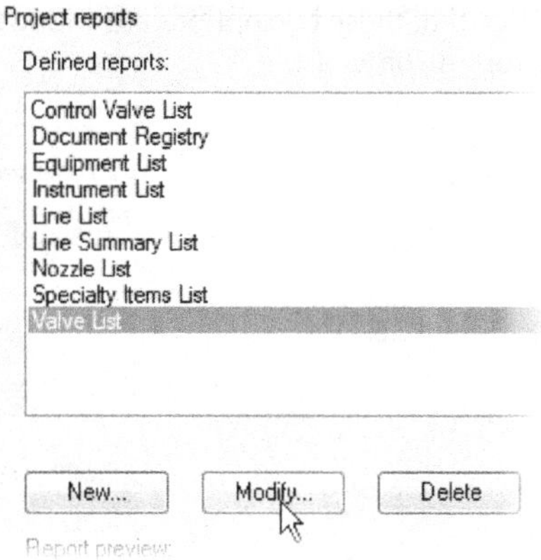

14. In the Modify Report - Valve List dialog box, expand P&ID Object Properties, and expand Hand Valves.

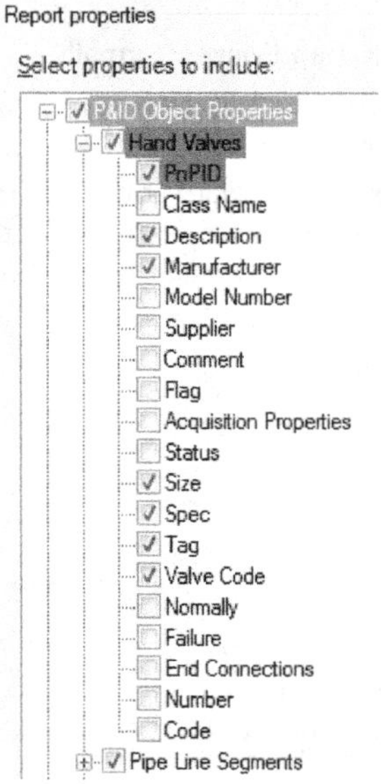

15. To add data to the report:

- Under Hand Valves, check Normally.
- Check Failure.

Note that those two options are added to the Property order list.

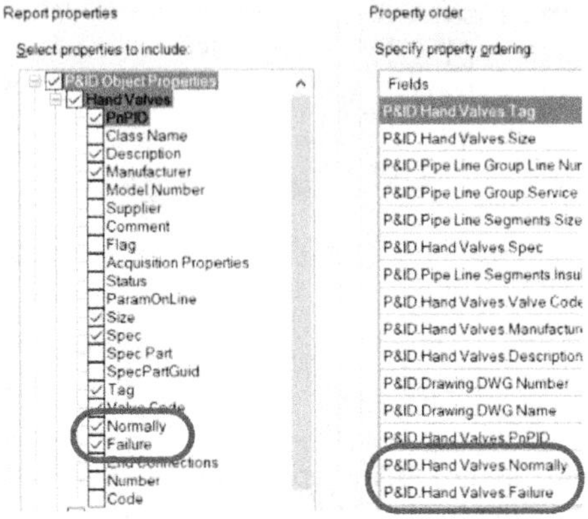

16. To reorder the properties, in the Property order list:

- Click P&ID.Hand Valves.Normally.
- Using <Ctrl>, click P&ID.Hand Valves.Failure.
- Click Move Up (upward arrow) such that both the selected properties are at the location shown in the illustration below.

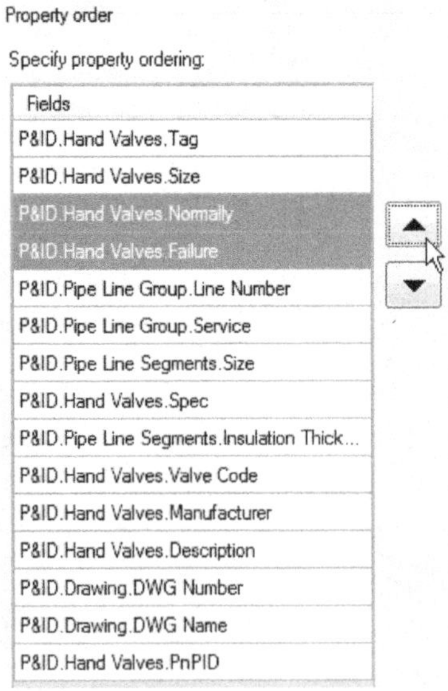

17. To remove a property:

- Under Property order, locate P&ID.Pipe Line Segments.Insulation Thickness.
- Under Report properties, expand Pipe Line Segments.
- Locate Insulation Thickness and clear the checkmark.

Note that the P&ID.Pipe Line Segments.Insulation Thickness under Property order is removed.

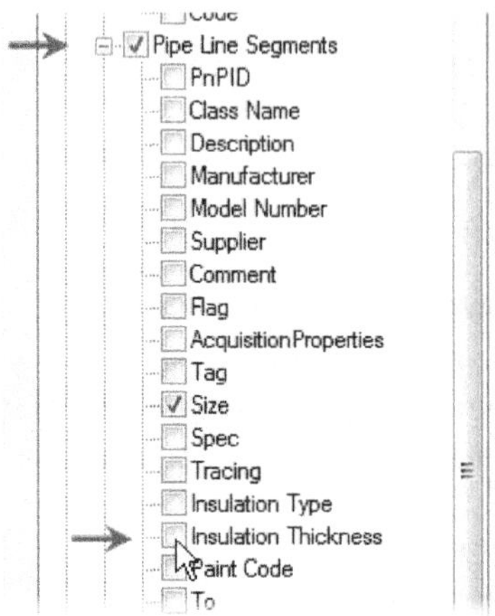

18. In the Modify Report dialog box, click OK. Note the updated display in the modified Valve List report.

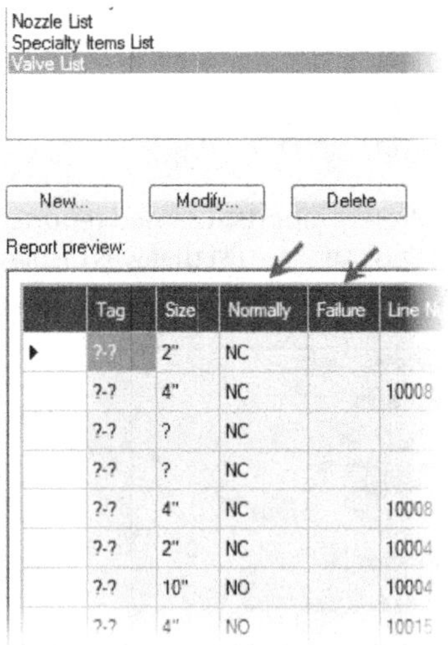

19. To accept the modification, in the Project Setup dialog box, click OK.

20. To view the report in the Data Manager:
    - Open the Data Manager.
    - From the drop-down list, select Project Reports.
    - Under Project Reports, click Valve List and note the Normally and Failure columns have been added.

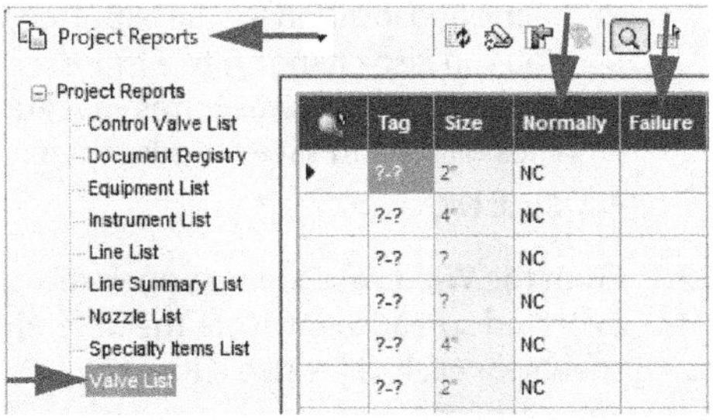

21. Close the Data Manager.

Configure the Data Manager Display

In this section of the exercise, you customize the Data Manager to display specific data.

1. Open the Project Setup dialog box.

2. In the Project Setup dialog box, expand P&ID DWG Settings. Click Data Manager Configuration.

   Note that there are currently no Customized views and the list is empty.

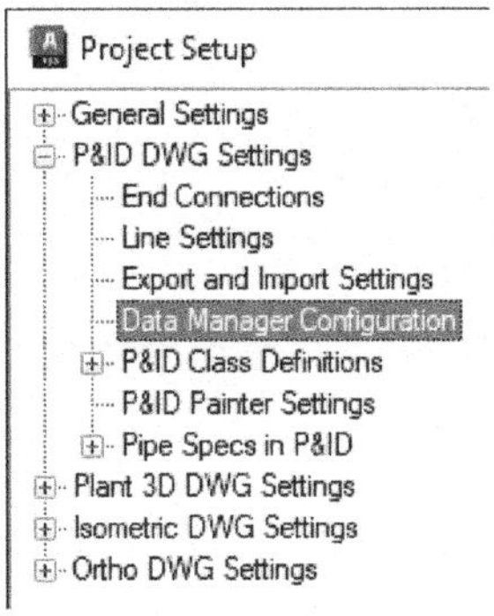

3. To create a new view:
    - Under Customized views, click Create View.
    - For Name, enter **Valve List by Vendor**.
    - For Scope, select Project Data.

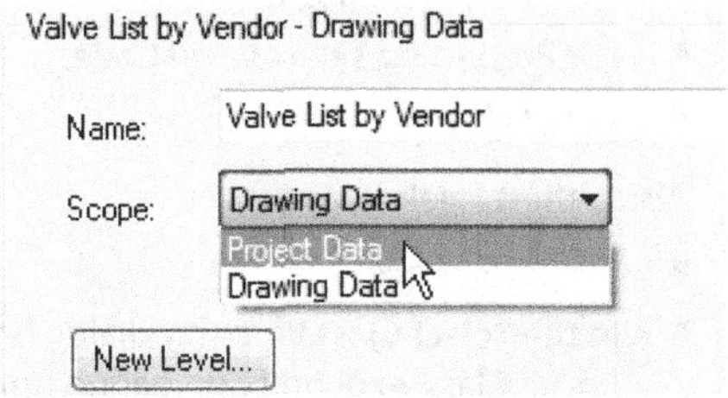

4. Note that the view is added to the Customized views list.

5. To add a level to the customized view:
    - Under Valve List by Vendor - Project Data, click New Level.
    - In the Select Class Property dialog box, under Class, expand Engineering Items, and expand Inline Assets.
    - Click Hand Valves.
    - Under Properties, click Manufacturer.
    - Click OK.

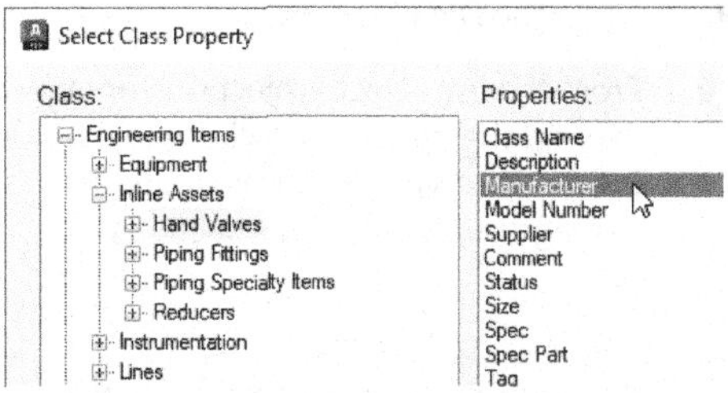

6. Add another level:
   - Click New Level.
   - In the Select Class Property dialog box, under Class, expand Engineering Items and expand Inline Assets.
   - For Class, select Hand Valves.
   - For Properties, select Valve Code.
   - Click OK.
7. Add a third level:
   - Click New Level.
   - In the Select Class Property dialog box, under Class, expand Engineering Items and expand Inline Assets.
   - For Class, select Hand Valves.
   - For Properties, select Size.

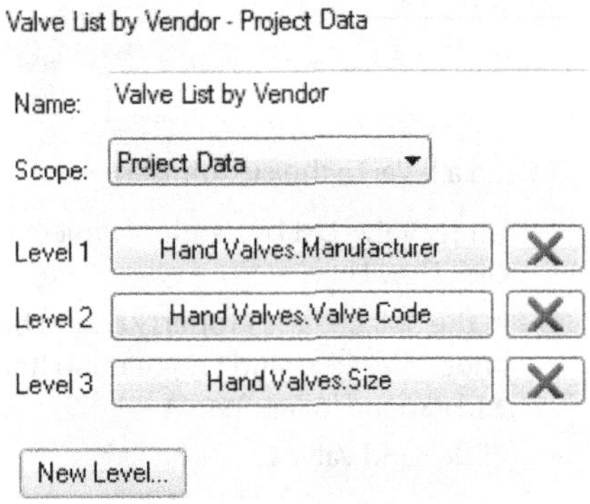

8. In the Project Setup dialog box, click OK.
9. Open the Data Manager.
10. From the list, select Project Custom Views. Expand the options and click the different levels. Observe the display of the Data Manager with different selections.

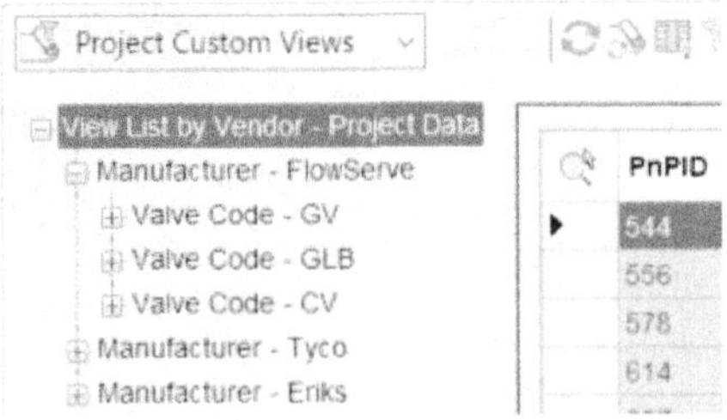

11. To export a custom report:
    - In the Data Manager, with Project Custom Views active, expand Manufacturer - FlowServe.
    - Click Valve Code - GV.
    - On the Data Manager toolbar, click Export. You might need to expand the Data Manager for all the tools in the toolbar to be visible.
    - In the Export Data dialog box, note the name and location for the exported data. You can also change it to a more convenient location, such as your Practice Files folder and save the .xlsx there.
    - Click OK.
12. From the Windows Explorer, open the exported spreadsheet. Note the different sheets for each valve size. Close the spreadsheet.

    Note: The following illustration shows the Size 10 sheet in the spreadsheet.

A	B	C	D
PnPID	Class Name	Description	Manufactu
844	Gate Valve	Gate Valve	FlowServe
898	Gate Valve	Gate Valve	FlowServe
1311	Gate Valve	Gate Valve	FlowServe
1432	Gate Valve	Gate Valve	FlowServe
1790	Gate Valve	Gate Valve	FlowServe
2047	Gate Valve	Gate Valve	FlowServe
2081	Gate Valve	Gate Valve	FlowServe

13. In the software, close the Data Manager.

Configure a Custom Report

In this section of the exercise, you set up a custom report to view a specific component in the project.

1. Open the Project Setup dialog box.
2. Expand General Settings and click Reports.

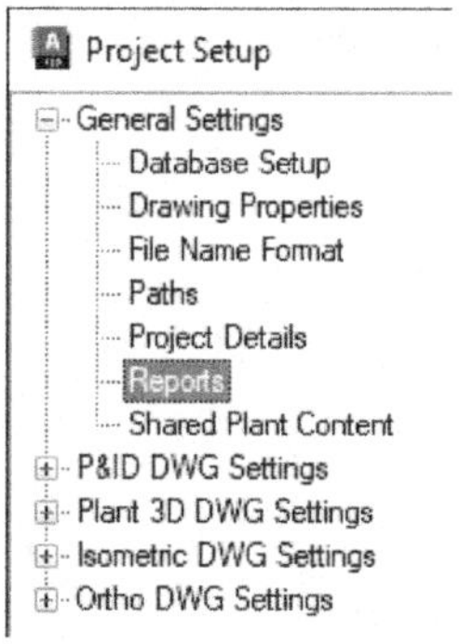

3. In Project reports>Defined reports, click Equipment List.
4. Under the list of defined reports, click New.

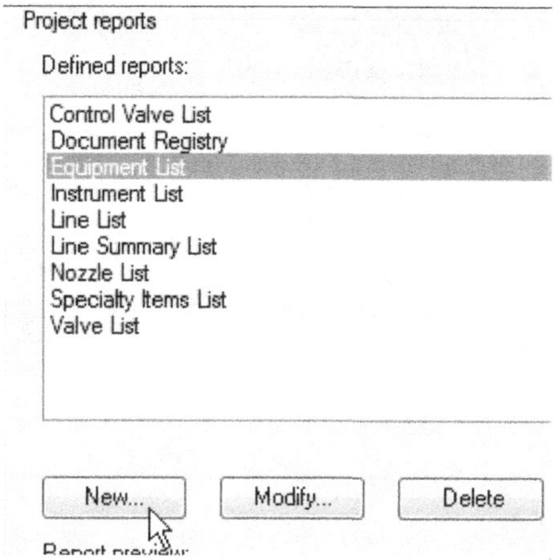

5. To define the new list:
   - In the New Report dialog box, for New Report Name, enter **Pump List**.
   - Click Replace Table(s).
   - In the Replace dialog box, click Equipment.
   - In the Equipment List, select Pumps.
   - Click Continue.
   - In the New Report dialog box, click Continue.

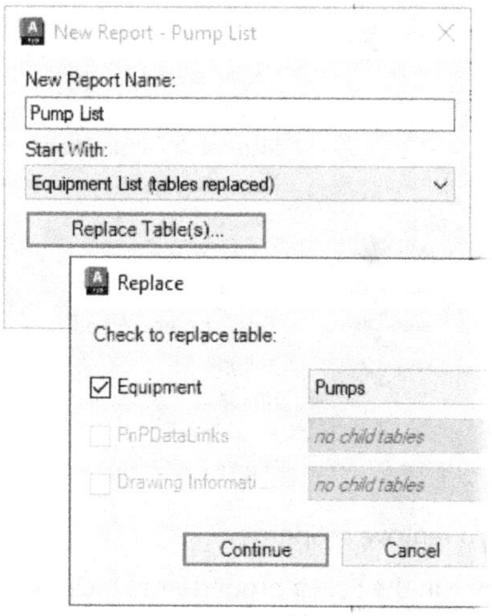

6. To view the newly created report:
   - In the New Report -Pump List dialog box, under Report properties, expand P&ID Object Properties.
   - Expand Pumps.

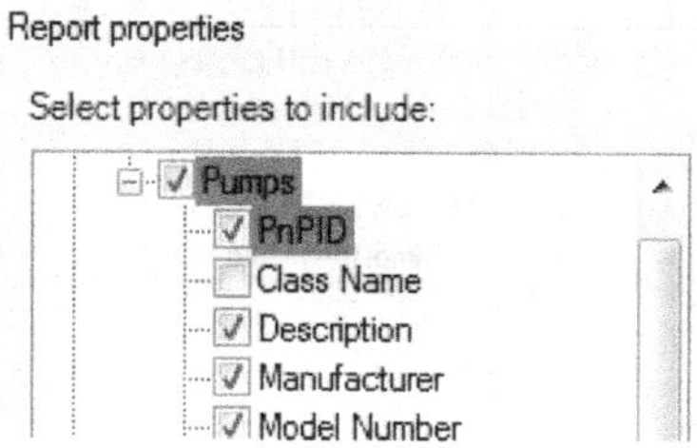

7. To add specific properties to the list, select the properties: Type, Flow Capacity, Power, Total Dynamic Head, and Voltage, as shown in the following illustration.

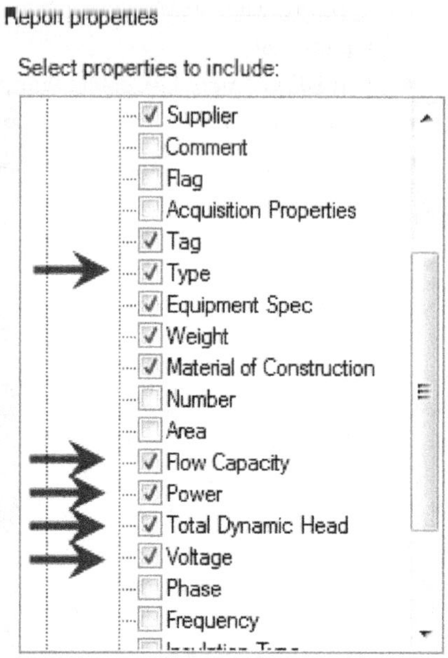

8. To remove properties:

- In the Select properties to include list, expand P&ID Drawing Properties.
- Clear the checkmark for DWG Name.

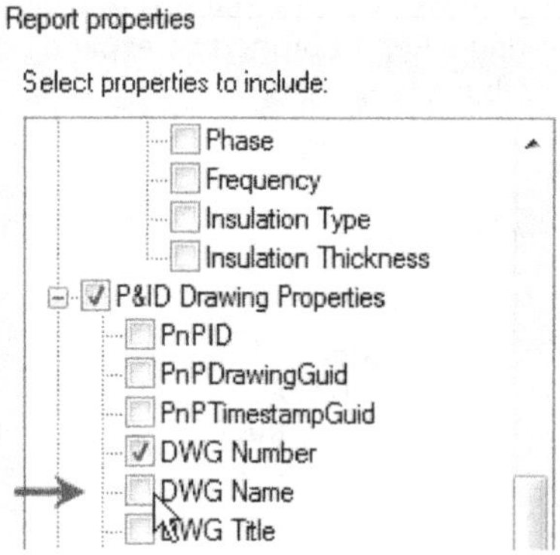

9. To reorder the list:

- Under Property order, select P&ID.Pumps.PnPID.
- Press <Ctrl> and select P&ID.Drawing.DWG.Number.
- Press the down arrow to the right of the list until the two selected properties are at the bottom of the list.
- Click OK.

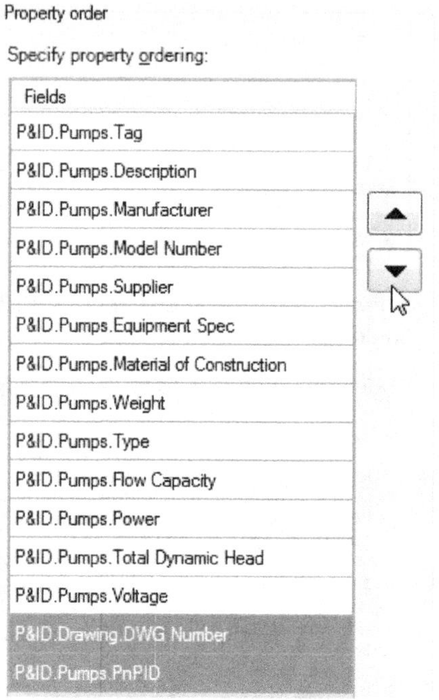

10. In the Defined reports list, note that Pump List is added to the list.

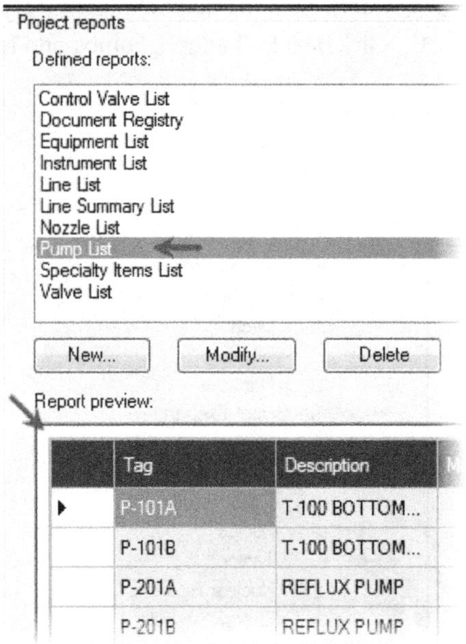

11. In the Project Setup dialog box, click OK.

12. To view the report in the Data Manager:

- Open the Data Manager.
- Select Project Reports.
- Click Pump List.

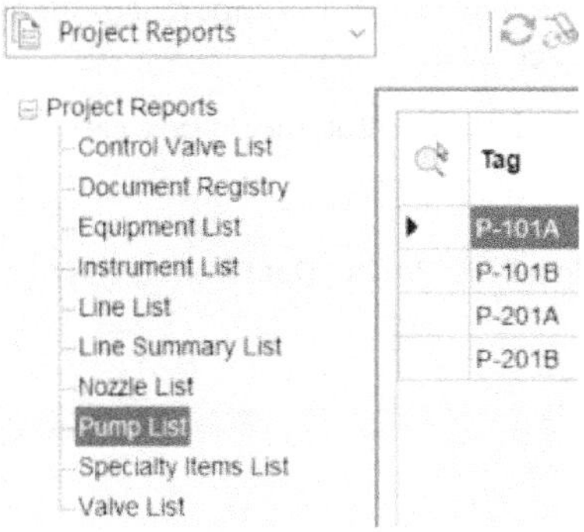

13. Close the Data Manager.

Set Up Import and Export Settings

In this section of the exercise, you set up import and export settings to create a report for all the equipment in the project.

1. Open the Project Setup dialog box.

2. In the Properties list, expand both P&ID DWG Settings and Plant 3D DWG Settings. Note that both headings contain Export and Import Settings. The processes are the same for both classes.

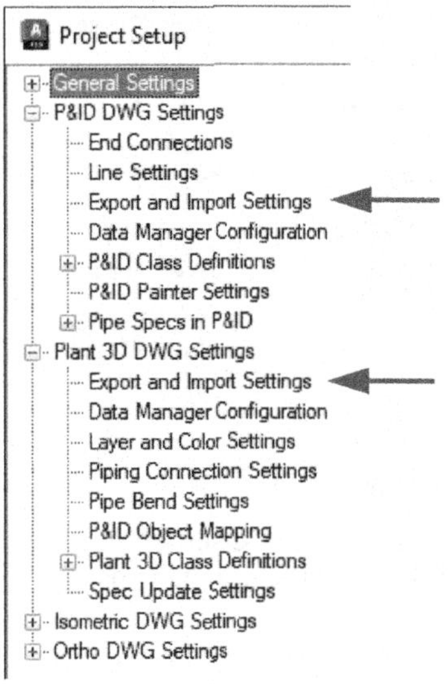

3. To begin to create new settings, under P&ID DWG Settings:

- Click Export and Import Settings.
- Click New.

4. To define the settings:

- For Name, enter **Master Project List**.
- For Description, enter **Shows all components**.

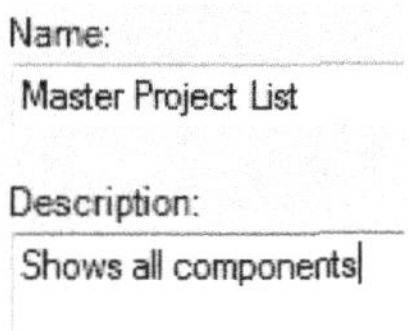

5. To add specific data from a class:
   - Under P&ID classes, click Engineering Items.
   - Under External data mapping, Properties list, check or clear the selections as shown in the following illustration.

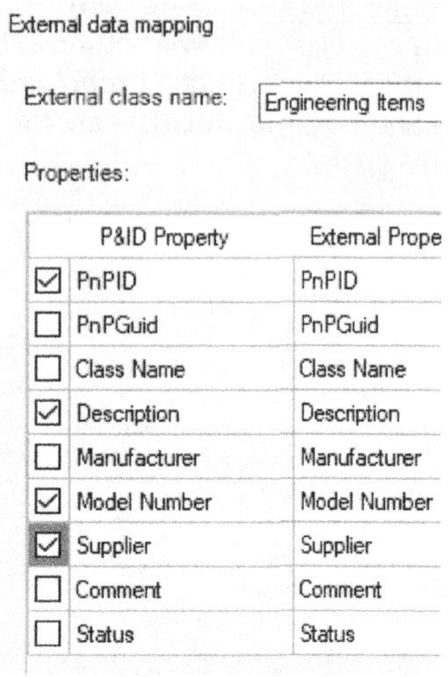

6. To add UID:
   - For the above selected P&ID Properties, click their UID checkmarks as well.

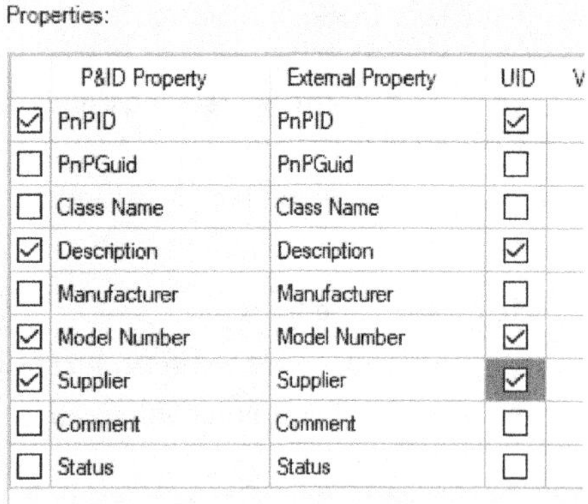

7. To add specific information:
   - Under P&ID classes, under Engineering Items, expand Equipment.
   - Click Heat Exchangers, Pumps, and Tanks.

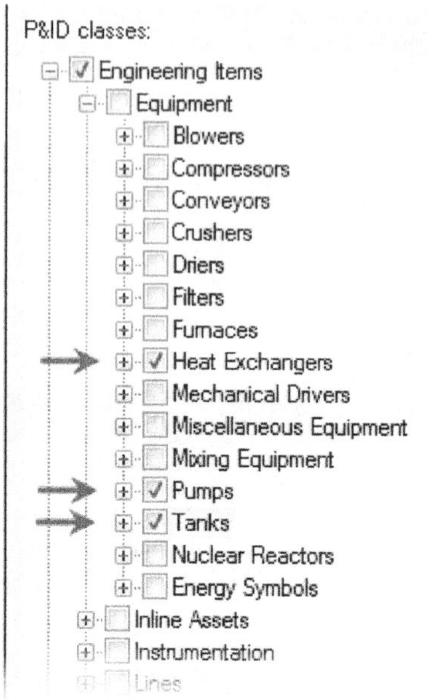

8. Under External data mapping, clear checkmarks for Manufacturer, Comment, Area, Insulation Type, and Insulation Thickness.

9. In the New Export and Import Settings dialog box, click OK.

10. In the Project Setup dialog box, click OK.

11. Open the Data Manager.

12. Select P&ID Project Data from the list.

13. To access the report:

- On the Data Manager toolbar, click Export.
- In the Export Data dialog box, for Select export settings, select Master Project List.
- In the Export Data dialog box, note the name and location for the exported data. You can also change it to a more convenient location, such as your Practice Files folder.
- Leave the name as is and note it.
- Click OK.

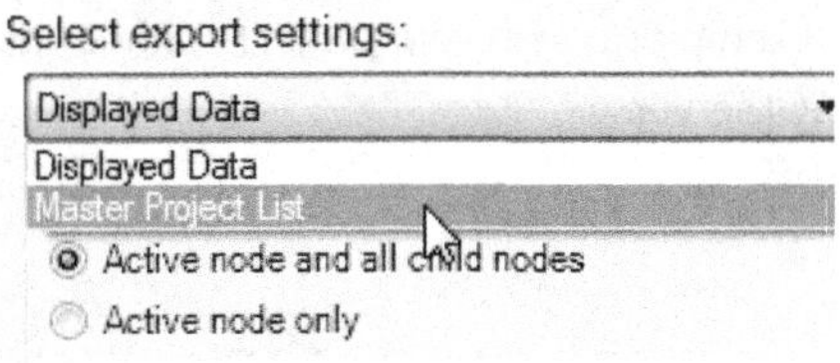

14. Using Windows Explorer, open the exported spreadsheet. Review the document. Note the different tabs created. Close the spreadsheet.

Note: The following illustration shows the Pumps sheet in the spreadsheet.

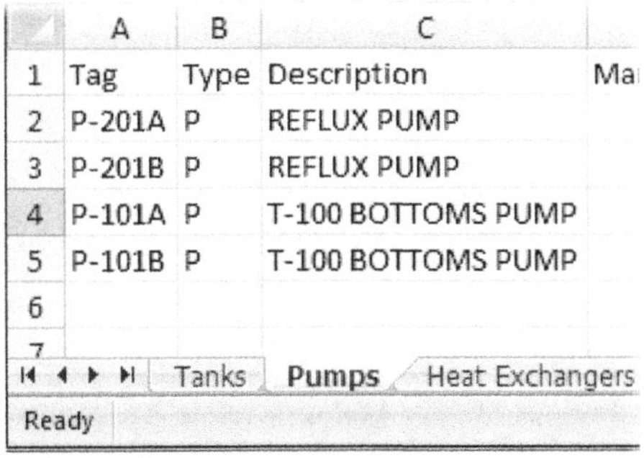

	A	B	C	
1	Tag	Type	Description	Ma
2	P-201A	P	REFLUX PUMP	
3	P-201B	P	REFLUX PUMP	
4	P-101A	P	T-100 BOTTOMS PUMP	
5	P-101B	P	T-100 BOTTOMS PUMP	
6				

15. Close the Data Manager.

16. Close the project.

Lesson Review Questions

1. A difference between a Data Manager view and a report is that reports only show one specific class, while the Data Manager view can show multiple classes.
   a. True
   b. False
2. Is it possible to add drawing and project information to your reports?
   a. Yes, but you have to enter the values manually.
   b. Yes. All information, drawings, project, and class can be part of a report.
   c. No, only class information can be shown.
3. Can you set up an export in such a way that multiple classes are exported at the same time?
   a. You can do this using the import and export setup option in your project configuration.
   b. This can only be done if you use Microsoft SQLserver.
   c. No, this cannot be done.

Lesson: Creating and Editing Drawing Templates and Data Attributes

Overview

In this lesson, you create a template that uses AutoCAD Plant 3D and P&ID layers and properties to drive information in a title block.

Objectives

After completing this lesson, you will be able to:

- Describe how property fields are used in title blocks.
- Explain how to create custom properties.
- State the process to change a template from the standard AutoCAD software to the AutoCAD Plant 3D software and AutoCAD P&ID software.
- Create a new template for the AutoCAD Plant 3D software and AutoCAD P&ID software.

About Property Fields

Projects and drawings have several properties that can be used to drive text in a title block. This is very similar to using block attributes in the standard AutoCAD software, except in this case, the fields are dynamic in nature, and their values update when the properties of the project or drawing change. In the following example, the project description field is used to drive the text in the title block. Any changes made to the value for the project description in the project properties are reflected in the title block of the drawings.

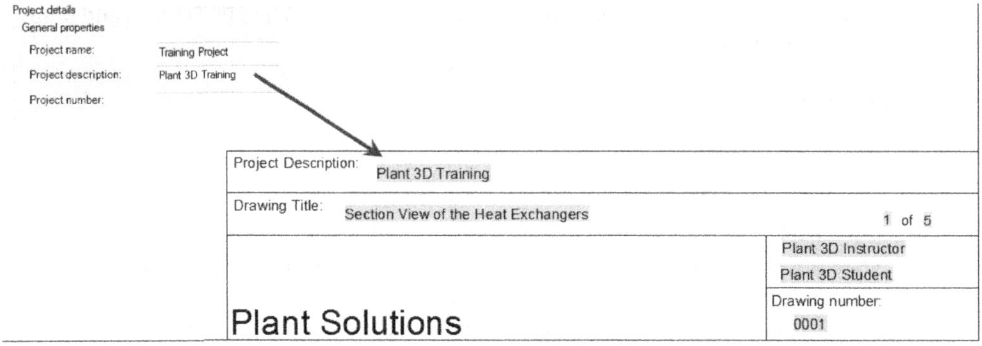

Project Properties and Drawing Properties

When a project property is used in a field, every drawing in the project that uses that field is populated with the same text. This is a common scenario, as most of the time the same template and the same title block values are used in a project. Because of this, you can dynamically update all the drawings in a project by changing only the property definition value in the project properties.

Drawing properties are specific to each drawing. When you enter drawing properties that are mapped to fields in that drawing, other drawings in the project are not affected. A title block can contain fields that are driven by both project and drawing properties. This enables a rich and sophisticated system of annotation that dynamically drives the information in the drawings.

There are two different ways of having project or drawing properties display in a drawing. You can insert a standard field that uses the property or you can configure a block attribute to use a field. The main difference between the two is if you want to override the property value. By creating a block attribute with a default field value from a project or drawing property, you can have the value in the block display the project or drawing property or you can override the value in the block. When you override the attribute value, that block attribute no longer uses a field.

When configuring a block attribute to use a field, you specify it as part of its default value. You specify the property for the field similar to when you directly insert a field.

Custom Properties

By default, there are several properties, such as project and drawing descriptions, that you can use in both the project and the drawings in the project. You can also create custom property categories and fields in those categories for both the project and the drawings. In this way, any information that you want to drive in the titles of the drawings can be created and mapped into fields in the templates. For example, a custom category called Additional Project Information has been added to the project, as shown in the following illustration. The values in the two rows can be used to drive text in the project drawings.

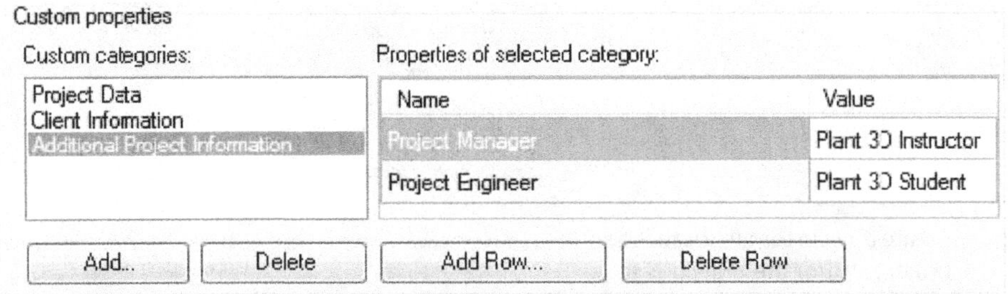

Custom Drawing Properties Behavior

When you create custom project properties, you enter the values once, or make changes to the values, as required. These values are used as the single source of values to populate the fields for all the drawings in the project. On the other hand, when you create custom drawing properties, you essentially create fields in the Drawing Properties dialog box that you then populate individually for each drawing. For example, the Drawing Information is a custom category, and Sheet and Total Sheets are rows in that category, as shown in the following illustration.

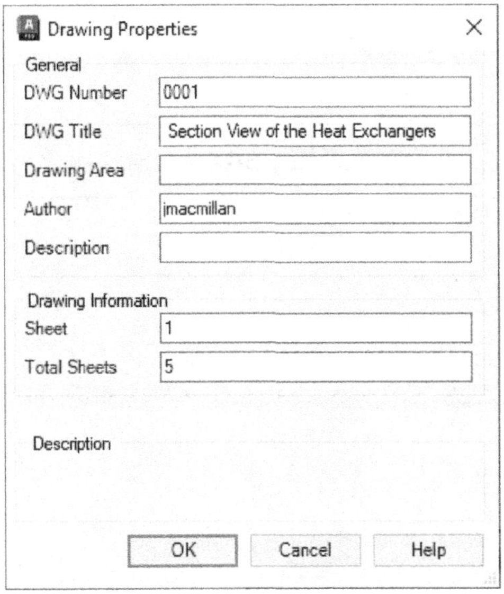

Process of Moving AutoCAD Templates to Plant 3D Templates

In many cases, you might have company templates that have been in use for some time and are well designed specifically for your purposes. In these cases, the process to change these over is fairly straightforward.

1. Use Design Center to add Plant 3D-specific layers.

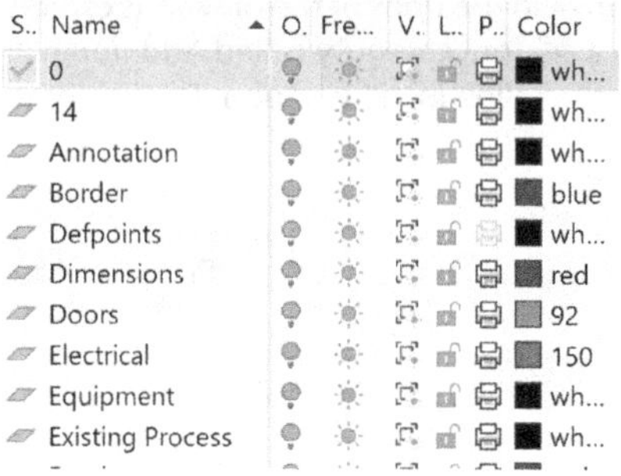

2. Create any custom fields for the project and/or the drawings to match the information you have used in the past.

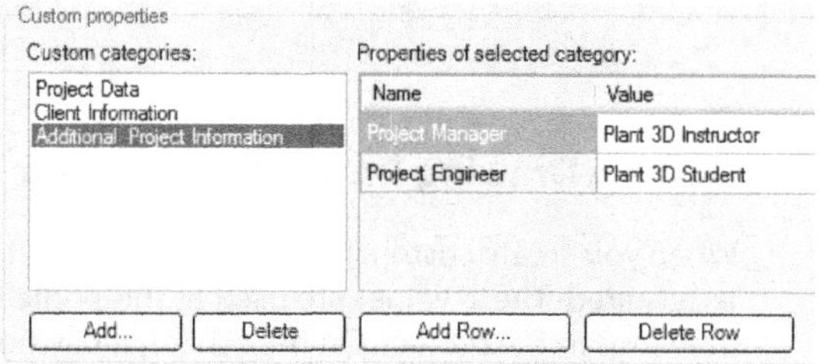

3. In your existing template, delete the existing block attribute tags.

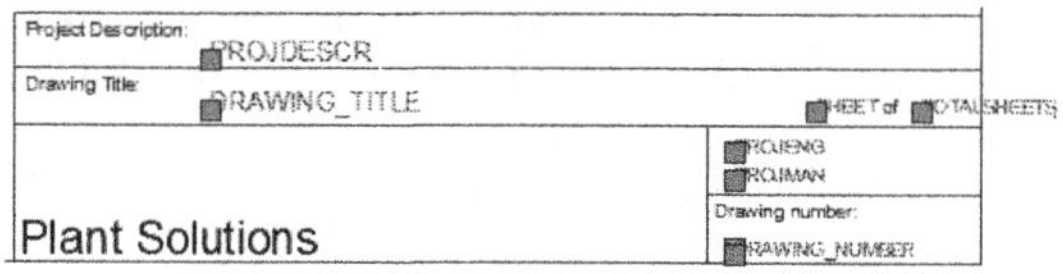

4. Replace the tags with fields from the project.

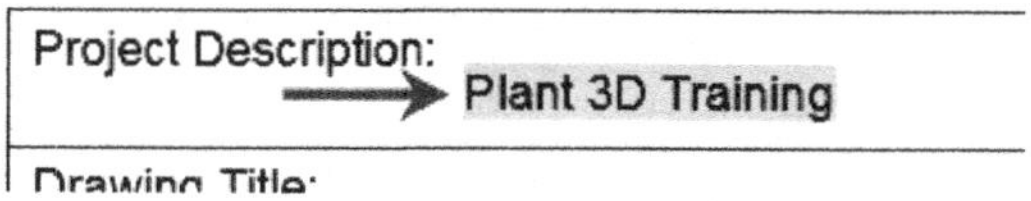

Exercise: Create a Template for AutoCAD Plant 3D

In this exercise, you start with a typical template and make changes to convert the template for Plant 3D. You will:

- Add Layers.
- Create custom properties. Edit the existing attributes.
- Edit the existing attributes.
- Add fields.

Open an Existing Template and Add Layers

In this section of the exercise, you open a drawing that might be a typical template used in a company for standard AutoCAD drawings. You examine the title block content, and add new layers specific to the AutoCAD P&ID software and the AutoCAD Plant 3D software.

1. Start the AutoCAD Plant 3D software, if not already running.
2. Open an existing project by doing the following:
   - In the Project Manager, Current Project list, click Open.
   - In the Open dialog box, navigate to the folder *C:\Plant Design 2024 Practice Files\Create and Set Up a Border with Title Block.*
   - Select the file *Project.xml.*
   - Click Open.
3. Open *D Layout (template source).dwg.*
   - On the Quick Access Toolbar, click Open.
   - Navigate to the folder *C:\Plant Design 2024 Practice Files\Create and Set Up a Border with Title Block\Past Company Templates.*
   - Select *D Layout (template source).dwg.*
   - Click Open.
4. Examine the contents of the title block and existing layers in the drawing.

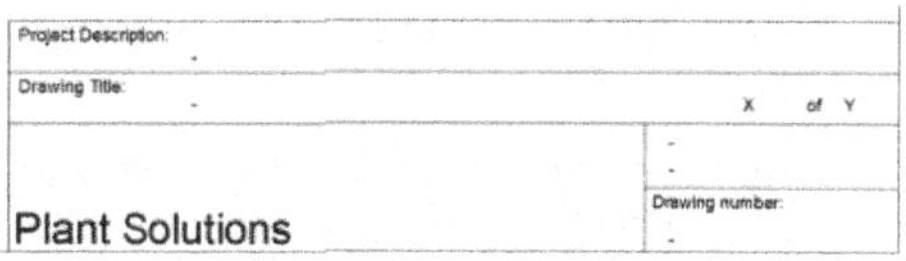

5. To import additional layers, on the View tab, on the Palettes panel, click Design Center.
6. On the Design Center, Folders tab, navigate to *C:\Plant Design 2024 Practice Files\Create and Set Up a Border with Title Block.*
7. Expand the *projSymbolStyle.dwg* drawing. Select Layers.

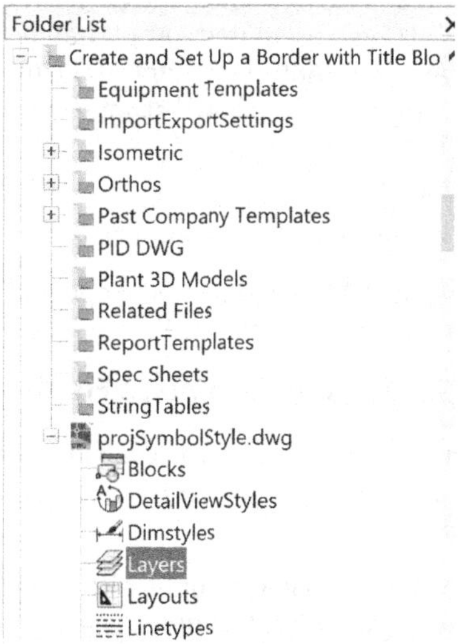

8. In the layer list, select all the layers and drag and drop them onto the drawing screen.

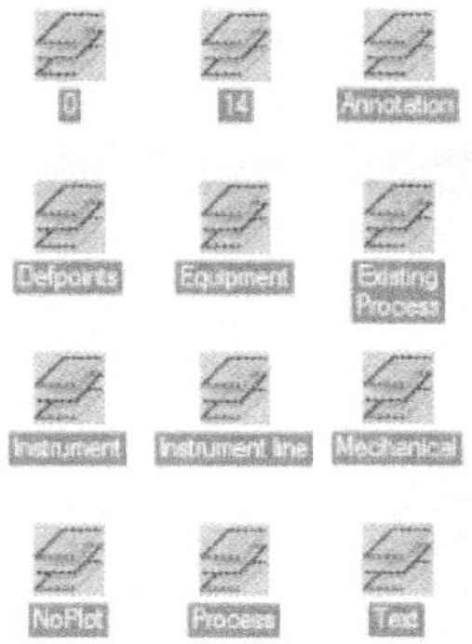

9. Close Design Center.

10. Open the Layer Properties Manager and examine the new layers in the drawing. Close the Layer Properties Manager.

    At this point, you could set the bylayer properties, such as color, etc.

11. To save the drawing as a template in the default templates folder, do the following:

    - On the Application menu, expand Save As, and click Drawing Template.
    - In the Save Drawing As dialog box, Files of type list, ensure that AutoCAD Drawing Template (*.dwt) is selected.
    - For File Name, enter **P3D D**. Note the default file location (generally, C:\Users\<username>\AppData\Local\Autodesk\Autodesk AutoCAD Plant 3D <release>\<Revision>\<Language>\Template).
    - Click Save.
    - In the Template Options dialog, click OK.

12. Leave the **P3D D.dwt** template open for the next section of the exercise.

Project Settings for Template Fields

In this section of the exercise, you examine existing fields and add custom fields that can be used in the title block.

1. In the Project Manager, right-click on the project. Click Project Setup.

2. In the Project Setup dialog box, under General Settings, click Project Details.

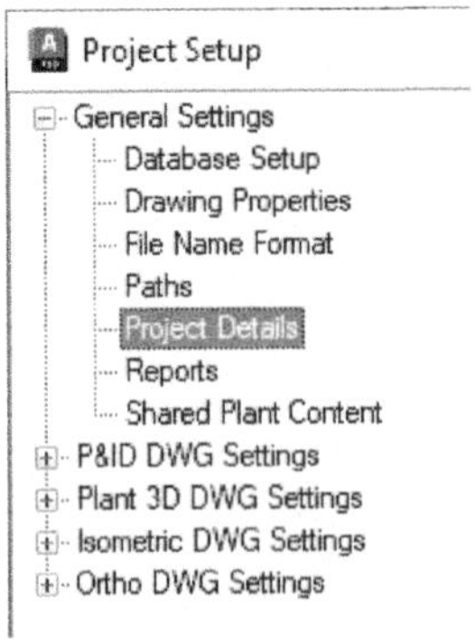

3. In the Project details, in the Project description, enter **Plant 3D Training**.

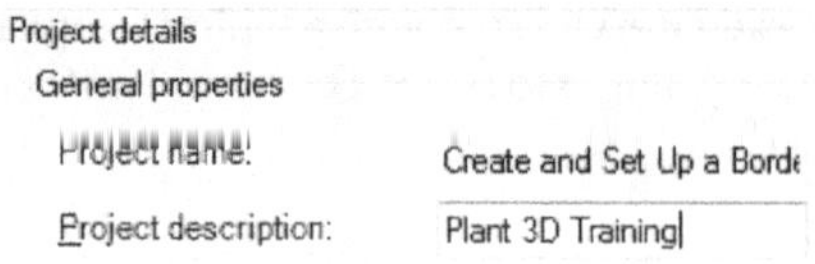

4. Under Custom properties, click Add.

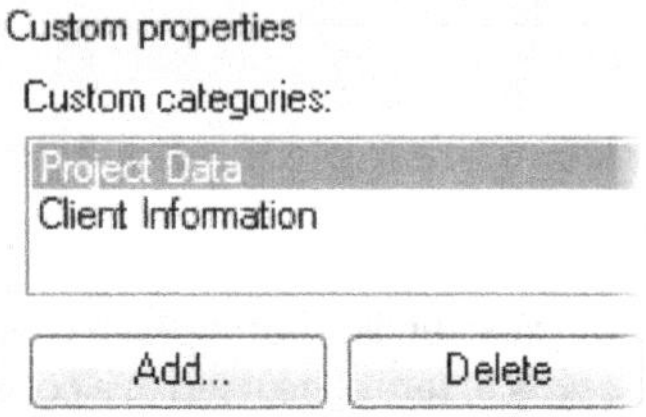

5. In the Add Category dialog box:

   - Enter **Additional Project Information**.
   - Click OK.

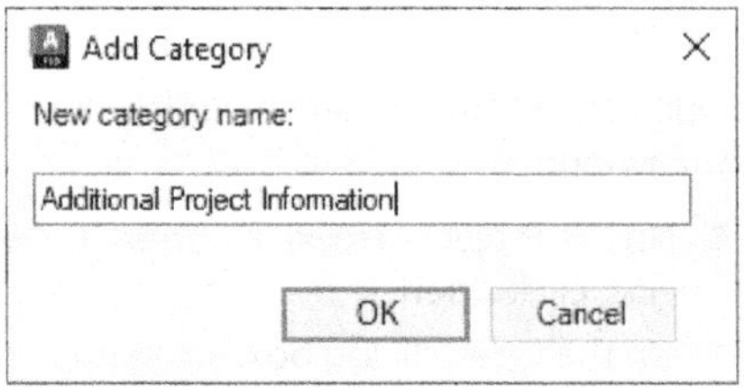

6. With Additional Project Information selected under Custom categories, click Add Row.

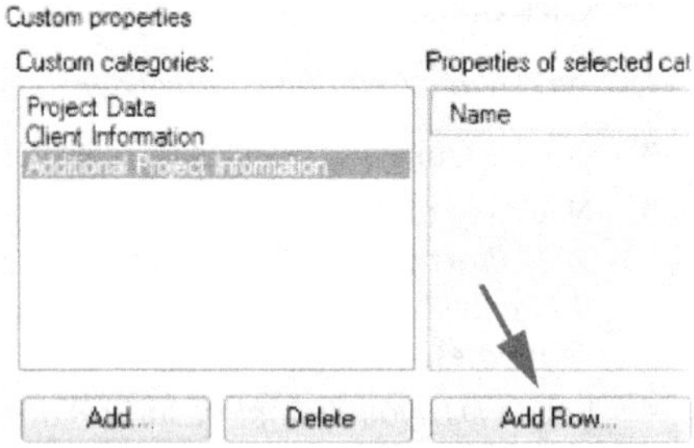

7. In the Add Row dialog box:
   - For Name, enter **Project Manager**.
   - For Value, enter **Plant 3D Instructor**.
   - Click OK.

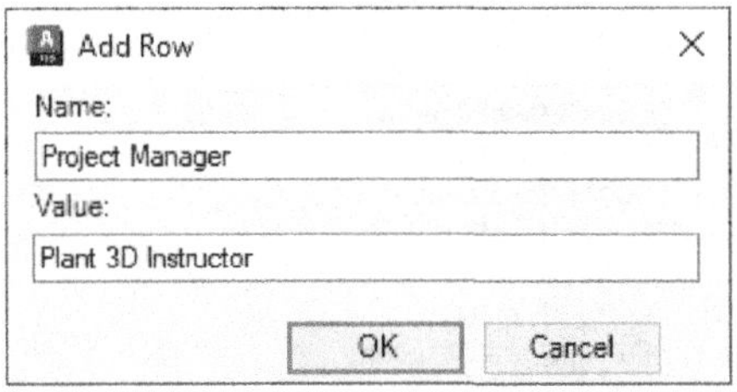

8. Add a second row with the following values:
   - Click Add Row.
   - Name: **Project Engineer**.
   - Value: **Plant 3D Student**.
   - Click OK.

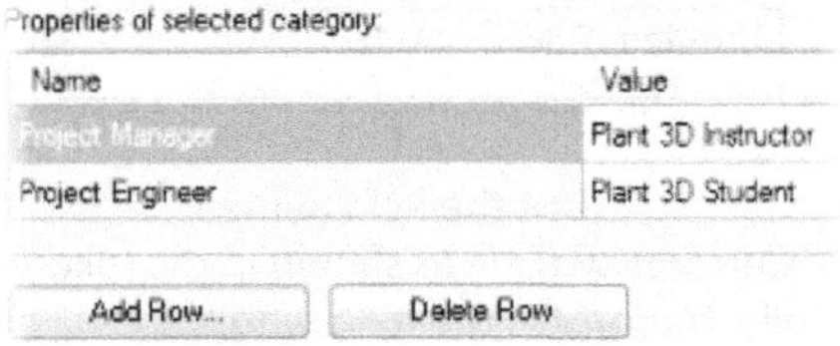

9. Under General Settings, click Drawing Properties.

10. On the Drawing properties page, click Add.

11. In the Add Category dialog box, enter **Drawing Information**. Click OK.

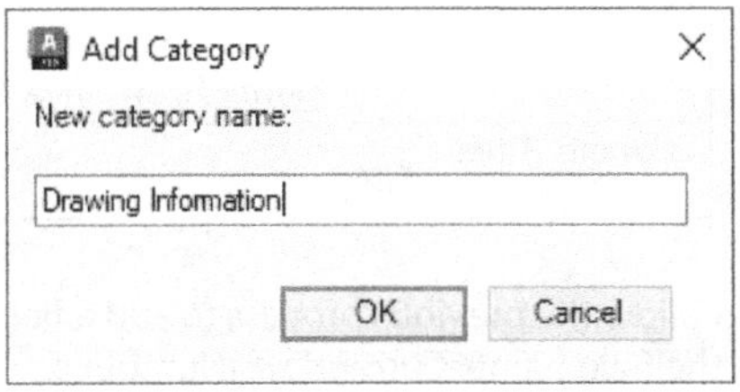

12. Add a row to the Drawing Information category with the following values:
   - Click Add Row.
   - Name: **Sheet**.
   - Description: **Enter the sheet number**.
   - Click OK.

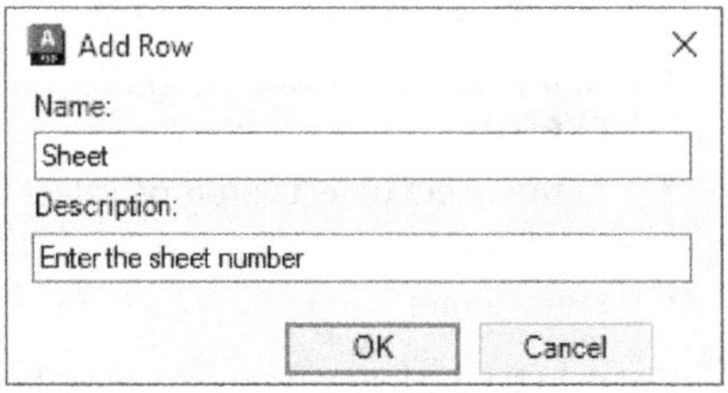

13. Add a second row with these values:
   - Name: **Total Sheets**.
   - Description: **Enter the total number of sheets**.

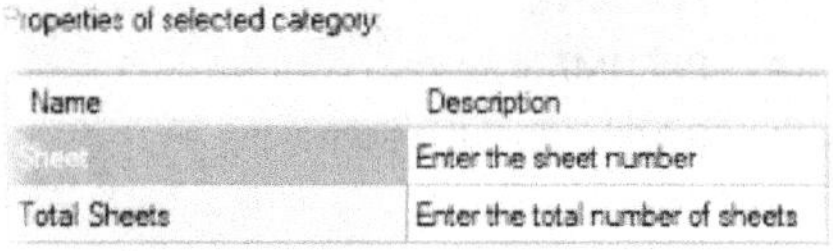

14. In the General Settings, click Paths.

15. To set the template and path as defaults, under P&ID, for the Drawing template file, select the P3D D template that you saved in the last section of the exercise.

    (For example, C:\Users\<username>\Local\Autodesk\Autodesk AutoCAD Plant 3D <release>\<Revision>\<Language>\Template)

16. In the Project Setup dialog box, click Apply. Click OK.

Insert Fields in the Title Block

In this section of the exercise, you replace existing attributes with fields from the project and drawing properties.

1. You should be in the **P3D D.dwt** template. To fully purge the old attributes, you explode the existing block. To explode the existing block:
   - At the command prompt, enter **EXPLODE**.
   - At the select objects prompt, select the title block.
   - Press <Enter>.
2. Zoom in on the lower right corner of the titleblock.
3. Delete all of the existing attribute tags:
   - PROJDESCR
   - DRAWING_TITLE
   - PROJENG
   - PROJMAN
   - DRAWING_NUMBER
   - SHEET
   - TOTALSHEETS

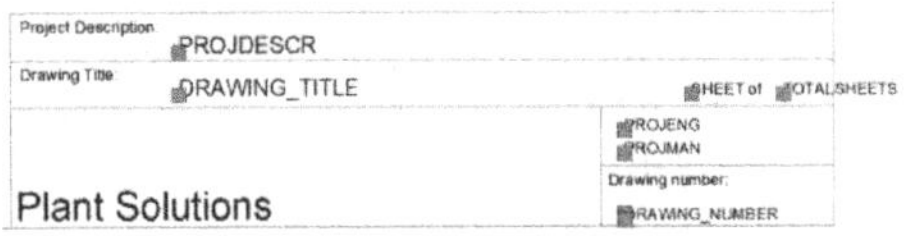

4. To begin adding fields to the new block, on the Insert tab, on the Data panel, click Field.

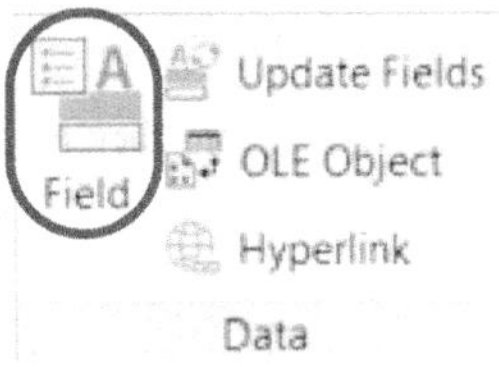

5. In the Field dialog box:
   - For Field category, select Project.
   - For Field names, select CurrentProjectDescription.
   - Click OK.

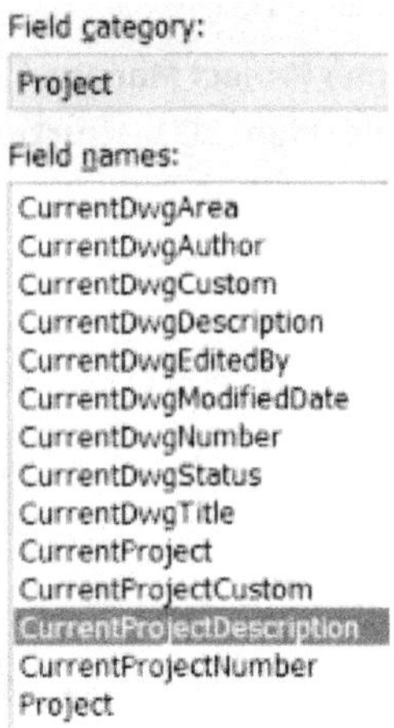

6. Place the field in the title block as shown in the following illustration.

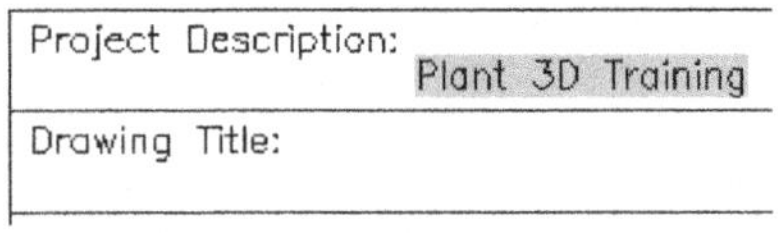

7. Add a field for the field name CurrentDwgTitle as shown in the following illustration. Do the following:
   - On the Insert tab, on the Data panel, click Field.
   - For Field names, select CurrentDwgTitle.
   - Click OK.
   - Place the field in the title block as shown in the illustration.

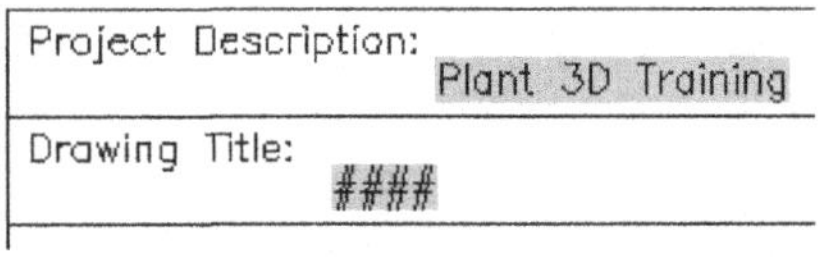

8. Follow the previous process to add a field for the field name, CurrentDwgNumber as shown in the following illustration.

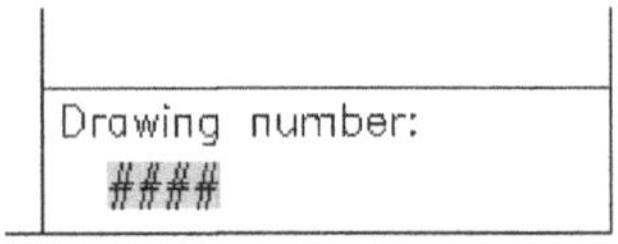

9. To begin to add a field for the custom project properties, on the Data panel, click Field.

10. In the Field dialog box:

- For Field names, select CurrentProjectCustom.
- For Custom property category, select Additional Project Information.
- For Custom property name, select Project Manager.
- Click OK.

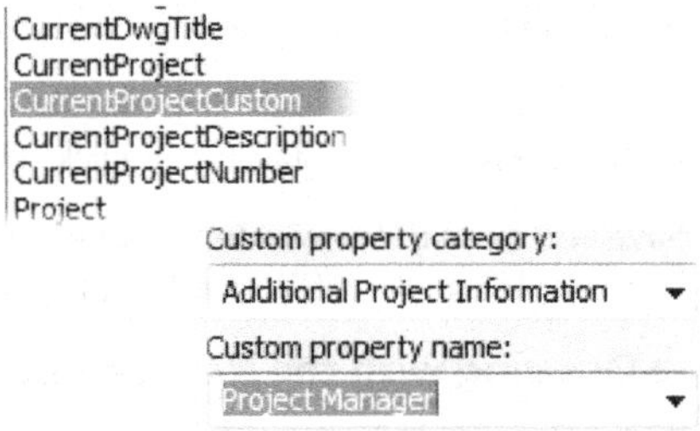

11. Place the field in the title block as shown in the following illustration.

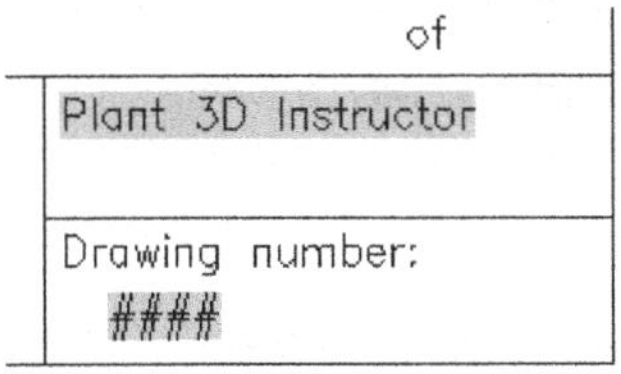

12. Follow the previous process to add a field for the Project Engineer custom project property as shown in the following illustration.

- Field names: CurrentProjectCustom.
- Custom property category: Additional Project Information.
- Custom property name: Project Engineer.

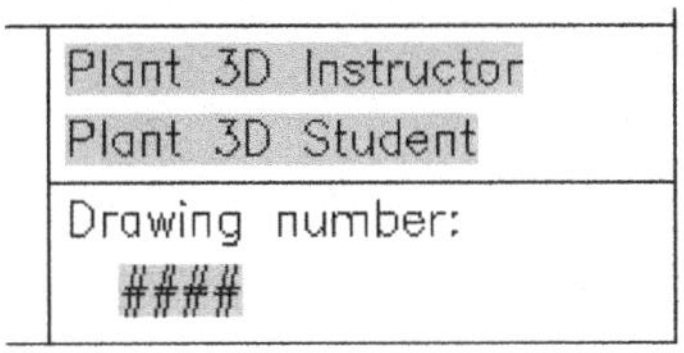

13. To begin to add an attribute with a field to a custom drawing property, on the Insert tab, on the Block Definition panel, click Define Attributes.

14. In the Attribute Definition dialog box:

- Tag field, enter **SheetNo**.
- Prompt field, enter **Sheet number**.

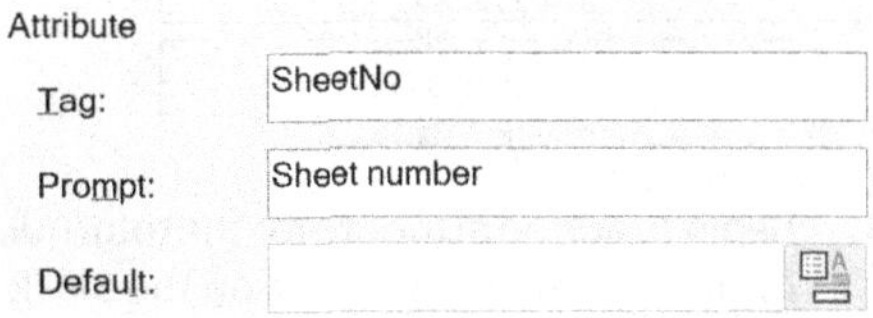

15. To the right of the Default field, click Insert Field.

16. In the Field dialog box:

- For Field names, click CurrentDwgCustom.
- In the Custom property category list, select Drawing Information.
- In the Custom property name list, select Sheet.
- Click OK.

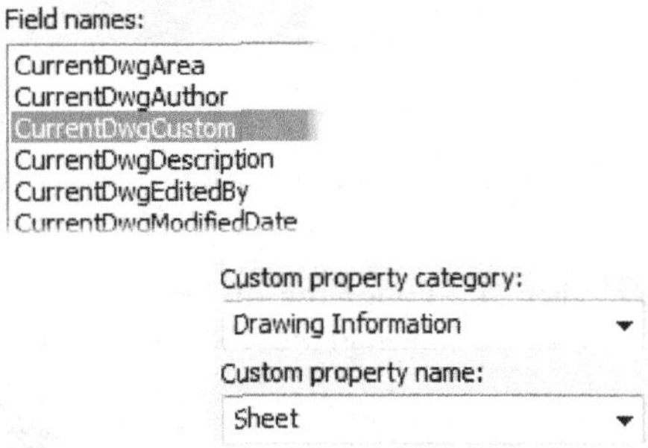

17. In the Attribute Definition dialog box:

- In the Text Settings area, Justification list, verify Left is selected.
- Click OK.
- Place the attribute in the title block as shown in the following illustration.

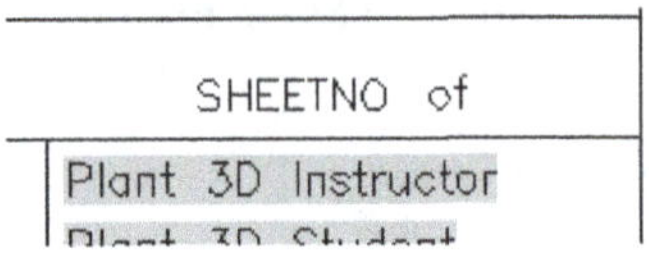

18. Begin to add an attribute for the total number of sheets, on the Insert tab, on the Block Definition panel, click Define Attributes.

19. In the Attribute Definition dialog box:

- Tag field, enter **TotalSheets**.
- Prompt field, enter **Total sheet count**.
- Default field, select Insert Field.
- Field names: CurrentDwgCustom.
- Custom property category: Drawing Information.
- Custom property name: Total Sheets.
- Click OK.

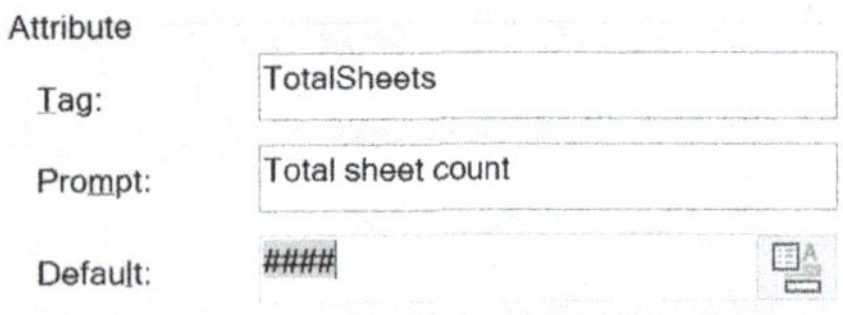

20. Click OK. Position the attribute in the title block as shown in the following illustration.

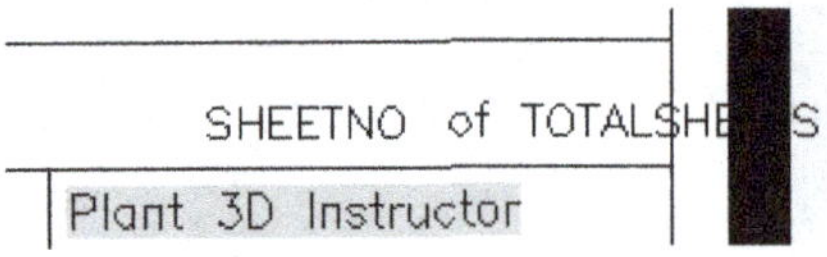

21. Review the fields and attributes added to the title block. It now displays as shown in the following illustration.

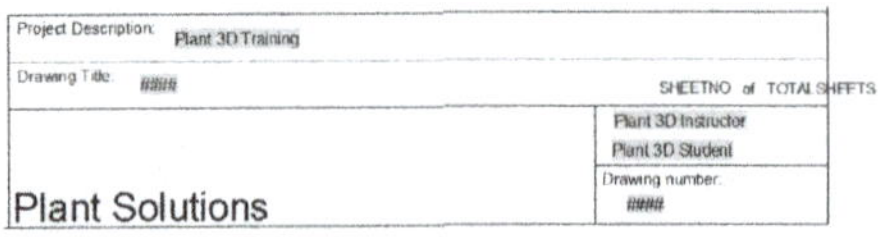

22. To begin to recreate the block of the border and title block, on the command prompt, enter **BLOCK**.

23. In the Block Definition dialog box:

- For Name, select Tblock-D.
- Under Objects, click Select objects.
- At the Select objects prompt, enter **All**.
- Press <Enter> after all the objects are selected.
- Click OK.

24. In the Blocks - Redefine Block dialog box, click Redefine.

25. In the Edit Attributes dialog box, click OK.

26. Save and close the template. Select AutoCAD Drawing Template (*.DWT) as File of type.

Start a Drawing with the New Template

In this section of the exercise, you start a new drawing using the template that you created in this exercise and make changes to some of the properties.

1. In the Project Manager:

- Right-click on P&ID Drawings.
- Click New Drawing.

2. In the New DWG dialog box:

- For File Name, enter **0001**.
- Ensure that the new P3D D template is set as the default DWG template. If not, browse and open it.
- Click OK.

3. In the Project Manager:

- Right-click on the 0001 drawing.
- Click Properties.

4. In the Drawing Properties dialog box:

- For DWG Number, enter **0001**.
- Scroll down to the Drawing Information area.
- For Sheet, enter **1**.
- For Total Sheets, enter **5**.
- Click OK.

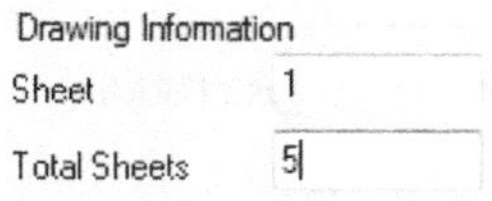

5. In the drawing, verify that all fields are now populated with the new values. If required, update the fields by selecting the title block and clicking Update Fields in the Insert tab>Data panel.

6. To change the value of a field for a custom drawing property:

- In the Project Manager, right-click on the 0001 drawing.
- Click Properties.

7. In the Drawing Properties dialog box:

- For DWG Title, enter **Section View of the Heat Exchangers**.
- Click OK.

8. Verify that the drawing title in the title block was updated to reflect the new value. Update the field if required.

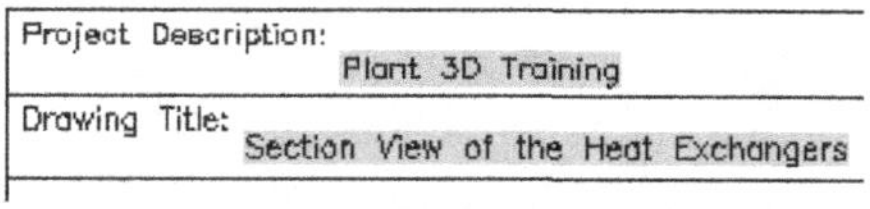

9. To override the total sheet attribute that is currently driven by the field value:

- In the drawing, double-click on a line in the title block.
- In the Enhanced Attribute Editor dialog box, with the attribute TOTALSHEETS selected, in the Value field, enter **3**.
- Click OK. The title block values now display, as shown in the following illustration.

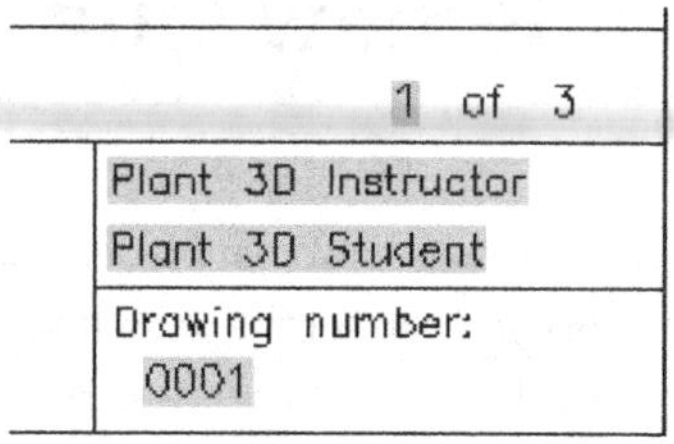

10. To begin to change the title block text for a field that displays custom project information, in the Project Manager, right-click on the current project. Click Project Setup.

11. In the Project Setup dialog box:

- Under General Settings, select Project Details.
- In the Custom properties area, Custom categories, select Additional Project Information.
- In the Project Manager field, change the Value to **Autodesk Instructor**.
- Click Apply and OK.

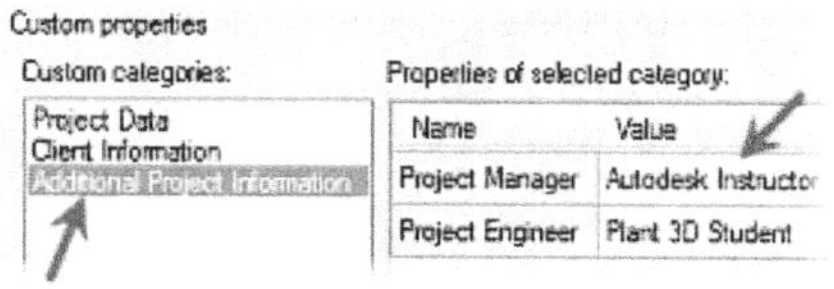

12. Review the values in the title block. The Project Manager name has updated as shown in the following illustration. Update the field if required.

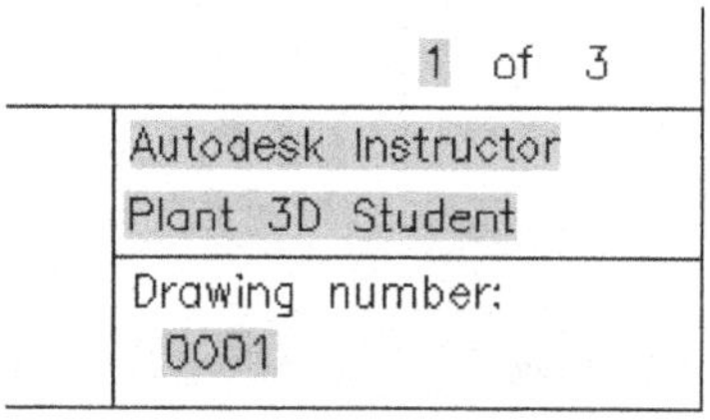

13. Save and close all drawings.

Lesson Review Questions

1. Can you use a combination of attributes with fields?
   a. Yes, you can set the default value of an attribute to use field information.
   b. Yes, but the field needs to be part of the same block as the attribute.
   c. No, fields and attributes are totally different functionalities.
2. What is a benefit of combining attributes with fields?
   a. There is no real benefit, attributes and fields are completely different ways of adding information to your drawing.
   b. When combining attributes with fields, you get the maximum flexibility of both options. You can pick up any information from the project and drawing properties, and can overwrite this data when necessary.
3. What is the big difference between using project and drawing properties?
   a. The property types are the same, but they have different names.
   b. Project properties can appear on each drawing, using the same value over and over, while drawing properties can differ from drawing to drawing.
   c. Project properties and drawing properties cannot be used at the same time.
4. Custom project properties are populated once and are the same for all drawings in the project while custom drawing properties are populated individually for each drawing.
   a. True
   b. False

Lesson: Specs and Catalogs

Overview

This lesson describes the basic concept of the spec and catalog editor. You learn the techniques required to edit and create your own specs and to create and duplicate components to build your own components. You also learn how to change a spec configuration in an existing project and update that project's 3D models.

Objectives

After completing this lesson, you will be able to:

- Describe the uses of the spec and branch table editors.
- Explain the process for editing parts.
- Describe catalogs and how to use the catalog editor to customize them.

Spec Editor

You use the Spec Editor to view and edit spec sheets and catalogs, as shown in the following illustration. You can also convert AutoPlant or CADworx specs to Plant3D specs.

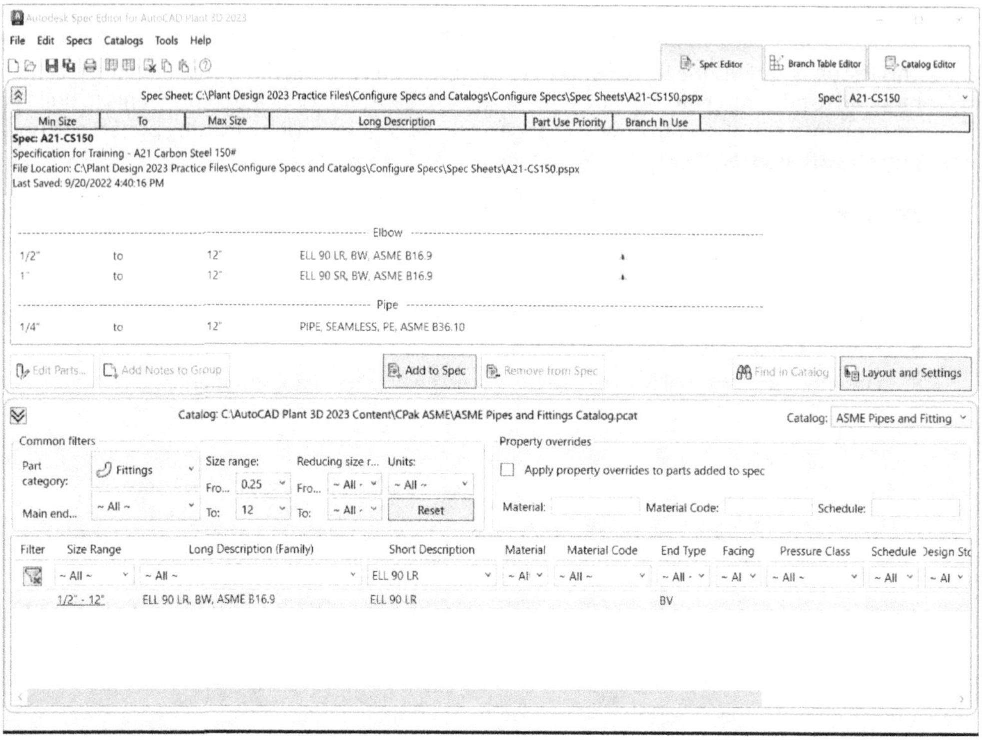

Spec Sheets

When you open a spec sheet, you see a list of components that you can use while routing, as shown in the following illustration. The components are listed in groups. Equipment cannot be included in a spec. When more than one of the same size component is listed, you can specify which one has the highest priority; that is, which one is used most often. The green dot next to the part indicates that the part has a priority assigned.

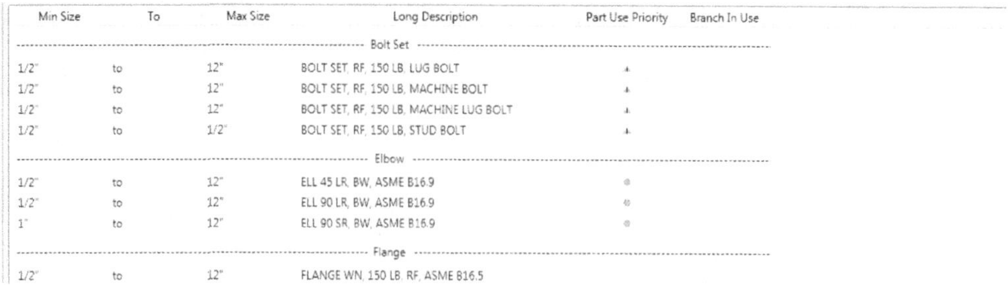

Spec Sheet Naming

When you create a new project using the AutoCAD Plant 3D software, several spec sheets are created by default. They are named with specific codes that indicate what components are contained in the spec sheet.

The US Standard spec sheets are named with codes as follows: CS150, SS300

- CS - Carbon Steel
- SS - Stainless Steel
- 150, 300 - Pressure Class, measured in pounds. The higher number can handle higher pressure and temperatures.

The European Standard spec sheets are named with codes as follows: 2HC01, 16HS01

- HC - High Carbon
- HS - High Stainless Steel
- 2, 16, etc. - Pressure Class

Branch Table Editor

A green checkmark next to the part in the Spec Editor indicates that the part is also listed in the branch table. You use the branch table to determine which branch fittings are used when connecting a branch in the AutoCAD Plant 3D software, as shown in the following illustration.

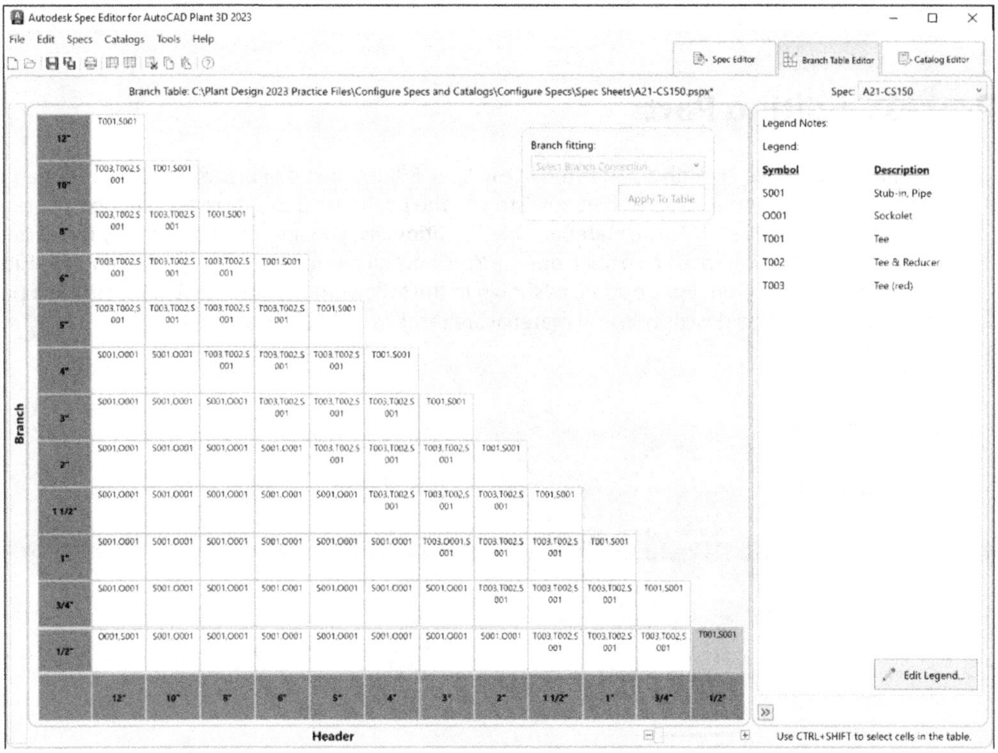

You edit the legend using the settings in the Branch Table Setup dialog box, as shown in the following illustration. You open the dialog box using Edit Legend below the legend in the Branch Table Editor. If you try to assign connections to branches that are not possible, you receive a warning message with the option of selecting the valid branch fitting(s) for the sizes.

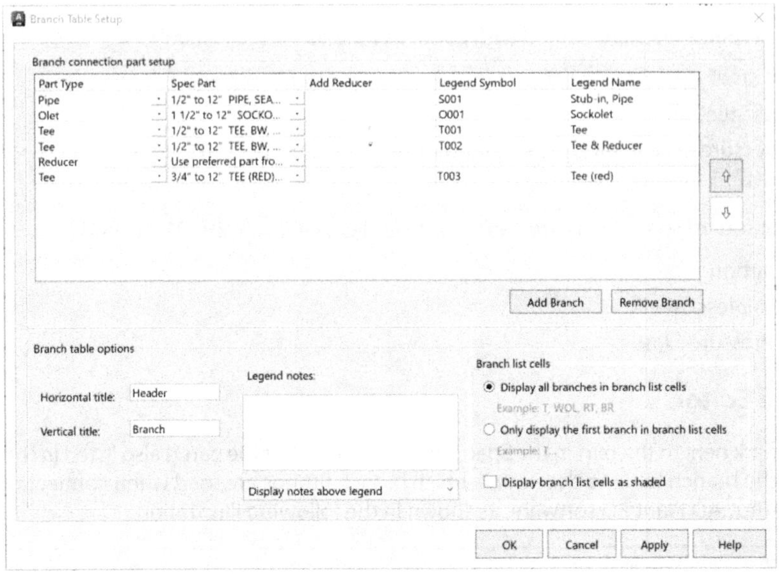

Process: Editing Parts

When you double-click on a part listed in the Spec Editor, the Edit Parts dialog box opens and all the sizes available for the selected part are listed. In the Edit Parts dialog box, you change any required properties values, such as the material code. Additionally, you limit the user to only use certain sizes by selecting the Remove From Spec option. You view all hidden part sizes by clearing the Hide parts marked Remove From Spec option, as shown in the following illustration. When you edit a part, properties, such as description and material are reset to the default values.

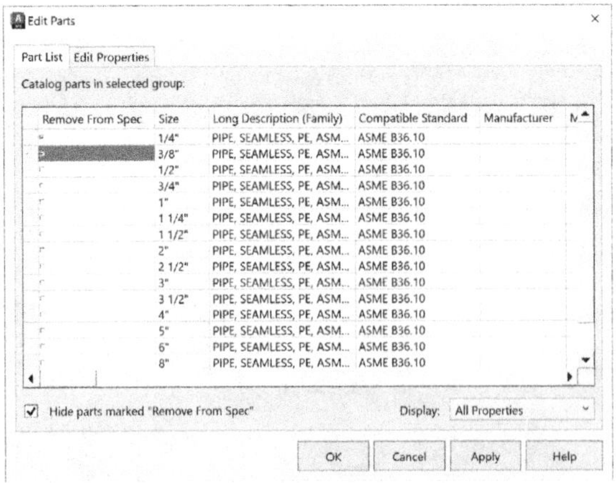

Catalogs

The entire library of components is loaded in catalogs. In a catalog, each component has a name, end type, facing, and other properties, as shown in the following illustration. The end type, such as FL, defines how parts are connected to each other. The facing defines how the gasket is clamped together. Facing values of THDM and THDF indicate threaded male and threaded female, respectively. You use filters to list only the parts that fit a particular criterion. Multiple catalogs can be combined in one spec.

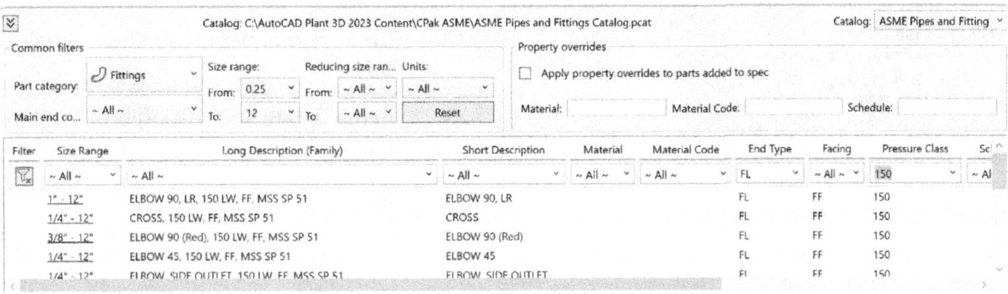

Catalog Editor

The Catalog Editor shows everything that is listed in a specific catalog, as shown in the following illustration. You can use the Catalog Editor to create, edit, or duplicate components.

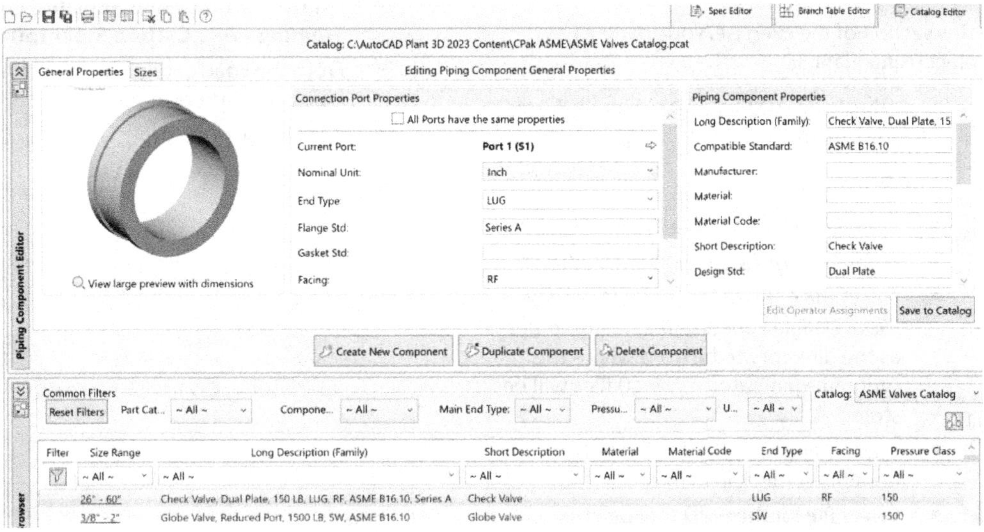

Exercise: Configure Specs and Catalogs

In this exercise, you create a new spec sheet. You add and edit the components in a spec sheet using the Spec Editor and Branch Table Editor. You also use the Catalog Editor to duplicate a component in a catalog and add it to the spec sheet.

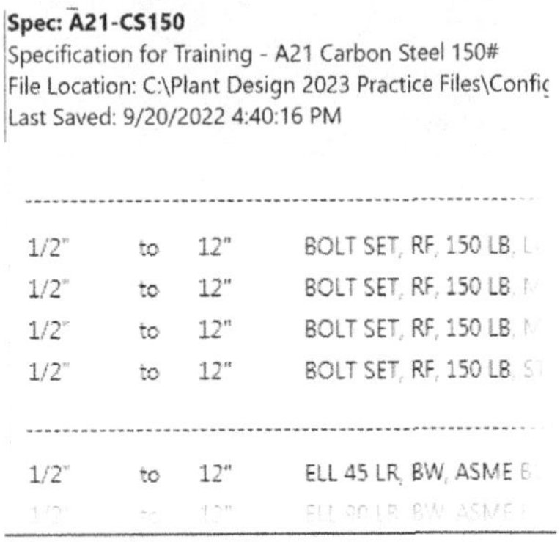

Create a New Project

In this section of the exercise, you create a new project using Plant 3D.

1. Start the AutoCAD Plant 3D software, if not already running.
2. Create a new project:
   - Click New Project in the Project Manager.
   - Enter **Configure Specs** as the name.
   - Select the *C:\Plant Design 2024 Practice Files\Configure Specs and Catalogs* folder as the directory to be used where the program-generated (project) files will be stored.
   - Use Imperial units that will report Imperial content in Inches.
   - Select PIP for the P&ID tool palette content.
   - Accept the remaining defaults to create the project.
3. Exit the AutoCAD Plant 3D software.

Create a New Spec

In this section of the exercise, you create a new spec.

1. Start Autodesk Spec Editor for AutoCAD Plant 3D 2024. Close the Welcome Screen.
2. Click File menu, expand New, and click Create Spec.
3. In the Create Spec dialog box, for New Spec name, click Browse.
4. In the Save As dialog box:
   - Navigate to the project folder *C:\Plant Design 2024 Practice Files\Configure Specs and Catalogs\Configure Specs\Spec Sheets*.
   - For File name, enter **A21-CS150**.
   - Click Save.
5. In the Create Spec dialog box:
   - For Description, enter **Specification for Training - A21 Carbon Steel 150#**.
   - From the Load catalog list, select ASME Pipes and Fittings Catalog.
   - Click Create.

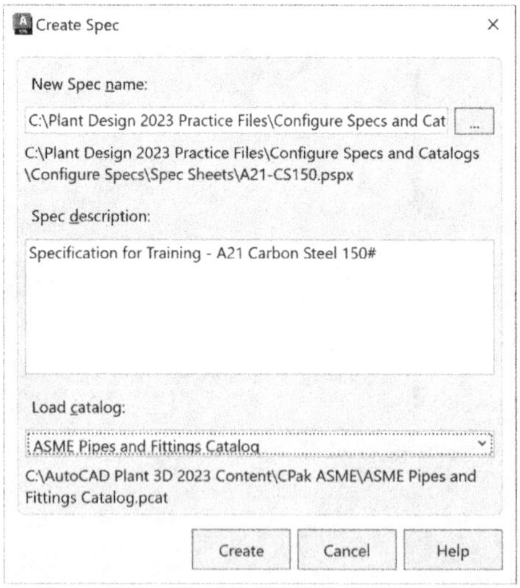

Add Components to a Spec Sheet

In this section of the exercise, you add components from a catalog to a spec sheet.

1. In the bottom pane of the Spec Editor, under Common filters, from the Part category list, select Pipe.

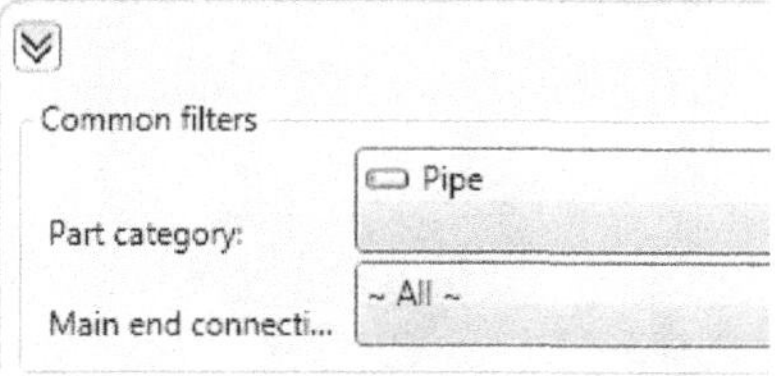

2. To filter the information based on size parameters:
   - Under Size range, from the From list, select 0.25.
   - Under Size range, from the To list, select 12.

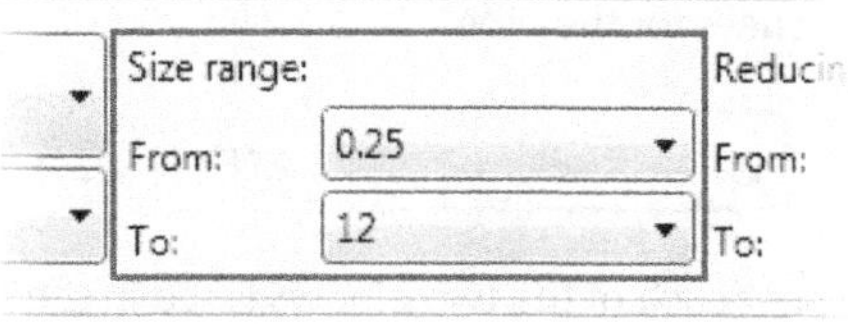

3. To add a Spec:
   - In the Catalog, under Long Description (Family), select PIPE, SEAMLESS, PE, ASME B36.10 from the Part list. One component is listed.
   - Select the part and click Add to Spec.

4. The B36.10 pipe is added to the spec sheet in the top pane.

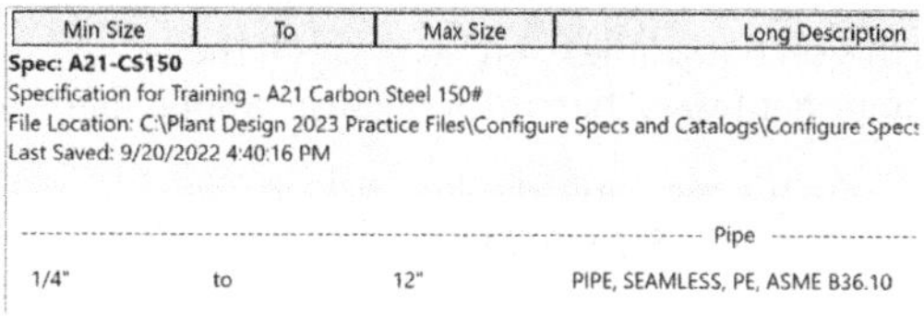

5. In the bottom pane of the Spec Editor, under Common filters, from the Part category list, select Fittings.

6. In the Filter row, from the Short Description list, select ELL 90 LR. One elbow component is listed. Add the elbow to the spec.

7. In the Filter row, from the Short Description list, select ELL 45 LR. One elbow component is listed. Add the elbow to the spec.

   Note the warning symbols that appear in the Part Use Priority column next to each elbow.

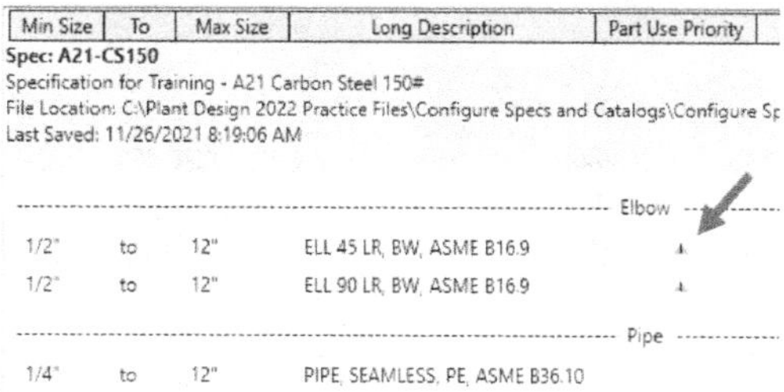

Edit the Component Sizes Available in the Spec Sheet

In this section of the exercise, you edit the component sizes that are available in a spec sheet.

1. In the top pane, double-click on PIPE, SEAMLESS, PE, ASME B36.10.

2. To take away the sizes that are not used frequently, in the Edit Parts dialog box:

   - Select the check boxes in the Remove From Spec column for the following sizes: 1/4", 3/8", 1 1/4", 2 1/2", 3 1/2".
   - Verify that the option Hide parts marked "Remove From Spec" is selected.
   - Click Apply.

   The selected part sizes are removed from the list.

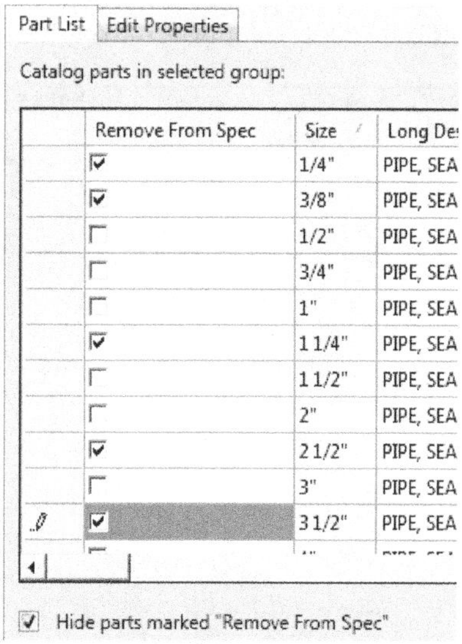

3. In the Material column, for the 1/2" pipe, enter **CS**.

4. Select the value that you just entered. Press <Ctrl>+<C> to copy the value.

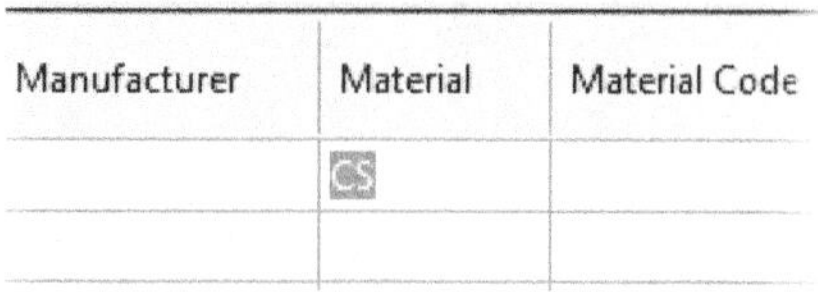

5. To copy the value to all the remaining fields:

   - Select the Material value field for the 3/4" pipe.
   - Hold <Shift> and click the value field for the 12" pipe to select all of the fields between the two sizes of pipes.
   - Press <Ctrl>+<V> to paste the value.

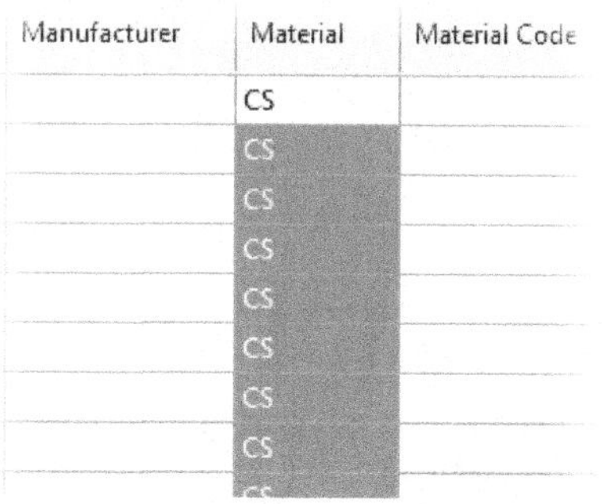

6. Click OK to exit the Edit Parts dialog box.

   Note the Min and Max sizes listed in the spec sheet for the pipe.

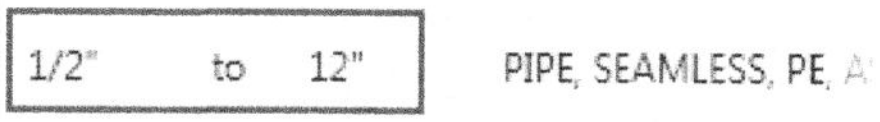

7. For each of the two elbows listed in the spec sheet, repeat the steps to remove 1 1/4", 2 1/2", and 3 1/2" from inclusion. For the Material of each size, enter **CS**.

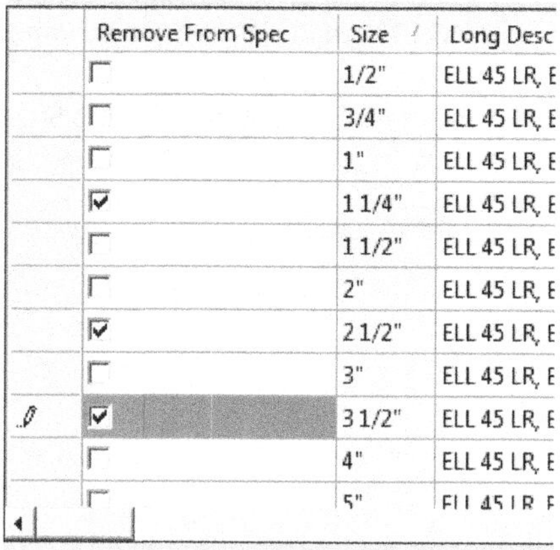

Edit the Part Use Priority of Components

In this section of the exercise, you edit the part use priority for each size of a component.

1. In the top pane, in the Part Use Priority column, next to ELL 45 LR, click the warning symbol.

2. In the Part Use Priority dialog box, under Assign part use priority:

   - Under Size Conflicts, select 1/2".
   - Under Spec Part Use Priority, verify that ELL 90 LR is listed for number 1. If it is not listed for number 1, click it and click Up Priority to move it to the number 1 position.
   - Select Mark as resolved.

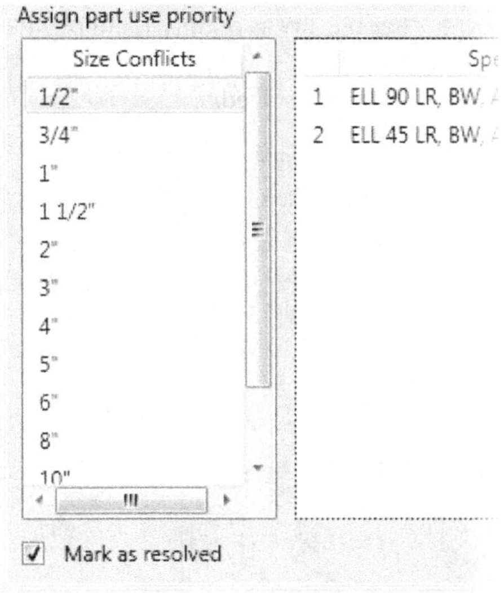

3. Under Assign part use priority, do the following:

   - Under Size Conflicts, select 3/4".
   - Under Spec Part Use Priority, verify that ELL 90 LR is listed for number 1. If it is not listed for number 1, click Up Priority to move it to the number 1 position.
   - Select Mark as resolved.

4. Under Assign part use priority, do the following:

   - Under Size Conflicts, select 1".
     i. Under Spec Part Use Priority, verify that ELL 90 LR is listed for number 1. If it is not listed for number 1, click Up Priority to move it to the number 1 position.
   - Select Mark as resolved.

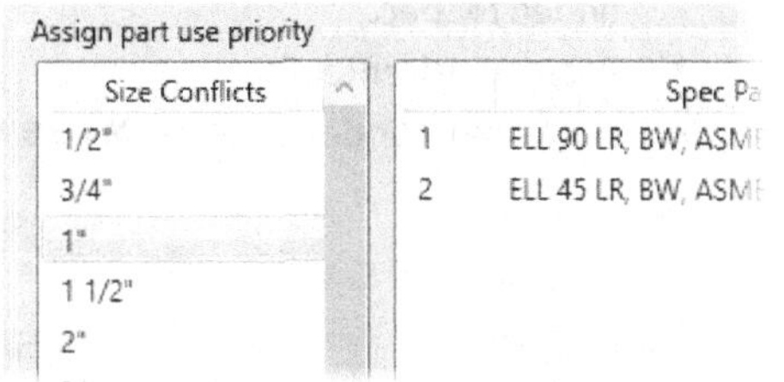

5. Repeat the steps for each of the remaining sizes. Mark each as resolved.

6. Click OK to exit the dialog box.

   In the Spec Sheet Parts list, note that the warning symbols under Part Use Priority for each elbow are replaced with green dots to indicate that the priorities are resolved.

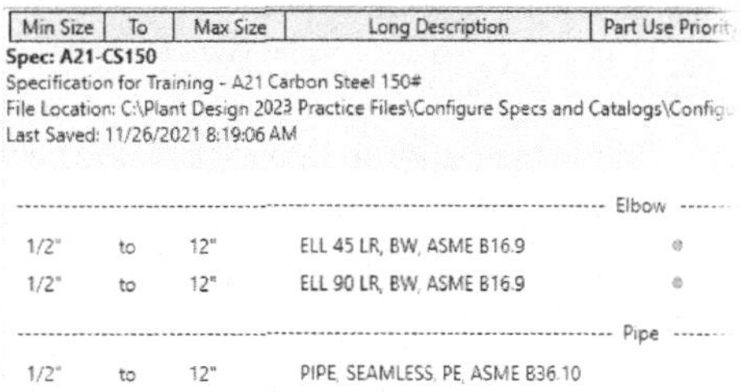

7. Click File menu, and click Save.

Apply Property Overrides

In this section of the exercise, you apply property override values to components as they are added from a catalog to the spec sheet.

1. In the bottom pane of the Spec Editor, under Common filters, verify that Fittings is selected from the Part category list.

2. In the Filter row, from the Short Description list, select TEE. Several tees are listed.

3. In the bottom pane, under Common filters> Size range:
   - In the From list, select 0.5.
   - In the To list, select 12.

   The number of parts for each component listed is reduced.

4. Under Property overrides:
   - Select Apply property overrides to parts added to spec.
   - For Material, enter **CS**.
   - For Material Code, enter **ASTM B36.10**.

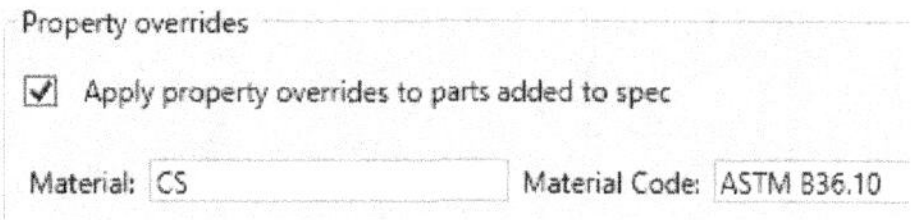

5. Select TEE, BW, ASME B16.9 from the component list. Add it to the spec and note it gets added to the top pane.

6. In the top pane, double-click on the newly added Tee to edit it.

7. In the Edit Parts dialog box:
   - Verify that the Material and Material Codes are added to each part size listed.
   - Remove the following sizes from being included in the spec: 1 1/4", 2 1/2", 3 1/2".
   - Click OK.

8. In the bottom pane, in the Filter row, from the Short Description list, select TEE (RED).

9. Select TEE (RED), BW, ASME B16.9 from the component list. Add it to the spec.

10. For TEE (RED), BW, ASME B16.9, repeat the steps to remove all sizes that reference 1/4", 3/8", 1 1/4", 2 1/2", and 3 1/2". Once selected, click OK to close the Edit Parts dialog box.

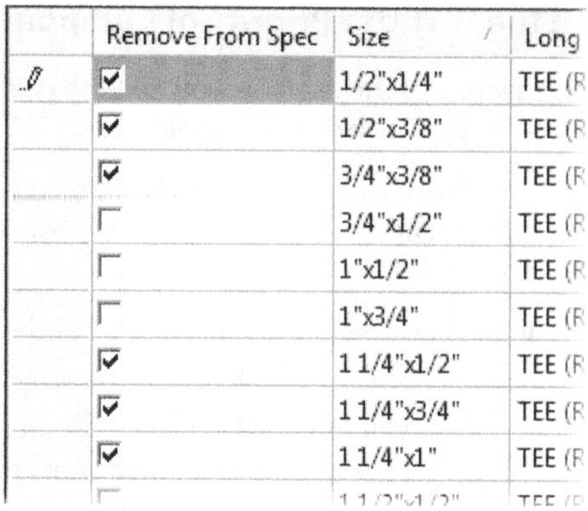

11. In the top pane, in the Part Use Priority column next to TEE (RED), BW, ASME B16.9, click the warning symbol.

12. For each size:
   - Set TEE, BW as priority 1 and TEE (RED) as priority 2.
   - Mark as resolved.

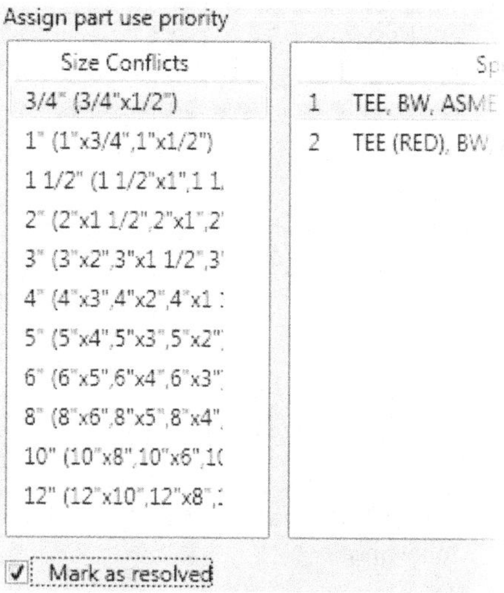

13. Click OK. The tees are marked as resolved.

14. In the bottom pane, under Property overrides clear (uncheck) Apply property overrides to parts added to spec option.

15. Click File menu, and click Save.

Add Additional Components

In this section of the exercise, you add additional components to the spec sheet.

1. In the bottom pane of the Spec Editor, in the Filter row, from the Short Description list, select REDUCER (CONC).
2. Add REDUCER (CONC), BW, ASME B16.9 to the spec.
3. Under Common filters, from the Part category list, select Flanges.
4. In the Filter row:
   - From the Short Description list, select FLANGE WN.
   - From the End Type list, select FL.
   - From the Facing list, select RF.
   - From the Pressure Class list, select 150.
   - One flange is listed. Add it to the spec.
5. Under Common filters, from the Part category list, select Olet.
6. In the Filter row, from the Short Description list, select SOCKOLET. Several components are listed.
7. Select SOCKOLET, 3000 LB, BWXSW, 13/16" LG, ASME B16.11 from the component list. Add it to the spec.
8. Under Common filters, from the Part category list, select Fasteners.
9. In the Filter row:
   - From the Short Description list, select BOLT SET.
   - From the Facing list, select RF.
   - From the Pressure Class list, select 150.
   - Add all four bolt sets that are listed to the spec.

   Note: You can select multiple components at one time by holding <Ctrl> while selecting them.

   Note: If you get an error, hold down <Ctrl> till it goes away.

				Bolt Set
1/2"	to	12"	BOLT SET, RF, 150 LB, LUG BOLT	
1/2"	to	12"	BOLT SET, RF, 150 LB, MACHINE BOLT	
1/2"	to	12"	BOLT SET, RF, 150 LB, MACHINE LUG BOLT	
1/2"	to	12"	BOLT SET, RF, 150 LB, STUD BOLT	

10. In the Filter row, from the Short Description list, select GASKET, FLAT. Add the 1/16" THK and 1/32" THK components to the spec.
11. In the Filter row, from the Short Description list, select GASKET, SWG. Add the 1/8" THK and 1/4" THK components to the spec.

				Gasket
1/2"	to	12"	GASKET, FLAT, 1/16" THK, RF, 150 LB, ASMI	
1/2"	to	12"	GASKET, FLAT, 1/32" THK, RF, 150 LB, ASMI	
1/2"	to	12"	GASKET, SWG, 1/4" THK, RF, 150 LB, ASME	
1/2"	to	12"	GASKET, SWG, 1/8" THK, RF, 150 LB, ASME	

12. Click File, and click Save.

Assign Connections in a Branch Table

In this section of the exercise, you use the branch table editor to create a legend and assign connections in a branch table.

1. In the top right corner, click the Branch Table Editor tab.

2. In the bottom right corner, click Edit Legend.
3. In the Branch Table Setup dialog box, click Add Branch.
4. Under Branch connection part setup, for the branch you just added:
   - From the Part Type list, select Pipe.
   - From the Spec Part list, select 1/2" to 12" PIPE, SEAMLESS, PE, ASME B36.10.
   - For the Legend Symbol, enter **S001**.
   - For the Legend Name, enter **Stub-in, Pipe**.

Branch connection part setup

Part Type	Spec Part	Add Reducer	Legend Symbol	Legend Name
Pipe	1/2" to 12" PIPE, SEAM...		S001	Stub-in, Pipe

5. Click Add Branch.

6. Under Branch connection part setup, for the branch you just added:
   - From the Part Type list, select Olet.
   - From the Spec Part list, select 1 1/2" to 12" SOCKOLET, 3000 LB, BWXSW, 3/8" LG, ASME B16.11.
   - For the Legend Symbol, enter **0001**.
   - For the Legend Name, enter **Sockolet**.

7. Add the remaining branches (three Tees) with the following settings.
   - 1/2" to 12" TEE, BW, ASME B16.9; T001; Tee
   - 1/2" to 12" TEE, BW, ASME B16.9; check Reducer; T002; Tee & Reducer. **Note:** The reducer is automatically added when the box is checked in the Add Reducer column.
   - 3/4" to 12" TEE(RED), BW, ASME B16.9; T003; Tee (red).

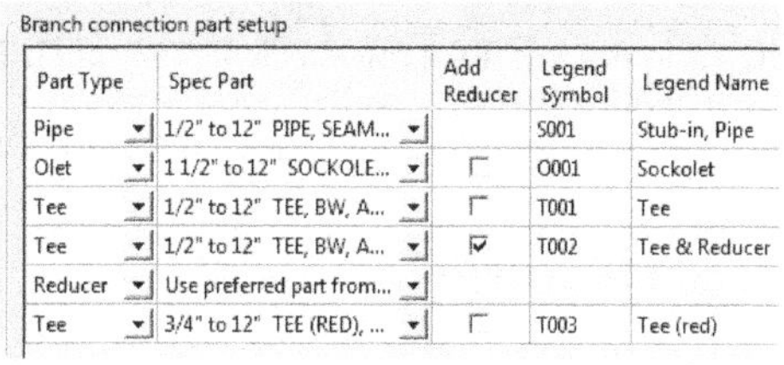
Branch connection part setup

Part Type	Spec Part	Add Reducer	Legend Symbol	Legend Name
Pipe	1/2" to 12" PIPE, SEAM...		S001	Stub-in, Pipe
Olet	1 1/2" to 12" SOCKOLE...	☐	0001	Sockolet
Tee	1/2" to 12" TEE, BW, A...	☐	T001	Tee
Tee	1/2" to 12" TEE, BW, A...	☑	T002	Tee & Reducer
Reducer	Use preferred part from...			
Tee	3/4" to 12" TEE (RED), ...	☐	T003	Tee (red)

8. Click OK to exit the dialog box. The legend is displayed in the right pane.

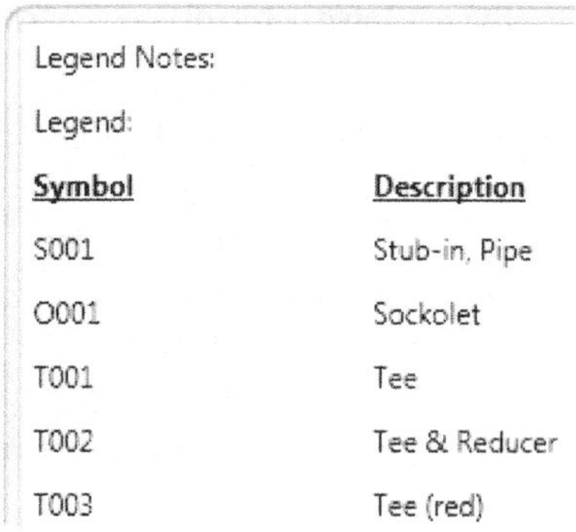
Legend Notes:

Legend:

Symbol	Description
S001	Stub-in, Pipe
0001	Sockolet
T001	Tee
T002	Tee & Reducer
T003	Tee (red)

9. In the left pane, hold <Ctrl> and select the top branches of each row as shown in the following illustration.

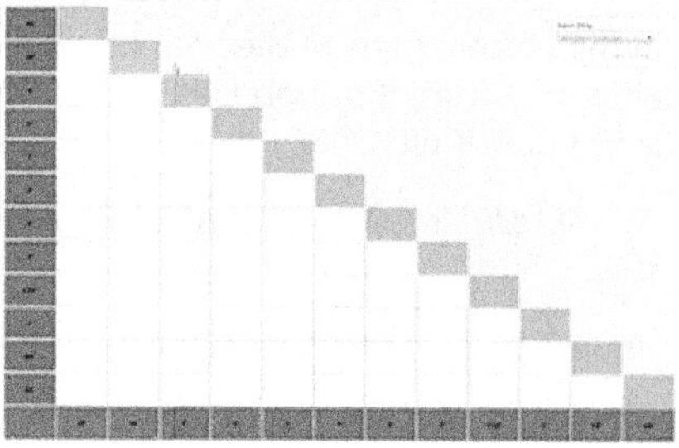

10. Right-click on any one of the selected branches. Click Multi Branch Selection.

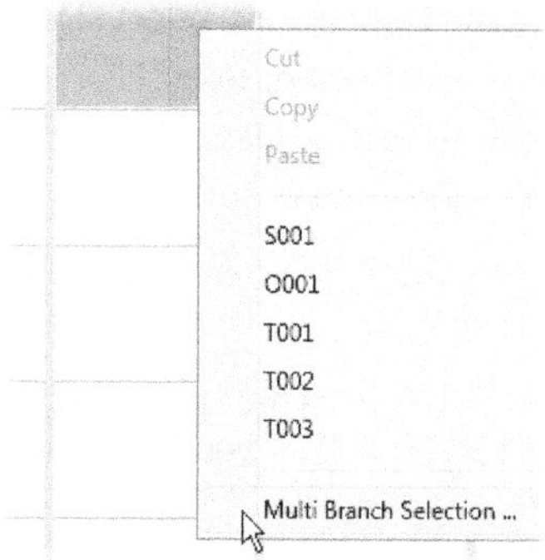

11. In the Select Branch List dialog box:
    - Under Use Branch, select S001 and T001.
    - Select the T001 row.
    - Under Priority, click Up until T001 is listed as Priority 1.

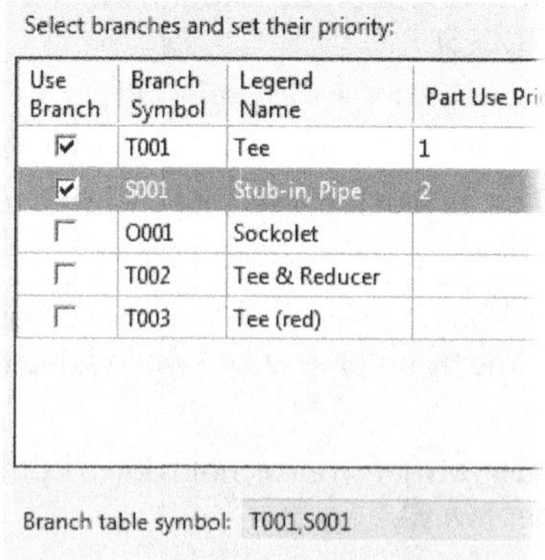
Select branches and set their priority:

Use Branch	Branch Symbol	Legend Name	Part Use Pri
☑	T001	Tee	1
☑	S001	Stub-in, Pipe	2
☐	0001	Sockolet	
☐	T002	Tee & Reducer	
☐	T003	Tee (red)	

Branch table symbol: T001,S001

12. Click OK to exit the dialog box. The branch table symbols are listed in each of the selected branches.

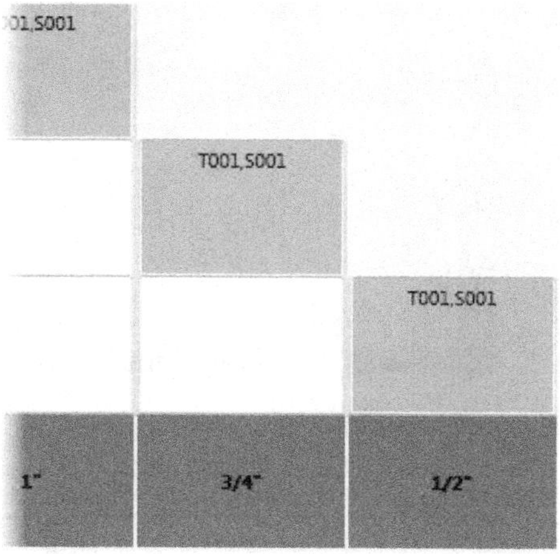

Assign Unavailable Branch Sizes

In this section of the exercise, you assign branch sizes that are unavailable to specific branches. After receiving a warning, you select a valid branch fitting for the sizes.

1. Select the first 1/2" x 12" branch as shown in the following illustration. Right-click and select Multi Branch Selection.

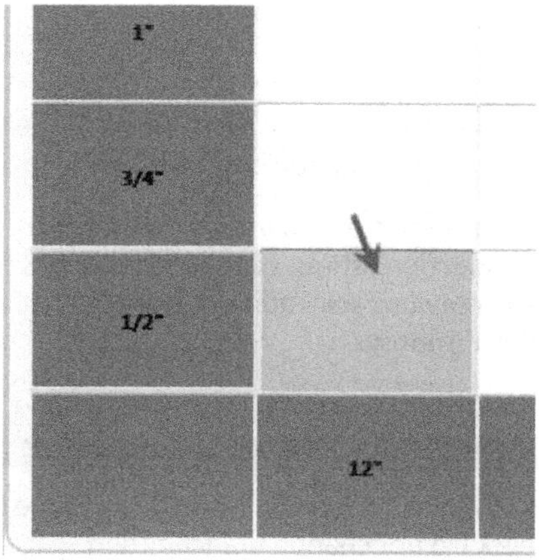

2. In the Select Branch List dialog box, under Use Branch, select S001, T002, T003. Click OK.
3. In the Branch Size Unavailable message box, click Select a valid branch fitting for these sizes.
4. In the Select Branch Connection dialog box, select O001. Click OK.
5. Select the same branch. Right-click. Click Multi Branch Selection.
6. In the Select Branch List dialog box, under Use Branch, select O001 and S001. Click OK.
7. Use <Shift> to select all remaining unassigned branches along the 1/2" row (Do not select the first and last assigned branch). Right-click anywhere on the selected branch and click Multi Branch Selection.

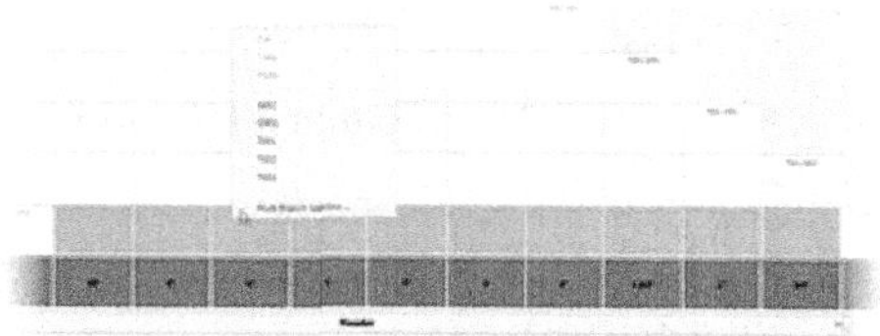

8. In the Select Branch List dialog box:
   - Under Use Branch, select S001, T002, T003.
   - Move T003 up so that it has a Priority of 1.
   - Move T002 up so that it has a Priority of 2.
   - S001 becomes Priority 3.
   - Click OK.
9. In the Branch Size Unavailable message box, click Do not change branch fitting. The Branches from 10" to 2" are highlighted in red, indicating that the assigned fittings are not available for these sizes.
10. Select the 1/2" x 2" branch as shown in the following illustration. Right-click. Click Multi Branch Selection.

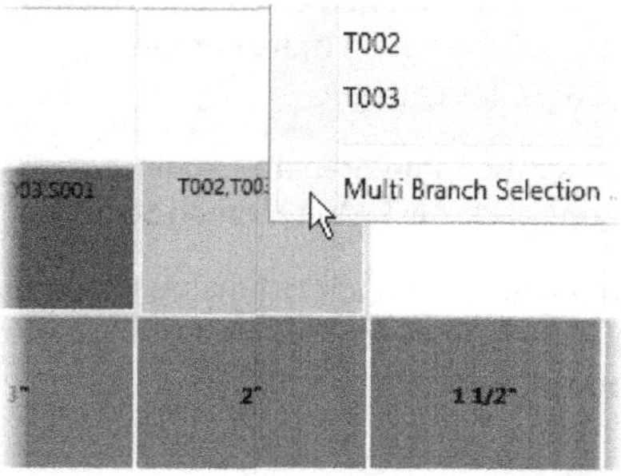

11. In the Select Branch List dialog box, click OK.

12. In the Branch Size Unavailable message box, click Select a valid branch fitting for these sizes.

13. In the Select Branch Connection dialog box, note that the valid branches are S001, O001, and T003. Click Cancel.

14. Select the 1/2" x 2" branch again. Right-click. Click Multi Branch Selection.

15. In the Select Branch List dialog box:

- Under Use Branch, select S001and O001.
- Clear all others.
- Move S001 up so that it is Priority 1.
- Click OK.

16. Click another branch to see that the 1/2" x 2" branch is no longer red.

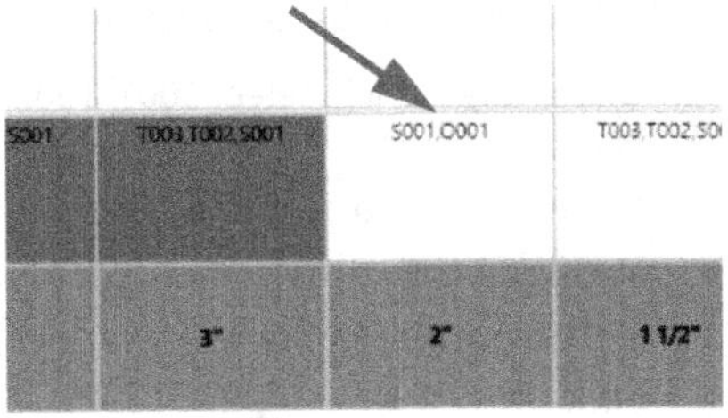

17. Use <Shift> to select the red branches and right-click on any one. Click Multi Branch Selection.

18. In the Select Branch List dialog box, click OK.

19. In the Branch Size Unavailable dialog box, click Select a valid branch fitting for these sizes.

20. In the Select Branch Connection dialog box, note that the valid branches are S001 and O001. Click Cancel.

21. Select the same branches again, if required. Right-click. Click Multi Branch Selection.

22. In the Select Branch List dialog box, under Use Branch, select S001 and O001. Clear all others. Click OK.

23. Using <Ctrl>, select the top three branches of each column and select the branches for the last two columns as shown in the following illustration.

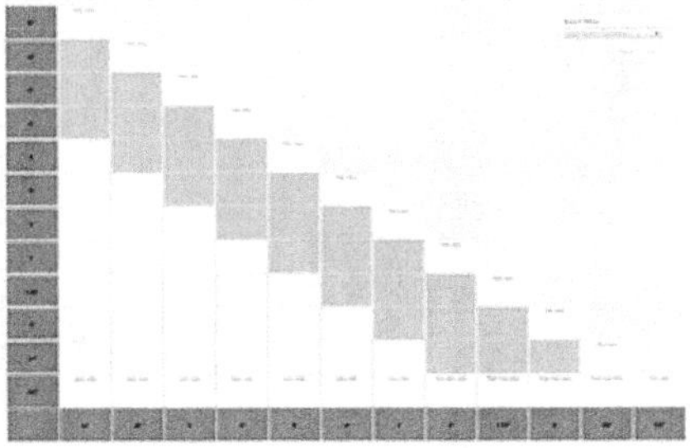

24. Assign the branch symbols with the priority as shown in the following illustration.

Use Branch	Branch Symbol	Legend Name	Part Use Prio
☑	T003	Tee (red)	1
☑	T002	Tee & Reducer	2
☑	S001	Stub-in, Pipe	3
☐	O001	Sockolet	
☐	T001	Tee	

Branch table symbol: T003,T002,S001

25. In the Branch Size Unavailable message box, click Do not change branch fitting.

26. Repeat the steps to assign the correct connection fittings to the red branches from the previous selection set. Use T003, O001, S001 priority.

27. Assign S001 and O001 to the remaining unassigned branches.

28. In the Branch Size Unavailable message box, click Do not change branch fitting.

29. Repeat the steps to assign the correct connection fittings to the red branch (T003, T002, S001).

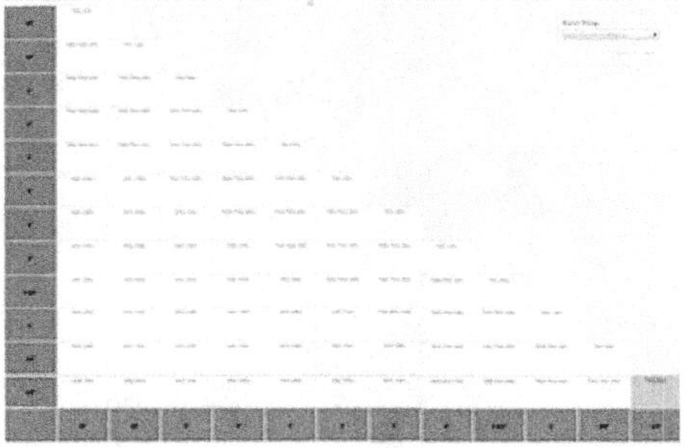

30. Click File menu, and click Save.

31. Exit Autodesk Spec Editor for AutoCAD Plant 3D.

Use the Parts from a Spec Sheet

In this section of the exercise, you use the parts from a spec sheet to build a model in the AutoCAD Plant 3D software.

Optional - If you did not successfully complete the Spec portion of this exercise, you can use a previously created Spec to complete this exercise.

- Go to Windows Explorer and locate the folder *C:\Plant Design 2024 Practice Files\Configure Specs and Catalogs\ConfigureSpecs\Spec Sheets*. Rename the Spec Sheets folder to **Spec Sheets Working**.
- Locate the folder *C:\Plant Design 2024 Practice Files\Configure Specs and Catalogs\Spec Sheets Backup*. Rename the Spec Sheets Backup folder to **Spec Sheets**.
- Move the newly named Spec Sheets folder into the *C:\Plant Design 2024 Practice Files\Configure Specs and Catalogs\ConfigureSpecs* folder.

1. Start the AutoCAD Plant 3D software.

2. Open the ConfigureSpecs project (*C:\Plant Design 2024 Practice Files\Configure Specs and Catalogs\ConfigureSpecs*).

3. In the Project Manager, expand the Pipe Specs node. Note that the new A21-C150 spec is not listed.

4. Right-click on the Pipe Specs node and select Copy Specs to Project. Browse to *C:\Plant Design 2024 Practice Files\Configure Specs and Catalogs\ConfigureSpecs\Spec Sheets*.

5. Select A21-CS150.pspx and click Open. The new spec has been added to the project.

6. Under Plant 3D Drawings, create a new drawing called *0001.dwg*.

7. Activate the 3D Piping workspace, if required.

8. On the Home tab, on the Part Insertion panel, click Spec Viewer. In the Pipe Spec Viewer, from the Spec Sheet list, select A21-CS150.

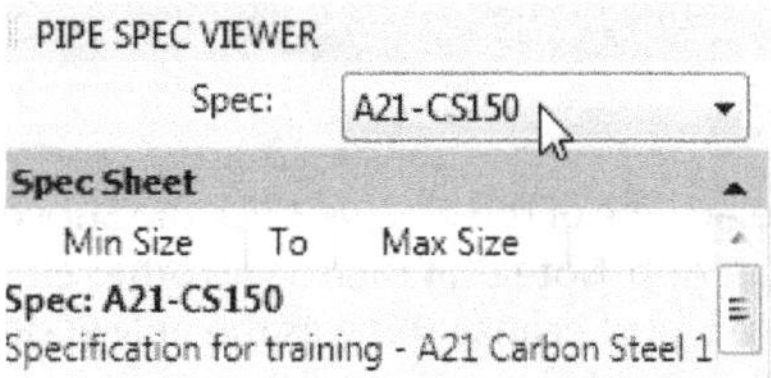

9. On the Home tab, on the Part Insertion panel, on the Spec Selector list, click A21-CS150.

   From the Pipe Size list, note that you can select from the sizes specified in the spec sheet. Select 4".

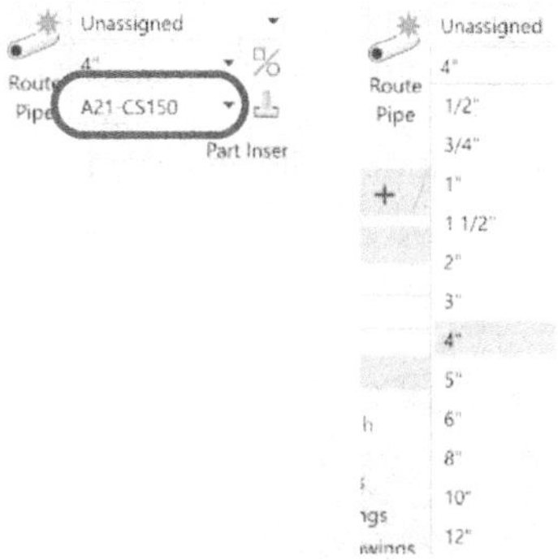

10. Close the Pipe Spec Viewer.

11. Use the Route Pipe tool to create a pipe run similar to the one shown.

    Note: Use <Ctrl>+right-click to change the planes when creating the pipeline.

    Note: Your display color might be different.

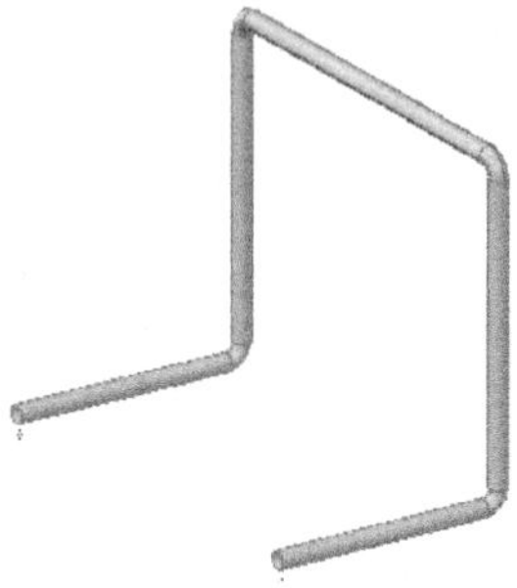

12. Select one of the elbows. Click the Substitute Part grip. Note that there is no other elbow available because this was the only 90deg elbow added to the spec sheet.

13. On the Tool Palette, select the Flange and place it at the end of the open pipe.

14. Press <Ctrl> and select the connection symbol as shown in the following illustration. The grips should display as yellow.

    Hint: If you are not seeing the tear icon, enable the Toggle Disconnect Markers option on the Visibility panel, on the Home tab. The tear icon indicates a disconnection.

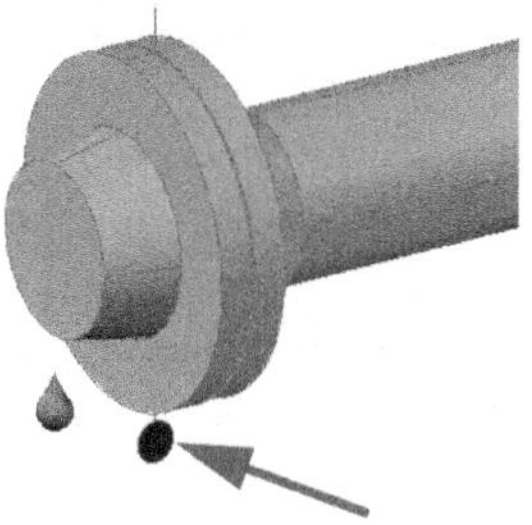

15. Click the Substitute part grip. Note the options you have for substituting the Bolt Set.

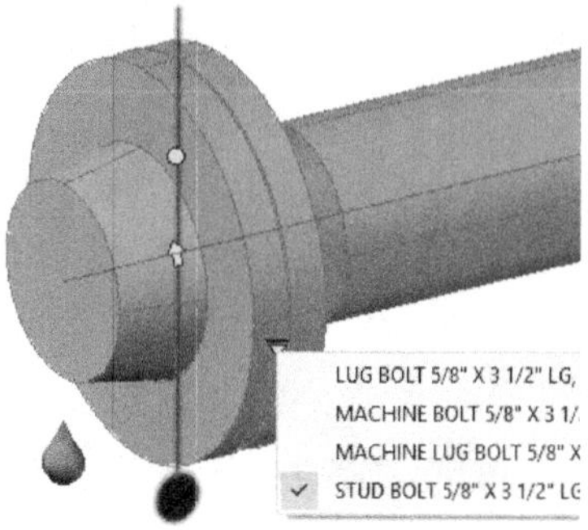

16. Press <Esc> to clear the selection.

17. Use the Tool Palette to place a sockolet in the top of the pipe shown. (Use rotation to move into position).

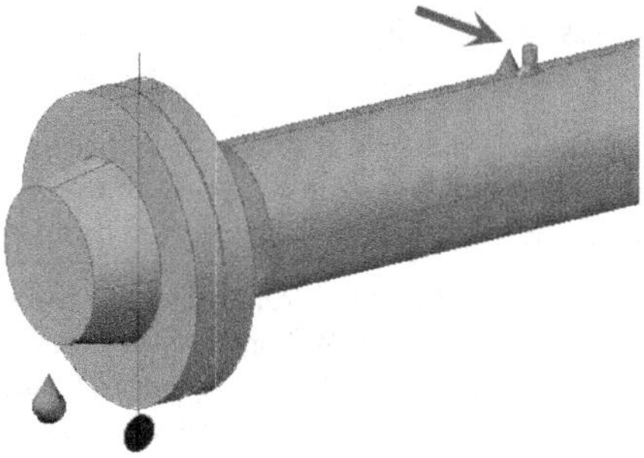

18. Use the Substitute Part grip to change the Sockolet to 4" x 1 1/2".

19. Use the Continue Pipe grip to add a vertical pipe as shown in the following illustration.

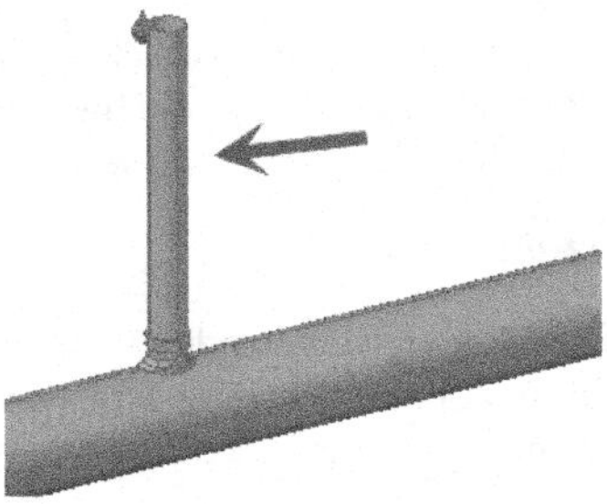

20. Between the two horizontal pipes, use the Route Pipe tool on the Home tab to add a horizontal pipe (4"pipe), as shown in the following illustration.

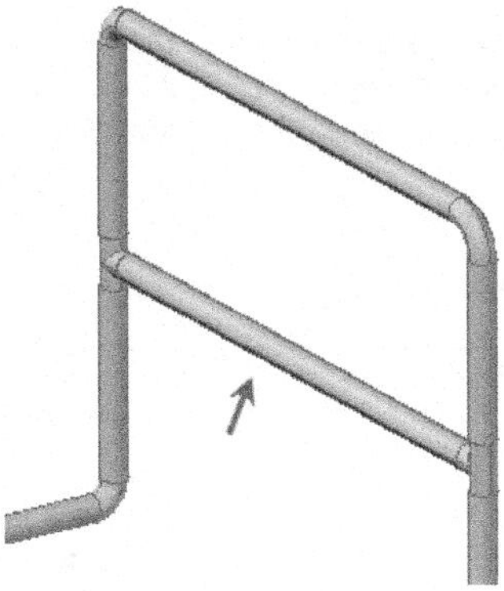

21. Use the Properties palette to change the size of the horizontal pipe to a 3" pipe. A reducer is used.

22. Select the tee and use the Substitute grip to change to a 4" x 3" reducing tee.

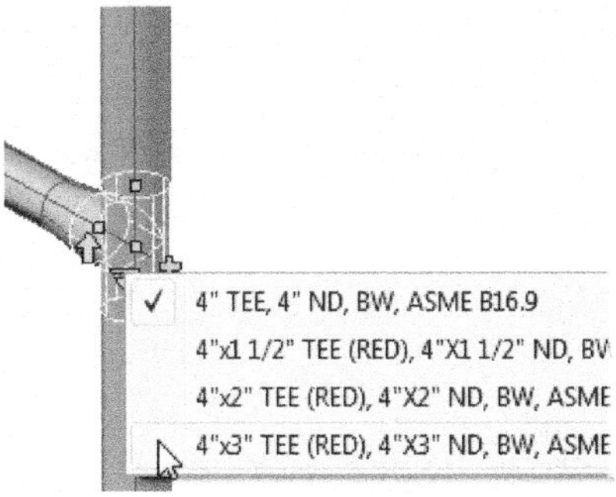

23. Use the Route Pipe tool on the Home tab, to place a 2" pipe on the top horizontal portion of the pipe, as shown in the following illustration. Note the tee used.

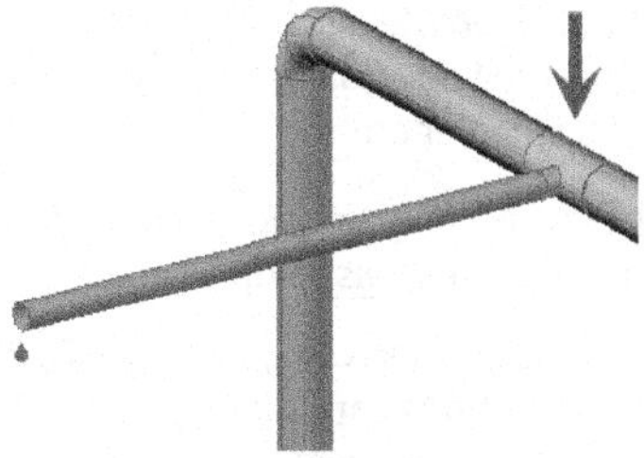

24. Select the 2" pipe and then on the Part Insertion panel, click Route Pipe.

25. Right-click in the drawing area. Click STub-in.

26. To specify a start point, select a point as shown in the following illustration.

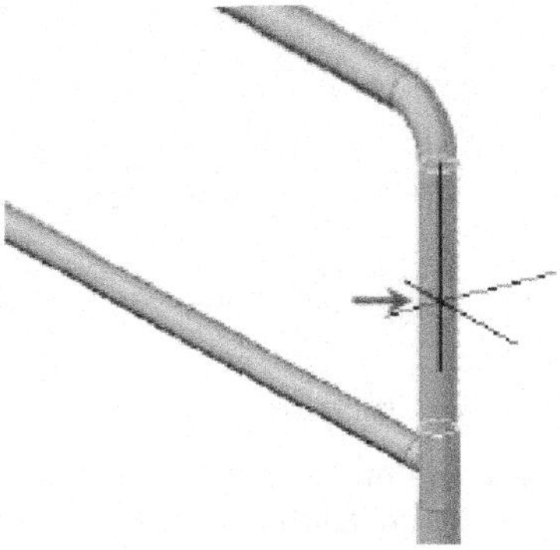

27. Select a rotation to the side. Note the stub-in created.

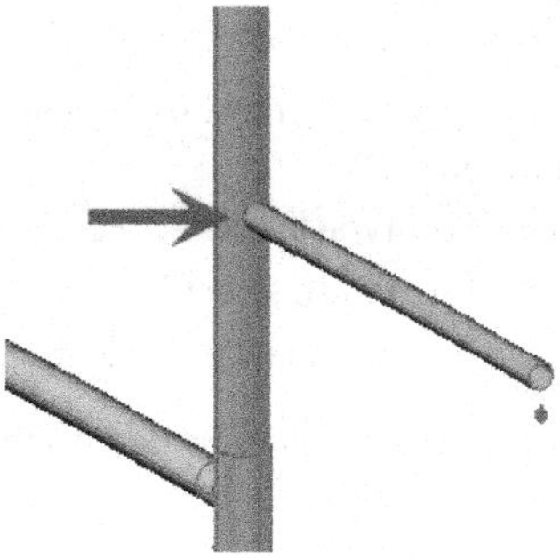

28. Save the drawing.

Add Values to the Spec Sheet

In this section of the exercise, you add values to the spec sheet.

1. In the Project Manager, under Pipe Specs, right-click on A21-CS150. Select Edit Spec to launch the Spec Editor and load the A21-CS150 spec for editing.

2. If the Catalog Not Found opens, complete the following; otherwise skip to step 3.
   - Click Browse. Navigate to the ASME Pipes and Fittings catalog in *C:\AutoCAD Plant 3D 2024 Content\CPak ASME.*
   - Select the file *ASME Pipes and Fittings Catalog.pcat.*
   - Click Open.

3. In the bottom pane, upper right corner, note that ASME Pipes and Fittings is displayed. In the Catalog list, select Open Catalog.

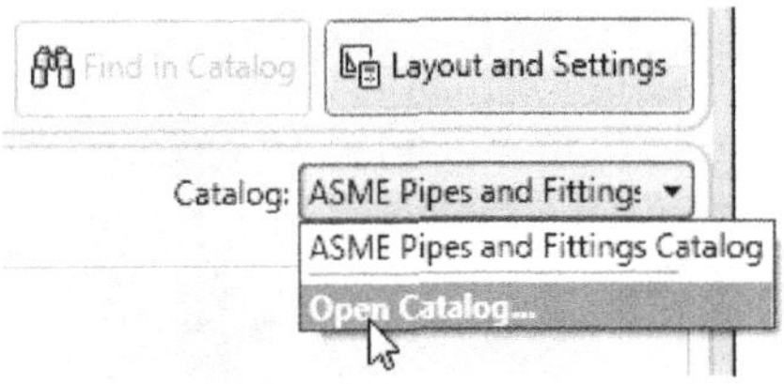

4. In the Open dialog box:
   - Navigate into the folder *C:\AutoCAD Plant 3D 2024 Content\CPak ASME.*
   - Select the file *ASME Valves Catalog.pcat.*
   - Click Open. Note that ASME Valves Catalog is listed as the new Catalog.

5. In the bottom pane, in the Filters row:
   - From the Short Description list, select GLOBE VALVE.
   - From the End Type list, select FL.
   - From the Facing list, select RF.
   - From the Pressure Class list, select 150.
   - One Globe Valve is listed. Add it to the Spec.

6. From the Short Description list, select BUTTERFLY VALVE. Two valves are listed. Add both to the spec.

7. From the Short Description list, select BALL VALVE. Four valves are listed. Add the Series B and Short Pattern ball valves to the spec.

Edit Pipe Sizes

In this section of the exercise, you edit the pipe sizes available in the spec sheet. The ASME Pipes and Fittings Catalog.pcat catalog should have been loaded.

1. In the top pane, listed under Pipe, double-click on PIPE, SEAMLESS, PE, ASME B36.10.

2. In the Edit Parts dialog box, clear the Hide parts marked "Remove From Spec" check box.

3. Scroll down the list and clear the Remove From Spec option for the ¼", 2 ½", and 3 ½" sizes, to add those sizes. Click Apply.

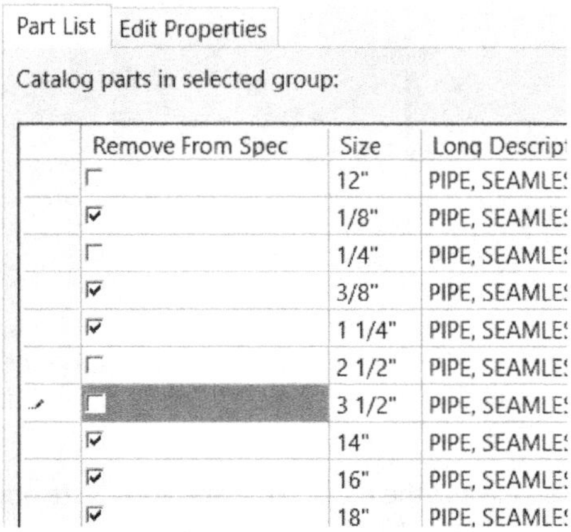

4. Select the Hide parts marked "Remove From Spec" option.

   Note that the Material values for the parts just included are blank.

Size	Long Description (Family)	Materi
1/4"	PIPE, SEAMLESS, PE, ASME B36.10	
1/2"	PIPE, SEAMLESS, PE, ASME B36.10	CS
3/4"	PIPE, SEAMLESS, PE, ASME B36.10	CS
1"	PIPE, SEAMLESS, PE, ASME B36.10	CS
1 1/2"	PIPE, SEAMLESS, PE, ASME B36.10	CS
2"	PIPE, SEAMLESS, PE, ASME B36.10	CS
2 1/2"	PIPE, SEAMLESS, PE, ASME B36.10	
3"	PIPE, SEAMLESS, PE, ASME B36.10	CS
3 1/2"	PIPE, SEAMLESS, PE, ASME B36.10	
4"	PIPE, SEAMLESS, PE, ASME B36.10	CS

5. For the Material of the 1/4" pipe, enter **Carbon Steel**.

6. Select and copy the text value that you just entered.

7. Use <Shift> to select the Material field for all of the remaining sizes. Paste the material.

ption (Family)	Material	Material Code
ESS, PE, ASME B36.10	Carbon Steel	
ESS, PE, ASME B36.10	Carbon Steel	
ESS, PE, ASME B36.10	Carbon Steel	
ESS, PE, ASME B36.10	Carbon Steel	
ESS, PE, ASME B36.10	Carbon Steel	
ESS, PE, ASME B36.10	Carbon Steel	
ESS, PE, ASME B36.10	Carbon Steel	
ESS, PE, ASME B36.10	Carbon Steel	
ESS, PE, ASME B36.10	Carbon Steel	
ESS, PE, ASME B36.10	Carbon Steel	

8. Repeat the steps to enter **DIN1.4407** for the Material Code for each size.

9. Click OK to exit the dialog box.

10. Click File menu, and click Save.

Duplicate a Component Using the Catalog Editor

In this section of the exercise, you use the Catalog Editor to create a custom component. You duplicate an existing valve and change the values of the new one. Then you add it to the spec sheet.

1. In the top right corner, click the Catalog Editor.

2. In the bottom pane, in the Filters row:
   - From the Short Description list, select BUTTERFLY VALVE.
   - From the End Type list, select FL.

   Two Butterfly Valves are listed: Narrow and Wide.

3. Select the Narrow valve. Click Duplicate Component.

4. In the Duplicate Part family dialog box, in the Enter new part family name, enter **Butterfly Valve, Long Shape Body - CS150 FL RF**. Click Create.

   The new component is added to the list. Note that since it is a duplicate of the other component, the Design Std is Narrow.

Long Description (Family)
~ All ~
Butterfly Valve, Narrow, 150 LB, RF, ASME B16.10
Butterfly Valve, Wide, 150 LB, RF, ASME B16.10
Butterfly Valve, Long Shape Body - CS150 FL RF

5. In the bottom panel, select the new butterfly valve.

6. In the top panel (Editor), under Piping Component Properties, for Design Std, enter **Long Shape Body**. Click Save to Catalog. Note that in the bottom pane (Browser), in the Design Std column the value for the valve changes.

7. In the top left corner of the top pane, click the Sizes tab.

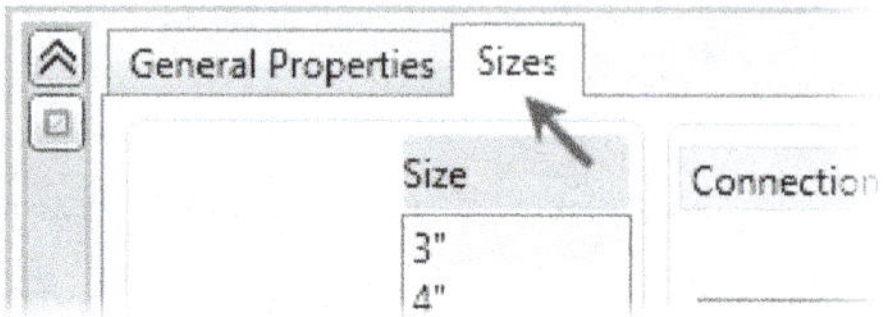

Here, you can edit the values for each size of the component individually.

8. Click Show Advanced Editing Table.

9. In the editing table, in Long Description (Size) column, for the 3" part, change NARROW to LONG SHAPE BODY.

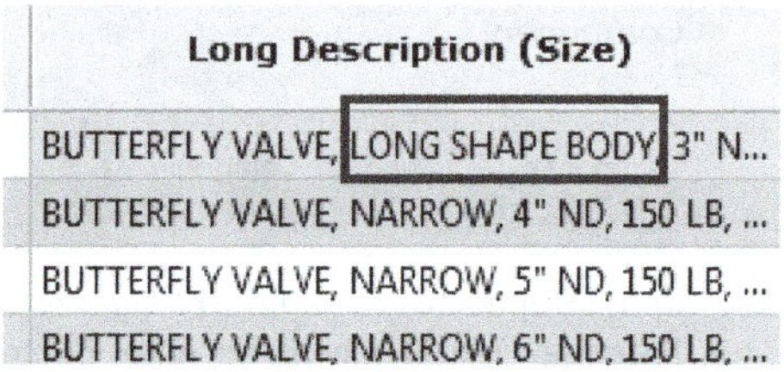

Long Description (Size)
BUTTERFLY VALVE, LONG SHAPE BODY 3" N...
BUTTERFLY VALVE, NARROW, 4" ND, 150 LB, ...
BUTTERFLY VALVE, NARROW, 5" ND, 150 LB, ...
BUTTERFLY VALVE, NARROW, 6" ND, 150 LB, ...

10. Repeat this for each size in the table.

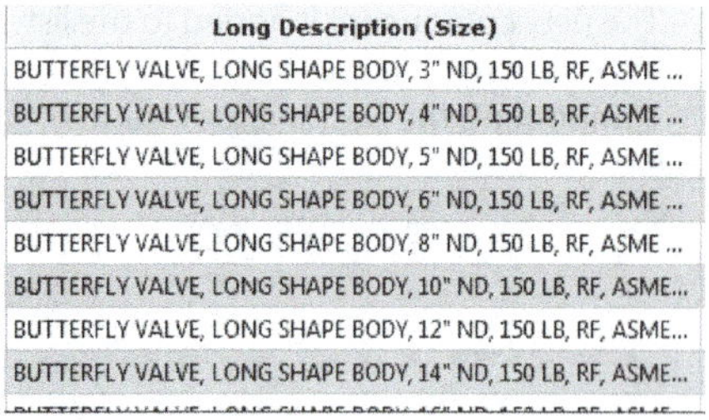

Long Description (Size)
BUTTERFLY VALVE, LONG SHAPE BODY, 3" ND, 150 LB, RF, ASME ...
BUTTERFLY VALVE, LONG SHAPE BODY, 4" ND, 150 LB, RF, ASME ...
BUTTERFLY VALVE, LONG SHAPE BODY, 5" ND, 150 LB, RF, ASME ...
BUTTERFLY VALVE, LONG SHAPE BODY, 6" ND, 150 LB, RF, ASME ...
BUTTERFLY VALVE, LONG SHAPE BODY, 8" ND, 150 LB, RF, ASME ...
BUTTERFLY VALVE, LONG SHAPE BODY, 10" ND, 150 LB, RF, ASME...
BUTTERFLY VALVE, LONG SHAPE BODY, 12" ND, 150 LB, RF, ASME...
BUTTERFLY VALVE, LONG SHAPE BODY, 14" ND, 150 LB, RF, ASME...

11. Click Save to Catalog.

12. Click Hide Advanced Editing Table.

13. Under Sizes, verify that 3" is selected.

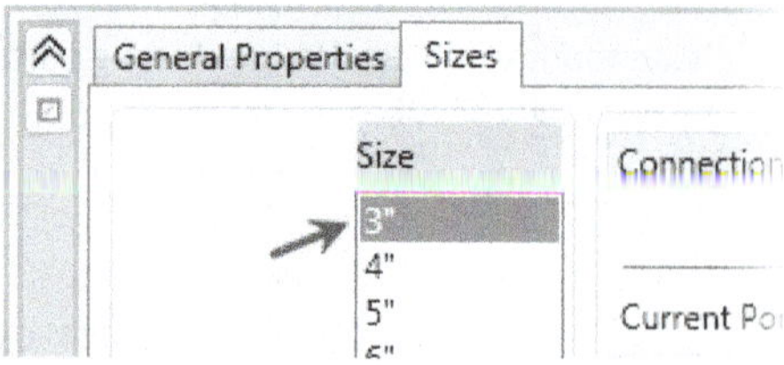

14. Under Size Parameters, for L, enter **6**.

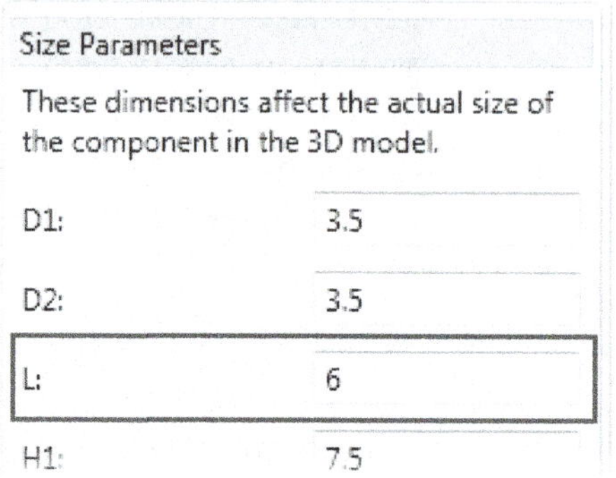

15. Select each size and add 1" to the length value (L) for each.

16. Click Save to Catalog.

17. Save the spec sheet. Exit Autodesk Spec Editor for AutoCAD Plant 3D.

Update a Drawing

In this section of the exercise, you update a drawing with the changes you made to the spec sheet.

1. Return to the AutoCAD Plant 3D software.

2. Verify that *0001.dwg* is open.

3. In the Project Manager, right-click on the Pipe Specs node and select Check for Spec Updates.

4. In the Spec Update Available message box, click Update pipe specs (Recommended).

5. In the Tool Palettes, at the bottom of the Dynamic Pipe Spec tab, note that the Valve tools are now included.

   Note: If you do not see them, change the active spec on the Home tab to a different spec and then change it back to the A21-CS150 to see the new tools.

6. On the Home tab, on the Project panel, click Data Manager.

7. In the Data Manager, left pane, select Pipe Run Component.

8. Verify that the Material and Material Code for the pipe has been updated from the changes made to the spec sheet.

9. Save and close all drawings.

Lesson Review Questions

1. Select the types of specs that the Spec editor can edit. (Select all that apply.)
   a. Inline Components
   b. Equipment Nozzles
   c. Instrumentation Components
   d. Equipment
   e. Pipe Supports
2. It is possible to combine multiple catalogs in one specification.
   a. True
   b. False
3. In the specification, you can have similar components. How do you know which one is going to be used by default?
   a. It is not possible to know, you must select the component while routing pipe.
   b. Each class in the specification has a priority setting. This way you can set which component should be used while routing pipe.
   c. You cannot have multiple similar components in one specification.
4. Is it possible to add equipment to your piping specification?
   a. Yes, you can add all types of components to the specification.
   b. Yes, but only if you also add nozzles to the specification.
   c. No, equipment is not part of the specification.
5. The Spec Editor can edit a spec file or a catalog file.
   a. True
   b. False

Lesson: Isometric Setup

Overview

This lesson describes how to create a custom isometric setup and how to add additional information to your drawing when generating the Iso.

Objectives

After completing this lesson, you will be able to:

- Describe what Iso styles are and how they are used.
- Explain the basic categories of customization that can be used in an Iso style.
- Describe the components of a bill of materials.
- Create and configure a new iso style for use in the active project.
- Configure a custom drawing template with a custom title block for use for Iso drawings.

About Iso Styles

The AutoCAD Plant 3D software installs with multiple Iso styles and paper sizes by default. The following are the default Iso styles:

- Check
- Stress
- Final
- Spool

Custom Iso Styles

You can add custom Iso styles to the project to meet the specific needs of your project. When you create an Iso drawing, you can use the customized Iso style to control the type of data you want to include: attributes, styles, formatting, etc. For example, a new Iso style called Company_D has been added to the list of available Iso styles, as shown in the following illustration. You can customize this without affecting the rest of the Iso styles.

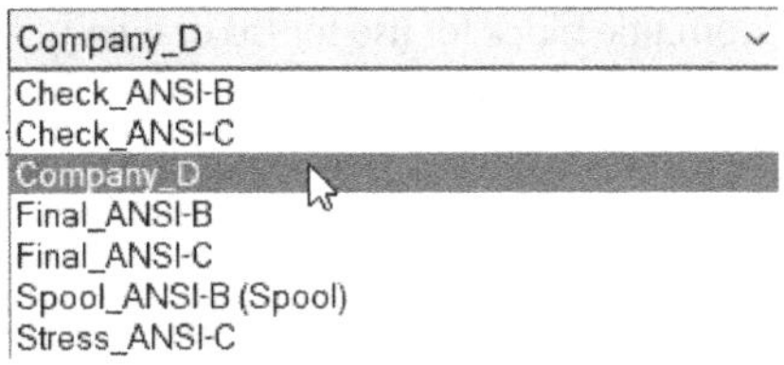

Iso Style Customization

You can customize an Iso style using the following settings (as shown in the following illustration):

- Symbols and Reference
- Iso Style Setup
- Iso Style Default Settings
- Themes
- Annotations
- Dimensions
- Sloped and Offset Piping
- Title Block and Display
- Live Preview

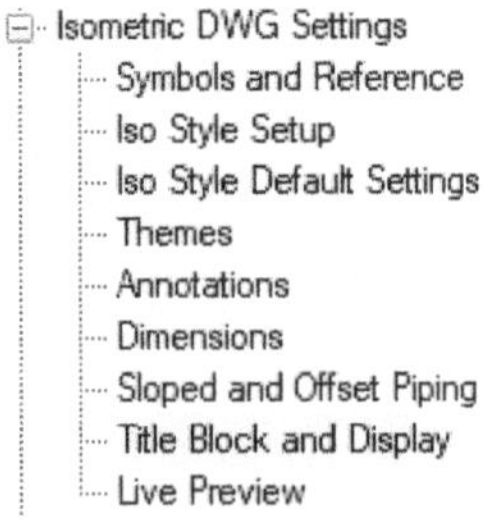

Symbols and Reference

The Iso Symbols and Reference controls how to edit the symbols used during the creation of isometric drawings. You can also set the default properties for the Iso reference dimensions, as shown in the following image.

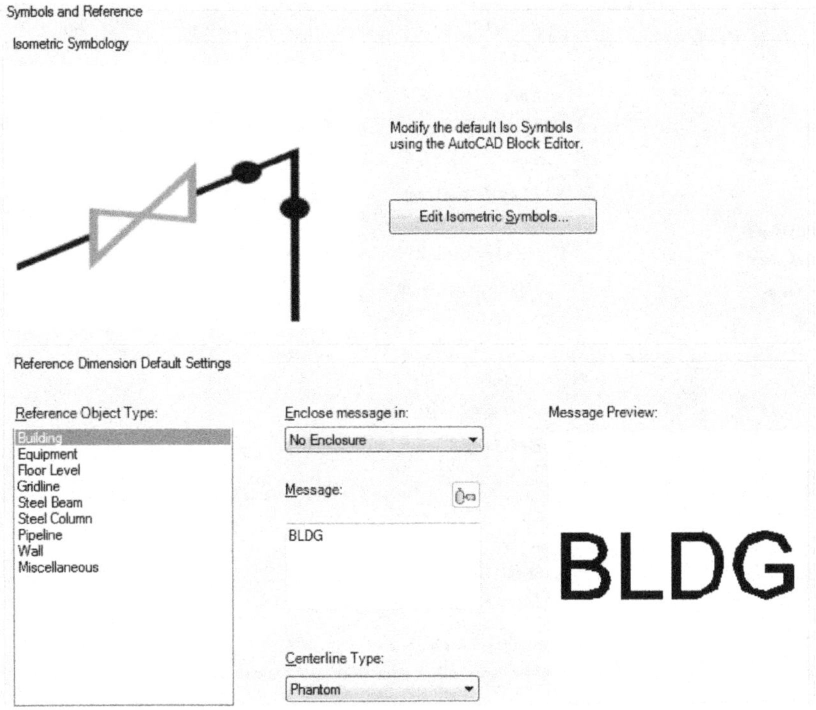

Iso Style Setup

The Iso Style Setup controls a number of features, such as style information, automatic field weld control, field fit weld makeup, file naming, spool naming, and content paths. The Iso Style Setup area of the Project Setup dialog box is shown in the following illustration.

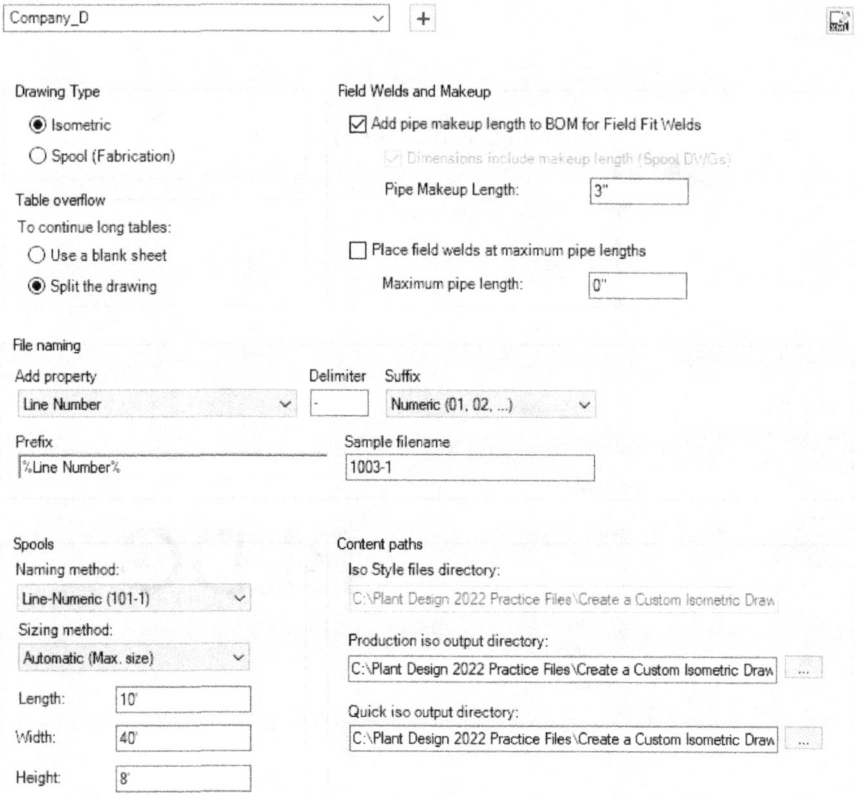

Iso Style Default Settings

The Iso Style Defaults Settings controls many of the default options that are available when creating an Iso drawing along with the defaults for exporting. The Iso creation defaults enable you to set preferences for overwriting, creating DWFs, and splitting the Iso drawing.

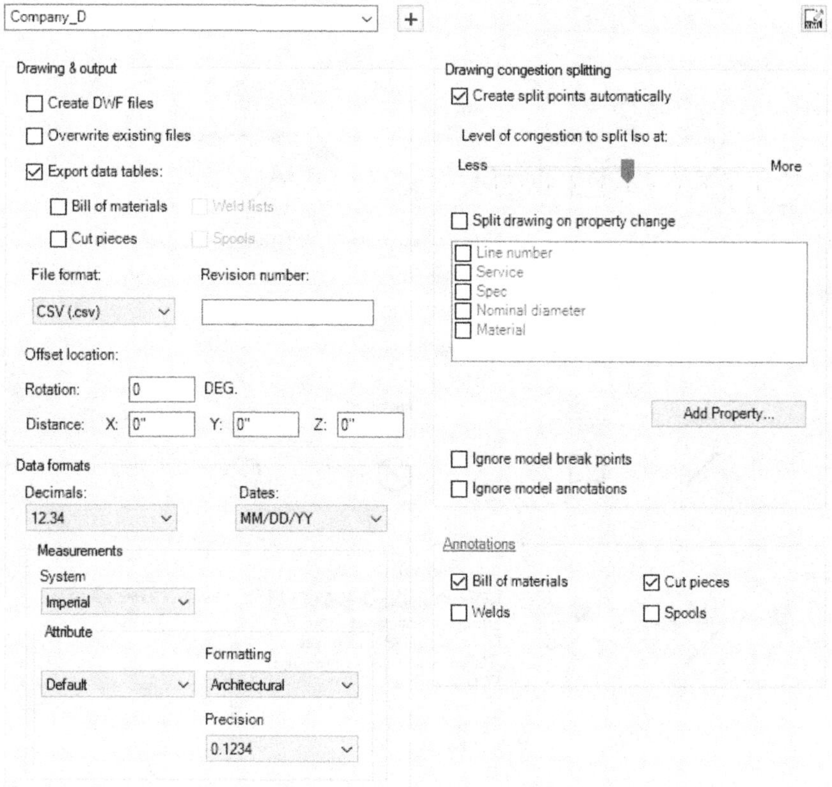

Annotations

Annotations provide the ability to control different portions of the output text on an Iso, including bill of materials (BOM), numbering, and enclosure, cut piece annotations, weld annotations, valve annotations, and end connection annotations, among other things. A portion of the Annotations area of the Project Setup dialog box is shown in the following illustration.

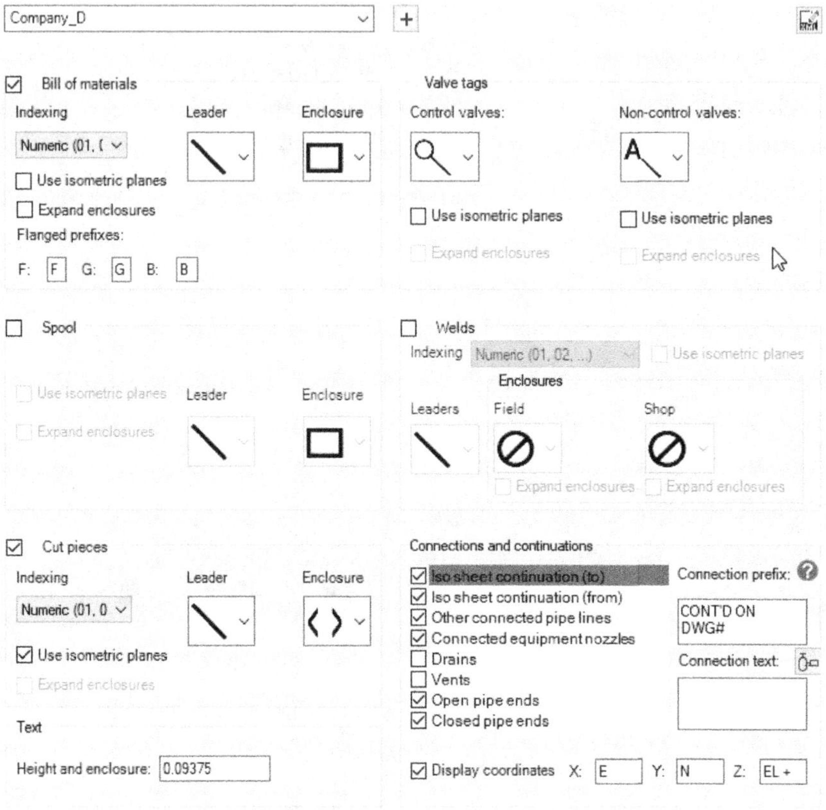

Dimensions

Dimensions enables you to control how not only the overall dimensions are handled, but specific case overrides for items, such as valves, gaskets, and other items. The Settings tab of the Dimensions area is shown in the following illustration.

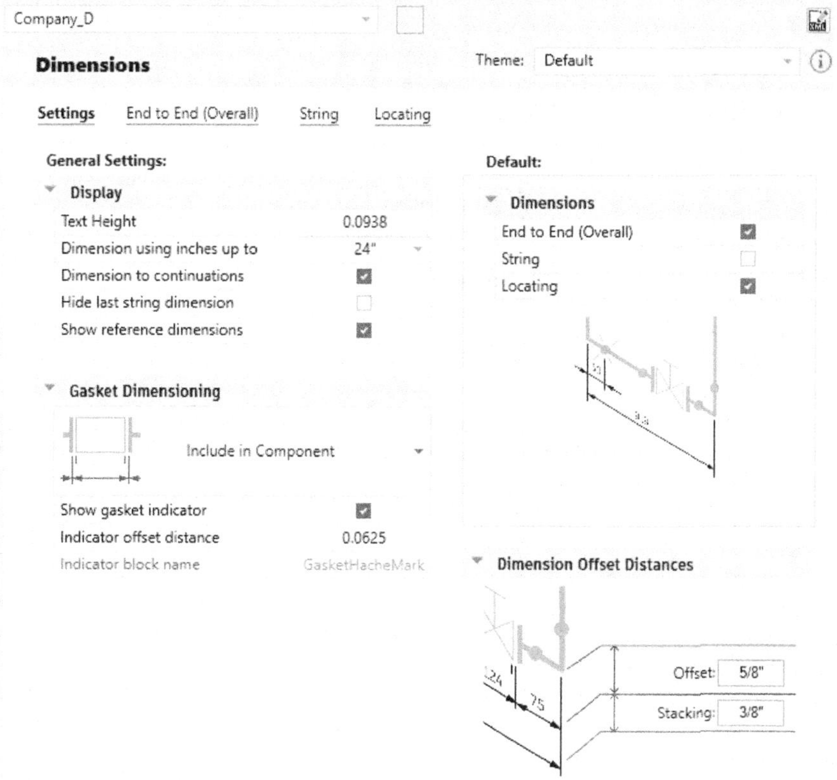

Themes

Themes enables you to control how to display dimensions, annotations, and bill of material reports. The Override and Branch Piping tabs enable you to target specific systems with the customization. The Default Piping tab in the Themes area is shown in the following illustration.

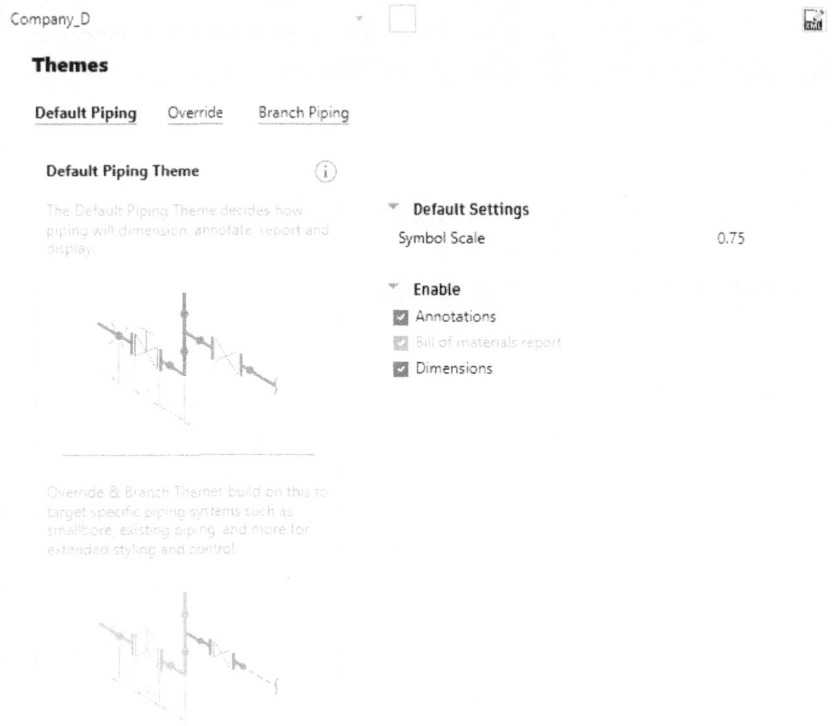

Sloped and Offset Piping

Sloped and Offset Piping provides settings that control how sloped lines are annotated in the Iso drawing. You can control how to show falls, set 2D and 3D skews, and designate the minimum slope to be represented in the isometric drawing. The Sloped and Offset Piping area is shown in the following illustration.

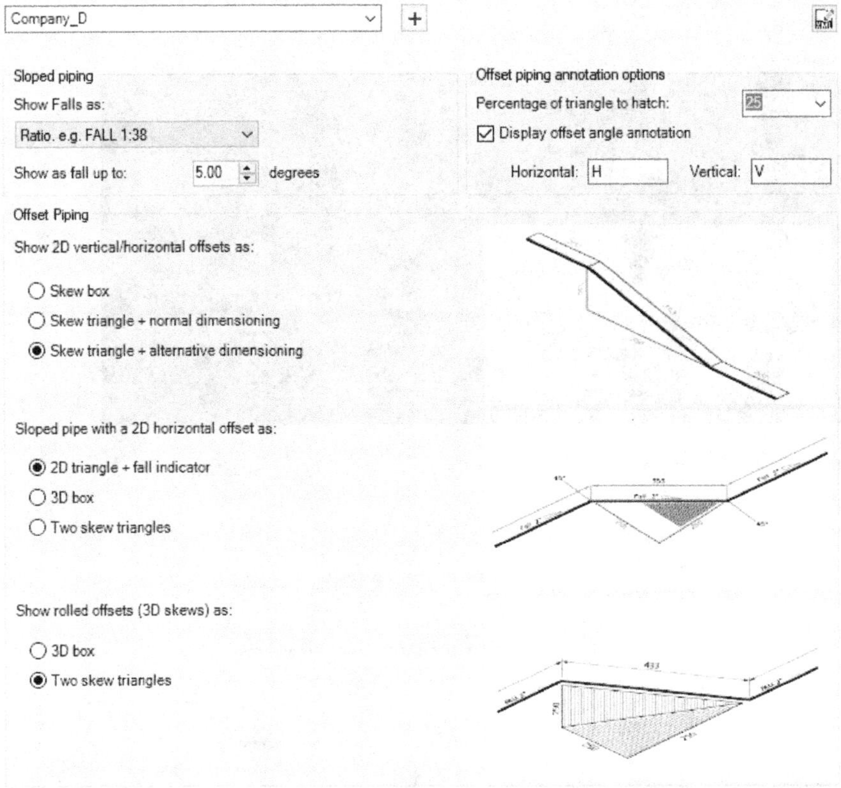

Title Block and Display

Title Block and Display enables you to modify and set up new title blocks, as well as the symbols used on your isometrics. Title blocks are handled as an AutoCAD drawing template, using block references to control the Title Block and North Arrow. The Title Block & display area of the Project Setup dialog box is shown in the following illustration.

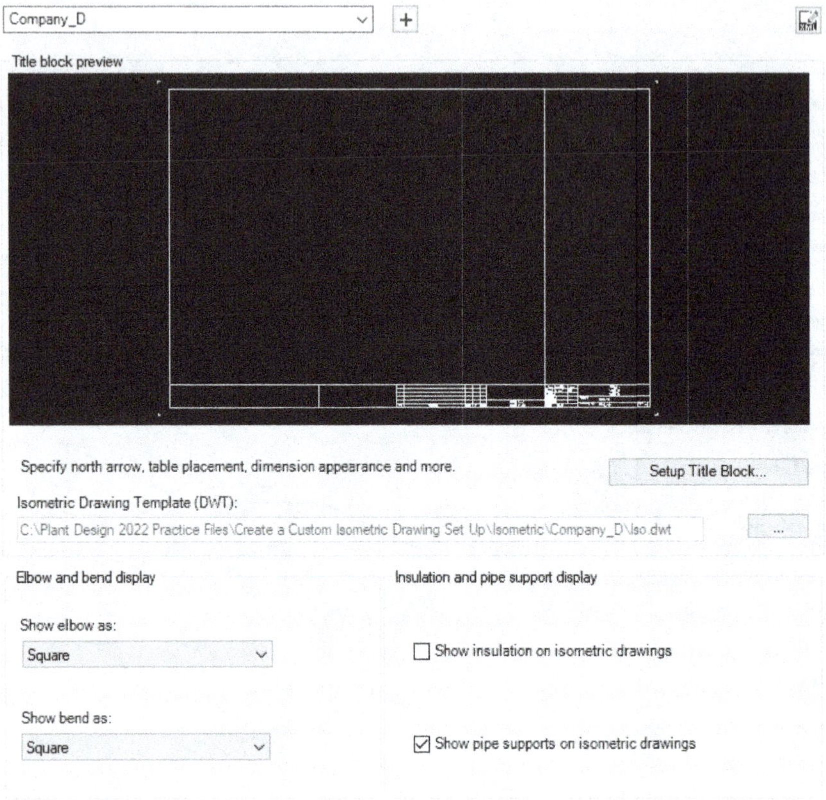

Live Preview

The Live Preview node enables you to view a preview of an Iso style. The preview file is a PCF file. This preview can be used to review style changes made to the Isometric DWG Settings.

Setting Up the Bill of Materials (BOM)

When you create an isometric drawing, one of the components of that drawing is a bill of materials (BOM). The formatting and placement of this is already set up in the Iso styles that are installed with the AutoCAD Plant 3D software. If you create a custom isometric drawing, you probably need to make adjustments to the BOM.

BOM settings are controlled through the Setup Title Block option in the Title Block and Display settings in the Project Setup dialog box. The Table Setup dialog box that is opened from the Title Block Setup tab, on the Table Placement & Setup panel is shown in the following illustration. For each table, bill of materials, Cut Piece list, Weld list, and Spool list, you can control the table layout and settings.

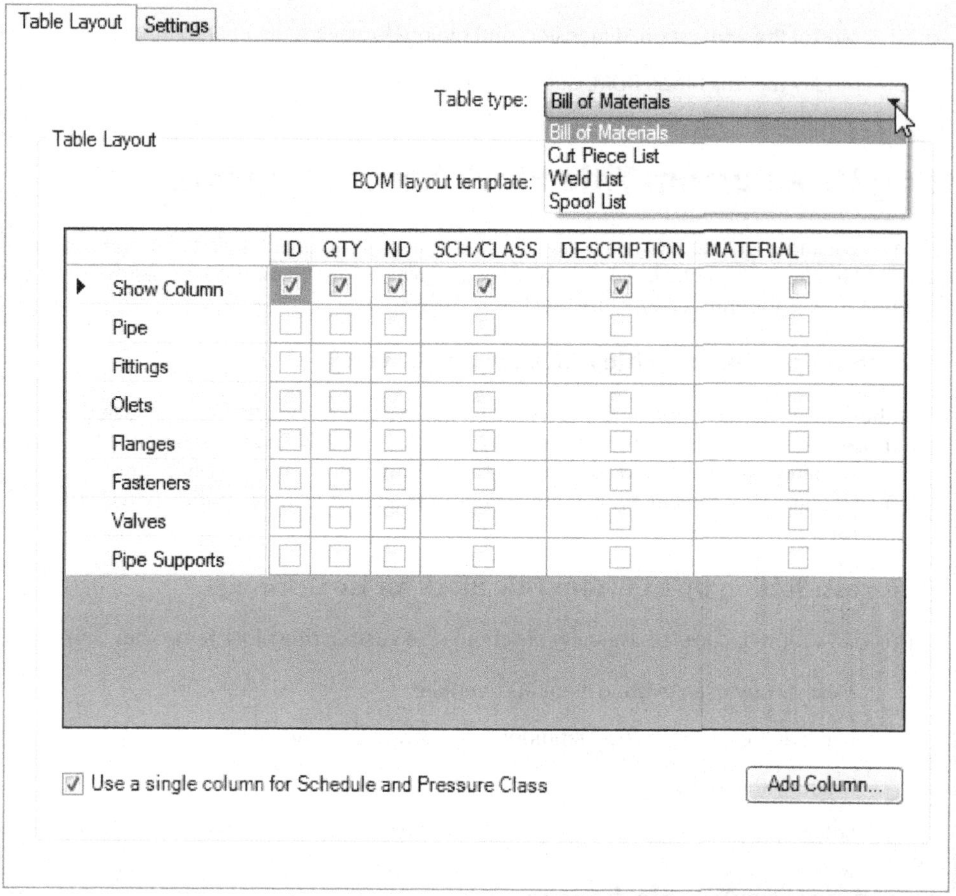

Creating and Configuring a New Iso Style

Creating a new Iso style is key to developing good working Isos that require minimum cleanup. To obtain good working Isos, you need to understand the process of creating and configuring a new Iso style in your project. Note that Iso styles are project-specific, and need to be copied either to the default project folder or to each project after completion.

Process: Creating and Configuring a New Iso Style

The following steps give an overview of creating and configuring a new custom Iso style:

1. In the Project Setup, create a new Iso style based on an existing style.
2. Modify the annotation, dimension, and piping display for the new style.
3. Modify the title block, BOM, Cut list, Weld list, and Spool list.

Setting Up a Custom Title Block for Iso Drawings

The most important step to generating an Iso is to have a custom title block for the company or client. To obtain the custom title block that you need, you must understand the necessary steps and requirements for entering any title block into the system.

Setting Up a Custom Title Block for Iso Drawings

Rather than inserting a title block, there are steps involved to ensure that you have the correct template defined for use with your system. This includes modifying the template file with a new title block definition and redefined coordinates to encompass the larger drawing. Correct creation of the drawing template enables easy customization throughout the system when adding the BOM and other lists.

Process: Setting Up a Custom Title Block for Iso Drawings

The following steps give an overview of setting up a custom title block for Iso drawings:

1. Make a copy of an existing Plant 3D template.
2. Remove the existing block definition information and purge.
3. Insert the new title block and rename the block definition.
4. Set up the Draw Area, No Draw Area, North Arrow Location, and BOM and list information.

Guidelines for Title Block Setup

Follow these guidelines when setting up a custom title block for use with Iso drawings:

- Title Block can start with any name, but the block reference in the template must be "Title Block".
- North Arrow, similar to the title block, has to be defined in the template.

Exercise: Create a Custom Isometric Drawing Setup

In this exercise, you create a new Iso style based on the Final_ANSI-B style. You customize this with a custom user border, along with new dimension styles and annotations.

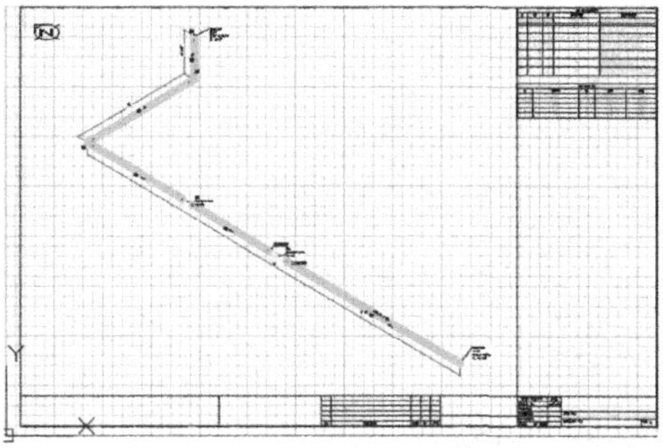

Open a Project and Create a New Iso Type

In this section of the exercise, you create a new Iso style based on Final_ANSI-B. Then, you create an Iso drawing and examine the results. **Do not save changes**.

1. Start the AutoCAD Plant 3D software, if not already running.
2. Open an existing project by doing the following:
   - In the Project Manager, Current Project list, click Open.
   - In the Open dialog box, navigate to the folder *C:\Plant Design 2024 Practice Files\Create a Custom Isometric Drawing Set Up.*
   - Select the file *Project.xml.*
   - Click Open.
3. Open the Project Setup dialog box.
4. In the Project Setup dialog box, under Isometric DWG Settings, select Iso Style Setup.

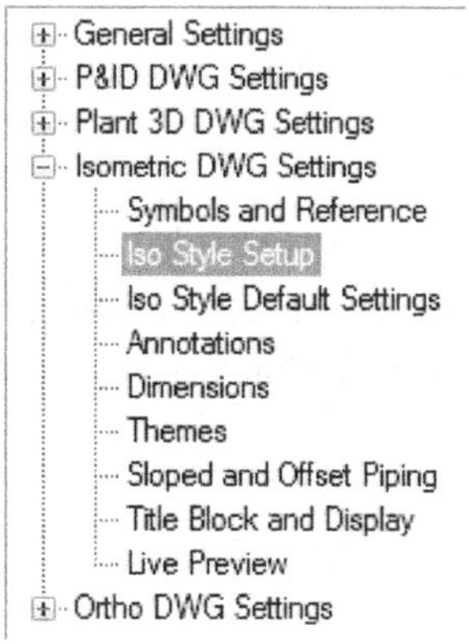

5. In the Iso Style Setup page, click Create a new Iso style based on an existing one (plus button).

6. In the Create Iso Style dialog box:
   - For New style name, enter **Company_D**.
   - In the Select an existing style list, select Final_ANSI-B.
   - Click Create.

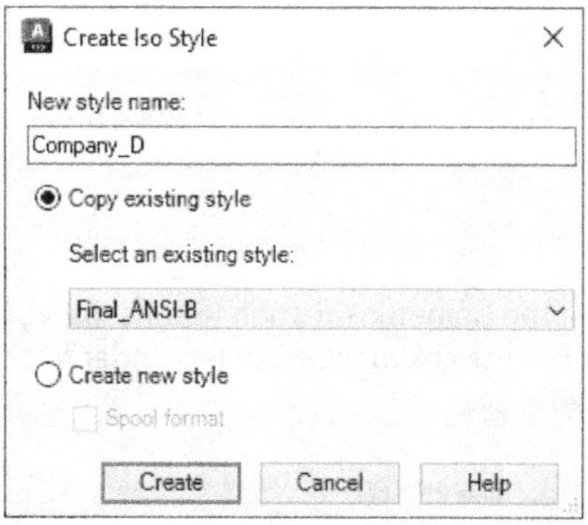

7. In the Project Setup dialog box, click OK.
8. In the Project Manager, open the Piping drawing.

9. To run a test of the new Iso style, on the Isos tab, on the Iso Creation panel, click Production Iso.

   Note: Change the workspace to the 3D Piping workspace, if required, to access the Isos tab.

10. In the Create Production Iso dialog box:

    - From the Line Numbers list, select 2031.
    - From the Iso Style list, select Company_D.
    - Click Create.

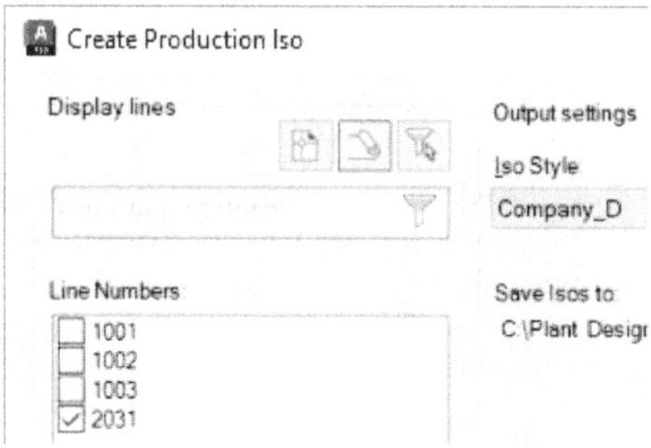

11. When the creation is complete (Iso icon turns blue in the Status bar), click the Click to view isometric creation details option in the pop-up balloon.

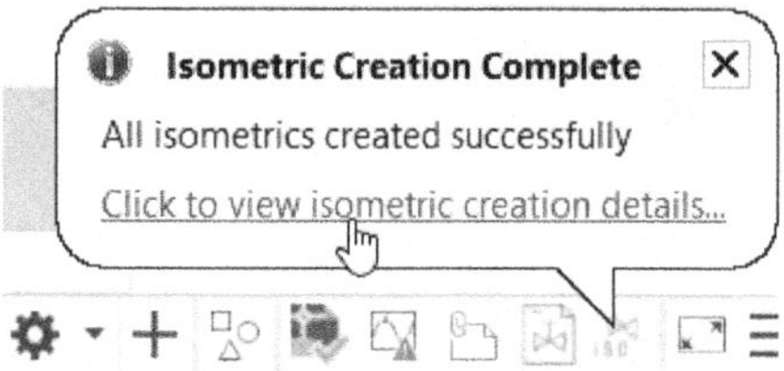

12. In the Isometric Creation Results dialog box, click the link to the file listed under from 2031.pcf.

13. In the isometric drawing, examine the results. This drawing represents the same default settings as the Final_ANSI-B Iso style because it was created based on that style. Close the isometric drawing.

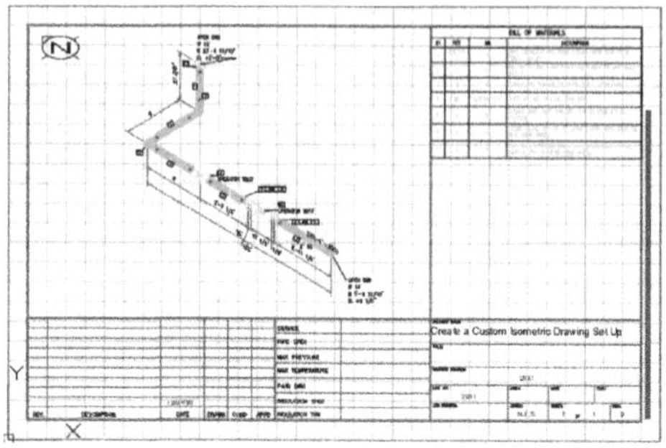

Customize the Settings

In this section of the exercise, you change various settings for the Company_D Iso style and recreate the Iso drawing to examine the results of the changes.

1. Open the Project Setup dialog box.

2. In the Project Setup dialog box, under Isometric DWG Settings, select Dimensions.

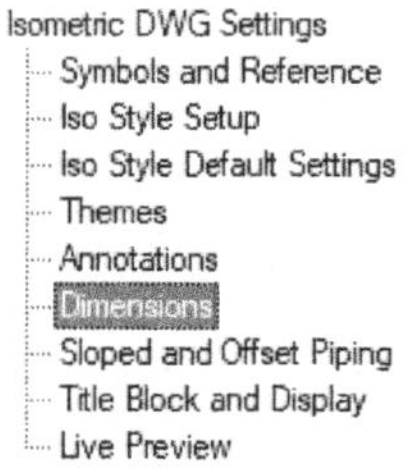

3. Ensure that the Iso Style is set to Company_D.

4. On the Settings tab:

   - Under the Default area, clear the String type dimensions check box.
   - Click Apply.

5. Remaining on the dimension page:
   - In the Gasket Dimensioning area, select Do not Dimension Gaskets from the drop-down list.
   - Click Apply.

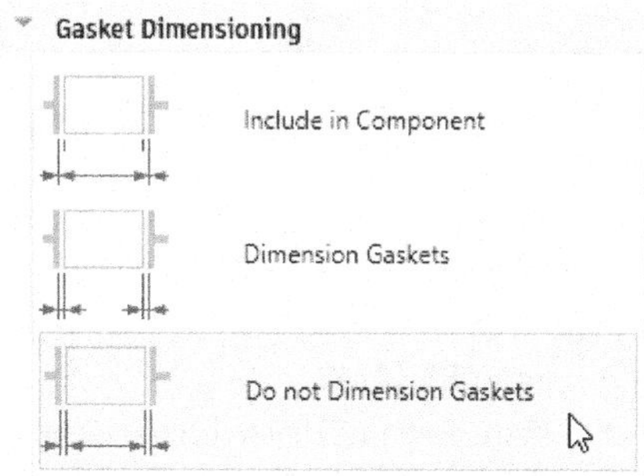

6. Click OK.
7. Recreate the 2031 Iso drawing by clicking Production Iso tool in the ribbon. In the Create Production Iso dialog box, select 2031 and select Overwrite if existing.
8. Open the to view isometric creation details by clicking the file from 2031.pcf. Examine the results of the settings by comparing the two Iso drawings. Note that only one dimension is along the edge with the valves. The individual gaskets were not dimensioned because of the new settings.

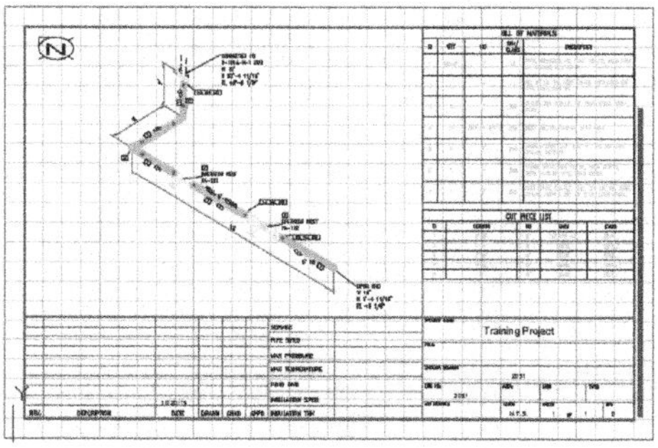

Note: When you recreate an Iso from the same line, the AutoCAD Plant 3D software creates a new Iso drawing name with a unique suffix. For example, 2031 (2). To overwrite the existing Iso when creating the Iso, click Overwrite if existing in the Create Production Iso dialog box.

Establish a Custom Iso Template

In this section of the exercise, you modify the Iso drawing template for the custom style so that it uses a custom company title block.

1. To open the *iso.dwt*:
   - On the Quick Access Toolbar, click Open.
   - In the Select File dialog box, Files of type list, select Drawing Template (*.dwt).
   - Navigate to the folder *C:\Plant Design 2024 Practice Files\Create a Custom Isometric Drawing Set Up\Isometric\Company_D.*
   - Select and open *iso.dwt.*
2. Delete all of the geometry, hatched areas (like the North Arrow and tables), and the title block that are displayed in the graphics window.
3. To purge the definition of the original title block from the template:
   - Enter **PURGE**.
   - In the Purge dialog box, under Blocks, right-click on Title Block. Click Purge Title Block.
   - In the Purge - Confirm Purge dialog box, click Purge this item. Do not purge the other items in the Blocks list.
   - The Blocks list now displays, as shown in the following illustration. Click Close.

   Note: Only purge the title block definition. Do not purge the North Arrow. If you do, it will not be available for placement later in the exercise.

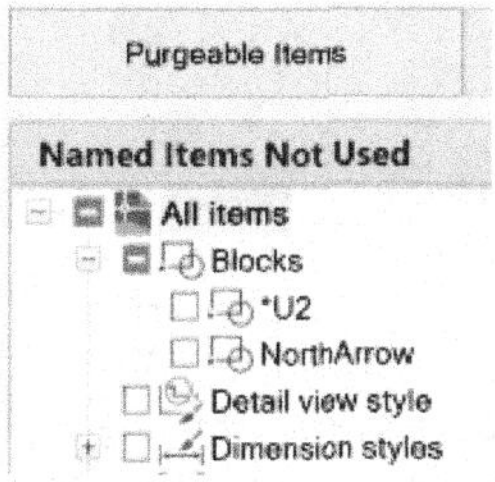

4. To begin to insert a custom company D-size border into the template drawing:
   - On the Insert tab, on the Block panel, expand Insert and click Blocks from Libraries.
   - Using the Navigation tool, navigate to the folder *C:\Plant Design 2024 Practice Files\Create a Custom Isometric Drawing Set Up\Company Drawing Templates*.
   - Select and open *Company_Dsize.dwg*.

5. In the Blocks palette, set the following:
   - In the Options area, clear Insertion Point and set the X,Y,Z values to 0,0,0.
   - Verify that the scale is set to 1 in the X, Y, Z edit box.
   - Verify that the Rotation Angle to 0.
   - Clear Explode if checked.

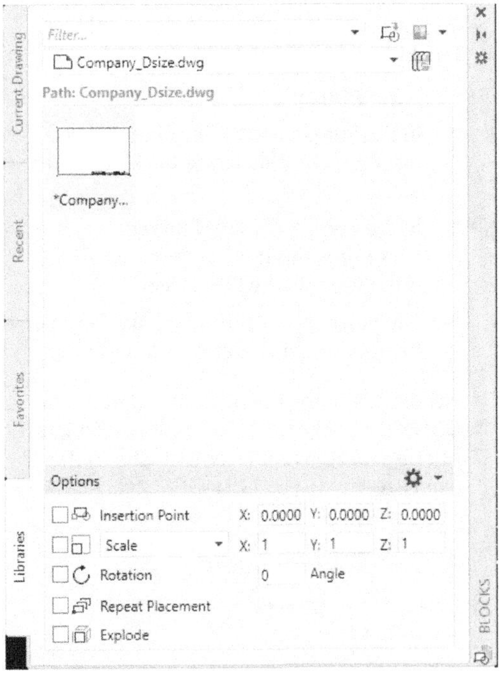

6. Double-click on the *Company_Dsize*. In the Edit Attributes dialog box, click Cancel. The drawing now displays as shown in the following illustration.

   Close the Blocks palette.

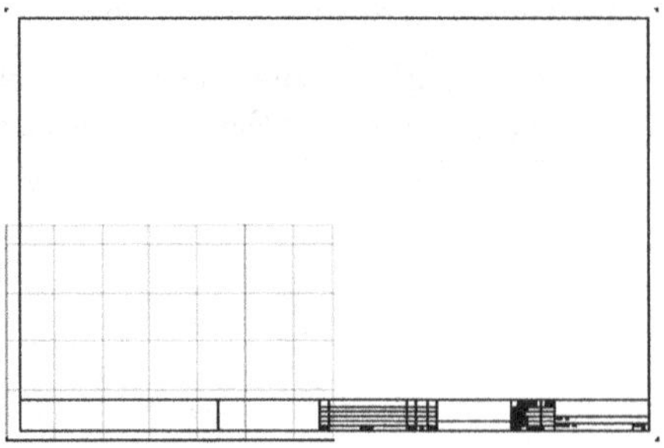

7. To rename the custom block definition for the title block and border so that it will be identified as an Iso title block:
   - Enter **RENAME**.
   - In the Rename dialog box, select Blocks in the Named Objects list.
   - In the Items list, select Company_Dsize.
   - In the Rename To field, enter **Title Block**.
   - Click Rename To.
   - Click OK.

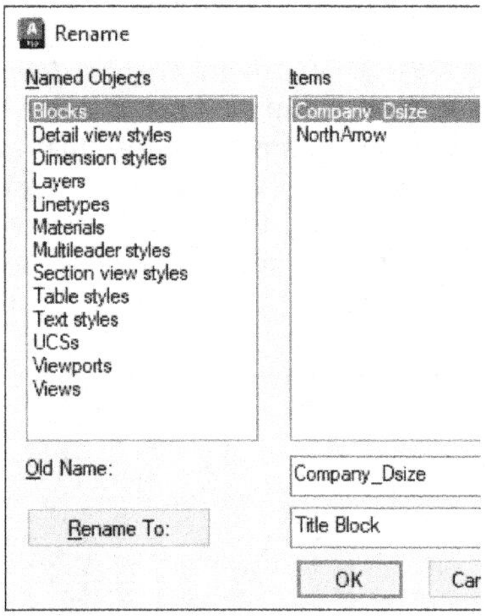

8. To set the drawing limits to match trim marks in the border block:
   - Enter **LIMITS**.
   - For the lower left corner, press <Enter>.
   - For the upper right corner, use the endpoint object snap to snap to the uppermost top right corner endpoint outside of the title block. The drawing displays as shown in the following illustration.

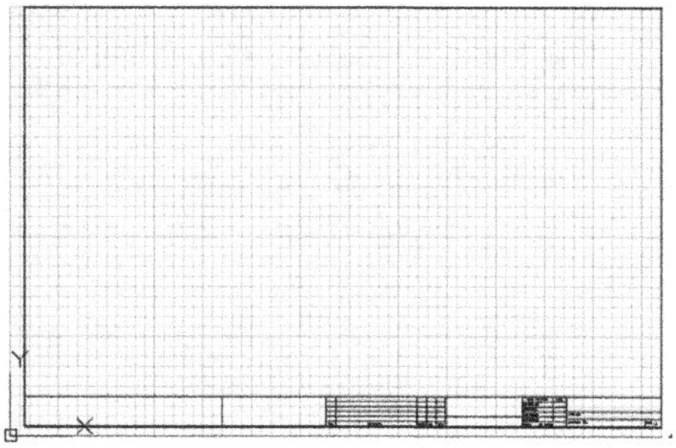

9. Save and close *iso.dwt*.

Set Up the Custom Iso Title Block

In this section of the exercise, you define the drawing and BOM area of the custom Iso title block.

1. Open the Project Setup dialog box.
2. Under Isometric DWG Settings, select Title Block and Display.
3. In the Title block & display page:
   - Ensure that Iso Style is set to Company_D.
   - In the Title block preview area, click Setup Title Block.
4. Modify the title block by right-clicking on the existing title block and selecting Block Editor. This opens the title block in the Block Editor.
5. Zoom into the title block near the bottom and select the left vertical line along the ENG RECORD label as shown in the illustration.

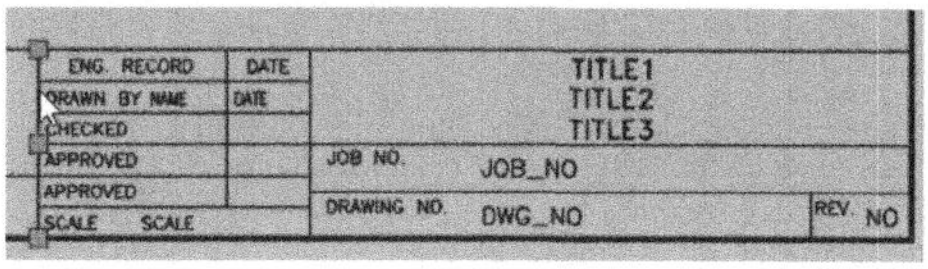

6. Click on the top-most grip and stretch the line up, till it is perpendicular with the top horizontal line of the border. (Use Perpendicular Object Snap)

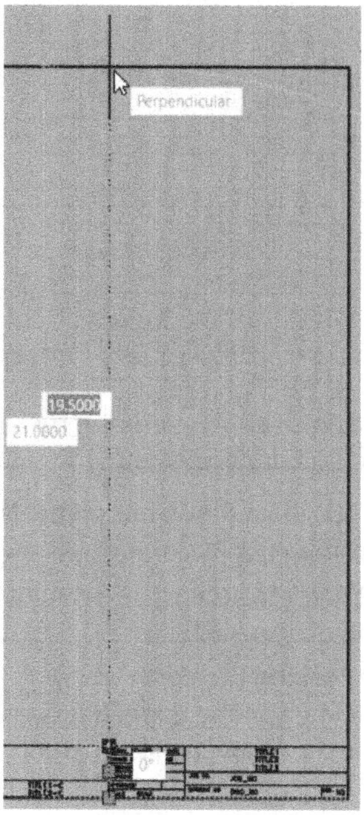

7. Close the Block editor and click Save the changes to Title Block. This provides a clean boundary between the drawing area and the table area.
8. To begin to set the drawing area in the border, on the Title Block Setup tab, on the Isometric Drawing Area panel, click Draw Area.

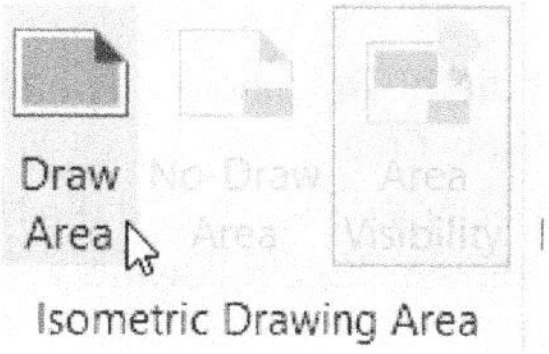

9. In the left side area, select two opposite points to define the drawing area as shown in the following illustration. Do not snap to any of the borders.

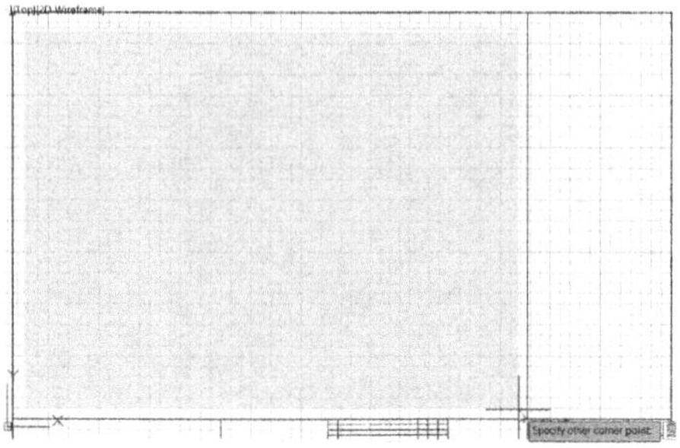

10. To insert the north arrow symbol in the upper left corner of the drawing area:

- On the Title Block Setup tab, on the North Arrow panel, click Place North Arrow.
- Press <Enter> to accept the default arrow direction of upper left.
- Click to position the north arrow approximately in the upper left corner as shown in the following illustration.

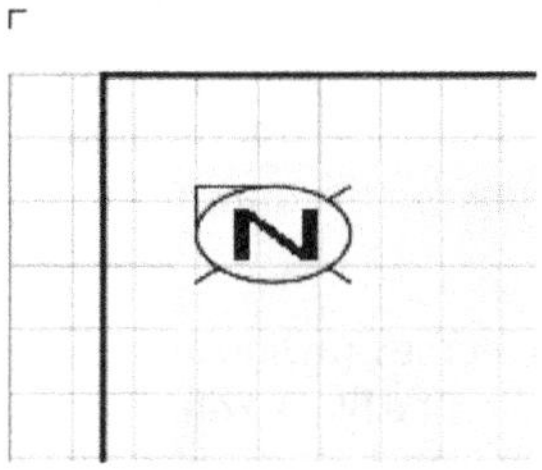

11. To set the area around the North Arrow as a no-draw area:

- On the Isometric Drawing Area panel, click No-Draw Area.
- Click to specify an area around the North Arrow as shown in the following illustration.

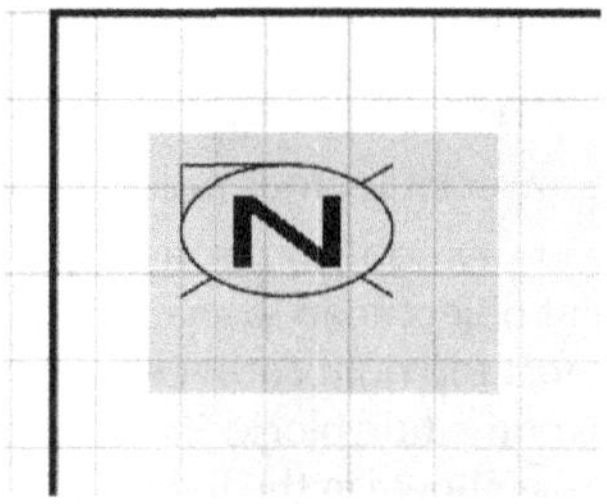

12. To begin to specify where the BOM should go, on the Title Block Setup tab, on the Table Placement & Setup panel, click Bill of Materials.

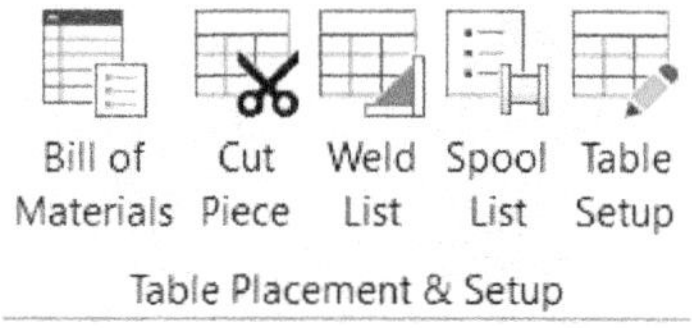

13. Using the Endpoint Object snap, click the upper left endpoint of the newly extended line and the right corner above the title bar, as shown in the following illustration.

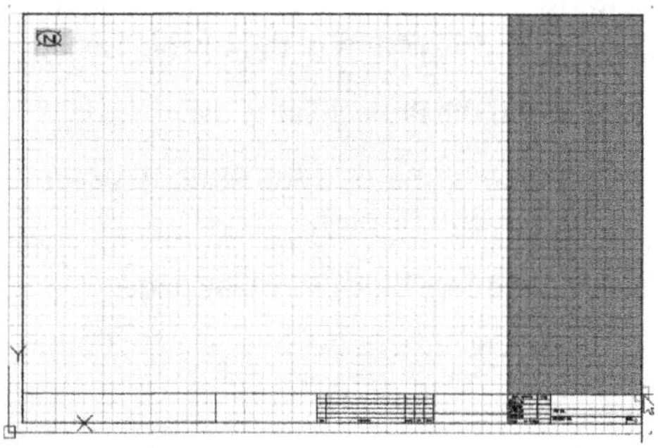

14. Note that the BOM table is now at the top of the specified area.

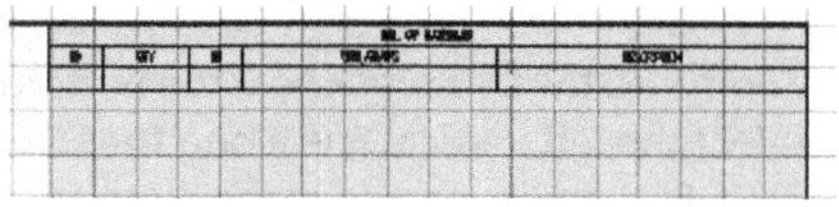

15. To define the area for a Cut Piece list:

- On the Table Placement & Setup panel, click Cut Piece.
- Open the down-arrow list or in the Command Line, select Add to existing area and then select inside the Bill of Material area. It places the new table just below the BOM.
- Press <Esc>. The completed setup now displays similar to shown in the following illustration.

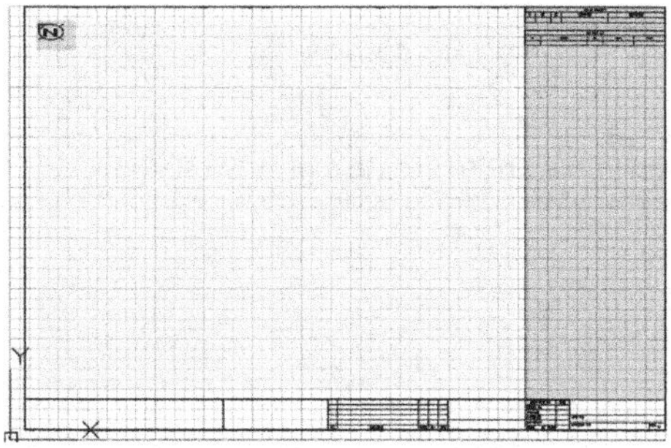

16. On the Title Block Setup tab, on the Close panel, click Return to Project Setup.
17. In the Block-Changes Not Saved dialog box, click Save the changes to "iso.dwt".
18. In the Project Setup dialog box, click OK.
19. Recreate the 2031 Iso drawing and examine the results of the settings.

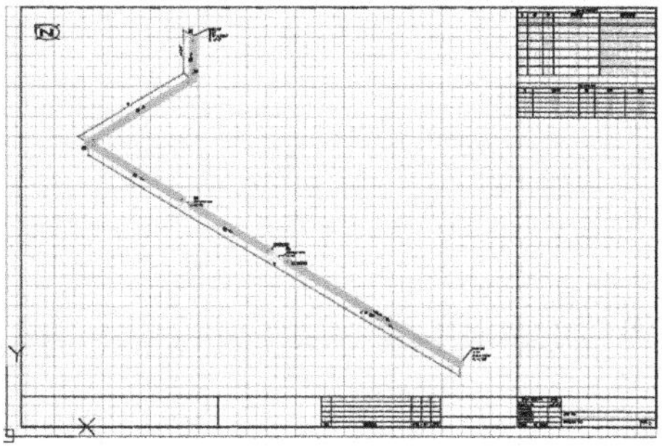

20. Save and close all drawings.

Lesson Review Questions

1. Where do you access the Isometric DWG Setting?
   a. AutoCAD Options
   b. The Isos tab on the ribbon
   c. Project Setup
   d. The Install folder of Plant 3D
2. What does the block definition need to be named for the Title Block to work?
   a. Anything you want, the software recognizes it
   b. Title Block
   c. Border
   d. The same as the Style Name
3. Which Project Setup section do you go to when you want to create a new Iso style?
   a. Annotations
   b. Title Block and Display
   c. Iso Style Setup
   d. Dimensions

Lesson: Troubleshooting

Overview

In this lesson, you learn what options there are to recover drawings and solve error messages when working with the AutoCAD Plant 3D software.

Objectives

After completing this lesson, you will be able to:

- Describe the process to validate components in a drawing or project.
- Describe the process for auditing Plant 3D drawings.
- List the tools used to create an Iso drawing from components that do not have a line number.
- Identify where the Iso creation options for controlling drawing congestion are located.

Validating Drawings

Before you hand off a P&ID project or drawing, you want to be sure that all connections and annotations are labeled. To do so, you can run a Validation Check on your project or drawing. To validate a project, on the Home tab, on the Validate panel, click Run Validation. Keep in mind, if a project is large, validating the entire project can take a very long time. It might make more sense to validate a drawing when you feel it is complete.

To validate a drawing, in the Project Manager, you right-click on the drawing and click Validate. The AutoCAD P&ID software analyzes the drawing and displays a Validation Summary. In the Validation Summary palette, you can select to Ignore specific errors, or click on the error to have the display zoom to the specific component.

The Validation Summary palette for the drawing PID001 is shown in the following illustration.

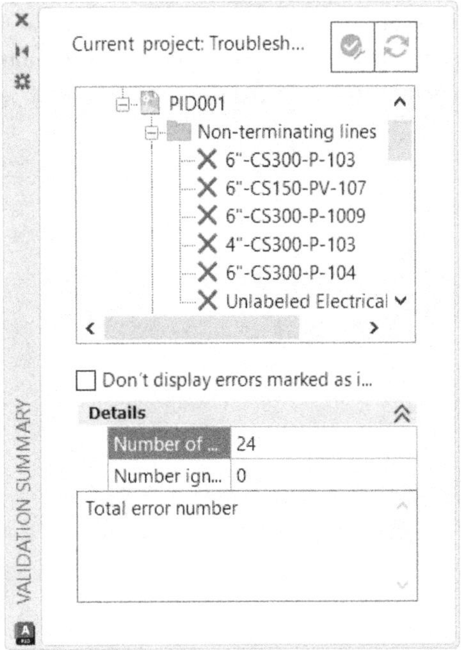

The Validation Progress dialog box opens while the validation is being performed, as shown in the following illustration.

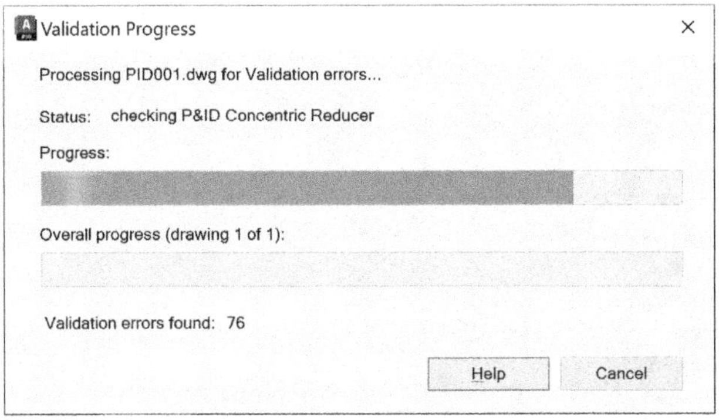

Process: Validate P&ID Projects and Drawings

The following steps give an overview of validating P&ID drawings and projects.

1. To validate a project, on the ribbon, on the Home tab, on the Validate panel, click Run Validation. To validate a drawing, in the Project Manager, right-click on the drawing and click Validate, as shown in the following illustration.

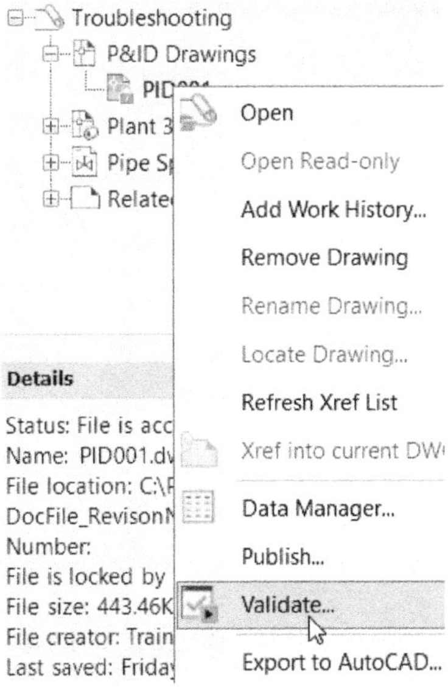

2. Review the results in the Validation Summary palette, as shown in the following illustration.

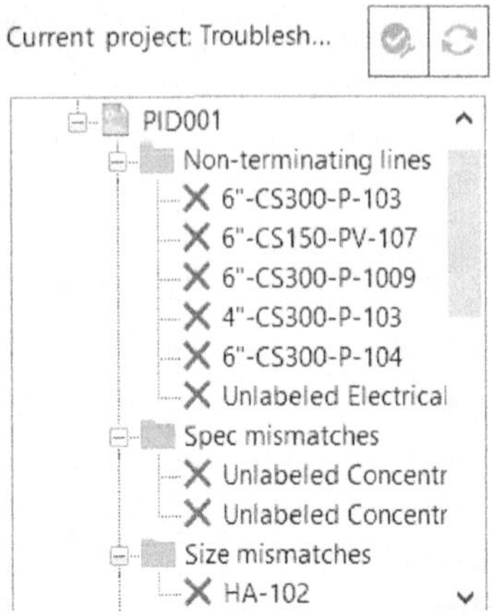

3. To see an issue in the drawing, select the error notification on the Validation Summary palette. The drawing automatically zooms and pans to the location.

4. To remove validation issues from further analysis, right-click on the issue and click Ignore or resolve the issue and rerun the validation, as shown in the following illustration. Ignored issues are moved to the Errors Marked as Ignored folder. To return them to the error list, right-click on them and click <Unassigned>. Rerunning the validation does not return them as unassigned.

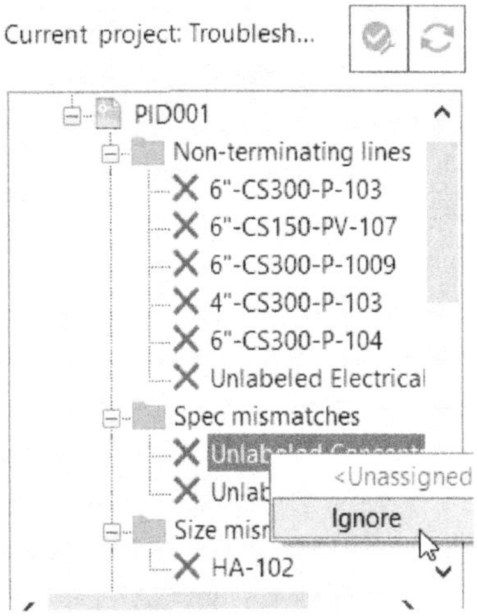

Validation Settings

To change the validation settings, right-click on the project name and select Validation Settings. The P&ID Validation Settings dialog box enables you to specify which conditions between specific objects are reported as errors during a validation, as shown in the following illustration.

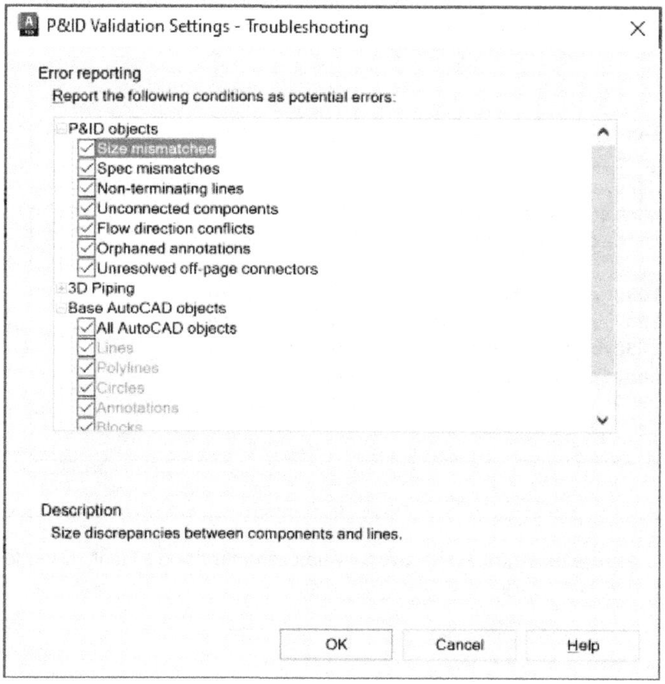

Auditing Drawings

Additionally, you can use the AUDITPROJECT command to repair all the drawings in an entire project.

If a project crashes, corrupting the Plant 3D model, you use the PLANTAUDIT command to repair the model in a single drawing. Enter **PLANTAUDIT** at the command line in the current drawing to run the command, as shown in the following illustration.

```
Command: plantaudit
Command:
The auditing process is starting.
Updated cache connection data for part 6BA.
Updated cache connection data for part 6CE.
Updated cache connection data for part 6D3.
Updated cache connection data for part C09.
Erased component 10AD not linked to project database.
Erased component 10B2 not linked to project database.
Erased component 10B7 not linked to project database.
Erased component 10BC not linked to project database.
Updated cache connection data for part 1309.
Erased component 1320 not linked to project database.
The auditing process is complete.

Command:
```

Important: Do not use the AutoCAD Recover or Audit commands on a Plant 3D model drawing.

Quick Iso

If you need to create an Iso drawing with components that do not have a line number assigned, you use the Quick Iso tool, as shown in the following illustration. This tool enables you to select the components in the drawing that you want to include in the Iso drawing that it creates. The selected components are included in the Iso drawing even if they do not have line numbers assigned. For more information on the Quick Iso tool, see AutoCAD Plant 3D Help.

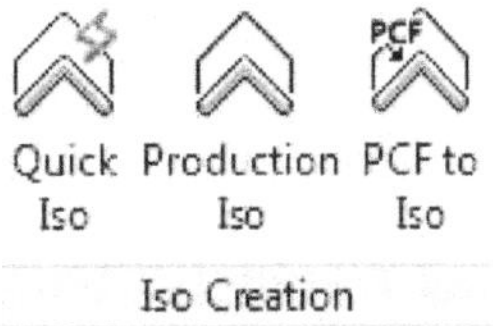

Iso Congestion

If you create an Iso and wish to force more onto one sheet, or force a less congested split, consider using the advanced options.

The Advanced Iso Creation Options dialog box is shown in the following illustration. To open this dialog box, start the Create Quick Iso tool and select the components to Iso. In the Create Quick Iso dialog box, click Advanced. Under Drawing congestion splitting, adjust the slider to specify the level of congestion.

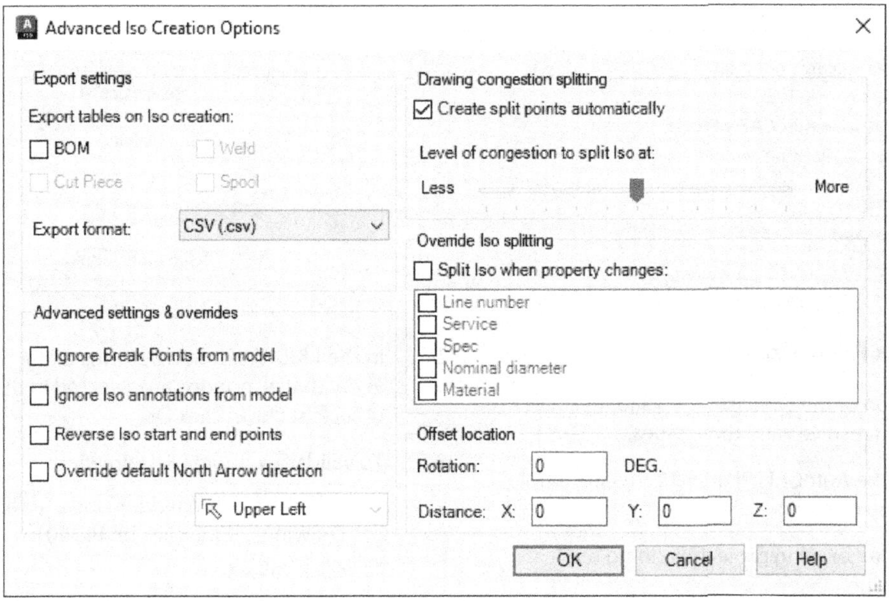

Note: The Advanced Iso Creation Options are also available if you are creating a Production Iso.

Exercise: Troubleshooting

In this exercise, you validate a P&ID drawing and fix some of the errors. You also modify the Advanced Iso Creation options to reverse the direction of an Iso.

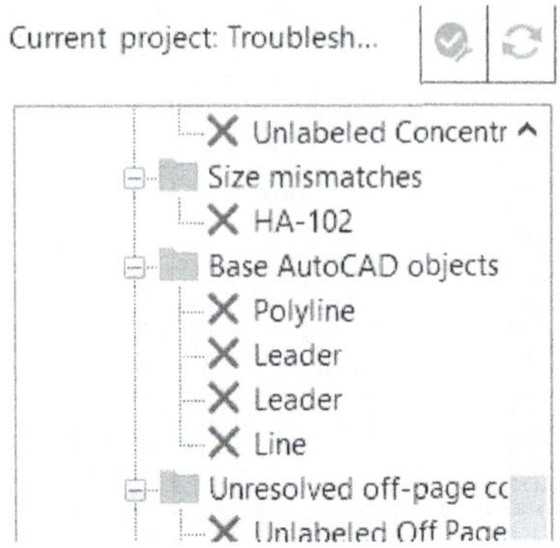

Validate a P&ID Drawing

In this section of the exercise, you validate a P&ID drawing and resolve validation issues.

1. Start the AutoCAD Plant 3D software, if not already running.
2. Open an existing project by doing the following:
   - In the Project Manager, Current Project list, click Open.
   - In the Open dialog box, navigate to the folder *C:\Plant Design 2024 Practice Files\Troubleshooting*.
   - Select the file *Project.xml*.
   - Click Open.
3. Under P&ID Drawings, open *PID001.dwg*
4. To specify validation settings:
   - In the Project Manager, right-click on the Project node.
   - Click Validation Settings.

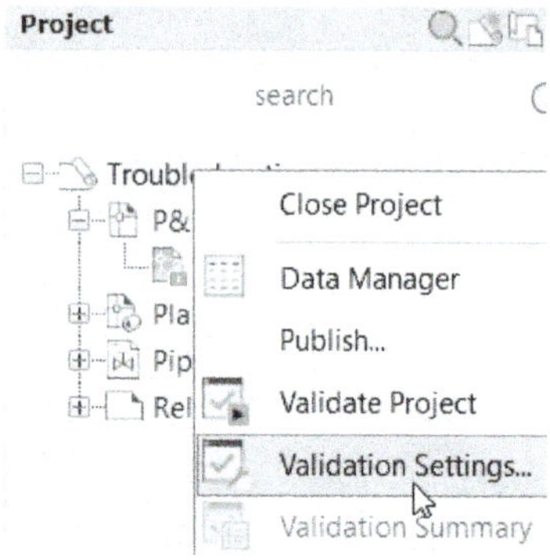

5. In the P&ID Validation Settings dialog box, verify that all options are selected in the P&ID objects section. Click OK.
6. To validate a single P&ID drawing:
   - In the Project Manager, under P&ID Drawings, right-click on PID001.
   - Click Validate.

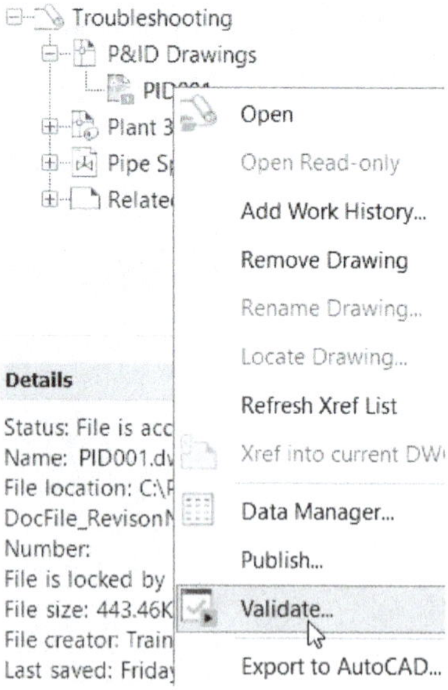

7. On the Validation Summary palette, under PID001, expand Base AutoCAD objects, and click Block Reference. In the drawing area, the software automatically zooms the display to the area.

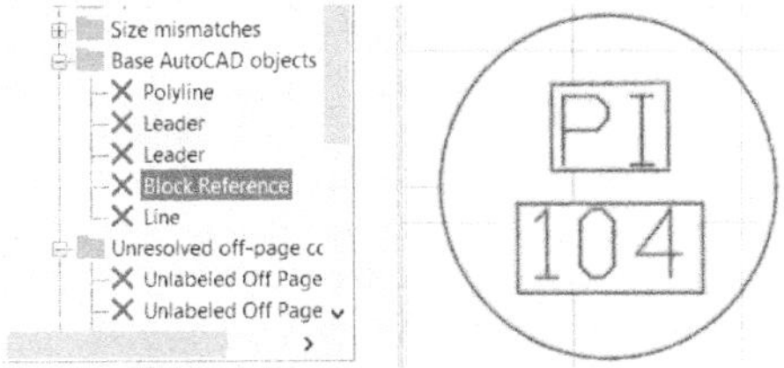

8. In the drawing area, select and right-click on the symbol. Click Convert to P&ID Object.

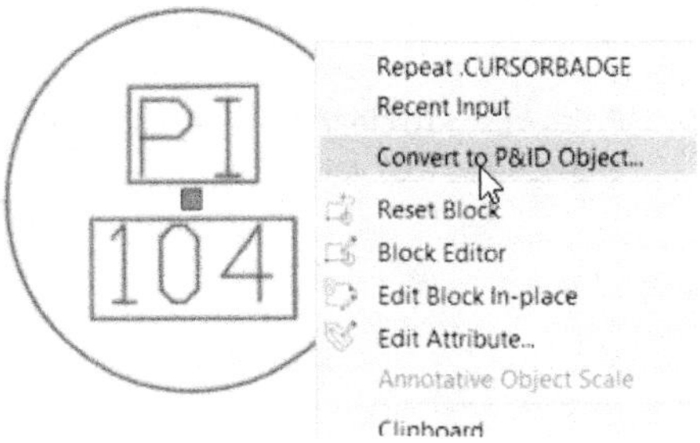

9. In the Convert to P&ID Object dialog box, expand Engineering Items> Instrumentation>General Instrument Symbols. Click Field Discrete Instrument. Click OK.

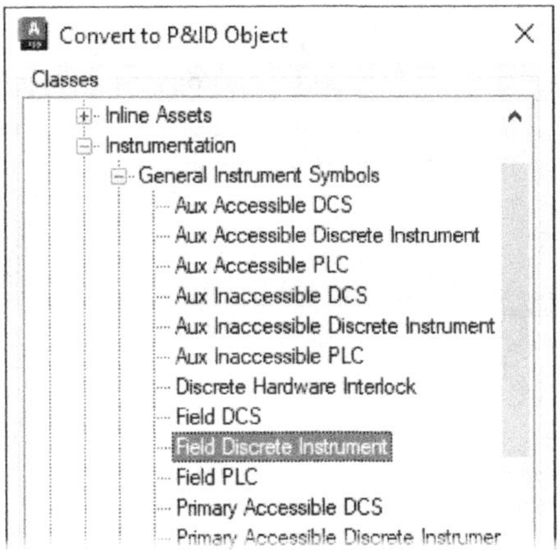

10. Select and right-click on the blank symbol. Click Assign Tag.

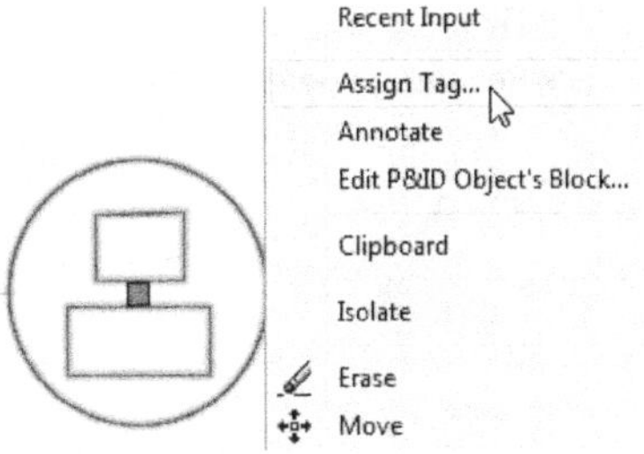

11. In the Assign Tag dialog box:
   - For Area, enter **10**.
   - From the Type list, select PI - Pressure Indicator.
   - For the Loop Number, enter **104**.
   - Click Assign.

12. To refresh the symbol values:
   - Select the symbol.
   - Select the Substitute with another Component grip.
   - Click Field DCS.

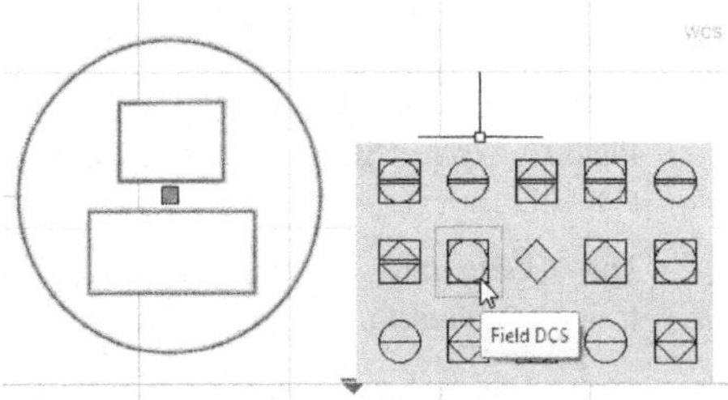

13. Set your WIPEOUTFRAME to 0 and note that the symbol is refreshed and displayed with the correct values.

14. To rerun the validation:
    - On the Validation Summary palette, click PID001.
    - Click Revalidate Selected Node.

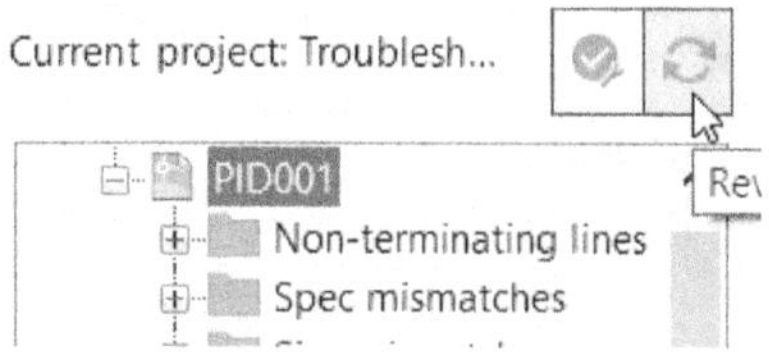

15. Note that Block Reference is no longer listed in the Base AutoCAD objects folder.

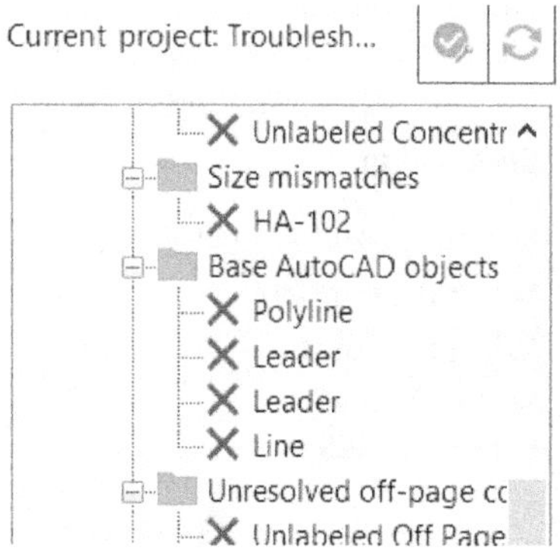

16. On the Validation Summary palette, under PID001, expand Size mismatches, and click HA-102.

    The 4" Gate Valve is highlighted and zoomed to in the drawing.

17. In the drawing area, select the gate valve and open its Properties.

18. On the Properties palette, under P&ID, expand the General section:
    - Click in the Size field.
    - Click Override mode symbol.
    - Click Acquire mode: from Pipe Line Segments.Size.

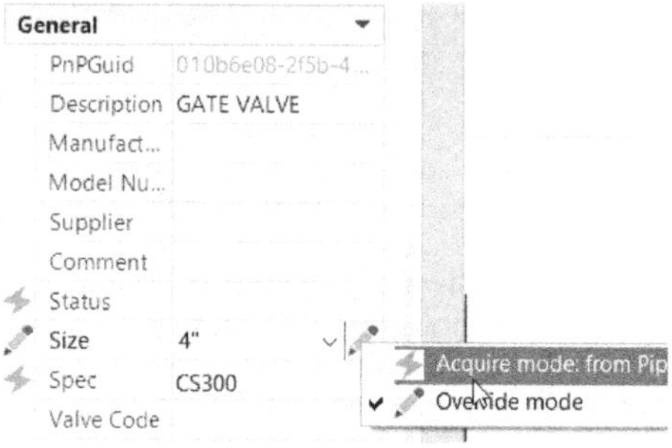

19. Press <Esc> to clear the selection. The Valve is changed to a 6" valve.

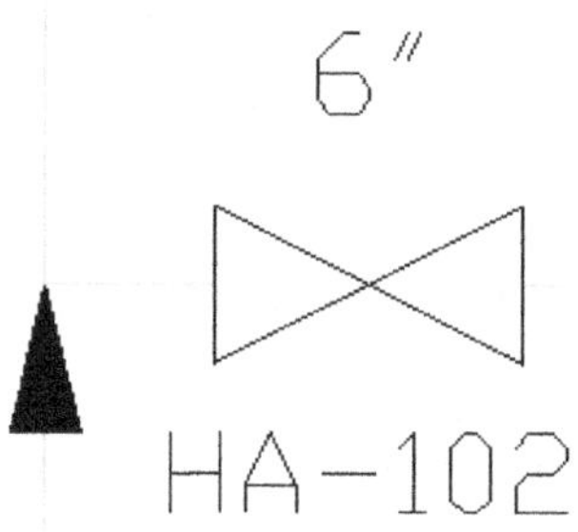

20. Rerun the validation (In the Validation Summary palette, select PID001 and click Revalidate Selected Node). Note that there is no Size mismatch in the list.

21. On the Validation Summary palette, under PID001, click Orphaned annotations:

- Click the first Unlabeled Annotation. Note the annotation that is highlighted below the pump.
- Under Details, note that the Allowed Distance is set to 25 and the Actual Distance is 27.5.

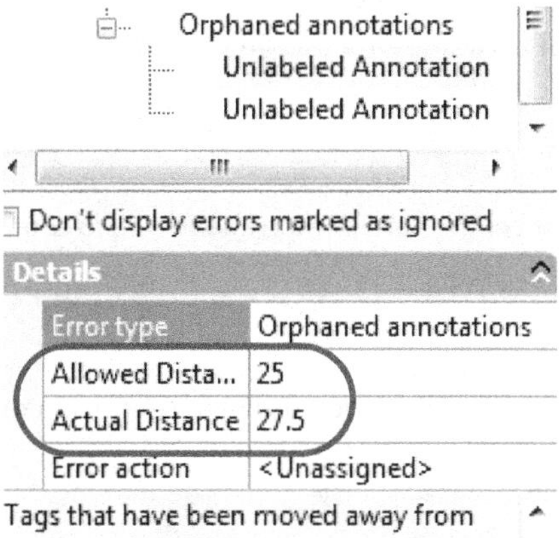

22. Click the second Unlabeled Annotation. Note that under Details, the values are the same.

23. In the drawing area, select the labels under both pumps.

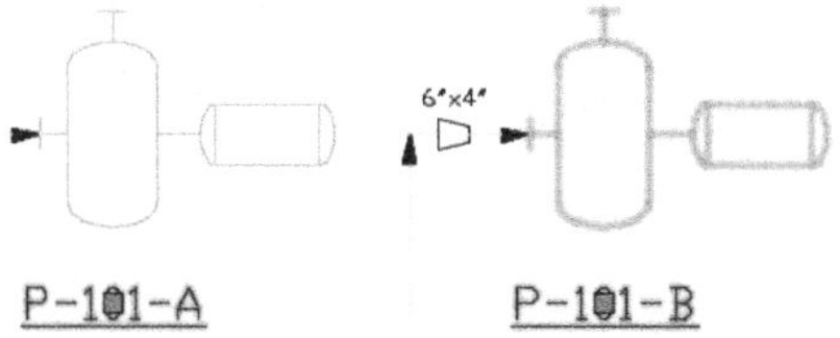

24. Use the Move command to move the labels closer to the pumps.

25. Rerun the validation. Note that there are no Orphaned annotations left.

26. Save and close the drawing.

Audit a Drawing

In this section of the exercise, you audit a Plant 3D drawing to correct an issue with orphaned fasteners.

1. In the Project Manager, under Plant 3D Drawings, expand Piping, and open the Piping drawing.

2. Use Zoom to display the drawing extents.

3. If the Orphaned Fasteners Detected message balloon is displayed, click the Click here to remove orphans link.

   Note: If the message balloon does not display, continue to the next step. It has resolved itself.

4. To ensure that the drawing database is cleaned up, on the command prompt, enter **PLANTAUDIT**.

5. Press <F2> to review the auditing information in the Text Window. You can review this list. The issue with orphaned fasteners was resolved.

```
Updated cache port data for part 10AD.
Updated cache connection data for part 10AD.
Updated cache port data for part 10B2.
Updated cache connection data for part 10B2.
Updated cache port data for part 10B7.
Updated cache connection data for part 10B7.
Updated cache port data for part 10BC.
Updated cache connection data for part 10BC.
Invalid pipe center of gravity 1105
Invalid pipe center of gravity 111F
Invalid pipe center of gravity 112F
Invalid pipe center of gravity 1148
Invalid pipe center of gravity 117A
The auditing process is complete.
Command:

Command:
The structural auditing process is starting.
The structural auditing process is complete.

Command:
```

6. Save and close the drawings.

Lesson Review Questions

1. How can you check whether your P&ID is consistent?
   a. Use the Data Manager to check whether everything is connected.
   b. Use the Project Manager to activate the validation setting and validate the drawing.
   c. Print the drawing and check it manually.
   d. There are no options for checking the consistency of your P&ID.
2. If a validation error is ignored, there is no way to return to the error list without having to rerun the Validation.
   a. True
   b. False
3. The Advanced Iso Creation Options that control the congestion splitting enable you to control the level of detail on a sheet.
   a. True
   b. False
4. If the AutoCAD Plant 3D software crashes, which command can you use to check the integrity of your Plant drawings (2D and 3D)?
   a. AutoCAD Recovery
   b. AutoCAD Audit
   c. PlantAudit
   d. AuditProject

Lesson: Creating and Managing Report Configurations

Overview

This lesson describes the creation and management of report configuration files. This includes determining file location, creating and customizing report information, and determining how the report is going to look.

The advantage of using piping design software with a database is the ability to get the reports you need for your clients. Because the fields that need to display might differ for each customer, you configure custom reports to include new fields or remove old fields. The Report Creator makes it easy to configure a report with customized fields and filtered values. The other advantage of Report Creator is that you can predefine a layout template, meaning that you do not have to format your spreadsheet or other reports after the fact; your reports are produced exactly as you need them every time.

A Major Equipment list in Adobe PDF format is shown in the following illustration.

Major Equipment List

Project: Training Project

Tag	Description	Model Number	Supplier	Area	Drawing Name
P-101-	HORIZONTAL CENTRIFUGAL PUMP				PID001
P-101-	HORIZONTAL CENTRIFUGAL PUMP				PID001
E-101-	TEMA TYPE AEL EXCHANGER				PID001
E-101-	TEMA TYPE AEL EXCHANGER				PID001
T-101	VESSEL				PID001
V-101	VESSEL				PID001

Major Equipment List

Project: Training

Tag	Description	Model Number	Supplier	Area	Drawing Name
P-101-A	HORIZONTAL CENTRIFUGAL PUMP				PID001
P-101-	HORIZONTAL CENTRIFUGAL PUMP				PID001
E-101-A	TEMA TYPE AEL EXCHANGER				PID001
E-101-	TEMA TYPE AEL EXCHANGER				PID001
T-101	VESSEL				PID001
V-101	VESSEL				PID001

Friday, September 02, 2011 Page 1 of

Objectives

After completing this lesson, you will be able to:

- Describe what report configuration files are used for and what they control.
- Identify the three settings for specifying the location of the report configuration files and where those settings are accessed and set.
- Identify where report configuration files are customized and describe the process of customizing them.
- Describe the role of queries in creating reports and the process of configuring a custom query.
- Customize a report by adding fields and changing the layout.
- State the difference between default fields and calculated fields and identify where to access the expression for a calculated field.
- Identify where to change the style sheet for a report configuration and style of a cell in the report.

About Report Configuration Files

Each project contains information about pumps, tanks, instruments, valves, pipe, steel, and more. Professionals that are working on the project need to see information about their particular field. To create reports that display information related to a particular discipline, you need to understand how report configuration files prepare reports for export.

Definition of Report Configuration Files

Report Configuration Files are a collection of settings that define the scope of your data, the type of data included, and how the data is formatted when it is exported. Configuration files can be shared between projects or users.

Example of Report Configuration Files

You create a configuration file for each type of report that you export. For example, the instrumentation group requires an instrument report, which includes fields, such as Tag, Loop, Drawing, or Area. Generally, for each project, you also need an Equipment list, which might include fields, such as Tag, Drawing, Descriptions, or Area. Because the Instrument list and the Equipment list require different fields, you need to create a separate report configuration for each one.

Location of Report Configuration Files

Working in a multi-user environment requires that you share your report configurations to avoid recreating the same report formats. Report Creator has built-in settings that enable you to determine the location of report configuration files.

Report Configuration Settings

You open the Settings dialog box to specify the location of the report configuration files by clicking Settings in the Report Creator dialog box, as shown in the following illustration.

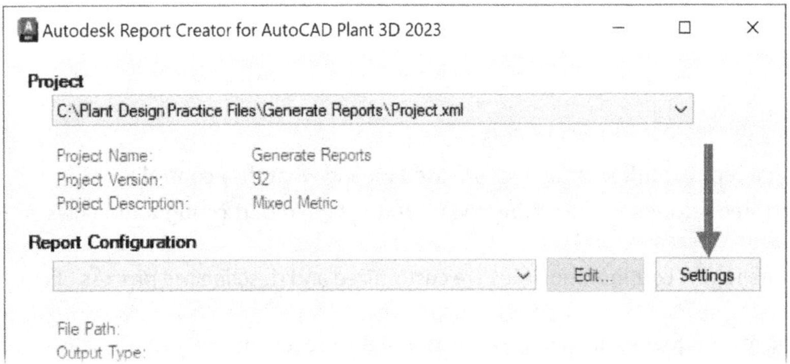

Report Creator has three different locations for storing report configurations, as shown in the following illustration:

- **General** - When this option is selected, the report configuration files are stored in the default Program Data folder (*C:\ProgramData\Autodesk\Autodesk AutoCAD Plant 3D 2024\<revision>\enu\ReportCreator\ReportFiles*). Use this option for reports that are created and used by an individual.
- **Project** - Use this option when you have custom reports specific to a project. The report configuration files are accessed and stored in a subfolder to the project file.
- **Custom Path** - Use this option to specify the folder in which you access and store common company reports. These are the reports that do not vary with clients or projects.

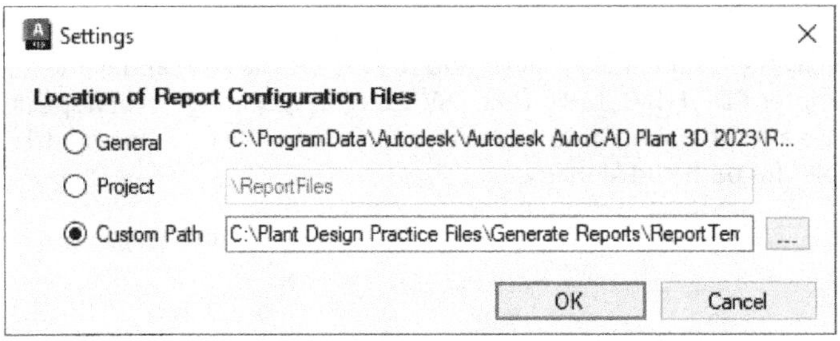

Creating and Editing Report Configurations

To customize the information contained in a report and its presentation, you must first learn how to access areas to change the underlying report query, the layout, and the export options.

Report Configuration Access

The majority of report configuration editing is done and accessed from the Report Configuration dialog box. You open the Report Configuration dialog box from in the Report Creator dialog box. To edit a report configuration, you must first select an existing report configuration from the Report Configuration list or click New from that same list. If you select an existing report, you then click Edit, as shown in the following illustration.

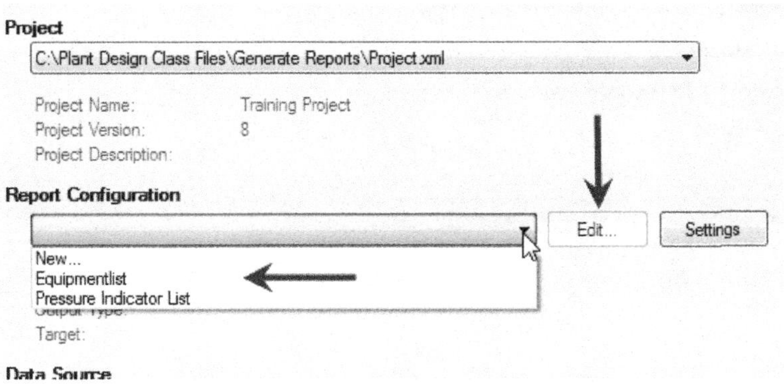

Description of Report Configuration

The Report Configuration dialog box has three main areas with a total of six key options, as shown in the following illustration. The workflow for customizing a report is to work through the dialog box from the top down.

In the Report Configuration area, you select which report configuration you want to modify (1) and then save or delete the current configuration. You use the Edit Query option (2) to configure the tables included in the report and filter the rows for specific values. The Edit report layout option (3) opens the Report Designer, where you control the display of the report fields and the overall look of the report.

The Output Type options (4), specify whether there is one report per project, one per drawing, or one per object.

Under Target, you first specify the target file format (5) and the Export File Path and name (6). The export target options are Printer, PDF, HTML, MHT, Text, CSV, Excel, RTF, or Image. When specifying the Export File Path, you can use a combination of variables and set values. The question mark button (?) details the available variables for path and filenames.

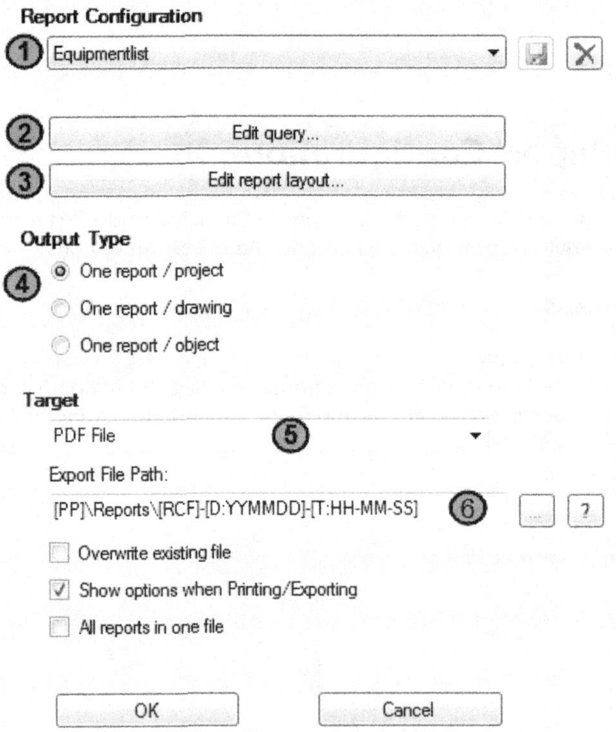

Process: Customizing the Report

The following steps give an overview of customizing a report:

1. Create a new report configuration or select to edit an existing report configuration.
2. Edit the query underlying the report.
3. Edit the layout of the report.
4. Specify the output type of one report per project, drawing, or object.
5. Set the target report file format and path for the report.
6. Save changes.

Assigning the Export File Path

Report Creator includes formatting functionality to enable customizing the storage location of the reports, as well as the filename they are created under. When deciding what format to use, it is important to visualize how the end user is going to access them. Using filenames that sort in a group often helps users find the report they are looking for and communicate the purpose of the reports.

For example, reports are often created for a particular discipline or group. You can create a reports folder for that group and put all of their reports in that folder. Alternatively, sometimes there are multiple reports for various areas in a plant. If you create reports that begin with the area name and then include a description of the report, someone looking for information on that area can see which reports are included. For example, assume that you have two areas in a tank farm (Area 1, Area 2). You also have to produce an equipment report for each area, an instrument report by area, and a valve report by area. You can name your files so that Windows groups them together as follows:

- Area 1 - Equipment
- Area 1 - Instruments
- Area 1 - Valves
- Area 2 - Equipment
- Area 2 - Instruments
- Area 2 - Valves

The Report Creator includes some variables that might be used in the Export file path to automate naming conventions and filename creation. Use the question mark (?) button next to the export file path to view help on available values.

Notable options are project name [PN], project path [PP], formatting value for date [D:x], formatting value for time [T:x], and [RCF], which is the name of the current report configuration. With the variables, you can create the file structure that you need.

Configuring Report Queries

The query determines which data is used to populate your report. To produce reports, you need the ability to change the tables for your report configuration.

Access Query Editor

To continue customizing your report, you can change the query by clicking Edit query on the report configuration dialog box, as shown in the following illustration.

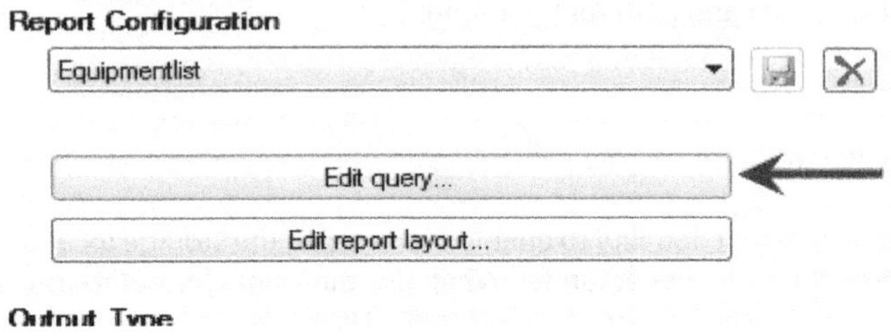

Queries and the Query Editor

The Query Configuration dialog box enables you to select information from a project by using a query. To ensure that the database understands what you need to see, the program uses Structure Query Language (SQL). Although different database formats can have their own dialect of SQL, they use a similar format.

A query is a method of describing a selection of items in a database. A query can have one or more tables or queries as its base. The basic query consists of three main parts: the SELECT statement, the FROM statement, and the WHERE statement. The SELECT statement specifies which columns to include. The FROM statement tells the database which table or query to read. The WHERE statement limits results from the table.

Example of a Query

A simple example of a query is as follows:

The result of using this query is that only pressure instruments with a type that equals "PI" are selected.

Editing Queries

The Query Configuration dialog box has five main sections, as shown in the following illustration. The section at the top (1) changes the classes that are available to use as a basis of the query. The section to the left (2) lists the available classes (or tables) that can be used in the query. The top right panel (3) specifies which classes are included (the FROM statement). The bottom right panel (4) enables input of filters on the included classes (the WHERE statement). The program selects all of the available columns in the included classes (SELECT statement). The bottom right button (5) enables you to view the results of your query.

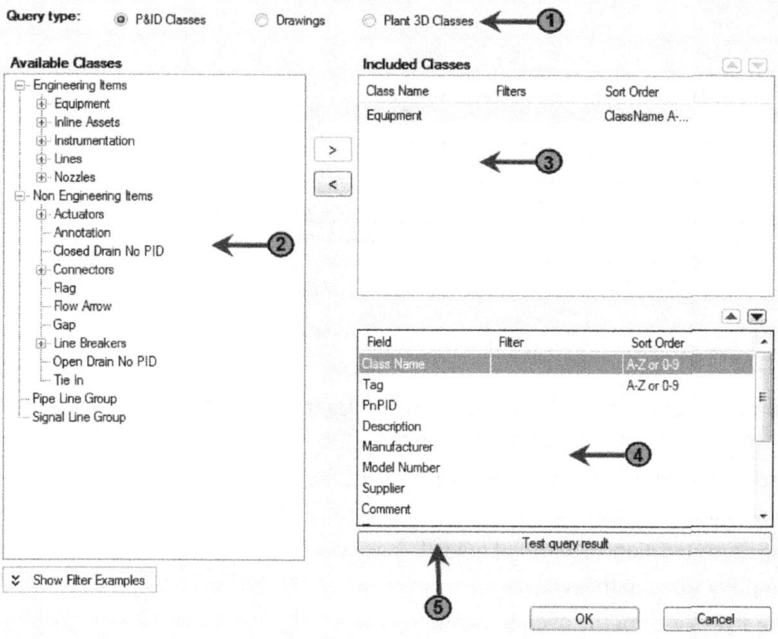

Process: Configuring a Report Query

The following steps give an overview of configuring a query for a report configuration:

1. With the report configuration file selected in the Report Configuration dialog box, click Edit query.
2. In the Query Configuration dialog box, select the query type.
3. Include the required class or classes for the query.
4. Enter the required filter information.
5. Set the sort order for the included classes and their properties.
6. Test the query results. Accepting the changes with the test results displays the information as required.

Customizing the Report Layout

To produce reports that match your company standard, you need to learn the formatting options in the report layout. By saving your standard styles, you can quickly create additional report configurations that match your company standard.

Access Report Designer

Layout customization is done in or initiated from the Report Designer. You access the Report Designer by clicking Edit report layout in the Report Configuration dialog box, as shown in the following illustration.

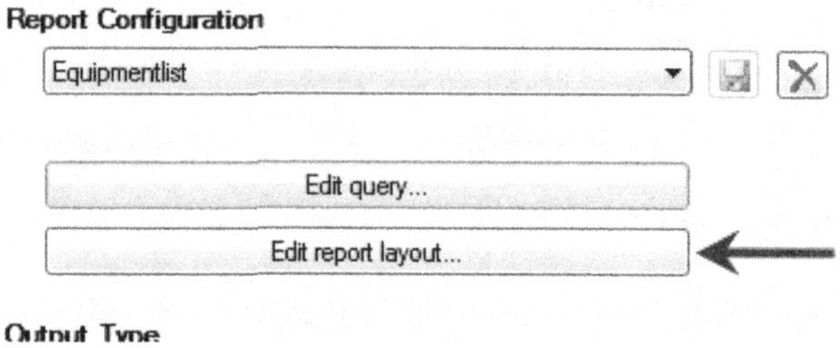

Types of Layout Customization

There are a number of things that you can do to customize the layout of a report. The most common changes include:

- Create fields with expressions that calculate a value.
- Modify which fields to display.
- Modify the order, location, or width of fields.
- Add and modify labels in the report.
- Specify the style sheet for the overall report.
- Modify cell styles.

Report Designer

To modify the layout, you need to become familiar with the Report Designer. Report Designer enables you to move report fields, change layout items, such as images, lines, or grids, and add new fields from the underlying query to your report. Report Designer consists of six main components, as shown in the following illustration.

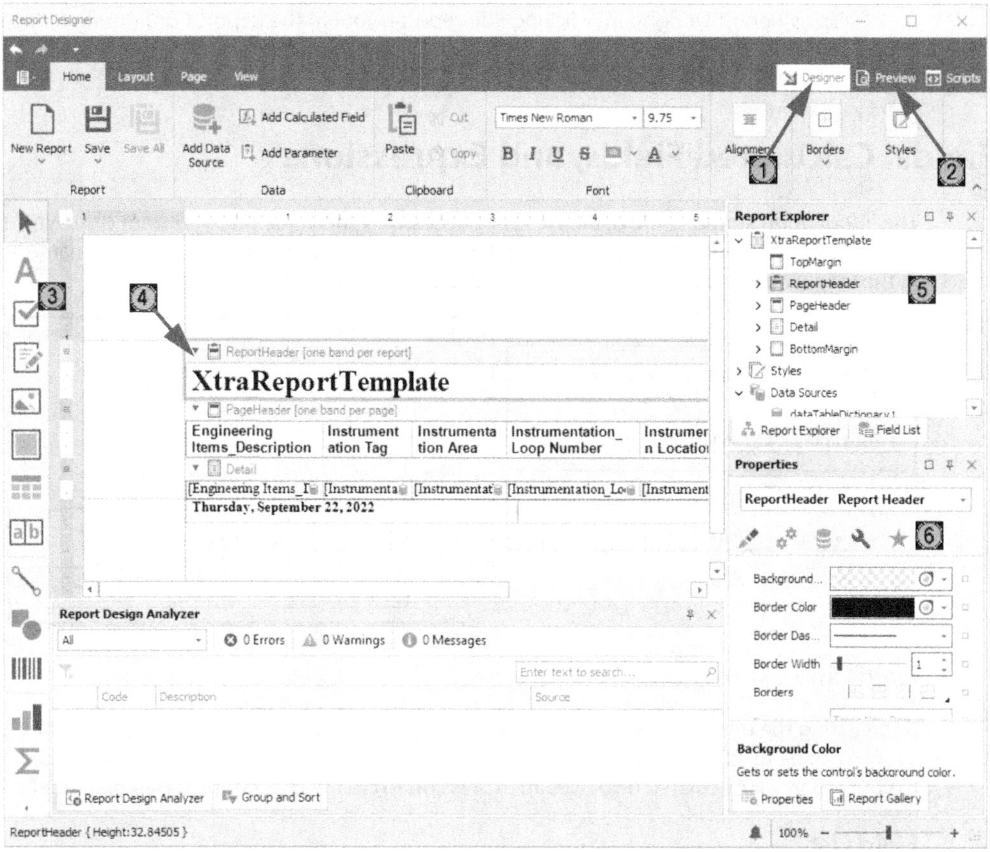

1 The Designer tab contains general commands, such as Save, New, and minor editing tools, such as Font Style.

2 The Preview tab opens a preview of what your report template looks like populated with data from your report. By using the Print Preview tab, you can get a glimpse of the final product.

3 This toolbar contains objects you can place in the report.

4 In the design window, you change the layout using tools, such as the standard controls to configure your template according to your standards.

5 Report Explorer and Field List. In these two views, you can alternate between viewing the report structure or the data structure.

6 This palette changes display based on the object(s) selected and enables you to modify object properties.

Process: Customizing the Layout of a Report

The following steps give an overview of customizing a report configuration file's layout:

1. Start AutoCAD Plant Report Creator.
2. Select the report configuration file that you want to customize and initiate its editing.
3. Display Report Designer by clicking Edit report layout in the Report Configuration dialog box.
4. In the Report Designer, make changes to the report layout.

Fields, Calculated Fields, and Expressions

The information stored in the database is not necessarily the value that you want displayed. For example, some companies might not want to show the .dwg extension in the drawing name, as shown in the following illustration. A calculated field can be used to change the value.

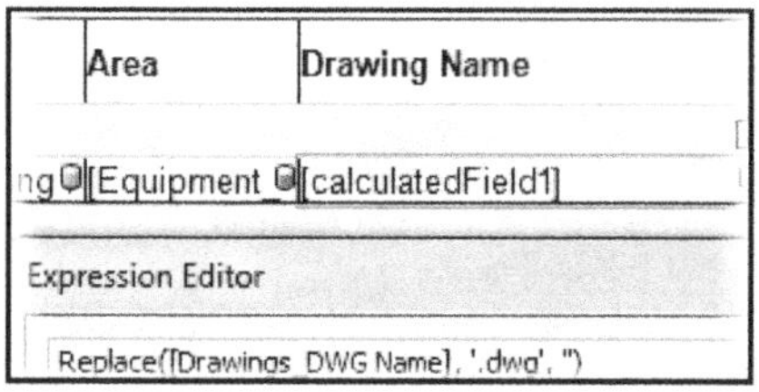

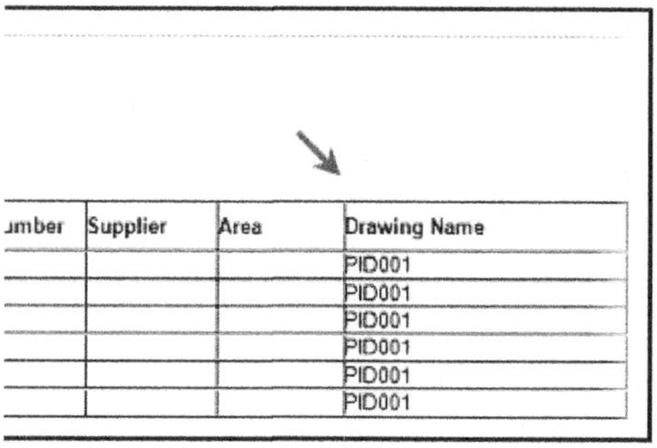

Fields and Expressions

By changing the query for the report configuration, you change the predefined fields that are available to be used in Report Designer. In addition to predefined fields, you can add calculated fields to your reports. A calculated field uses an expression to create a new value based on predefined fields.

Field List

The fields available to be placed in your report are listed in the Field List tab. By default, the Field List tab is available in the right pane with Report Explorer. To create a calculated field, right-click on an existing field and click Add Calculated Field, as shown in the following illustration.

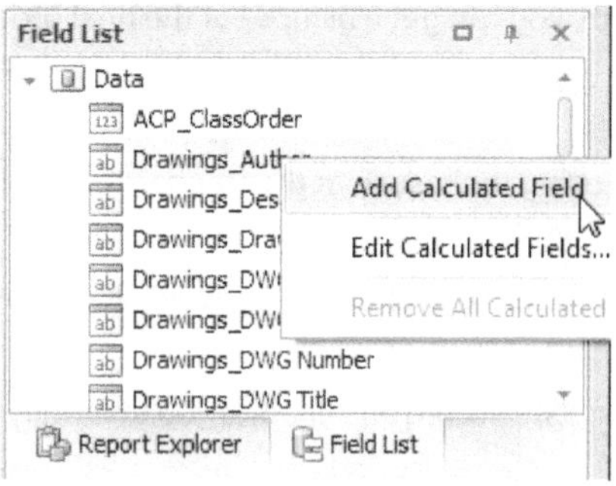

Expression Editor

Expression Editor enables you to create a value that the program executes to get the calculated value. Expression Editor includes some program logic, constants, mathematical expressions, and other data fields. Expression Editor is directly available by right-clicking on the calculated field in the Field List, and clicking Edit Expression, as shown in the following illustration.

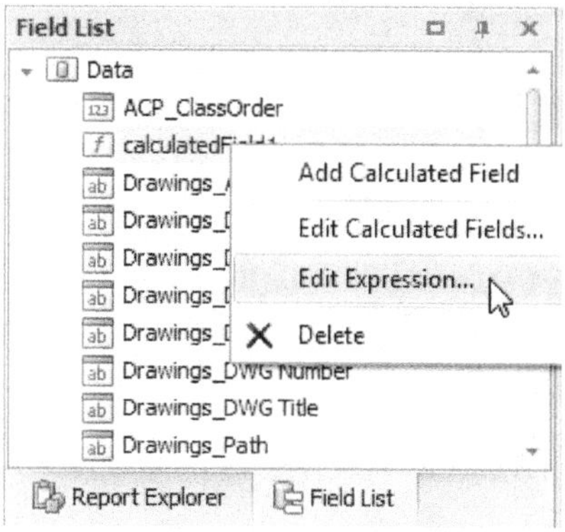

The expression can also be edited when editing calculated fields. In the following image, the properties for the calculated field, calculatedField1, are shown because it is selected in the Members list. The expression for this field can be edited in the Expression field or the Expression Editor can be opened to edit the expression, as shown in the following illustration.

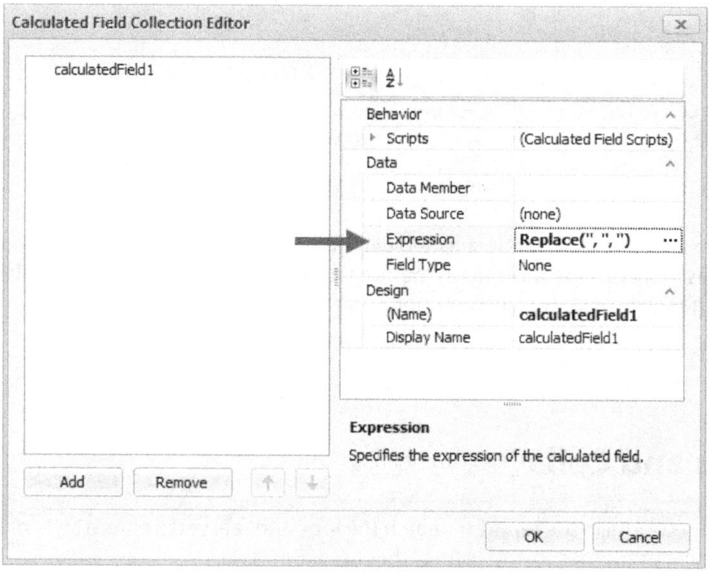

The Expression Editor has five main areas, as shown in the following illustration.

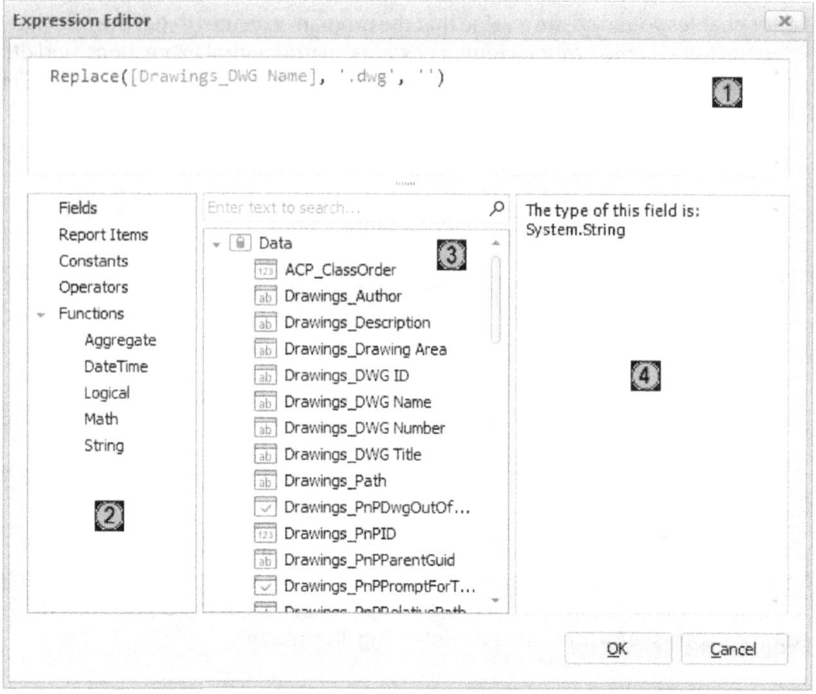

1 In this area, you can enter values or type freely. The value stored in this area is the expression that the software executes to retrieve the calculated value.

2 List of the categories of items that you can use in the Expression Editor.

3 Contains the items from the currently selected category. The software contains built-in functions, such as Replace, Operators (as in mathematical operators), extra fields available from the query, general constants, and additional parameters.

4 Lists help information on the currently selected item.

Styles for Reports and Cells

While you can edit every control in the report to match the look and feel you desire, a style provides a quick way to apply similar properties to any control that uses that style.

Report Style Sheet

On the Property Panel with the current report template selected (xtraReportTemplate) is a Style Sheet property. Select the ellipsis button in the Style Sheet row to launch the Styles Editor, as shown in the following illustration. When you edit styles, the changes take effect on any control that currently uses that style.

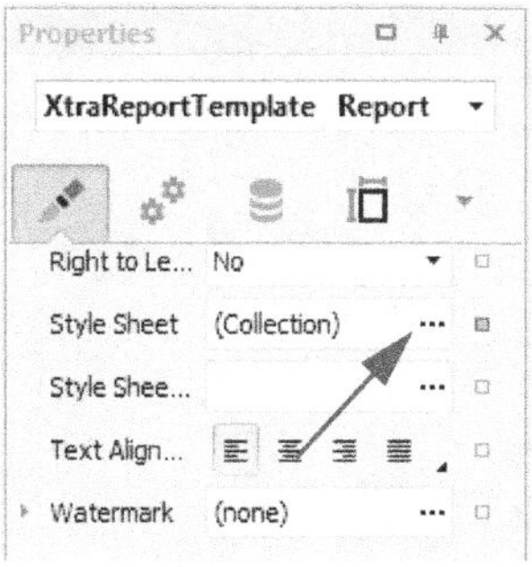

The Styles Editor has three main areas, as shown in the following illustration.

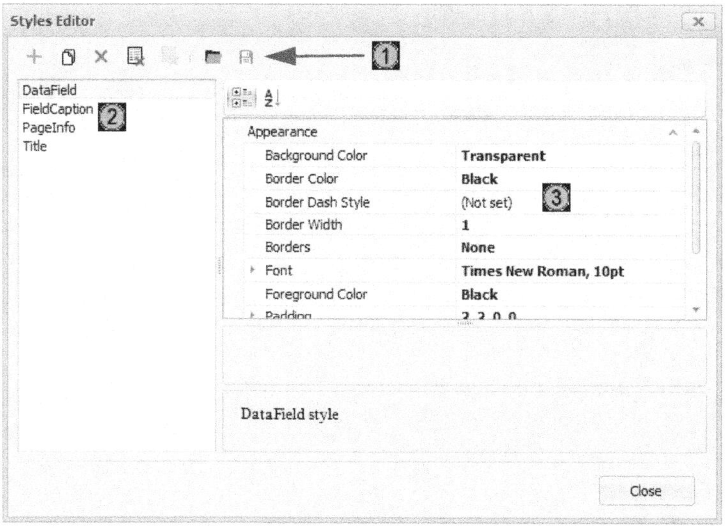

1 Command buttons to add a new style, delete a style, clear all styles, clear unused styles, open styles from a file, and save styles.

2 Lists available styles.

3 Lists properties for the current style.

Styles can be saved to an external file for future use via the save button and loaded via the open folder icon.

Control Style

Each item that you place in the design window is called a control. The Appearance properties of each control can be governed by a style, individually, or by overriding the style.

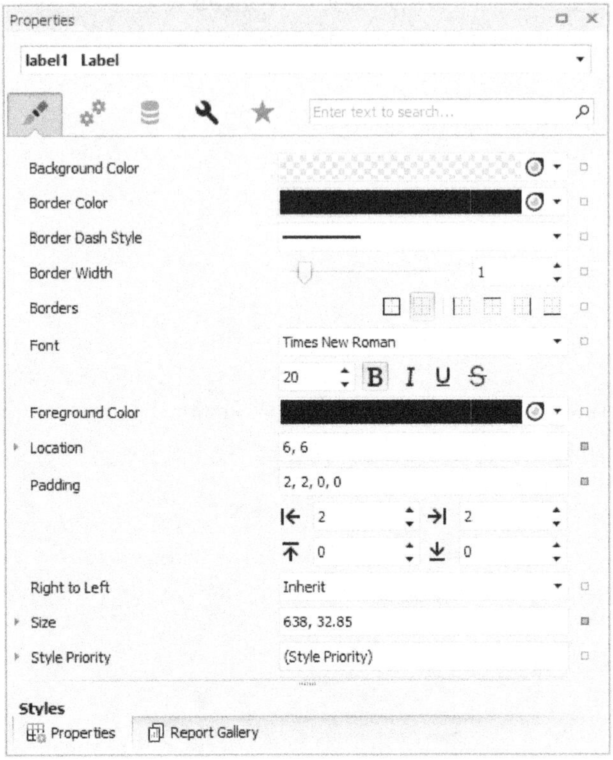

Exercise: Create and Manage Report Configuration Files

In this exercise, you create a custom report configuration for a Pressure Indicator List.

Pressure Indicator List

Training Project

Tag	Drawing Name	Area	Loop	Location	Type
10-PI-104	PID001	10	104		FIELD DISCR
10-PI-105	PID001	10	105		FIELD DISCR

Set the Report Configuration File Location

In this section of the exercise, you set the location of report configuration files to a custom path.

1. Start Autodesk Report Creator for AutoCAD Plant 3D.
2. To set the project:
   - In the Report Creator dialog box, Project drop-down list, click Open.
   - In the Open dialog box, navigate to the folder *C:\Plant Design 2024 Practice Files\Create and Manage Report Configuration Files\P_Aug-11210*.
   - Select the file *Project.xml*.
   - Click Open.
3. Under Report Configuration, click Settings.
4. In the Settings dialog box:
   - Select Custom Path.
   - Click Browse for Folder (ellipses button).
   - In the Browse for Folder dialog box, navigate to the folder *C:\Plant Design 2024 Practice Files\Create and Manage Report Configuration Files\Server\Plant 3D\Company Reports*.
   - Click OK to exit the Browse for Folder dialog box.
   - Click OK to exit the Settings dialog box.

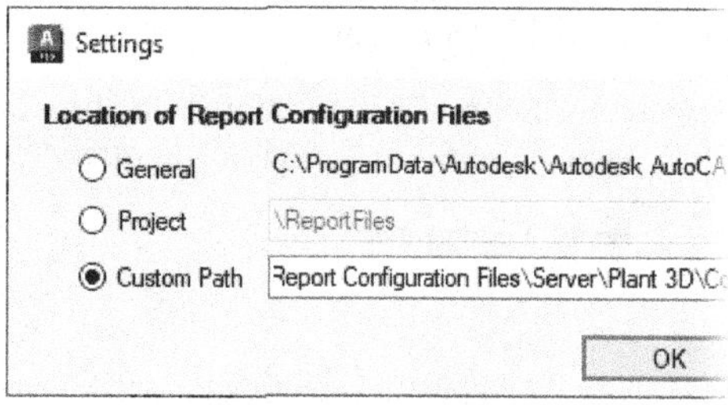

Create a New Report

In this section of the exercise, you create a new blank report.

1. From the Report Configuration drop-down list, select New.

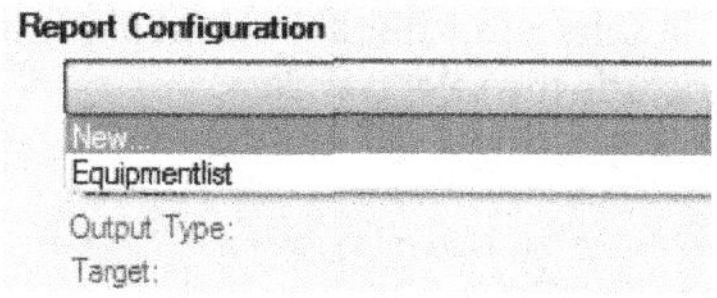

2. In the New Report Configuration dialog box:
   - Select New blank report.
   - Click OK.

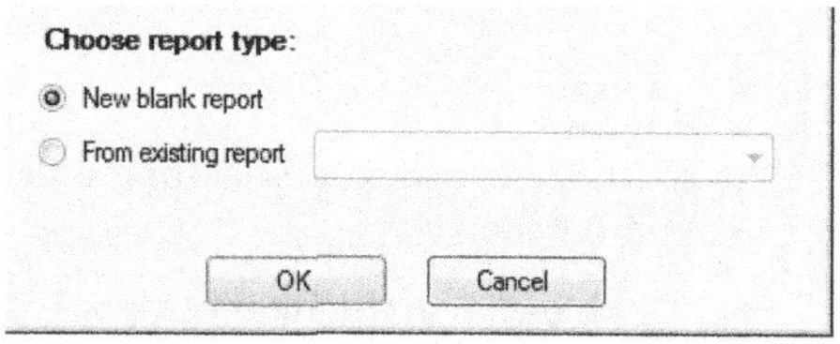

3. In the Report Configuration dialog box, under Report Configuration, enter **Pressure Indicator List**.

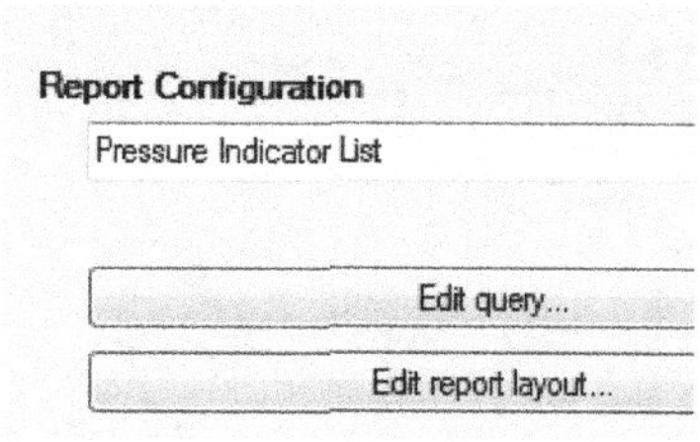

Create a Query

In this section of the exercise, you create a new query for the custom report.

1. In the Report Configuration dialog box, under Report Configuration, click Edit query.

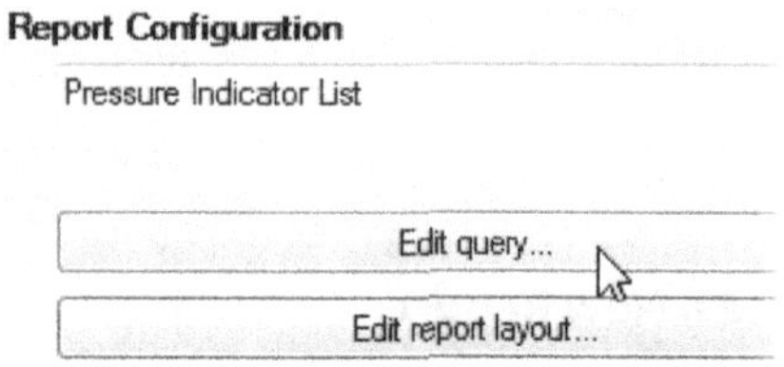

2. In the Query Configuration dialog box:
   - From the Available Classes list, select Instrumentation under Engineering Items.
   - Click the > button to the right of the list to include the selected class.

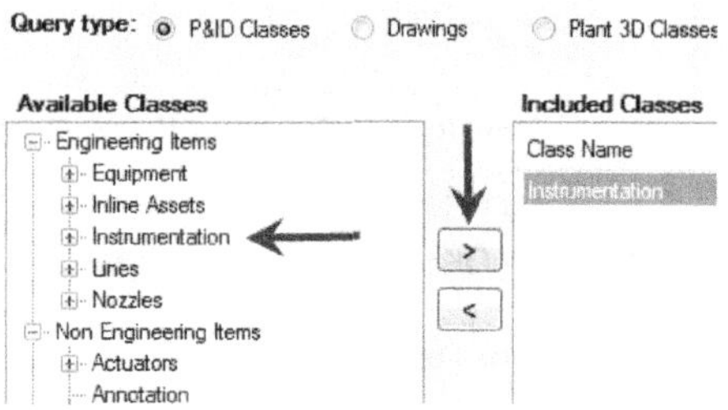

3. To set the filter and sort order for the Instrumentation class:
   - Double-click in the Filter field for Type, and enter **='PI'**.
   - Double-click in the Sort Order field for Tag to set the sort order by **A-Z or 0-9**.

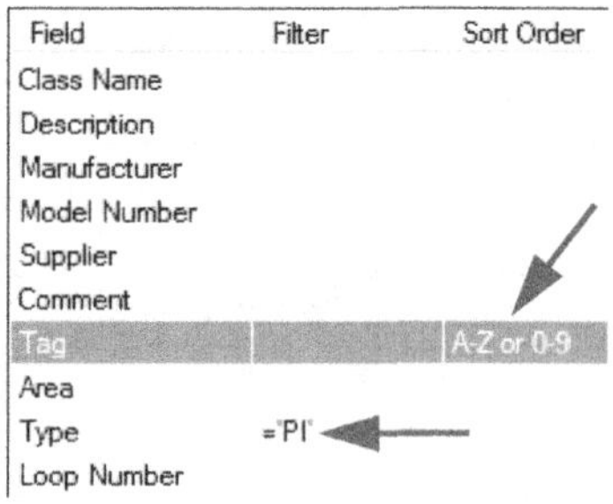

4. To test and review the query results:
   - Click Test query result.
   - In the Query result dialog box, scroll to view the information for the results. The query returned only two instruments that have the PI Instrumentation Type.
   - Click Close.

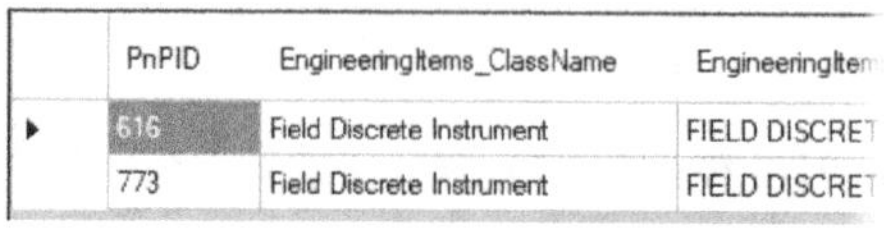

5. In the Query Configuration dialog box, click OK.

Create the Report Layout

In this section of the exercise, you create a new report layout using the Report Wizard.

1. In the Report Configuration dialog box, click Edit report layout.

2. In the Report Wizard, select the following fields. Click the > button to include them in the Fields to display in a report list.
   - Engineering Items_Description
   - Instrumentation_Tag
   - Instrumentation_Area
   - Instrumentation_Loop Number
   - Instrumentation_Location
   - Drawings_DWG Name

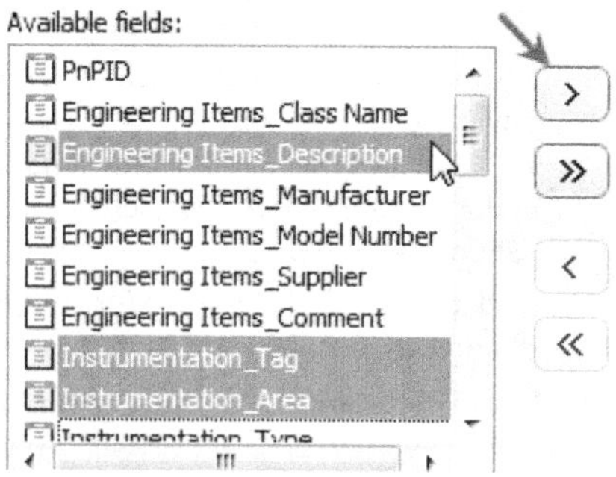

3. With the Fields to display in a report list displayed, click Next.

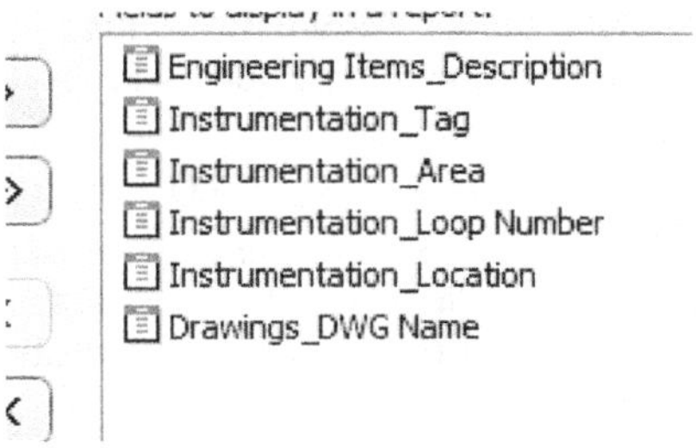

4. On the Grouping levels page, click Next.

5. On the Layout page of the wizard:
   - Under Layout, select Tabular.
   - Click Next.

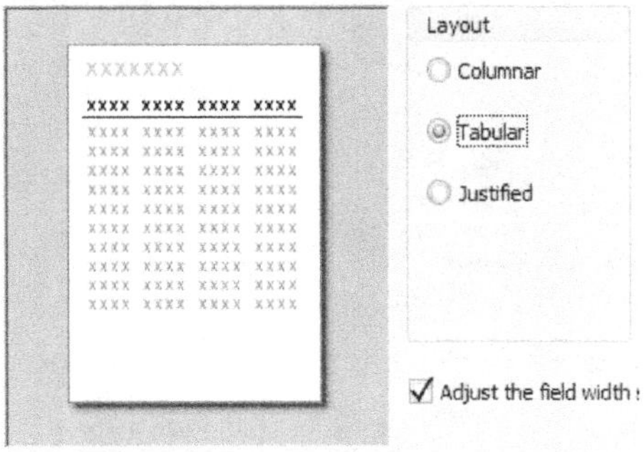

6. On the Style page, with Bold selected, click Next.

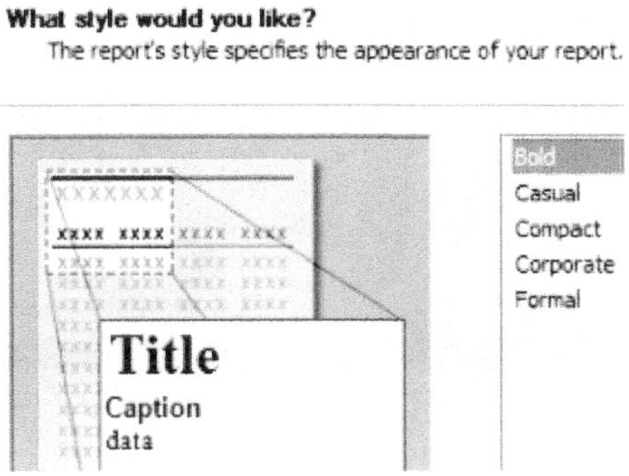

7. To accept the default name, XtraReportTemplate for the report, click Finish.

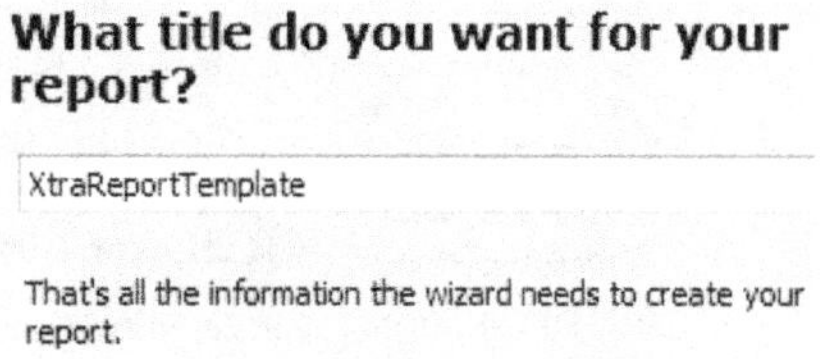

8. To preview the output of the new report, in the Report Designer, click the Preview tab. Note that the drawing name includes the .dwg extension.

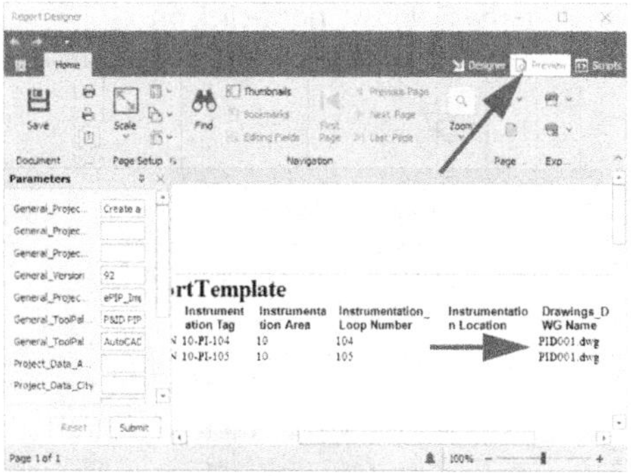

9. In the Report Designer, click the Designer tab.

Create a Calculated Field

In this section of the exercise, you create a calculated field and then define an expression for the field.

1. In the Report Explorer panel, click the Field List tab.

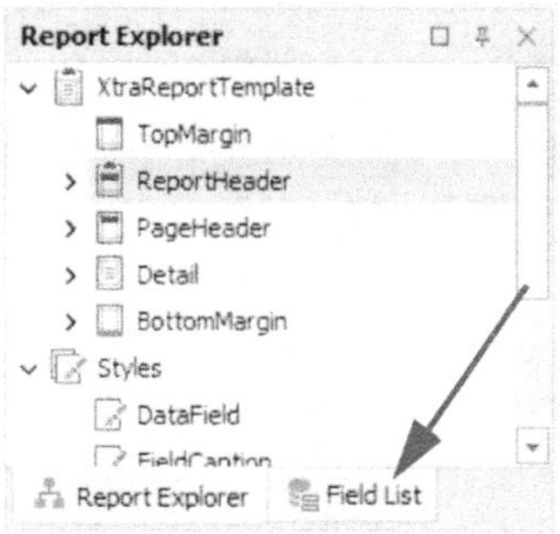

2. In the Field List tab, right-click on a field. Click Add Calculated field. A field named calculatedField1 is added to the Field list.

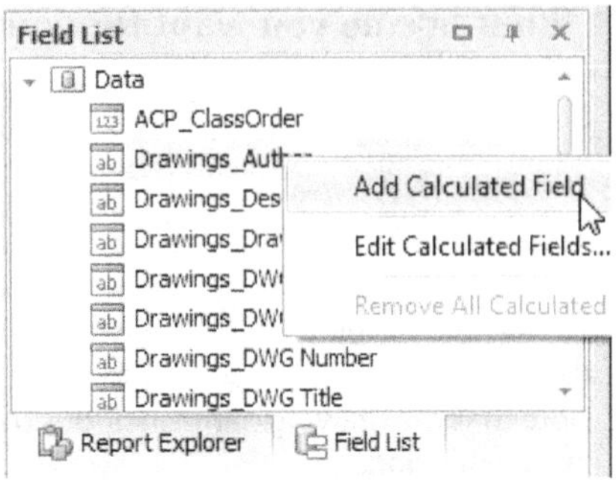

3. In the Field List, right-click on calculatedField1. Click Edit Expression.

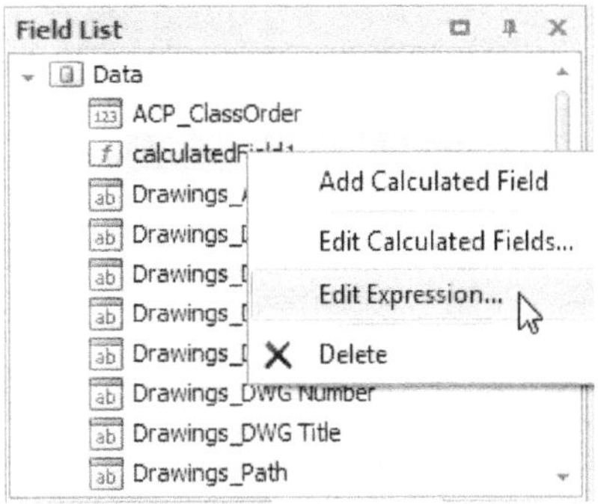

4. In the Expression Editor, in the Category list, note that the Functions category is expanded. Select String. Scroll down in the middle pane and find Replace. Double-click on Replace to add it to the Edit window at the top.

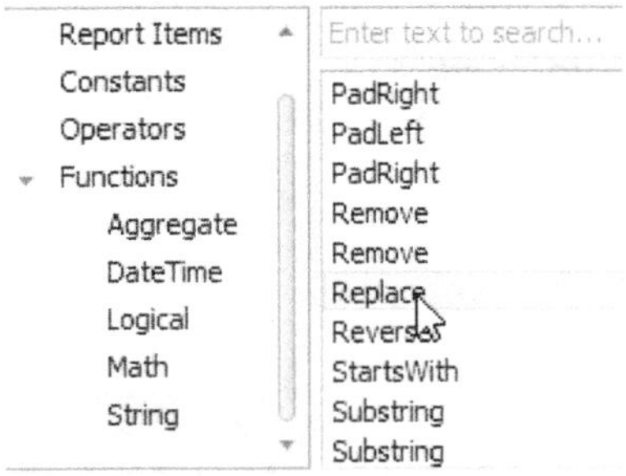

5. To specify the first parameter of the Replace function:

- Position the cursor between the first two apostrophes (single quotes) to the left of the first comma.
- In the Category list, select Fields.
- Double-click on Drawings_DWG Name. Note that it gets added between the first two apostrophes which is the position of the cursor.

6. Click OK in the Expression Editor.

7. To replace the previous field name for the drawing name with this new calculated field, from the Field List, drag and drop calculatedField1 onto the Drawings_DWG Name field in the Detail section of the report, as shown in the following illustration.

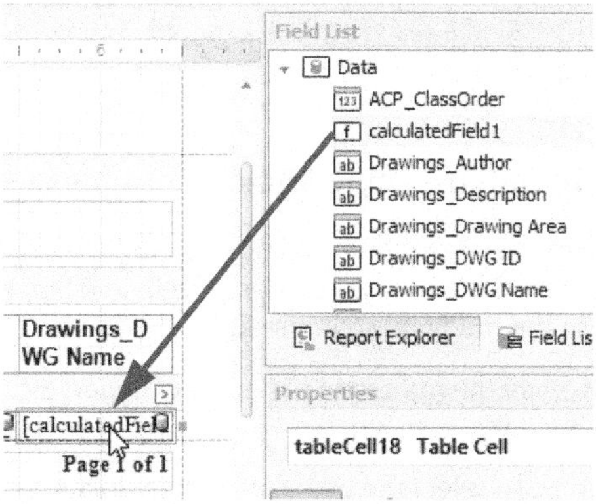

8. On the Report Designer tab, on the Report panel, click Save.

Modify Fields

In this section of the exercise, you modify the properties and layout of fields.

1. From the Field List panel, drag and drop the Instrumentation_Tag field onto the first data field on the left in the Detail row, as shown in the following illustration.

2. From the Field list, drag and drop Drawings_DWG Name onto the second position from the left in the Detail row.

3. From the Field list, drag and drop Engineering Items_Description onto the last position in the Detail row, as shown in the following illustration.

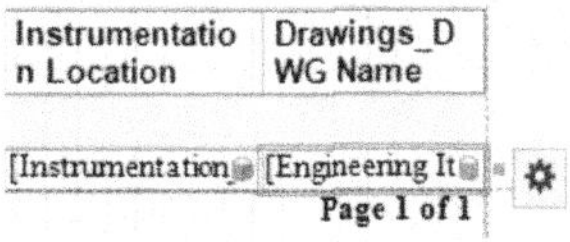

4. Double-click on each header and change the title of the fields as follows: **Tag, Drawing Name, Area, Loop, Location,** and **Type**.

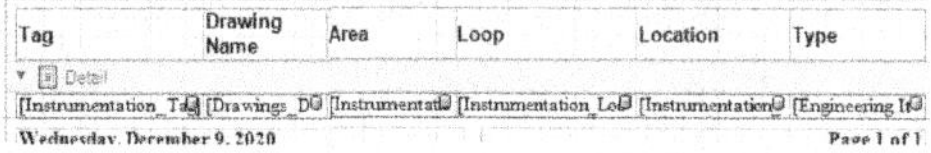

5. Change the title of the report to **Pressure Indicator List**.

6. To expand the Header Band so that there is room for another label under the title, click and drag the edge approximately as shown in the following illustration.

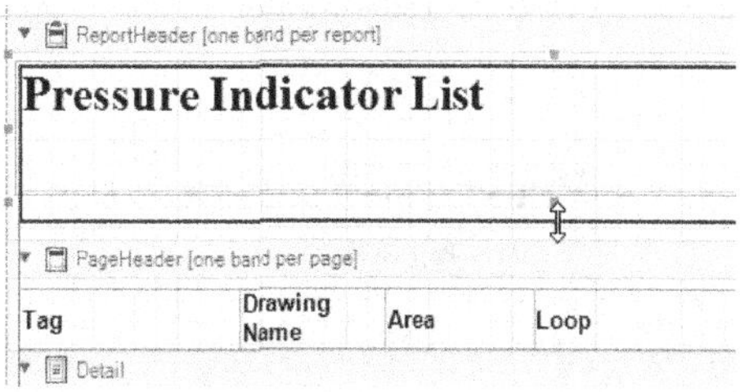

7. From the Standard Controls panel, drag and drop the Label control under the title as shown in the following illustration.

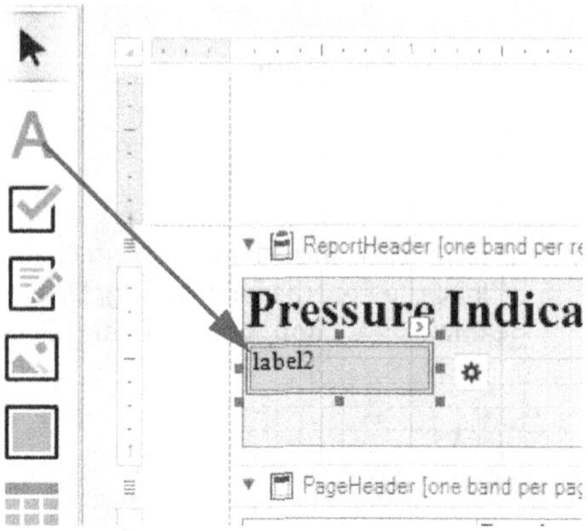

8. In the Field List, expand Parameters.

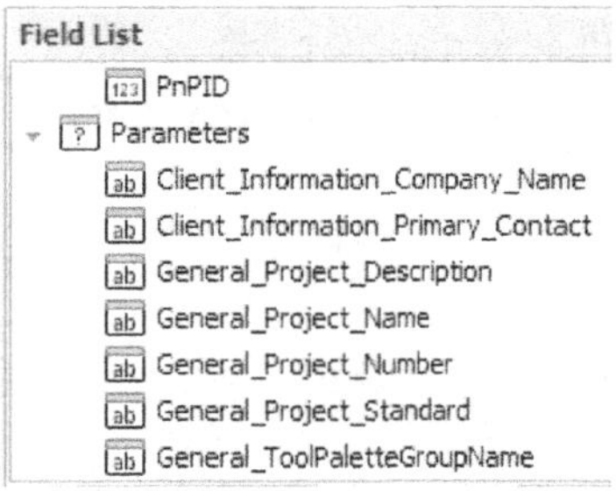

9. Drag and drop the parameter General_Project_Name onto the previously added label to create the result as shown in the following illustration.

10. Expand the label to the right to ensure that there is ample room for the project name to be displayed.

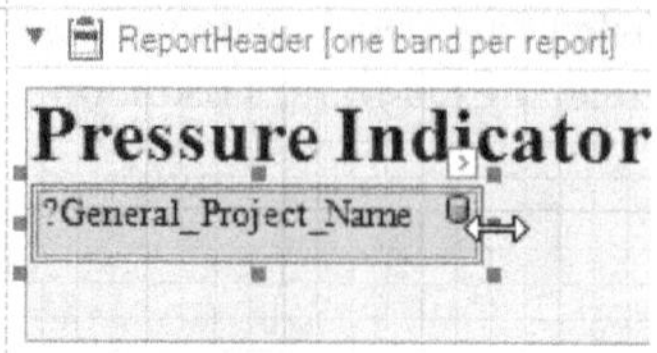

Change the Style Sheet

In this section of the exercise, you modify the style sheet and then assign different cells and labels to use the modified style sheet.

1. In the right-side pane, select Report Explorer tab.

2. To select the overall report template, on the Report Explorer tab, at the top of the list, click XtraReportTemplate.

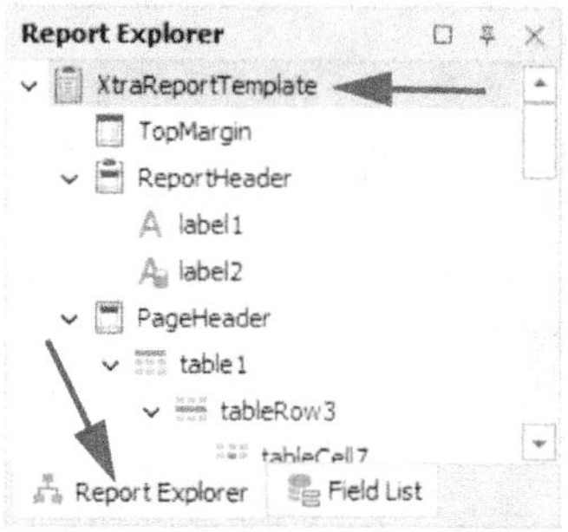

3. To open the Style Editor, on the Properties panel, Appearance area, select the Style Sheet field, and click the ellipsis button.

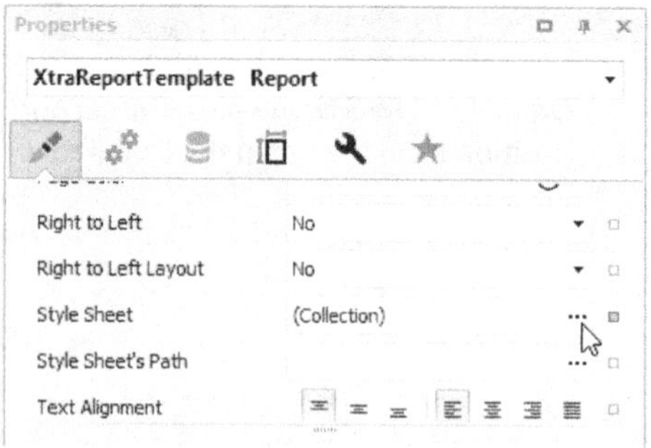

4. In the Styles Editor list of styles, select FieldCaption.

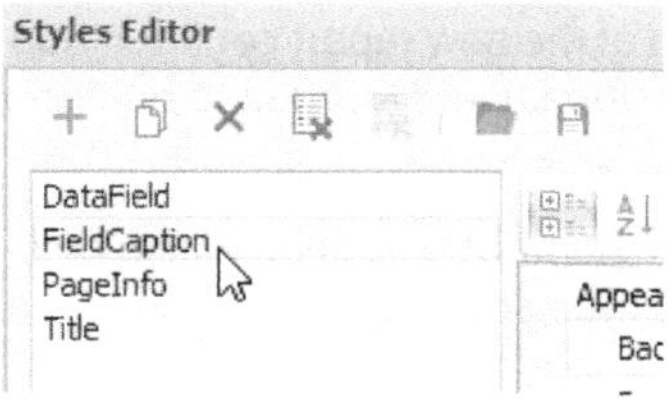

5. In the Appearance area, from the Foreground Color list, select Black.

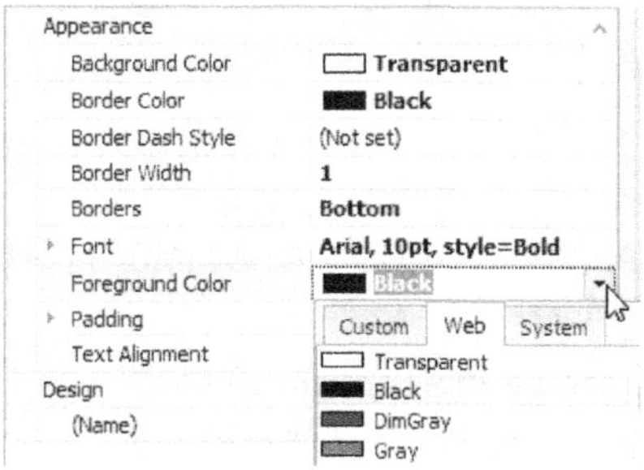

6. For Text Alignment, select Middle Center.

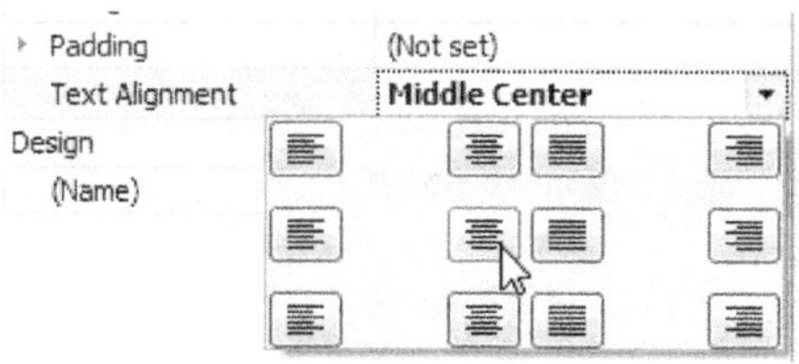

7. Select the DataField style and change the Text Alignment to Middle Center.

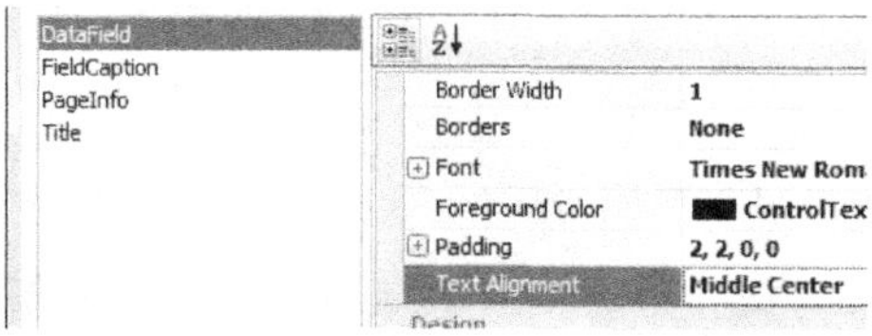

8. Select the Title style and change Foreground Color to black.

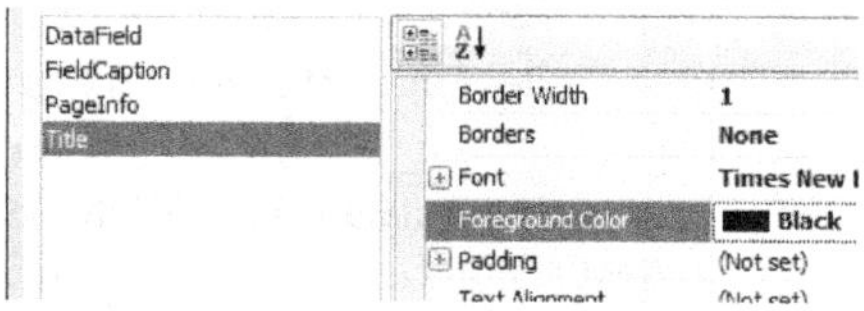

9. To begin to add and configure a new style, click Add.

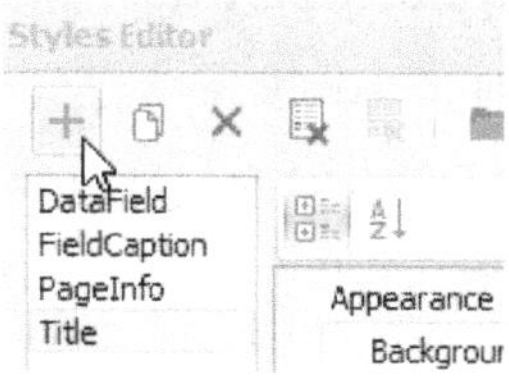

10. In the Design area, in the (Name) field, enter **HeaderProperty**.

11. For the HeaderProperty style:

- For Foreground Color, select Black.
- For Text Alignment, select Middle Left.

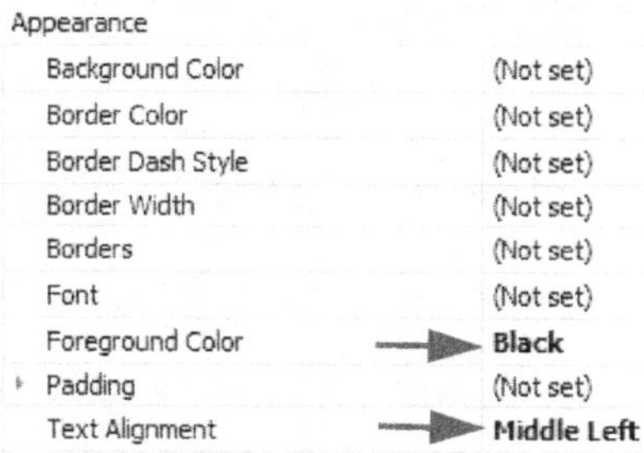

12. Set the font style to Arial 12 pt, Bold.

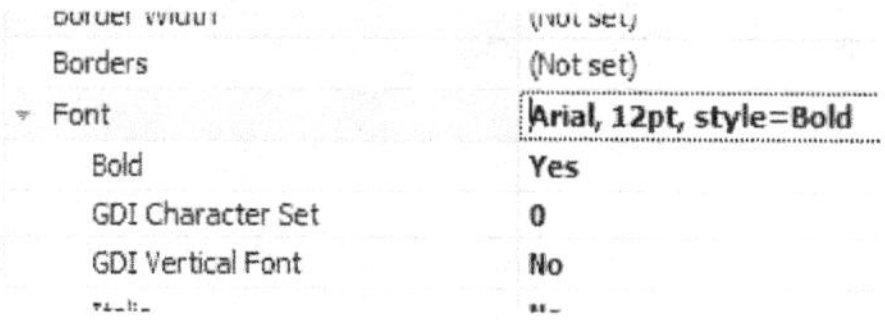

13. To save the changes to a Report StyleSheet file so it can be imported in the future in a different template:
    - In the Styles Editor, click Save styles to a file.
    - In the Save As dialog box, navigate to the folder *C:\Plant Design 2024 Practice Files\Create and Manage Report Configuration Files\Server\Plant 3D\Company Reports.*
    - Save the file to the selected folder with the name **TypicalReport-1**.
14. In the Styles Editor, click Close.
15. Select the label [? General_Project_Name].

16. In the Properties panel, Appearance area:
    - Expand Styles.
    - In the Style field, select HeaderProperty.

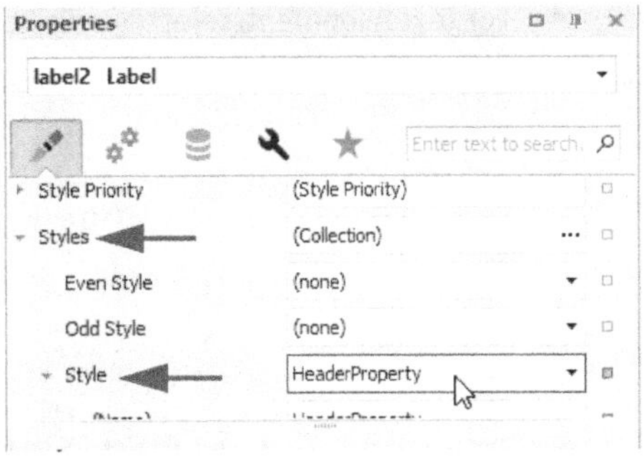

17. On the Report Designer tab, on the Report panel, click Save.
18. Close Report Designer.

Set the Publish Format and Location

In this section of the exercise, you complete the configuration of the new report configuration file by setting the format and location to publish the report.

1. In the Report Configuration dialog box, Output Type area, verify that One report / project is selected.

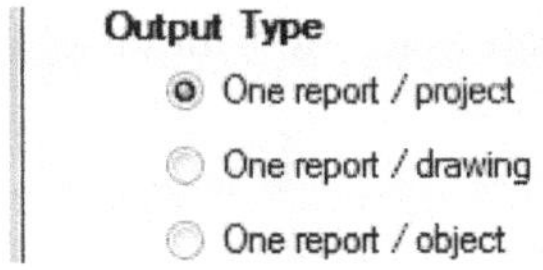

2. From the Target list, select PDF File.
3. For Export File Path, enter **[PP]\Reports\[RCF]-[D:YYMMDD]-[T:HH-MM-SS]**
4. Clear the Show options when Printing/Exporting check box.

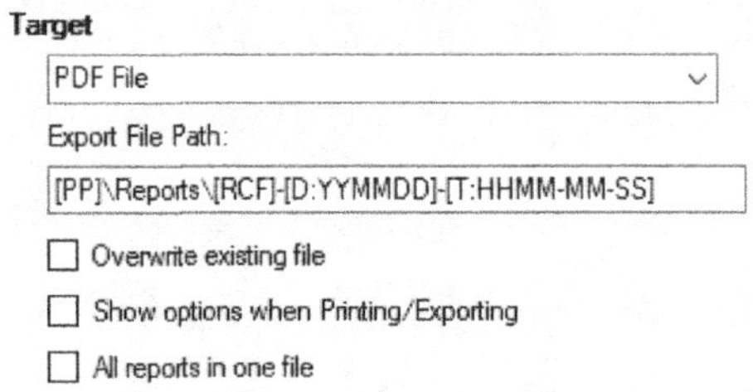

5. Under Report Configuration, click Save.

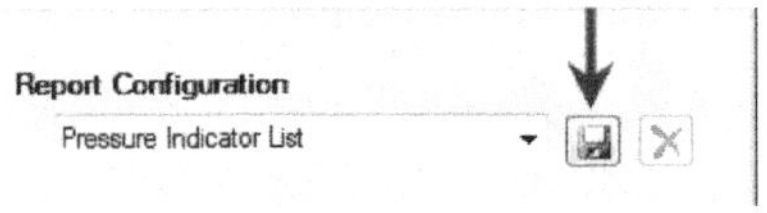

6. Click OK.

Test the Report Configuration

In this section of the exercise, you test the report configuration by exporting the data for the selected project.

1. In the Autodesk Report Creator for AutoCAD Plant 3D dialog box, verify that the Data Source is set to Project Data.

2. Click Print/Export.

3. In the Export results dialog box, double-click on the listed file.

4. In the PDF viewer, review the configuration and order of information in the report.

   Note: In this case, the column width for Type is wide enough for the data. To adjust the column widths so that all of the information displays, you must return to the Report Designer.

   Pressure Indicator List

   Create and Manage Report Configuration Files

Tag	Drawing Name	Area	Loop	Location	Type
10-PI-104	PID001.dwg	10	104		FIELD DISCR
10-PI-105	PID001.dwg	10	105		FIELD DISCR

5. Close the PDF viewer, Export Results dialog box, and Report Creator.

Lesson Review Questions

1. Which of the following setting types are saved in a report configuration? (Select all that apply.)
   a. The number of valves in the project
   b. Fields to display
   c. Project name
   d. The font used in the report
2. Which of the following statements about report configuration files is true?
   a. You have to use the reports included with the program.
   b. You have to create new ones for every project.
   c. You can customize the file output type.
3. Which panels in the Report Designer contain fields that are available to use in the report?
   a. Standard Controls
   b. Field List
   c. Properties
   d. Report Explorer
4. Select the statement about calculated fields that is true.
   a. Calculated fields are based on predefined fields.
   b. Calculated fields must include math operations.
   c. Calculated fields use expressions to create new values.
   d. Values returned by calculated fields are stored in the database.
5. What is the best way to manage the appearance of a report?
   a. Use the same template for all of your reports.
   b. Set up standard styles.
   c. Use a macro to format the report.
   d. Copy/Paste from existing reports.

Lesson: Setting Up SQL Server for AutoCAD Plant 3D

Overview

For large projects, the default database, SQLite, might not be robust enough to handle the load. This lesson gives an overview of how to connect a current AutoCAD Plant 3D project to the new server database.

Objectives

After completing this lesson, you will be able to:

- Explain the different database configurations that can be used in a Plant 3D project.
- Explain the overall process for setting up a server database with SQL Server Express.
- Create a new Plant 3D project and configure it to use an SQL Server Express database.
- Convert an existing Plant 3D project that uses a local database to use an SQL server database.

Prerequisites

Before taking this lesson, you should be able to:

- Install applications on your computer.
- Have rudimentary IT knowledge.

About Plant 3D Databases

To be used in a scalable environment, the AutoCAD Plant 3D software must be used with an SQL Server or SQL Server Express database. By default, the AutoCAD Plant 3D software uses a local SQLite, which is suitable for smaller projects without many users.

Database Options in Plant 3D

Plant 3D projects use either a local database or a server database. A local or file-based database is one that does not require services running to access the database. A server database requires a Windows service to run in order to access data.

Using SQLite

When creating a project, the AutoCAD Plant 3D software uses a popular database format called SQLite (*http://www.sqlite.org/*). SQLite is a file-based format, meaning that an application does not have to be running or launched to maintain a connection to the database. Because of the open format, developers, using many types of technology, have created methods for interacting with an SQLite database (for example, C++, .Net). SQLite provides excellent performance for small-scale projects.

Using SQL Server Express

SQL Server Express is a free version of the Microsoft enterprise database server, Microsoft SQL Server. SQL Express has fewer features compared to SQL Server, but it is able to handle virtually any project that uses the AutoCAD Plant 3D software. Also, once the move to SQL Server Express is complete, no data migration is required to use SQL Server.

SQL Server Express can be installed on desktop operating systems, such as Windows 7, XP, or Vista. SQL Express is free, and can use databases up to 10 gigabytes (GB). For projects that are larger than 10 GB, using a full SQL Server instance is mandatory.

The server can be connected to the user's workstation via local area network (LAN). While other connection types are possible, more complicated setups are better left to IT professionals experienced in domain permissions, wide area networks (WANs), and general network configuration protocol.

Guidelines for Selecting a Database

Because database performance can fluctuate based on a wide variety of factors, only guidelines for use can be established. For example, projects that might perform well in one location, might suffer in another due to differences in servers, connection cables, or even the speed at which users work.

Lab tests have been conducted with up to ten users working simultaneously on a project. In a working environment, the number of active users might be lower, perhaps six to ten simultaneous users.

When using the SQLite database, file size is not an issue, as files can hold up to 2 terabytes of data. However, because SQL Server Express is free, it is the preferred method for handling projects that require multiple users.

Setting Up to Use a Server Database

Because the lesson transitions from a file-based database to a server database, the server database is put on a computer. Technically, you can install SQL Server on any machine. However, because the server is usually the only computer guaranteed to be on and accessible, SQL Server Express is usually installed there.

Server versus Client Workstation

The computer that has the SQL Server instance installed and that holds the databases is referred to as the server. Computers that connect to the server and do not host the databases are referred to as client workstations or clients.

Process: Setting Up to Use a Server Database

The following steps give a high level overview of setting up a server database for use with Plant 3D.

1. Install SQL Server Express or SQL Server on a server computer.
2. Set up the SQL Server network configuration. This includes configuring SQL Server or Server Express to enable connections, and configuring the firewall on the server computer to enable connections for other computers.
3. Determine the authentication method to use for secure access to the database. Select either Windows Authentication or SQL Server Authentication.

Security Considerations

An SQL Server implementation must cover many details to ensure that the security of your network is not compromised. This lesson only offers a few guidelines that might be of use. If you are not versed in network security for your production environment, an IT professional should be consulted.

Questions to address for limiting access to your SQL Server installation:

- Can the server be closed to the Internet (not hosting a website)?
- Have you changed the default passwords and user names to make them custom?
- Are you using strong passwords?
- Have you changed the default ports?

Creating a New Plant 3D Project that Uses SQL Server Database

Multiple users working simultaneously on different aspects of Plant and P&ID projects must be working in a project configured to use an SQL Server database configuration. To have a project configured to use SQL Server, you need to know how to create a new project and configure it to use an SQL Server database.

Specifying SQL Server Database

The steps for creating a new plant project that uses an SQL Server Database database configuration is almost identical to the steps for creating one that uses the default SQLite local database configuration. The difference is on the Specify Database Settings page of the Project Setup Wizard.

When creating a new plant project that uses SQL Server, on the Specify Database Settings page of the Project Setup Wizard, you:

1. Select the Multi-User - SQL Server database option.
2. Select the server and SQL server name.
3. Enter a name for the database. Typically, you enter the same name as the project name you entered on the first page of the wizard, which is often a recognizable project number.
4. Select the authentication method to use for logging in to the SQL server. Select between Windows Authentication and SQL Server Authentication.
5. If you set the authentication method to SQL Server Authentication, enter the SQL Server user name and password login information, as shown in the following illustration.

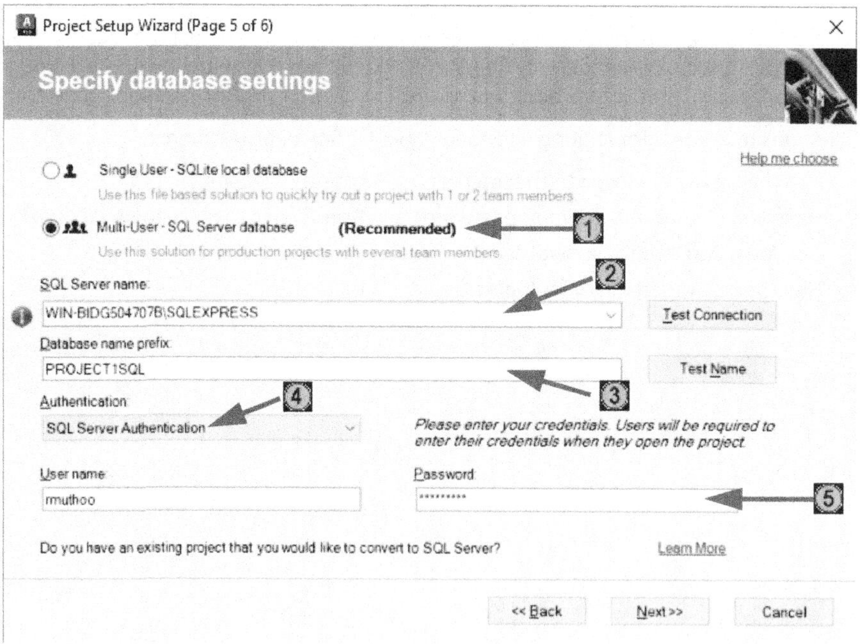

When the project is being created, corresponding databases are automatically created and configured in the SQL Server for that project. Each database has the project name as its prefix and has either Iso, Misc, Ortho, Piping, or Pnld as its suffix. Two projects (ap3d and Project1SQL) created in the SQL server are shown in the following illustration.

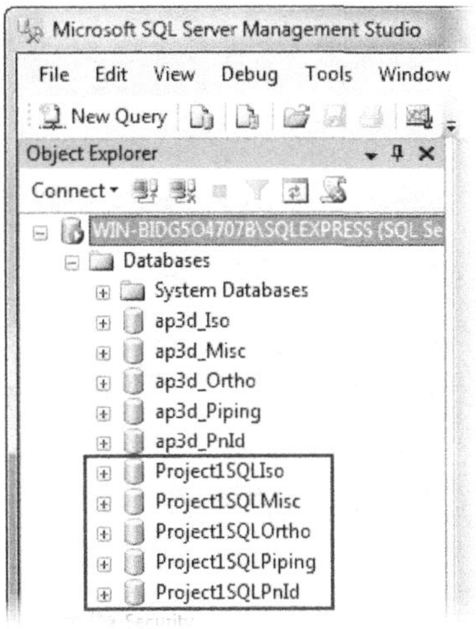

Converting a Project to SQL Server

Projects set to use a file-based database are not conducive to simultaneous access by multiple users. If you have a situation in which you have an existing file-based database project that needs to be accessed by multiple users, you need to know how to convert it to use a SQL Server database.

Project Maintenance Utility

You use Project Maintenance Utility to convert a file-based database project to one that uses an SQL database configuration. Along with converting a project, you can use the utility to move or copy a project. When you start the Project Maintenance Utility, the initial dialog box lists the options Convert a Project to SQL Express, Move a Project Database, or Copy a Project Database, as shown in the following illustration. You select the option that you need and click Next.

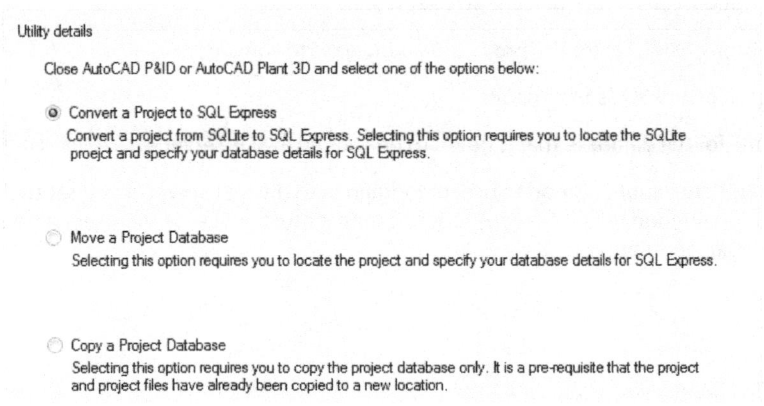

After you select the Convert option and click Next, the Project Maintenance Utility - Convert a Project to SQL Express dialog box opens, as shown in the following illustration. This is where you specify the project to convert and the new location and database name after conversion.

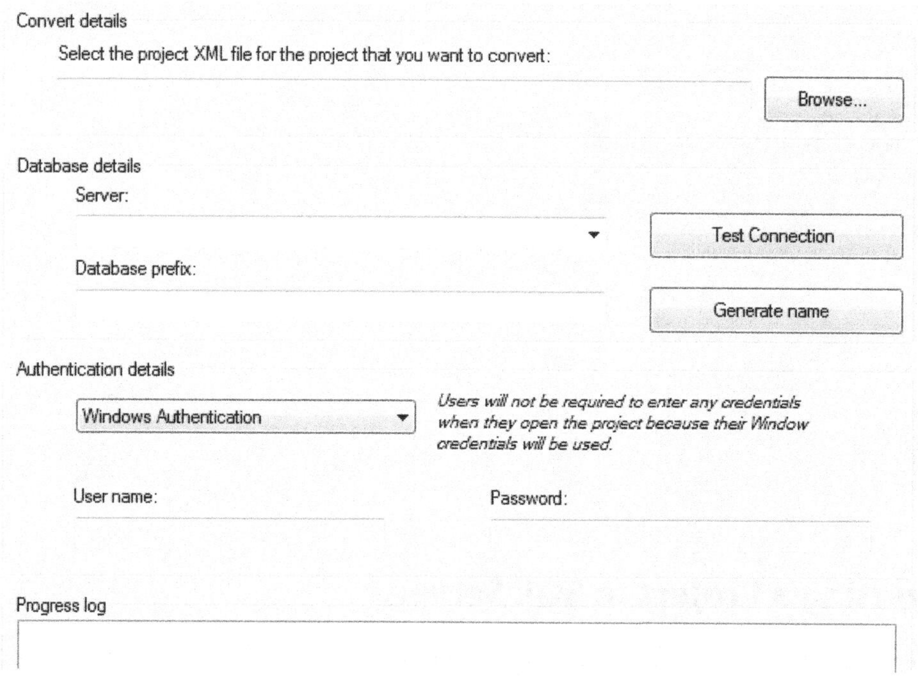

Process: Converting an Existing Plant 3D Project to Use SQL Server

The following steps give an overview of converting an existing Plant 3D project that uses the default file database to use a SQL Server Express database:

1. Ensure that the AutoCAD Plant 3D software is closed.
2. Start Project Maintenance Utility by clicking *C:\Program Files\Autodesk\AutoCAD 2024\PLNT3D\PnPProjectMaintenance.exe*.
3. Select the option Convert a Project to SQL Express.
4. Select the project XML file for the project that you want to convert.
5. Select the server and SQL server name.
6. Enter a name for the database that is going to be created in SQL server.
7. Select the authentication method to use for logging in to the SQL server. If you set the authentication method to SQL Server Authentication, enter the SQL Server user name and password login information.
8. Click Convert.

Lesson Review Questions

1. What type of database is SQLite?
   a. A server-based database
   b. A file-based database
2. What is the main limiting factor on SQLite performance when used with the AutoCAD Plant 3D software?
   a. The file size
   b. The number of items in each drawing
   c. The number of concurrent users
   d. The number of files in the project
3. Select the factors that contribute to a secure implementation of SQL Server. (Select all that apply.)
   a. A good internet connection
   b. Standard ports for connections
   c. Custom user names
   d. The SQL Browser service
   e. Strong passwords

Chapter Summary

In this chapter, you learned the skills and knowledge for setting up and administering a plant project. This included tasks like setting up the project file for large projects, controlling the project structure and file location, customizing the data manager, and creating and editing drawing borders to name just a few.

Having completed this chapter, you can:

- Create a new project and structure it to your needs.
- Explain how projects are structured in the AutoCAD Plant 3D software and the AutoCAD P&ID software and identify where the project files are located.
- Set up and maintain a project that can be used for larger projects with multiple users.
- Set up the tagging scheme and place symbols on the correct layer with the required color.
- Set up any report or view in the Data Manager and use that set up to export data from the project.
- Create drawing templates and use data from the project and the drawing in your title block.
- Create, modify, and convert a spec and create and duplicate components to build your own components.
- Create a custom isometric set up and add additional information to your drawing when generating the Iso.
- Troubleshoot issues by recovering drawings and solving error messages.
- Create and manage the report configuration files that are used to generate reports.
- Set up SQL Express for the AutoCAD Plant 3D software.

Made in United States
North Haven, CT
05 November 2026

21764583R00293